PENGUIN BOOKS

THE LONDON HANGED

Peter Linebaugh, historian and educator, was born in Washington, DC. Educated in Cattaraugus (New York), London, Bonn, Frankfurt and the Karachi Grammar School (Pakistan), he received degrees from Swarthmore College and Columbia University and a Ph.D from the University of Warwick, where he attended the Centre for the Study of Social History under E. P. Thompson, with whom he helped to write *Albion's Fatal Tree* (Penguin 1977).

He has taught at several American universities, at the Attica Correctional Facility in New York and at the Federal Penitentiary in Marion, Illinois. He has been a Fulbright Scholar at the University of Campinas, Brazil, and a fellow at the Max Planck Institute in Göttingen. With Marcus Rediker he is writing *The Many-Headed Hydra*, a history of the Atlantic working class in the seventeenth and eighteenth centuries.

He is married, lives in Brookline, Massachusetts, and helps to care for his baby daughter.

PETER LINEBAUGH

THE LONDON HANGED

CRIME AND CIVIL SOCIETY IN THE EIGHTEENTH CENTURY

PENGUIN BOOKS

PENGUIN BOOKS

Published by the Penguin Group
Penguin Books Ltd, 27 Wrights Lane, London W8 5TZ, England
Penguin Books USA Inc., 375 Hudson Street, New York, New York 10014, USA
Penguin Books Australia Ltd, Ringwood, Victoria, Australia
Penguin Books Canada Ltd, 10 Alcorn Avenue, Toronto, Ontario, Canada M4V 3B2
Penguin Books (NZ) Ltd, 182–190 Wairau Road, Auckland 10, New Zealand

Penguin Books Ltd, Registered Offices: Harmondsworth, Middlesex, England

First published by Allen Lane The Penguin Press 1991
Published in Penguin Books 1993
1 3 5 7 9 10 8 6 4 2

Printed in England by Clays Ltd, St Ives plc

To my mother, Ann S. Linebaugh,
and to the memory of my father, J. David Linebaugh

Contents

List of Illustrations ix

List of Tables, Figures and Maps x

Abbreviations xi

Acknowledgements xiii

Introduction xv

Part One: Pandaemonium and Finance Capitalism,
1690–1720

Chapter One   'The Common Discourse of the Whole
Nation': Jack Sheppard and the Art of
Escape   7

Chapter Two   'Old Mr Gory' and the Thanatocracy   42

Chapter Three   Tyburnography: The Sociology of the
Condemned   74

Part Two: The Pedagogy of the Gallows under Mercantilism,
1720–50

Chapter Four   The Picaresque Proletariat During the
Robinocracy   119

Chapter Five   Socking, the Hogshead and Excise   153

Chapter Six   'Going Upon the Accompt': Highway
Robbery under the Reigns of the
Georges   184

Part Three: Industry and Idleness in the Period of Manufacture, 1750–1776

CHAPTER SEVEN   The Cat Likes Cream: The Waging Hand in Five Trades   225

CHAPTER EIGHT   Silk Makes the Difference   256

CHAPTER NINE   If You Plead for Your Life, Plead in Irish   288

Part Four: The Crisis of Thanatocracy in the Era of Revolution, 1776–1800

CHAPTER TEN   The Delivery of Newgate, 6 June 1780   333

CHAPTER ELEVEN   Ships and Chips: Technological Repression and the Origin of the Wage   371

CHAPTER TWELVE   Sugar and Police: The London Working Class in the 1790s   402

BIBLIOGRAPHY   442
INDEX   475

LIST OF ILLUSTRATIONS

p. xxii: On the Way to Tyburn (Mansell Collection)

p. 32: Jack Sheppard (reproduced by courtesy of the Trustees of the British Museum)

p. 36: Jack Sheppard's escape from Newgate (reproduced by courtesy of the Trustees of the British Museum)

p. 76: The Sessions House (Mary Evans Picture Library)

p. 129: The press-gang at work (Hulton Picture Company)

p. 139: Sailors and friends drinking grog on board ship (Mary Evans Picture Library)

p. 146: 'The idle 'prentice returned from sea and in a garret with a common prostitute', by Hogarth, from *Industry and Idleness* (Mary Evans Picture Library)

p. 165: An African-American cooper at work (Collection of the Maryland Historical Society, Baltimore)

p. 188: The King's Highway (Hulton Picture Company)

p. 199: Honour buys no meat (Hulton Picture Company)

p. 208: Turpin leaps Hornsey tollgate (Mary Evans Picture Library)

p. 293: An Irish street-seller (from Henry Mayhew, *London Labour and the London Poor*)

p. 305: Coal-porters filling wagons at Coal Wharf (from Henry Mayhew, *London Labour and the London Poor*)

p. 312: A gang of coal-whippers at work (from Henry Mayhew, *London Labour and the London Poor*)

p. 335: The burning, plundering and destruction of Newgate (Mary Evans Picture Library)

p. 350: A crippled black sailor (Mary Evans Picture Library)

p. 369: 'Albion rose from where he labour'd at the Mill with Slaves', by Blake (reproduced by courtesy of the Trustees of the British Museum)

p. 384: A sawyer (Mary Evans Picture Library)

p. 421: A cooper

LIST OF TABLES, FIGURES AND MAPS

TABLES

1 Punishment and property (p. 80)
2 Punishment and money (p. 81)
3 Birthplaces of the London hanged, 1703–72 (p. 92)
4 Birthplaces of London emigrants, 1718–59 (p. 93)
5 Occupations of the Irish hanged at Tyburn, 1703–1772 (p. 95)
6 Occupations of the English born outside London and hanged at Tyburn, 1703–1773 (p. 97)
7 The ten most numerous trades in three groups (pp. 105–6)
8 Birthplaces of the women hanged at Tyburn, 1703–1772 (p. 143)
9 Sites of hangings of those who took part in the riots of 6–7 June 1780 (p. 364)
10 Old Bailey prosecutions against misappropriations by employees during the 1790s (p. 405)

FIGURES

1 The structure of trades (p. 104)
2 London indictments and the employment of London seamen, 1715–55 (p. 124)
3 The seasonal spread of indictments before the Middlesex Sessions of Peace and Oyer and Terminer, 1699–1754 (p. 132)
4 Tobacco imports to England and Wales, 1700–1750 (p. 157)

MAPS

1 Clerkenwell and New Prison in 1746 (p. 26)
2 The parish or ward of birth of the London hanged in the eighteenth century (pp. 108–9)
3 Principal highways in and about London (p. 194)
4 Shadwell and the Pool in 1768 (p. 315)

ABBREVIATIONS

Brit. Lib.
  Add. MSS   British Library, Additional Manuscripts
C(H)MSS   Cholmondeley (Houghton) Manuscripts, Cambridge University Library
CLRO   Corporation of London Record Office
DNB   *Dictionary of National Biography*
GLCRO   Greater London Record Office
JHC   *Journals of the House of Commons*
KRO   Kent Record Office
MRO   Middlesex Record Office
OED   *Oxford English Dictionary*
PRO   Public Record Office

In the footnotes and the bibliography the place of publication is London unless otherwise given.

ACKNOWLEDGEMENTS

In the writing of this book I have received the generous cooperation of many libraries, institutions and individuals. I am deeply grateful to all who have helped me. I thank the staffs of the following archives and libraries: the Institute of Historical Research, the Harvard Law Library, the Kress Collection of the Harvard Business School, the Guildhall, the British Library, the London Library, the Henry E. Huntington Library, the Middlesex Record Office, the Bodleian Library, the Westminster Record Office, the Corporation of London Record Office, the Boston Public Library, the Library of Congress, the Newberry Library, the Public Record Office, the House of Lords Record Office, Lincoln's Inn Library, the Folger Shakespeare Library, the William L. Clements Library at the University of Michigan, and the Cambridge University Library.

I gratefully thank the Graduate History societies of Columbia University and the University of Pennsylvania, the Mid-Atlantic Radical Historian's Organization, the Ruskin History Workshop, the Centre for the Study of Social History at the University of Warwick, the Society for the Study of Labour History, the Centre for Metropolitan [London] History, the International Roundtable on History and Anthropology, the Workers and Industrialization Section of the Social Science Research Council, the African-American Study Group of the New York Penitentiary at Attica, New York, the Critical Legal Studies Conference, the American Society for 18th Century Studies, the Union of Radical Political Economists, the Hibernian Society (Rochester, New York), the Universidade de Campinas (Brazil), and the Max Planck Institut für Geschichte.

I thank the following individuals for their assistance, criticism, encouragement and support. Indispensable, all. My teacher, Edward Thompson; my editor at Penguin Books, Charles Drazin; Richard Andrews, John Beattie, Bettina Berch, Leon Botstein, Lisa Brennan, Michaela Brennan, Joseph Harry Brown, Nick Builder, George Caffentzis, Bruno Cartosio, Bryn Clark, Randall Conrad, Dan Coughlin, Doug Deal, Stan Engerman, Carl Estabrook, John

Fairfield, Silvia Federici, Fred Fleron, John Flym, Carol Flynn, Ferruccio Gambino, John Gillis, Allen Ginsberg, David Hardisky, Robert Harmon, Royden Harrison, Doug Hay, Joe and Joan Hendrick, Selma James, Jeff Kaplow, Geoff Kaye, Duncan Kennedy, Jesse Lemisch, Andrew Daniel Linebaugh, Kate Linebaugh, Nick Linebaugh, Alf Lüdtke, Rick McGahey, Tom McGrath, Johnny Mañana, Clement Mararaj, Shula Marks, Gene Mason, Hans Medick, John Merrington, David Montgomery, Jim Morrice, Roger Murray, Jeannette Neeson, Monty Neill, Pat O'Malley, Paulo Sérgio Pinheiro, George Rawick, Marcus Rediker, Dave Riker, Nick Rogers, John Roosa, John Rule, Leslie Rowland, Raphael Samuel, Bob Scally, Cardell Shaird, Michael Sonenscher, Amy Dru Stanley, Malcolm Thomas, Dorothy Thompson, Bethia Waterman, Igor Webb, Gwyn Williams and Bill W.

INTRODUCTION

In criminology as in economics there is scarcely a more powerful word than 'capital'. In the former discipline it denotes death; in the latter it has designated the 'substance' or the 'stock' of life: apparently opposite meanings. Just why the same word, 'capital', has come to mean both crimes punishable by death and the accumulation of wealth founded on the produce of previous (or dead) labour might be left to etymologists were not the association so striking, so contradictory and so exact in expressing the theme of this book. For this book explores the relationship between the organized death of living labour (capital punishment) and the oppression of the living by dead labour (the punishment of capital).

The intensification of capital punishment has become a worldwide trend since the mid 1970s precisely when capital, reacting to the prior period of colonial emancipation, unprecedented wage demands and cultural revolutions, gained a new lease on life. Considering five of the countries that have utilized it most frequently or broadened its application, we find that South Africa has executed more than a hundred a year since 1980; that Iran since 1979 has tripled the annual number of executions, now measured in the thousands; that Nigeria between 1974 and 1977 extended the death penalty to include crimes against money; that large numbers have been executed in China since 1980; and that in the United States, following an unofficial ten-year moratorium, the execution of the death penalty was resumed in 1977. All told, according to Amnesty International, there have been about a thousand executions a year since 1985, a figure that excludes unofficial deaths that governments have nevertheless acquiesced in – the 'disappeared', the assassinations, the victims of death squads. Thus, the tendency to capital punishment has been clear, alarming and specific to a historical period that has been reactionary in every sense.[1]

---

[1] In opposition to this world trend, the movement against capital punishment has grown. Eighty countries have abolished it by law or in practice. In February 1987

In contrast to eighteenth-century London when news of hangings, the last words of the condemned, their biographies and descriptions of their behaviour were widely published, remarkably little is known about the recent victims of capital punishment, or about the attitudes of their peers. This is unusual considering that nineteen countries permit public executions. The international press is strangely silent, and the national press is terse. One reason for such silence is suggested by a Pakistani journalist who, following a public execution in 1988 before 10,000 people, observed 'Such punishments will project the image of the state as a perpetrator of violence.'[2] Occasionally, such violence has met a violent response, despite unequal forces. The prisoners of the Virginia State Penitentiary rioted unsuccessfully in April 1985 to prevent the execution of James Briley.[3] Very few condemned have had their last words recorded. In China, it is said, a choke cord around the neck of the condemned prevents the uttering of sounds during the 'public humiliation' ceremonies that precede execution. An exception to this silence was provided by Dr Nawal el Saadawi, who recorded the words of Firdaus, executed in Egypt in 1974. Firdaus had declined to plead for a pardon when asked to do so by the warden. 'Everybody has to die,' she explained. 'I prefer to die for a crime I have committed rather than to die for one of the crimes which you have committed.' Thus did she express a contradiction inherent in capital punishment and which poses a problem that must be faced by all who contemplate it. Free alike of hope and fear, Firdaus approached her fate with concentrated fortitude. 'This journey to a place unknown to everybody on this earth fills me with pride.'[4]

While I have not attempted to elucidate the moral or political contradiction as stated by Firdaus, I have sought to consider such

---

the USSR as part of *glasnost* announced its intention to restrict the death penalty, and a public debate about the abolition of capital punishment began. The German Democratic Republic abolished the death penalty on 17 July 1987. In December 1988 Prime Minister Benazir Bhutto, whose father had been hanged in April 1979, commuted over 2,000 death sentences in Pakistan. In March 1988 Colonel Gaddafi of Libya called for the abolition of the death penalty, and in June he intervened to commute all existing death sentences. See, *The Death Penalty: Amnesty International Report* (1979), and *When the State Kills . . . The Death Penalty: A Human Rights Issue* (Amnesty International, 1989).

[2] *Dawn*, 12 March 1988.
[3] *The Boston Globe*, 19 April 1985.
[4] Nawal el Saadawi, *Woman at Point Zero*, trans. Dr Sherif Hetata (London, 1983), pp. 101 and 11.

problems within the social and economic context of eighteenth-century London. This book has its origins in 1965, when Malcolm X was assassinated and when I first read Edward Thompson's *The Making of the English Working Class*. Referring to the eighteenth century, he had written, 'One may even see these years as ones in which the class war is fought out in terms of Tyburn, the hulks and the Bridewells on the one hand; and crime, riot, and mob action on the other.' When he wrote of the eighteenth-century inarticulate that 'it is tempting to follow them into the archives of crime', it was a temptation that I, as a young scholar, accepted.[5] Having met Edward Thompson at a Columbia University Students for a Democratic Society meeting I shook the dust from my feet, matriculated at the Centre for the Study of Social History at the University of Warwick, and lived in London to study crime. The present book is the fruit of that research.

At first I delved into the judicial records of London, Westminster and Middlesex, taking statistical soundings of indictments, but eventually, encouraged by my colleagues at the Centre, I became more interested in the thousands of men and women who died upon the Tyburn gallows at the then westernmost extremity of London. There were two reasons for this. First, in contrast to other judicial records, the documentation about the hanged people was unusually rich and had never been systematically studied. Second, the hanging was the terrible pinnacle in the landscape of available punishments. I concluded that the Tyburn hangings were the central event in the urban contention between the classes, and indeed were meant to be so.

Before I could publish the evidence and reasons for this conclusion two other matters connected with the hangings had to be established. First, I needed to dispel the lazy characterization that the public Tyburn hanging was merely a raucous spectacle. I would like to say that my contribution to *Albion's Fatal Tree*, 'The Tyburn Riot Against the Surgeons', accomplished this by describing the earnest battle of loved ones against the surgeons for possession of the condemned corpse, and that it showed the scorn evinced in word and deed by the Tyburn crowd against law and authority.[6] But this view has recently been challenged. Professor Thomas Lacqueur

---

[5] *The Making of the English Working Class* (New York, 1964), pp. 55 and 60.
[6] Douglas Hay, Peter Linebaugh, Edward Thompson (eds), *Albion's Fatal Tree: Crime and Society in Eighteenth-Century England* (1975), pp. 65–119.

believes that the crowd at London hangings was 'titillated', that it enjoyed the 'exquisite pleasure of venting power on the powerless', and it viewed the hanging as 'light entertainment' whose carnival atmosphere reinscribed 'a deeper community'. Despite these assumptions, he has produced neither argument nor evidence that requires significant revision of the evidence in *Albion's Fatal Tree*.[7]

That book, and its companion, *Whigs and Hunters* by Edward Thompson, since they were published in 1975, seem to have stimulated the growth of an academic sub-field and certainly provoked critical contributions by other scholars.[8] However, what the subsequent discussion gained in methodological sophistication and breadth of contributions, it lost in conceptual timidity and the narrow rejection of historical imagination, as the history of crime was increasingly transformed into the history of administration or 'the machinery of justice'. A recent survey of the workhouse from the sixteenth to the nineteenth century, for instance, does not even mention the factory or the enclosure movement.[9] A conservative orientation towards the subject that regarded it as a police problem, that considered methods of preventing crimes rather than the circumstances giving rise to them, that accepted the inert inexorability of the legal juggernaut as it ground its victims into finer particles, that fascinated itself with state power, and that doubted the existence of classes and even of the Industrial Revolution itself had the effect of denaturing men and women who fell foul of law and of displacing the historiographic discussion we had tentatively opened.

[7] Thomas W. Laqueur, 'Crowds, Carnival and the State in English Executions, 1604–1868', in A. L. Beier, David Cannadine and James M. Rosenheim (eds), *The First Modern Society: Essays in English History in Honour of Lawrence STONE* (Cambridge, 1989), pp. 305–55.

[8] See in particular, J. S. Cockburn (ed.), *Crime in England, 1550–1800* (Princeton, 1977); John Brewer and John Styles (eds), *An Ungovernable People: The English and their Law in the Seventeenth and Eighteenth Centuries* (1980); J. A. Sharpe, *Crime in Early Modern England, 1550–1750* (1984); and J. M. Beattie, *Crime and the Courts in England, 1660–1800* (Princeton, 1986).

[9] Joanna Innes, 'Prisons for the Poor: English Bridewells, 1555–1800', in Francis Snyder and Douglas Hay (eds), *Labour, Law, and Crime: An Historical Perspective* (1987); Joanna Innes and John Styles, 'The Crime Wave: Recent Writings on Crime and Criminal Justice in Eighteenth-Century England', *Journal of British Studies*, 25 (October 1986); John Langbein, 'Albion's Fatal Flaws', *Past and Present*, 98 (1983); G. R. Elton, 'Introduction: Crime and the Historian', in J. S. Cockburn (ed.), *Crime in England, 1550–1800* (1977), p. 2; Peter Linebaugh, '(Marxist) Social History and (Conservative) Legal History: A Reply to Professor Langbein', *The New York University Law Review*, vol. lx, no. 2 (May 1985).

One might argue, indeed, that *Albion's Fatal Tree* and *Whigs and Hunters*, far from initiating historical research, were rather the culmination of a historiography that had considered crime within a broader framework of social history. We built upon earlier studies by E. J. Hobsbawm and George Rudé, who, in introducing the fertile notions of 'social banditry' and the 'crowd', helped to open agrarian crime and urban disorder, respectively, to new sources and analysis. In addition, we reached deeper to the studies of the Industrial Revolution found in Paul Mantoux and M. Dorothy George, who described the corruption and cruelty of those punishing crimes, as well as the social and economic circumstances that provided historical specificity to particular crimes.[10] As expressed in 1975 our research prevented us from making that tidy distinction between 'social crime' and 'crime without qualification', where the former receives popular support and the latter is merely deplored. On this issue, indeed, our significant differences remained unexplored, as the academic field, now less about life and criminals than law and police, prospered.

Second, in arguing that Tyburn was at the centre of urban class contention, I needed to show that the literature describing the hangings was a credible source of historical information, for it had either been ignored or dismissed as ephemeral; and in fact it lay scattered and uncatalogued in libraries throughout the English-speaking world. So two years later I published a second essay about Tyburn that provided a critical guide to an eighteenth-century periodical called *The Ordinary of Newgate, His Account of the Behaviour, Confession, and Dying Words of the Malefactors who were Executed at Tyburn*.[11] These biographies of the condemned men and women provide a unique and inestimable source of knowledge of the poor people who were hanged. Nothing like them has been published before or since. I was able to demonstrate that the biographies supplied information that could be corroborated from other, more familiar historical sources, such as parish and apprenticeship records, and that the historian may therefore be justified in relying upon the

---

[10] George Rudé, *Wilkes and Liberty: A Social Study of 1763 to 1774* (1962); E. J. Hobsbawm, *Primitive Rebels* (1959); Paul Mantoux, *The Industrial Revolution in the Eighteenth Century* (1928); M. Dorothy George, *London Life in the Eighteenth Century* (1925).
[11] 'The Ordinary of Newgate and His *Account*,' in J. S. Cockburn (ed.), *Crime in England, 1550–1800* (Princeton, 1977), pp. 246–70.

short biographies printed in the *Account* as records of the truth. But what is the truth that they tell?

Most important, it was a dramatic truth. Drama depends upon conflict, and in this it needs to be contrasted with the spectacle, whose appeal is to every sense but the understanding. But as drama, each hanging was different. The hanging of a malefactor was a carefully managed affair, as Professor Douglas Hay has shown.[12] The crime was well-known; the culprit was selected as an 'Example'; each of the condemned would be known to different sorts of Londoners according to his or her trade, neighbourhood, age and past. The agony of the hanging stirred various emotions – rage, glee, pity, terror and fear – with their own potentialities of action, and these emotions were aroused by different means according to the malefactor and the crime.

The hangings were permitted and ordered by men of a ruling class who had studied the applications of death throughout human history and had power to apply that knowledge. The hanging was one of the few occasions (coronations were another) that united the several parts of government (monarch, courts, Parliament, City and Church). Equally important to the meaning of these awful dramas was the renewal of the 'social contract'.[13] Most of those hanged had offended against the laws of property, and at the heart of the 'social contract' was respect for private property. It could therefore be argued that, just as each hanging renewed the power of sovereignty, so each hanging repeated the lesson: 'Respect Private Property.' So, if the hangings are to be considered as dramas, the conflict that they represented was the conflict of the Powerful and the Propertied against the Weak and the Poor – a futile, unchanging conflict whose lesson, it seemed, was never learned. Malcolm X, a prisoner at the Norfolk Correctional Facility in Massachusetts, recognized this in 1949. He was a member of the debating team that defeated MIT. In arguing the affirmative to the proposition, 'The Death Penalty is Ineffective as a Deterrent', he reminded the judges that the eighteenth-century pickpocket plied his trade within the crowd at the hanging of another pickpocket.[14]

[12] 'Property, Authority and the Criminal Law', *Albion's Fatal Tree: Crime and Society in Eighteenth-Century England* (1975), pp. 17–64.
[13] Louis P. Masur, *Rites of Execution: Capital Punishment and the Transformation of American Culture, 1776–1865* (1989), shows that in the early American republic the lesson taught was 'public order'.
[14] The prison newspaper, *The Colony*, vol. xxi, no. 1 (1 January 1950).

While this view contains an important truth, it is an over-simplified one, for the population was not so stupid that it needed so many 'examples' to teach the same lesson. Actually, the lesson changed, because the meaning of 'property' changed. The *production* of property in the eighteenth century underwent changes of such magnitude that they are appreciated by comparison with the neolithic revolution of 4,000 years earlier (hence the phrase 'Industrial Revolution'). The *uses* of property expanded to such a degree of refinement and luxury that it amazed contemporary thinkers, who based their definition of civilization upon it. The *laws* of property underwent revision, statutory expansions and codification. Finally, the *value* of property underwent huge changes, as the labour producing it expanded in geographical mass, in temporal duration and in the intensification of work. As a result of these changes questions of making and questions of getting were continually being raised and tested, requiring ever fresh lessons from the 'triple tree'.

The present volume, therefore, considers the individual cases as incidents of a drama, and in that, it is similar to the Ordinary's *Account*. Such history by the neck gives us a history of the eighteenth-century class struggle that includes both the expropriation of the poor from the means of producing (resulting in 'urbanization') and the appropriation by the poor of the means of living (resulting in 'urban crime'). To state the central thesis of this book, we can say, first, that the forms of exploitation pertaining to capitalist relations caused or modified the forms of criminal activity, and, second, that the converse was true, namely, that the forms of crime caused major changes in capitalism. In short, people became so poor that they stole to live, and their misappropriating led to manifold innovations in civil society. From this it follows that we can no longer regard the casualties at Tyburn as the lamentable victims of historical development, to be cast, forgotten, on the dustheap of time. The criminalized population of London was a force, in itself, of historic changes. Research revealed the difficulty of distinguishing between a 'criminal' population of London and the poor population as a whole. That is why we can say of the hanged that they belonged to the *poor*. Furthermore, the hanged, like the labouring people in London as a whole, worked with their hands and expended the energies of their bodies to make the civilization of the eighteenth century. That is why we can say that they were of the *labouring poor*. Finally, the struggles of the hanged, like those of their class, inspired their rulers to initiatives of their own. It is from this pattern

On the way to Tyburn: No longer can the casualties of Tyburn be regarded as the lamentable victims of historical development, to be cast, forgotten, on the dustheap of time.

of struggle, initiative and response that an historic dialectic was created. That is why we consider the history of the condemned as part of an eighteenth-century *working class*. With that argument this book takes up the problem with which *Albion's Fatal Tree* closed, namely, what was the relationship between crime and the working class?

It is an old question of course, but since 1975 the emphasis in the discussion, even among those writing from a critical perspective, has been less upon the working class than upon state power. Professor Duncan Kennedy, the critical legal theorist, takes up the problem:

There is a long Marxist tradition characterizing the state under capitalism as the executive committee of the ruling class, thereby reducing executive, legislative, or judicial action as a raw expression of class interest. There is also a long tradition of insisting that executive officers and judges under capitalism often twist, or plain break the rules in order to do in oppressed groups, thereby furthering their class interests.[15]

[15] Duncan Kennedy, 'The Role of Law in Economic Thought: Essays on the Fetishism of Commodities', *The American University Law Review*, vol. xxxiv, no. 4 (Summer 1985), p. 998.

What are the implications of this manner of presenting the problem to our question about the working class?

If the law is only a mask for class interest, then the working class scorns as hypocritical the laws pretending to universality. The working class adopts either an antinomian viewpoint – there is no law – or one of cynical, individualistic materialism. In either case it commits crime-crimes and in doing so its debasement descends to resemble those monkey Yahoos who beshat themselves upon Gulliver. If, on the other hand, the law indeed expresses ideals of justice which transcend the corruptions of the rulers of society to break them, then the working class in prophetic wrath may turn the world upside down and justify its social crimes as part of the movement towards that rational, benevolent society Gulliver found among the horse Houyhnhnms. In sum: the former created justice, and the latter restore justice to its ideal.

This antimony *can* be a useful way to understand the problem. *Whigs and Hunters*, for instance, may be expounded in the second of these traditions. A book that relentlessly demonstrated the corrupt venalities of Sir Robert Walpole and his regime concludes with an epilogue that speaks of law as an absolute human good. In contrast, *Albion's Fatal Tree* argued that law was central to ruling–class authority, replacing in some respects the role formerly played by religion, and its studies of the labouring poor showed them as both dirty Yahoos and kindly Houyhnhnms. But this antimony is limited and false, if not comic. Its starting-point is law and its idol-like power to entrance the intellect. Our starting-point is neither law nor 'critical law' but the hanged men and women whose views and actions continually challenged both law and their own class. If we categorize them too quickly as social criminals taking from the rich, or criminal-criminals stealing from the poor, in the process of making these judgements we cloud our attentiveness to theirs.

At the fulcrum of eighteenth-century class relations was the exchange between living labour and those who exploited it. This relationship is usually regarded as a monetary, or wage, relationship: on the one hand, employers buy labouring activities, and on the other hand working people purchase what is required to survive, more or less, in order to continue working. Yet in eighteenth-century London the relationship was sometimes not monetary in theory, and often not so in practice. The nature of class relations, therefore, concerned other things. The form of such exchanges could not be universal; they were particular to each situation. Whether the worker derived the wherewithal of life from the workshop, ship or land (sites of production where materials and tools were at hand), or whether the worker derived his or her means of living from the street, market or household (places of consumption where food, drink, love and raiment were available), cannot be determined theoretically or in advance of actual investigation. An earlier formulation of this argument has recently been criticized by Professors Joanna Innes and John Styles, who believe that 'wage labour was often embraced with enthusiasm' and who question 'whether capitalism can be usefully portrayed as having specific needs'.[16] There is truth to both of these views though not perhaps the truth intended. It is true that only rarely did workers actually reject money, even when they believed that other incomes were to be removed in consequence. Men and women of the eighteenth century wanted money, most certainly. This is not quite the same, however, as the enthusiastic embrace of wage-labour which was so often accompanied by the kiss of death. As for 'the needs of capitalism' one might recall, indeed, the words 'Capital is dead labour, that, vampire-like, only lives by sucking living labour, and lives the more, the more labour it sucks', or 'Accumulate, accumulate! That is Moses and the prophets!'[17] Yet these 'needs of capitalism' can be described only as they emerge from the antagonism provided by the counterforce of living labour.

Unlike the historian of class relations in the nineteenth or twentieth centuries, whose subject-matter is studied through the glass of money, the eighteenth-century historian needs sources of information that are as particular as the things of the eighteenth century and as concrete as the labouring history of eighteenth-century persons. The eighteenth-century historian has greater reason than those of subsequent periods to search for evidence of the organizational and technical aspects of the labour process, since these decided both the value and use of what was produced and the ability of the living worker to take, in exchange for work, what was necessary to live, whether such taking was 'allowed', or 'customary' or otherwise.

Only then can we be in a position to understand the contentious

[16] Peter Linebaugh, 'Eighteenth Century Crime, Popular Movements, and Social Control', *Bulletin of the Society for the Study of Labour History*, 25 (1972). Joanna Innes and John Styles, op. cit., pp. 397–9.
[17] Karl Marx, *Capital*, trans. Ben Fowkes (1976), pp. 600 and 216.

exchange between living, labouring people and their rulers. Since the exchange was disputed, it was very often disputed at law, and therefore, for London, there are fewer sources of information better than the vast documentation left by the criminal courts. The archives of the criminal jurisdictions of London and the printed *Proceedings* of the Old Bailey give us a history of misappropriated things. From them we may derive *a history of taking*. Rarely do they provide information permitting us to understand how things were made or the exact combinations of materials, tools and expenditure of labouring creativity. For that information we need to begin with the biographies of the men and women who were hanged – from these we may obtain *a history of making*.

Together, the histories of taking and making propel us inexorably to the idea of contradiction in the social relations of production. The resolution to this contradiction is suggested by two tendencies at the end of the century. First was the tendency to remove the central place of public hangings in the panoply of rule. This tendency begins with the abolition of the procession to Tyburn in 1783. Second was the tendency – discerned most clearly during the repression of the 1790s – to introduce the wage relation as a variable, dynamic means of dividing the working class while simultaneously acceding to one of its most insistent demands.

This book is organized in three ways. First, the chapters are divided into four chronological periods of twenty-five or thirty years each. While it has proved impossible to present all of the evidence exactly in temporal sequence (the chapter on the Irish, for instance, contains many examples from earlier periods at odds with its placement under the 'Period of Manufacture'), in general the subject-matter of this book is presented in accordance with the advance of time.

Progress through the eighteenth century has traditionally been measured by the accumulation of wealth, so the second principle of organization has been loosely derived from the concepts of economic history. Thus, the early period is about money or finance capitalism; the second period is about commerce ('mercantilism'); the third period is about manufacture; and the concluding period of the century is about industrialism and machine production. These designations are limited even in their own terms and I here intend them to be suggestive only. By calling attention to the dominant economic trend of the periods, the others are by no means excluded; on the contrary. Theoretically, this is clear as we realize that the accumulating social product takes several forms – as commodity, as exchange, as money, and as production. Historically, it becomes evident too: the finance capitalism of the 1690s was also a period of major changes in commerce and production; the factory production a century later corresponded to a money and trade crisis.

The limitation of the economic concepts, their focus on the externalities of accumulation, is partly rectified by the third principle of organization, which leads us into the internal secrets of accumulation. That organizing principle arises from the procedure of selection that emerges from the sociology of the hanged presented in Chapter 3. In that chapter there is shown to be an important relationship between particular trades (such as butchers or weavers) or groups of people (such as sailors and the Irish) and the people hanged. This relationship suggested the need for separate study, which then appears in subsequent chapters.

In addition to these guides of organization, other themes appear and recur among the chapters. The theme of freedom as its significance changed from the seventeenth century to the 1790s is one of these. Freedom is treated literally to mean escape from confinement; it is as much a matter of action as it is of words. Such 'excarceration' is introduced in Chapter 1 with the discussion of a gaol-breaker, Jack Sheppard, and recurs in Chapter 10, where it is discussed as a collective, even international, action. A similar transition from the particular to the general is important in considering the theme of work. In some chapters we consider men and women as they were organized by particular trades, and these chapters owe much to the methods of labour history, while in others we see how workers organized themselves, informally and culturally, against the exploitation inherent in the conditions of labour, and these chapters owe much to social historians. The material exchange between labour and capital is a theme virtually present in every chapter because, as I argue it, it is essential to understanding the who, when, and why of the Tyburn hangings, but its full consequences are addressed only in Chapter 11. Finally, the theme of police suppression, whose failure is considered in Chapter 5, recurs in the final chapter when it became successful.

A final word. Hanging, even a hanging 200 years old, is a powerfully emotive subject. While I have spoken with people who have witnessed the execution of the death penalty, I have not done so myself. 'Woe unto Woe!' exclaimed Luke Hutton, a Newgate prisoner in 1596, at the 'rueful sight'. His spirits sank. He was left aghast. It forced him to 'bethink'.[18]

[18] Luke Hutton, *The Black Dog of Newgate* (1596?), reprinted in A V. Judges, *The Elizabethan Underworld* (1930), p. 275.

PART ONE

PANDAEMONIUM
AND
FINANCE CAPITALISM
1690–1720

An important meaning of liberation with continuities to the Revolution of 1640 is suggested in the first chapter: namely, the growing propensity, skill and success of London working people in escaping from the newly created institutions that were designed to discipline people by closing them in. This tendency I have dubbed 'excarceration' because I wish to draw attention to the activity of freedom in contrast to its ideological or theoretical expressions. I see that activity as a counter-tendency to a recent historiographical trend exemplified by Michel Foucault, who stresses incarceration in 'the great confinement' and who makes the rulers of government and society seem all-powerful.

Chapter 1 discusses one exemplifier of this counter-tendency, Jack Sheppard, because not only did he become that 'example' of the majesty of his country's laws which hangings were designed to produce, but also his prior escapes were a legend that survived him in pantomime, on vase paintings, at Bartholomew Fair, in ballad, story and play.[1] Such forms of expression were popular and proletarian, and it was from them therefore that people to some extent formed their understanding of freedom. Sheppard's escapes were compared to the revolutionary activities of the Levellers. Sheppard's partner went on to help found the Sons of Liberty, the revolutionary organization in New York.

Chapter 2 provides the reader with the background of economic and political history that is necessary to understanding the subsequent chapters. 'A new world burst upon the horizon of mankind in those days,' wrote the German sociologist Werner Sombart, referring to the end of the seventeenth century. He found that the spirit of trade and colonial conquest was the same as the spirit of robbery. Rapacity and idleness belonged to the entrepreneur and the robber alike.

---

[1] Brit. Lib., Add. MSS. 27 825. Place MS; fols. 62–3. 'This notorious fellow was held in memory, spoken of and sung of with applause when I was a boy.'

Dishonesty was the presumption, among workers, businessmen and family members.[2]

On the one hand, labour was the source of wealth; on the other, the wages of labour were to be kept as low as possible. Sir Henry Pollexfen calculated that £500,000 would be gained for every holiday that was abolished. Writing in 1704 Daniel Defoe noted 'a general taint of slothfulness upon our poor'. William Petty observed that a plentiful harvest resulted in labour that was expensive and scarce. Josiah Child noted that when corn was cheap the poor would not work more than two days a week, as that was enough to maintain them in the 'condition to which they have been accustomed'. Roger North found it was the same: the poor preferred not to work if they did not have to, than to work to accumulate or to save.[3]

The chapter is organized with the help of John Milton's poem, *Paradise Lost*. Milton, it has been suggested, preferred allegory to history because in allegory questions are not closed in the way that a historical defeat can seem to end a question.[4] The Restoration of 1660 and the Compromise of 1689 seemed to have put an end to the English Revolution. Therefore, despite the historical closure of the counter-revolution, allegorical presentation may open our investigation to ways in which the revolution still lived. The relation of allegory or epic to history arises again at the end of the eighteenth century in the poetry of William Blake. Both poets were poets of freedom, and the Samson story was an archetype of liberation to them both.

Chapter 3 treats the hanged people of London in dramatic and in aggregate terms: 'Tyburnography'. The court room is considered a drama: the Old Bailey is the scene; black letter law is the script; the players are judge, jurors and defendants; the audience is cockney London. This helps us to understand the political or moral exemplification that the eighteenth-century hanging represented. But hundreds upon hundreds were hanged, and we need, therefore, to consider the individual dramas in the aggregate, using methods

[2] Werner Sombart, *The Quintessence of Capitalism: A Study of the History and Psychology of the Modern Business Man*, trans. M. Epstein (New York, 1967), pp. 77–88.
[3] Edgar S. Furniss, *The Position of the Laborer in a System of Nationalism: A Study in the Labor Theories of the Later English Mercantilists* (New York, 1920).
[4] Christopher Hill, *The Experience of Defeat: Milton and Some Contemporaries* (1984).

more akin to sociology than to theatre. Aggregation may appear to destroy what is dramatic, but this is necessary since the only way we can determine what was significant to the mass of Londoners about particular offenders is to know what kind of people they were. Aggregation permits us to understand the similarities and the differences between the condemned malefactor and those who had come to witness the hanging. What may appear incidental or anecdotal in the individual case may attain from an aggregated study a significance that puts it close to the essence of class relations in civil society.

CHAPTER ONE

'THE COMMON DISCOURSE OF THE WHOLE NATION': JACK SHEPPARD AND THE ART OF ESCAPE

> Who can avoid drinking when there comes such a
> Glut of Company to see this Fellow, this Sheppard?
> To tell you the Truth, Master Rust, he's worth to us
> as much as a Rebellion, and may turn to a very good
> Account.
>
> Thomas Walker, *The Quaker's Opera; Or, the Escapes
> of Jack Sheppard* (1728)

> Some of the children have never heard the name of
> Her Majesty, nor such names as Wellington, Nelson,
> Buonaparte. But it is to be especially remarked, that
> among all those who had never heard such names as
> St Paul, Moses, Solomon, etc. there was a general
> knowledge of the character and course of life of Dick
> Turpin, the highwayman, and more particularly of
> Jack Shepherd, the robber and prison-breaker.
>
> R. H. Horne, Children's Employment Commission,
> quoted in Frederick Engels, *The Condition of the
> Working Class in England* (1845)

I

Jack Sheppard, housebreaker and gaol-breaker, was once the single most well-known name from eighteenth-century England.[1] His fame spread across oceans and the centuries. When the bandit Ned Kelly was alive, the Australian press was full of comparisons between him and Sheppard. At the same time on the other side of the globe, in Missouri, Frank and Jesse James wrote letters to the *Kansas City*

---

[1] Horace Bleackley, *Jack Sheppard* (Edinburgh, 1933) is a scholarly biography of Sheppard whose epilogue by S. M. Ellis describes the dramatic and narrative literature on Sheppard and provides a useful bibliography.

Star signed 'Jack Sheppard'. In England his name cut deep into the landscape of popular consciousness. Henry Mayhew noted that Cambridgeshire gypsies accepted Sheppard stories as the archetype of 'blackguard tales'. Among English sailors anyone with the surname of 'Sheppard' was automatically called 'Jack'. Within the Manchester proletariat of the 1840s his name was more widely known than that of the Queen herself. One of these lads said, 'I was employed in a warehouse at 6s. 6d. a week, and was allowed 6d. of it for myself, and with that I went regularly to the play. I saw Jack Sheppard four times in one week.'[2]

Ignored, not to say disdained, by academic historiography, he has belonged clearly to an 'other history' of histories, pantomime and song. The oral history of Sheppard has *maintained* his memory within human contexts where books were scarce and working-class resources for an independent historiography were non-existent. Moreover, that memory was kept in contexts of social struggle in which a continuity, if not a development, with earlier moral and political conflicts was suggested. Falling halfway between the apparent death of popular democracy in 1649 and its revival in the 1790s, the life of this malefactor raises questions about the relationship between 'criminality' and the working-class movement. Likewise, questions are raised about the relationship between ruling-class plunder and the depredations of the poor, because he lived at a time when imperialist conquest and domestic expropriations had few checks. At a time when economists have been hard put to explain how the labouring people could actually live given the wage rates that prevailed, Sheppard's life can raise the question of the relationship between thievery and survival.

Even while he was alive, one extended biography was published, and within a year it was followed by several others, each evidently having independent sources of information.[3] These were not

[2] The Melbourne *Argus* (18 December 1878), p. 16, a reference that I owe to Professor Pat Malley of Monash University; Henry Mayhew, *London Labour and the London Poor*, iii (1861), pp. 388–90; Frank C. Bowen, *Sea Slang: A Dictionary of the Old-Timers' Expressions and Epithets* (c. 1920s); *6th Report of the Inspector of Prisons for the Northern Districts of England*.

[3] Anon., *A Narrative of All the Robberies, Escapes, &c. of John Sheppard* (1724) was published before his hanging and went through six editions before the year was out. 'G. E.', *Authentick Memoirs of the Life and Surprising Adventures of John Sheppard by Way of Familiar Letters from a Gentleman in Town*, 2nd edn (1724), and Anon., *The History of the Remarkable Life of John Sheppard* (1724), have been my two

especially concerned with his early years except as these could be seen as the cause of his later ruin. Yet more is known of these years than for most members of his class. He was born in White's Row, Spitalfields, on 4 March 1702, the year in which Queen Anne came to the throne. His father, grandfather and great-grandfather were carpenters. His father died while Jack was a child. Jack had a sister who died young, and a brother, Tom, who left home to become a footboy in a 'Lady's Family' and whose future career was to be as motley as his brother's, though he ended up, not 'dangling from the Triple Tree' but as one of 'His Majesty's Seven Years' Passengers'. Widowed young and without a pension, his mother placed Jack in the newly opened Bishopsgate workhouse, and herself went into service across town in the Strand, where she worked for Mr Knee-bone, a woollen-draper. After a year and a half Jack was removed from the workhouse and placed under the charge of Kneebone, who taught the boy to read and 'cast Accompts'. In April 1717 he was apprenticed to Mr Wood, a Wych Street carpenter at the bottom of Drury Lane.

Extraordinary, even marvellous, as his later actions appeared, they would not have stirred such excitement, such passion, such fundamental discussion, had he not shared in the central experiences of his class and generation. These were three. Born and raised a Spitalfields' lad, he belonged to the industrially most dynamic part of London, if not of England. Having been in the workhouse, he had direct, pioneering experience inside the fastest growing institutional innovation of social control. Breaking his indentures with Mr Wood, he became an 'idle apprentice', a social figure every much as threatening to the established order as the 'sturdy rogue' of the sixteenth century, or the 'sectary' of the seventeenth century or the 'factory proletarian' of the nineteenth century.

II

Silk had become proverbial as the class insignia of idleness, artifice and deception. 'Silks and satins put out the kitchen fire,' said Benjamin Franklin's Poor Richard. 'In silk and scarlet walks many a harlot,' warned Hazlitt at the end of the century. Silk was the fabric

other principal sources of information. I abbreviate these texts as *A Narrative, Authentic Memoirs*, and *The History* respectively.

of haughty command, and silk was a labour of cringing subservience. It expressed the central moral topic of the day – the gulf between Luxury and Necessity. It underlay the main topographical division of London, between the West End and the East End. It expressed the contrast of classes. 'We are all Adam's children, but Silk makes the Difference' went a bitter proverb of 1732.

The accumulation of silk capital may be expressed as an increase in the volume of trade, which doubled between 1664 and 1713, and as the lucrative and dynamic investment that Defoe, Postlethwayt and Charles King extolled.[4] It is seen in the increase of the number of houses between 1675 and 1737 from 1,336 to 2,244, and in the creation of new parishes (Stratford Bow, Christ Church, St Luke's, St Matthew's), where only one, Stepney, had existed before. By the 1720s Spitalfields had become, with Lyons and Nanking, one of the great silk centres of the world.

Accumulation of capital means accumulation of the proletariat. Just as the industry spread into new suburbs outside the jurisdiction of the City of London, so its weavers, throwsters, pattern-makers and drawboys worked without the protections or paternalism of guild control. The labour force was 'free' in the economic senses: free from apprenticeship and wage regulation, free as to the hours of work, free to quit, free to starve. The silk proletariat reflected in its diverse origins – Norwich, Kent, the French Huguenots, the Irish, some Palatinates – a regional and ethnic heterogeneity whose exact proportions were constantly in motion and were reflected at the gallows.[5] There was 'French Peter', born in Poitou: he became a Spitalfields weaver, then robbed in Moll Raby's gang, stealing fabric from shops, and was hanged in 1704. Quite a number of Irish weavers were hanged: John Cannon in 1733, James Falconer in 1737, Philip Murray in 1738. Nathaniel Jackson, originally a Doncaster man, served in the Norwich textile trade before coming to Spitalfields, getting in trouble and finishing his days at Tyburn.[6] Despite immigration and despite gallows' discipline, the Spitalfields weavers maintained their historical traditions. They were the heirs to a

[4] Daniel Defoe, *The Complete English Tradesman* (1727); Charles King, *The British Merchant or Commerce Preserv'd* (1721); Malachy Postlethwayt, *The Universal Dictionary of Trade and Commerce*, 3rd edn (1766), article on 'Silk'.
[5] Daniel Defoe, *The Review*, I, 7 (1705).
[6] The Ordinary's *Account*, 25 October 1704, 6 October 1733, 3 March 1736/7, 26 May 1738, 18 July 1722.

history of heresy that included the Lollards, the Anabaptists, the Familists, as well as the egalitarian and millenarian sects that had burst forth during the English Revolution. William Walwyn, the radical Leveller who believed that hell was nothing but a bad conscience and who opposed the invasion of Ireland, was apprenticed to a London silkman.[7] John Lilburne in 1648 pleaded the cause of the wives and children of the ribbon-weavers at the bar of the House of Commons against the City oligarchy which had attempted to prevent them from peddling.[8] Silk-weavers and throwsters took an active part in Venner's plots of 1657 and 1661. They participated in the Army debates in Monmouth's rebellion, and one of them was implicated in the theft of the crown. Professor Capp, who has made a careful study of the occupational composition of the Fifth Monarchy people, found that millenarian ideas were particularly popular among the suburban journeymen weavers.[9] The association between the radical, gathered churches and the weavers persisted into the eighteenth century. A list of Anabaptist meeting-houses published in 1735 shows that most of them were to be found in the silk suburbs of the north-east (Moorfields, Shoreditch, Spitalfields) or in the eastern river parishes.[10]

Sheppard's paternal ancestors built Spitalfields. They would have been touched by these traditions. Jack was born in White's Row, only a few hundred yards from Bishopsgate, where 'Arise' Evans, the Welsh tailor and self-appointed prophet, had proclaimed himself Christ in 1647, where Cromwell and Fairfax failed to convince a mutinied regiment to assemble for the Irish expedition. It was only a stone's throw from Sheppard's birthplace to Artillery Lane, where the Particular Baptists suffered secessions in 1700 and 1706.[11] Jack Sheppard was no spokesman for these traditions. Indeed, it is difficult to find anybody who was, for they did not survive in their original forms, but experienced a mutation under the twin influences of direct repression and the recomposition of the silk labour market.

Bishopsgate workhouse was built only a few years before

---

[7] A. L. Morton, *The World of the Ranters: Religious Radicalism in the English Revolution* (1970), p. 144.
[8] H. N. Brailsford, *The Levellers and the English Revolution* (Stanford, 1961), p. 105.
[9] B. S. Capp, *The Fifth Monarchy Men: A Study in Seventeenth Century English Millenarianism* (1972), *passim*.
[10] Michael R. Watts, *The Dissenters: From the Reformation to the French Revolution* (Oxford, 1978).
[11] Capp, op. cit., p. 42; Brailsford, op. cit., p. 46.

Sheppard's birth.[12] It was situated a few steps from the boundary between Spitalfields and the City. Although there had been much talk of such an institution in the 1640s,[13] it was not until the weavers' disturbances of August 1675 that planning became serious. That 'insurrection' consisted of dozens of bands of weavers, dispersed throughout London, but concentrated in the north-east, and clothed in the Levellers' colour green, who, with drums a-beating and flags a-waving, set upon all those masters who employed the recently imported engine loom, a machine that allowed one ribbon-weaver to do the work of seven.[14] One of the participants, John Mason, had been a Fifth Monarchist who looked to a time when men would not 'labour and toyl day and night . . . to maintain others that live . . . in idleness'.[15] Neither the constabulary nor the militia was reliable, so the Army was deployed to suppress the 'insurrection'. The result of the struggle was mixed: on the one hand mechanization (in London) was delayed for more than a century; on the other hand, the workhouse was realized.

What was it like in the workhouse? The recollections of Robert Blincoe, raised in the St Pancras workhouse in the 1790s, describe an experience that would have been similar to Sheppard's in Bishopsgate workhouse. Cooped up in gloom, surrounded by sullenness and discontent among inmates and by dissimulation and hypocrisy among overseers, Blincoe dreamed of escape.[16] The heartfelt longing for freedom, the detestation of confinement, the silent observation of gates, locks and walls, were Sheppard's reactions too.

[12] Norman Longmate, *The Workhouse* (1974), covers the nineteenth century; Georg Rüsche and Otto Kirchheimer, *Punishment and the Social Structure*, English translation (1939); Joanna Innes, 'Prisons for the Poor: English Bridewells, 1555–1800', in Francis Snyder and Douglas Hay (eds), *Labour, Law, and Crime: An Historical Perspective* (1987), pp. 89 ff.

[13] Valerie Pearl, 'Puritans and Poor Relief: The London Workhouse, 1649–1660', in Donald Pennington and Keith Thomas (eds), *Puritans and Revolutionaries: Essays in 17th Century History* (1978).

[14] Richard M. Dunn, 'The London Weavers' Riot of 1675', *Guildhall Studies in London History*, vol. i (October 1973–April 1975). Anon., *A True Narrative of All the Proceedings Against the Weavers* (1675), describes the behaviour of some of those who were arrested: only three confessed and humbled themselves before the court: 'The rest stood upon their Tryal.'

[15] Capp, op. cit., p. 149.

[16] John Brown, *A Memoir of Robert Blincoe, an Orphan Boy: Sent from the Workhouse of St Pancras, London, at Seven Years of Age, to Endure the Horrors of a Cotton-Mill* (Manchester, 1832), and republished by Caliban Books, 1977, pp. 12–13.

The workhouses were institutions of incarceration and places for punishment. The purpose of the punishment was both to scare people on the outside and to produce docility on the inside. 'The advantage of the workhouse to the parish,' wrote Matthew Marryott, a Buckinghamshire magistrate who hoped to make a fortune from the workhouse, 'does not arise from what the poor people can do towards their own subsistence, but from the apprehension the poor have of it.'[17] Bellers had written, 'A Rebellious temper must be subdued by Correction (far better be Unlearned than Ill-bred).' John Freame, a governor of the Quaker workhouse, argued that, it 'being easier to bend a Twig while 'tis Young ... therefore we should endeavour to break their Wills whilst they are Little, and as soon as ever they are capable, to make them sensible that Their Wills ought to be entirely subject to ours'.[18] There was opposition within the workhouses. At the Quaker workhouse the old people went 'out when they wished and without permission'. In 1711 the steward complained: 'Some who have dined at our table have several times told us we were but their servants.'[19] 'These Workhouses tho' in Appearance Beneficial,' warned Defoe, 'yet have in some Respects an evil Tendency for they mix the Good and the Bad; and too often make Reprobates of all alike.'[20] The children, it seems, learned from the old, and complaints were frequent of their running away and 'telling divers notorious lies'. In 1712 the steward of the Quaker workhouse described the activities of one of its inmates, John Gordon, the son of a Ratcliff cordwainer. He picked pockets and spent the money. He woke at midnight and 'took four pounds of plumb pudding' from the storeroom. He stole the key to the street door, which was discovered in his bed.[21] Within a few years of their establishment, the London workhouses, then, had become locations of struggle.

Sheppard left the workhouse after a year and a half. The 'Epitomy of the World', as John Bellers termed it, was not for him. Perhaps his mother's request was sufficient to obtain his freedom. Perhaps the intercession of Kneebone was sufficient. What we do know is

---

[17] Matthew Marryott, *An Account of Workhouses* (1730). See also, Michael Ignatieff, *A Just Measure of Pain: The Penitentiary in the Industrial Revolution 1750–1850* (New York, 1978), ch. 1 particularly.
[18] Bolam, *Unbroken Community* (Saffron Walden, 1952), pp. 24–5.
[19] Beck and Ball, *The London Friends' Meetings* (1869), p. 369.
[20] Daniel Defoe, *Giving Alms No Charity* (1704).
[21] Bolam, op. cit., pp. 22–3.

that an institution designed to instil habits of industry and obedience among its incarcerated inmates and whose origins were closely associated with the repression of the Spitalfields weavers produced Jack Sheppard, a master of escape whose imaginative daring was at least as great as the bold vision of the creators of the workhouse. His dazzling feats were to provide an example of resourcefulness and freedom to the London weavers and labouring poor that answered the slavish designs of the workhouse.

A new morality became triumphant among the capitalist class at the end of the seventeenth century. Christopher Hill contrasted it with the religious attitudes prevailing earlier: 'Labour, the curse of fallen man, had become a religious duty, a means of glorifying God in our calling. Poverty had ceased to be a holy state and had become presumptive evidence of wickedness.'[22] By the eighteenth century 'idleness' had become one of those terms that encapsulated the widest variety of attitudes within the ruling class, serviceable to trustees of the Society for the Reformation of Manners, magistrates on the Middlesex bench, financiers in Cornhill, as well as master manufacturers of Spitalfields. In all three contemporary biographies of Jack Sheppard idleness is a decisive concept in what are otherwise differing interpretations of the origins of his criminality.

The first six years of his apprenticeship were exemplary. 'He was very Ingenious at his Trade, and knew his Business very well, and very early in his Time, in which he far exceeded most of his Years.' The concept of idleness was thus independent of skill or constancy in completing a task. Idleness meant the refusal of discipline, subordination or obedience. The commentaries on Sheppard always made clear that in necessary labour few were as hard-working as Sheppard. Indeed, on the stage a 'Gentleman' found in Sheppard's escapes a new standard of socially necessary labour time: 'What he has done in the compass of one Night, wou'd take up a Month's time for any Artificer to Perform.' He had learned as much as he could, ahead of his peers in ingenuity, 'weary of the Yoke of Servitude'; the conditions of rebellion were present.

We have three theories explaining Sheppard's transition from industry to idleness. They can be summed up under the headings 'Bad Company', 'Sabbath Breaking' and 'Lewd Women'. The bad company of the first theory was a button-mould-maker who left the trade and established a public house which Sheppard began

[22] Christopher Hill, *Puritanism and Revolution* (1958), p. 218.

to frequent and where he became 'Headstrong, Disobedient, and Vicious'.[23] According to the second theory, although Mr Wood and family were strict Sabbatarians, they allowed Sheppard to spend 'the Lord's Day as I thought convenient'.[24] 'If less Liberty had been allowed me then, I should scarce have had so much Sorrow and Confinement after.' The Lewd Woman theory focused on his acquaintance with Elizabeth Lyon, also known as Edgworth Bess, who 'laid the Foundation of his Ruin'. She undermined his habits of docility. At the Sun alehouse in Islington where he worked, Sheppard is said to have beat Mr Wood 'in a most barbarous and shameful manner'. 'Perpetual Jarrings and Animosities; these and such like, were the Consequences of his intimacy with this she Lyon; who by the sequel will appear to have been a main load-stone in attracting of him up to the fatal Tree.'[25]

For six years he was a precocious, steady, almost masterful carpenter; but in the spring of 1723, only ten months before the completion of his indentures, he fled his master. He did this at a decisive point in the life cycle, a point full of danger and explosiveness. The crisis of apprenticeship was part of a deeper, structural recomposition of the London proletariat. There existed a tension between, on the one hand, those journeymen, small masters and apprentices in trades that no longer enjoyed the protection of guild organization and thus were exposed to the ravaging shocks of divisions of labour and experimentations in industrial organization, and, on the other, all those whose social existence was defined by their refusal to accept the new conditions of exploitation. The circulation of experience between those two poles was characteristic of the late seventeenth and early eighteenth century. Many apprentices, journeymen and small masters would have experienced substantial periods in which they were without wage work and would therefore have sought out other expedients, such as the sea, gaming, the tramp, 'going on the Account'. Similarly, those who lived from day to day as paupers, sharpers, footpads or beggars will almost surely have had some direct acquaintance with the structures of production, such as apprenticeship to a trade or service to a rich family. The zone of circulation between these two poles is what the new institutions of Queen Anne's reign – the workhouse, the charity school, the Society

[23] 'G. E.', *Authentic Memoirs*, p. 173.
[24] Anon., *A Narrative*, p. 160.
[25] Anon., *The History*, p. 139.

for the Reformation of Manners, the new punishments of the penal code – sought to demarcate and control.

If Jack were late at night Mr Wood locked him out, but Jack 'made a mere jest of the Locks and Bolts and enter'd in, and out at Pleasure'. He took to pilfering from his master and then to thieving and housebreaking. The first felony he committed was the stealing of two silver spoons from his job site at the Rummer tavern in Charing Cross. His second and more famous felony was also committed as a result of an opportunity provided by work. He robbed Mr Baines of a 24-yard piece of fustian by removing the iron bars from the cellar windows, which he later replaced so smartly that it was thought that a household servant had stolen the cloth. Jack could not find a buyer for the cloth. A fellow apprentice reported the theft to Mr Baines, and Jack constructed an alibi. He persuaded his mother to say that she had bought the fustian from a Spitalfields weaver, a story she was willing to back up by spending a day with Mr Baines walking about Spitalfields in search of 'the pretended weaver'.

It was shortly after this episode that Jack left Wood never to return. He went to Fulham, wrought as a journeyman carpenter, and cohabited with Edgworth Bess. Soon a warrant was out for him and he was brought before the Chamberlain's court in Guildhall for having broken his apprenticeship. He was able to settle out of court with Wood, and from then on 'he fell to robbing almost every one that stood in his way'. The years between 1717, when Sheppard started his apprenticeship industriously, and 1723, when he ended it idly, saw another transition, that of the consolidation of a new dynasty. Three themes of this period of consolidation are essential to an understanding of the London populace which was soon to follow Sheppard's escapes with avid interest. They are: repression, finance capitalism and the weavers' struggle.

III

Of the Hanoverian accession of 1714 we can say that it represented peace among the European imperialist powers, slavery for Africa and America, and repression at home. The repression is suggested by the key legislation of the period: the Riot Act, the Transportation Act, the Combination Act, the Workhouse Act and the Black Act. The Riot Act of 1715 provided the ruling class with its most simple, pliant and oft-used legal weapon against working-class collective action in the eighteenth century.[26] If twelve or more persons were unlawfully, riotously and tumultuously assembled, if a proclamation of the riot were read by any magistrate and if the persons failed to disperse within an hour of the reading, then they were guilty of felony without benefit of clergy. The Transportation Act of 1719 helped to resolve a contradiction within the practices of punishment. The courts had been forced either to hang a felon or to brand him on the thumb and let him go. The policy of sending felons to the West Indies or to the North American plantations for a period of slave labour had developed in the seventeenth century as both an intermediary punishment and an expedient for satisfying the hungry demand of those places for forced labour. The Act, by authorizing a sentence of fourteen years' transportation for those pardoned of capital offences and by mandating seven years' transportation for those guilty of felony without benefit of clergy, did not greatly disturb penal policy towards forced labour. However, it does appear to have provided the courts with a more flexible response to crime, making it a hanging offence to return early from transportation. In 1720 Sam Whittel, a Whitechapel weaver's son, and Steven Delaforce, a Stepney weaver, were hanged under this provision. In America 'the Lady [Delaforce] was slave to, had given him his Freedom'.[27] The Combination Act of 1721 made it illegal for the journeymen tailors to enter 'into combinations to advance their wages to unreasonable prices, and lessen their usual hours of work'. This is the earliest Act of British history designed to stop the formation of trade unions, and it was passed at the behest of master tailors against some 15,000 journeymen tailors who had struck for better pay and shorter hours. Imprisonment and impressment forced them into submission.[28] Two years later the Workhouse Act was passed. Sponsored by Sir Edward Knatchbull, it authorized any parish to set up its own workhouse, and within a few years many

[26] 1 George I, c. 5 (1715). M. G. Collison's unpublished paper, 'Eighteenth Century Public Order: a Study of the Riot Act', Centre for Criminological Studies, Sheffield University (1976); John Stevenson, *Popular Disturbances in England 1700–1870* (1979).

[27] 4 George I, c. 11 (1717). J. M. Beattie, *Crime and the Courts in England, 1660–1800* (Princeton, 1986), pp. 450–520; The Ordinary's *Account* for 26 October 1720 and 3 April 1721.

[28] 7 George I, c. 13 (1721). F. W. Galton, *Select Documents Illustrating the History of Trade Unionism: I. The Tailoring Trade* (1896).

scores of these were built. In the same year the most notorious criminal statute of the eighteenth century was passed, the Waltham Black Act: its historian has written that it 'signalled the onset of the flood-tide of eighteenth-century retributive justice'.[29] Although it created more than 200 capital offences, it did not cause the carnage of the gallows to increase particularly. This was already high: in 1721 it was said 'there is hardly a day of Execution passes without an Instance of some condemn'd Criminal, who, by solemn Protestations in the last Moments of his life, does not endeavour to persuade the World that he dies Innocent.'[30] But the Black Act remained on the books as an instrument of last resort.

Looking at all five of these Acts we can see that two of them affected the criminal sanction, making it at once more terrifying and more effective; two of them prohibited the most obvious means by which the collective power of the working class might manifest itself, in public assembly or in trade union; and one of them (the Workhouse Act) was a mixture of criminal policy and labour policy. The Workhouse Act, by generalizing the principle of incarceration, and the Transportation Act, by regularizing the supply of forced labour to the plantations, were bold attempts to find means of creating and encouraging new modes of production. The Combination Act and the Riot Act assured, in principle, that these could grow without countervailing organization.

Theatre has always been a better guide to London than law. In spite of the Duke of Newcastle's repression of the West End stage, the plebeian theatre at Bartholomew Fair kept Londoners laughing. Bankers, politicians, nonconformists and parsons, the beau monde and the cyphering cits were all made fun of before the thousands of common Londoners who in the summer the South Sea Bubble burst (1720) attended the two weeks of the fair held at Smithfield. In *The Broken Stock Jobbers: Or, Work for the Bailliffs* they would have seen Mr Pluckwell, a Director, and Mr Transfer, a Banker, swindle first Lord Equipage, then Sir Frippery Upstart, Dr Sine-Cure, and Headless, before themselves succumbing to the crash.[31] The sailors, the veterans, the weavers and throwsters, the former

[29] 9 George I, c. 22 (1723). E. P. Thompson, *Whigs and Hunters: The Origin of the Black Act* (1975), p. 23.
[30] Anon., *Select Trials at the Sessions House in the Old Bailey* (1742), vol. i, p. 81.
[31] Sybil Rosenfeld, *The Theatre of the London Fairs in the 18th Century* (Cambridge, 1960), ch. 2, describes these years at Bartholomew Fair, its 'theatrical heyday'.

slaves would have laughed heartily at these scenes where the hypocrisy of rulers pretending to motives of pure benevolence was exposed
as ruthless egotism. Not only could this audience recognize the noise
of capital's money circuit – the chatter of speculators, the whispers
of rumour-mongers, the chink of the teller – but it had heard the
explosion of cannon, the cry of the ship's wounded, the pigeon talk
of slaves such as were transported aboard the *Liberty* or the *Hope*,
the names of two of the South Sea Company's slavers. If the theatre
at Bartholomew Fair staged greed as comedy, across town at the
Tyburn Theatre it was presented as tragedy, and it was the same
at Execution Dock in Wapping, where many of the 400 to 500
pirates hanged between 1716 and 1726 suffered.[32] One unfortunate
malefactor hanged at Tyburn in 1717 had his last speech recorded:
'Men, Women, and Children, I come hither to hang like a Pendu-
lum to a Watch, for endeavouring to be Rich too Soon.' He was
guilty of nothing more than 'out-witting the Directors of the
Bank of England by a sort of Collusive Practice, and that Body
Corporate has play'd the same Game in their Turn, by over-
reaching the Bankers, and establishing themselves by an Act of
Parliament'.

While greed and repression had thus attained new meaning to
people of Sheppard's generation, the experience of effective, collective direct action was also renewed despite legislative repression.
As in 1675 and 1697, the Spitalfields weavers rebelled once again in
1719–20 to defend their interests. As on the previous occasions, a
distinct pattern may be detected of fruitless petitioning to Parliament, recourse to direct action, military repression and finally legislative reconciliation.

In 1717 the East India Company began to import, besides the raw
silk from India and China upon which the Spitalfields industry
depended, printed cottons and calicoes which directly threatened
the silk industry.[33] In June 1719 the weavers assembled in Spitalfields
and the Mint. A magistrate, John Lade, leading a force of twenty
constables, entered the sanctuary, proclaimed the Riot Act, and

[32] Marcus Rediker, '"Under the Banner of King Death": The Social World of
Anglo-American Pirates, 1716 to 1726', *The William and Mary Quarterly*, 3rd
Series, vol. xxxviii (April 1981), p. 226.
[33] John Entick, *A New and Accurate History and Survey of London, Westminster,
Southwark and Places Adjacent* (1766), pp. 376 ff.

arrested two weavers, John Colson and Isaac Shard, both of Spital-fields. Lade wrote to the Secretary of State:[34]

I shall only add that the Vox Populi, or the Rumour of the Mob, was not disrespectful to his Majesty or His Government, but the word was Must the Poor Weavers Starve? Shall the Ingy (meaning East India) Callicoes be worne whilst the Poor Weavers and their Families perish?

In the autumn the weavers petitioned Parliament against 'Ingy' calicoes. Papers brought to the attention of the House of Lords showed that Indian weavers got only 2d. a day. 'There will be thousands out of work before Winter,' they were told. In May 1720 the weavers assembled in 'extraordinary Numbers in the Old Palace Yard, Westminster ... begging the Lords as they pass'd by to commiserate the poor Weavers'. A lord met the weavers

just at the door, and asked whither those fellows were going? 'Going, my Lord,' answered one of them pertly, 'why we are going to be starved.' [The Horse Guards were called out] and with the flats of their Swords oblig'd 'em to retire, which they did in good Order, only as they went off they unrigg'd a few Callico Ladies.[35]

Episodes of 'callico unrigging' became more frequent. Vials of aqua fortis were thrown upon calico gowns, petticoats and mantuas. It was an effective action, for Parliament quickly acted to prohibit the use of calicoes and to expand domestic silk markets to buttons and buttonholes. In the next year another Act was passed to encourage the silk industry, granting silk exporters a drawback upon the tariffs they had paid on imported raw materials.[36] Mass direct action thus led to legislative compromise; the later custom of 'nailing people' maintained the threat. Francis Place, perhaps the century's most well-known 'industrious apprentice', recollected this Twelfth Day custom. Armed with hammers and a quantity of nails, apprentice boys hammered the silk skirts and coat-tails of the Quality into the wooden fronts of the pastry shops where they had paused to examine

[34] For most of the eighteenth century there were two 'Secretaries of State', one for northern and one for southern affairs. By the end of the century these two offices had evolved into 'Foreign Secretary' and 'Home Secretary' respectively.
[35] The Original Weekly Journal, 7 May 1720; The Daily Post, 5 May 1720; The Weekly Journal or Saturday Post, 7 May 1720.
[36] 8 George I, c. 15 (1721).

the holiday cakes.[37] For an instant, the rage of the well-dressed met the exultation of the ragged children, a temporary reversal of the class emotions provoked by status designations of clothing. Jack Sheppard understood and expertly manipulated these appearances. His escapes may now occupy our attention.

IV

The first escape we consider was not Jack's at all, but one in which he helped. Once Edgworth Bess had brought him the spike end of a halbert that almost enabled him to break out of St Anne's Roundhouse. So when, in the spring of 1723, she found herself confined in the St Giles's Roundhouse, he assisted her escape. 'I have sometimes procured her Liberty, and she at others had done her utmost to obtain mine, and at other times she has again betrayed me into the hands of Justice.' They robbed together, they were confined together, they escaped together. Following his break with Mr Wood, she helped him set up in Fulham and later in Spitalfields. One source says that she lived with him as a common-law wife, another that she was 'always look'd upon as the Wife of John Sheppard'. The courts and the prisons tended to treat them as if they were married: they were confined together in the same apartment in New Prison, and in March 1726, two years after Sheppard was hanged, when Bess came up to trial, the court reporter listed 'Sheppard' as the first among her several aliases.[38]

They formed a partnership of unsteady mutual assistance that had to be continuously renewed. She was a 'froe' or a 'mort' – that is, a wife or a mistress.[39]

> Here's a Health to all the prigs who pike about
>   the rum-start
> And spend all they get on the froes and the morts
> And think not of a rope or a cart

was the popular drinking toast. Jack certainly paid for the services of his female companions. They generally fenced his stolen goods.

---

[37] Mary Thale (ed.), *The Autobiography of Francis Place (1771–1854)* (Cambridge, 1971), pp. 64–5.
[38] *The Proceedings*, 2–7 March 1726.
[39] Anon., *A New Canting Dictionary* (1725).

First his mother, and then his morts did this, though they treated the goods as gifts rather than payments. During the 1720s several women found themselves accounting in court for the possession of stolen goods by entering the plea, 'Jack gave it to me.' When Kate Cook was tried in December 1725 for burglary she defended the possession of a stolen silver-handled knife, fork and spoon, all hidden in her stockings, by saying she 'had them from Jack Sheppard'. She added, 'with a vulgar double Entendre, that she was Jack Sheppard's Washerwoman, and had many a time wash'd his three Pieces betwixt her –.' Kate Keys, tried under the same indictment, defended herself by saying that she was a seamstress who had worked for two years as a neighbour to Jack Sheppard when he was an apprentice in Wych Street. Charged with receiving nine ells of stolen holland cloth, she said, 'Sheppard brought it to her to make some Shirts.' When Elizabeth Lyon came to trial in March 1726 on a charge of stealing six silver spoons from a Clerkenwell hog butcher's house she defended herself similarly. Kissing the spoons, she said, 'These were left me by my dear, John Sheppard, and I have just fetched them out of pawn.'[40] But Jack's gifts could not infallibly confer immunity: Edgworth Bess was found guilty of felony and transported to the plantations, and although Kate Keys was acquitted, Kate Cook was fined and imprisoned on the charge of receiving stolen goods. She earned the court's scorn when she 'pretended to be ignorant of his ever being in *Newgate*, tho' his twice escaping from thence had been the common Discourse of the whole Nation'.

Sheppard ended up in the St Giles's Roundhouse because he was betrayed first by his brother, Tom, and then by his friend, James Sykes. Tom, who besides having been a lady's servant had been to sea and had become something of a carpenter himself, was committed to Newgate for robbing a house in Clare Market. Hoping to procure his release he impeached his brother and Elizabeth Lyon. However, to be impeached was one thing, to be apprehended another. Sykes lured him into a trap. They were friends, 'brothers in Iniquity'. 'Hell and Fury', as he was known, was one of the greatest runners of the day, a well-known athlete at both long and middle distances.[41]

---

[40] *The Proceedings*, 4–9 December 1724, 2–7 March 1726.
[41] Gerald Howson, *The Thief-Taker General* (1970). For running footmen see Montague Shearman, *Athletics and Football* (1887), ch. 1. For an association between foot racing and footpads see Anon., *Tricks of the Town Laid Open: Or, a Companion for Country Gentlemen* (1747), 12th letter.

This champion appealed to Sheppard's sporting instincts and bowling skills, saying that he knew of 'two Chubs' from whom they might win some money playing skittles at a victualling house in Seven Dials. One of these fish was not a chub but a shark: he took Sheppard to Justice Parry, who confined him to the Roundhouse.

In less than three hours he was out. He was confined in the top floor. He cut through the ceiling, untiled the roof, and with the aid of a sheet and blanket lowered himself into the churchyard, climbed a wall, and joined a gathering throng which had been attracted to the scene by the falling roof tiles. That was in April 1724. From then until the end of November the saga of his escapes grew, astounding ever-increasing numbers of people for their daring and dexterity. Even in April some of his talents were manifest: his skills already appeared marvellous; he seemed to embody the magic of the 'cunning artificer'. One European scholar has characterized this period as an age of 'the great confinement'.[42] Doubtless, incarceration, in its many forms and for many purposes, was a major theme that can easily and exactly be particularized for London in the early eighteenth century. Yet the theme of incarceration brought with it a counter-theme of excarceration. As the theme of incarceration was played out in workhouse, factory, hospital, school and ship, so the counterpoint of excarceration was played out in escapes, flights, desertions, migrations and refusals.

The first English textile factory was built near Derby between 1718 and 1721, and William Hutton provides us with the first voice from inside the factory.

To this curious, but wretched place I was bound apprentice for seven years, which I always considered the most unhappy of my life ... My parents through mere necessity put me to labour before Nature had made me able. Low as the engines were, I was too short to reach them. To remedy this defect, a pair of high pattens were fabricated, and lashed to my feet, which I dragged after me till time lengthened my stature.

The factory employed 300 people, mostly children. Their task was to mend the threads. 'From the fineness of the materials, the ravelled state of the slips and bobbins, and the imprudence of children, much waste is made, which [offered] another motive of correction; and when correction is often inflicted, it steels the breast of the inflictor.'

[42] Michel Foucault, *Discipline and Punish: The Birth of the Prison*, trans. Alan Sheridan (1977).

Hutton was not impressed by the single automaton that wound, twisted and doubled the silk in five huge rooms: it was the cold that he remembered, for the factory was warmed by a single stove. The 26,000 moving wheels did not matter to him except in so far as they provided the environment where cruelty could flourish, whose scars he carried to his grave.[43]

Why was this factory not placed in London? The transcript of a murder trial held in London in January 1724 provides a partial answer, in that it enables us to see the class relations of work from the inside. In 1724 Richard Coats of Stepney was tried for the murder of Alexander Tailor. He had heaved a 'Throwster's Star' (a wheel or pulley-block attached to a drive-shaft) at Tailor's head, giving him a mortal wound. The crime took place in a Stepney throwing mill (throwing was to silk as spinning was to wool). Tailor was a servant hired to knot broken threads. When he refused to obey the mill turner's command to repair three threads, Coats, a journeyman, told him

not to treat a Man who was his Better, with saucy Language; that upon this the Deceased gave him very saucy and reviling Language, and persisting in his saucy Carriage, he followed him to catch him; but the Boy, the Deceased, running round the Mill, and still reviling him, and then being stooping, and raising up his Head, received the Blow on his Head.

A jury had no trouble in altering the charge to manslaughter: at that time 'sauciness' meant not a venal kind of impertinence or cheekiness but the kind of violation of subordination worthy of serious reprobation. 'The hired Servant' was punished, it seems clear, less for his lax response to his task than for his assumption of equality in manner and speech with his 'Betters'. The refusal of subordination was a characteristic of the London labour force, and it explains why new experiments in industrial organization, such as the factory, were placed outside of London. And it led to the delight that greeted Sheppard's escapes.

Jack was confined again. One evening in front of the Prince of Wales' palace in Leicesterfields a crowd gathered around a quarrelling gentleman and 'a Woman of the Town', enabling Jack to

[43] W. Hutton, *The History of Derby* (1791).

pick the gent's pocket of his watch. In the confusion following the discovery of this fact, the Serjeant of the Guards at Leicester House seized Jack, who was carried off to New Prison in Clerkenwell. Edgworth Bess was detained at the Roundhouse, where she had visited Jack, so she was also taken to New Prison. They were secured in what was reckoned the safest part of the prison, 'Newgate Ward', and Jack was loaded down with a pair of double links and basils weighing 14 lbs. each. But he sawed off his fetters, and with 'unheard of Diligence and Dexterity' cut through an iron bar. He then bored through a muntin, or oak bar 9 ins. thick, another work 'of great Skill and Labour'. Then he fastened sheets, gowns and petticoats together, enabling Elizabeth Lyon to descend safely to the grounds, 25 ft beneath them, where he joined her, only to realize that they had escaped from one prison to land in another. New Prison and Clerkenwell Bridewell were contiguous. Jack drove his gimblets and piercers into the 22-foot wall and, using these for steps and hand-holds, he and his companion were free again in the early morning light of Whit Monday 1724.

The escape was remarkable in two respects. First, among the *cognoscenti*, it was regarded as his masterwork. While the escape from the condemned hold of Newgate made 'a far greater Noise in the World', the London gaolkeepers regarded the New Prison escape as the most 'miraculous' ever performed in England, so they preserved the broken chains and bars 'to Testifie, and preserve the Memory of this extraordinary Event and Villain'. Second, the escape occurred at an important juncture in the development of the class differentiation of urban space. 'London is essentially a city of antithesis,' Henry Mayhew wrote of the nineteenth-century city. In the eighteenth century this 'topographical essence' was being formed, as we can see in the urban struggle of which Sheppard's escape was an instance.

New Prison was a recent addition to a concentration of carceral institutions in Clerkenwell, a part of town through which livestock passed to the city and through which the Quality passed to the country (Sadler's Wells, Bagnigge Wells, the London Spa and Merlin's Cave). In the midst of these movements stood the walled and forbidding buildings designed for coercion and incarceration: the Quaker workhouse, Clerkenwell workhouse, Bridewell, New Prison, the madhouse and the charity school. The committees governing the Quaker workhouse suggested calling the place a 'Colledge, which comprehands both hospitall, workhouse and

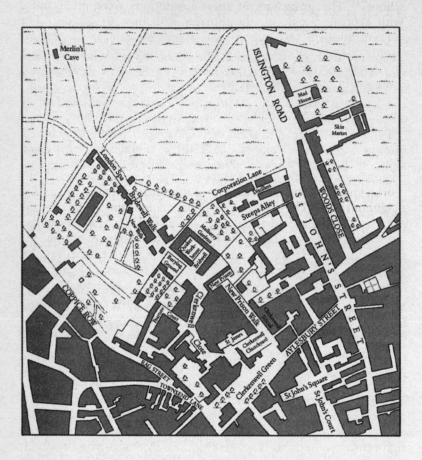

Map 1:   Clerkenwell and New Prison in 1746

school'.[44] The governors of these institutions were preoccupied with keeping people in, the inmates with how to get out. The concentration of such places in Clerkenwell amidst the pleasure haunts of the bourgeoisie defined it as an upper-class zone of the city hostile to the labouring poor. This would have added to the dramatic impact of Sheppard's feat.

Newly escaped from New Prison, Jack had three months of liberty. He robbed on the highway. He robbed in Hampstead. He stopped coaches. He broke into shops. A detail from one of these robberies anticipates a major theme of the eighteenth century. In June he joined an apprentice mathematical-instrument-maker (whose son became the first secretary of the Sons of Liberty in New York) and a cooper in order to rob a master tailor in his old neighbourhood. They entered the house at night and Sheppard took for his own use a 'Padesuoy Suit of Cloathes' (fashionable Italian corded silks that would enable him to 'make a Figure among the Beau Monde'). He was then 'employ'd in Ransaking the Trunks, Boxes, &c. for Taylor's-Cabbage which, to his agreeable Surprise, consisted of Cash, Bonds, Notes, and other easy Moveables as amounted to the value of Three Hundred Pounds'. Jack was surprised to find 'cash'; we are surprised that he expected 'cabbage'. Boxed wealth took the form of 'cabbage' (a technical term of various definition but denoting some by-product of the tailor's labour), not of money.

The robbery that got him in trouble again took place in mid-July. With William Field and Blueskin he robbed his old master, Mr Kneebone; Jack had surreptitiously cut the bars of the cellar windows in the days preceding the break-in. Inside the house he picked the locks of doors and cupboards while Blueskin, his partner, stood by with tinder and candles. They made off with '108 Yards of Broad Woollen Cloth, five yards of blue Bays, a light Tye-Wig, and Beaver-Hat, two Silver Spoons, an Handkerchief and a Penknife', all to the value of £50.

Upon discovery of his losses Kneebone advertised for the stolen goods in the newspapers and notified Jonathan Wild, the 'thief-taker General', whose complex and parasitic system of training thieves and impeaching thieves, of receiving stolen goods and returning lost property had become in these years a system of

[44] Beck and Ball, op. cit., p. 365.

municipal policing.[45] Wild fulfilled the warnings uttered by Gerrard
Winstanley two generations earlier: 'Indeed this Government may
well be called the Government of highwaymen, who hath stolen
the Earth from the younger brethren by force, and holds it from
them by force.'[46] Wild gave contemporary meaning to that query
addressed by William Walwyn to the troops who led the Bishopsgate mutiny in 1649: 'Whether Julius Caesar, Alexander the
Great, William Duke of Normandy or any other great conqueror
of the world were any other than great lawless thieves, and whether
it be not as unjust to take laws and liberties from our neighbours as
to take goods one from another of the same nation?'[47] Sheppard had
refused to cooperate with Wild, never using his receiving networks,
never begging his influence with the Old Bailey. Yet, 'impeach or
be hanged' was the name of the game. Jonathan Wild found Edgworth Bess at a brandy shop in Temple Bar. He threatened, she
wheedled. A warrant was obtained, and one of Wild's men was sent
to capture Sheppard in a chamber in Rosemary Lane, owned by
Blueskin's mother. After an exchange of pistol-fire Sheppard was
retaken and confined to Newgate, where in the middle of August
he awaited trial on a triple felony indictment. He was found guilty
and although 'he beg'd earnestly for Transportation to the most
extream Foot of his Majesty's Dominions' he was returned to the
Condemned Hold, under sentence of death by hanging for robbing
a shopkeeper.

In the eighteenth century Newgate was a stinking, deathly place.
In 1719 Captain Alexander Smith wrote, 'Newgate is a dismal
prison ... a place of calamity ... a habitation of misery, a confused
chaos ... a bottomless pit of violence, a Tower of Babel where all
are speakers and no hearers.'[48] About thirty people died in it a year.
Physicians refused to enter it. Pedestrians in passing the gateway
held their noses. Prisoners might urinate from the upper windows,
passing citizens might be doused with the contents of a chamber-pot.

[45] The Proceedings, 12–14 August 1724, gives details of the Kneebone robbery.
Howson, Thief-Taker General (1970).
[46] Gerrard Winstanley, The Law of Freedom in a Platform or True Magistracy Restored
(1652) in George Sabine (ed.), The Works of Gerrard Winstanley (Ithaca, NY,
1941), pp. 526, 529.
[47] William Walwyn, The English Soldier's Standard (1649), quoted in Brailsford,
op. cit., p. 499.
[48] Alexander Smith, A Complete History (1719). Robin Evans, The Fabrication of
Virtue: English Prison Architecture, 1750–1840 (Cambridge, 1982), pp. 34–41.

Foul-mouthed women, 'a troop of hell cats', diverted themselves by cursing through a grate adjoining the foot-passage. Yet, Newgate contained a society whose intricacies were of vital importance, and they were by no means under the absolute control of guards. In fact, the guard-to-prisoner ratio was 1:90 in 1724, which may be contrasted with a 1:6 ratio in Attica in 1982. Therefore, access to exercise, music, visiting, drink, food, sex, dancing, cards, dice and books was more favourable to the prisoners than it would be today. Let us look more closely.

Newgate was a five-storey structure dating from the fifteenth century. After the Great Fire of 1666 it was restored at a cost of £10,000 with an ornate, sumptuous exterior. At the base of one of its pilasters was a sculpture in bas-relief of Dick Whittington's famous cat: thus did that archetypal familiar of social mobility and accumulation come to overlook the City's malefactors, and therefore popular irony dubbed the place 'the Whit'.[49] According to a description of 1724 there were four parts to Newgate: the Keeper's Lodge, where ale, stout and tobacco were sold; the Master's Side, which consisted of thirteen common charity wards each holding thirty prisoners in a 26 ft by 32 ft confinement; the Press Yard, where prisoners of conscience and rebels were confined – Quakers, Jacobites – but terrible enough to cause the historian of Newgate to wonder how man could have been made in God's image; and the Condemned Hold in the cellars.

Wives could stay overnight. 'The Female Gentry of the Hundreds of Drury' could solicit custom. Children lived there. Pets, pigs, pigeons and poultry were permitted until 1792. Newspapers were delivered daily. A gymnasium of sorts provided a place for exercise on the second floor. A 'Free and Easy Club' with by-laws to 'promote tumult and disorder' organized drink and hops for singing and dancing. One of the strong drinks brewed in the Whit, a place as noted for the variety of its potions as the irony of its expressions, was called 'South Sea'. The gin brewed in Newgate was called 'Cock-my-Cap', 'Kill-Grief', 'Comfort', 'Poverty', 'Meat and Drink' or 'Washing and Lodging'. All these could be obtained in the prison for money. Hard cash – 'rhino' – governed. In *The Quaker's Opera*, a play about Sheppard's escapes, the two turnkeys,

---

[49] H. D. Kalman, 'Rebuilding Newgate Prison', *Architectural History*, vol. xii (1969); Anon., *A New Canting Dictionary* (1725).

Careful and Rust, agree, 'You and I know the Sweets of touching the Rhino.'[50]

In 1649 Winstanley asked, 'Did the light of Reason make this Law, that if one man have not such abundance of the earth as to give to others he borrowed of, that he that did lend should imprison the other, and starve his body in a close room?' And he wrote, 'For talking of love is no love, it is acting of love in righteousnesse, which the Spirit Reason, our Father delights in. And this is to relieve the oppressed, to let goe the prisoner, to open bags and barns that the earth may be a common treasury.' The tradition of excarceration was strong; moreover, it was one preserved more by acting than by talking. Everyone would have known about John Meffs, a Spital-fields man and son of a French weaver, because he was the man in the tumbril who was saved from a hanging in 1719 after the hangman was arrested for debt. Meffs was reconfined in Newgate. He escaped in 1721.

Three years later in 1724 a more rigorous regime was established in Newgate. Four trusties called the 'Partners' maintained order among the prisoners by exacting the worst enormities: they con-fiscated gifts from visitors, they broke into the charity-box and took the money, they stole the bread ration, they refused to allow visitors to bring beer in. It was in the midst of this regime that Sheppard made his fourth escape. It was beautifully timed: not only was the internal government of the prison under unusual stress, but the Royal Court was in Windsor, so the 'nine unhappy Wretches' in the Condemned Hold had a longer respite, and Bartholomew Fair was opened, so the streets were fuller than usual of noise, bustle and disguising. He had planned to escape with two others, a Radnor teacher and a Cambridge man, but their death warrants arrived too soon. On the day his death warrant came down he managed to obtain some privacy from the eye of the turnkey, which enabled him to get a 'Spike asunder'. He inserted himself into a small aperture that he had enlarged in the wall and with the help of visitors on the other side was dragged into freedom. 'Then like a Freeman [he] took his Ramble through the City and came to Spitalfields and there lay with Edgworth Bess.'[51]

The following day Sheppard met a friend, William Page, a

---

[50] Thomas Walker, *The Quaker's Opera* (1728).
[51] He stayed at the Paul's Head in Spitalfields; *The Proceedings*, 4–9 December 1729.

butcher's apprentice in Clare Market. Dressed in blue butcher's frocks Sheppard and Page took to the northern drove roads and made for Northamptonshire, where, in Chipping Warden, Page had relatives who were poor and welcoming. In 1724 Chipping Warden was an unenclosed parish whose poor subsisted upon pastoral common rights. It was also a minor point within the web of routes that supplied calves and cattle from Yorkshire to London markets. 'If a fellow need a place at once remote yet connected to London, this was it.'[52] But because of their poverty, the relatives were not able to keep Sheppard and Page, who consequently returned to London after three days. Edgworth Bess had again been apprehended by Jonathan Wild. The shopkeepers of Drury Lane and the Strand, especially Kneebone who had refused to sign a petition of mercy for Sheppard, were all under the greatest apprehension. The 'Quaker' declaimed against Sheppard, 'Woe to England, for Sheppard is escaped; Woe to the Shopkeepers, and woe to the Dealers in Ware, for the roaring Lion is Abroad, and their Goods will not lie on their Hands.'[53] The shopkeepers fortified their houses and hired guards.

It was a Drury Lane bailiff, one Ireton, who was to organize the hunt for Sheppard. A cobbler in Bishopsgate and a milkman in Islington had recognized Sheppard and the news spread. Page and Sheppard saw a watchmaker's shop open that evening in Fleet Street with only a boy to guard it. 'Jack Sheppard ... bade him stick to his Tools, and not use his Master to such ill Habits of working so late.'[54] Later, they robbed the shop, pawned one of the watches, went out drinking, and then sought out the milkman and upset his pans and pipkins, covering him in cream. But it was too late to rectify the damage of their discovery, so once again, with money in their pockets this time, they left London, going north to Finchley Common. A posse pursued them and soon they were apprehended. Taken back to London in a coach-and-four, Sheppard tried once to escape by springing from the Keeper's grip at the door of Newgate. He failed and was once again in Newgate, this time taken to the 'Castle' and fastened to the floor with double fetters.

Now began the heady days of his fame. His deeds became 'the

---

[52] Dr Jeanette Neeson, the modern historian of agrarian relations in eighteenth-century Northamptonshire, has informed me of this.
[53] *The Quaker's Opera* (1728).
[54] *The Proceedings*, 4–9 December 1724, trial of William Page.

JACK SHEPHERD
Drawn from the Life

A. the Hole he made in the Chimney when he got loose

Printed for and Sold by T. Bowles Print Seller next the Chapter House in St Pauls Ch Yard & I. Bowles Print Seller over against St Books Mkt

Jack Sheppard

Common Discourse of the whole Nation'. The 'common People' went 'Mad about him'. It was a week of the greatest 'idleness among Mechanicks that has been known in London'. Porters were unavailable. Butchers, shoemakers and barbers crowded the ale houses. Ballad writers subsisted 'very comfortably'. Women and children kept watch at the gallows lest Jack be hanged 'Incog.' at night.[55] The great, the fast, the strong, the talented and the beautiful sought his company in Newgate and, if they could pay the Keeper, they got it. James Figgs, a powerful six-footer, since 1719 the first generally acknowledged English heavyweight boxing champion, was one of the first visitors. Sheppard promised to drink a glass with him along the Tyburn procession. A young woman and friend of his mother did a daily washing for him and brought him beer and 'necessaries'. When several divines finished remonstrating with him, he declared them all 'Ginger-bread Fellows' who were visiting merely 'to form Papers and Ballads out of his Behaviour'. Mr Wagstaff, the Ordinary of Newgate, urged him to concentrate on the hereafter rather than upon devising methods of escape. Sheppard answered in proletarian materialist philosophy: 'One File's worth all the Bibles in the world.' To the visiting journalists he passed his opinion of the criminal-justice system. He deplored the practice of thief-catching and of offering awards for stolen goods. Thief-takers deserved the gallows just as much as thieves did: 'They hang by Proxy, while we do it fairly in Person.' He declared himself against 'whidling' or impeachment. In chapel one Sunday a man belonging to the Lord Mayor asked one of the turnkeys which one was Sheppard. Jack called out, 'Yes, sir, I am the Sheppard, and all the jailors in the town are my flock, and I cannot stir into the country but they are all at my heels baughing after me.'

Jack used to say that if his frequent robberies were 'ill in one respect, they were as good in another; and that though he cared not for working much himself, yet he was desirous that others should not stand idle, more especially those of his own trade, who were always repairing of his breaches'. His acumen as a political economist was no less than his respect for brother craftsmen. He told Mr Robbins, the City smith, that he'd procured him a small job, and that whoever it was that put the spikes on the Condemned Hold was an honest man, 'for a better piece of metal I never wrought upon in my life'. The most original economist and moralist of the time was Bernard Mandeville, whose 'remarks' in *The Fable of the Bees* might seem as if they had been part of such discussions as Sheppard was leading. In 1705 Mandeville had written:

> The Worst of all the Multitude
> Did something for the common Good

[55] Anon., *The History*, p. 148.

remarking that thieves and housebreakers maintain the employment of 'half the Smiths in the Nation', who produce the abundance of ornamental and defensive workmanship of locks, gratings and bars. In 1723 Mandeville extended the 'remarks' by eight pages to show how the thief who robs the miser increases the volume in circulation, or how the highwayman who new rigs a harlot from top to toe in satin employs a hundred different tradesmen. They are passages of vitality in a work that observes the beneficent operations of self-interested egoism. He is the precursor of both Adam Smith and Rousseau in discovering that contradiction was the motor of capitalist accumulation. 'The short-sighted Vulgar in the Chain of Causes seldom can see further than one link, but those who can enlarge their View, and will give themselves the Leisure of gazing on the Prospect of concatenated Events, may, in a hundred Places see Good spring up and pullulate from Evil.'[56]

Sheppard's comments on political economy, theology and the justice system caused a traffic that maintained his courage, confused his guardians and provided him with money. Still he complained, 'But I wanted still a more useful Metal, a Crow, a Chisel, a File, and a Saw or two, those Weapons being more useful to me than all the mines of Mexico.' Late in September he was removed from the Condemned Hold because it was suspected that he was in communication with his brother, who, since his trial and sentence to transportation in August, was confined in one of the common wards above. After a file was discovered, he was taken to the 'Stone Castle' almost at the top of the prison and chained with two iron staples to the floor. The turnkeys observed and checked his irons regularly. They constructed new leg-irons and added handcuffs. Never had he been so thoroughly secured.

On 9 October Blueskin was apprehended. Animated by Sheppard's examples, the felons on the common side had cut several bars asunder. Some sawed off their chains, 'the rest Huzzaing, and making Noises ... to prevent the Workmen being heard; and in two Hours time more, if their Design had not been discovered, near One Hundred Vilains had been loose into the World'.[57] The next day Jack Sheppard's brother, chained with ninety-five other felons, was marched from Newgate down to the docks for transportation to

---

[56] Mandeville, *The Fable of the Bees: Or, Private Vices, Publick Benefits*, ed. Philip Harth (1970), pp. 68, 118; Lucio Colletti, 'Mandeville, Rousseau, and Smith' is a remarkable essay in *From Rousseau to Lenin* (New York, 1972).
[57] Anon., *The History*, p. 152.

Annapolis. On 14 October the Sessions at Old Bailey opened. Blueskin was brought to trial and, stopping to have a glass of wine with Jonathan Wild in the court house, he said, 'You may put in a word for me, as well as for another Person.' Wild replied, 'You are certainly a dead Man, and will be tuck'd up very speedily.' Whereupon Blueskin drew his penknife and lunged for Wild's throat. While he failed to kill Wild, the attempt inspired a great ballad and the confusion resulting from the attempt contributed to Sheppard's most spectacular escape.[58]

For Jack, meanwhile, it was 'Now or Never, Neck or Nothing.' In the afternoon of 14 October one of the turnkeys who made daily inspections of his irons escorted the Keeper of Clerkenwell Bridewell, the Clerk of the Westminster Gatehouse and Captain Geary, Keeper of New Prison, and two others on an inspection tour of Jack's handcuffs, leg irons and cell. Following their departure Jack went to work overcoming a series of obstacles that would become as deeply ingrained in one part of the memory of the English working class as those obstacles that stood in the way of the *Pilgrim's Progress* in another. Christian trespassed at Doubting Castle, whose owner Giant Despair put him in a dungeon where Christian lamented until he remembered Promise, the key in his bosom, that opened door after door.

Sheppard got out of his handcuffs. Then with 'main strength' he twisted asunder a small link in the chain binding his legs. He drew up the fetlocks tight about his thighs. He reached up the chimney, removing an iron bar from it with the help of parts of the broken leg links. The bar enabled him to remove some of the chimney masonry, and so he ascended to the room above, the Red Room, where the Preston rebels had been kept and whose door had not been opened in seven years. He found here a large nail that enabled him to break the wall, dislodge the bolt and enter the chapel. There he broke off a spike from one of the railings in the chapel which helped him wrench off the bolt-box of the next door. This and the next two doors were all bolted on the other side. He was working in the pitch-black. A final door allowed him access to the lower leads of the roof. The city lay below him. He knew 'that the smallest Accident would still spoil the whole Workmanship', so he did not

[58] 'Blueskin's Ballad' or 'The Newgate Garland'. Sometimes attributed to Swift, sometimes to Gay, it exists in several versions (*A New Canting Dictionary*, for instance, prints some stanzas not found elsewhere; Song XIV).

Jack Sheppard's escape from Newgate

risk leaping on to one of the adjoining houses, but retraced his steps
through the doors, the chapel, the Red Room, the chimney, back
into the Stone Castle where he retrieved his blanket. Once again on
the roof, he drove the chapel spike into the wall, attached the blanket
to it, and gently lowered himself on to a neighbouring roof. He
stole softly down two flights of stairs. 'I was once more, contrary
to my Expectation and that of all Mankind, a Freeman.'

He tore his cap, coat and stockings, so as a 'Beggar-Fellow' he
visited a cellar ale-house in Charing Cross to hear the talk, and wish
'that a Curse might fall on those who should betray him'. The next
day he heard the ballads about him. He robbed a clothes-dealer in
Monmouth Street and cut a figure as a 'Botcher'. The talk was that

he was with the smugglers, and his mother, to be sure, begged him heartily to leave the kingdom. Dressed now as a porter he paid a visit to Mr Appleby, the printer of 'last Dying Speeches'.

On 29 October he robbed a pawnshop in Drury Lane to furnish himself with a black suit, a silver sword, diamonds, watches and 'other pretty little Toys'. He hired a coach and, accompanied by his 'sweethearts', he began his triumphant tour through the city that had been his home and now became the theatre of his climactic and defiant last act. Through the densely populated weaving suburbs of Spitalfields, Sheppard rode. Along Bishopsgate with its thick traffic his coach carried him, passing the sombre workhouse. His coach drove through Newgate itself, an itinerary of 'idleness' and 'sauciness'. Sheppard spent that day, the last of his free life, parading himself through the ale-houses and gin-shops of Clare Market to an audience of hundreds of curious and attentive ears. Late in the evening he was retaken, after fifteen days of flaunting his liberty in the face of London.

How did he do it? One historian of his life said 'that the Devil came in Person and assisted him'. Another compared him to Fortunatus, whose magical cap could make him invisible. A third compared him to Proteus, the ancient one of the sea who, as described in the *Odyssey*, eluded captors by assuming different shapes. The comparisons are mythical or magical; but Sheppard's techniques were practical and characteristic of the eighteenth-century London human being. His excellence lay in the manipulative genius with the tool and the extraordinary dexterity of hand and limb that were much prized in this metropolis of skilled craftspeople. His elusiveness and attraction alike relied on apparel (a beggar, a botcher, a butcher, a carpenter, a porter, and finally a spark indeed), which was the city's major amusement and industry, as well as the major social and economic signifier of its individual persons. Thus his magic was of his time and place.

Back in Newgate Sheppard was painted handsomely by James Thornhill, Hogarth's father-in-law, and the official court painter to George I.[59] Daniel Defoe probably visited him at this time. The attention isolated him from the other prisoners, who complained,

---

[59] Bleackley, op. cit., writes that Thornhill set up his easel in the dungeon and painted Sheppard emphasizing the strong, sensitive hands. Bleackley also reports the rumours that the portrait ended up in a bar on Pennsylvania Avenue, Washington, DC, but I have not been able to verify this.

'we have been hindered from going to chapel because the keepers
... make a show of the condemned prisoners in the chapel by which
they raise great sumes of money'.[60] On 10 November Sheppard was
conveyed to the Court of King's Bench 'thro' the most numerous
Croud of People that ever was seen in London'. He told Justice
Powis that he never had 'Opportunity to obtain his Bread in an
honest Way'. He refused to wheedle on any who had assisted him.
He was reprimanded for profanity. He offered to demonstrate his
art: if they would put handcuffs on him, he would take them off
before their eyes. Sheppard had become a hero, to be used for bitter
political satire or to be admired for tenacity and indomitability. His
elevation to fame was a rise neither with, nor without, his class.
Almost as a figure of sport, he attained an 'individual fame' that
united 'the mob'.

'Mob' was an abbreviation of a Latinate neologism devised by
the ruling class in the early eighteenth century to describe the labouring poor beneath it: *mobile vulgus* was the cognate term. In
contrast to earlier designations of social groups two aspects of this
one require emphasis. First, its grandiloquence expressed the new
tone of imperious superiority which older terms, such as 'multitudes'
or 'host', did not. Second, despite the abbreviation, which purists
like Addison and Swift alike deplored, 'mob' retained the con-
notations with motion expressed by its cognate. In fact one might
as easily translate the term as 'the movement'. The 'mob' that
followed Sheppard's escapes was both an audience (for the ballads,
the papers, the book-makers) and a constellation of a world working
class. One historian of the eighteenth-century mob in England and
America sees a direct connection between Sheppard's accomplice
(the mathematical-instrument-maker who was transported) and the
revolutionary organizations formed in New York against the
Crown.[61] At the classic and most massive presence of the eighteenth-
century London working class, the Tyburn hanging, when Hero
and Mob looked at each other for signs of mutual recognition, when
Hero and Mob assessed one another's 'social contract', we may pause
for a final glance at the living Sheppard. The day of his hanging
was 16 November. Some customs of a hanging were allowed (he
could ride in an open cart), and others were not (he wore handcuffs

---

[60] CLRO, Sessions Papers, December 1724.
[61] Lloyd I. Rudolph, 'The Eighteenth Century Mob in America and Europe',
American Quarterly, vol. xi, no. 4 (winter 1959), pp. 466–7.

instead of the symbolic white gloves). Escape was on everyone's mind. In the previous June William Parkinson, a Leeds cloth-worker who had scoffed at Newgate religion, 'especially the Prayer for his Majesty', had attempted an escape along the route to Tyburn.[62] A penknife was confiscated from Sheppard in the Press Yard. None of the escape rumours materialized. Sheppard dangled in the 'Sheriff's picture frame' for fifteen minutes before a soldier cut him down and others tried to resuscitate him. For the balance of the day there were running skirmishes and subtle stratagems for the control of his corpse. The anatomists failed to possess it and he was decently buried.[63] This, if not the hanging that launched him into eternity, may count as his sixth and final escape. Not since the funeral of Robert Lockyer, seventy-five years earlier, when thousands of men and women wearing the Leveller green attended the execution of this leader of the Bishopsgate mutiny against service in Ireland, had such a vast proportion of the London population assembled.[64]

In the winter of 1725 the *British Journal* published a dialogue between Julius Caesar and Jack Sheppard. Sheppard complained that an account of his life would not be credited, yet he did not ravage the East or plunder the West. 'All my Actions were enterprized upon a justifiable Score.' Caesar cannot answer the arguments: 'I perceive by your Discourse, that you are a Leveller, and not to be conversed with upon such Subjects.' In the 1720s such 'discourse' was beyond the pale of polite or printed conversation. The important debates about liberty and the 'earthly Treasury' in the English Revolution could only be skirted in the 1720s. 'Levelling' could be referred to, but only to shut up any discussion. Yet the indication is that Sheppard's escapes had revived the conversation in impolite and vulgar contexts.

The printed and dramatic interpretation of his career appeared almost immediately, and was raucous and vigorous. John Thurmond's *Harlequin Sheppard* opened in Drury Lane two weeks after the hanging. Then, too, the famous 'Newgate Garland' was first heard:

[62] The Ordinary's *Account*, 15 June 1724.
[63] See my article, 'The Tyburn Riot Against the Surgeons', in Douglas Hay, Peter Linebaugh, Edward Thompson (eds), *Albion's Fatal Tree* (1975).
[64] S. R. Gardiner, *History of the Commonwealth and Protectorate 1649–1656*, vol. i (1903), p. 46.

Some say there are Courtiers of highest Renown
Who steal the King's gold and leave him but a Crown
Some say there are Peers and Parliament-men
Who meet once a Year to rob the Courtiers again.
        Let them all take a swing
        To pillage the king
And get a Blue Ribbon instead of the string,
        For Blueskin's sharp penknife hath set you at Ease,
        And Ev'ry Man round me may rob if he please.

Knaves of old, to hide Guilt by cunning Invention
Called Briberies Grants and plain robberies Pensions
Physicians and Lawyers (who take their Degrees
To be learned Rogues) call their Pilfering Fees
        Since this happy day
        Everyone may
Rob (safe as in office) upon the Highway
        For Blueskin's sharp penknife hath set you at Ease,
        And Ev'ry Man round me may rob if he please.

A few months after the hanging, the Earl of Macclesfield (who, as Lord Chancellor, had interviewed Sheppard in Westminster) was impeached from office, guilty of bribery and embezzlement in excess of £100,000. In *The Beggar's Opera*, Jeremy Twitcher asked, 'Why are the laws levelled against us? Are we more dishonest than the rest of mankind?' To which Mat of the Mint replied, 'We retrench the superfluities of mankind. The world is avaricious and I hate avarice.' The popular theatre of Southwark or Bartholomew Fair kept cockneys laughing at themes of repression and resistance. Amid the balladeers, acrobats, African animals and Merry Andrews, they could watch *Wat Tyler and Jack Straw; Or, the Mob Reformers* or *The Comical Humours of Justice Wantbrains. Robin Hood and Little John* was revived in the late 1720s at the fairs. In 1729 *The Beggar's Wedding; Or, Rackall the Gaol Keeper Outwitted* played at Southwark Fair, and at Bartholomew Fair a year earlier *The Quaker's Opera* opened. Interpretations of the Sheppard hanging, then, quickly fell into either a vulgar, carnival-fair tradition, or into a high-brow critique of the Walpole regime that depended on the classic conceit that compared the conqueror (Caesar, Alexander) to the criminal. While each could raise moral and even general historical questions, neither could do so in the context of the actual recent experiences of Londoners: the weavers' riots, the recomposition by immigration of the working population, the political repressions of the second decade, the new enclosed structures of coercion and discipline. Yet, Sheppard's became a legend that was important to English speakers for more than a century afterwards, because it, no less than the Samson story, which 'Free-Born' John Lilburne invoked during his imprisonment of 1647 and which Milton chose as his last poem to invoke regenerative sacrifice against slave-labour and imprisonment, was a story of freedom.

CHAPTER TWO

'OLD MR GORY'
AND THE THANATOCRACY

Did the light of Reason make this law, that some part
of mankinde should kill and hang another part of mankinde, that could not walk in their steps?

Gerrard Winstanley,
The New Law of Righteousness (1649)

One may destroy a man who makes war upon him,
or has discovered an enmity to his being, for the same
reason that he may kill a wolf or a lion; because they
are not under the ties of the common law of reason.

John Locke, *Second Treatise of Civil Government* (1690)

Milton's *Samson Agonistes* was written in the Restoration. It was a
defence of the revolution: 'Milton had lost confidence in the people,
and in the middling sort whom he had previously regarded as
natural leaders. He now put his hope in the efforts of regenerate
individuals,' writes Christopher Hill.[1] The genres presenting Sheppard's struggle for freedom were the burlesque and the ballad, yet
they succeeded in raising epic themes from the English Revolution
of 1640–60.

Broadly speaking, the English Revolution was a conflict among
three social forces. The bourgeoisie, led by Oliver Cromwell and
organized in Parliament, aroused the English proletariat to make
war against Charles I, the High Church and the aristocracy. Having
vanquished them, Cromwell then turned against his erstwhile class
ally, the many-headed multitude, which during the course of the
struggle against the King had developed a movement of teeming
freedom that was antithetical to the capitalist order that Cromwell
and Parliament sought to impose. The scale of these upheavals can
scarcely be exaggerated: an army electing its own officers; the first
democratic political party in world history; a complex discussion of

---

[1] *Milton and the English Revolution* (1977), p. 446.

the franchise; huge mobilizations in street and field; the provocative and stirring intellectual ferment of 'mechanick preachers'; the practical questioning of all form, manner and type of authority, whether of God, King or patriarch. While the struggle against the most prominent organizations of the proletariat, the Levellers and the Diggers, quickly led to their annihilation as a force in contention for the leadership of society, their influence was by no means crushed in the resistance to expropriation, uniformity of belief, and Puritanical concepts of work discipline. The restoration of Stuart kingship in 1660 seemed to represent a compromise in the class leadership of society, as traditional aristocratic virtues (toleration, cakes and ale, holidays) were welcomed by the poor. In fact the Restoration added to the scourges of war and dearth of the 1650s, the disasters of plague (1665) and fire (1666). Organizationally, the 'third culture' was driven underground, forced into exile or emigration, or petrified in sectarian rigidity.

John Milton had been a spokesman of freedom during the revolution, and he did not compromise during the counter-revolution. He had defended regicide; he had been actively engaged in understanding the thought of the English communists who opposed private property, kingly rule, patriarchal authority and 'gibberish laws'. He sought to explain the failure of revolution in the Christian story of the Fall. Composed between 1658 and 1663, when Milton was isolated, imprisoned and targeted by assassins, his *Paradise Lost* may be understood as an epic interpretation of the counter-revolution of the late seventeenth century. We may treat it allegorically to introduce themes in our history of the eighteenth century.

By Satan's command of 'Sovran power' hundreds and thousands assembled in war council at Pandaemonium in order to devise a strategy for the conquest of Heaven, from which the fallen angels had recently been expelled. In the first two books of *Paradise Lost* Milton describes their deliberations. Lucifer listened with deep concentration to the advice of his major counsellors Moloch, Belial and Mammon. 'After May 1660 Satan was not trying to recover power in England: he had won it,' writes Christopher Hill.[2] Let the three demons represent three forms of rule.

[2] ibid., p. 366.

I

Moloch was the first to speak. He was

> ... the fiercest Spirit
> That fought in Heav'n; now fiercer by despair;
> His trust was with the Eternal to be deem'd
> Equal in strength, and rather than be less
> Car'd not to be at all; with that care lost
> Went all his fear: of God, or Hell, or worse
> He reck'd not ...

(II, 44–50)

He advocated open war, the immediate mobilization of millions, a direct assault armed with hellish cannon, infernal thunder and the 'Almighty Engine' against Heaven. Under Cromwell and Charles II the English state was reorganized for war. Cromwell had 207 men-of-war built; three-quarters of the state's revenues was paid to the Navy. Charles II instituted a standing army of 19,000. By 1694 it had grown almost fivefold to 90,000 soldiers. Of 'King William's War' Sir George Clark wrote, 'It was the longest foreign war [England] had waged since Queen Elizabeth; it was the bloodiest and most costly. It was the first war of what may be called the modern type.' David Ogg had this to say of the Army: 'As for the ordinary soldier and sailor, they were still barely distinguishable from the criminal ... Indeed there was this to be said for active service: that it supplemented the gibbet as a means of keeping down the number of undesirables.'[3] The first drill book of an infantry regiment appeared in 1686. The first Mutiny Act was passed in 1689. Moloch is found in the great commanders of the day: in Cromwell, in Rupert, in the Duke of York, in Marlborough, in the Campbells, and in William Wolseley, whose family crest bore the motto: *homo homini lupus.*[4] Moloch fought against Spain (1656–9), the Netherlands (1652–4, 1665–7, 1672–4) and France (1689–97, 1701–14) in five European theatres of war. Moloch fought upon four continents, in Brazil, the Caribbean, New England, Africa, India, Scotland and Ireland.

[3] G. N. Clark, *The Later Stuarts, 1660–1714* (1944), p. 159; David Ogg, *England in the Reigns of James II and William III* (1955), p. 328.
[4] G. N. Clark, op. cit., pp. 170–81; Joseph Lehmann, *The Model Major-General: A Biography of Field-Marshal Lord Wolseley* (Boston, 1964), p. 13.

The English Moloch had to defeat the Dutch in order to control Surinam and to show the Portuguese that it had no other options than English clientage. This was made urgent by the gold rush occurring in Minas Gerais and Bahia at the end of the century. Brazilian gold entered England in the West Country, where it paid for Portuguese purchases of broad cloths. Then quickly, if not safely, the gold made its way to London in the shape of the moidore, a coin whose value was fixed in 1712 by Sir Isaac Newton at 27s. 8½d. There men and women were hanged for taking it: Thomas Charnock, a box-maker in 1720, Edward Joyce, a ship's sawyer in 1724, William Lipsat, a Dubliner in 1725, Edmund Neal, a tailor in 1722 who thought 'that London was built of Gold and Silver'. Mary Taylor, a prostitute in Whitefriars (a London sanctuary or 'alsatia'), stole 12 moidores from a client and knocked loose one of his teeth so 'it was hung by Geometry ever since'.[5]

The Caribbean was the cockpit of the European powers where the struggle among the fighting cocks of the imperialist gamesters – the freebooters, filibusters and buccaneers – was most fast, furious and vicious. Barbados, Bermuda and the Bahamas were English conquests that on the one hand provided the dumping ground for the vanquished of the British class wars (the Irish, the Quakers, the Monmouth rebels) and, on the other hand, produced a sugary arch of economic accumulation. Jamaica, since its conquest from Spain in 1655, was its keystone.

Moloch's want of fear 'of God, or Hell, or worse' was no more apparent than in the 'Company of Royal Adventurers' founded by the King's brother, the Duke of York, in 1663 to 'trade' with Africa. The slaves of the newly organized trade were branded on the forehead by the letters 'DY'. The King chose to exhibit his glory and to advertise the 'Royal Adventurers' by issuing a new coin, the gold guinea whose purity was so great that the coin's value soon rose to 30s. on the exchange. In the London vernacular it was called 'Old Mr Gory', partly because of its provenance and partly because of the circumstances of its production.[6] The period between 1690 and 1721 is notable in the history of the English slave trade because in 1713 England gained possession of the licence to sell slaves to the

[5] The Ordinary's *Account*, 29 January 1720, 29 April 1724, 1 February 1725, 31 December 1722 and 20 May 1728.
[6] Richard S. Dunn, *Sugar and Slaves: The Rise of the Planter Class in the English West Indies, 1624–1730* (Chapel Hill, 1972), p. 230.

Spanish Empire. As a result trade flourished. New ports like Liverpool were created and old ones like Bristol gained new life. England
took control of the entire Guinea coast. Where the annual number
of slaves transported in the seventeenth century had been 27,500, in
the eighteenth century it was between 40,000 and 100,000.[7]

Of the East India Company H. G. Wells wrote: 'It had come to
buy and sell, and it found itself achieving a tremendous piracy.' A
premature military adventure against the Mogul Emperor, Aurang-
zeb, resulted nevertheless in a peace that permitted the fortification
of a new factory at Calcutta in 1690. Three years later the company
bribed the 'great men' of England to the amount of £90,000. Besides
these 'great men' the East India Company owned a substantial part
of the Bank of England, which in turn owned debts on the King
and Parliament. The Company financed the *Dadni* merchants and
encouraged them to organize the putting-out system among Indian
weavers. After 1698 the company gained the right in Calcutta to
collect produce and to administer justice, including the power to
hang Indians, a power exercised 'with no tiresome restrictions'.[8]

In Scotland during the 1690s Moloch dealt with two profoundly
different societies. In the Lowlands, there was an urban society
whose rulers, through the Kirk, were able to make this area one
of the most dynamic and enterprising of capitalist zones. In the
Highlands, however, material and social life was not only pre-
capitalist, it was pre-feudal; Gaelic culture and clan organization
were militarist and pastoral without notions of private property.
Following the Massacre of Glencoe (1692), Highland society consisted of a huge pauperized and landless population, a growing
clique of English clients living upon confiscated estates, and the
bellicose remnant of the autonomous chiefs who would lead the
eighteenth-century Jacobite rebellions until they permitted themselves to be co-opted into the formation of Scottish regiments in the
mercenary service of the English Crown.[9] Meanwhile the Lowlands

[7]K. G. Davis, *The Royal African Company* (1957); W. E. B. DuBois, *The Suppression of the African Slave Trade* (New York, 1896), ch. 1.
[8]H. G. Wells, *The Outline of History, Being a Plain History of the Life of Mankind*
(1920), ch. 35, section 9; Ramakrishna Mukherjee, *The Rise and Fall of the East
India Company* (New York, 1974), pp. 24, 236, 238; Philip Woodruff, *The Founders
of Modern India* (New York, 1954), pp. 59, 74.
[9]T. C. Smout, *A History of the Scottish People, 1560–1830* (1969), chs. 9 and 14;
David Ogg, *England in the Reigns of James II and William III* (1955), p. 265; the
DNB.

produced Calvinist cadres of capitalist accumulation, such as William Patterson, a former missionary and buccaneer who founded the Bank of England (1694), or John Law, a goldsmith and convicted murderer, whose financial genius reached its apogee in the 'South Sea Bubble' affair of the 1720s. In 1698 Fletcher of Saltoun, the republican and prison escapee, proposed that a system of enforced, hereditary servitude be imposed on Scotland's 200,000 vagrants.[10]

If Moloch's motto in Scotland was 'Divide and Rule', in Ireland it was 'Woe to the Vanquished'. During the campaign of 1690 the 'loyalty and military competence' of the English regiments were so dubious that in action they had mostly to be put in the second line behind Dutch and Huguenot soldiers.[11] Eleven million Irish acres (52 per cent of the land mass) that William Petty had surveyed in the 'Down' survey (so-called because Ireland was put down on paper) went to Catholic *gentlemen*. Otherwise the confiscations were distributed to the victorious Protestant captains, adventurers, provisioners, and the aristocratic plunderers in King William's immediate entourage in the biggest land grab in the century preceding the Louisiana 'Purchase'. While the ruling class quarrelled within itself over the disposal of the forfeited estates, it was united upon two cardinal points of Irish policy. First, the majority of the Irish people ought to be kept subjugated by a penal code directed against the Catholic religion. This policy was 'intended to make them poor and keep them poor', according to W. E. H. Lecky. It was William Petty who dreamed that 'that vast Mountainous Island [would sink] under Water', thus expropriating its inhabitants from their land and livelihood, forcing them to migrate to England where they could be exploited efficiently, 'a pleasant and profitable Dream indeed'.[12] But Moloch was not a dreamer; that was more in Belial's line. So, Moloch sat down. By the 1690s his sulphurous thunder, having scented the planet's atmosphere in five continents and seven seas, had produced an empire.

[10] Andrew Fletcher, *An Account of a Conversation Concerning a Right Regulation of Governments for the Common Good of Mankind* (1703), and also his *Two Discourses Concerning the Affairs of Scotland* (1698).

[11] James Connolly, *Labour in Irish History* (Dublin, 1910), p. 9; Ogg, op. cit., p. 251; G. N. Clark, op. cit., p. 284, writes 'It was indeed something like the Norman Conquest of England.'

[12] W. E. H. Lecky, *A History of Ireland in the Eighteenth Century* (New York, 1893), vol. 1, p. 152; William Petty, *Political Arithmetick* (1690), reprinted in C. H. Hull (ed.), *The Economic Writings of Sir William Petty* (1899), vol. 1, pp. 285–7.

II

Belial rose to address the demons and advise Satan. In contrast to
Moloch, he was

> ... in act more graceful and humane;
> A fairer person lost not Heav'n; he seem'd
> For dignity compos'd and high exploit:
> But all was false and hollow, though his Tongue
> Dropt Manna, and could make the worse appear
> The better Reason, to perplex and dash
> Maturest Counsels; for his thoughts were low;
> To vice industrious, but to Nobler deeds
> Timorous and slothful: yet he pleas'd the eare.
>   (II, 109–17)

So with persuasive accent he rejected war and advised instead simply
enduring the *status quo*. War, open or concealed, would result in
utter annihilation. 'In reason's garb' he counselled ease. Belial had
been the proverbial devil of aristocratic vice, and during the English
Revolution his name was synonymous with the Cavaliers. Milton
presents him more interestingly: he stresses persuasive qualities of
good breeding, study and 'reason'. He was an intellectual as opposed
to a soldier.

We may introduce the 'reason' of Belial through William Petty
and John Locke, who both waited prudently until 1690 to publish
their thought – Petty's *Political Arithmetick*, and Locke's *An Essay
Concerning Human Understanding* and *Two Treatises of Civil Government* – because after that date James II had been deposed by Parliament, and William of Orange, a Protestant, had become king. Petty
had written *Political Arithmetick* in Ireland, where he had been paid
for his cartographical services with a 50,000-acre estate in County
Kerry. He found in Ireland that people were not willing to work
more than two hours a day. By expropriating the people from the
land and forcing them to migrate to England 'Spare Hands to
Superlucrate Millions of Millions' would be created. He could not
have more vividly expressed the new economic axiom of the English
bourgeoisie – that work, not land, was the source of value. However,

it was not this that makes him 'the father of political economy'.[13]

He was shocked by his dream (a 'Distemper of my own mind') because it violated his epistemology, which was to discard all argument of 'comparative and superlative Words' and to use only such reasoning as can be expressed 'in Terms of *Number, Weight,* or *Measure*'. Only such reasoning could make profit from the labour of the poor. Petty introduced to the analysis of class relations the method of quantification, and to the understanding of society the notion of abstract aggregation, both of which became essential techniques of the new government in its tax policies and its maritime recruitment policies. Petty's technique of computational abstraction allowed the mind to concentrate on instruments of measurement that appeared to possess their own objectivity, so that social relations among people would appear as reified relations among things. Arising from this process was a new abstract universal – namely, 'the economy'. 'Political arithmetick' and 'political economy' were the new sciences, the manna 'dropt' from Belial's tongue. Moreover, Petty understood that his observations 'if they are not already true, certain, and evident, yet may be made so by the Sovereign Power'.

Petty was a rough intellectual tailor. 'Reason's garb' found a far more brilliant and fashionable tailor in John Locke. 'Never perhaps has a wiser, more methodological mind, a more precise logician existed than Mr Locke,' wrote Voltaire. Christopher Hill called him one of 'the backroom boys of the Whig Junto' (Newton was the other), and Paul Hazard, historian of the European mind, said Locke was 'decidedly a gentleman'.[14] 'The great and chief end ... of men's uniting into commonwealths .. is the preservation of their property' is the well-known conclusion of his theory of the social contract. Less known but of equal importance to his political theory is his apodictic insistence upon capital punishment. Locke argued reasons to kill a man for a coat: 'Thus a thief, whom I cannot harm but by appeal to the law for having stolen all that I am worth, I may kill when he sets on me to rob me but of my horse or coat.' The animus in this direct expression should not be overlooked, for the personal wealth of the possessing class was often endangered by marauders,

[13] ibid., pp. 244, 261, 273, 307; Joyce Oldham Appleby, *Economic Thought and Ideology in Seventeenth Century England* (Princeton, 1978).
[14] Christopher Hill, *The Century of Revolution 1603–1714* (1961), p. 295; Paul Hazard, *The European Mind, 1680–1715* (New York, 1963), p. 241.

freebooters and highwaymen. In the winter of 1692 thirteen men entered the Duke of Ormond's mansion in St James's Square and 'all but succeeded in carrying off his magnificent plate and jewels'. The Duke of Marlborough was stopped outside St Albans by a highwayman and compelled to deliver 500 guineas. Robbers some years later stole the Duchess of Marlborough's chair. The Royal Chapel at Whitehall was broken into and the communion-plate stolen. A London dyer and an Irishman stole the King's crown and jewels from the Tower.[15] Certainly Locke would not have been unsympathetic to these 'victims'. Locke's aggressive edge may also be partly explained by the Jacobite sympathies of the highwaymen of the Interregnum and the 1690s.[16] Yet, as a philosopher of the new regime, Locke did not write from a spirit of vengeance. Sovereignty is given a new meaning in Locke.

Political power, then, I take to be a right of making laws with penalties of death, and, consequently, all less penalties for the regulating and preserving of property, and of employing the force of the community in the execution of such laws ... and all this only for the public good.

The movement of ideas is from property to law, from law to death, and from death to the public good. The aptness of this theory to the realities of the Whig regime, as well as Locke's prominent influence within it, leads me to adopt the term 'thanatocracy' to characterize a government that ruled by the frequent exercise of the death penalty. English sovereignty had exercised the death penalty before, indeed it appears to have done so more often and more vigorously. For example, during Elizabeth I's reign in Middlesex an average of 45 people were capitally convicted each year (2,045 people from 1558 to 1603), and an average of 20 were actually hanged.[17] The average number hanged in Middlesex during the eighteenth century was less than this, and since the population of Middlesex had increased severalfold between Elizabethan and Hanoverian times the per capita hanging rate diminished considerably. However, it is not the rate of hanging but the definition of sovereignty in terms of it and its exercise in close calibration with money that requires emphasis. Furthermore, as the killing of a single

---

[15] Andrew Browning (ed.), *English Historical Documents, 1660–1714* (1953); Anon., *The Life of Jonathan Wild* (1725).
[16] Lincoln B. Faller, *Turned to Account: The Forms and Functions of Criminal Biography in Late 17th and Early 18th Century England* (Cambridge, 1987), app. 2.
[17] John Cordy Jeaffreson, *Middlesex County Records*, vol. ii (1887), pp. 246–87.

individual is justified and accepted as the norm of sovereignty, the habit is extended in manifold ways to war and genocide.

John Locke was also a practical man. He joined the supporters of William of Orange in the Netherlands and reached the heights of the new regime with the help of Charles Montague, the Chancellor of the Exchequer.[18] He became the 'chief director' of the Council of Trade and Plantations when it was founded in 1696. As such he surveyed an empire in its macrocosm and its microcosm. He considered paupers in the parishes, slaves in Jamaica, the sailors in the Baltic trade, as well as the advantages of coercing children in Ireland to labour in workhouses from the age of six to fourteen, ten hours a day at a double-wheeled spinning machine. Locke was among many who regarded the poverty of the 1690s 'as a man's fault rather than his misfortune'.[19]

In 1696 the Coinage Act was passed. Professor Caffentzis, in his study of Locke's philosophy of money, noted that 'the English monetary system had slowly driven itself into a sort of collective madness'. The clippers, the coiners and the counterfeiters had physically crippled the coin of the realm. In the summer of 1695, during the Siege of Namur, Locke wrote, 'Clipping is the great leak which for some time past has contributed more to sink us than all the forces of our enemies could do.'[20] The Coinage Act was a victory for Locke's theory of commodity money.[21] The detokenization of the currency, making the 'real' and nominal value of the coinage identical, can only be interpreted as an immense transfer of value from tenants and debtors to landlords and creditors. The Coinage Act and its allied Acts provided a universal principle for the measurement of socially necessary labour time. The financial innovations of the 1690s, especially the foundation of the Bank of England in 1694, established a credit market that must be understood as a trust in the future stability of the state, and a faith that the fictitious value thus

[18] H. R. Fox Bourne, *John Locke: A Biography* (1876), 2 vols.

[19] Brian Inglis, *Poverty and the Industrial Revolution* (1971), p. 17.

[20] John Locke, *Further Considerations Concerning Raising the Value of Money* in *Works* (1823), vol. v, p. 198.

[21] For the recoinage, see Pierre Vilar, *A History of Gold and Money, 1450–1920* (1976), ch. 23; Ming-Hsun Li, *The Great Recoinage of 1696 to 1699* (1963); Sir Albert Feavearyear, *The Pound Sterling: A History of English Money* (1963), pp. 94–152; Max Beloff, *Public Order and Popular Disturbances, 1660–1714* (1938), ch. 5; and Appleby, op. cit., ch. 8. See, as fundamental, C. G. Caffentzis, *Clipped Coins, Abused Words, and Civil Government: John Locke's Philosophy of Money* (New York, 1989).

advanced in the form of credit monies would be realized by the future value produced by a labour force not yet under the command of English capital. The five statutes passed in the 1690s against clipping and coining culminated in the Act of 1697 which made coining high treason. Sir Isaac Newton, as the aggressive Warden of the Mint, took credit for this Act.

Money and law became the two languages of Belial. Each was abstract in the sense that it provided to a greater or less extent its own system of reason, one about 'value' and the other about 'justice'. Money governed exchange, law contract. Together they composed the intricate appearance of wealth in its commodity form. It was this that Bunyan, writing *Pilgrim's Progress* in Bedford gaol, denounced in his satire of Vanity Fair where

all are such merchandise sold as houses, lands, trades, places, honours, preferments, titles, countries, kingdoms, lusts, pleasures, and delights of all sorts, as whores, bawds, wives, husbands, children, masters, servants, lives, blood, bodies, souls, silver, gold, pearls, precious stones, and what not.

We will consider first law then money.

'The Restoration may be said to open a new period in the history of English law,' wrote F. W. Maitland.[22] But while Professor Beattie notices that after 1660 the pardoning power was exercised far more strictly (as well as other sovereign acts of mercy: Bunyan's wife complained to Judge Hale that her husband was not included in the 'releasement of divers prisoners' that usually accompanied 'the coronation of kings'), he seems to consider 1689 as a more significant date: it was after the 'Bloodless Revolution' that (1) the system of rewards ('Blood Money') became an established element in the system of criminal administration; (2) summary jurisdiction, especially in London, expanded; (3) new gaols and houses of correction were encouraged; and (4) the 'new capital offences' were created.[23] An insular and administrative perspective favours the latter date; an imperial and substantive perspective favours the former. The year 1661 saw the promulgation of the first slave code in English history, enacting that human beings become 'real chattels'. First passed in Barbados it was soon copied in Jamaica, Antigua and the

[22] F. W. Maitland and F. C. Montague, *A Sketch of English Legal History* (1915), p. 131.
[23] J. M. Beattie, *Crime and the Courts in England, 1660–1800* (Princeton, 1986), pp. 51, 269, 292, 423 and 475.

Carolinas, whose 'astonishingly reactionary constitution' was drawn by Locke.[24] The code became a durable basis of the economic and social life of the islands for 150 years. Also in 1661 the thirty-six Articles of War were promulgated. In these the death penalty recurs as often as do the curses in the Commination Service of the Church of England. One might say with equal justice that the 'wealth, safety, and strength' of His Majesty, the Defender of the Faith, owed more to these Thirty-six Articles, twenty-two of which provide the death penalty, than to the Thirty-nine Articles of the Church of England, though every one of them promised eternal salvation.[25] Besides that thanatocratic code, discipline in the Navy was maintained by 'customs of the sea' that had been recently enlarged by Dutch contributions: the spread eagle, ducking, mastheading, keel-hauling, marrying the gunner's daughter, and the cat-of-nine-tails.[26] In addition to the slave codes, the military codes and the Irish penal code, the criminal code with its 'new' capital offences formed the defining characteristics of this era of substantive British law.

That the death penalty defines sovereignty and that the protection of property defines the end of government were related propositions, as James Fitzjames Stephens emphasized in his *History of the Criminal Law in England*, and as Locke had successfully argued. The courts and Parliament determined the relationship partly by the statutory device of removing 'benefit of clergy'. Matthew Hale in his *Pleas of the Crown* (1682) called it 'one of the most involved and troublesome titles in law', and he spent more than ten years trying to reconcile it with his 'methodological summary' of law.[27] In practice the idea poses few difficulties. If you stood condemned, but could recite the 51st Psalm (the 'neck verse') to prove your literacy, you were saved from the gallows. Benefit of clergy originated in the Middle Ages when clerics were subject to dual jurisdiction, secular and ecclesiastical. Although the Hanoverians added significant laws to the 'bloody code', it was during the Restoration and particularly during the 1690s that the most important capital statutes were passed. The criminal code of William III laid the

[24] Dunn, op. cit., pp. 239–45; Peter King, *The Development of the English Economy to 1750* (1971), p. 403.
[25] Noticed by John McArthur, *Principles and Practices of Naval and Military Courts Martial* (1792).
[26] Theodore Thring, *Thring's Criminal Law of the Navy*, 2nd edn (1877), pp. 38–49.
[27] Chs. 24–54.

foundation of the eighteenth-century thanatocracy.

We may group the 'new' capital statutes in five classes. First, were those protecting Crown revenues (the Forgery Acts). Second, were those protecting money (the Clipping and Coining Act, the Bank of England Note Act and the South Sea Bond Acts). Third, were those protecting the state's monopoly of violence (the Conscription Act, the Naval Stores Act, the Piracy Acts and the Mutiny Acts). Fourth, were those designed to enforce the criminal code (the Blood Money Act, the Parish Office Exemption Act, and those provisions in the Clipping, Burglary and Shoplifting Acts that offered a £40 reward for the apprehension of offenders). Fifth, and finally, were those that revised the law of larceny (the Robbery Act, the Shoplifting Act, the Burglary Act and the Larceny from a Dwelling House Act). The revised law of larceny may be simplified thus: stealing (taking and carrying away the goods of another) is divided into simple larceny and compound larceny. Larceny is 'grand' when the value of the stolen goods exceeds 12d. and 'petty' when the value is less than 12d. Larceny becomes 'compound' when it is aggravated by specified circumstances concerning taking from a person or from a location. The Williamite code tended to remove benefit of clergy from the varieties of compound larceny.

Of decisive importance to the life of the offender was thus (1) the physical location of the misappropriated goods; and (2) the monetary value of the goods. The Williamite criminal code established an ever more refined relation between money and the death sentence. If measurement of such objectives as value is accepted as 'reason', the code is eminently reasonable, although even John Locke considered the thief 'not under the ties of the common law of reason', who therefore may be instantly killed.[28] The murderous character of Belial's 'reason' was expressed in an antithetical vocabulary between the two classes as they contemplated death by hanging at Tyburn. To Matthew Hale hanging was 'suspendatus per collum quousque fuerit mortuus'. To the vulgar Londoners hanging was 'the cheat'.

Money was Belial's other language. It had not yet become the exclusive lash of the discipline. On the one hand, too much money led to idleness: as Defoe observed, 'There's nothing more frequent than for an Englishman to work until he has got his pocket full of money, and then to go and be idle.' On the other hand, too little

---

[28] *Second Treatise of Civil Government* (1690), III, pp. 16–18.

money led to desperation. As Mandeville said of the poor, 'They have nothing to stir them up to be serviceable but their Wants, which it is prudence to relieve, but Folly to cure. The only thing then that can render the Labouring Man industrious is a moderate Quantity of Money.'[29] Money must both excite and hurt. The point of quantitative equilibrium between these apparently opposite purposes became the subject of inquiry. Matthew Hale, in 1683, calculated that 10s. a week, or £26 a year, could provide a small family with a level of maintenance that guaranteed continual working. William Petty found the realities to be beneath this standard: 8d. a day for husbandmen and 16d. a day for tradesmen.[30] David Ogg, a modern historian, concluded, 'Modern economists have not been able to explain how the poor lived.'

The poverty of London reached crisis proportions in the 1690s. Depressions in the cloth markets in 1689, 1693–4 and 1696–7 put many textile workers out of gainful employ. Arrears in pay to sailors and their families was the cause of mutiny as well as widespread hardship. There was a major shortage of coal in 1691. High bread prices in 1693–4 and 1696–8 meant going without and starvation. Beggars, hawkers, pedlars filled the streets.[31] The justices at Hick's Hall, where Quarter Sessions for Middlesex sat, considered more than 2,000 indictments in 1699 (2,159) and again in 1700 (2,108), substantially more than they would for any of the next fifty-five years, even though the urban population over the same period increased by a third.[32]

People made their own money. Clipping, coining and counterfeiting threatened the stability of the kingdom. Even the coinage crisis of the 1690s could not put an end to what was the practice of monetary democracy. Sir Isaac Newton, the Warden and Master of the Mint, spent fifty days a year prosecuting clippers and coiners on behalf of 'Old Mr Gory'.[33] Richard Dove, a silversmith in

[29] Bernard Mandeville, The Fable of the Bees, ed. Philip Harth (1970), p. 209.
[30] Hale, A Discourse Touching Provision for the Poor (1683), p. 6; Petty, op. cit., pp. 267–8.
[31] Steven Macfarlane, 'Social Policy and the Poor in the later Seventeenth Century', in A. L. Beier and Roger Finlay, London 1500–1700: The Making of the Metropolis (1986), p. 259.
[32] GLCRO (Mddx Div.), Calendar of Indictments, MJ/CJ.
[33] J. F. Scott (ed.), The Correspondence of Isaac Newton, vol. iv (Cambridge, 1967), p. 201; Frank E. Manuel, A Portrait of Isaac Newton (Cambridge, 1968), pp. 230–44, and Richard S. Westfall, Never at Rest: A Biography of Isaac Newton (Cambridge, 1986), pp. 554–70.

Blowbladder Street, was hanged in 1709 for counterfeiting coin. Jane Houseden, three years later, was hanged for the same offence. She made 'false money in Newgate at the time when other Prisoners were in the Chapel'.[34] A coiner by the name of Goodman understood exactly the relation between money and sovereign power. Sentenced to death for coining, in Newgate he petitioned Charles II, begging that he might be allowed once more to perform the role of Alexander the Great in a play before His Majesty. His petition was granted, and his performance was so successful in giving to the sovereign power a mirror of its own image that Goodman was reprieved.[35] Many forms of money existed besides 'Old Mr Gory' and the paper notes of the financiers – for example, private minted tokens, the tally-sticks of the public house or victualler's shop, navy tickets and the tickets of 'mine uncle's'. Some were stores of value, others means of purchase or payment. These were credit monies that brought with them their own systems of violence. Of some 150 lock-ups of early eighteenth-century London most were designed for the safe keeping of one or the other.

The working class of London regarded money as an abstract grid of value, but its vocabulary used concrete expressions of particular powers. Each denomination had its own name: 'jack' ($\frac{1}{4}$d.); 'mopus' and 'make' ($\frac{1}{2}$d.); 'winnings' (1d.); 'threpps' and 'thrums' (3d.); 'kick', 'sice', 'simon' and 'pig' (6d.); 'loon-slatt' (1s. 1$\frac{1}{2}$d.); 'slate' and 'trooper' (2s. 6d.); 'ounce' (5s.); 'smelt' ($\frac{1}{2}$ guinea); 'heart's ease' (20s.); and 'yellow boy' (1 guinea). Different qualitative forms of money were distinguished: 'ribbin' (money); 'rhino' (ready money); 'quidds' (cash); 'witcher' (silver); 'spanks' (gold or silver), and 'Old Mr Gory' (gold). Money was a prize or the result of it was called 'win' or 'winnings'. It was power, 'clout'. It represented food and warmth: 'grannam', 'cole', 'provender', 'seed' and 'bread'. Its association with military violence was preserved in 'prey', 'flag' and 'recruits'. Its links with waste and excrement were suggested by 'garbage', 'muck' and 'crap'.[36]

New forms of coercion were introduced in the 1690s. The sergeants and bailiffs, a money police, gave rise to a vocabulary of denunciation as powerful as the prophetic utterances of old. They

---

[34] The Ordinary's *Account*, 18 May 1709 and 19 September 1712.
[35] Theophilus Lucas, *Authentick Memoirs Relating to the Lives ... of the Gamesters and Sharpers*, 2nd edn (1744), p. 138.
[36] Anon., *A New Canting Dictionary* (1725).

were 'setters' and 'bums'. They were called 'catchpills' after Roman tax collectors, 'pursuivants' after the Privy Council messengers, 'janissaries' after the renegade guards of the Ottoman Sultan, and 'Philistines' and 'Moabites' who, as Jeremiah foretold, would wallow in vomit. There were some areas of London, 'the pretended privileged places', where their writs did not run: Whitefriars, the Savoy, Salisbury Court, Rum Alley, Mitres Court, Fullers Rents, Baldwin's Gardens, Montague Close, the Minories, the Mint, the Clink and Deadman's Place.[37] In such places the money police, if caught, were forced to grovel in dirt. Thomas Shadwell describes a 'pumping'.[38] John Gay describes a setter 'plunged in miry ponds, he gasping lies, Mud chokes his mouth'. Thomas D'Urfey tells how they were 'forc'd to drink against their Will'.[39] The financial crises of 1696 and 1721 led to legislation designed to abolish the sanctuaries.

By 1724 the inhabitants of the last remaining money sanctuary, the Wapping Mint, had organized themselves. The names of the Minters were kept in a book, thus obliging them 'to the utmost extent of their Power to rescue and set at Liberty any Person on the said List, whenever he was arrested or imprison'd'.[40] The book was kept at 'The Seven Cities of Refuge'. The reference is to the communism of Hebraic Law: 'And of these cities which ye shall give six cities shall ye have for refuge ... both for the children of Israel, and for the stranger, and for the sojourner among them.' The battle between the bailiffs and Minters continued through the year. One bailiff was 'duck'd in a Place in which the Soil of Houses of Office had been empty'd'. Another was forced to lie in a pit 'like a Sow in hot weather'. A third was whipped to a degree that 'Sixpenny of rods [were worn] to the stumps'. A fourth was marched around in a nocturnal parade of 200 torch-bearing people, the man forced to keep a turd in his mouth. In the winter of 1725 'Captain' Towers, a leader of the Minters, was hanged at Wapping before 'a very great Concourse of People who with Tears lamented his Condition'.[41] At

---

[37] 8 & 9 William & Mary III, c. 27 (1697), 9 George I, c. 28 (1722), and 11 George I, c. 22 (1724).

[38] Whitefriars originally was a sanctuary for the Carmelites. Its immunities were confirmed by James I in 1608. Shadwell, an opium addict whose father lost his property during the Revolution, had once lived there himself.

[39] John Gay, 'Trivia, or the Art of Walking the Streets of London' (1716) in *The Poetical Works of John Gay*, ed. G. C. Faber (1969); D'Urfey, *Collin's Walk Through London and Westminster* (1690), p. 59.

[40] *The Proceedings* 15–19 January 1725.

[41] The Ordinary's *Account*, 4 January 1725.

his trial he had said it was better to reside in the Mint 'and live honestly, than go upon the Highway for Money to pay his Debts'. The conception of honesty implied by the preference was venerable, if submerged, because it denied the universality of money. It hearkens to Bunyan's description of Vanity Fair and behind Bunyan to Winstanley and his denunciations of 'the crafty art of buying and selling'. The revolutionary traditions of the 1640s were kept alive in the London sanctuaries. Shadwell considered them 'in Rebellion still'. Under Charles II they protected 'the Enthusiasts, call'd *Levellers* and *Fifth Monarchy Men*'. In 1725 the Minters were thought to harbour Ranters and members of the Family of Love.

In addition to the money police (which included the Riding Officers of 1698, to be discussed in Chapter 5), a moral police and a thief police were created in the 1690s. The former was a London creation. At first known as 'ye Society of Informers' it quickly changed its title to others of greater sanctimony: the Society for the Reformation of Manners (1691) and the Society for the Propagation of Christian Knowledge (1701). It hired informers, prosecuted offenders and published lists of reprobates ('Black Rolls'). Its invigilations were directed against cussers, drinkers, tipplers, besporters of 'unlawful exercise of pastime' and lovers. 'Great number of subjects that in time of war might defend their country are effeminated, debauched, diseased and made incapable of bearing arms; fitter for an hospital than an army,' declaimed one of their sermons in 1694.[42] These outriders of the Puritan work and family ethic prosecuted between 200 and 900 prostitutes a year.[43]

> The mercenry Scouts in every Street,
> Bring all that have no Money to your Feet,
> And if you lash a Strumpet of the Town,
> She only smarts for want of Half a Crown:
> Your Annual lists of criminals appear,
> But no Sir Harry or Sir Charles is here

wrote Defoe in 1702. Of the 298 leaders of the societies, 297 were men. Their first object of attack in 1690 were the brothels of Tower Hamlets; names of women outnumber men on the 'Black Rolls'.

---

[42] T. C. Curtis and W. A. Speck, 'The Societies for the Reformation of Manners: A Case Study in the Theory and Practice of Moral Reform', *Literature and History*, vol. iii (1976), p. 52.
[43] Sir Leon Radzinowicz, *A History of Criminal Law and Its Administration*, vol. ii, pp. 431–3.

In the 1690s the judicial attack on women was especially severe, not only by these informal means. Professor Beattie informs us that 'the jails in London were filled with women pardoned from the death sentence on condition of transportation'. Yet the colonies did not want them. In 1697 the Government agreed to pay £8 a head to get fifty women shipped to the West Indies. Still the Recorder of London had to release some of the women from the crowded gaol at Newgate.[44] One reason for the extraordinary repression of women, prostitutes particularly, was undoubtedly the encouragement they gave to sailors to desert: the desertion rate trebled in the first eighteen months of William's reign. Women often took the lead in opposing the press-gang.[45]

A third form of police coercion is described by Bunyan at Vanity Fair: 'And moreover, at this fair there is at all times to be seen jugglings, cheats, games, tools, apes, knaves and rogues, and that of all sorts. Here are to be seen, too, and that for nothing, thefts, murders, adulteries, false swearers, and that of a blood-red colour.' The Blood Money Act of 1692 offered a reward of £40 for the apprehension, prosecution and conviction of any highway robber. Another Act of 1698 rewarded those who brought a thief to a prosecution leading to conviction, a certificate exempting them from having to undertake any office in the parish or ward where the felony was committed. Furthermore, the same Act promised a thief who gave information leading to the conviction of two other like offenders a free royal pardon. Thus was a thief set to catch a thief. The system of blood money reached its apogee under Jonathan Wild, 'the Machiavel of Thieves', who used these laws together with the laws of stolen goods to build an urban mafia of thieving, receiving, and deceiving that became an essential prop of metropolitan authority between 1715 and 1725. Thereafter too, the *Proceedings at the Old Bailey* are replete with expostulations against them: 'This Rogue ... will swear any Body's Life away for a Farthing'; 'These Thief-Catchers will do any Thing for Money'; 'They live by nothing but taking Men's Lives away'.[46]

---

[44] M. Beattie, *Crime and the Courts in England, 1660–1800* (Princeton, 1986), pp. 481–2.

[45] G. Hinchcliffe, 'Impressment of Seamen During the War of Spanish Succession', *Mariner's Mirror*, 53, no. 2 (May 1967); J. S. Bromley (ed.), *The Manning of the Royal Navy: Selected Public Pamphlets, 1693–1873: A Social Survey* (1968).

[46] *The Proceedings*, 27 June, 15 July, and 31 August 1733.

The manna that dropped from Belial's tongue easily found its way from the 'ideological superstructure' of society to its 'material base', from the abstractions of philosophy to who'd put the kettle on in the workhouse. Since in the geography of conquest there were actually many 'bases', Belial assisted in uniting them in practice through 'Old Mr Gory', for it was by means of an internationally recognized metallic standard that the value of internationally produced goods as well as the international productivity of labour could be measured. In Locke's vast philosophical treatise on empiricism, the *Essay Concerning Human Understanding*, few animal, vegetable or mineral creations are actually named; of all the earth's things, it is 'gold' that recurs most often. Newton had 'consecrated England to Gold'.[47] Belial rested.

III

Mammon, the humblest and most profound of Lucifer's counsellors, was the last to speak at Pandaemonium. He was

> ...the least erected Spirit that fell
> From Heav'n, for ev'n in Heav'n his looks and thoughts
> Were always downward bent, admiring more
> The riches of Heav'n's pavement, trod'n Gold,
> Than aught divine or holy else enjoy'd
> In vision beatific: by him first
> Men also, and by his suggestion taught,
> Ransak'd the Center, and with impious Hands
> Rifl'd the bowels of their mother Earth
> For Treasures better hid.
>
> (I, 679–88)

He advocated neither war nor peace. Milton presents him in 1674 neither as an emblem of greed nor a demon of usury but as one who has understood the 'skill and art from whence to raise Magnificence'. His is the counsel of toil and productivity. It is Mammon whom we see in the Protestant planter overlooking his fields of cane and slaves, in the Christian philanthropist counting the yarn spun by seven-year-olds, in the well-fed cit thrashing his 'prentices, or in the Bible-toting interloper who cheated Moguls.

[47] William Shaw, *Select Tracts and Documents Illustrative of English Monetary History, 1626–1730* (1896), p. 133.

His counsel advised making the best out of *contradiction*. Thus did he anticipate an active principle of historical development,

> ... Our greatness will appear
> Then most conspicuous, when great things of small,
> Useful of hurtful, prosperous of adverse
> We can create, and in what place soe'er
> Thrive under evil, and work ease out of pain
> Through labour and endurance.
>
> (II, 257–62)

Work was the medium through which contradiction between great and small, useful and hurtful, prosperity and adversity, ease and evil was resolved. Moloch did not fight wars: soldiers and sailors did, and they mutinied. Belial's smooth tongue did not become the national idiom: people talked back even though their vernacular was profane, licensed, watched, and rarely allowed into print. Likewise, it was not Mammon who made useful things from hurtful: workers did and they devised many conditions to ensure that what greatness their labours yielded was not taken out of their hides without a price. Labour took several forms – forced labour, slave labour, bonded labour, convict labour, indentured labour, incarcerated labour, craft labour, and 'free' labour or service. A longer working day, a longer working week, the abolition of holidays, the attack on fairs, mechanization, reduced wages, provided Mammon with renewed weapons of accumulation.

We may outline a typology of work, distinguishing the modes of production available in the 1690s by several criteria. These criteria include: (1) the ownership of the tools, materials and product of labour; (2) the extent of the division of labour and the form of cooperation; (3) the architectural and geographical setting of production; (4) the source of energy and power and the mode of transportation; (5) the forms of reproducing the labour; (6) the kinds of self-organization of workers within each mode of production; and (7) the organization of time and the durations of labour. With these criteria in mind we may distinguish five modes of production in the 1690s. Over-simplified as such a typology must be, it may help us distinguish the period under investigation from the preceding and the following periods.

First, handicraft. In this mode of production, simple hand tools owned by the artisan were applied to animal or vegetable materials for fabrication into his own food, clothing and shelter. The division of labour was simple, the artisan performing almost every operation. The location of fabrication was the artisan's dwelling. Recompense for labour arose either from the sale of the product, or by its exchange for something more useful. The reproduction of the artisan occurred in the craft household. The 'art and misterie' of the craft was often passed from parent to child. Such people did not distinguish between work and life, and lived according to a sacred or rural calendar. Handicraftspersons were organized juridically into apprentices, journeymen and masters.

Since two-fifths of those hanged at Tyburn in the eighteenth century had started an apprenticeship, it is important to examine the meaning of that term. Apprenticeship was a means both of entering the urban patriciate ('free' of a municipal corporation) and of learning a trade in order to practise it. The two functions began to diverge during the English Revolution of the 1640s. The process was hastened by the Plague and the Fire. By the early eighteenth century apprenticeship in the first sense 'had really entered its last phase'. By 1720 the London guilds had lost 'their power to control trade as well as industry'. One cannot assume, therefore, that an eighteenth-century London 'apprentice' belonged to a juridically controlled, urban system of guild mutualism.[48] Nor, can it be assumed that an apprentice was a 'skilled' as opposed to 'unskilled' worker. Apprenticeship was less likely to involve the development of highly qualified, skilled labour power than to be the means of organizing the exploitation of young labour power. Hence, dishonesty was the presumption. When John Cloggs was apprenticed to his uncle, his father 'gave a bond for my Honesty for what I steale or pilfer away'.[49] R. Campbell, writing in *The London Tradesman* (1747), called it 'a tedious Seven Years Slavery'.

Second, putting-out. In order to escape the guild and corporate

[48] O. Jocelyn Dunlop, *English Apprenticeship and Child Labour: A History* (New York, 1912), pp. 107–133 and 224; J. R. Kellett, 'The Breakdown of Guild and Corporate Control over the Handicrafts and Retail Trade in London', *Economic History Review*, 2nd series, vol. x, no. 3 (1958); Stella Kramer, *The English Craft Gilds: Studies in their Progress and Decline* (New York, 1927), pp. 385–90; A. L. Beier, 'Engine of Manufacture: The Trades of London', in A. L. Beier and Roger Finlay (eds), *London 1500–1700: The Making of the Metropolis* (1986), pp. 156–9.
[49] Max Beloff, 'A London Apprentice's Notebook, 1703–1705', *History*, new series, vol. xxvii (June–September 1942), p. 38.

regulation of production typical of handicrafts, merchants began to put out the materials and tools of production to workers dispersed in their own homes outside the municipal franchises of the large towns. This was the origin of 'suburbs'. In relation to the 'freemen' of the towns, these workers were, juridically speaking, 'foreigners'. The simple equipment and uniform materials of production were generally (at first) for the fabrication of new products (the 'new draperies', silk, etc.), so that they did not initially compete with existing handicrafts. The conduits of 'the sensuous human activity' of the labourers were often neither quite owned nor quite not owned by those who worked them. This ambiguity required significant revision in the law of property, which was supplied by Chief Justice Holt, who more than any other jurist adapted law to finance capitalism. In *Craggs* v. *Bernard* (1703) he formulated the modern English law of bailments (the delivery of goods in trust for a specific purpose), an essential law to such a transitional mode of production as putting-out.[50]

These workers were part of a much larger market, with respect to both the sources of their supplies, put out to them by international merchants, and the destination of their products, which became part of national and international markets. Recompense took two main forms in addition to time wages: the price-form (the ancestor of piece-wages) was common; or it might consist in direct appropriations governed by a pattern of customary negotiations. This triple form of recompense (wage, price and custom) has puzzled economic historians, who are not quite sure whether to classify putting-out as a 'firm' or not.[51] The reproduction of this working class (men *and* women, adults *and* children) was the direct result of the expropriation of those who had owned their own means of subsistence and production, an expropriation that could be either direct and violent or accomplished through price, market and taxation policies. The duration of labour was determined by the worker. This characteristic, together with the considerable street life (coming and going between shop and warehouse), lent to its workers an appearance of idleness. Consequently, the rise of putting-out in London corresponds to the Acts of Tudor times enforcing a working day from sun-up to sundown. Self-organization by such workers

---

[50] 2 Lord Raymond 909–920; Blackstone, *Commentaries*, bk. II, ch. 24.
[51] R. Millward, 'The Emergence of Wage Labour in Early Modern England', *Explorations in Economic History*, 18 (1981), pp. 21–39.

depended upon this urban mobility and its link with porters, wagoners, carters and itinerants.

Third, manufacture. In this, the tools remained extensions of the hand or eye, distinguishing it from factory production and establishing a continuity with handicraft and putting-out. However, by the eighteenth century the tools had become highly specialized and refined, as a glance through the illustrations of Diderot's *Encyclopédie* might attest. The same may be said of the materials of production, which were mined, gathered or harvested from ever vaster areas of the earth's surface. The principle of the division of labour had become the manifest cause of differential productivity, and already in the 1690s was being extolled by political economists. William Morris, writing after its demise, was less optimistic:

The unit of labour is a group, not a man; the individual workman in this system is kept life-long at the performance of some task quite petty in itself, and which he soon masters, and having mastered it has nothing more to do but to go on increasing his speed of hand under the spur of competition with his fellows, until he has become the perfect machine which it is his ultimate duty to become, since without attaining to that end he must die or become a pauper.[52]

What chiefly characterized manufacture as a mode of production was its location – the central workshop – which removed the labour process to a site owned and controlled by the boss, who was able consequently to maintain control over both the tools and materials of labour that he owned and over the labouring activity of the workers employed. They received recompense for their creative activity by a wage of account, though this might still be supplemented in numerous traditional ways. This working class was reproduced on an urban basis – that is, it was recruited through a labour market that actually consisted of (1) an urban pool of labour; (2) migrants from the countryside; and (3) people from other parts of the world. Within the city both the public house and the brothel, with their 'networks of loose and transitory alliances', helped to organize informally the labour market of manufacture.[53] Self-

[52] 'The Hopes of Civilization', a lecture to the Hammersmith Branch of the Socialist League, 1885, and published in *Signs of Change* (1888).
[53] John L. McMullan, *The Canting Crew: London's Criminal Underworld, 1550–1700* (New Brunswick, 1984), p. 129.

organization by this working class consisted of incipient trade unionism, the Friendly Society or Box Club, and strong links with particular public houses. Morris, the handicraftsman, had studied our period with a practical eye, deeply regretful for what it had destroyed. He noted that when the woes of the poor press most dangerously upon the rich, then an age searches most energetically to pierce the future for hope. He wrote: 'The eighteenth-century artisan must have been a terrible product of civilization, and quite in a condition to give rise to hopes – of the torch, the pike, and the guillotine'.

Handicraft, putting-out and manufacture could lead to confusion as to the ownership of the means, materials and product of production. The Williamite criminal code sought to clarify the confusion. The privilege of benefit of clergy was removed from the following offences: robberies of 5s. or more in a dwelling-house, shop or warehouse (Robbery Act of 1691); stealing goods of 5s. or more in the day or night from a shop (Shoplifting Act of 1699); stealing goods of 40s. or more from a dwelling or outhouse (Larceny from a Dwelling House Act of 1713). Of cardinal significance to these statutes was the *locus operandi*.[54] New modes of the circulation of commodities (shopping) and new modes of their production (putting-out and manufacture) that emphasized physical locations were reflected in these revised definitions of robbery, breaking and entering, burglary and shoplifting.

Fourth, the plantation. This was characterized by its huge scale: in land, many acres; in labour, many hundreds; in equipment, large investments, though the hand tools remained simple and rough. The planter owned tools, land, materials and, according to the planter's law, the workers themselves. Methods of cultivation were politically efficient, if economically inefficient; the planter 'had to keep his labourers fully occupied in the slow months, as well as in crop time, to forestall mischief and rebellion. So he put them to work in the fields with hoes instead of horse-drawn plows.'[55] There the workers cooperated in massive gangs and were therefore quick to appreciate the power of collective labour: 'They were closer to a modern proletariat than any group of workers in existence at the time,' wrote C. L. R. James.[56] They produced tobacco and sugar

[54] Also emphasized by Radzinowicz, op. cit., vol. i, pp. 666–72.
[55] Dunn, op. cit., p. 198.
[56] C. L. R. James, *The Black Jacobins*, 2nd edn (New York, 1963), p. 86.

destined for a mass, world market whose clearing house was the Port of London. The duration of labour was from can-do in the morning to can't-do at night. It was reproduced only through the most vicious struggle: the refusal of reproduction by those women bought precisely as 'breeders' and the tendency to suicide of the most desperate had to be compensated for by the trading from the African coast of ever new thousands for the hated 'middle passage' and the breaking-pens of the West Indies. Recompense consisted of near-worthless 'garden plots' or whatever masters chose to dish out in intervals between work. Self-organization of these workers began at sundown: nocturnal, flightful, conspiratorial, magical and exotic, what it lacked in velocity it more than made up for in mass. Since this multitude was dispersed among plantations in continental America and in the Caribbean Antilles, a basis was established for the emerging pan-African civilization and cycles of rebellion that bore increasingly interesting relationships with struggles in Ireland and London.[57] In 1688 Aphra Behn wrote the first English novel. Its hero was an African slave, Oroonoko, the leader of a slave rebellion, who was inspired by English emigrant Quakers and by the memory of Hannibal.[58]

Fifth, the ship. This was the mode of production that provided communication among the others, from the handicrafts of India to the plantation in America to manufactures and putting-out in London. Technically, it differed from the others in that the location and instrument of production were identical – the most complex contrivance of nearly 1,000 years of European civilization. A first-rate ship-of-the-line carried a crew of between 700 and 900; a second-rate was manned by about 600; a third-rate, 500. The labour that a ship organized combined the necessities of large-scale co-operation such as was found on the plantation with the intricacies of the division of labour such as was found in manufacture and the versatility of individual skills such as might be found in handicraft. Characteristics of the slave, the artisan and the labourer were therefore to be found in the sailor. Nominally a wage worker, the sailor was in fact often lucky to be fed. The crews of two frigates off the

[57] Carl and Roberta Bridenbaugh, No Peace Beyond the Line: The English in the Caribbean, 1624–1690 (New York, 1972), pp. 351–61.
[58] Aphra Behn, Oroonoko (1688); Angeline Goreau, Reconstructing Aphra: A Social Biography of Aphra Behn (New York, 1980).

coast of Ireland petitioned the Admiralty, stating that they were naked, homeless and hungry, 'there being above fifty-two months' pay due to them'. Even when payment was made, it might not be what it seemed: £10,000 in shillings and sixpences to pay off the Fleet in 1696 was 'rejected by ye lower Order of People' because it was unsound coin.[59] Nominally free, the sailor was coerced for long periods of service. By the 1690s the press-gang had become the chief means of recruitment. Labour discipline, as with manufacture, consisted of constant surveillance and corporal punishment, apparently made necessary by the cooperation needed where one life depended on the whole. That the work was fully incarcerated and that in many tasks the 'machine' controlled the worker rather than the worker the tool, lent to the ship an objective principle similar to the factory.[60] The labour was continuous, 'around the clock', but organized by the bell. This working class was fully international. By 1700 the Navigation Acts had been amended to permit up to three-quarters of the merchant complements to consist of foreigners. Both the merchant marine and the Royal Navy drew upon the strolling and vagabond population to fill their manning requirements. Sailors were held in lock-ups, gaols, crimping houses and the hated hulks.[61] Self-organization of the nautical proletariat consisted of mutiny, 'running' and malingering. Indeed, in the sailors' slang, terms denoting malingering were exceeded only by those denoting punishments.[62] And these punishments, when combined with the violence of the profession and the isolation from other kinds of people, produced a worker who was on shore perhaps the most volatile, dangerous and creative of eighteenth-century working-class subjects. In 1728 James Oglethorpe argued that impressment violated the Magna Carta. He heard a man expostulate who had been closed into a Thames press smack, 'I that am born free, are not I and the greatest duke in England equally free born?'

[59] 'Petition for Arrears of Pay', *Calendar of State Papers Domestic*, p. lx; Marcus Rediker, *Between the Devil and the Deep Blue Sea: Merchant Seamen, Pirates, and the Anglo-American Maritime World, 1700–1750* (Cambridge, 1987).
[60] Elmo Paul Hohman, *Seamen Ashore* (New Haven, 1952), p. 224.
[61] Ogg, op. cit., p. 328. Between the summer of 1701 and the spring of 1702 thirty-two of those convicted at the Old Bailey were allowed to join the military in commutation of their punishment. See Godfrey Davis in *The Journal of the Society for Army Historical Research*, vol. cviii, no. 116 (1950).
[62] Frank C. Bowen, *Sea Slang: A Dictionary of Old-Timers' Expressions and Epithets* [n.d.].

Seven years earlier the Minters took up 'Arms in Defence of LIBERTY' and expelled the press-gang from Southwark.[63]

The workhouse might 'work ease out of pain' as well as these five modes of production. Indeed, it prepared workers for them. Often compared to the factory, it could be compared to school. Yet, it differs from them in that it was a direct result of government planning. The workhouse in London was the child of the Spitalfields riots of August 1675 when the weavers successfully rioted against the introduction of imported engine-looms.[64] One of the participants looked to a time when men would not 'labour and toyl day and night . . . to maintain others that live . . . in idleness'.[65] The following year Thomas Firmin, a City mercer and friend of Locke, started a workhouse in Aldersgate that employed 1,700 spinners – as young as five years old – at sixteen hours a day for 6d.[66] Matthew Hale wrote in praise of the workhouse after the 1675 tumults; he hoped it would produce the orderliness among the London poor that he had observed on a Barbados slave plantation. Workhouse advocates often had practical experience with Irish, African and American labour conditions – John Cary, the founder of the Bristol workhouse, was a slaver – and by 1696 some began thinking of India, whence materials and patterns were imported for English workers. The Spitalfields weavers again rose in rebellion in 1697 against the threat of imported Indian silks. They threatened the house of Joshua Childs, 'the father of modern banking' and the absolute dictator of the East India Company. Frightened by such tumults, John Bellers was stimulated to throwing the 'Mechanics of England' into 'Colledges of Industry', where it would be easier to manage them than if they were 'scattered each at their own Homes'. For its first eighteen months the London workhouse trained children and then sent them

[63] Quoted by J. S. Bromley in his collection, *The Manning of the Royal Navy: Selected Public Pamphlets, 1693–1873* (Navy Records Society, 1974); *Applebee's Original Weekly Journal*, 8 April 1721; James Edward Oglethorpe, *The Sailor's Advocate* (1728).
[64] Valerie Pearl, 'Puritans and Poor Relief: The London Workhouse, 1649–1660', in Donald Pennington and Keith Thomas (eds), *Puritans and Revolutionaries: Essays in 17th Century History* (1978); Richard M. Dunn, 'The London Weavers' Riot of 1675', *Guildhall Studies in London History*, vol. i, (October 1973–April 1975).
[65] B. S. Capp, *The Fifth Monarchy Men* (1972), p. 149.
[66] Joyce Oldham Appleby, *Economic Thought and Ideology in Seventeenth Century England* (Princeton, 1978), p. 140.

to parishes that were supposed to put out yarn to them. As this failed, the workhouse modelled itself more upon the manufactory.[67] In 1700 Bishopsgate workhouse was opened with a ward for 'poor Children' and a ward for 'Vagabonds, Beggars, Pilferers, lewd, idle, and disorderly Persons'. They were occupied beating hemp and picking oakum.[68] In 1702 the Quaker workhouse in Clerkenwell, partly patterned on the Bishopsgate institution, opened its doors to the first inmates; Bellers was one of its most active councillors. The children in it wound Bengal silk.[69] John Locke, an advocate of state workhouses, thought that children should be obliged to enter the workhouse at the age of three.

Mammon's understanding of contradiction, or how to thrive under evil, was unbounded by nation, place or ocean. The world centre of the modes of production was London, for in it the wealth, the money and the 'abstract labour' of the continents were concentrated; in London too were the modes of production and experiences of the worldwide producers. The wards of the City contained the workshops of handicraft production. Its growing suburbs were full of impoverished people trying to make ends meet by working in the materials put out to them. Near its rivers (the Thames, the Lea, the Fleet) were manufactories requiring wind or water and employing proletarians. Its port and river contained the moored vessels of plunder, war and transportation. To be sure, there was no plantation in the metropolis, but (as we shall find) many an ex-slave made it home: 'Black Tom's' adventures around London's docks were a popular subject for chap-books as early as the 1680s.[70]

[67] Macfarlane, op. cit., p. 262.
[68] Max Beloff, *Public Order and Popular Disturbances, 1660–1714* (1938), pp. 84–7; John Bellers, *Essays About the Poor, Manufactures, Trade, Plantations and Immorality* (1698); C. J. Ribton-Turner, *A History of Vagrants and Vagrancy and Beggars and Begging* (1887), pp. 186–91.
[69] William T. Beck and T. Frederick Ball, *The London Friends' Meetings: Showing the Rise of the Society of Friends in London* (1869), ch. 24.
[70] Anon., *Black Tom* (1686), reprinted in Roger Thompson (ed.), *Samuel Pepys' Penny Merriments* (New York, 1977).

IV

By 1700 the techniques of Belial had joined to serve the ambitions of Moloch to satisfy the cravings of Mammon. We bring our allegorical interpretation of Milton to a close. The ruling élites of Britain were not seeking the conquest of Heaven; they sought world power. They sought not the riches of Paradise, but to command the wealth of labour. It was not Divinity but empire and labour whose submission they desired. 'Political arithmetic' and the 'bloody code' of law had provided taxation policies dependent on demography; a statistically studied recruitment policy for the Army and Navy; an unprecedented flexibility of law and law enforcement; and a monetary policy that was internationally recognized, centralized and boundless in its futurity. These had been of huge assistance to the Crown and its commanders in the Nine Years War and would stave off the dangers of the 'many headed monster', transforming it through several modes of production into the labour power that might 'superlucrate millions of millions'.

London was a place where workers might find a historical definition that did not exclusively depend on the mode of production organizing their labour, and this was made possible precisely because here was a centre for circulation of worldwide experiences. Outcasts, runaways, mariners, castaways, the disinherited and the dispossessed found in it a place of refuge, of news, and an arena for the struggle of life and death. Many experiences were shared. The most noticed was the growth of the town. The migration of young adults from the country and from abroad exceeded in number the mortalities of war, famine and pestilence. The working people were ever renewed by outlandish migrations. The Huguenots brought a fractious tradition. The French Camisards brought their millenial aspirations and their experience of guerrilla fighting against Royalist Dragonnards. German Palatinates brought a Rhenish spirituality which was maintained through the Moravians, a remnant in London that would become stitched to Methodism.[71] The Irish, the Americans and the Africans formed an essential presence within the eighteenth-century London proletariat.

[71] Hillel Schwartz, *The French Prophets: The History of a Millenarian Group in Eighteenth Century London* (Berkeley, 1980); Daniel Defoe, *A Brief History of the Poor Palatine Refugees* (1709), republished in J. R. Moore (ed.), The Augustan Reprint Society, no. 106 (Los Angeles, 1964).

However, there were some continuities, as we shall find by considering John Bunyan's trial in November 1660. He was indicted for not going to church. By 'church' the judges meant the parish church of the Church of England, while Bunyan said he was 'a frequenter of the church of God' — a reference to the unlawful meetings that in the view of the judges 'made people neglect their calling' and which had been such a revolutionary force in the preceding years. Bunyan and the court disagreed about prayer: was it to be according to the 'many elegant, or excellent words' of the Common Prayer Book, or according to the spirit, an outpouring of the heart 'with sighs and groans'? They disagreed about the interpretation of 1 Peter 4:10–11, Bunyan saying that it made it 'lawful for me *and such as I am*, to preach the word of God' (emphasis added). Justice Keelin construed the verse 'as every man hath a trade, so let him follow it', and applying this to Bunyan: 'If any man hath received a gift of tinkering, as thou has done, let him follow his tinkering.'

The trial illustrates an instance of that 'criminalization of the poor' which characterized labour policy from Tudor times. Indeed, it had been thought of tinkers, the 'roughest members of the roadside fraternity', that they made more holes than they mended.[72] The Punishment of Vagabonds Act of 1572 had specifically mentioned tinkers. Criminalization as a social process not only entailed hostile legislation, but also was supported by a deeper ideological campaign. The Elizabethan prose writers attempted to marginalize a significant part of the poor to a criminal subculture of deviance with its own institutions, territory, division of labour, and language. Thomas Harmon, the Elizabethan Kent magistrate, translated their 'lewd, lousy language' which 'they term pedlar's French or canting'. Thomas Dekker wrote that he heard an initiation oath into the 'Ragged Regiment': 'Henceforth, it shall be lawful for thee to cant, that is to say, to be a vagabond and beg, and to speak pedlar's French, or that canting language which is to be found among none but beggars.'[73] So, when Bunyan disputed with his judges about the ministry of prayer, one of them contemptuously interrupted to ask

[72] Gamini Salgado, *The Elizabethan Underworld* (1977), p. 137.
[73] John L. McMullan, *The Canting Crew: London's Underworld, 1550–1700* (New Brunswick, 1984), p. 49; Thomas Harmon, *A Caveat or Warning for Common Cursitors* (1566), reprinted in A. V. Judges (ed.), *The Elizabethan Underworld* (1965), p. 113; Thomas Dekker, *The Bellman of London* (1608), in ibid., p. 308.

'Who is your god? Beelzebub?' And, after Bunyan gently explained that they 'had the comfortable presence of God among us', Justice Keelin 'called this pedlar's French saying that I must leave off my canting'. The process of criminalization included such semantic manœuvres to deny voice and reason to the powerless.

The dictionaries of 'thieves' cant' continued to appear in the late seventeenth century and in the eighteenth century, inviting their readers to imagine a vigorous, threatening underworld or an 'out-lawed deviant population'.[74] And despite Bunyan's twelve years' imprisonment and threatened hanging ('You must stretch by the neck,' Justice Keelin said), the radical theology of his Pilgrim with his egalitarian class hatred would persist too as an underground presence among the London poor. Bunyan, the tinker, wrote against the thieving and pilfering of the purported underworld. Yet he was not unattracted to its energy, as when he wrote of old Tod, 'the veriest rogue that breathes upon the face of the earth', who came into court, 'clothed in a green suit, with his leather girdle in his hand, his bosom open, and all in a dung sweat'. In *The Life and Death of Mr Badman* (1680) Bunyan understands that the long unreasonable hours, the pitiless driving, and the absence of time to read or pray, and masters 'such as mind nothing but their worldly concerns', contributed to the drinking, cursing, pilfering and whoring of their apprentices. One reads this great plebeian moralist in vain to find confirmation of a hermetically sealed underworld of crime that middle-class authors attributed to the poor. On the contrary, as we see at his trial, his faith was tested by imprisonment and the criminalization of his doctrines and ideas. The court pretends these are incomprehensible as spoken in an unknown, forbidden language, and thus it is spared the embarrassment of reasoning with them. It was left to his wife, who had miscarried their fifth child as a result of Bunyan's arrest, to summarize them: he was condemned 'because he is a tinker, and a poor man, therefore he is despised, and cannot have justice'.

There were other continuities, especially those represented in the pregnant phrase, 'the free-born Briton', whose meaning was a matter of the necessities and creativities of successive generations. We find its meaning in the law and traditions of *habeas corpus*. We find it in the deeply held suspicion of a standing army. We find

[74] McMullan, op. cit., p. 96.

it in the rejection of the workhouse, the factory, impressment, involuntary apprenticeship, indoor relief, slavery and involuntary servitude. At its most dangerous the struggle of the English Revolution was a struggle against expropriation from the 'earthly treasury'. By the 1690s the struggle was against the appropriation of surplus labour. If the struggle at mid-century had been against buying and selling as such, that at the end of the century was a struggle for money and what money could buy. Against these abiding struggles of freedom, Lucifer (to turn to Milton once again) as a last resort relied upon the gallows at Tyburn. Formerly there had been a debate about the death penalty. Winstanley wrote:

It is not for one creature called man to kill another, for this is abominable to the Spirit, and it is the curse which hath made the Creation to groan under bondage; for if I kill you I am a murderer; if a third come, and hang or kill me for murdering you, he is a murderer of me; and so by the government of the first *Adam*, murder hath been called Justice when it is but the curse.[75]

That debate had been silenced. We now shall attempt to quantify the 'curse', following a course proposed by William Petty, who in 1670 advocated that the 'annual totals of corporal sufferings and persons imprisoned for crime' should be collected in order 'to know the measure of vice and sin in the nation'.[76]

[75] Gerrard Winstanley, *The New Law of Righteousness* (1649), reprinted in George Sabine (ed.), *The Works of Gerrard Winstanley* (Ithaca, NY, 1941), p. 193.
[76] V. A. C. Gatrell, Bruce Lenman and Geoffrey Parker (eds), *Crime and the Law: The Social History of Crime in Western Europe since 1500* (1980), p. 3.

CHAPTER THREE

Tyburnography:
The Sociology of the Condemned

Hetherto gentle Reader we have remembred a great
nomber of lamentable and bloudy tragedies of suche
as have been slayne through extreme crueltie.

John Foxe, *The Actes and Monuments of These Latter
and Perilous Dayes* (1563)

I perceived a slender Gentleman address himself to one
of the Criminals in a low tone to this Effect, That he
would tip him as handsome a Coffin as a Man need
desire to set his A-se in, if he would come down but
half a dozen more Pages of Confession.

Anon., *A Trip Through the Town* (c. 1735)

I

The authors of the death statutes belonged to the ruling and propertied classes. Those who suffered at Tyburn belonged to the
propertyless and the oppressed. Yet, an understanding of the class
dynamics of the eighteenth-century judicial process in London
cannot be gained by walking, so to speak, between only Westminster
and Tyburn, the two most prominent sites of West End power,
because the laws created in Westminster causing 'examples' to suffer
at Tyburn were adjudicated some miles east at Newgate and the
Old Bailey, where a third social class, small property-holders, neither
as numerous as the poor nor as powerful as the oligarchs, met 'to
hear and determine' offences. From a large number of malefactors
they selected a handful to hang every six weeks in what Doctor
Johnson called the 'legal massacre' at Tyburn.

We may examine a single Session at the Old Bailey. The January
1715 Sessions was one of eight annual Sessions that tried cases for
the City of London and the County of Middlesex on commissions
of gaol delivery and oyer and terminer. It thus tried all cases of
felony for metropolitan London with the exception of felonies

committed south of the river outside Southwark. In January 1715 there were 52 indictments brought before the judges and juries. Of these 5 were multiple indictments, so 57 persons were actually put on trial; 25 were acquitted, 32 found guilty. Of the guilty, 1 was sentenced to stand in the pillory, 8 to be whipped, 17 to be branded in the hand, and 6 to be hanged. These decisions were made over three days, the court sitting from 6.30 in the morning until 9 o'clock at night.[1] It is useful to think of the Old Bailey proceedings as a drama. The setting was carefully and theatrically arranged. The script consisted of the black-letter law of the criminal statutes, the unlettered and unrecorded whisperings of the jurors, and occasional expostulations or pleadings by the defendants. The *dramatis personae* may be put into three groups: the judges, the jurors and the defendants.[2]

The Old Bailey was situated only a few score yards from the Fleet Prison and the Bridewell in the west, Newgate Prison and the Smithfield pens in the north, Newgate Market and its adjacent slaughter-houses in the east, and Ludgate Prison, Dung Wharf and Puddle Dock in the south. It was at the centre of an animal ecology of the metropolis where two-footed and four-footed creatures came to meet their destiny and be dispatched.[3] The Old Bailey was off rather than on a busy thoroughfare connecting Newgate Street and Ludgate Street. Its complex spaces of courtyards, outbuildings and the Sessions House itself, a three-storey, Italianate structure completed after the Fire in 1673, could be approached only by a single alleyway. Thus its business was isolated from the thick urban traffic around it.

Having entered this alley, three different spaces would appear to the eye. First a large gathering place, called the Sessions House Yard, in which the various actors of the drama – the witnesses, court attendants, turnkeys, prosecutors, compurgators, jurors, judges and defendants – would sort themselves out and distinguish themselves from those who came to watch. A bail dock, or low wall with short spikes affixed to the top, marked the boundary between the yard

[1] John H. Langbein, 'The Criminal Trial before the Lawyers', *University of Chicago Law Review*, vol. xlv (1978), pp. 277–8.

[2] *The Proceedings*, 14–17 January 1715; Gerald Howson, *The Thief-Taker General: The Rise and Fall of Jonathan Wild* (1970), pp. 27, 50, and app. 4.

[3] Peter Linebaugh, '(Marxist) Social History and (Conservative) Legal History: A Reply to Professor Langbein', *New York University Law Review*, vol. lx, no. 2 (May 1985).

The Sessions House: The scene has been compared to 'a giant Punch and Judy show'; it might just as well be compared to the amphitheatre of Greek tragedy.

and the second space of the Old Bailey. After 1714, when a turnkey had been murdered, the prisoners were kept fettered near this dock, from where, exposed to the elements, they could see and hear what transpired during the proceedings in the Sessions House. After 1716, following a just-convicted highwayman's vaulting escape into the safety of the crowd, iron crossbars were installed.[4] On the other side of this dock was a plain Doric portico whose nether side was entirely open (save four rows of supporting columns) to the ground floor of the Sessions House. Stone steps, railings and a balustrade provided entryways on either side of the portico. Within, elevated several feet above the yard, covered by the upper part of the House, was the judges' bench. On either side were partitions enclosing the

[4]Howson, op. cit.; *The Proceedings*, 13–14 January 1716.

jurors, and above these were small balconies for court officers and well-placed observers. The scene as a whole has been compared to 'a giant Punch and Judy show'; it might just as well be compared to the amphitheatre of Greek tragedy. Yet in the mixture of exposed and protected areas, in the promiscuous proximity of most of the actors (and the spectators) of the judicial drama, in the gaping front of the Palladian structure, there were violations of that harmony of eighteenth-century architecture that depended upon the separation of the classes.

Presiding over this scene was a combination of the bourgeoisie of the City in the person of the Lord Mayor, Sir William Humphreys, and the legal representatives of the newly installed Hanoverian oligarchy. In January 1715 these were leaders of empire and principal officers of state. They were: (1) Robert Tracy (1655–1735), a baron of the Exchequer, formerly on the King's Bench in Ireland, 'a complete gentleman'; (2) John Pratt (1657–1725), a judge of the King's Bench and a former advocate of the new East India Company, who would later become known for his brutal usage in court of Christopher Layer, the Jacobite; (3) Samuel Dodd (1652–1716), who had only recently been elevated to the office of Lord Chief Baron of the Exchequer; he made his mark during the Restoration when he successfully represented the London bankers in arguing for Crown liability on the interest of loans taken by Charles II, and he led the negotiations that fused the two East India Companies; (4) Peter King, Chief Justice of Common Pleas, a man who as Recorder of London and as Lord Chancellor had a legal reputation for incompetence and inattention. As the husband of Locke's niece and pall-bearer at Newton's funeral he was connected perhaps to the most competent and attentive thinkers of Whig England.[5]

As a group they were not as bad as some who had recently served the needs of the regime. 'Hanging' Judge Jefferies, the virtual dictator of London in his day and the most consummate bully known in the history of the English bench, had been dead for twenty-six years. Salathiel Lovell, a recent City Recorder, who was 'distinguished principally for his want of memory' and was rewarded some forfeited estates on the 'ground that he had been more diligent in the discovery and conviction of criminals than any other person in the kingdom', had also gone west. Tracy, Pratt, Dodd and King were not to attain the personal notoriety attached to those names. Nor

[5] DNB; Edward Foss, The Judges of England (1864), vol. vii, pp. 58, 231, 232.

did they need to profit excessively from the court calendar, or the 'Bill of Fare', as a later Old Bailey judge called it. These four were loyal servants in a Whig judiciary led by William Cowper (Lord Chancellor, 1714–1717), who would 'hang a man first, and then judge him', according to one of his victims.

Flanking the bench, between it and the defendants, was the second group of the Old Bailey *dramatis personae*, the jurors. These were twenty-four in all, organized in two panels of twelve, one for the City of London and the other for Middlesex. Theirs was 'the one institution ... which stands between the people and the abuse of authority by the state', to quote a manual on jury work by twentieth-century specialists. Or, to quote a frequently published eighteenth-century guide to the jury, it was a 'Bank' that held back 'an ocean of oppression'.[6]

Jurors were not, as we understand the term 'peers' of the defendants. They were landowners – small landowners to be sure, but landowners nevertheless.[7] By a law of Henry VIII they had 'to dispend £10 by the Year of Freehold for a term of Life'. Under Charles II the property qualification was raised to £20. In 1692 it reverted to '£10 by the Year at least above Reprizes of Freehold or Copyhold Land or Tenements, or rents in Fee-simple [or] fee-tail'. Blackstone wrote that they were 'chosen by lot from among those of the middle rank', but if they were 'middle' this was only in a social or political sense, not a demographic or democratic sense. Recent studies of income stratification of eighteenth-century London show that two-thirds of the inhabitants were too poor to even pay taxes, much less own freehold lands or tenements. 'Middle class' or 'middle rank' actually refers to the weakest part of the powerful minority of the propertied. It was precisely this rank, as Professor Rogers has shown, that was most susceptible to the crippling ties of clientage and dependency characterizing municipal politics.[8] Such people had more face-to-face dealings and neigh-

---

[6] Beth Bonora and Elissa Krauss, *Jurywork: Systematic Techniques* (New York, 1979), p. 2; John Hawles, *The Englishman's Right: A Dialogue Between a Barrister-at-Law and a Juryman*, 8th edn (1771), p. 10.

[7] Thomas A. Green, *Verdict According to Conscience: Perspectives on the English Criminal Trial Jury, 1200–1800* (Chicago, 1985); J. M. Beattie, *Crime and the Courts in England, 1660–1800* (Princeton, 1986), p. 410.

[8] L. D. Schwarz, 'Social Class and Social Geography: The Middle Classes in London at the End of the Eighteenth Century', *Social History*, vol. vii, no. 2 (May 1982); Nicholas Rogers, 'Popular Protest in Early Hanoverian London', *Past and Present*, no. 79 (May 1987), p. 70–101.

bourly ties with the 'loose and disorderly' than their richer brethren. The social class of the juror will also have been the social class of the creditor, the landlord, the masters, the employers, the constables and the overseers of the defendants. That social class, too, will have provided many of the victims of thefts and misappropriations.

In January 1715 the jurors found thirty-two people guilty of their indictment. Of these twenty-nine were crimes against property, but did not involve the theft of money. The first thing that is mentioned in the printed *Proceedings* (following the name of the accused) is a description and list of the particular properties that were stolen – a copper bed warmer, a silver tankard, a bag of sugar and so forth. This is followed by the prosecutor's evaluation of the goods in money. It is a suggestive sequence of presentation. The legal anti-quary, Daines Barrington, made one of the first and more interesting attempts to understand the social history of the law of larceny;[9] he relied not upon the evasive abstractions subsequently favoured ('rapidly increasing trade and wealth', 'new forms of economic activity'), but made reference to use-values – such as furniture, linen, wood and plate – that were prominent as stores of wealth and instruments of power or emblems of status during the different phases of English history.[10] The jurors of January 1715 would have had a knowledge of the social meanings of particular properties that we do not, whether they were goods of consumption or means of production, things for use or for sale, necessities or luxuries, insignia of office or means of survival. A hint of these meanings arises from Locke's view of a coat. Property's universal equivalent, money, was the object of few thefts, only four in the January 1715 Sessions. Of these, three resulted in acquittals (thefts of a 5-guinea piece, 9s. and 3s. in unspecified coinage). A guilty verdict was returned against Robert Williams, who forged a bill of exchange worth £60 1s. and was sentenced to stand twice in the pillory and fined one mark (13s. 4d.), a unique crime and a unique punishment. Otherwise, the relationship between punishment and misappropriated property at this Sessions may be tabulated as follows:

---

[9] *Observations on the More Antient Statutes* (1766).
[10] James Fitzjames Stephen, *A History of the Criminal Law in England*, 3 vols. (1883), vol. i, p. 468; John Langbein, 'Albion's Fatal Flaws', *Past and Present*, no. 98 (February 1983), p. 119.

TABLE I:

Punishment and property (Old Bailey Sessions, January 1715)

Whipped (7 offences)	Burnt in hand (13 offences)	Hanged (5 offences)
15 yds linsey-woolsey	25 yds drugget	silver tankard and silver
100 lbs hemp	15 lbs whalebone	spoon
1 silk handkerchief	3 holland smocks	'a large quantity of
groceries (1 quartern loaf,	2 cloth coats	Cambricks'
2 lbs cheese, $\frac{1}{2}$ lb bacon,	4 gold rings	600 lbs sugar
$\frac{1}{2}$ lb sugar)	1 gold ring	4 pewter spoons and a
2 holland shirts	3 diaper tablecloths	copper furnace
1 huckaback tablecloth	1 pair of shag breeches	1 bed, 2 blankets and a rug
4 canes	1 feather bed and flaxen	
	sheets	
	3 silver spoons and 1 silver	
	mug	
	1 cloth coat	
	1 russet waistcoat	
	2 coach seats	

The relationship between the punishment and the material of the stolen property is not really evident at this Sessions. Someone looking for a pattern might discern a relationship between death and metal, between a branded hand and fibre products, between a whipping and foodstuffs, but only the study of the evidence of other Sessions could convincingly establish this.[11] A clearer relationship between punishment and property arises when we consider its quantitative relationship to money. The stolen property was given two different monetary magnitudes in five cases out of twenty-five, and in another six cases a double valuation is implied. The first monetary evaluation is that of the prosecutor, and the second is that of the jury.

[11] Michel Foucault, *Discipline and Punish: The Birth of the Prison*, trans. Alan Sheridan (1977), writes of 'a political technology of the body in which might be read a common history of power relations and object relations'.

TABLE 2:

Punishment and money (Old Bailey Sessions, January 1715)

Whipped	Prosecutor's Valuation	Jury's Valuation
linsey-woolsey	15s.	4s. 10d.
hemp	–	10d.
silk handkerchief	6d.	–
groceries	–	10d.
holland shirts	8s.	10d.
tablecloth	–	10d.
canes	–	10d.
Burnt in Hand		
drugget	–	4s. 10d.
whalebone	30s.	–
holland smocks	10s.	4s. 10d.
2 cloth coats	–	–
4 gold rings	60s.	–
1 gold ring	–	4s. 10d.
tablecloths	10s.	–
pair of breeches	15s.	–
feather bed and sheets	–	–
silver spoons and mug	70s.	39s.
1 cloth coat	4s.	–
russet waistcoat	10s.	–
coach seats	40s.	4s. 10d.
Hanged		
silver tankard and spoon	£10	–
Cambricks	£90	–
600 lbs sugar	£10	–
pewter spoons and copper furnace	–	–
bed, 2 blankets and rug	–	–

We observe a relationship between 10d. and a whipping, between 4s. 10d. and a branded hand, and between large sums of money and a hanging. From the point of view of money the relationships are unreal because the properties were never actually exchanged for those amounts; they are only imagined figures of account. From the point of view of people, the consequences of these sums upon the bodies of the offenders were very real. The statute law made them so. We recollect that a larceny was petty larceny when the value of the stolen goods was less than 12d. Hence, 10d. appears often as the value of goods stolen by those who were whipped. Benefit of clergy was allowed in cases of larceny from a shop, stables or warehouse, if the goods stolen were valued at less than 5s. Hence, the frequency of the sum of 4s. 10d. in the Burnt in Hand column. The sum of 39s. is signally important too (though appearing only once at this Sessions): when the goods taken from a shop or dwelling-house without breaking in and without a person being put in fear therein were greater than 40s., benefit of clergy was excluded.

This form of evaluating property has been given various names such as 'down-charging', 'under-valuing', and 'pious perjury'.[12] The terms are suggestive and misleading. They suggest common knowledge of the monetary value of things, and they suggest that the jurors ignored that knowledge from motives of merciful humanitarianism. But the terms are equally misleading inasmuch as an imagined quantitative value has an objective reality. Yet, the market prices of things, especially small and second-hand things, were as changeable and as various as the number of buyers, whether these were pawnbrokers, fences of stolen goods or open markets. The 'humanitiarianism' of the Old Bailey jury could not have existed without the imagined reality of a commodity-producing society. The discussion about commodity society that took place during the English Revolution occurred at a time of fundamental discussion about law and the jury. At his trial, 'Free Born' John Lilburne addressed the court with these words:[13]

The jury by law are not only judges of fact, but of law also; and you that call yourselves judges of the law, are no more but Norman intruders; and in deed, and in truth, if the jury please, are no more but cyphers, to pronounce their verdict.

[12] Beattie, op. cit., pp. 419–27.
[13] As quoted in Joseph Tower, *Observations on the Rights and Duty of Juries in Trials for Libels* (1784), p. 27.

Thus he enunciated a major theme of constitutional liberty, which, despite the repression of the Restoration, remained the subject of a serious, sensitive debate that generally flourished at times when questions of libel, public assembly, freedom of the press or seditious utterance were put on trial.

At such times (1670s, 1770–1790s) the legal question at issue was whether the jury decided questions of law, and behind the eloquent, impassioned debate about that lay even deeper issues about law – was it 'made' by judges or 'discovered' by jurors? Sir John Hawles, in one of the most frequently republished guides to the jury, *The Englishman's Right: A Dialogue Between a Barrister-at-Law and a Juryman* (1680, 1731, 1752, 1763, 1770, etc.), argued that since 'all matters of law arises out of matter of fact' and since 'law ... is no other than a superstructure on fact' jurors decided both, and in the tense relationship between them and the judges their views and decisions should be pre-eminent. In the vast majority of cases the significant decision made by jurors was *neither of law nor of fact but of value*. Even in the few cases of political as opposed to property offences, it took an extraordinarily courageous, conscientious juror to defy the judge's directions as to the law and the evidence, because not only did the theatre, costuming, make-up and 'staging' of the Old Bailey drama give the bench the advantage, but material or economic advantage was with the judges too. They could dispense small favours and payments to jurors, excuse them from panels or allow them to serve again, and keep them from their dinners.[14]

Sir John Hawles wrote from experience about the political consequences of this uneven balance of forces. Some made 'a trade of being a Juryman', seeking office or preferment by refusing to 'give a disobliging verdict'. Others were motivated by 'particular picques, and a humour of revenge'. When picqued they would cry, 'Hang him, find him guilty, no punishment can be too bad for such a fellow.' These jurors would stretch the evidence or strain the law 'because they fancy it makes for the interest of government'. What Hawles called 'ancient jurors' lived by 'careless custom' or 'slavish fear' and merely 'echoed back' the judges' preferences. They rendered verdicts based upon the size of estates 'or to avoid the trouble of disputing the point, or to prevent the spoiling of dinner by delay'.

[14] Hawles, op. cit., pp. 13, 34. Edward Bushel was such a courageous juror. See also, John Langbein, 'The Criminal Trial before the Lawyers', *The University of Chicago Law Review*, vol. xlv (winter 1978).

'Antient Jurymen' or 'standing Jurors', those who actively sought to become jurors or to remain in the jury pool for several panels, were favoured in *voir dire* proceedings by prosecutors and distrusted by the defence, because experience had shown that their willingness to sit in judgement tended to a greater number of guilty verdicts than were rendered by those who accepted the responsibility only with reluctance. One of the reasons why jurors were supposed to be selected 'by lot' (Blackstone) was to avoid the presence of those who actually liked the job. Another reason was to prevent too great a familiarity with the judges.[15]

The nature of the two jury panels of January 1715 was this. One half of the City jurors, including the foreman, were exactly the type of 'standing Juror' whom Hawles warned against. On the Middlesex panel six jurors, including the foreman, would serve again, most of them at least twice – furthermore, this figure was a little smaller than was usual for the nineteen juries empanelled between December 1714 and December 1717; during this period the average number for each jury of those who, on the evidence of their repeated appearance, actively sought the duty was closer to seven than six.[16] In a population of nearly 650,000, of whom perhaps a quarter might meet the jurors' property qualification, this is evidence of the failure of random selection and of exactly that kind of corrupting relationship with the law that Sir John Hawles had warned against. Even the preambles to the Williamite and Hanoverian jury statutes acknowledged the susceptibility of juries to corruptions. A 1696 Act referred to the 'Partiality and Favour of Sheriffs' and 'the Corruption of Officers', among 'many other evil Practices'. A 1730 Act referred to the 'evil Practices . . . used in corrupting Jurors' and the 'Neglects and Abuses . . . in making up lists of Freeholders'. Judge Jefferies ordered the Sheriffs to exclude all 'sectaries' from the London panels.

---

[15] Hawles op. cit., pp. 44–6; Bonora and Krauss, op. cit.
[16] I studied 456 jurors on 38 panels in 19 different Sessions. There were 36 duplicants in City panels, 126 on Middlesex panels. On a City panel the average number of 'standing Jurors' was 1.9, and in Middlesex 6.6. On five of the Middlesex panels almost all the jurors were these practised ones. See *The Proceedings* for 8–11, 13 December 1714; 14, 15, 17 January 1715; 23–5 February 1715; 27–30 April 1715; 2–4 June 1715; 13–16 July 1715; 7–9 September 1715; 12–15 October 1715; 7–10 December 1715; 13, 14 January 1716; 22–5 February 1716; 5–8 November 1716; 11, 12, 14 January 1717; 27, 28 February, 1–4 March 1717; 6–8 June 1717; 17–18 July 1717; 11–14 September 1717; and 4–7 December 1717.

The moral character of jurors is suggested by Bunyan's allegorical account of a trial presided over by 'Lord Hate-good'. In his summation to the jury he cited as legal authority the Pharaoh, Nebuchadnezzar and Darius, who were accepted without demur by a jury consisting of Mr Blind Man, Mr No-good, Mr Malice, Mr Love-lust, Mr Live-loose, Mr Heady, Mr High Mind, Mr Enmity, Mr Lyar, Mr Cruelty, Mr Hate-light and Mr Implacable.

The typical juror of Hanoverian London, we may hazard, was a tradesman in three senses. First, having to possess a freehold in land or tenements of at least £10 per annum would most likely have made him one. Defoe wrote about and for such people, taking an interest in their difficulties, offering useful advice, helping them to retain the strengths of the Dissenting traditions while forgetting the Good Old Cause. Second, the Hanoverian juror would have been likely to have made 'a trade of being a Juryman', seeking preferment or future associates of business through the networks he could establish among the robe-wearing grandees and their servants of petty officialdom. It was the Sheriff who chose him, and since every Lord Mayor had first to be Sheriff, a juror might make important City connections. Third, in the practice of his duties the Hanoverian juror would have exercised a tradesman's knowledge in appraising little properties and assessing what these would be worth. His 'humanitarianism' was filtered through a legal–monetary sieve.

Half the women in January 1715 Sessions were acquitted; the jury exercised 'pious perjury' in half the guilty verdicts returned on the women. Two-fifths of the men were acquitted; of the guilty the jurors exercised 'pious perjury' in only a quarter of the cases. When the jurors closeted themselves (which they did not often do!) to determine their verdicts, their conversations would have been a kind of weighing of the exchange values of property and the mutilations upon the bodies of the wrongdoers. Even if we assume, against evidence such as Hawles' or the criticisms of Bunyan, that they set about their deliberations earnestly and conscientiously, they would have to reconcile two profoundly different types of reasonings, an assessor's art and a judicial–punitive judgement that would have consequences upon the defendant's hand, back or neck. Between 10d. and 1s. was the difference between a lashed back and death, between 4s. 10d. and 5s. the difference between a branding and a hanging. Thus, it was also through this legal–monetary process, not only the 'free market' of labour, that the price of life and limb was determined. Perhaps no other group in the eighteenth century was forced to make such direct calculations of law, money and human blood – which may help explain why in popular belief it was thought that neither surgeons nor butchers could sit on a jury. One of the 'idle and disorderly crew' who loitered around the Sessions Yard may have consoled the Tyburn children (sired by judges, birthed by juries) with the proverb that Shylock's servant passed to Antonio's friend: 'You have the grace of God, sir, and he hath enough.'[17]

II

The third space of the Old Bailey was filled with people who, in being excluded from an official role in the proceedings, acted as spectators to the drama of oyer and terminer, but who nevertheless produced a counter 'hearing and determining' of their own. In 1732 a book was published with a title for the times: *The Tricks of the Town; Or, Ways and Means of Getting Money*. Its description of the Old Bailey Yard possesses the virtues and authenticity of the distant, cynical observer. 'The Old Bailey Yard is crouded with an idle and disorderly Crew of Persons of both Sexes, who have no other Business but to obstruct those who have any unwish'd for Avocation to the Place.' Evidently, the author has business at the Old Bailey, but business not so serious that he cannot spend time watching the 'disorderly Crew' obstructing his way. He glances around the Yard. 'In one Corner stands a Circle, compos'd of, perhaps, a Baker's-Boy, a Journeyman-Shoemaker, a Butcher's-'Prentice, and a Bailiff's-Follower, telling how it was; By what means such a Robber was taken; who his Relations are, One boasting of being his near Neighbour; and another of an intimate Acquaintance with him.' The visitor has approached near enough to overhear the conversation: he detects their eager sympathy and the note of hero-worship for the defendants. These are the youths who delight in the ballads extolling highwaymen and footpads. The observer leaves their corner, and sees 'In another, a heap of Earthen-ware Women,

---

[17] *The Merchant of Venice*, II, ii, 158–160.

with Straw Hats, and their black and blue Eyes and swoln Faces, lamenting the Fate of poor Bob, or Jemmy, hoping the L—d will deliver him out of the hands of his Adversaries; meaning the Laws of his Country,' the observer finds it necessary to add, upbraiding the dusty potters for their ignorance, as if they didn't know that their adversaries were the Law. Their outlook is at once resigned and hostile. While the well-to-do ate, drank, pissed and defecated in china, the poor used the unglazed, unpainted vessels made by these women. The visitor turns his head to another corner of the Yard. 'In a third, a row of Spittle-fields Weavers, with the Lice passing in Review over their Shoulders, before two or three lazy Silver-button'd Ale-house Fellows at their Elbows; near whom, are four or five old Women, shaking their Heads at the Wickedness of the Times.' What news, pointed joke, telling silence, critical observation might a taproom fellow have picked up from weavers? And among the old women, were the times just as wicked in their youth as now? 'A yard farther two or three Grenadiers together, with a red-faced Serjeant or Corporal of the Footguards, ready to rap a Reputation for some offending Brother.' This was a familiar Old Bailey story. In the winter of 1715, for example, a soldier, Thomas Smout, had refused to lift his mug to toast the new dynasty: 'G—d d—n King G—e, I'll fight for another Man as soon as for him.' Two fellow soldiers rapped him a reputation in Court, but they 'not being credited', Smout was found guilty and fined 5 marks, a sum equal to more than three months' pay.[18] Having noticed the idle 'prentices, the earthenware women, the weavers and the soldier, the 1732 observer completes his survey of the sociology of the Yard:

These together with two or three Dozen of Whores and Thieves from Rosemary-lane and St Giles's, and a Company of idle Sailors from Wapping, resolve themselves into Committees of threes, fours, and fives, all over the Sessions-house-yard, and there debate on the Fates and Circumstances of the Criminals, till the latest Hour of the Court's sitting.

These committees and debates were the counter-theatre of the Old Bailey. Theirs was neither the complacent, haughty hermeneutics of the Bench, nor the hurried agreements of jurors who couldn't avoid

[18] *The Proceedings*, 7–10 December 1715.

a Shylock reasoning. To the latest hour they debated, which would have been 9 o'clock, a significant hour in the diurnal rhythm of the city. After 9 it was forbidden for singing or revelling to take place, or the beating of wives; it was forbidden for hammermen, smiths, founders or other noisy artificers to work; it was forbidden to 'cast any Urine-Boles, or Ordure-Boles into the Streets'.[19] Then the sailors, the 'Whores and Thieves' made their way across the City to Rosemary Lane and Wapping, where, if their 'committees' remained constituted, they continued their 'debates' in more familiar settings.

However, instead of following the street people, our observer appears to have stopped off for a drink. He has joined another kind of people. 'Nor are the Taverns, Ale-houses, and Brandy-shops in the Neighbourhood less fill'd with idle Spectators: for, besides the Prosecutors and their Witnesses (which must necessarily attend) there are infinite Numbers of Watch-makers, Poulterers, Barbers, Engravers, and other Artizans and Handicraft-Tradesmen, who have no other Business there, but to hearken to the Stories of the Newgate Solicitors, and their Companions.' In crossing from the road to the tavern, the observer crosses perhaps a sociological line of status, of property, or of skill, but it is not a class line, and certainly it is not a line reflected by an analysis of those hanged at Tyburn. This we may prove by analysing the life histories of 1,242 men and women hanged from the fatal tree.

III

The sociology of the condemned studies by the technique of aggregation those who suffered at the gallows. In methodology the study is not dissimilar to that invented by Petty, Graunt and Davenant, founders of 'political economy', and practised by Gregory King, the first demographer, because the social significance of the individual is expressed only in so far as he or she is aggregated with others to form statistical generalizations. What Gregory King did for the population as a whole in his *Natural and Political Observations and*

---

[19] W. Bohum, *Privilegia Londini*, 3rd edn (1723), pp. 107–109.

Conclusions upon the State and Condition of England (1696), we may do for the condemned. King's statistics were based upon the poll-tax and hearth-tax reports, new records of the 1690s; ours are based also upon a new type of evidence – the periodically printed pamphlet entitled *The Ordinary of Newgate, His Account of the Behaviour, Confession, and Dying Words of the Malefactors who were Executed at Tyburn.* As King's methods became known as demography, so we may call ours 'Tyburnography'. As demography originated in records designed to take private property under the sanction of public law (taxation), Tyburnography is based on records designed to warn people to respect property when privately taken against public law (hangings).

'The great Bishop of the Cells' (as the Ordinary was called) talked to the condemned malefactors in their last days. He summarized these conversations and published them in his *Account* along with his sermons. It was then sold in the streets before, during and after the hanging for the edification of his readers and for his own profit. In the nineteenth century those who sold 'Last Speeches and Dying Confessions' were familiar figures known as 'paperworkers', 'flying stationers', 'running patterers' and 'death hunters'. Some did 'board work' by supporting a placard at customary pitches; others practised 'burking' in pubs, bars and taprooms. The 'Last Dying Speech Man' sold literature that was part of a broader library of the street, whose other purveyors included the reciters of dialogues, litanies and squibs, taletellers and balladmongers.[20] And they rubbed shoulders with bear-wards, buffoons, charlatans, clowns, acrobats, fencers, jugglers, hocus-pocus men, merry andrews, players, minstrels, mountebanks, showmen, tumblers, puppeteers, quacks and rope-dancers, who in turn were part of an ancient urban culture of street-sellers of fruits, fish, vegetables, game, potions, medicines, drugs, toys, buttons etc.[21] Since much of that street culture has disappeared, there is a tendency to overlook differences in its evolution, and particularly to identify the 'Last Dying Speech' of the nineteenth century with the Ordinary's *Account*. However, the Ordinary's *Account* belonged to a recent medium of communication, print, and

[20] Henry Mayhew, *London Labour and the London Poor* (1861), vol. i, pp. 213 ff, especially the chapter called 'Of the Street Sellers of Stationary, Literature, and the Fine Arts'.
[21] Peter Burke, *Popular Culture in Early Modern Europe* (New York, 1978), p. 94.

its form introduced several elements distinguishing it from the traditional ballads that supported a mythic presentation of the malefactor.

One of these new elements consisted in the theological demands on the reader. This required more attention than did the homilectic and moral sensationalism of the nineteenth-century 'Last Dying Speech', which produced only responses of ironic dismissal or pathetic resignation.[22] A second novel element of presentation was the verifiability of time and place in each of the stories. The Ordinary's *Account* was history, not legend. That distinguished it from the timelessness of the ballad and the sentimentality of Victorian expression. This documentary quality of the eighteenth-century *Account* lent to it a wider range of uses – as tavern gossip, as a schoolmaster's text, as legal–social discussion, as practical investigation. Further, not only could readers judge the malefactors, but because the *Account* and the Old Bailey *Proceedings* prominently printed the names of judges and jurors, these in turn might be judged too, lauded, criticized or derided.

What went into the *Account* was subject to restrictions. After James Shepeard, the Jacobite conspirator, was hanged in 1718, a pamphlet was published called *Some Reasons Why It Should Not be Expected the Government Wou'd Permit the Speech or Paper of James Shepeard which he Delivered at the Palace of Execution to be Printed*, in which it was said:

The Sheriffs generally, according to their Duty on such Occasions, carry such Paper to the Secretary's Office, where they are laid before the Council, or before such Persons concern'd in the Administration, as are proper to judge and appoint whether the said Paper shall be publish'd or no.

The author of this pamphlet was at pains to destroy what he called 'the Sanction of a dying Person's Words'. Eighteenth-century Sheriffs and Secretaries of State kept an attentive ear to these gallows' utterances, and were prompt to intervene when the words spoken might question the Hanoverian Succession, the doctrine of private property, the sovereignty of money or approved norms of sexual

---

[22] Lincoln B. Faller, *Turned to Account: The Form and Functions of Criminal Biography in Late Seventeenth- and Early Eighteenth-Century England* (Cambridge, 1987); J. A. Sharpe, '"Last Dying Speeches": Religion, Ideology and Public Executions in Seventeenth Century England', *Past and Present*, no. 107 (1985), pp. 144–67.

conduct. When the 'New Minter', Charles Towers, was hanged in 1725, the publication of his last words was prevented by ministerial authority.[23] Censorship, therefore, limited what might be expressed in the *Account* and while we might speculate as to what was left out, our Tyburnography must stick to what was allowed in.

Our sociology relies, then, on the apparently insignificant facts of the birth, geography and occupation of the condemned, facts unaffected by commercial considerations of publishing, government censorship or the tangled and contradictory motivations of a condemned person speaking for the last time. The facts of date of birth, apprenticeship training and occupational history can be corroborated from independent sources in parochial, apprenticeship and judicial records.[24] These are as individual as a signature, and as authentic. When aggregated they may help us write the history of the times.

IV

I have studied 237 different issues of the *Account* describing 1,242 men and women hanged on 243 hanging days in London between 1703 and 1772. This is not a comprehensive figure. It amounts to an average of 3 or 4 hanging days a year, when, in fact, sometimes there were as many as 8 in a single year (excluding special hangings), though 6 would be more common. Nor does my study include hangings that took place near London, such as those Surrey hangings performed on Kennington Common.[25] But although the sample is not absolutely comprehensive, it is large enough that patterns derived from it would not be much altered were the lacunae in the evidence filled.[26] Let us now examine these patterns as they concern

[23] The Ordinary's *Account*, 4 January 1725.
[24] Peter Linebaugh, 'The Ordinary of Newgate and his *Account*', in J. S. Cockburn (ed.), *Crime in England 1550–1800* (Princeton, 1977), pp. 246–70.
[25] Beattie, op. cit., pp. 452–6, studies Surrey hangings between 1663 and 1694.
[26] A bibliographical guide to the *Account* and a location list of the whereabouts of individuals therein is contained in my thesis, 'Tyburn: A Study of Crime and the Labouring Poor in London during the First Half of the Eighteenth Century', Ph.D., Centre for the Study of Social History, University of Warwick, 1975, vol. ii, pp. 844–8.

the geography, apprenticeship, occupations and urban topography of the condemned.

Table 3 summarizes the geographical origin of the condemned.

TABLE 3:
Birthplaces of the London hanged, 1703–72

Place	Number	Percentage
London	483	38.9
England (outside London)	429	34.5
Ireland	171	13.8
Scotland	30	2.4
Wales	21	1.7
Elsewhere	42	3.4
Unknown	66	5.3

We note that a surprisingly high number were not English, more than a quarter of the total. Of these most were Irish (171). We also note that among the English almost half were born outside London. How unusual was this pattern? We can compare it to that supplied by the London emigrants to the American colonies on whose indentures place of origin was noted.[27] Table 4 summarizes this information. We note that among the London emigrants also, a high proportion were born outside the city, and the concordance of the two tables suggests a general pattern for the London populace as a whole.

This migratory movement into London is one that recent demographic studies have led us to expect. London maintained, and actually increased, its population during the first half of the eighteenth century by an annual net migration to the town, it has been calculated, of something like 9,000 or 10,000 people.[28] A primary

---

[27] Jack and Marion Kaminkow, *A List of Emigrants from England to America, 1718–1759* (Baltimore, 1964).

[28] All commentators are agreed that the vital index was negative; the extent to which the mortality rate exceeded that of births varies from author to author depending on whether they work backwards from the 1801 census (M. D. George;

TABLE 4:

Birthplaces of London emigrants, 1718–59

Place	Number	Percentage
London	1203	37.0
England (outside London)	1714	52.7
Ireland	69	2.1
Scotland	160	4.9
Wales	64	2.0
Elsewhere	42	1.3

social experience of the inhabitants of the metropolis, reflected in novels, drama, poetry and paintings, as well as in the judicial and parochial archives, was the arrival in town of people born outside it. A 1757 observer put the proportion of London adults 'from distant parts' at two-thirds. The records of the Westminster General Dispensary show that of 3,236 admittances between 1774 and 1781 only a quarter were born in London. The records of the Chamberlain's Court in 1690 show that 73 per cent of those given the freedom of the City by apprenticeship were born outside London.[29] The proportion of native Londoners among the hanged was about as small as it would be in the populaton of London as a whole.

Let us study the differences in origin between the London hanged and the London emigrants. A higher proportion of Scots and Welsh became bonded servants than were hanged. On the other hand, a

Deane and Cole) or forwards, projecting from the Gregory King estimate based on the hearth-tax returns, as does E. A. Wrigley in 'A Simple Model of London's Importance in Changing English Society and Economy, 1650–1750', *Past and Present*, 37 (1967), pp. 44–70. See also, Roger Finlay and Beatrice Shearer, 'Population Growth and Suburban Expansion', in A. L. Beier and Roger Finlay (eds), *London 1500–1800: The Making of the Metropolis* (1986), pp. 37–59.

[29] George Burrington, *An Answer to Dr William Brakenridge's Letter* (1757), p. 37; 'Midwifery Reports of the Westminster General Dispensary', *Philosophical Transactions*, vol. lxxi (1781), p. 355; D. V. Glass, 'Socio-economic Status and Occupations in the City of London at the End of the Seventeenth Century', in A. E. J. Hollaender and William Kellaway (eds), *Studies in London History* (1969), pp. 385–7.

very high proportion of the hanged were Irish, almost 14 per cent, while only 2 per cent of the migrant servants were Irish. From the relatively high concentration of the country migrants who came from Bristol, Liverpool and Portsmouth, it would appear that they were a more maritime group than the hanged. Of the Irish, a very large percentage of the hanged came from Dublin. Excluding Ireland, the hanged appear to have been from the Midlands, the West Country, and East Anglia, areas of declining textile production, and from the Thames Valley and the London provisioning areas. These differences can call attention to some of the specific patterns of eighteenth-century London migration. London was the vortex of English imperialism, which began in the Irish Sea. London also had a changing place within the social division of labour in two respects — agricultural provisioning and textile production.

Since about 60 per cent of the Irish who were hanged came from Dublin their migration to London was less an aspect of the town/country relation than it was the town/town relation. The penal code imposed after the Williamite *coup d'état* imposed many restrictions upon Irish commerce and industry: cattle trade and woollen manufacturing were crushed. Colonial trade and shipping were severely curtailed. As Swift wrote, the 'conveniency of ports and harbours which Nature bestowed so liberally on this kingdom, is of no more use to us than a beautiful prospect to a man shut up in a dungeon'.[30] The occupational histories of the Irish hanged at Tyburn show their concentration in non-agricultural employments. Table 5 shows less than 9 per cent were country labourers; most were apprenticed workers, sailors or qualified artisans.

A table like this can be misleading, as it may suggest a permanence of employment or fixity of experience at odds with the actualities of uncertainty and mobility that a few individual cases quickly illustrate.

Take Humphry Angier, for instance, a Dublin cooper. He enlisted in 1715 in the British Army at the time 'of the late Rebellion in Scotland. He was in expectation of being ordered thither where he had hopes of improving his Fortune.' Instead, he was sent to Spain, where he profited from the British sacking of Vigo. As a result he was able to set up as an alehouse-keeper in Charing Cross and made

---

[30] *A Short View of the State of Ireland* (1727–8).

TABLE 5:
Occupations of the Irish hanged at Tyburn, 1703–1772

Occupation	Number	Percentage
Apprentices	58	27.2
Qualified artisans	44	20.6
Sailors	39	18.3
Soldiers	17	8.0
Country labourers	18	8.5
Servants	14	6.6
Clerks, lawyers and merchants	13	6.1
Unknown	10	4.7

his establishment a headquarters for Westminster highwaymen. He was hanged in 1723. Or Martin Newland, who brought his wife and children to England to work in harvest and hay-making time. During the rest of the year he found money – and good money – in recruiting Irishmen off the London quays for service in the Irish regiments in France. He promised recruits 'five Pence Halfpenny a Day and four Loaves a Week, every one as big as a three penny Loaf'. Perhaps he recruited Thomas Dwyer and James O'Neal, who served in the Irish regiments at Philipsburg, Fontenoy and Dettingen. Both were agricultural workers in Tipperary who joined the spalpeen gangs of the English harvests. O'Neal had spent time working the Newfoundland fisheries, and Dwyer had sailed in Guinea slavers. When they were examined for highway robbery, they both said they were lace pedlars. James Ryan was born to poor cottiers in the west of Ireland. Being 'wearied of staying at Home' he went to sea and served on a Guinea slaver making runs to the West Indies. He fought in the Walloon Guards for Spain at Gibraltar, and then 'serv'd in General Buckley's Regiment in the late Wars at the siege of Fort Keil and Philipsburgh, where finding there was little to be had but Red Hot Cannon Ball Bullets, he thought fit to desert, and then he came over to London'. He was hanged for highway robbery. In London 'he provided for his wife and children by working about the river, going on Errands as a Porter, or any

Way he could honestly earn a Penny under the Masons, Bricklayers, Carpenters'. He worked in the hay harvest around London. But for most of his years in the metropolis he cushioned the insecurity of seasonal and casual labour by silvering over copper farthings and passing them off as six-penny bits. He was hanged in 1743.[31]

Thus, even for those Irish without apprenticeship training or experience in urban manufacturing, the route to London was via a wide variety of jobs. They came as veterans, sailors, pedlars, illegal recruiting officers, builders, masons, harvesters and counterfeiters. They did *not* land in London as country bumpkins, to be preyed upon by the sophisticates of the town. Far from being products of self-enclosed, 'organic' communities of traditional society, most were cosmopólitans of several European countries, and sometimes of three continents, whose roots were not in village life, though some were born in villages, but in the defensive institutions they created to sustain themselves in a hand-to-mouth existence. Arrivals in London did not suffer traumatic shocks through their inability to adapt to the contractual and impersonal role-playing of modernity. In London other institutions, in the form of night-houses, brandy-cellars, bawdy-houses and receiving kens harboured the wisdom born of fighting the Hanoverian empire (or surviving in spite of it) in Ireland, Spain, France, Flanders and Germany, as well as the west coast of Africa, the West Indies and North America. It was a wisdom and an experience that found its way into the pores of London, from which it would occasionally emerge, as in the river strikes of 1768, to make the London working-class experience cosmopolitan.

If we examine Table 6 we can find that the dynamic of English urban migration shared similarities with the Irish. We can see from the table that about 12 per cent of the English born outside London had been sailors or soldiers. Their experience had been with organized and forcible expropriation on an international level. For them the road to London passed through the sea lanes dividing five continents or along muddy marches up the Rhine, across Flanders to Bergen-op-Zoom, Maestricht, Dettingen and Fontenoy. These men had experienced the realities of eighteenth-century English capitalism long before their sociological debut in urbanized London. The world they lost upon coming to London was very

[31] The Ordinary's *Account*, 9 September 1723, 7 April 1742, 27 September 1736, 3 March 1737 and 13 April 1743.

TABLE 6:

Occupations of the English born outside London and hanged
at Tyburn, 1703–1773

Occupation	Number	Percentage
Apprentices	153	26.4
Qualified artisans	188	32.4
Sailors	37	6.4
Soldiers	33	5.7
Country labourers	77	13.3
Servants	51	8.8
Unknown	41	7.0

much like the world they found once they got there. Of course, one wears a different face on the quarterdeck than in the forecastle. Of course, one comports oneself differently while being reviewed by the Duke of Cumberland than while arranging with an innkeeper to desert. To this extent these migrants into London were well-acquainted with the 'role-playing' required of them in the city. And, as on the field or on ship, in London cash bought most anything: Old Mr Gory spoke clearly in Europe without having to take language lessons.

To the lover of eighteenth-century novels, London will be less known as the hub of imperialism than as the 'Town' with its 'Fashions' and its 'Season'. The expansion of the mercantilist metropolis, Werner Sombart wrote, was 'essentially due to the concentration of consumption', a judgement expressing a partial but essential truth. 'Wherever capital predominates, industry prevails: wherever revenue, idleness,' wrote Adam Smith.[32] Rentier wealth exhibited itself at the gaming-tables, cockpits, theatres, coffee-houses, flesh-pots and drawing rooms. Mannered, conspicuous consumption provided the comic subject of the great novels of the time.

[32] Werner Sombart, Luxury and Capitalism (Ann Arbor, 1967), p. 24; Adam Smith, The Wealth of Nations (1776), bk 2, ch. 3.

A constant and studious visitor to the gallows during our period of study would have observed that 8 per cent of its victims were household servants to the Quality – 65 of the non-London born. How prominent the theme is in the literature of the day! We remember Joseph Andrews, a parish child, who becomes a footman, accompanies his mistress to London and becomes a little too forward in riots at the playhouses and assemblies. The paternal protection of his master, Sir Thomas Booby, saves him from further corruption and a rake's nemesis. Similarly with Humphry Clinker, 'a poor Wiltshire lad' and workhouse boy, who is taken into service by Matthew Bramble, and then to London. There all is 'rambling, riding, rolling, rushing, jostling, mixing, bouncing, cracking, and crashing in one vile ferment of stupidity and corruption'. Bramble complains, 'They desert their dirt and drudgery and swarm up to London, in hopes of getting into service, where they can live luxuriously and wear fine clothes, without being obliged to work; for idleness is natural to man.' In London Humphry Clinker learns to aspire to a spiritual equality with his benefactor, which almost causes him, but for the timely intervention of his master, to be hanged. The paternal care of Sir Thomas Booby and Matthew Bramble is contrasted with the impersonal forces of Quarter Sessions, prison discipline and the gallows. The eighteenth-century novel, with its paternalist good feeling, expresses the viewpoint of a genteel *rentier* come to town to spend money. The question of labour discipline and labour supply therefore appeared to the parasitic and leisured class of the London gentility as above all else a 'servant problem', and few were the Augustan writers who did not flatter their patrons by writing about the insubordination, insolence and ambition of household servants. Tyburnography reminds us that this viewpoint was a selective one.

Of more significance were the London migrants who had started life as apprentices or country labourers. They comprised about 40 per cent of the migrants hanged at Tyburn. London was a centre of manufactured productions. In this, it did not stand in contradiction to the rest of England; the class relations of particular trades were more developed in London than in other English towns, but were not in qualitative opposition. Moreover, the integration of London manufactures within the social division of labour of the national market was on the whole harmonious, though of course from the standpoint of investors it might be more or less profitable to invest in other areas, according to circumstances.[33] In textile production these 'circumstances' changed profoundly, with regional specialization undergoing rapid shifts: (1) decline in the East Anglia and West Country trades; (2) experimentation with modes of production in London; and (3) massive restructuring in the North. In Chapter 9 we examine this process more closely. As for the country labourers, they remind us that London was still a country town.

John Middleton, an 'improving' Middlesex farmer writing at the end of the century, asks us to imagine the relation of London to the immediately surrounding countryside as a series of concentric orbits. The first of these, surrounding London, consists of towns and villages dominated by garden and nursery farming for the London grocery markets. Outside this is a ring composed of the villas, country houses and retreats of the wealthy citizenry. Finally, the largest orbit consists of Middlesex farmers supplying London, and these are of three kinds: those for whom farming is secondary to their business in the City; those who have gathered their capital elsewhere and to whom farming is a retirement; and those who are farmers by profession.[34] The complementary division of labour between town and country was not new to the eighteenth century. London's effect on regional specialization of agricultural production began in Tudor times. What is surprising is that 200 years later a harmony in the exchange of agricultural commodities is said to coexist with an antagonism in the movement of labour, even when that movement was an essential aspect of the movement of eggs, milk, peas, berries, grain, turkeys, cattle and apples to the city, and then from it back to the country – the night-soil and wastes that fertilized the cycle.

'Their parent, Earth, has in a manner banished them from her bosom; they have her no more to suckle them in idleness; industry has gathered them together, labour must support them, and this must produce a surplus for bringing up children.' Thus, Steuart's remarkable formulation of the development of expropriation and accumulation in agriculture. 'When thou tillest the ground, it shall not henceforth yield unto thee her strength; fugitive and a vagabond shalt thou be in the earth.' Thus, the Ordinary of Newgate applies God's curse on Cain to the agricultural workers pining in Newgate.

---

[33] John Chartres, 'Food Consumption and Internal Trade', in Beier and Finlay, op. cit., pp. 168–96; F. J. Fisher, 'The Development of the London Food Market, 1540–1640', *Economic History Review*, vol. v (1934–5).
[34] *A View of Agriculture in Middlesex* (1798), p. 51.

Indeed, the agricultural labourers who ended their days at Tyburn were fugitives and vagabonds in the earth, but it was not the just wrath of the Lord that separated them from their parent, Earth, but the statutes and judicial decisions of the newly propertied, the enclosure of fields, the taking away of commons and wastes, the penal code against Irish pastoral farming, the turbulence in the Highlands and the 'scissors' of rents and prices. Henry Grover was bred a day labourer. He worked on daily or monthly contracts in Luton, Hampstead and Hertford before he was caught selling a stolen brown gelding in Southwark. He was hanged in 1751.[35] For most of his life he 'did his Business, eat his Meat and rubb'd on, as People thus brought up are us'd to do'. The move to London for 13.3 per cent of those hanged, the agricultural workers, was rubbing on in search of work. As London 'sucks the vitals of trade in this island to itself', so the quest for employment led there too. Wagoning, carrying, carting, droving, higgling, threshing, podding, gardening, hopping, hay-making and milking were agricultural tasks that belonged to a London setting just as smithing and milling, for instance, belonged to the country.

As there were islands of the city in the surrounding countryside – mills, manufactories, pleasure gardens, merchant suburbs – islands of the country were found in the city, often clustered around the terminals of the main western, eastern and northern roads. At these points (Clerkenwell, Piccadilly, Smithfield, Stepney, Southwark) coach-houses, stables, saddlers, farriers, pounds, inns, lodging-houses and wheelwrights were found. St Giles-in-the-Fields was known in the nineteenth century as a thieves' rookery. This reputation was preceded by one for its transient population; because it marked the intersection of the main north–south route along Tottenham Court Road and the main west–east route along Oxford Street and High Holborn, it was a centre for cheap rooming-houses, gin-shops and taverns for the country population. John Burton was born in Croydon and bred to country work in Surrey. He drove carts and wagons of farm produce to London from time to time. He lodged in St Giles, where he 'contracted acquaintance with all manner of wickedness', as the Ordinary observed. We also learn that his wages were 4s. a week without victuals. He was hanged for stealing two woollen caps.[36]

[35] Sir James Steuart, *An Inquiry into the Principles of Political Oeconomy*, ed. A. S. Skinner, vol. i (Edinburgh, 1966), p. 67; The Ordinary's *Account*, 25 March 1751.
[36] The Ordinary's *Account*, 17 February 1744.

Temporary, unstable employment as the background to a robbery or theft reflected the highly seasonal labour requirements of the agriculture surrounding London. Virtually all of it was labour-intensive at certain times of year, particularly during the August and September hay-making periods, but also earlier when the podding season and the demands of fruit and vegetable-tending in Chelsea, Kensington, Lambeth, Knightsbridge, Hammersmith and Richmond commanded labour from as far away as north Wales.

William Holloway was able to get work outside the seasons when the demand for agricultural labour was heavy in Middlesex. He was born in Berkshire to labouring parents. When he was unable to get country work, he carried a sedan chair for Lady Weymouth and Lady Grey in London. He was hanged for a highway robbery between Marylebone and Hampstead.[37] He was twenty-six. The only statistically significant difference that we have found between the malefactors born in London and those born outside is the difference in their average age at death. The London-born tended to be in their early twenties. Those born outside London tended to be a few years older – in their late twenties or early thirties. It is a finding that is not especially surprising, since we might expect that those who rubbed on in search of work to London would more often pick up and go later in life: the reasons propelling them to such a major decision might occur at any time in their life.

The urban–rural conjuncture of the eighteenth century was characterized by the imperial functions of the metropolis; by the concentration of parasitic, non-productive revenues in it; and by a complementarity between the class relations of the division of labour in it and the country. The social relations of urban production we touched on only in relation to the work of provisioning agricultural produce. The fundamental relation of early eighteenth-century production was apprenticeship, and it, as the evidence of the gallows shows, was in crisis.

V

Forty-eight per cent of the Irish hanged at Tyburn had started an apprenticeship, as had 58.8 per cent of the English born outside London. The rate of completion for both was 81 per cent. Of the 625

---

[37] ibid., 21 December 1739 and 24 August 1763.

Londoners hanged, 252 (40 per cent) had started an apprenticeship. Altogether, we find that 498 (40 per cent) of the 1,242 men and women hanged in Tyburn in the first half of the eighteenth century for whom we have biographies had been apprenticed to a trade. By comparing these to two other lists of apprenticed people – those whose indentures were taxed and those who sold themselves into temporary servitude in order to obtain passage to America – we can consider how the social composition of the hanged differed from that of the poor and working population of London as a whole.

The first list is derived from the 1709 statute called 'An Act for laying certain duties upon candles, and certain rates upon monies to be given with clerks, and apprentices, towards raising Her Majesty's supply'. It was passed to raise money for the war, but in 1710 it was made 'perpetual' and was repealed only a century later. A quarter of a million entries were made between 1710 and 1762. These have been alphabetically arranged in thirty-three volumes by the Society of Genealogists.[38] I have made a random sample of 1,000 cases from these volumes. In two respects a comparison of this information with the list of hanged apprentices will give an incomplete picture. Firstly, although I have not been able to determine precisely the extent of under-registration or avoidance of payment under this Act, it may have been considerable, especially in trades that did not require the 'freedom' of a corporate municipality.[39] Secondly, the 1709 Act pertained to apprentices throughout Great Britain, and so comparison will be inexact to the extent that the pattern of trades in London deviated from that of Britain as a whole.

The second list of trades is derived from the surviving records of bonded emigrants to America between 1718 and 1759.[40] Of the 3,117 'Agreements to Serve in America' approximately half included a description of the trade that the emigrant had exercised. I have abstracted the trades only of those who said that they were from London, 618, and from this sum I have subtracted 63 (11 per cent) who were listed simply as 'labourers'.

[38] Guildhall, Society of Genealogists, *The Apprentices of Great Britain, 1710–1762, extracted from the Inland Revenue Books at the Public Record Office*, 33 vols. (typescript, 1921–8).
[39] Surrey Record Society, *Surrey Apprentices from the Registers in the Public Record Office, 1711–1731* (London, 1726), vol. x, introduction.
[40] Kaminkow, op. cit. See also, A. Roger Ekrich, 'Bound for America: A Profile of British Convicts Transported to the Colonies, 1718–1775', *The William and Mary Quarterly*, 3rd series, 42 (1985), pp. 184–200.

Among the hanged 112 different trades are mentioned; among the emigrants, 89; and among the taxed apprentices, 110. There were 180 different trades in all. How can we compare the three lists? Two methods suggest themselves: we may classify the trades into groups, or we may consider only the most numerous trades in each list.

The problem with classification is that substantial assumptions about the division of labour must be made, and these may predetermine important questions about the nature of class relations in social production. Professor Pound in his study of the trade structure of sixteenth-century Norwich classified trades by the materials of labour and the use of the product of labour.[41] It is his typology of trades that I've employed in Figure 1. It is important to remember that behind each column category lies a myriad of different callings:

Food and Drink: Victuallers, poulterers, grocers, gardeners, fishermen, distillers, butchers, bakers, wine-dealers, millers and chocolate-makers.
Building: Plumbers, glaziers, masons, chimney-sweeps, bricklayers, carpenters, plasterers, brickmakers, house-painters, slaters, glass-grinders, glass-cutters and sawyers.
Textiles: Weavers, spinners, sailmakers, hotpressers, dyers, silk-winders, stocking trimmers, linen-printers, calico-printers and flaxters.
Metal and Allied: Founders, ironmongers, gunsmiths, silversmiths, blacksmiths, sword-cutlers, goldsmiths, watchmakers, locksmiths, pin-makers, needle-makers, silver-trimmers, buckle-makers, sieve-makers, silver-spinners, braziers and surgical-instrument makers.
Leather and Allied: Glovers, tanners, saddlers, curriers, collar-makers, shoe-makers, patten-makers, cordwainers and heel-makers.
Health and Service: Surgeons, apothecaries, cooks, wig-makers, lawyers and clerks.
Clothing: Tailors, stay-makers, mantua-makers, hatters, button-makers, needle-workers and breech-makers.
Transport: Wagoners, wheelwrights, farriers, coach-carvers, carters, watermen, coachmen, cab-makers and shipwrights.
Furnishing: Upholsterers, turners, joiners, chair-makers, carvers and cabinet-makers.

[41] J. F. Pound, 'The Social Structure and Trade Structure of Norwich, 1525–1575', *Past and Present*, no. 34 (July 1966), p. 57. Besides the material of the product and the use of the product, Porphyre Petrovitch, 'Recherches sur la criminalité à Paris dans la seconde moitié du XVIIIe siècle', in *Crimes et criminalité en France 17ᵉ–18ᵉ siècles*, eds A. Abbiateci et al., *Cahiers des Annales*, vol. xxxiii (Paris, 1971), uses two other criteria in developing his classification of the trade structure, namely the employer, and the legal owner of the labour power.

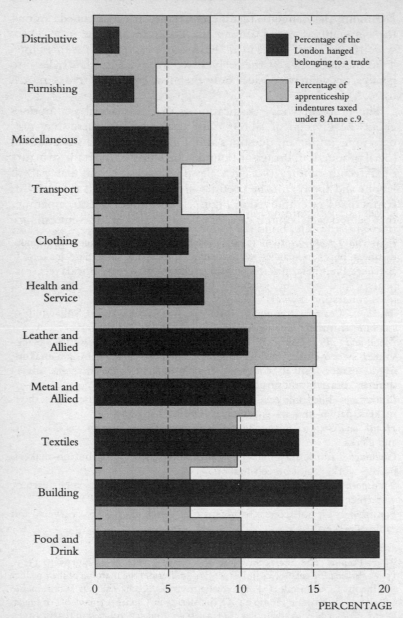

Figure 1: Breakdown of trades. The London hanged versus taxed apprenticeship indentures in England

Distributive: Linen-drapers, clothiers, mercers, haberdashers and tallow-chandlers.

Miscellaneous: Jewellers, ivory-turners, box-makers, coopers, potters, packers, colliers, pipe-makers, map-makers, block-makers, printers, card-makers and papermakers.

These people *made* eighteenth-century London: its streets and markets, its bricks and spires, its ships and wagons, its swords and rifles, its tables and chairs, its pastries and beers, waistcoats and boots – all the immense materiality of that metropolis was the work of their collective hands. This was the century of *homo faber*. These were the men and women of its *making* class.

Let us now examine Figure 1. The proportion of hanged apprentices in the textile, building and food-and-drink trades was greater than the corresponding proportions among the taxed apprentices. Perhaps this may be accounted for by the fact that such groups would predominate in an urban sample as opposed to one that was nationwide. The differential in the food-and-drink group is caused by the differential in a single trade, the butchers. Of the hanged apprentices 10 per cent were butchers, while only 3.3 per cent of the taxed apprentices and 1.6 per cent of the bonded emigrants belonged to this trade. Similarly, the differential in the textiles category is caused by the relative predominance of weavers. These differentials are of considerable interest and we will come back to them later (Chapter 6 and Chapter 8).

The study of particular trades raises fewer problems. Table 7 avoids problems of classification.

TABLE 7:

The ten most numerous trades in three groups

Trade	Number	Percentage
Hanged		
Weaver	46	9.6
Butcher	45	9.4
Shoemaker	34	7.1
Barber and wig-maker	23	4.8
Carpenter	21	4.3

Trade	Number	Percentage
Blacksmith	17	3.5
Waterman	15	3.1
Brickmaker	14	2.9
Baker	14	2.9
Gardener	12	2.5
TOTAL	241	50.4
Taxed		
Cordwainer	90	8.9
Tailor	63	6.2
Barber and wig-maker	54	5.3
Weaver	50	4.9
Carpenter	45	4.4
Mercer/merchant	38	3.7
Cooper	37	3.6
Butcher	34	3.3
Baker	29	2.8
Joiner	23	2.2
TOTAL	463	45.3
Bonded Migrants		
Carpenter	53	8.7
Weaver	50	8.2
Cordwainer	39	6.4
Bricklayer	33	5.4
Tailor	30	4.9
Clerk/bookkeeper	24	3.9
Joiner	18	2.9
Barber and wig-maker	18	2.9
Cooper	17	2.7
Smith	16	2.6
TOTAL	298	48.6

Two similarities among the three groups stand out. First, in each group the ten most numerous trades account for about half the number of people designated by that group as a whole. Second, there are a large number of trades common to the three groups. Three of them (weaver, carpenter and barber/wig-maker) appear in all three samples. When we consider these four trades as a proportion of the ten most numerous trades within each group, we get the following figures: Hanged, 51 per cent; Taxed, 54 per cent; and Bonded Migrants, 52 per cent. Three or four trades appear in the Taxed and Bonded Migrants groups, but not the Hanged. The trades of butcher and baker appear under Hanged and Taxed but not under Bonded Migrants. This measure of overlapping suggests that the samples are representative of the trade structure of the population in London as a whole. What is the significance of this finding?

The history of eighteenth-century working and poor people has been deeply influenced by the assumption that their internal stratification was characterized by a deep rift between artisans, apprentices and journeymen on the one hand, and on the other, vagrants, criminals and 'riff-raff'. The work of the great London historian, George Rudé, has done most to establish the validity of this view, yet it is one which the results of our investigations force us to qualify.[42] Dr Rudé's interest in the London labouring poor focuses on such extraordinary moments in its activity as 1736, 1768–9 and 1780, when it engaged in widespread, collective direct action. He discovered that participants in popular disturbances were 'wage-earners' and 'rarely criminals, vagrants, or the poorest of the poor'. He distinguishes three groups within the London 'lower orders'. First, 'the small shopkeepers and craftsmen, both masters and journeymen'. Second, 'the unskilled workers in more or less regular employment: the porters, watermen, water-carriers, day-labourers, and domestic servants'. Third, the 'destitute, beggars, homeless, vagrants, part-employed, seamstresses, and home-workers, criminals, prostitutes, and lumpenproletarians (Marx's later term), whom the more respectable workers . . . thoroughly despised and rejected'. In so far as this stratification rests upon the actual occupations of different parts of the labouring poor it is difficult to sustain. If there is any means of studying those whom he calls variously 'down-and-outs', 'lay-abouts', 'riff-raff', 'slum dwellers' and 'criminal elements', surely it is the Ordinary's *Account* of those hanged. Yet a study of this clearly shows that the occupational structure of the 'criminal elements' was more similar than not to that of the London 'lower orders' as a whole. Nominal, occupational differentiation,

---

[42] *Wilkes and Liberty: A Social Study of 1763 to 1774* (1962), p. 15, and *Paris and London in the 18th Century: Studies in Popular Protest* (1970), pp. 50–51.

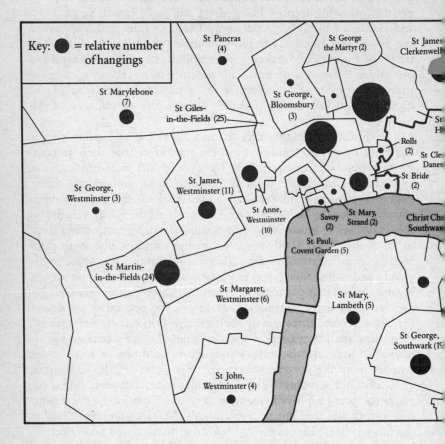

Key: ● = relative number of hangings

St Pancras (4)

St George the Martyr (2)

St James Clerkenwell

St Marylebone (7)

St Giles-in-the-Fields (25)

St George, Bloomsbury (3)

St H

Rolls (2)

St Cle Dane

St Bride (2)

St James, Westminster (11)

St George, Westminster (3)

St Anne, Westminster (10)

Savoy (2)

St Mary, Strand (2)

Christ Ch Southwa

St Paul, Covent Garden (5)

St Martin-in-the-Fields (24)

St Margaret, Westminster (6)

St Mary, Lambeth (5)

St George, Southwark (19

St John, Westminster (4)

Map 2:   The parish or ward of birth of the London hanged in the eighteenth century

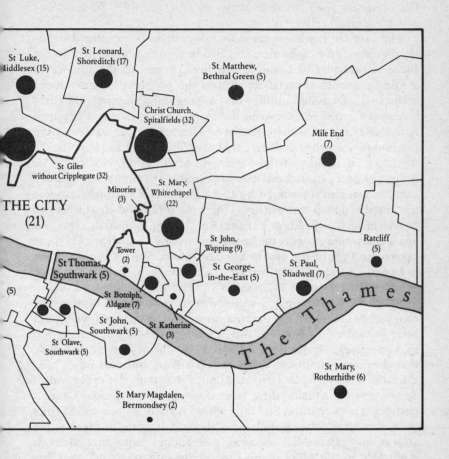

St Luke,
Middlesex (15)

St Leonard,
Shoreditch (17)

St Matthew,
Bethnal Green (5)

Christ Church,
Spitalfields (32)

Mile End
(7)

St Giles
without Cripplegate (32)

THE CITY
(21)

Minories
(3)

St Mary,
Whitechapel
(22)

St John,
Wapping (9)

Ratcliff
(5)

Tower
(2)

St Paul,
Shadwell (7)

St Thomas,
Southwark (5)

St George-
in-the-East (5)

(5)

St Botolph,
Aldgate (7)

St John,
Southwark (5)

St Katherine
(3)

St Olave,
Southwark (5)

St Mary,
Rotherhithe (6)

St Mary Magdalen,
Bermondsey (2)

The Thames

therefore, is not in itself sufficient reason for finding the house of the labouring poor divisible between a 'respectable' ground floor and a 'criminal' cellar.

The case Dr Rudé argues does not rest on occupational stratification alone: the distinction can also be seen, it is suggested, in the social topography of London, but here, owing to the absence of studies of parochial social structures, the problem is rather more conjectural. Dr Rudé implies that a geographical separation characterized the division between the wage-earning part of the population and the 'criminal elements'. The former are said to have predominated in the northern parishes of Shoreditch and Spitalfields; the latter, in St Giles-in-the-Fields and St Andrews, Holborn. The subject of occupational and class topography in eighteenth-century London was also considered by O. H. K. Spate.[43] His findings were presented in a map that pictures Holborn, St Giles-in-the-Fields and St Martin-in-the-Fields as parishes combining 'industrial areas and artisans' dwellings' with the 'amusements and vice areas'. Of those hanged at Tyburn for whom we have biographies, 625 were born in London. Of these, the Ordinary failed to specify further the place of 150, noting it simply as 'London' or 'Town'. The areas of London in which the remaining 475 were born are indicated in Map 2. The two parishes in which the greatest number of the hanged were born were St Andrew's, Holborn, and St Giles-in-the-Fields, with 33 and 25 respectively. From these figures it would be easy to conclude that they were the most 'dangerous parishes', but two other considerations ought to be born in mind. First, with the exception of St Martin-in-the-Fields, these were the two most populous London parishes at mid-century, St Andrew's with about 30,000 and St Giles with almost 35,000 − populations about half again as great as the 20,000 in Spitalfields.[44] Second, we should note that after St Andrew's and St Giles come supposedly safe areas such as Clerkenwell, Spitalfields and Whitechapel, where, respectively, 17, 18 and 15 of the hanged were born. The parochial origins of the hanged show no striking difference between what are said to have been the safe and 'industrious' parts of town as against the dangerous and 'idle' parts.

[43] O. H. K. Spate, 'The Growth of London', in H. C. Darby (ed.), *Historical Geography of England Before 1800* (Cambridge, 1936), pp. 529–48.
[44] M. D. George, op. cit., app. 3 (B), 'The Growth of London: Houses and Population'.

VI

The aggregative methods of Tyburnography have taught us that the hanged were more international in their composition than other samples of the London population. They were a mobile group of people, in terms of both land and oceans. Particular groups among the hanged (the Irish, sailors, servants, butchers and weavers for instance) stand out as anomalous by the methods of Tyburnography. They require other contexts of investigation and other kinds of evidence than the Ordinary's *Account.* One such context is suggested when it is recalled that such groups belonged to the labouring poor or the class of proletarians. We need to understand them in the context of the labour market, and the buyers of labour power. That is to say, the social history of Tyburn must also be an economic history of the trades and working conditions of its victims.

PART TWO

The Pedagogy
of the Gallows under
Mercantilism,
1720–50

During the first half of the period 1720–50 Robert Walpole was Prime Minister. He favoured peace and pursued a policy of expanding trade and acquisition of foreign markets. During the second half of this period Pelham and Newcastle led the 'broad bottom ministry', and then Pitt, a manic depressive, thrust England into wars of violent aggression. Historians both then and now were dismayed by the corruption of the time. Smollett, for example, wrote: 'This was the age of interested projects inspired by a venal spirit of adventure; the natural consequence of that avarice, fraud, and profligacy, which the monied corporations had introduced. This, of all others, is the most unfavourable era for an historian.' The Tory Opposition (Swift, Pope, Gay) criticized the rule of money. Their pens could be savage. In 1729 *The Craftsman*, the principal paper of the Opposition, coined a new word, 'Robinocracy', to characterize the regime of Robert Walpole. The Robinarch 'rules by Money, the root of all evils, and founds his iniquitous dominion in the corruption of the people'.[1]

The Fable of the Bees, perhaps the most interesting economic work of the period, has a subtitle, *Private Vices, Public Benefits*, that neatly summarizes the essential contradiction of the time. Another important tract of the period is *Money Answers All Things*. Both accept the labour theory of value that had been developed in the previous period 1690–1720, and both show that as money comes to answer more things the labouring class increases in size. Indeed, it does so as a proletariat because its labour is increasingly abstracted in the money form.

Chapter 4 examines the proletariat of the Robinocracy, which it shows to be picaresque. The emphasis is upon sailors because mariners supplied a considerable proportion of those dying on the

[1] Tobias Smollett, *A Complete History of England*, 3rd edn (1760), vol. x, pp. 259–60; *The Craftsman*, 18 October 1729; Isaac Kramnick, *Bolingbroke and His Circle: The Politics of Nostalgia in the Age of Walpole* (Cambridge, Mass., 1968).

gallows and because their labour brought the international products that gave to London its cosmopolitan sophistication. As things are answered by money they become commodities and must, therefore, have quantifiable standards of measure. The standardization of these, and the creation of them, is what gives to the period its mercantile characterization.[2]

Chapter 5 describes a class struggle in the tobacco trade that shows how measure actually came about. The struggle was carried out partly in terms of 'custom', thus bringing to our subject a notion often associated exclusively with agricultural production. There were hangings on one side and river murder on the other. Walpole attempted to introduce a *police* (then a French word) to monitor and crush the struggle but failed. International markets required international labour. Despite the heterogeneous composition of this working class, already it was beginning to cooperate in its own interests.

In the British Isles a home market was being formed during this period. We see this clearly in the provisioning of protein to London – that is, in the meat trades. Provisions originated from the far reaches of Scotland, Wales and Ireland; they were realized in sale at many markets; they were consumed in London. A transportation infrastructure was created; roads were built; capitalist methods of marketing were imposed; people were expropriated from traditional ways. In Ireland and in Scotland banditry prevailed; in London, highway robbery. Bandits and highwaymen conducted their affairs with distinct, living memories of a regulated moral economy.

Behind the abstracted 'corruption' noted so often then and since as being typical of the period, there were monied corporations insinuating an avaricious tone into society. An aggressive dialectic existed between two forces: one established commodities, organized labour and provided discipline at the gallows; the other consisted of an unusual conglomeration of people with different ideas and experiences of property – from the Irish 'fairies', to the shambles butcher, to the riverside porter, to the 'common People' of Guinea.[3]

It was precisely during these early conflicts in the formation of British markets that the symbols of the British nation came into

[2] Eli F. Heckscher, *Mercantilism*, 2 vols. (1935).
[3] William Snelgrave in *A New Account of Some Parts of Guinea and the Slave Trade* (1734) writes (p. 3), 'the greatest Inconvenience we were exposed to was the thievery of the common People'.

being. The cross of St George and the cross of St Andrew were combined to become the flag of the nation. The words of the National Anthem, 'God Save the King', were introduced in 1744, and 'Rule Britannia' (in whose first eight notes Wagner found the whole character of the British nation) was composed in 1740. In that decade the rules to the national pastimes were published. The rules of cricket were promulgated by the London Club in 1744, and in the following year Edmund Hoyle published *The Polite Gamester, containing short treatises on the games of Whist, Quadrille, Backgammon and Chess*. In 1744 the first of many editions of *Tommy Thumb's Pretty Song Book* appeared, containing lines whose explication would require a volume of social history:

> Nanty Panty
> Jacky Dandy
> Stole a piece of
> Sugar Candy
> From the Grocer's
> Shoppe Shop,
> And away did
> Hoppe Hop.

THE PICARESQUE PROLETARIAT DURING THE ROBINOCRACY

> The sailors, seeing things in a desperate situation, according to custom broke up the chests belonging to the officers, dressed themselves in their clothes, drank their liquors without ceremony ... [The purser] complained bitterly of the injustice done to him, and asked the fellow what occasion he had for liquor, when in all likelihood he should be in eternity in a few minutes. 'All's one for that,' said the plunderer, 'let us live while we can.' 'Miserable wretch that thou art!' cried the purser. 'What must be thy lot in the other world, if thou diest in the commission of robbery?' 'Why, hell, I suppose,' replied the other with great deliberation.
>
> Tobias Smollett, *Roderick Random* (1748)

I

'Picaresque proletarian' is a useful expression for distinguishing a part of the London working class and for describing a mode of its existence. What does 'picaresque' mean? It is derived from *piquero*, Spanish for pikeman. It is thus associated with the huge demographic movement that the Spanish Habsburgs caused by heaving Spain's vagabond and pauperized population into the boiling cauldron of the Flemish civil wars. The survival of such a person was an accomplishment.

It became the subject of a new literary form, the 'picaresque'. F. W. Chandler defines the form:

The picaresque novel of the Spaniards presents a rogue relating his adventures. He is born of poor and dishonest parents ... Either he enters the world with an innate love of the goods of others, or he is innocent and learns by hard raps that he must take care of himself or go to the wall. In either case the result is much the same: in order to live he must serve somebody, and the gains of service he finds obliged to augment with the gains of roguery.[1]

[1] F. W. Chandler, *The Literature of Roguery* (New York, 1907), vol. i, p. 45.

The literary form represented a European-wide experience – the survival of those without a station in life, the early proletariat. Such persons were observed in the bitter engravings of Callot, described in the objective light of Georges de la Tour, and profoundly acknowledged by Rembrandt. In England the dramatists of the early seventeenth century welcomed such figures on to the stage with hilarity and bloody-mindedness. By the late seventeenth century the picaresque had become fully Anglicanized from its Spanish origin; indeed it was transformed by Puritan moralism and by the concentration in the metropolis of those it described. On the one hand, it was transformd into non-fictional periodicals such as *The Ordinary of Newgate, His Account of the Behaviour, Confession, and Dying Words of the Malefactors Who were Executed at Tyburn*, and, on the other hand, it reached an apogee in the publication of *Moll Flanders* in 1722.

By that time the picaro had become a social type, the 'sharper' or 'blade'. Such a person exploited with surgical precision the new joints in the social body where pretence and fashion were the skin, exact incisions into which might result in profitable blood-letting. From the chimney-sweep, John Cottington, who robbed the republican pay-wagon of £4000, who attempted to pick Oliver Cromwell's pocket, and who succeeded in robbing Charles II of his silver plate, to Bampfylde-Moore Carew, who played to advantage the failed farmer, Tom of Bedlam, a Non-Jurying Clergyman, a tin-miner from Cornwall, a ship-wrecked Quaker, a Newfoundland trader and a blacksmith, disguise became a means of deceit and robbery. Jonathan Wild, the most powerful criminal of the Robinocracy, is reported to have said: 'The mask is the *summum bonum* of our sanction, a mask that may be put on at any time without incurring the displeasure of the Black Act or any other trammels of the law.'[2] Indeed, under the Waltham Black Act of 1723, disguising had become a capital offence.

Masking, costume, disguise and fashion developed rapidly in the

---

[2] George L. Phillips, 'Two Seventeenth-Century Flue-Fakers, Toolers, and Rampsmen', *Folklore: Transactions of the Folk-Lore Society*, vol. lxii, no. 2 (June 1951); Bampfylde-Moore Carew, *The Life and Adventures of Bampfylde-Moore Carew noted Devonshire Stroller and Dog-stealer during his passage to the Plantations in America* (1749), and the Ordinary's *Account*, 18 March 1741; reprinted in Frederick J. Lyons, *Jonathan Wild: Prince of Robbers* (New York, 1936), pp. 88 ff. See also John Ramsay, *Account of the Life, Adventures, and Transactions of Robert Ramsay, alias Sir Robert Gray* (1742).

eighteenth century in direct proportion to the new urban settings of show and promenade. The coffee-houses, the chocolate-houses, the gaming-houses, the gin-shops and the tea-garden were open to all who could pay and were policed by hired bullies or 'captains'. The tea-gardens particularly provided the locale for the intermixture of social classes eating, drinking, gaming and flirting. By mid-century twenty-five tea-gardens had been established. Such places were entirely for show, pretence and appearance (fireworks, air balloons, 'illuminations'), and in that they are to be distinguished from market, fair or pump. They became one of the urban stages for the ambitious, resourceful picaro. 'Take care of your pockets!' was the sign that the lights were about to go out and the show begin.[3]

What does proletarian mean? The word appeared in English in the 1660s shortly after the defeat of those very people who, during the English Revolution, had opposed the greed and ambition of the rising Moloch by their own antinomian theologies and resistance against the development of private property. 'Either poverty must use democracy to destroy the power of property, or property in fear of poverty will destroy democracy,' Thomas Rainborough had said. A word which at the end of the nineteenth century had attained all the nobility pertaining to the class that would bring to birth a new society from the ashes of the old, actually had its origins in the counter-revolution of a class that went to Roman history to find a term adequate to express its contempt (and fear) of those 'lawless' or 'loose and disorderly' persons whom it had just vanquished. The recourse to Classical history is significant because, in this case, it suggests both the militant confidence of a new imperial power, and an understanding that the basis of this power depends, ultimately, upon having ever new labour to command. Under the Roman constitution of Servius 'plebeian' denoted a working class of limited property, and 'proletarian' one that was good for nothing but the production of workers, or the women's labour of parturition. Hence, the appearance of 'proletarian' in the English vocabulary corresponds to the simultaneous discovery of 'the labour theory of value'.[4]

[3] Warwick Wroth, *The London Pleasure Gardens* (1896), *passim*; Richard Altick, *The Shows of London* (Cambridge, Mass., 1978).

[4] *OED*; G. E. M. de Sainte Croix, *The Class Struggle in the Ancient Greek World from the Archaic Age to the Arab Conquest*, Ithaca, NY, 1981), pp. 98 ff.; and Joyce Oldham Appleby, *Economic Thought and Ideology in Seventeenth Century England* (Princeton, 1978).

'Proletarian' was a term for the lowest of the low – whoever was 'mean, wretched, vile, or vulgar', to quote Samuel Johnson's *Dictionary* (1755). The ruling class held this 'proletariat' in unremitting contempt that was so consistent in its violence both of expression and deed that it suggests also a profound respect for this 'many-headed monster'. Its history was very much 'from below': in ruling-class imagination, proletarians belonged in Hell, where, as in Tom Brown's *Letters from the Dead to the Living* (1702), they were governed by Ethiopians and Blacks amid dirt and ugliness with the outcasts of the world, Jesuits, merry andrews and James Nayler, the antinomian communist of the English Revolution.

'This gray army . . . of socially shipwrecked and homeless elements composed the beginnings of the proletariat,' wrote the French historian of the subject.[5] He added another defining characteristic to the term. Like the serf and unlike the slave the proletarian had 'legal freedom'. But also the proletarian had 'economic freedom', in that he was tied down by neither the tools nor the materials of production. However, there is another sense to 'freedom' which needs emphasis, a sense that William Blackstone provides in his *Commentaries on the Laws of England* (1765–9) when he defines 'liberty'.[6] 'This personal liberty,' he writes, 'consists in the power of locomotion, of changing situation, or removing one's person to whatsoever place one's own inclination may direct, without imprisonment, or restraint, unless by due process of law.' The 'power of locomotion, of changing situation' was characteristic both of the picaro and the proletarian in the eighteenth century.

The picaresque as a prose narrative with its episodic structure, its individualist attention to the protagonist, its structural resolution by accident, fate or fortune, was ill-suited to showing the collective power of the proletarian in the face of its many enemies or through the course of its history. Still, it remains a valuable and symptomatic source of evidence. The contradiction between the individualism of picaresque *presentation* and the collectivism of proletarian *experience* is nowhere more evident than in the life of a sailor, especially one about to be hanged, where the individual mind can concentrate, as Dr Johnson observed, 'wonderfully'.[7]

---

[5] Alfred Meusel, 'Proletariat', *International Encyclopedia of the Social Sciences*, 1st edn (New York, 1936).
[6] Vol. i, bk. 1, p. 134.
[7] James Boswell, *Life of Johnson* (1791), 19 September 1777.

II

As a characteristic example of such picaresque concentration of proletarian experience we may summarize the history of John Meffs, who was hanged at the age of forty in 1721. Meffs was born in London to French Huguenot parents. He served his time as an apprentice to a weaver, but the vicissitudes of the London silk-weaving trades made it impossible for him to maintain his wife and children, and so he took to thieving. He might have been hanged four years earlier, but, in the confusion resulting from the bailiffs serving a writ against the hangman for debt, the mob pounced on the hangman 'and beat him to death'; Meffs was transported to America instead.[8] The transport ship carrying him to the plantations was taken by pirates. While most of the felons signed articles aboard the pirate ship (which included in its complement the legendary Anne Bonny and Mary Read), Meffs did not and was marooned on a desert island. He stole 'an Indian canoe' and made his way to the mainland, where he entered ship again, sailing between Virginia and South Carolina and Barbados and Jamaica. He then returned to England, fell into his 'former wicked Practises' and was imprisoned in Newgate. With the assistance of a bricklayer he escaped and fled to Hatfield, where he was betrayed into the hands of Jonathan Wild, who turned him in to the authorities for 'a very handsome Sum'. Departing this 'restless and tumultuous World', he hanged conscious of the 'Misfortunes' of his life. He hoped that his father, currently a gardener in Amsterdam, would provide for the children of his first wife, and that his industrious second wife would care for her children. He regretted that he had not run once more, to Ireland, for that 'regular and sober life' that everywhere else had eluded him.

Meffs' story is the picaresque presentation of a large and historic experience of 'the deep-sea proletariat', the labour force of mercantilism. Its size can be estimated by a government office – the Receiver-General of the Sixpences from the Merchant Seamen – which was established in 1695 to collect a tax from each merchant

---

[8] There are two sources for Meffs' life: *Select Trials at the Sessions-House in the Old Bailey* (1742), vol. i, pp. 70–73, and the Ordinary's *Account*, 11 September 1721; *Reade's Weekly Journal*, 9 November 1717, and *Applebee's Original Weekly Journal*, 2 November 1717. See also Horace Bleackley, *The Hangmen of England* (1929), pp. 30 ff.; Anon., *A Trip from St James to the Royal Exchange* (1744).

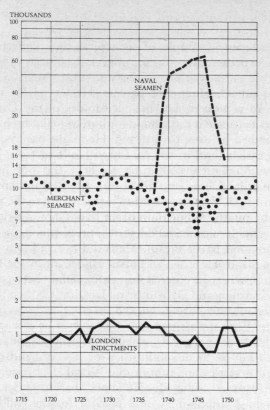

Figure 2: London indictments and the employment of London seamen, 1715–55

Note: The number of naval seamen (total complements of ships in commission) is supplied in Daniel A. Baugh, *British Naval Administration in the Age of Walpole* (Princeton, 1965), table 13, 'The Manning Level, 1739–1749', p. 205. Ralph Davis, 'Seamen's Sixpences: An Index of Commercial Activity, 1697–1828', *Economica*, new series, vol. xxiii, no. 92 (November 1956), provides a basis for estimating the number of employed merchant seamen. An Act of 1696 (7 & 8 William III, c. 21) specified that every seaman pay sixpence a month for the maintenance of Greenwich Hospital for Disabled Seamen. By dividing the annual revenues for London by twelve and multiplying them by forty (the accounts are in pounds sterling) we can estimate the number of London merchant seamen.

seaman of 6d. a month in order to maintain the disabled seamen at Greenwich Hospital. While inshore fishermen, apprentices and small boatmen were exempted from the tax, the records of the office indicate levels of annual employment in the merchant marine. Since £1 equals the employment of 40 seamen for one month, we can obtain the total annual employment by dividing the annual sum of receipts by 12 and then multiplying by 40. In this way we reach a figure of 20,533 men who sailed the merchant ships in 1721.[9] This is a large number of people to be employed in a single industry; it probably exceeded most others, excepting only agriculture and textiles. London was the largest port in the world and in the 1720s the number of its merchant seamen exceeded all other British ports combined.

Figure 2 shows the fluctuation of annual employment in both the London merchant marine and the Royal Navy (the sharp rise in the number of sailors attached to the latter was caused by the outbreak of the War of Jenkin's Ear in 1739). It also depicts the annual movement of the indictments for all London jurisdictions.[10] A comparison of the two will give quantitative, 'global' indication of that inverse relationship between sailoring employment and urban criminality which the picaresque presents in such an 'accidental' way, as if fate, and not commercial necessities, determined life. Tyburn was the 'fate' that awaited many of these sailors.

John Masland was a man who had spent most of his working life in the Guinea trade, and he looked it. A hatchet scar across his face was the result of a mutiny and shipboard slave rebellion. When he

[9] Ralph Davis, 'Seamen's Sixpences: An Index of Commercial Activity, 1697–1828', *Economica*, new series, vol. xxiii, no. 92 (November 1965).
[10] Indictment levels have been compiled from MRO, MJ/CJ, *Calendar of Indictments*, vols ii (1689–1709), iii (1709–1724), iv (1724–1740) and v (1740–1754). Where lacunae exist in the Calendar I have made use of *Sessions of the Peace and Oyer and Terminer Books*, MJ/SBB, vol. ix. City and Southwark indictments have been compiled from CLRO, Index to London Indictments, 1714–1755, vol. i. The technical problems posed by these sources and my suggestions for their resolution may be found in Peter Linebaugh, 'Tyburn: A Study of Crime and the Labouring Poor in London During the First Half of the Eighteenth Century', Ph.D., Centre for the Study of Social History, University of Warwick, 1975, vol. i, chs. 1 and 2. The statistical relationship between crime and the demobilization of the fleet in London was first noticed by Stephen Theodore Janssen, *Tables of Death Sentences* (1772). The total complements of the Royal Navy in these years is supplied by Daniel A. Baugh, *British Naval Administration in the Age of Walpole* (Princeton, 1965), table 13, 'The Manning Level, 1739–1749', p. 205.

became too old for the work (he was forty-four when hanged) he 'straggled up and down the Town', selling what he called 'French Brandy'. Henry Johnson alternated between working as a bricklayer and sailing in the merchant fleets. He took to stealing roofing lead at building sites because 'the Number of Sailors made it difficult to get Employment even at Sea'. He was hanged on 14 March 1739. Robert Legrose served in both the Royal Navy and the merchant fleets. Ashore he wrought for the brickmakers, bricklayers and slaters. 'He was a poor, simple, ignorant, naked Creature, having undergone a vast Number of Hardships.' He stole clothes from haberdashers and sold them to Margaret Frame in Rag Fair. He was hanged on 18 March 1741. When Richard Eades was discharged from a man-of-war, having been first impressed thereon, he was 'reduc'd to extreme Poverty'. So he took to street robbing. 'He commonly resided about Rag Fair, and kept Company with a Parcel of the most abandon'd Wretches too many of whom are in that Neighbourhood.' He stole the buckles, watches, wigs and money of wealthy people in Cable Street. He was hanged on 31 July 1741. James Ryan served the masons and bricklayers in London whenever he disembarked from his many voyages to the Mediterranean, the Guinea coast, the West Indies or the East Indies. But, it being a wicked world in all meridians, he took to highway robbery not many miles from the prime meridian. At his trial he was willing to admit that he had been a 'great Transgressor', though he did not think that it was justice that transpired at the Old Bailey.[11]

These men hanged as examples to other sailors whose lives were valuable precisely to the extent that their labours brought to England the wealth of nations. 'The Labour of Seamen', William Petty had written, 'and freight of ships, is always of the nature of an Exported Commodity, the overplus whereof, above what is imported brings home Money.'[12] In 1721 the oceanic proletariat exported more than £8½ million worth of commodities, and it brought to England £6 million of imports, arriving in London at the rate of twenty-four ships a day. Exports in 1721 included brass, candles, coals, copper, cordage, pilchards, herrings, glass, earthenware, nails, ordnance, lead shot, thread, wrought and thrown silk, cottons, linens and woollens;

---

[11] For these cases see the Ordinary's *Account* for 14 March 1739, 18 March 1741, 3 July 1741 and 3 March 1737; *The Proceedings*, 14–17 January 1737.
[12] Petty, op. cit., republished in C. H. Hull (ed.), *The Economic Writings of Sir William Petty* (1899), vol. i, p. 260.

imports included flax, hemp, coffee, corn, oil, pitch, tar, tea, brandy, rum, sugar, tobacco, cotton, linen, mohair, iron, wine and wood.[13] These were the commodity-forms of the sailors' labour.

A sailor's 'overplus' could be augmented in three distinct ways. First, progress in ship design and sailing techniques might increase the tonnage served per man. And this occurred: in 1686 each sailor served 8 tons; in 1736, 10 tons; and in 1766, 13 tons.[14] Second, the ship's turnaround time might be reduced to allow more frequent sailings, thereby increasing the turnover of the advanced capital. As the century progressed capitalists paid increasing attention to this possibility, because the third method of increasing overplus – namely, reducing Jack Tar's wages – so often ran into trouble.

Wages varied considerably. In the 1690s they were 55s. a month, a level not reached again until 1748. In the 1720s they were 30s. a month.[15] An Act of George II attempted to place a ceiling on wages of 35s. against a rising labour market. If the 20,000 merchant sailors of 1721 each received 30s. a month (£18 a year), then the total annual wages bill would amount to £360,000. When that sum is set against the value of the combined imports and exports of 1721 (£14½ million), we obtain only a rough indication of the value of the eighteenth-century sailor's work because we do not include costs of constructing or maintaining the sailing vessels, yet such calculations may suggest the labouring basis of mercantile wealth.

Some shipmasters were willing to advance wages in money or goods to satisfy the sailor's creditors (often the crimp). In the first two decades of the century this was generally limited to between a quarter and a third of the anticipated total earnings. The costs of rum, brandy and tobacco purveyed on shipboard were deducted from wages. Other deductions were made against the aggregate wages bill of the crew for damage done to the cargo in loading, stowage and unloading.

In addition to the quantitative calculations of this proletarian wage, there are some qualitative aspects to it. The crew possessed customary rights to carry some cargo freight-free. These were of various importance. The 'Privilledge' or 'Benefitt' (as these customs

[13] Elizabeth Boody Schumpeter, *English Overseas Trade Statistics, 1697–1808* (Oxford, 1960).

[14] Ralph Davis, *The Rise of the English Shipping Industry in the 17th and 18th Centuries* (1962), ch. 4.

[15] ibid., pp. 146, 171, 153.

were called) was fixed at 5 per cent of the chartered tonnage in the seventeenth century. In 1772 it amounted to 25 tons per ship for outward voyages and 15 tons for homeward journeys. A sailor who might make £2 or £3 in wages on a Jamaica run could supplement this by £10 or £20 from the rum he brought back to London. These forms of self-payment went under different names in sailors' talk: they were 'shakings', 'rumbo', 'forking', 'rabbit', 'plush' or 'blessing'. The sailor in the Royal Navy used a variety of expressions to signify what he took directly: 'To use the wee riddle', 'to sweat the purser', 'to tosh', 'to sling', 'to cut out', 'to knock off', 'to drop', 'to manarvel', 'to fork' and 'to earn' expressed different forms of directly appropriating things in a manner that to the Admiralty was nothing more than stealing. 'To tap the Admiral' meant to insert a goose quill into a wine or brandy barrel and drink at the King's expense.[16]

The sailor's 'earnings' thus had a double aspect: customary and legal, picaresque and proletarian. And he might receive a third kind of remuneration in the form of 'prize-money' – if his ship had indeed taken a 'prize' – which meant only what his ship had plundered from the vessels of other seafaring nations. Prize-money was often delayed, and in any case was available only at the Navy Pay Office in London. John Clarke, after sixteen years sailing out of Liverpool, had to 'pike to the start' in order to collect his prize-money. Necessity drove him to robbing, and the law drove him up Holborn Hill to his hanging. He had stolen a gold ring. A Norwich orphan boy, James Newton, by turns a coal-heaver, able seaman in the Holland trade and a sailor for twelve years in the West India trade, quit seafaring altogether after he was cheated of his prize-money. He took to street-robbing under the tutelage of Spanish Jack, and followed the lyric advice of a young Spitalfields dyer: 'Go with me and do as I do, and Money shall never be wanting. I live well upon the Lay, and have everything at Command. We cannot be hanged more than once, and there's an End.'[17]

Neither wage-payment, nor prize-money, nor 'Privilledges' and

[16] Frank C. Bowen, *Sea Slang: A Dictionary of Old-Timers' Expressions and Epithets*, n.d.; William Falconer, *An Universal Dictionary of the Marine* (1769).

[17] See the Ordinary's *Account* for 6 August 1740 and 11 November 1751; Anon., *The Whole Life and Conversation, Birth, Parentage, and Education of John Sutton* (1711); Anon., *The Genuine and Authentick Account of the Life and Transactions of William Parsons, Esq.* (1751).

The press-gang at work: Neither wage-payment nor 'Privilledges' were sufficient to solve the perennial problems of recruitment.

customs were large enough to solve 'the perennial problems of recruitment', so the merchant marine, like the Navy, had to rely on various statutory and coercive devices to recruit labour. An Act in 1704 (2 & 3 Anne, c. 6) allowed parish officials to bind young boys to shipmasters for seven to nine years at sea without pay, a relationship that anticipated the poorhouse–factory cycle by seventy years. The conditions of the nautical proletariat may be compared in other respects to the factory proletariat. Professor Rediker has written that the sailor can be considered 'the first collective labourer'.[18] Crew sizes varied. In the Baltic or Portuguese trade a ship might sail with a crew of little more than half a dozen. On the other hand a slaver rarely sailed with a complement of less than twenty. A majestic East Indiaman, a vessel of 450 tons, six times that of a Baltic trader, shipped a crew of ninety men and boys or more. A huge degree of cooperation was required between the men

[18] Marcus Rediker, *Between the Devil and the Deep Blue Sea: Merchant Seamen, Pirates, and the Anglo-American Maritime World, 1700–1750* (Cambridge, 1987).

on board, as is suggested by the specialization of tasks in the ship's hierarchy: navigation for the captain and mates, ordnance and ballistics for the gunnery crew, repairs for the carpenter, sailmaker and cooper, and so forth. A seaman possessed a medley of individual skills. He was expected to be proficient in knots and the intricacies of the running and standing rigging; to have the navigational skills required for reading the weather and coastlines, as well as the sun, the moon and the stars; and to know the languages needed for trade and survival in a world of intercontinental communication. The sailor had to be agile and dexterous, he had to possess stamina and endurance, and he needed immunological powers too, because typhus, malaria, scurvy and the yellow fever were his deadliest enemies. Only half the men sailing with Anson around the world (1740–44) survived. Despite Dr James Lind's discoveries in 1747 of the antiscorbutic qualities of oranges and lemons, 133,708 sailors died of scurvy and other diseases (compared to 1,512 killed in action) during the Seven Years War.[19]

The working and living conditions of the eighteenth-century sailor were as confined, dangerous and noisome as the factory or prison. The stench, the grime and the dark caused Rattlin the Reefer to lose his mind. Fourteen inches' breadth was the permitted space for a man to sling his hammock. When Roderick Random was shown his berth he was 'filled with astonishment and horror. We descended by divers ladders to a space as dark as a dungeon.' Doctor Johnson was adamant in his view that their situation was worse than prison: 'No man will be a sailor who has a contrivance to get himself into a gaol; for being in a ship is being in gaol with the chance of being drowned.'[20] Shipboard discipline was, if anything, worse than factory discipline. At its most personal and sadistic discipline on board eighteenth-century sailing vessels left marks upon veterans that were not easily forgotten or forgiven. Such brutality was often noticed by the Ordinary of Newgate in his conversations with the condemned. On 14 March 1722 James Appleton, alias Appleby, alias John Doe, was hanged for stealing three wigs. He first went to sea as a twelve-year-old Holborn lad. Until he was hanged seventeen

[19] Dr James Lind, *Treatise of the Scurvy* (1753) and *Essay on Diseases Incidental to Europeans in Hot Climates* (1768). See also, Christopher Lloyd (ed.), *The Health of Seamen: Selections from the Works of Dr James Lind, Sir Gilbert Blane and Dr Thomas Trotter*, Navy Record Society, vol. cvii (1965).
[20] Tobias Smollett, *Roderick Random* (1748), ch. 24; Boswell, op. cit., March 1759.

years later he had passed his life before the mast with brief inter-
missions ashore. Once he was transported to 'HM American Dominions' and another time he indented himself as a servant there. The
Ordinary commented that he was

scourged and lashed and salted which hardn'd his Mind, and made him
hate and defy almost all Mankind. So that returning to England ... he
cast his Mind how most easily to keep himself at the Expense of others,
and by spoiling and preying on all whom he thought he could with
security.

Thomas Wilson, hanged later that year in September, joined the
Baltic fleet at the age of thirteen. He was lashed, salted and hanged
by the heel. Later he was hanged at Tyburn, where he questioned
the 'Being of God, and would talk as if there was no Futurity'.[21]
   The proletarian aspect of the eighteenth-century sailor thus arose
from his relationship to money, from the cooperative experience of
seafaring, from the close supervision and brutal discipline, and from
the close confinement of the working environment. This was aboard
ship. On shore the picaresque aspect of the eighteenth-century sailor
was revealed in his revels and riots 'with greater Licentiousness than
is Customary to be allow'd to others', as Bernard Mandeville wrote,
who had observed these 'Lords of Six Weeks' between sailings.
'You may ... see them accompanied with three or four Lewd
Women, few of them Sober, run roaring through the streets by
broad Daylight with a Fiddler before them: And if the Money, to
their thinking, goes not fast enough these ways, they'll find out
others, and sometimes fling it among the Mob by handfuls.'[22] The
cyclical rhythm of the sailor's life, between regimentation and
freedom – 'Lords of Six Weeks' and slaves of forty-six – helps to
explain the seasonality of London indictments. In Figure 3 we note
that the seasonal distribution of London indictments is characterized
by two cycles: a winter–spring cycle in which indictments from a
winter low of around 75 rise to around 125 in the spring; and a
summer–autumn cycle in which indictments, having fallen remarkably early in the summer to about 100, suddenly rise to heights of
200 or more in the late summer and early autumn.[23] The time of

---

[21] The Ordinary's *Account*, 14 March 1722 and 25 September 1722.
[22] Bernard Mandeville, *The Fable of the Bees*, ed. Philip Harth (1970), p. 207.
[23] Seasonal reporting of indictments can be obtained from MRO, *Process Registers
of Indictments*, MJ/SBP, vols. xi–xiv. See also Linebaugh, op. cit.

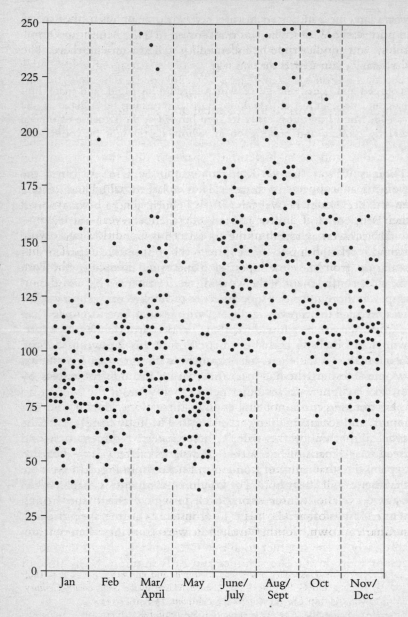

Figure 3:   The seasonal spread of indictments before the Middlesex Sessions of Peace and Oyer and Terminer, 1699–1754

year when most indictments are recorded corresponds to the arrival in port of the West Indian and East Indian fleets, when thousands of sailors were discharged. The seasonality of these annual indictment rhythms is one of the recurring statistical patterns of eighteenth-century London social life. It is not explained exclusively by the characteristics of the maritime labour market. In building labour 11 man-days were worked in December and 37 in June. In the agriculture around London, spring was time for podding, autumn for hops and orchard work. The rebuilding of London following the Great Fire and its architectural expansion into the surrounding countryside was the work of many thousands of brickmakers working in cooperative gangs called 'stools' (earthmaker, carter, up-striker, moulder, off-bearer, up-ganger). The gallows awaited their missteps, as it did for James Robert, a forty-year-old Devonshire bricklayer who, 'thinking to better his Condition in Town', trekked to London only to find no work to support himself or his wife (she took to street-selling) or his son (he enlisted in the East India Company), and was 'cheated' at Tyburn for stealing four silver candle snuffers.[24] Podding, hop-picking, cherry- and apple-gathering in the gardens and orchards around London relied on migratory workers from all over the British Isles, who found in the hedges and roads in and about the city little rest or comfort from their labours. A child 'dyed by the way as it was carrying home by its Grandmother who had been at Harvest work in Kent', noted the Vicar of St Pancras in his burial book.[25]

London was cosmopolitan because of the sailors. The ships' crews comprised men from all over the world. The historian of the Navy under William III writes that the 'interchange of seamen between the different maritime countries was widespread and deep-rooted a custom' and that 'English seamen continued throughout the war to serve under all colours'.[26] The origin of the crews can partly be suggested by the documents produced during the trials of the various mass hangings of pirates. In 1718, for instance, 31 men were hanged in Charles Town, South Carolina: 6 were from London, 5 from

[24] John Houghton, *Husbandry and Trade Improv'd*, 2nd edn (1728), vol. i, p. 189; Douglas Knoop and G. P. Jones, *The London Mason in the Seventeenth Century* (Manchester, 1935), p. 88; The Ordinary's *Account*, 13 April 1743.
[25] GLCRO, St Pancras, *Register of Burials*, 1689–1729, P90/PAN/1/3.
[26] John Ehrman, *The Navy in the War of William III, 1689–1697* (Cambridge, 1953), pp. 111–15.

Jamaica, 4 from North Carolina, 3 from South Carolina, 3 from Aberdeen, 2 from Glasgow, and 1 each from Newcastle, Guernsey, Dublin, Oporto, Holland, Antigua and Bristol. In 1723 in Newport, Rhode Island, 24 pirates were hanged: 7 were from London, 3 from Liverpool, 3 from Wales, and 1 each from Rhode Island, Virginia, Connecticut, Limerick, Londonderry, the Isle of Man, New York, Devon, Exeter, Suffolk and Durham.[27] Two aspects of this experience need emphasis.

First, 'the ship was not only the means of communication between continents, it was the first place where working people from the continents communicated'.[28] Needless to say, the medium of communication could not be the King's English; instead 'vehicular languages' were created – creole, pidgin and 'all-American'.[29] These drew upon parent languages of north-eastern Europe (English, French, Dutch) and western Africa (Yoruba, Fanti). To Ned Ward the sailor's language was 'all Heathen Greek to a Cobbler'. Much of the lexicon was a jargon – that is, the specialized vocabulary of the intricate, particular tasks necessary to the technique of sailing. But much of it was not. A 'manany' puts off work, a 'javel' was a loafer, 'scrovy' and 'cosier' were names for useless sailors. 'Sogering' meant malingering. A 'King's Bencher' preferred to hold forth at the galley than do a job of work. Someone 'in Everybody's Mess and Nobody's Watch' was equally incapable of work. 'Tim Potter' was the nickname of such a person. To perform 'Tom Cox's Traverse' was to give all the appearance of work with none of its effort, like taking 'two turns around the longboat' or a 'pull at the scuttlebutt'. To go 'up one hatchway and down another' was the dodge of a shirker. 'Keeping one hand for your self, and one for the ship' summed up the contradictory nature of the work and its social relations. The language was not only a jargon; it was part of an 'oppositional culture' that expressed its own motive of justice. Readers of *Roderick Random* will remember the readiness with which an unknown sailor rescues Miss Williams from a Drury Lane bawdy-house-keeper who threatens her with Newgate ('You shan't go to

---

[27] Captain Charles Johnson, *A General History of the Pyrates* (1724), pp. 104 and 330.
[28] Peter Linebaugh, 'All the Atlantic Mountains Shook', *Labour/Le Travail* (winter 1982).
[29] Louis-Jean Calvet, *Les Langues Véhiculaires* (Paris, 1981), and J. H. Dillard, *All-American English* (1975).

the bilboes this bout!'), or with which another seafaring man helps Rory to take vengeance upon a tyrannical schoolmaster: 'Ah, God help thee, more slip than ballast, Rory. Let me alone for that – leave the whole to me – I'll show him the fore-topsail, I will.'[30]

To the authorities this culture was opaque. Here is the magistrate John Fielding, for instance:

When one goes into Rotherhithe and Wapping, which places are chiefly inhabited by sailors, but that somewhat of the same language is spoken, a man would be apt to suspect himself in another country. Their manner of living, speaking, acting, dressing, and behaving are so peculiar to themselves.[31]

His half-brother, Henry Fielding, also a magistrate, wrote with great irritation:

It is difficult, I think, to assign a satisfactory reason why sailors in general should, of all others, think themselves entirely discharged from the common bands of humanity, and should seem to glory in the language and behaviour of savages![32]

If by the term 'savages' Henry Fielding referred to the Africans and Afro-Americans who comprised a significant portion of ships' crew during the eighteenth century, or to the bi-racial and tri-racial communities that were springing up upon the edges of the Atlantic, then it would appear that rather than breaking 'the common bands of humanity' the sailors of the British Isles were broadening those bands, and not just of that species, for with the traffic of animals and plants they were creating the biosphere. Fielding refers not only to the language of 'savages' but also to their behaviour. The London-centred international nautical proletariat had learned on shipboard other means of communication, such as the fiddle, the drum, the banjo and dances like jigs and clogging.

By the second quarter of the eighteenth century the Atlantic maritime culture, and particularly the African and Afro-American elements of it, had already had an impact on proletarian existence in London. This is the second point that needs emphasizing. Isaac George was a black man who fell afoul of the law in London. He was a sailor, born in New England, his father from Guinea, his

---

[30] Smollett, *Roderick Random* (1748), ch. 5.
[31] John Fielding, *A Brief Description of the Cities of London and Westminster* (1776), pp. 28–9.
[32] Henry Fielding, *A Journal of a Voyage to Lisbon* (1754).

mother a mulatto. Before he was hanged at the age of twenty-two in July 1738, he had made more than ten transatlantic voyages. He was literate. Charles Wesley, the evangelist's brother, visited him in Newgate. John Cross was a black man hanged on 18 October 1749 for robbing a man on the highway of 6½d. He was a gentleman's servant and had spent many of his twenty-five years at sea. His companion in this robbery as well as at the fatal tree was Thomas Robinson, a Virginia man, marked by smallpox and a sometimes sailor on the Jamaica–London sugar run. Edward Ward, an Irish sailor and cutler (18d. a day), robbed with a Negro before suffering at the tree.

Shipboard communication was decisive to the formulation of the eighteenth-century pan-Africanism – it was an American mariner who taught Olaudah Equiano to read *Paradise Lost* on shipboard during the 1760s – and the combination of European knowledge conveyed in books with African–American experience conveyed in mass labour was to produce a revolutionary force. Sailors were among the first to study slavery and abolition. Henry Woolford was bred to the sea. Although he could not read or write, 'he fear'd not an Argument'. Transported for stealing three bags of nails, he returned early and was sentenced to hang. 'He seem'd most to resent his Dying', the Ordinary wrote of him, 'and said that if he had not returned for the sake of his Family, he thought he had just Reason to come Home; because the Law was not, he said, that they should be in such a manner sold for Slaves, which was worse than Death, being Christians by Baptism; and that the Negroes after they were Baptised were no longer Slaves.' They were sold for £50 apiece, and had 'to walk into the Sea to the middle to find Oysters in Winter time, and the like'.[33]

Such pan-Atlantic interchanges, and the communities built upon them on ship and in port, are often regarded as 'marginal'. The contrary may be true: they were the essence of the proletariat of merchant capital, and they were the basis of the circulation of rebellion in widely differing geographical and cultural settings. The New York insurrection of St Patrick's Day 1741 was the work of Africans, Irishmen, a Londoner, North American Indians and Spaniards. Robert Barrow, alias Runwell, alias Barbadoes, was born

[33] The Ordinary's *Account*, 3 April 1721, 19 July 1738, 18 October 1749 and 25 March 1751. See also Olaudah Equiano, *The Interesting Narrative of the Life of Olaudah Equiano or Gustavus Vasa, the African, Written by Himself* (1789).

in Liverpool and hanged in London. In between he had lived in
Guinea, Virginia and Barbados for more than a quarter of his life.
He deserted the English slaver in which he first sailed, and lived
with a colony of runaway Negroes in Antigua, perhaps participating
in the Antigua Revolt of 1736. In the West Indies he sailed under
Dutch and Spanish colours for short periods before running again.
He sailed to London, where he was paid off, and, as he told the
Ordinary of Newgate before he was hanged on 15 October 1737,

After I had received my Wages, Captain Crawford would have had me
to have gone again with him, but it was too soon – my Money was not
gone, and I never could bear the Thoughts of Working, or taking Pains,
while my Money lasted.

So, he lived in the Minories, became a thief and fenced his goods
to Margaret Poland, or Irish Peg, in Rosemary Lane.[34]

Experience of slave rebellion on the plantations and in urban
colonial insurrections was thus already becoming available to the
proletariat of London, where they received their own translations,
according to circumstances, and where they met their own forms
of official repression. In September 1731 the Lord Mayor proclaimed
that 'for the future no *Negroes* or other *Blacks* be suffered to be
bound Apprentices at any of the Companies of this City to any
Freeman thereof' and the wardens of the various guilds were
appointed to see that the proclamation was enforced, in an attempt
to limit or control the political and ethnic characteristics of the
London population.[35] The 'St Giles's Blackbirds', as they were
already called, had became a force to be reckoned with by the rulers
of the metropolis.

The early history of London Methodism, itself a part of the
transatlantic 'Great Awakening' in the 1740s, was part of a new,
unofficial repression, which owed, at least in some of its salient
cadres, not a little to experience aboard slavers. Slavery was a
turning-point in the life of Silas Told. In 1724, at the tender age of
fourteen, Silas was apprenticed aboard *The Prince of Wales*, destination Jamaica with a stop at Cork. Outside Kingston the ship
foundered in a hurricane, and Silas fell victim to a 'pestilence', which

[34] The Ordinary's *Account*, 15 October 1737; Daniel Horsmanden, *The New York
Conspiracy, Or, a History of the Negro Plot* (1810).
[35] Quoted in James Walvin, *The Black Presence: A Documentary History of the Negro
in England, 1555–1860* (New York, 1972), p. 65.

was healed with doses of Jesuit's bark administered to him by an African conversant with its anti-malarial properties. He sailed next with Captain Timothy Tucker aboard *The Royal George*. For having been thought wasteful in taking bread from the Gun Room, Silas was whipped with such energy that his clothes were cut to shreds and the crew declared that they could see the white of his bones. *The Royal George* was a slaver whose captain drove the cook to suicide and who shot a sick African in cold blood. This provoked a mutiny and Silas and others nimbly betook themselves to the cannon and repelled the uprising. Many of the mutineers jumped overboard, and others were locked below decks. Upon opening the hatches the next morning it was discovered that forty of the eighty who had stayed aboard had suffocated. In view of such sights passed the early manhood of this famous Methodist. When he returned to London his faith underwent revitalization by submission to the passionate injunctions of John Wesley. Inured to the brutality required to discipline the newly organized mass labour of the Atlantic, he easily found himself a prominent place at the recently erected gallows at Kennington Common and Moorfields, and in the Newgate cells. He joined the condemned in the tumbril on the way to Tyburn, a zealot who preached an authoritarian piety to the 'outcasts of men'.[36]

III

The London nautical proletariat did not come into this world, like the Venus of old, in a sea shell or upon the ocean's foam. Orphaned, wayward, bastards, loose upon the world perhaps, nevertheless they were all mothers' sons. Periodically, they returned to London and to particular settings of female society where they might find such companionship, care and pleasure as they might have or pay for. The reproduction of the total seafaring proletariat required more than initial recruitment such as might be accomplished by impressment or via the workhouses and prisons; it also depended on the maintenance of the existing sailoring population – and, in the long run, the creation of a new one.

[36] Silas Told, *Life*, 3rd edn (1796). See also the biographical essay about Told in Austin Dobson, *Eighteenth Century Vignettes* (Oxford, 1923). William Snelgrave, *A New Account of Some Parts of Guinea and the Slave Trade* (1734), describes other slave mutinies.

Sailors and friends drinking grog on board ship.

Generally, the proletariat of mercantilist production depended on the organization of demographic reproduction. Etymologically, the term 'proletariat' meant precisely this — those whose value was nothing more than the production of new workers (*proles*). This is why the discovery of the labour theory of value and the beginnings of quantified demographic analysis constituted two intellectual pillars of the early eighteenth-century mercantilist state.

The eighteenth-century maritime labour force and the demographic pools whence it was recruited were the creation of as specific social practices of reproduction as those producing other parts of the eighteenth-century labour market. As the 'family' producing the slaves of the colonial plantations had characteristic kinship, ceremonial and naming practices; as the 'proto-industrial' family producing the workers within the English domestic system had its practices of inheritance and work-sharing; as the manufacturing workshops drew upon coerced child and female labour available from specific 'family' and property relations; so did the seafaring proletariat have its characteristic forms of reproduction.[37] Tyburn

[37] Herbert Gutman, *The Black Family in Slavery and Freedom, 1750–1925* (New

was a place where such 'reproductive workers' were disciplined and taught examples.

A great many London women had material relations with the London mariner, for he might become for her a source of maintenance and money, even if for only the time he was 'Lord of Six Weeks'. The relations were reproductive and sexual; they included washing, sewing (at sea the sailor called his sewing-kit his 'housewife'), nursing and provisioning. We can discern such relations in some of the women topped off at Tyburn. Anne Hazard, termed a 'prostitute', who married a sailor and was hanged in 1743, had been a 'Bomb-Boat Woman' – that is, one who plied small craft alongside the moored ocean-going vessels to sell groceries and other wares. Deborah Hardcastle was a sailor's widow who worked in a Thames-side victualler's house before becoming 'reduced to great Poverty and Want'. Mary Dutton, hanged in 1742 for stealing a watch in Piccadilly, was the widow of a sailor killed at Cartagena. Ruggety Madge, the famous Dublin lady of Rag Fair and Drury Lane, former inhabitant of the Mint, often passed as an Indiaman's widow. Hannah Dagoe, also Irish, 'wrought and dealt in the millinery way'. She was married to a Spanish sailor whom she met in a debtor's spunging house in Wapping. Elizabeth Fox was hanged for stealing £9 and five Portugal pieces from a dwelling-house. She was literate, a former servant, and the wife of a sailor. She was described by the Ordinary of Newgate as one who 'walk'd the Streets, robbed, stole, and taking every Thing she could lay hold on, being one of the most scandalous Creatures, and notorious Pickpockets in Town'. The Ordinary characterized the male companions of such women as herself as 'their Cullies whom they call Husbands'.[38]

The Ordinary's confusion reminds us that many forms of working-class marriage and conjugality, based neither on the doctrine of *femme covert* nor on ecclesiastical or government sanctions of 'true love', flourished in the eighteenth century, and persisted into the nineteenth century among isolated communities – communities

---

York, 1976); Hans Medick, 'The Proto-industrial Family Economy: The Structural Function of Household and Family during the Transition from Peasant Society to Industrial Capitalism', *Social History*, vol. iii (October 1976); John Gillis, *For Better, For Worse: British Marriages, 1600 to the Present* (New York, 1985).
[38] The Ordinary's *Account*, 23 August 1743, 31 January 1713, 13 January 1742, 24 November 1740, 4 May 1764 and 18 March 1741.

based on 'waste' and scavenging, and mobile employments. In London these 'marriages' took place with little formality, such as that alliance described in *Roderick Random* between the prostitute, Miss Williams, and her friend the sailor ('we lived in great harmoney together'). There was a practice known as 'leaping the sword', in which the partners step over a sword placed on the ground to the words: 'Leap rogue and jump whore/And then you are married for evermore.'[39]

Neither simple wedding customs nor 'great harmoney' between the couple could, in themselves, impose legal monetary relationships between man and woman. This is why the Fleet marriages were so important. Such marriages were cheap; they could be performed at any time of day, any day of the week, in any building within the precincts or the 'Rules' of the Fleet Prison, without banns or licensing, and without a clergyman. Records of the marriages were kept, and they were recognized by administrative and legal authorities of the cash economy. Women married insolvent debtors there in order to rid themselves of their own debts. Parish overseers might pay a man to marry an unwed mother in order to relieve them of supporting a pauper. Several of the women hanged at Tyburn were Fleet brides: Mary Dyman of Rotherhithe, Deborah Churchill, alias Miller, Catherine Conner of Ireland, and Hannah Wilson, a Bethnal Green vendor of peas and beans. She was married at the Fleet, once at the age of fourteen and once again at the age of eighteen. She was hanged at the age of twenty-five for stealing clothes worth 18d.[40]

The attack on the Fleet marriage, and its abolition in 1753, stressed the abuses that such clandestine marriage led to for women of some means or property, and it is tempting to consider these marriages in that light. However, we need to remember that for many of the London poor such weddings were the only feasible kind and – far from being clandestine – provided an occasion of noisy street celebrations that brought together a cross-section of the urban

---

[39] Francis Grose, *A Classical Dictionary of the Vulgar Tongue* (1785).
[40] The Ordinary's *Account*, 18 October 1749, 17 December 1708, 31 December 1750 and 1 October 1753. See also John Ashton, *The Fleet: Its River, Prison, and Marriages* (1887); John Burn, *History of Fleet Marriages* (1933); and William Connor Sydney, *England and the English in the Eighteenth Century: Chapters in the Social History of the Times* (1891), vol. ii, ch. 20. Between October 1704 and February 1705 almost 3,000 marriages were performed. Marriage might be entered into the registers for a shilling, and removed for half a guinea.

proletariat who rough-musicked the couple with shouts, hollering and the banging of pots and pans. The ballad 'The Bunter's Wedding' shows how Ben the basketman and Kitty, a coney wool-cutter, were married at the Fleet in a large celebration that included Joe the sandman, Ned the drover, Fanny the 'pretty match maker', Dolly the rag woman's daughter, Jenny the quilter, Roger the chimney-sweep, Ralph the grinder, bandy-legged Susan, Nan the tub woman, Peggy the mop-yarn spinner, 'draggle tail'd Pat with no shoes on, Who pins and laces doth cry', as well as a crowd of sailors and butchers.[41]

The advantage of marrying a seafaring man was that in the event of his disappearance or demise, the wife might take possession of the wages due to him. The Fleet marriage was thus an institution that would provide money to the female friends of sailors, and as such it was a necessary aspect of the seafarer's 'family wage'. It was transmuted in the nineteenth century; 'widow's men' signified imaginary naval seamen, about 2 per cent of the ship's complement, who drew pay for the benefit of sailor's widows.

Demographically speaking, London in the early eighteenth century was a killer because deaths far exceeded births. Therefore, as a labour pool, from which sailors, like other workers, were recruited, it had to be maintained by migration into the city. Many of these migrants were single women – widows, deserted wives, unmarried mothers. The centralization of agricultural holdings, the enclosure movement, the demise of the cottager's family wage, the limitations on the rural domestic by-employments, the famines in Ireland were some of the forces driving women to the metropolis.[42] The experience is reflected in Tyburnography: of the 92 women hanged at the triple tree only a third were born in London, as the table opposite summarizes.

Some refused a transatlantic existence. Mary Standford, for instance, who was hanged for picking a pocket of a handkerchief and 4 guineas, said 'she preferred hanging at home to Transportation Abroad, and that she was of Opinion, that her living in foreign parts was worse than a disgraceful and shameful Death at Home'.[43] The migratory experience helped shape the picaresque character of

[41] Quoted in Ashton, op. cit., pp. 365–9.
[42] Ivy Pinchbeck, *Women Workers and the Industrial Revolution, 1750–1850*, 3rd edn (1981), pp. 2 ff.
[43] The Ordinary's *Account*, 3 August 1726.

TABLE 8:

Birthplaces of the women hanged at Tyburn, 1703–1772

Place	Number	Percentage
London	32	35
England (outside London)	40	43
Ireland	17	19
Scotland	2	2
Wales	1	1

the London woman. The women who reproduced the city's 'loose and disorderly' persons were often themselves picaresque proletarians, although their field of action was smaller, and their opportunities for monied employment far fewer. Mary Young, alias Jenny Diver, is perhaps the most famous since she became a heroine in both Gay's and Brecht's *Beggar's Opera*. She was born in the north of Ireland of indigent parents who nevertheless instructed her in reading, writing and needlework. In London she was tutored by Anne Murphy in the skills of pocket-picking in 'a kind of club' near St Giles-in-the-Fields. Her 'superior address' was quickly recognized. She designed a pair of false arms and hands which she could manipulate from beneath her clothing. Appearing as a pregnant woman, accompanied by an accomplice guised as a footman, she robbed the gentry during prayers at church. She was quick and subtle, a mistress of manual dexterity; these were qualities highly prized in this period of history and she shared them with Jack Sheppard. She exercised her skills of timing, disguise, wit and dissimulation at 'Change Alley, the theatres, St Paul's, London Bridge, the fairs and the tea-gardens, those urban locations of bourgeois traffic. After her hanging her memory was preserved by the hawkers of 'Dying Speeches', ballads and stories, and in this way she came to the attention of the young apprentice, Francis Place, forty years later.[44]

Because of restrictions in the employment of women, their conditions of life were difficult and extreme hardship was their lot. The

[44] ibid., 18 March 1741.

historian of women workers before the Industrial Revolution notes that it was their dependence upon the casual and pauper trades that explains the large number of suicides, prostitution, starvation and crime among London women. Many thousands were engaged in the needle trades as milliners, seamstresses, mantua-makers, embroiderers and the like. A great many others – a 'whole army' of 30,000 in 1807 – were employed in the seasonal employments of fruit and vegetable gardening, walking with heavy burdens to London markets twice a day. The milkmaids were mainly Irish, and it was 'a slavish trade demanding physical strength and endurance'.[45]

In subsequent chapters we shall examine textile workers and the workers in domestic service to the well-to-do. Here we need to examine prostitution and street-selling, since they figure so frequently in the histories of the women hanged at Tyburn.

The cries of the street-sellers echoed throughout the day and some of the night. A deck of playing-cards of 1754 called 'The Cries of London' depicts women crying sheep's hearts, livers, matches, musk melons, shrimps, damask roses, cotton laces, peaches, apricots, nectarines, broken bottles, hot-cross buns, cucumbers, eels, periwinkles, crab, and, of course, 'Milk Maids, come quick for I'm a going.' This street life was predatory. As the King of Hearts says:

> The Cat does on the Cock with Fury Fly
> And many reasons urged that he must dye
> The cock deny'd the fact; in Vain thou plead'st
> Replyed the cat for right or wrong, thou bleed'st.

Mary Goddard, hanged for picking a pocket, had once escaped from the Clerkenwell House of Correction. She sold old broken glass bottles and 'worked hard for her own and her children's livelihood'. Elizabeth Price, hanged for burglary, 'had follow'd the Business of picking up Rags and Cinders and at other times that of selling Fruit and Oysters, crying Hot Pudding and Grey Peas in the Streets'. Susan Perry, alias Dewy, who was hanged for murdering a child whose clothes she stole (she denied the charge to the end), 'betook herself to cry, some times Newspapers, and at other times Fruit, &c., about the Streets'. Sarah Clifford, alias Arkins, who was hanged for stealing £13, cried flounder and mackerel in the streets when those fish were in season.[46]

---

[45] Pinchbeck, op. cit., p. 61.
[46] The Ordinary's *Account*, 3 March 1708, 31 October 1712, 13 March 1713, 25 September 1713.

Women's hold on London street-selling was not simply an economic matter of shopping or petty commodity trade. There were two other important aspects. First, such street activities were closely related to subversive communication. London cries might become London ballads. Ann Mudd, for instance, hanged for murdering her husband ('Why said she, I stabb'd him in the Back with a Knife for Funn'), amused herself in the condemned cell by singing obscene songs she had picked up in the streets. Mary White, or – to give her the name she was known by in both street and court – Mary Cut-and-Come-Again, was hanged for stealing an apron worth 6d. The Ordinary of Newgate said of her: 'She was queen of the blackguards, pilferers and ballad-singers, universally known amongst them, and partaker in most of their villainies; she acquired the cant name by which she stood indicted for her dexterity in cutting off women's pockets.'[47]

Second, there was a criminal connection. A statistical analysis of all London indictments (Westminster, Middlesex, Southwark and the City) for the year 1740 shows that the *only* felony for which a greater number of women were indicted than men was the offence of receiving stolen goods. Male thieves frequently formed partnerships with female receivers. We saw this with Jack Sheppard, and we can note such relationships over and over again. In the eighteenth century marriage was a business partnership. In the proletarian life of London as revealed by felony records it is interesting that the most frequent male–female relationship was that between the thief and the receiver. In chapters 7 and 8 we shall find that this criminal relationship was, in fact, closely related to a dominant urban mode of production.

It is difficult to analyse what was called prostitution because many eighteenth-century sources, especially those associated with criminal sources, assume rather than explain what was meant by the term. The Ordinary of Newgate, being a clergyman, was moralizing and prejudicial in his use of the term, applying it to most of the women he interviewed before their hanging. He did not explore the social, conjugal or sexual relations of those people he chronicled. That a variety of social/sexual relations did exist is suggested by the large number of names for those called prostitutes: 'bunter', 'smut', 'trumpery', 'crack', 'mawkes' at the poorer end of the trade; 'buttered

[47] ibid., 29 June 1737 and 7 June 1745. See also, *The Proceedings*, part 2, May 1745.

'The idle 'prentice returned from sea and in a garret with a common prostitute', by Hogarth: The only felony for which a greater number of women were indicted than men was the offence of receiving stolen goods.

bun', 'buttock', 'squirrel', 'mackerel', 'cat', 'moll', 'froe' or 'vrow' at the richer end.[48]

Bernard Mandeville, in his *Defence of Public Stews* (1724), contrasted parochial policies to prostitution in London unfavourably with the municipal regulations developed in Amsterdam, which he thought were both healthier and less dangerous. The more flexible and ambiguous policies in London reflected, I believe, the nature of family relationships within the urban poor. In Covent Garden, along the Strand and in Goodman's Fields householders might be defeated in attempting the suppression of bawdy-houses by riotous combinations of women and sailors. Women who worked out of houses experienced more favourable conditions than those who solicited in the streets. Doubtless, the working conditions in those places called 'cavaulting schools', 'Academies', 'nanny houses' or 'nunneries' varied considerably. They provided apparel. They might provide some restraint upon the practices of defloration, sado-masochism

[48] Francis Grose, *A Classical Dictionary of the Vulgar Tongue* (1785).

and sexual assaults on young girls. They provided contraceptive information and means of abortion. Some perhaps may have provided nursing to those with work-related diseases.[49]

Those who worked in the streets without such places of minimal protection had to be quick, deft and hard. A client to Constantia Jones, 'a three-penny upright', described her method of work: 'As I stood against the Wall, the prisoner came behind me, and with one hand she took hold of — and the other she thrust into my Breeches Pocket and took my Money.' The money she stole amounted to 36s. and a half-guinea, and so at the age of thirty, after twenty previous stays in Newgate, she suffered at the tree. Disputes about payment were resolved, if they went to court, in favour of the client, and he generally prosecuted for theft. When Susan Brockway and Mary Gardner declined to 'shew him Postures' or 'to whip him to make him a good Boy', their client called a constable and swore a robbery against them.[50] Only if justice transpired in the streets did the working prostitute have a chance, as happened when neighbourhood crowds formed to protect Isabella Roe and Grace Weedon, who were apprehended following a dispute about payment for services in Drury Lane.[51] Solidarity among prostitutes is suggested in their slang. The 'game' or 'town' was the name of their work. 'One of my cousins', 'one of us' and the 'company' were names for fellow workers. In general, as they said, they belonged to the 'sisterhood'.

Pregnancy meant disaster not only to the prostitute but to domestic servants, most of whom were hired on condition of remaining both single and childless. It prevented the woman from earning money, and brought a time-consuming burden in the form of nursing and minding. Moreover, confinement and childbirth posed a threat to her health and even her life. Unwanted infants were 'starved at nurse' or 'over-laid' according to Dr Cadogan, whose *Essay on the Nursing and Management of Children* (1750) argued that 'the ancient Custom of exposing them to Wild Beasts or drowning them would certainly be a much quicker way of despatching them' than the slow deaths of neglect. In the worst years infant mortality

[49] Dr Ivan Bloch, *Sexual Life in England*, trans. William H. Forster (1958), chs. 5, 12, 14.
[50] *The Proceedings*, 27–31 August 1725.
[51] ibid., July 1736; the Ordinary's *Account*, 22 December 1738 and 16 March 1753; Peter Linebaugh, '(Marxist) Social History and (Conservative) Legal History', *New York University Law Review*, vol. lx, no. 2 (May 1985), pp. 224–5.

was 74 per cent. Among parish children and workhouse children, it was closer to 80 or 90 per cent, according to Thomas Hanway. It appears from Thomas Coram, the founder of the Foundling Hospital in 1742, that even when birth was successful many women could not afford to nurse or rear their children and preferred to put them out to 'wicked and barbarous nurses' (Moll Flanders and Mother Midnight understood this kind of transaction), or to expose them as foundlings in the street, or, finally, to kill them.[52] 'If you happen to let the Child fall, and lame it, be sure never confess it; and, if it dies, all is safe,' Jonathan Swift 'advised' the nurse.[53]

Of the women hanged at Tyburn, ten (12 per cent) were hanged for infanticide. Mary Ellenor, a gentleman's servant debauched by an apprentice coach-maker, and Agatha Ashbrook ('she was very stubborn and would not give any particular Account of her Life') were both hanged in 1708. Phoebe Ward, a domestic servant who 'took a mighty disgust at Things of Religion', was hanged in 1711. Judith Leford, the daughter of a French weaver and herself a silk-winder for eleven years, was hanged for killing her new-born in the workhouse in 1734. The next year Elizabeth Ashbrook, a servant in Lincoln's Inn, was hanged for infanticide. Jane Cooper 'was very sick during her Confinement and so poor and naked that at last she lost her Sight. She seemed not to be of compassionate Temper, but hard-hearted, and was not to be made sensible of her Crimes.' She was hanged in 1737. Sarah Allen had been forced to leave her serving position at a Westminster public house when she became pregnant. She suffocated her infant in the workhouse, and was hanged in 1738. Elizabeth Harwood 'got Work in Gardens about the Town not understanding Women's Work having been constantly employed in Gardening and Hay-making about Richmond, Twickenham, and other Villages near London, and never came to Town but to sell Fruits or Greens'. She gave birth in a Twickenham field one night, and drowned the infant in Powder Mills River. She was hanged in 1739. In 1743 Sarah Wilmshurst suffered at the tree for infanticide. She had already had ten children, fathered by a house-painter. The child she threw into a bog-house was fathered by a watchmaker. Finally, in 1752 Ann Wallsam, a butcher's widow and serving maid, hanged for the same offence.[54]

[52] M. D. George, *London Life in the Eighteenth Century* (1965), pp. 55–9.
[53] *Directions to Servants* (1745).
[54] The Ordinary's *Account*, 27 October 1708, 22 December 1711, 8 March 1734,

We find with these ten victims of the tree similar familiar themes –
poverty, loss of employment, hostility towards the Ordinary of
Newgate, and irreligion. Further, the chronology of the hangings
is suggestive, for only three were hanged during the first third of
the century, while the remaining seven were hanged in the two
decades just before mid-century. Yet, it was widely known and
accepted that both parish nursing and the workhouse virtually meant
certain death for the infants in their charge.

From the War of Jenkin's Ear (1739) until the cessation of hostilities in the Seven Years War (1763) there occurred in London an
important series of changes in family and demographic policy.
Orphanages were established in London for the purpose of meeting
the manning needs of the Navy. The infant mortality rate was
drastically reduced by the reforms of midwifery and the establishment of the Foundling Hospital and numerous lying-in hospitals – the London Lying-in Hospital (1749), the City Lying-in
Hospital (1750), Queen Charlotte's Hospital for Unmarried Mothers
(1752), the Royal Maternity Hospital (1757) and the Westminster
Lying-in Hospital (1765). In 1767 the 'Act for Keeping Children
Alive' was passed, which directed wage rates for nurses (2s. 6d. a
week for each child). In 1753 Hardwicke's Marriage Act, which
put an end to Fleet marriages, was passed. That these measures
immediately followed the increased number of hangings for infanticide suggests that capital punishment was part of the preparation
for a new organization of reproduction in the London labour
market.

IV

Urban proletarians lived in dirt; they lived by an economy of wastes;
they were part of a 'marginal' or 'disposable' population; they lived
without the discipline of either the patriarchal family or schools and
hospitals. A yahoo proletariat could be a dangerous population –
and one with its own territorial autonomy within the metropolis,
as the Black Boy Alley gang illustrates. The women in the gang were
Ann Gwyn, an orphaned washerwoman; Margaret Greenaway, the
receiver; Ann Wells, born in the Whitechapel workhouse; and Ann

---

3 March 1737, 18 January 1738, 21 December 1739, 18 May 1743 and 23 March
1752.

Duck, daughter of a Negro sword-maker. The men were Barefoot, Gentleman Harry, Captain Poney, Long Will, Nobby, Scampey, Dillsey, Jack the Sailor, Ninn and Country Dick. They lived amid the dung and refuse of the nearby Smithfield cattle and sheep pens. They were said to control about 7,000 others in Southwark, the Mint, St Giles-in-the-Fields and the City. Street-walkers attempted to lure difficult clients to those areas, where they could count on finding swift assistance. In 1744 several assassination attempts against the constabulary and the magistracy originated in Chick Lane and Black Boy Alley, and as a result of the counter-attack that followed many were hanged.[55]

London proletarians, excluded from its hegemony, held the law in contempt. Indications of this appear in the Old Bailey *Proceedings*. With insistent, repeated, ironic servility, James Ryan, a sailor, interrupted the court:

My Lord, with humble Submission that Fellow will swear that a Cow is a Jack-ass. With humble Submission, you must understand the Evidence; I don't know what they are, not I, the Thief-takers instruct them for the sake of the Reward – and that's every thing. My Lord, with humble Submision, look at that Fellow's Face while he talks.

Mary Cut-and-Come-Again, the ballad-singer, pulled out her breasts when the watchmen came to apprehend her 'and spurted the milk in the fellows' faces, and said, d—m your eyes, what do you want to take my life away?' At her trial she kicked the prosecutrix and spat on the judge's seat. The only reason we know her given name is that she bargained the information with the court, which unfettered and unhandcuffed her in exchange. This proletariat amused itself by mocking the law. A mock court held by sailors in the Caribbean is transcribed in Captain Charles Johnson, *A General History of the Pyrates* (1724):[56] 'And how should a Man speak good Law that has not drank a Dram?' 'If the Fellow should be suffer'd to speak, he may clear himself, and that's an Affront to the Court.' It was a venerable tradition. In the trial scene in *Pilgrim's Progress* Lord Hate-good brings three witnesses – Envy, Superstition and Pickthank – to testify against the pilgrim for speaking ill against the Lord Luxurious, Lord Desire for Vainglory and Sir Having Greedy.

[55] ibid., 7 March 1764, 7 November 1744, 24 December 1744, 9 July 1745 and 26 July 1745.
[56] *The Proceedings*, 14–17 January 1737; ibid., part 2, May 1745; Johnson, op. cit., pp. 292–40.

This picaresque proletariat was not completely lawless, however much it may have detested the courts and law-learning. When necessary it developed its own kinds of written self-organization. Some of these, like the 'articles' that John Meffs refused to sign when his transport ship was seized by pirates, were democratic and egalitarian, in which 'the supream Power lodged with the Community', in which disputes were settled by jury, officers elected, prizes distributed equally, and 'Every Man has a Vote in Affairs of the Moment'.[57] Others may have owed more to the guildsman's oath or club rules, such as the 'honourable Society' to which Jenny Diver belonged. It had four 'articles': (1) admittance was to be by consent; (2) no one was 'to presume to go upon any thing by him or herself', (3) the 'Cant Tongue' was to be spoken; and (4) if any member were incarcerated, 'a sufficient Allowance was to be given to him or her in Prison'. At the 'Hempen Widow's Club' near the Black Boy Alley the 'articles of confederation' included these three provisions: (1) everyone was to be prepared to swear anything 'to save each other from being *Scragg'd*', (2) everyone was to be prepared to swear one another to be substantial housekeepers 'in order to bail any Member', and (3) an allowance of 7s. a week was to be made 'out of the Box' for persons in prison.[58] The criminals' oaths resemble the self-help of friendly societies, the pirates' 'articles' resemble some of the 'agreements' of the Levellers. The London proletariat was not incapable of self-government; yet because it needed to be mobile in order to find work and was scattered throughout the city, it could not, at least in this period, develop broader or more durable instruments of self-rule. Such, indeed, would contradict the very notion of the picaresque proletarian.

To sum up, we may compare the picaro and the proletarian. Like the picaro, the proletarian has nothing: neither a mess of pottage today nor the land and tools to work with that he or she may fill his or her bowl tomorrow. Unlike the picaro, who is defined by shunning work, the proletarian is defined as being a worker. The scene of action of the picaro is the road, the market, the inn or the tea-garden – places of public exchange. The proletarian in contrast operates in places of private production: beneath decks or in a garret. Like the proletarian, the picaro is held in contempt by those who

---

[57] See the recent edition of *A General History of the Pyrates* by Manuel Schonhorn (South Carolina, 1972), pp. 148, 165, 211, 308.
[58] The Ordinary's *Account* 18 March 1741 and 21 October 1743.

lord over him or her. While the picaro's stance towards the world is active and resourceful – qualities promoted by the literary forms that arose from the individuality of the protagonist – the proletarian as an individual is often left passive and dumb by the historical records, more like a drone or a brute. However, since the proletarian's experience in life is dominated by cooperative action in the production and reproduction of the world, it is within collective experience that his or her individuality is realized. That the world can be hostile and capricious the proletarian knows, but he or she also knows that this need not always be so, because it is the work of his hands and the labour of her body that have created it in the first place. Therefore, destiny does not arrive as the necessary corollary of axiomatic forces. On the contrary, history is made by a series of collective battles, now defeats, now victories, as the following chapters suggest.

CHAPTER FIVE

SOCKING, THE HOGSHEAD AND EXCISE

> He did work upon the River, this is a very suspicious
> Way of Life, such People being generally looked upon
> as getting more Money by the bye than by their
> Labour.
>
> The Ordinary *Account*, 13 July 1752

> Of all the commercial articles which traverse the
> ocean, there are none, perhaps, which are more subject
> to wastage and depredation than the commodity we
> are speaking of.
>
> William Tatham, *An Historical and Practical Essay on
> the Culture and Commerce of Tobacco* (1800)

I

The proletariat is a useful class because it works. Indeed, its life is consumed in the producing of useful things. Consequently, the historian may learn less about this class by studying it directly than by studying the commodities resulting from its work, for these are the 'social hieroglyphs' of its existence. In this chapter we study tobacco as a dynamic commodity in the formation of the markets of the Atlantic empire, and as a paradigm of the labours of a cosmopolitan proletariat.

We may begin with James White. He was born in London of 'poor but honest parents'. He was educated at a parochial charity school, where he learned to 'Read, Write, and Cast Accompts'. Later he secured a position in one of the river societies of porters unloading freight from river craft to the quays and carrying 'Goods from the Thames in Carts'. In February 1722 he was convicted of stealing tobacco. Under examination by Sir Francis Forbes, he said that he lived south of London Bridge in Tooley Street and that he, with a red-headed man from the North, William 'Carrot' Langley, was accustomed to making off with parcels of tobacco from the London quays.[1] White was convicted of stealing 28 lbs of tobacco

---

[1] *The Proceedings*, 6–13 December 1721. Our knowledge of White comes from the Ordinary's *Account*, 6 November 1723; *The Proceedings*, 28 February–3 March 1721/2, 16–18 October 1723; and CLRO, Sesssions Papers, box 1721–1722, 'The Examination and Confessions of James White, 8 January 1721/2'.

belonging to Micajah Perry (who estimated the loss at 20s.) and 40 lbs. of tobacco belonging to William Dawkins (who estimated the loss at 30s.). These estimates were 2d. or 3d. a pound beneath the market, but well above the demarcation between petty and grand larceny. Five years earlier White would have been hanged, but the Transportation Act (4 George I, c. 11) substituted a punishment of seven years' transportation to the plantations.

In Newgate White waited for Jonathan Forward, the Government's contractor for carrying transported felons across the sea, to bring the ship *Alexander* up the river and to fill it with the 'King's Seven Years' Passengers', collected from the gaols of East Anglia and the Home Counties. The Treasury paid him £3–5 for each felon he transported. In Annapolis, Maryland, he could then sell them for £10 apiece.[2] His was a lucrative and dangerous business. Three months earlier, in December 1721, William Shaddon and nineteen other transportees surprised the ship's master, overcame the officers, and then 'made their Escape in the Ship's Long Boat and landed at Deal in the night'.[3] After White had finally embarked 'to cross the herring pond at the King's Expence' he was placed in the 'Close Hole', an enclosure between decks measuring 2 ft by 2 ft by 6 ft. There he subsisted on salted meat and water for the six weeks of the Atlantic passage. Thus he was 'marinated', a phrase of the day meaning 'transported'. In Jamaica he escaped and made his way to the mainland, where he lived for six months 'upon whatever he could get' before he was able to find passage home to England.

He returned to London during the winter, the harshest time of year for a river porter, when commercial activity on the Thames, with the exception of the coal trade, was virtually dead. For a time he hawked fruit about the London streets, but in December 1722 he was seen at Brewer's Quay 'taking tobacco out of a pair of Trowzers and putting it into a Shirt'. A month later he was seen 'loitering about Porter's Key'. He was apprehended. In October 1723 he was convicted again, this time of returning from transportation before his time was up, and so, according to law, he was hanged at Tyburn.

<hr />

[2] Prices of transported felons may be found in William Edolis, *Letters from America, Historical and Descriptive* (1792). See also Abbot Emerson Smith, *Colonists in Bondage: White Servitude and Convict Labor in America, 1607–1776* (New York, 1971), pp. 112–14.

[3] CLRO, Sessions Papers, box 1721–1722, 'Examination of William Shaddon, 20 December 1721'.

Both William Dawkins and Micajah Perry were substantial merchants in the international tobacco trade. Of Dawkins, we know little beyond the fact that he was a merchant and purchasing agent to one of the largest Virginia planters, Robert Carter, and that he aspired to operate on as grand a scale as Micajah Perry.[4] Perry was the grandson of the founder of a London tobacco dynasty. His dealings set in motion the labours of thousands of men and women in three continents. Scarcely a planter in Virginia was not in debt to him. In the year White was hanged, William Byrd, the Virginia magnate, confided that he had sold 'land and Negroes to stay the stomach of that hungry magistrate', referring to Perry.[5] Perry had majority control in the fortune of the Randolph family of Virginia. Perry was a leading banker in New York and Pennsylvania. Possessing large interests in shipping and the slave trade, a prominent member of the Board of Trade and Plantations, the father of a future Lord Mayor of London, himself an alderman of the City, a magistrate at Guildhall and the Old Bailey, he was both White's nemesis and the personification of the English Mammon.

Profits had fallen for this merchant prince. His father was used to a volume of trade ranging between 360 and 450 hogsheads of tobacco a year. By 1720 the family's dealings had sunk to 130 hogsheads.[6] In such circumstances he took a number of steps. He defrauded the King's Revenue by more than half by colluding with the Thames landwaiters to short-weight his imports, a practice known as 'hickory puckery', thereby reducing his duty, and then by bribing the searcher to long-weight the same consignment on re-export, thereby increasing his drawback, a practice known as 'puckery hickory'. Perry still took a loss of £1,500 in 1722 on the five ships he sent to Virginia. So he petitioned the House of Commons to investigate abuses in the tobacco trade. Perry's evidence to Parliament attacked the smuggling organized by his Scottish competitors. The rise to prominence of Glasgow was the most important

[4] Louis B. Wright (ed.), *Letters of Robert Carter, 1720–1727: The Commercial Interests of a Virginia Gentleman* (San Marino, Cal., 1940), *passim*.
[5] Elizabeth Donnan, 'Eighteenth Century English Merchants: Micajah Perry', *Journal of Economic and Business History*, vol. iv (1931–2), pp. 71–98.
[6] The profitability of Perry's firm (as well as others) may be found in *JHC* vol. xx (24 January 1722/23), pp. 102–109. See also, Alfred Rive, 'The Consumption of Tobacco since 1600', *The Economic Journal*, Economic History Series, vol. i (January 1926), pp. 69 ff, and Joseph C. Robert, *The Story of Tobacco in America* (New York, 1952), p. 17.

geographical change in the trade.[7] While shipment to Scottish ports avoided the troubled waters of the English Channel and reduced the length of the transatlantic passage by about a fortnight, historians of the Scottish trade agree that it was the smuggling, made convenient by the difficult coastline, and a widespread attitude that regarded Revenue 'officers as if they were thieves' that were responsible for the success of Scottish competition.

Perry also sought to reduce his freight costs. The prime cost of a pound of sweet-scented tobacco in Virginia was three farthings. Freight costs added a penny a pound, and the revenue duties fivepence farthing a pound. Freight costs meant payment to sailors, shipmasters, insurers, lightermen, porters and warehouse carters.[8] When ships needed unloading it meant to James White his daily toil, whose value he augmented by taking a cut in the product of his labour, opening up the 'snout' (hogshead) and taking 'cloud' or 'fogus'. In 1721 Robert Carter, the Virginia planter, wrote to a Member of Parliament complaining of a recently introduced 'custom of making us pay freight'. He also wrote reassuring letters to Perry to describe labour-saving methods of packing, to defend himself against complaints about the quality of his tobacco, and to inform him of the transition to slave labour: 'To save the charge of cooper's work we have employed a Negro belonging to the estate,' he wrote. In response, Perry provided him with the necessary credit for land purchases in the Northern Neck of Virginia and advised him to delay loading his tobacco aboard the ships moored in the Chesapeake until the captains reduced the freight charges. Carter also wrote to William Dawkins (White's other 'victim'): 'My overseers are under as strict orders and penal obligation as I can put them.'[9] In other words, the squeeze was on both sides of the Atlantic.

---

[7] *JHC*, vol. xx (24 January 1722/3), and Jacob M. Price, 'The Rise of Glasgow in the Chesapeake Tobacco Trade, 1707–1775', in Peter L. Payner (ed.), *Studies in Scottish Business History* (1967).
[8] Cost analysis of tobacco prices may be found in Price, op. cit., *JHC*, op. cit., and in the Cholmondeley Houghton Papers (hereinafter abbreviated C(H)MSS) at the Cambridge University Library, 33/1.
[9] Wright, op. cit., pp. 21, 71 and 74.

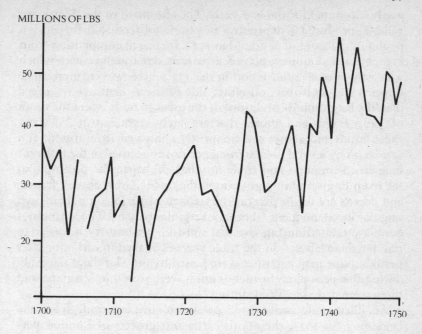

MILLIONS OF LBS

Figure 4:   Tobacco imports to England and Wales, 1700–1750

II

The relative decline of Micajah Perry's rate of profit was a symptom of a general price depression in the tobacco trade during the first thirty years of the century. There was a distinct reduction of tobacco imports during the first quarter of the century, as Figure 4 indicates.[10] About 38 million lbs of tobacco were imported annually at the end of the seventeenth century, a sum that fluctuated widely over the next twenty years – dropping to its lowest point of the century in 1712/13, recovering in 1721, only to fall again at the end of that decade. Higher freight charges, greater insurance premiums, and the partial loss of European markets, all consequences of the war,

[10] A general account of the slump and its causes may be found in W. E. Michinton (ed.), *The Growth of English Overseas Trade in the Seventeenth and Eighteenth Centuries* (1969). For tobacco imports by weight and price, from which the graph was drawn, see Elizabeth B. Schumpeter, *English Overseas Trade Statistics, 1697–1808* (Oxford, 1960), pp. 52–5.

partly accounted for the bad years. The aftermath of the 'South Sea Bubble' produced a depression in prices; tobacco sold for $11\frac{1}{2}$d. a pound in 1720 and $\frac{1}{2}$d. a pound in 1722. Increased competition from French trade doubtless played a part, as did bad weather, which adversely affected production in the 1720s.[11] However, merchants, shippers and legislators on either side of the Atlantic were agreed that 'the languishing conditions of the tobacco trade' were the result of 'gross frauds and abuses that are lately crept into it'.[12] 'Many great frauds and abuses are frequently contrived, committed, and carried on by several ill-designing persons concerned in the different branches of business and trade in tobacco,' began the preamble to the main English statute governing the trade. 'Great abuses, frauds, and deceits are dayly practiced by covetous persons for their own singular lucre and gaine,' began a Virginia statute.[13] The amount of new law created during the first third of the century in order to remove these 'abuses' in the trade was unequalled in earlier or later periods. Nine major statutes were passed by the Maryland assembly during this period; eight such statutes were passed in Virginia; and three were passed in Westminster.[14]

An illicit trade had existed parallel to the fair trade from the beginning. In 1625, the apothecaries and grocers of London petitioned against 'Lewd persons [who] under pretence of selling tobacco keep unlicensed alehouses and others [who] barter with

[11] Analysis of the crisis in the tobacco trade may be found in Lewis C. Gray, *History of Agriculture in the Southern United States to 1860*, vol i (Washington DC, 1933), pp. 259–77. More recent accounts are Arthur Pierce Middleton, *Tobacco Coast: A Maritime History of the Chesapeake Bay in the Colonial Era* (Virginia, 1953), and John Hemphill, 'Virginia and the English Commercial System, 1681–1733', unpublished Ph.D. thesis, Princeton University, 1964.

[12] *Calendar of State Papers, Colonial Series, America and the West Indies*, vols. xxxiii (1722–3), pp. 297–8, 254, 304; xxxiv (1724–5), pp. 123, 183; xxxv (1726–7), pp. 414 ff; xxxvii (1730), pp. 203 ff; xxxix (1732), pp. 18, 97–8, 173–8.

[13] William W. Hening, *The Statutes at Large Being a Collection of all the Laws of Virginia* (1823), vol. iii, pp. 31–2.

[14] For Maryland, see Vertrees J. Wyckoff, *Tobacco Regulation in Colonial Maryland* (Baltimore, 1936), pp. 103 ff, and William H. Browne (ed.), *Archives of Maryland: Proceedings and Acts* (Baltimore, 1894), xiii, 518; xxvi, 231–2; xxvii, 95, 157; xxx, 260–63, 348–55; xxxvi, 87, 507; xxxviii, 175. For Virginia, see Hening, op. cit., iii, 51–3, 435–40, 497–9; vi. 49–50; iv, 247–71, 381–93; v, 9–16, and also Arthur P. Scott, *Criminal Law in Colonial Virginia* (Chicago, 1930). The main English statutes were 10 & 11 William III, c. 21; 5 Geo. I, c. 11 (1718); 6 Geo. I, c. 21 (1719); and 9 Geo. I, c. 21 (1722).

mariners for stolen and uncustomed tobacco to the disadvantage of the petitioners'.[15] The spectacular boom in tobacco imports allowed the gigantic profits made by legitimate traders to coexist with a smuggling trade. With the decline in imports, the latent antagonism opened up: 'For the first time [it] became a highly organized and widely distributed trade, involving every class,' according to one authority on smuggling.[16] The uncustomed trade took increasing shares of the market, and the state created new law and new means of enforcement to eliminate it.

The Act of Frauds of 1662 established the basic law of the customs. Customs officials accepting 'any bribe, recompense, or reward in any kind whatsoever' were fined, but carmen, porters, watermen and any others who 'assist in the taking up, loading, shipping off, or carrying away' were punished with imprisonment.[17] In 1671 the Board of Customs and in 1683 the Excise Board were restored. Three years later the Board of Customs took over the administration of the customs in the plantations. Together with the military and naval establishments, it became one of the pillars of the mercantilist state. In 1698 protective departments of the Customs were created, divided between water and land jurisdiction. 'Riding Officers', men who patrolled the coasts to prevent the illegal export of wool and to suppress smuggled imports of tea, wine and tobacco, became the progenitors of a force that came to be called *police*. Payment of the Customs men depended on kickbacks. Malachy Postlethwayt estimated that more than half the revenues due to the Treasury from tobacco imports was lost in theft and smuggling. Customs officers were compensated by defalcation and peculation.[18] By 1785 in the import department of the Customs House the proportion of fees and gratuities to salaries was nearly four to one; in the export department it was seventeen to one.[19] The 1625 petition

---

[15] As quoted in Rive, op. cit., pp. 554–69.
[16] Lord Teignmouth and Charles G. Harper, *The Smugglers* (1923), p. 37. See also, John Spencer Basset, 'The Relation between the Virginia Planter and the London Merchants', *Report of the American Historical Association* (1901), pp. 553–75; and Stanley Gray and V. J. Wyckoff, 'The International Tobacco Trade in the Seventeenth Century', *The Southern Economic Journal*, vol. vii, no. 1 (July 1940), pp. 23–5.
[17] 14 Charles II, c. 11 (1662).
[18] Jacob Van Klaveren, 'Fiscalism, Mercantilism and Corruption', in D. C. Coleman (ed.), *Revisions in Mercantilism* (1969).
[19] George L. Sioussat, 'Virginia and the English Commercial System, 1730–1733',

distinguished 'stolen' from 'uncustomed' tobacco, though both were smuggled. It is an important distinction. In the case of the former, those *employed* in the trade take part of the tobacco and then run it through the Customs. In the case of the latter those who own title to the tobacco avoid by various devices payment of the duties.

We recall that James White and 'Carrot' Langley would take parcels of tobacco from off the quays. The manner of containing or 'unitizing' the tobacco was a crucial matter to all concerned – slaves and planters, porters and shipmasters – because both the security of the leaf and the measurement of its value depended on it. Parallel to the reorganization of the various customs authorities at the end of the seventeenth century was a revolution in packing and handling techniques. This began in 1687 with a merchants' and shipowners' petition and ended in 1699 with the passage of the Bulk Tobacco Act. The merchants wanted to prohibit the shipment of unenclosed parcels or bundles, 'bulk tobacco', in order that all tobacco might be encased in hogsheads.

Their petition of 1689, 'Some Reasons Why Bulk Tobacco from Virginia and Maryland Ought To Be Prohibited', and their pamphlet, *An Essay on Bulk Tobacco* (1692), agreed that bulk tobacco permitted 'every sailor and woman and little inconsiderable person ... [to] squeeze over by little design part of the duties if not wholly run it, and then carry it from ship to shop and sell it at easy and low rates'. Between a quarter and a third of the cargo was wasted. Some of this waste arose from water damage, dehydration and storage faults, but, they argued, these causes of waste would also be removed by enclosing the leaf in hogsheads. Furthermore, they estimated that the time of unloading would be reduced by containerization. These advantages to turnaround time and inventory preservation were secondary to the main purpose, however, which was to remove what they were careful *not* to call theft, but 'a presumptive Custom' or an 'accustomed privilege' of taking tobacco.[20]

The hogshead was a big barrel that could be rolled, hoisted, shifted or slid to and from wagons, carts, scows (flat-bottomed

---

Report of the American Historical Association (1905), pp. 75–97. See also Walter M. Stern, *The Porters of London* (1960), pp. 26, 32, 230 and 290.

[20] Anon., *An Essay on Bulk Tobacco* (1692), pp. 145, 155; Insurance Company of North America, *Ports of the World: A Guide to Cargo Loss Control*, 10th edn (Philadelphia, 1976).

Chesapeake river craft), ships and lighters. Once packed in the hogshead, the tobacco might travel by a half-dozen or more modes of transport without incurring the additional handling costs of packing and repacking with each transfer to a new type of transport. It tended to increase the size of ships, thus reducing unit freight costs because crew size did not increase in the same proportion as hold capacity. 'Many poor planters would lose by it,' the 1692 pamphlet noted, 'because Seamen buy their odd parcells, which are not fit to put in Casks.'[21] Quality would improve because the hogshead protected the leaf from wind, water and salt.

In 1699 Parliament responded to a decade's agitation by passing the Bulk Tobacco Act, which prohibited the import of tobacco 'but in a cask, chest, or case each containing two hundredweight of neat Tobacco'. Thereafter, tobacco, protected by the coopers' arts in the hogshead, travelled across the Atlantic apparently unavailable to porters, sailors, women, slaves, 'hands' and sea-officers.

As a result, smuggling became further centralized and concentrated. No longer based mainly on petty dealers, it was driven to larger forms of organization under the control of 'owlers', who employed their own attorneys and maintained their own armed squadrons. The Acts of Parliament 'did indeed make the rich ones leave off going themselves, but by their trusty Servants they hired stout fellows, to run ye bodily hazard', as one well-informed observer noted.[22] Eighteenth-century smuggling had entered its heyday, where quick steady profits, organized violence and adulteration characterized entrepreneurship. A Lambeth warehouse supplied the East End dealers with tobacco mixed with chestnut, walnut and hops leaves. In Glasgow a man who could disguise 'trash' as tobacco might earn £50. Walpole's hirelings kept him informed of how false weights were used on the quays.[23]

The 1722 Parliament unified the Scottish and English Customs administration. The intricate customs of allowing 'Abatement, Discounts, and Allowances for Waste and Damage' to the standard duties were abolished. Instead a flat allowance of 25 per cent was

---

[21] *An Essay*, p. 143 and *passim*.
[22] PRO, SP 35/78, part 1, fols. 132–4, 'The Originall, Rise, Progress and Present State of Those Enemies to England, the Owlers Describ'd'.
[23] HC, vol. xvii (March–April 1715–16), pp. 410, 414 and 420–21; Robert C. Jarvis, *Customs Letter-Books of the Port of Liverpool 1711–1813*, Chetham Society, 3rd series, vol. xi (Manchester, 1954), p. 25; Cambridge University Library, C(H) MSS, 43, 11/6.

granted across the board on the old subsidy (the first penny a pound duty). Another 25 per cent was granted for swift payment, and a final 7 per cent for discharging import bonds within eighteen months. Micajah Perry, who had access to large capital markets (he held the largest of the very few private loans that the Bank of England entertained, £8,000), could take advantage of these terms and reduce the tariffs by 40 per cent while medium-sized merchants without access to credit could not.[24] This attempt to remove the thicket of collusion and fraudulence betwen merchants and the Revenue officers came at the same time as the 'penal obligations' were enforced between the merchants and the shipping and dockside workers.

The state had intervened in two decisive ways at the turn of the century – one political in forming a large Customs bureaucracy and a police force and the other apparently technological in the legislation of containerization.

III

In the eighteenth century the science of metrology was as underdeveloped as the concept of the commodity. Indeed, the entire period of mercantilism has been defined by the fragmentation of measuring standards. A system of standardized metrology was hardly more than a dream of a few, and the economic theory of the commodity was similarly at an early stage of concoction. For most people, notions of metrology were determined by the practices of the 'moral economy', whose theory owed much to those Mosaic limitations upon commodity production found in the biblical commands against unequal weights, against taking more than can be used, and against reaping a field too cleanly.[25]

The class struggle in the oceanic tobacco trade took a metrological form, because the ambiguities of measure benefited the porters,

[24] The best contemporary account of the organization of the Customs is found in 'The Report of the Committee Appointed to Inquire into the Frauds and Abuses in the Customs', 7 June 1733, *Reports from Committee of the House of Commons*, vol. i, pp. 601–655. Elizabeth Hoon, *The Organization of the English Customs System, 1697–1786* (New York, 1938), provides a systematic modern account.

[25] Karl Marx, *Capital*, vol. i, trans. Ben Fowkes (1976), pp. 125–6, 164; Eli F. Heckscher, *Mercantilism*, vol. i (1935), p. 111; E. Chambers, *Encyclopaedie; Or, An Universal Dictionary of the Arts and Sciences* (1728) in words later repeated in Diderot's *Encyclopédie*, vol. xii (Paris, 1765); Bruno Kisch, *Scales and Weights: An Historical Outline* (1965), p. 1; Deuteronomy 25:13–16, 23:24, 24:19.

the crews, the slaves, the lightermen and the 'little inconsiderable persons'. Legislation attempted to standardize the hogshead. Maryland increased the authorized diameter of its top from 30 ins. to 32 ins., the diameter of the bulge to 37 ins., and the length of the staves to 48 ins.; it hoped that these modifications would make its crop more competitive by reducing freight rates. Virginia law set similar restrictions on the size of the hogshead. Both colonies regulated the tare. In Maryland the allowance for tare was set at 8 per cent 'of the Neat Weight of the Tobacco'. In Virginia every hogshead was to be branded with its tare and the initials of the cooper who made it. By 1704 in Maryland and 1705 in Virginia it had become a felony to tamper with these marks.[26]

After 1699 the coopers' work of fabrication, assembly, repair and breaking of bulk had become decisive to all systems of tobacco carriage, whether by land, river or sea. Well-seasoned white oak staves bound together by hickory hoops lent to the container its typical shape. Tapering ends with a bulge in the middle gave it an ability to be rolled; a higher centre of gravity for ease of handling; and the strength to withstand the shocks and stresses of long haulage. A skilful cooper could fit the headings of the hogshead so well into the staves by the characteristic join of the chime and croze that the container would resist the seepage of salt water to be encountered in the lower parts of the ship's hold. Specialized tools (adzes, axes, howels, chives, planes), expensive equipment (benches, blocks, the cresset), intelligence between the hand and eye, and years of training were necessary to cooperage.[27]

The skills might easily be turned to the advantage of labouring men. By all contemporary accounts the cooper was dilatory in the completion of orders, wilful in his mode of operation, and idle in the work itself.[28] The colonial authorities, with the approval of the London Board of Trade, sought to prevent the use of 'green and unseasoned timber', thin staves and insubstantial hoops ('flat hooping') 'as will not endure rolling to the water', by specifying the mode of seasoning, the thickness of staves and the materials of

---

[26] Browne, op. cit., vol. xxx, pp. 348–55; Hening, op. cit., vol. iii, pp. 435–40; and Wyckoff, op. cit., pp. 89–128.

[27] Franklin Coyne, *The Development of the Cooperage Industry in the United States, 1620–1940* (Chicago, 1940); R. A. Salaman, *Dictionary of Tools Used in the Woodworking and Allied Trades, c. 1700–1970* (1975); Bob Gilding, *The Journeyman Coopers of East London* (1971).

[28] Wyckoff, op. cit., p. 88.

hooping.[29] Such were the problems with paid labour in the 1720s that the incentives to use slaves as coopers and carpenters were considerable.[30] 'Every man who is concerned in the trade should be more or less a cooper himself,' wrote a leading eighteenth-century authority. After field work, coopering was the most common trade exercised by African slaves in early eighteenth-century Virginia.

'Checked' or 'dotty' wood used in making staves was sure to split or fall apart, thus providing employment to fellow coopers, and other workers with opportunities at the tidewater inspection houses or in the Thames moorings. A faulty chime and croze allowing the head to spring open would expose the tobacco to the carters and porters transporting the burden. Defective hooping might produce equally lucrative results. The manner of loading and stowing the hogsheads also offered opportunities.

In Virginia hoops were cut and staves stripped away so that the 'picker' might insert his hand-mall into the compacted mass for sampling. Even before this the hogshead remained open in the warehouse yard, 'where every man thinks himself privileged to take a handful as he passes, for the purpose of chewing or smoking, *according to established custom*' (my emphasis). When the hogshead was 'turned up' for inspection, the pickers, coopers and attendants became 'the most benefited of all men by a practice which has become a kind of calculable privilege through its frequent indulgence', for they took twists and rolls not only for their own consumption, but to supply sailors and 'small adventurers' for exportation. Thousands of pounds of tobacco were thus lost to the planter each year. Indeed, those who insisted on buying the finest tobacco wasted their time in legitimate markets, for the choicest

[29] L. C. Gray, op. cit.
[30] Allan Kulikoff, 'Tobacco and Slaves: Population, Economy and Society in Eighteenth Century Prince George's County, Maryland', unpublished Ph.D. thesis, Brandeis University, 1975, pp. 5–47. See also Marcus W. Jernegan, 'Slavery and the Beginnings of Industrialism in the American Colonies', *American Historical Review*, vol. xxv, no. 1 (October 1919), p. 220, and Leonard P. Stavisky, 'Negro Craftsmanship in Early America', *American Historical Review*, vol. liv, no. 2 (January 1949), p. 320; William Tatham, *An Historical and Practical Essay on the Culture and Commerce of Tobacco* (1800), p. 43; Philip Bruce, *Economic History of Virginia in the Seventeenth Century* (New York, 1896), vol. ii, p. 420, and Leonard Stavisky, 'The Origins of Negro Craftsmanship in Colonial America', *Journal of Negro History*, vol. xxxii, no. 4 (October 1947).

tobaccos were only to be had on application to the African attendants in the Virginia warehouses.[31]

Having been inspected, the hogsheads were removed from the warehouses down skids to the flats which carried them down the creeks to the ships for their stowage. In cropping, cutting away the bulge and drawing the staves 'great quantities of tobacco ... are *purloined* by the sailors' (my emphasis), according to a 1710 Virginia statute, which empowered shipmasters to fine such mariners £5. Stowage techniques were vital. Unlike the modern container, the hogshead did not possess an interlocking capability. To protect the hogsheads from sea water wedges were used that kept them away from the bottom and sides of the hold. They were to be stowed with regard to the disposition of the ship's trim and centre of gravity, for a lee-lurch might sink a ship. They were to be placed 'bung up, and bilge free'. However strong the individual container, or well-chocked with wedges, or protected by dunnage, few were able to withstand the great stresses imposed by the ship's pitch and roll through surging seas. Since it was the planter's interest to get his crop as quickly as possible to the London markets, he was not usually willing to cause further delay by arguing with the ship's mate about stowage techniques. The shipper, on the other hand, charged freight rates according to the number of hogsheads he carried, so the lever and the stowing jack were employed to compress them into as small a space as possible. 'They have a constant Method of Loading their Ships quite different from the English,' William Byrd complained against Scottish stowing in 1728.[32] Sometimes the hogsheads were actually split to fit around the ship's stanchions, more often bilges were forced flat, sides indented, and the interstices of the hold packed with smaller casks and, despite the 1699 Act, with loose bundles.

Not only did the haste of the planter and the avarice of the shipper cause damage to the cargo, but so too did the difficulties of manual handling. The ablest of sailors and slaves, expert at the task, united their labours to get the hogsheads aboard. First, the hogshead was rapped to find its emptier end ('taking off'), so that it might be manhandled into parbuckle gear or rolled down the skids into lighters. Then a 'purchase' of slings and blocks removed the hogs-head to the ship's hatches. The ship's crew forwarded the hogsheads

---

[31] Tatham, op. cit., pp. 96–8. See also G. Melvin Herndon, *William Tatham and the Culture of Tobacco* (Florida, 1969).
[32] Hemphill, op. cit., p. 198.

to the stowing gang, often African, that worked the hold.

On the other side of the Atlantic 'tacklehouse' and 'ticket' porters unloaded the ships. They were paid piece-rates that were high in comparison with many other rates in carrying work but low when regarded as part of their total annual earnings, since the porters' 'vintage time' was restricted to the few autumn months of the fleet's arrivals. Serious jurisdictional quarrels separated the ticket and the tacklehouse porters. The former had worked the Caribbean and North American vessels in the sixteenth century when tobacco commerce was small, while the latter possessed the privilege of carrying all the merchandise of City Freemen. As the North Atlantic trade increased the tacklehouse porters sought to re-establish their monopoly in a series of legal disputes. On the river front the tacklehouse contractors and the ticket gangsmen entered a price war of competitive fee reduction. As wages fell, embezzlement and pilfering increased proportionately. The threat 'from below' united the contractors.[33]

The porter's work was arduous and dangerous, and imposed a terrific toll on the lives of the men. The ship had first to be prepared for the breaking of bulk – sails needed unbending, running rigging needed to be unreeved, yards and topmasts to be struck. Then stages had to be built for cables, planks had to be laid out for rolling the hogsheads or derricks got up for slinging them by 'fall'. Finally, the force of cooperative labour, a dozen or so men, was brought to bear on the freight itself. They worked the hogsheads across the 'drift' (the distance in the hold between the freight and the hatch) to the scuttle, from the scuttle to the tending lighter, and from there to the wharf. Here it was lifted to the quay, inspected, weighed and then shifted to cart or wagon. Fractures, rope burns, lacerations and broken bones were common. The greatest dangers came from the sheer weight of the load. The gross weight of the hogshead might be 300 lbs. at the least, but in the 1720s it was likely to weigh half a ton, a tremendous burden for manual handling.[34] Porters were

[33] CLRO, 'The Case of the Ticket Porters against the Tacklehouse Porters presented to the Court of Aldermen' (1707), box 5, shelf 149; 'The Case of the Tacklehouse Porters of the Twelve Primary Companies' (1707), box 1, shelf 149; and 'The Porters Case Book, 1716–1724', pp. 91–3.

[34] In 1967 the International Labour Conference set 50 kilograms as the maximum permissible weight carried by one worker. *Maximum Permissible Weight to be Carried by One Worker*, International Labour Conference, 51st Session, report VI (1 & 2), Geneva 1966.

bent out of shape, crippled and disabled by hernias. A person labouring with these loads aged prematurely and could expect a working life of no longer than ten years. The fellowships of London porters were as concerned with injuries and sickness as they were with basic rates or demarcation disputes. Hogsheads and casks were damaged as if by routine. Spillage, spoilage and wastage were translated into income for the river worker, enabling him to eke out the thin months or to stretch out a job for a few more days.

The work was cooperative in several senses. The unloading of a ship required the coordinated labours of many men – hauling, signalling, rolling, heaving, coopering, etc. Upon this cooperation depended the turnaround time of the ship, the security of the unloaded cargo and the intensity of the day (working hours were 6 to 6 with half an hour for breakfast and an hour for dinner). Just as the dangers of the job could either maim men or break cargo, so cooperative labour could work two ways – to the advantage of either the shipper and merchant or the porters, coopers and sailors.[35] This was another meaning of cooperation. In Maryland and Virginia workers' appropriation was so complex and widespread that Tatham developed a systematic analysis, dividing such appropriations into two categories: those 'privileged by Custom' and those resulting from 'casual Exposure'. He further classified the 'plunder' according to its geographical site (barn, transit, warehouse, ship) and the degree of 'tacit assent of the crowd'. Tatham stressed the reliance of these 'customs' and 'privileges' upon the labour process. Tatham recognized the international character of labour. A variety of labours (coopering, carting, sailing, portering) cooperated in diverse geographical settings (plantation, creek, ocean, river). Once set in motion this international division of labour developed a mind of its own. 'Plunder' available in any section of this labour force depended directly upon the concrete labours of other parts of the whole. Thus the relation between the plantation cooper and the Thames lighterman, between the stowing gangs of the Chesapeake and the portering crews of the London quays, between the sailors and the London coopers might become cooperative.

---

[35] 'It is apparent that a system for the operation of pilferage exists, if by system we mean a set of interconnected parts organized together to perform a particular job with the boundary to the system being largely congruent with the work gang,' writes Gerald Mars in 'Dock Pilferage: A Case Study in Occupational Theft', in Paul Rock and Mary McIntosh (eds), *Deviance and Social Control* (1974), p. 220.

River work relied on temporary workers – the 'floating population' – despite the continued existence of the older porterage societies. The 'lumper' of the 1790s, or even the 'casual labourer' of Mayhew's day, was already characteristic.[36] The porter shifted as best he could from job to job. James White hawked fruit during the off-season. Patrick Kelly, a river porter who was hanged for coining in 1743, ran errands, assisted masons, bricklayers and carpenters, and in season went hay-making in Middlesex and Kent. Conversely, many, like Michael Grant who lost a weaving job after a wages dispute, were neither bred nor established in river work, but easily found casual employment, and Grant rolled tobacco hogsheads before he turned to highway robbery.[37]

James White was transported to tobacco plantations as a convict labourer. Of course, he took there his ideas and experiences and when he returned to London we may be sure he was a different man. Scottish, Irish, English, American and African men were forced by the whip, the transport ship, the crimp and the slaver to cooperate on the gangway, in the hold and in the rigging over the mortal dangers of the deep. By the 1720s we already find considerable evidence of African interchanges with the American and English parts of the proletariat. In 1724 an African, Thomas Gurnes, working with a Minories man, took tobacco from Micajah Perry's warehouse to sell in Ratcliff Highway.[38] In the late 1720s Job, son of Solomon, laboured in the Maryland tobacco plantations and translated the Koran three times.[39] A Fanti blacksmith boy from Nigeria, known to the masters and mates of the slave ships that transported him as Jacob or Michael, laboured 'weeding grass and gathering stones in a plantation'. His plantation master sold him to the captain of a 'fine, large ship loaded with tobacco', which shortly thereafter sailed for England. His new master, a lieutenant in the

---

[36] Henry Mayhew, *London Labour and the London Poor*, vol. iii (1861), p. 301. Charles Booth at the end of the century conducted a statistical study of the occupational histories of the workers in the West India Docks. Only 22 per cent had grown up in more or less river trades as dockers and sailors. Most had had other occupations: artisans and mechanics (20 per cent), labourers (16 per cent), soldiers (7 per cent), domestic servants (3 per cent), and so on. Quoted in E. C. P. Lascelles and S. S. Bullock, *Dock Labour and Decasualization* (1924), pp. 28–9.
[37] *The Proceedings*, 13 April 1743 and 12 July 1742.
[38] ibid., 26 February 1724.
[39] Thomas Bluett, *Some Memoirs of the Life of Job, the Son of Solomon* (1734).

Royal Navy, persisted in calling him Gustavus Vasa despite active opposition from the boy. The voyage was long. Towards its end, in the twelfth week, the provisions ran out. Gustavus Vasa was terrorized into believing that he was to be eaten. Another boy, Richard Baker, a few years older and an American, befriended the young slave. 'Many nights we had lain in each other's bosoms when we were in great distress.' For two years they were companions, Dick teaching the twelve-year-old that knowledge would conquer his fears – of the 'grampusses', of the white men, of the future. From Dick he learned to respect books. Thus did the African spokesman of Abolitionism, whom the world knows now as Olaudah Equiano – a musician, a Christian and a lover of Homer and Milton – start his political education as a slave aboard a tobacco ship.[40] The international character of the London proletariat was one aspect of the international capital that centred on London. This proletariat depended for its survival on what Equiano called 'trifling perquisites'.

IV

The transoceanic tobacco proletariat produced both colonial tobacco for London lungs and an economic and political crisis for the Walpole regime. To understand this we need to examine the two meanings of 'customs' in the 1720s: 'customs' and 'Customs'. One led to a crisis caused by the criminalization of compensation, and the other to a crisis of police authority in the Customs offices.

A usage of a locality or trade, which by long continuance has acquired the force of law or right, is one meaning of 'custom'. It would not *appear* that taking tobacco was either lawful or right, for our knowledge of the practice depends on criminal prosecutions for felonious stealing, and the records of such prosecution seem to individualize the actor and to remove him from any community that might sanction such a custom. James White's crime was not isolated, though his punishment was the severest meted out to the dozens of porters, coopers, watermen and seamen who were indicted for stealing tobacco in the 1720s.

[40] Olaudah Equiano, *The Interesting Narrative* (1789), reprinted in Francis D. Adams and Barry Sanders (eds), *Three Black Writers in Eighteenth Century England* (Belmont, California, 1971), pp. 134–40.

Let us look at these cases chronologically. In 1721 William Rippin, 'being in want', took and sold quayside tobacco. He was transported to Virginia. Benjamin Jones opened a hogshead with a knife, hid the tobacco under 'ye Gateway', and took it away in the morning. He was transported. Charles Allchorn, a cooper, took 'some Tobacco off the Ground' during the dinner-break. He was whipped. Edmund Ogden took tobacco – 'the Goods of Micajah Perry' – and sold it at an alehouse where he was betrayed by 'a scandalous drunken fellow'. He was acquitted. In 1722 Robert Friend, a wharfinger's servant, was accused of stripping the hoops from a hogshead and taking 'a Cake of Tobacco'. He was acquitted. In 1724 Richard Jennings and one Robinson, two ticket porters, were indicted for taking tobacco from a lighter and concealing it in their knee-breeches. In 1725 another ticket porter, John Winter, was accused of stealing tobacco from a lighter at Somers Key. In 1729 James Smith was transported for stealing a 'considerable Quantity' of tobacco from a frigate. John Brown and Thomas Mullings stole a large amount and were whipped only, the jury valuing the tobacco at 10d. Robert Nuttal, 'a Porter employed to land Goods', was whipped for taking 8 cwt. of tobacco. James Adams, a cooper, was found guilty of stealing 6 cwt. of tobacco. William Wood, John Edgings, Giles Rawlings, Thomas Wood, Richard Scott and Thomas Allen, all working on lighters, were indicted for stealing various amounts of tobacco. Allen Sawyer, a Billingsgate porter, was indicted and acquitted for taking 20 lbs. of tobacco.[41]

---

[41] CLRO Sessions Papers, box 1721–3, 'The Examination of William Rippin, 3 May 1721', 'The Examination of Benjamin Jones', 'The Information of John Skinner, 20 December 1723', 'The Information of John Skinner, 6 Feb. 1724/5', and 'The Confession of Richard Jennings, 20 December 1723'. Marion and Jack Kaminkow, *Original Lists of Emigrants in Bondage from London to the American Colonies, 1719–1744* (Baltimore, 1964) provide the name of the ship on which each transported felon sailed. *The Proceedings*, 11–14 October 1721, 6–13 December 1721 and 10–12 December 1722; *The British Journal*, 6 July 1723. Also see, *A Handlist of Proclamations Issued by Royal and other Constitutional Authorities 1714–1910*, Bibliotheca Lindesiana, vol. viii (Wigan, 1913); *The Proceedings*, 16–21 January 1728/29, 26 February–5 March 1728/29, 16–24 April 1729. The penal sanction made each of the individual labours along the 3,000 miles from the Shenandoah to Stepney interchangeable. Besides living, stealing, making, carrying, and breathing the stuff, men were often sold for it. Jesse Waldon, for instance, was transported to Annapolis, where he was sold for two hogsheads to a planter who took him to his Blue Ridge tobacco lands. The Ordinary's *Account*, 7 April 1742.

We may make several observations about these cases. The tobacco was generally enclosed in the hogshead. The appropriation took place in a group setting. Judging from the occupational designations, it appears that most of the taking was within the context of the labour process. Finally, we note the wide variety of punishments and the mixture of verdicts. Although Old Bailey jurors came from a different social class than river workers, they detested informants. Several notorious informers were active in the campaign on the docks – William Foster and John Skinner to name two.[42] One of Walpole's spies wrote to him that 'Juries would not always give credit to Evidences who had already broke their oaths of office'.[43] Whether the jurors accepted defence arguments based on 'custom' we cannot know, but they certainly had to consider them. They did not in the case of William Drinkwater and Samuel Hoy of Stepney, who were transported in April 1729 for taking 13 cwt of tobacco from the ship *Barwell*. The evidence against them stated: 'There was an Agreement among the prisoners, the first and second Mate, the Boatswain, Gunner, and Captain's servant to sock, that is, to take Tobacco out of the Merchant's Hogsheads, to sell it, and to share the Money among them, it having been said, it was an old Custom so to do.'[44] To the porters, coopers, seamen and lightermen 'socking' was an 'old Custom', and as such part of their income. To 'sock' meant to take or to pocket. It was a word of the London vernacular, and like 'funk' and 'fogus' (tobacco) or 'snout' (hogshead) it rarely appeared in print. The attack on socking may be seen then less as an attack on 'crime' than as an intensification of the exploitation of river workers.

'Socking' enjoyed the sanction of the London vernacular; to many workers it was a customary right. As such, it was not a use-right, because those taking the tobacco did so to barter or to sell it. It was their pockets or bellies that wanted filling, not their pipes. Socking bears some similarities to rural customs, particularly to common appurtenant.[45] How frequently it could be exercised, who might

[42] CLRO, Sessions Papers, box 1723–5, 'The Information of William Foster, 19 August 1723', and also *The British Journal*, 24 August 1723, which reported that a Customs House porter was committed to Newgate for 'unlawful freedom with some Hogsheads of Tobacco'.

[43] Cambridge University Library, C(H) MSS, 35/1–3.

[44] *The Proceedings*, 16–24 April 1729. Drinkwater joined Manning aboard the *Forward Sally*.

[45] Jeanette Neeson, 'Common Right and Enclosure in 18th Century Northamptonshire', unpublished Ph.D. thesis, University of Warwick, 1977.

exercise it, and how much might be socked, were vague. It was not a right of time immemorial. It might have been an old custom but it originated in recent memory. The creation of custom, just as much as its preservation, was a living struggle.[46] In the case of tobacco, a relatively new commodity, we should look less to agrarian relations in England than to other points in tobacco's circuit of production. On the other side of the Atlantic the growers of the leaf also had their vernacular of appropriation and justice – 'takee no stealee' and 'no catchee no havee'.[47]

For most products of transatlantic commerce, the social behaviour that might lead to accepted forms of customary appropriation was in gestation during the 1720s. A notorious informer supplied evidence against those taking sugar.[48] South Sea Company porters took cochineal, a Caribbean dye-stuff, to sell to Mrs Austin who made linen bags for the purpose.[49] John Field and Edward Wintland ('they worked on board of ships' the jury heard as exculpation) were acquitted of stealing indigo.[50] Tobacco, however, was the most contentious of the oceanic commodities in the 1720s.

By the end of the decade the conflicts on the Thames quays had intensified. In about 1726 the Customs House and thirty warehouses were burnt down. In 1727 Micajah Perry presided over a tobacco-dealers' association which decided to engross the market and raise prices. In 1728 a House of Commons committee came to the conclusion that pilfering tobacco from the rivers had increased 'to a very great Degree' among the tidesmen, porters, mates, coopers, ships' crews and lightermen. That year several Customs officers were suspended 'only for taking Care of their Families and making the most of their Places'. In 1729 a purge of the Customs took place; scores lost their jobs and more than a dozen were prosecuted in the courts. To understand these events we need to look more carefully at this second meaning of the word 'customs'.

Three types of officers were associated with the importation of

---

[46] See Chris Fisher, *Custom, Work and Market Capitalism: The Forest of Dean Colliers, 1788–1888* (1981).
[47] Folarin Shyllon, *Black People in Britain, 1555–1833* (1977), p. 88; Peter H. Wood, *Black Majority: Negroes in Colonial South Carolina from 1670 through the Stono Rebellion* (New York, 1974).
[48] *The Proceedings,* 16–24 April 1729.
[49] ibid., 5–7 June 1728.
[50] ibid., 26–8 February, 23–31 March, 1–4 April 1724.

tobacco. First there were the tidewaiters ('poor indigent & vile fellows') who sailed with the ship after its sighting at Rye. Four of these men would embark at the Gravesend boarding station to prevent illegal discharges, to search the ship and tally the cargo by checking each hogshead for the Virginia or Maryland cooper's mark of type, amount and quality of tobacco. The Customs employed 284 such men. After the ship reached its mooring and the cargo had begun to be unloaded into awaiting lighters, a second group of Customs officials, working the Legal and the Sufferance quays, took responsibility for the tobacco. This group consisted of 30 landwaiters, 19 King's waiters and 9 land surveyors. They were the most important Customs men on the quay, and were assisted by 40 to 80 watchmen, 5 searchers each with under searchers, several dozen noon tenders, 25 weighers in fee, and several hundred ordinary weighers.

Like the third class of Customs officials – the jerquers, comptrollers, collectors, tellers and their clerks and servants in the Long Room of the Customs House – the men down on the quays had everything to gain by delay. In addition to Sundays, Customs officials took forty-five holidays a year. They had three and a half hours for their midday dinner. It might take anywhere from three to six months, according to the author of *An Essay on Bulk Tobacco*, to discharge the whole cargo.

Travelling with the hogsheads, their inseparable companions, were the phantom-like representatives of the value that lay concealed within the dusty-packed tobacco hands of the hogshead – documents such as prime entries, post entries, inward clearing bills, landing accounts, ship's reports, manifests, etc. These were the visible, paper consequences of the lurking suspicions that haunted all parties in the trade. Paperwork, as a Parliamentary Committee discovered, encouraged fraud.[51] In the 1720s the Customs House reduced the yearly allowance to its officers in the Long Room to a maximum limit of 8 reams of paper and 6,000 pens. 'The grotesque fashion in which the Customs clerks stated matters of accompt, render the documents extremely puzzling to the direct thinker,' one authority concluded.[52] The arithmetics of the eighteenth century, 'casting Accompts', reflected the confusion: young scholars learned arith-

[51] *Parliamentary Reports,* vol. vi, no. 59.
[52] ibid., and Hoon, op. cit., p. 140.

metic by obedience to rules that were scarcely distinguishable from commerce (the Rule of Loss and Gain, the Rule of Bartering, the Rule of Alligation), and in the 1713 edition of Wingate's *Arithmetic* we learn that the Rule of Tret and Tare was 'call'd beyond the seas *The Courtesies of London*, because not practised in any other place'.[53]

The officers of the City were allowed by custom 'tret and clough' (an allowance of 4 lbs. in every 104) and 'tare' (an allowance equivalent to the weight of the container). The deputy meter took 'fillage'. 'Bailage' was paid for the inspection of Merchant Strangers' goods. For each hogshead 2 lbs. of 'sample' was allowed and a 'draft' of 8 lbs. was deducted from the suttle weight for the buyer.[54] The tobacco merchant paid lighterage, moorage, keelage, primage (payments to the ship's captain for use of cables and ropes and to the mariners for working them), cooperage, pesage (for weighing), porterage, tenage (for the use of the unloading area) and wharfage. The 'husband of the ship' worked closely with the landwaiter in assessing import duties and export drawbacks. Kickbacks in the form of tobacco were returned to the tidesmen and the landwaiters as part of 'hickory puckery'. The Act of Frauds generally allowed 5 per cent to the merchant 'for defects and damages'. The ship's 'portage' was an allowance made to the master for the correct entry of his cargo. The ship's captain enjoyed the privilege of stowing in his cabin and in the ship's upper works. The ship's mate might carry two hogsheads freight-free, the second mate and carpenter one each. The ship's officers also enjoyed the rights over broken stages, lockstocks and dunnage. At loading time the crew expected a consideration in tobacco. 'Each sailor carryes his particular venture which Amounts to between one or two hhds. a man,' wrote one of Walpole's informants. The lightermen and porters took 'spillage' and 'sockings'. The tobacco strewn around the ship as it was being unloaded was called 'gold dust'.

The division between legitimate and criminal transactions was never clear at any level. Purloining, bribery, fraud, collusion, embezzlement, wage-payment, perquisites, the purchase, the sale, taking, 'borrowing', London courtesies, the pay-off and the blind

---

[53] In addition, see William Webster, *Arithmetick in Epitome* (1715), and Edmund Wells, *The Young Gentleman's Course in Mathematics* (1714).
[54] Stern, op. cit., pp. 38–41, 70–71.

eye took forms that were barely separable in the daily traffic of the river. On the waterfront, the hidden hand was flesh and blood, dealing in gold and socking tobacco. The commodity-form of the products of human labour does not arise peacefully in history. 'Hands Off' is its slogan, as it enters the market, a slogan that fell on ears as deaf in eighteenth-century London as in twentieth-century Brazil or Indonesia, where *mordomia, korupsi, ngompreng* and *ngobyek* prevail and bring with them their violence – a violence that in the 1720s was by no means reserved exclusively to the merchant, magistrate and hangman.

In 1733 a Parliamentary Committee of Frauds in the Revenue reported that the number of Customs House officers who were 'abused and wounded since Christmas 1723' was more than 250. During the same period six officers had been murdered. Thomas Pearce, a river tidesman doubling as a government informer, caused the prosecution of 'several of the Tidesmen and some Lightermen, Porters, and others for stealing and running tobacco'. His evidence in 1729 brought 16 men to the Old Bailey: 4 were acquitted, 4 whipped, and 8 transported. One night in April three men with their faces blackened seized one William Pearce under the mis-apprehension that he was the Customs House informer. They dragged him to a river wherry, rowed him to mid-river and attempted to drown him. Fortunately the attempt failed and the guiltless Pearce survived.[55] But the lesson was not lost, and Walpole was notified that informers, willing enough in clandestine meetings to name names or set up their fellow workers, would refuse to confirm their privately given testimony in public trials. A deter-mined offensive swept across the waterfront in these years, sparing no expense to secure convictions. Work crews were infested with informers; hundreds of examinations were collected from frightened porters and labourers; 150 men were purged from the Customs service – and all this organized at the highest levels of the state under the close supervision of the Prime Minister himself.

[55] *The Proceedings*, 1729 entire; PRO, SP 36/11 fol. 12, 'Commissioner of His Majesty's Customs to the Lords Commissioners of His Majesty's Treasury', 15 April 1729; and Cambridge University Library, C(H) MSS, 35/1–3.

V

The crisis was international, affecting the colonies and the French competitors. In 1728 John Randolph of Virginia visited England to secure the repeal of the 1722 Tobacco Frauds Act. Among its provisions was one prohibiting the separation of the tobacco leaf from the stem and stalk, a provision that increased harvesting costs far beyond what was saved by making pilfering and false packing more difficult. Randolph was able to organize the repeal of this clause. In 1729 Governor Gooch wrote to the Board of Trade complaining of 'the fraudulent practice of breaking open of hogsheads' and of 'sailors who well know how to dispose of it without paying any duty'. 'The People of Virginia,' he wrote, 'know by woeful Experience that their most celebrated Crops are not free from embezzlement on Shipboard or after their Arrival in Britain.'[56] This governor responded to the crisis by reducing wages through the Virginia Tobacco Inspection Act. This statute not only reduced the money-wage by 30 to 40 per cent, but also, through its provisions designed to eliminate 'depredations', reduced real compensation even further. The Act prohibited the conveyance of bulk tobacco even in the tidewater creeks. Losses during stowage were to be minimized by forbidding the shipment of oversized and over-weighted hogsheads. These provisions were to be enforced by inspectors working from public warehouses.[57]

The Act prevented some frauds, but put much of the Northern Neck into a state of insurrection. The Northern Neck people 'always remarkable for their disobedience and mingled with many transported convicts' burnt down four new warehouses soon after the Act had been passed. Over the next two years sporadic outbreaks of arson by 'the most turbulent among the planters' were recorded in the Lieutenant-Governor's report to the Council of Trade and Plantations.[58] To many poor planters in Virginia the selling of 'trash' tobacco and the 'vile practice of false packing' were means of reducing their rents, which were paid in tobacco. The practice meant, even in Governor Gooch's opinion, the difference between

[56] Hemphill, op. cit., p. 150 ff; Calendar of State Papers, Colonial Series, America and the West Indies, vol. xxvii, pp. 202–204.
[57] Gooch's description may be found in Calendar of State Papers, op. cit. See also Sioussat, op. cit.
[58] Calendar of State Papers, op. cit., vol. xxxix, pp. 18, 97–8.

going clothed and going barely naked. The Act failed in its main purpose, 'being very much opposed by the Masters of Ships and such merchants as get by running and pilfering tobacco; which it is chiefly contrived to prevent', as a Virginia authority wrote in a letter to the Bishop of London.[59]

The French tobacco monopoly, a financial pillar of the Absolute State, had been substantially dependent upon English imports. The French authorities sought to regulate socking to 1 lb. of tobacco a person a month. Tobacco workers were searched upon leaving work. In 1729 a sit-in strike and serious riots occurred in Dieppe when a *gratification* that the workers had formerly enjoyed was removed. After 1733 a new manufactory was built in Dieppe whose manufacturing process was designed to eliminate socking. The hire of guards became a major expense.[60] In England a similar policy almost toppled the Great Man himself.

Walpole sought to introduce, in the Excise Scheme of 1733, a Bill that, had it been passed, would have revolutionized the material relations in the tobacco trade. In replacing the Customs duties on tobacco with a single excise tax that taxed consumption instead of trade, Walpole anticipated that higher revenues would accrue to the Treasury as that jungle of corruption, the Customs operations in the Thames, would be swept away at a stroke. Furthermore, the system of bonded warehouses envisaged by the bill would effectively make London a free port and therefore remove the main cause of smuggling. The scheme, he hoped, by increasing revenues, would permit him to pay more money to the King; reduce the land tax, so strengthening his position among the landed squires in Parliament; and improve his command over state administration by curtailing the semi-independent status of the Customs Board.[61]

Walpole's plan has fared better among subsequent historians than it did in his own day. Most have been content to repeat Adam

---

[59] Hemphill, op. cit., p. 217.
[60] Jacob M. Price, *France and the Chesapeake* (Ann Arbor, 1973).
[61] William Coxe, *Life and Administration of Sir Robert Walpole* (1800); J. H. Plumb, *Sir Robert Walpole* (1960); E. R. Turner, 'The Excise Scheme of 1733', *The English Historical Review*, vol. xlii (January 1927); Paul Langford, *The Excise Crisis; Society and Politics in the Age of Walpole* (1975); and William J. Hausman and John L. Neufeld, 'Excise Anatomized: The Political Economy of Walpole's 1733 Tax Scheme', *The Journal of European Economic History*, vol. x, no. 1 (spring 1981) have been my principal guides to the Excise Crisis, though the material discovered about 'sockings' obviously requires amendment of these accounts.

Smith's favourable assessment. His first biographer wrote that the Tobacco Excise Bill failed 'because it was perverted by the malignant spirit of party, and was not thoroughly understood by sober and impartial persons' – a judgement that later biographers have substantially accepted. Resistance to the Bill, according to the various accounts, began with the high-minded, though spurious, arguments that the leading Opposition newspaper, *The Craftsman*, began to develop in the autumn of 1732, six months before the Bill's collapse. These were to the effect that in establishing a permanent armed force empowered to search houses without warrant and to levy fines or seize property without judgement by jury, the constitutional settlement would be subverted and the rights of the free-born Briton destroyed. These lofty principles were used to excite 'the rage of the deluded multitude' in a deliberately instigated, vulgar propaganda war. Soon the satiric refrain of a popular ballad, 'Excise, Wooden Shoes, and No Jury', became the slogan of those out-of-doors mobs that surrounded Parliament during the debates and insulted the proponents of the Bill. Such is the conventional picture of the Bill's detractors: self-interested politicians hiring Grub Street scribblers to run its scurrilous propaganda campaign, and manipulating, if not actually buying, London mobs to run mayhem in the streets.

Did the Opposition organize the mob? Or did the mob inspire, stimulate and partly organize the Opposition? Modern accounts of the crisis do not even pose this question. Yet the scheme was 'the theme of Coffee-Houses, Taverns, and Gin-shops, the Discourse of Artificers, the Cry of the Streets, the Entertainment of Lacquies, the Prate of Wenches, and the Bugbear of Children'.[62] The discussion of liberty that characterized the opposition to the Excise Bill was immediately preceded by eloquent cries of freedom uttered by the oppressed in the London prisons. In 1731 one prisoner wrote:

There is so vast a majority of Lion-like Men among us possessed with the true English and Heroick Spirit, scorning to bow their Necks to Slavery and Oppression ... Let us consider we are a Little Community among ourselves, a Body Politik, whereof not a single Member should suffer but the whole should be concerned.[63]

[62] Anon., *A Letter from a Member of Parliament for a Borough in the West ... Concerning the Excise Bill* (1733), p. 10.
[63] Anon., *An Oration on the Oppression of Jailors which was Spoken in the Fleet Prison on the 20th of February 1731*, pp. 7–8.

Fees, extortion and the torture of prisoners in the Fleet, the King's Bench and the Marshalsea led to the organization of prisoners. In 1729 James Oglethorpe chaired a Parliamentary Committee that investigated the London Prisons. Concerning the Fleet Prison, he wrote:

The present Warden of the Fleet ... hath exercised an unwarrantable and arbitrary power, not only in extorting exhorbitant fees, but in oppressing prisoners for debt, by loading them with irons, worse than if the Star-chamber was still subsisting, and contrary to the Great Charter, the foundation of the liberty of the subject.[64]

Hogarth painted a picture of thirteen wigged MPs assembled in a prison and hearing testimony from a ragged black man. The MPs are depicted fingering the thumbscrews, choke collars and cranium pincers that Thomas Bambridge, the warden, employed in the interrogation of prisoners and which had been the cause of death of Thomas Bliss, a carpenter, in 1726. The revelations of this Committee led Oglethorpe to apply for a charter founding Georgia, which he obtained in 1733. Georgia became in its earliest years a buffer against the Spaniards in Florida, a forcing-house of Methodism, and a dumping-ground for incarcerated debtors. Such was one of the results of the prisoner movement of the late 1720s – a movement that drew heavily upon the traditions of the 'free-born BRITON'. In 1731 a Fleet prisoner wrote the following lines:

> The free-born BRITON to the dungeon chain'd,
> Or, as the lust of cruelty prevail'd,
> At pleasure mark'd him with inglorious stripes;
> And crush'd out lives by various nameless ways,
> That for their country would have toil'd or bled.[65]

There can be no doubt that Walpole and his party understood that the Excise Bill was an attack upon the river people, and intended it as such. In his opening speech in favour of the Bill, Walpole

---

[64] *The Parliamentary History of England from the Earliest Period to the Year 1803,* vol. viii (1722–33), p. 709.
[65] See Anon., *An Oration.* For other printed literature coming out of the prisons in the late 1720s see T. Bird, *Lieutenant Bird's Letter from the Shades to Thomas Bambridge in Newgate* (1729), and Matthew Pugh, *The Humble Petition of Matthew Pugh, Late Steward to the Poor Prisoners in the King's Bench* (1732?).

enumerated the frauds in the trade. After describing instances of hickory puckery, he came to

one of very great consequence, known by the name of *socking*, which is a cant term for pilfering and stealing tobacco from ships in the river. This iniquitous practice, which was discovered in 1728 and 1729, was chiefly carried on by watermen, lightermen, tidewaiters, and city-porters, called gangsmen

who then sold the tobacco to eminent merchants.[66] Sockings, he said, amounted to more than fifty tons a year, from London alone. When later he chastised the Opposition in his major speech for countenancing, if not encouraging, the clamouring mob at the doors of Parliament, he referred to these crowds as 'sturdy beggars'. There was far more to this Bill than innocent advantages to the free trader. 'Savagery and efficiency,' a sympathetic modern biographer has remarked of another context, 'became correlated in the minister's mind.' And it is true that in this same speech Walpole appeared to take pleasure in listing the convictions, the whippings, the sentences of transportation and the dismissal of officers that had already been accomplished at the Government expense in 1728 and 1729.

His interest in tobacco commerce had begun in the early 1720s. In 1724, the year when the duties on tea, coffee and chocolate were converted into excise, he had received from John Crookshanks a well-informed and closely argued 'Memorial Relating to Duties on Tobacco'. It demonstrated that the more complex the Customs duties the greater the opportunities for fraud. Walpole had made it his business to master the dodges and deceits practised by the merchants, even to the extent of taking data in his own hand of the weights of hogsheads on import and export at three ports so that he could compute the one with greatest corruption (London). He mastered the myriad of fees that were charged upon unlading. He followed from year to year the import bonds left outstanding by the tobacco merchants. Of thirty-nine bondholders in the spring of 1732, we have already met three – Micajah Perry (£6,418), Jonathan Forward, the contractor for transporting felons (£9,561), and John Hyde, the dealer who employed the informer named John Skinner (£2,077). To the uttermost farthing, Walpole tabulated the costs of Government prosecutions. Between 1723 and 1725 these amounted to about £600 a year. Over the next three years they almost doubled

---

[66] Plumb, op. cit., vol. ii, p. 237; Coxe, op. cit., vol. ii, pp. 205–231.

to £1,100 a year. His papers show that during the purge of 1729 he took a personal interest in at least the major cases.[67] In that same year he received 'A Representation of the State of the Tobacco Trade' and began his association with John Randolph, the Virginia spokesman of the planters, whose mission to London that year was so successful.

When Randolph arrived in London on a second mission in June 1732 he brought with him a petition from the planters for the conversion of the tobacco duties into an excise tax. He came on behalf of planters whose hostility to the merchants had intensified during the price depression of the 1720s, and who were persuaded that the customs – in both senses of the term – were to blame for the depression. In Walpole, Randolph found not only a master of the intricacies of the tobacco commerce but a close friend and ally to the planter's interest of extirpating sockings, smuggling and frauds from the trade. Their association, oiled by Horace Walpole, the Prime Minister's brother and Auditor-General of the Plantations, grew in intimacy.[68] In November Randolph was knighted. Many thought that he had drafted the Tobacco Bill that Walpole finally presented. Besides the threat of despotism implied by the Bill, it threatened the material interests of both merchants and proletarian dockers and sailors, throwing them into temporary alliance.

So, in the summer of 1733 the Bill was rejected. Randolph went home a knighted failure and Sir Robert Walpole met the first major defeat of his career, while Micajah Perry and Jonathan Forward continued to prosper. Bonfires were lit, effigies of ministers burnt, cockades worn, windows illuminated and the slogan 'Liberty and No Excise' sounded in the streets, signifying a victory against the Government, and a victory for those depending both on the customs of 'accompt' and on the custom of socking.

VI

We began with James White who could read, write and 'cast Accompts' as well as sock tobacco. He led us to Micajah Perry and to the slump in profits of commercial imperialism, to the transatlantic circulation of struggle, to the containerization of tobacco, to His

[67] Cambridge University Library, C(H) MSS 29/6/1; 29/12; 29/13, 16, 22; 41/11, 12; 41/18/3.
[68] Sioussat, op. cit.

Majesty's Customs and the mercantilist state, to working-class customs and the commodity-form, to dockside arson and insurrection in the colonies, to poetry in the prisons and William Hogarth, to arithmetic and the vernacular speech, and finally to the Prime Minister's personal efforts to introduce a paid, centralized police whose failure almost caused the downfall of the Robinocracy, ten years after James White was executed in November 1723.

CHAPTER SIX

'GOING UPON THE ACCOMPT': HIGHWAY ROBBERY UNDER THE REIGNS OF THE GEORGES

> Thou hast many bags of money, and behold now I
> come as a thief in the night, with my sword in my
> hand, and like a thief as I am, I say deliver your purse,
> deliver, sirrah! deliver or I'll cut thy throat.
>
> Abiezer Coppe, *A Fiery Flying Roll: A Word from the
> Lord to all the Great Ones of the Earth* (1649)

I

In Tyburnography we found that among those hanged who had been apprenticed to a trade, a disproportionate number had been butchers.

> *Butchers* whose Hands are dy'd with Blood's foul stain
> And always foremost in the Hangman's Train,

as John Gay wrote.[1] Many of the butchers hanged for highway robbery. In this chapter we shall find that the relationship between the meat trades and highway robbery needs to be explained in the context of the transition from a moral economy to capitalist marketing practices. In addition we shall find that the various meanings denoted by 'going upon the Accompt' correspond to a dialectic that abstracted capital even further in its money-form.

Many London butchers were more plebeian than proletarian. Such a plebeian butcher had been, generally, a tradesman owning a market-stall: he would have possessed his own tools and dealt with buyers and sellers as a small proprietor himself; he would have been married and tied to neighbourhood and kinship groupings, conscious of his 'independence', conscious too of the relationship between 'character' and credit; and he would have belonged to the

---

[1] John Gay, 'Trivia; Or, the Art of Walking the Streets of London', in G. C. Faber (ed.), *The Poetical Works of John Gay* (1969), p. 144.

culture of a specific trade with its particular urban locations, language and habits. These conditions changed in the first half of the eighteenth century, though the memory of them remained, and the butcher came to share increasingly experiences in common with the picaresque proletarian.

Cases of thwarted ambition, strivings for independence and even capital accumulation are frequent among the butcher highwaymen. Daniel Tipping completed an apprenticeship to a Newgate poulterer, then married into the trade, fattening ducks for his father-in-law. He was convicted of highway robbery in Stepney, and would most certainly have hanged had not a great many market people testified to his 'character', thus securing him a reprieve ten hours before he was due to be launched into eternity.[2] William Brown and Joseph Whitlock (hanged in 1733) had been cast off their lands in Wiltshire, but found that they could regain their lost independence by combining work for the Leadenhall and Newgate poulterers with robbery of the higglers and butchers as they returned from sales at these markets. George Robins, a Clare Market butcher, married the daughter of one of the market's richest butchers, but lost his dowry of £30, and then lost his 'character' by turning highwayman under the guise of a 'country tradesman'.[3] Henry Saunders, a Hertford butcher, 'dressed like a Country Farmer, with Boots and Spurs, as if just come to Town'. James Walker, an Aldgate butcher, 'accoutered with Boot and Silver Spurs', robbed on the highway, pretending to be 'a dealer in Horses'. A failed apprenticeship, as in the case of the Whitechapel butcher, William Meers, or a premature marriage, as in the case of Richard Shepherd, whose master 'claimed £2 and a bond of £28 more for the Remainder of his Time', might force a young man to the road.

The story of Henry Cook shows how such activities might be sympathetically received. He was raised by a leather-cutter in the Essex cattle trade and schooled to read, write and cast accounts. He married the beadle's daughter in Stratford Bow, fathering four children and falling into debt. He contracted intimacy 'with most of the loose and disorderly Sparks in and about Stratford', who taught him how to steal fowl from the farmers and estate-owners and sell them in London. At his first trial at the Old Bailey he was

---

[2] The Ordinary's *Account*, 21 December 1747 and 26 July 1732.
[3] ibid., 19 December 1733, 10 December 1735 and 7 November 1750; *The London Gazette*, 26 October 1750.

acquitted by an 'artful defence' that played on the jury's hostility to bailiffs. He then returned to 'raising Contributions upon the Publick'. A neighbouring chandler turned against him and he was caught in possession of five watches. Many of the poor in Stratford, the poulterers of Leadenhall, the porters about Moorfields, his brother-in-law, and some fellow tradesmen followed his recognizable figure in his gold-laced hat around the roads and inns of northeast London. Twice he raised enough to stock his business, and twice he was apprehended 'in the Profession of a Gentleman Collector'. 'What is got over the Devil's back is spent under his Belly,' he said on his hanging day.[4]

Sudden failure in trade preceded the decision of Edward Dixon, Smithfield drover and Whitechapel dealer, to go 'upon the Accompt'. He made this proposal to Jiffling Jack: 'Let us enter into Articles to have no others than ourselves concerned for the future.' And they lived in the woods of north London as highwaymen and smugglers. Imprisoned, Dixon plotted to escape Newgate but was discovered with his irons sawn off. William Gordon, a Leadenhall Market man, left money for the turnpike-keepers, tipped generously at inns, and did no harm to his victims. He and his partner, a Welsh farrier, went to their hanging in April 1733. They requested that the Ordinary sing the 16th Psalm. The seventh verse was a signal to escape: 'I will bless the Lord who hath given me Counsel; my reins also instruct me in the night seasons.' As the Ordinary sang it, they pulled themselves to the side of the cart, 'and jumpt over among the crowd in the twinkling of an Eye'. Although the crowd allowed them to flee, the Sheriff's officers retrieved them and the hanging continued without any more psalm-singing.[5]

Many of the butcher highwaymen were picaresque proletarians, like James Dalton who was three times caught, three times transported and three times returned to London before he was finally hanged in 1730; or Jesse Walden, a Houndsditch butcher, who had sailed to Portugal and the Carolinas and had been sold in Maryland for 1,600 cwt. of tobacco as a transported convict; or Robert Glasgow, a Newgate sheep-dealer, who had fought the Spanish aboard a man-of-war, and worked the London quays; or Edward

---

[4] The Ordinary's *Account*, 16 September 1741; *The Proceedings*, 28 August–1 September 1741.
[5] The Ordinary's *Account*, 24 November 1740, 29 January 1720, 29 July 1751, 25 April 1733 and 28 May 1733.

Mires, who was enchained as a transportee for the entire voyage to Maryland and escaped to Canada, where he worked with the Iroquois during the corn harvest; or Sam Ellard, a Spitalfields Market butcher, who was transported for robbing a cheesemonger of 18s. 9d. and escaped servitude in Philadelphia; or Robert Lake, a journeyman Bishopsgate butcher, who made three voyages to India and, when found guilty of highway robbery, 'insolently turned about and put on his hat uttering some taunting and opprobrious Words'.[6] Such men as these remind us that while the scene of action of the highwaymen was localized to the provisioning roads of London, and while their apprenticeship training might suggest incorporation in an ancient, corporate trade, in fact the individual highwaymen could be as cosmopolitan and as penniless as any proletarian.

Thomas Easter, a Norwich butcher, once stopped a gentleman on Putney Heath, who protested, 'Why, I took you for an honest man!' To which Easter replied, 'So I am because I rob the Rich to give to the Poor.'[7] It is the classic defence of the highwayman, and in this case it was uttered in a classic location for the early eighteenth-century highwayman, because in the commons, heaths, woods and fields surrounding London the contradictions between capitalist 'improvement' and the non-accumulative economies of the poor intersected. Scottish cattle enervated from their long trek, the black cattle of Norfolk, hogs from Rumford, calves from the Essex marshes, Leicestershire wethers fattened around Tilbury, droves of geese and turkeys — all waddled, gaggled, squealed and moaned across the muddy roads to London.[8] Interrupting the provisioning routes were meat markets for calves in Rumford, hogs in Finchley Common and dairy cattle in Islington, and staging areas where herds were formed at Brentford and Mile End. The social intercourse of these roads and the 'improvement' of the fields adjacent provided the geographical setting for London highway robbery.

Capitalists seeking to 'improve' agriculture, as well as those seeking to discipline the 'lower classes', complained frequently about

---

[6] Anon., *A Genuine Narrative of all the Street Robberies Committed since October last by James Dalton* (1728), and the Ordinary's *Account*, 20 May 1728; the Ordinary's *Account*, 29 July 1751, 7 November 1744 and 24 September 1722.
[7] ibid., 14 March 1739, 7 April 1742.
[8] ibid., 16 September 1741; Daniel Defoe, *A Tour through the Whole Island of Great Britain*, vol. i (1772), p. 15.

The King's Highway: Such roads, with their increasing traffic, provided the setting for London highway robbery

the connection between common lands and the practice of highway robbery. And they were quite aware that this relationship went well beyond robbery, objecting also to the nuisances of sport, gaming, 'idleness' and 'debauchery'. According to John Middleton, the poor cottagers to the north and east of London pilfered corn from the substantial farmers to feed their animals; the children brought up in common and copse learned to pilfer and be idle rather than to labour; and the inns provided not only an informal market, where ostlers, drovers, wagoners and cottagers traded goods taken from gardens, cornfields and hen-houses, but also a place where news of possible and actual 'depradations' might occur. Josiah Tucker wrote in 1755 that 'so many Heaths and Commons around London can answer no other End, but to be a Rendezvous for Highwaymen, and a commodious Scene for them to exercise their Profession'.[9]

[9]Josiah Tucker, *The Elements of Commerce and Theory of Taxes* (1755), p. 103; John Middleton, *A View of the Agriculture of Middlesex* (1798), pp. 85, 88; also William Pearce, *General View of the Agriculture in Berkshire* (1794).

These communities of woodland and commons that surrounded London are analogous to the colonial frontier zones, the forests and mountains to which servants, slaves and runaways fled. The comparison did not go unnoticed. At the beginning of the century the Lord Chief Justice signed a warrant allowing the Horse Guards to attack and disperse the communities of squatters in the woods and forests of north London. The communities were called 'maroon villages' after the liberated West Indian colonies founded by fugitive slaves.[10]

Artisanal independence was based on an income sufficient to maintain a family. Most of the butchers we have considered were husbands and fathers. A collapse of income might result in the destruction of these relations too, although it is by no means clear that the 'life of the pad' might restore them.[11]

> I keep my Horse; I keep my Whore;
> I take no Rents; yet am not poor;
> I travel all the Land about,
> And yet was born to ne'er a Foot.

The highwayman represented personal independence and power, a figure apparently who was neither an oppressor ('I take no Rents') nor limited by the life of service.[12] He aspired in part to the independence of the master artisan – that proud, muscular, bluff and hearty person with cleaver in hand and blood on his apron who figures in many of the images of the eighteenth-century London street.

Stephen Jenkins was a married man with four children who lived in Shoreditch and robbed the higglers returning from market. Constable Haines, acting on the information of a certain Mary Chaplain, discovered that he had 27s. in silver money. 'I ask'd him how he came by it, and he said he had sav'd it out of his Labour. I told him, if it was so, he had no reason for making me come after him so often for Money for the Watch.' Haines fetched the headborough and the two of them searched Jenkins' lodgings, where

---

[10] *OED*; William Fisher, *The Forest of Essex: Its History, Laws, Administration and Ancient Customs* (1887), p. 315.

[11] Anon., *A New Canting Dictionary* (1725), appendix 2.

[12] It was frequently noticed by foreign travellers in England, e.g., César de Saussure, *A Foreign View of England in the Reigns of George I and George II* (1725–30), trans. van Muyden (1902), and Béat Louis de Muralt, *Letters Describing the Character and Customs of the English and French Nations* (1726).

they found his market friend Thomas Pinks 'at Dinner with four Fowls on the Table ready dressed'. Pinks had been in trouble before. In March 1742 he escaped from Newgate, scrambling over the roofs and aided by a variety of people – a female witness to his escape who failed to raise the alarm; the cottagers of Shoreditch who concealed and protected him; and, finally, the people of Birmingham, 'where everybody made him welcome ... he walk'd the Streets publickly'. He returned to London and to the robbing of higglers and hen-houses, fencing the fowls to market friends 'used to that Business'. A reward of £100, a huge sum of money, was offered for Pinks' and Jenkins' capture, and it was then that Mary Chaplain, a former mistress of Pinks, betrayed them. In 1742 Pinks and Jenkins were hanged for stealing thirty-six fowls valued at £2 10s. The most telling evidence at their trial was a bad half-crown that a higgler had received several times from Pinks. This is a micro-economy in which stolen chickens can be bought for sixpence before dawn, and a single coin can betray a culprit.[13]

Jenkins left a 'hempen widow' and four children. Eight years earlier in 1734 Jacob Vanderlint, a Dutchman living in London, published a tract stimulated by the Excise debate. Called *Money Answers All Things*, it gave one of the very few contemporary budgets of a poor family. This was one for a 'labouring Man and his Family in London, consisting of a Man and his Wife and four Children'.

The budget helps us to understand one meaning of eighteenth-century subsistence; it indicates the necessity of savings and the inadequacy of prevailing wages rates.[14] Vanderlint listed the daily payments as follows:

Meat	6d.
Bread	$4\frac{1}{2}$d.
Butter	$1\frac{1}{2}$d.
Cheese	$\frac{3}{4}$d.
Roots, herbs, flour, oatmeal, salt, vinegar, pepper, mustard, sugar	$1\frac{1}{2}$d.
Milk	$\frac{3}{4}$d.

[13] The Ordinary's *Account*, 7 May 1742; William Robinson, *The History and Antiquities of the Parish of Hackney* (1842), vol. i, p. 240.
[14] Vanderlint believed that the principles requiring the reduction of wages 'are founded in the Nature of things, and Constitution of the World itself'. The budget is printed on pp. 77–8 of his tract.

Small beer..		3d.
Strong beer..		1½d.
Coals...		2d.
Soap..		¾d.
Candles..		¾d.
Thread, needles, pins, tapes, worsteds, etc..............		¾d.
Total daily payments.................................	1s.	11¾d.

The budget has no place for such items as tea, tobacco, chocolate or coffee, and, clearly, a dinner of 'four Fowls ready dressed' would have been a sumptuous one indeed. Each week daily expenses amounted to 13s. 10d. Then there were these necessary weekly payments:

Rent of two rooms.....................................	1s.	6d.
Schooling..		9d.
Repairs of household goods, bedding, linen, mops, pots, pans, brooms.................................		4¾d.
Total Weekly Payments............................	2s.	7¾d.

Jenkins' rent was three times as great as that in Vanderlint's budget: so he was certainly not living in 'the meanest Manner it can be decently done'. Savings would be necessary in order to meet the annual payments:

Women's victuals and wages in lying-in................	£2	
Physick for the family..................................		10s.
Clothes, linen, woollens, shoes and stockings for the man..	£2	10s.
Same for the woman....................................	£2	10s.
Same for four children..................................	£4	
Total annual payments..................................	£11	10s.
Total annual, weekly and daily payments..............	£54	10s. 4d.

Vanderlint estimated that without making deductions for illness or unemployment, a 'labouring Mechanick' can earn only 'about half what is necessary for the Support of such a Family'. The emphasis is on rhino. Credit was short and available only to the well-trusted. So the options open to the 'labouring Mechanick' were three: he might reduce expenses by reducing his needs (meat, beer, clothing, shoes?); he might ally with other income-earning workers (women's work was paid far less than men's); or he might step outside the money economy, and meet his needs in other ways. It was this third option that Vanderlint saw as the consequence of the 'too great a Scarcity of Money amongst the people':

Our Poor are so very much increased that we are obliged to transport many of them; and our Roads and Streets are so exceedingly infested with Highwaymen and Robbers, as perhaps the like was never.

The revenue obtained by the highwayman might be a means of personal survival or a means of restocking his business. Thus, in actuality as well as in popular representation, he shared attributes of both the plebeian tradesman and the proletarian victim of oppression. The ambiguity was also one of lifestyle: on the one hand, the highwayman appeared to have been accustomed to a lifestyle that put him above the 'labouring Mechanick', and, on the other hand, the lifestyle of the 'labouring Mechanick', according to Vanderlint, was such that he might be driven to highway robbery. Yet, there is a formalism to Vanderlint's view; it is the formalism of money which did not yet answer all things, at least not in the meat-provisioning of London. The punishment for the highway robberies of so many butchers in 'the Sheriff's picture frame' needs to be understood in precise relation to the actualities of the trans-formation of the London markets.

II

It was the century of the roast beef of old England, according to Dorothy George, the great historian of London.[15] No doubt an important history of the eighteenth century could be written just in terms of the new substances ingested by the London body: sugar, tobacco, tea, gin and meat altered the social complexion of eighteenth-century London. Meat not only supplied protein to the city, but also determined the hierarchy of status, the modes of land transportation, the city's nitrogen cycle, the municipal organization of waste, the nature of recreation, etc. An ideology of meat-eating (ennobling the heart, enriching the blood, encouraging the soldiers)

[15] M. D. George, *London Life in the Eighteenth Century* (1965), p. 173.

played its part in the formation of the eighteenth-century person. At the centre of this ideology was dinner.

The English eat a great deal at Dinner [wrote Misson, the French traveller]. I always heard they were great Flesh eaters, and I found it true... They chew the Meat by Whole Mouthfuls ... a Leg of roast or boil'd Mutton, dish'd up with Fowls, Pigs, Ox, Tripe and Tongues, Rabbits, Pidgeons, all well moistened with Butter.[16]

Meat was an essential part of even the proletarian diet. Vanderlint included it as a daily expense. Roderick Random dived into

the middle of a cook's shop, almost suffocated with the steam of boiled beef, and surrounded by a company of hackney coachmen, chairmen, draymen, and a few footmen out of place, or on board wages, who sat eating shin of beef, tripe, cowheel, or sausages, at separate boards, covered with cloths.

His reckoning for beef, bread and beer amounted to $2\frac{1}{2}$d.[17]

To feed this carnivorous population 74,000 sheep a day were sold at Smithfield (on average between 1740 and 1750). The growth of London meat consumption has been linked to the develop-ment of scientific breeding practices, the extension of turnpikes and highways, the draining of marshes, the cutting down of forests and the creation of regional specialization.[18] For those economists whose starting-point is 'demand', the London food market was the first cause of the creation of a 'home market' and the advance in the division of labour. A traditional version of the division of labour was as follows: the Highlander sold his Scottish runts at the great October Falkirk Tryst to the drovers; the drovers herded the cattle across England to the fattening pastures in Norfolk and Lincolnshire for sale to the graziers; the graziers brought the cattle all fat and fine to Smithfield, where they were sold to the cutting butcher; and the butcher then sold his joints to the house-holder. By the second decade of the eighteenth century this version bore little relation to reality.

[16] H. Misson, *Memoirs and Observations in his Travels Over England* (1719) quoted in John Ashton, *Social Life in the Reign of Queen Anne* (1883), p. 141.
[17] Tobias Smollett, *Roderick Random* (1748), ed. Paul-Gabriel Boucé (1979), p. 65.
[18] F. J. Fisher, 'The Development of the London Food Market, 1540–1640', *Econ-omic History Review*, vol. v, no. 2 (April 1935). See also, K. H. Burley, 'The Economic Development of Essex in the Later Seventeenth and Early Eighteenth Centuries', Ph.D. thesis, University of London, 1957. Eric Kerridge, *The Agri-cultural Revolution* (1967) summarizes the literature.

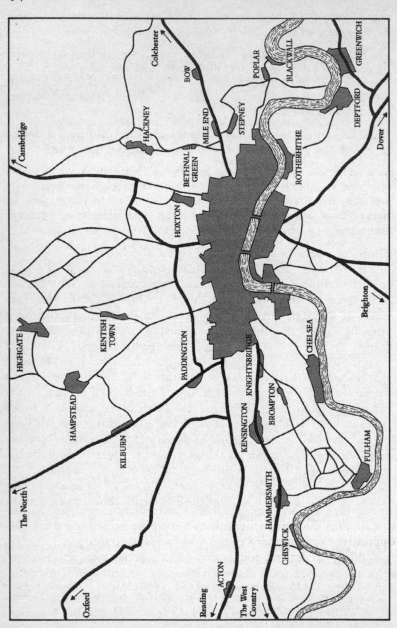

Map 3: Principal highways in and about London

Whereas 'cattle' and 'chattel' had recently obtained separate meanings in England – as livestock and movable property – in the pastoral societies of Ireland and Scotland they had not, cattle being a near thing to money. The conquest of both places, bringing them within the ambit of English mercantilism, had the effect of reversing the traditional relation between man and beast, as the latter replaced the former from the land.

The subjugation of Ireland and the Scottish Highlands was partly accomplished by legislation designed to promote the interests of English farmers, whose dominance depended upon the establishment throughout the British Isles of commodity trade in livestock. The Great Cattle Act of 1667 prohibited the export of Irish cattle, sheep, beef and pork to England, thus forcing Irish farmers to seek new markets in France, Spain and America. The Alien Act of 1705 threatened to prohibit the import into England of Scottish cattle.[19] In reaction to these subjugations, social banditry became endemic in Ireland and Jacobite in Scotland. The geographical space of social banditry – in mountain, bog or coast – is marginal to mercantile societies, but as regards historical time such banditry is a notable feature of the transition to capitalism.

Rob Roy (1671–1734), the Scottish bandit, reflected this opposition. On the one hand, he had been a drover himself, acting as an intermediary between the lowland dealers and their Highland clans. On the other hand, he plundered the Whigs and, more importantly, defended tenants in their struggle against higher rent. His banditry was a variation upon *blackmail*, a traditional form of tribute. Captain Edward Burt wrote of Scottish forms of exchange: 'The stealing of cows they call lifting, a softening word for theft.'[20] Rob Roy's knowledge of terrain, his ability to endure great fatigues, his prowess as a swordsman (his arms were of a length that it was said he could tie his garters without stooping), his generosity and largesse, and his occasional victories against both the English military and their allies among the clans, lent considerable lustre to that oft-sung protection that he provided to tenants and country people suffering from the oppressive expropriations of the new forms of commerce.

Banditry in Ireland took other forms, because the Irish chiefs

[19] Angus Calder, *Revolutionary Empire: The Rise of the English-Speaking Empires from the Fifteenth Century to the 1780s* (New York, 1981), pp. 283, 377, 419.
[20] Captain Edward Burt, *Letters from a Gentleman in the North of Scotland* (1754), and T. C. Smout, *A History of the Scottish People, 1560–1830* (1969), ch. 14.

were not invited to join the English élites and population policy was more ruthless. The tories and rapparees of Ireland were from the dispossessed military chieftains – men like John MacPherson ('he was a stranger to work and it was beneath him to beg'), or Redmond O'Hanlon who sought vengeance for the loss of his ancestral lands under such titles as 'Chief Ranger of the Mountains, Captain General of Irish Robbers, Surveyor General of the High Roads and Lord Examiner of All Passengers'. William Crotty, favoured by market folk, Richard Balf, a pedlar, or Chares, a drover, who organized 'men living wild in the Fields . . . stealing Horses, Kine, Sheep, and all other sort of Cattle', were popular men whose followers were known as 'satyrs' or as 'fairies'.[21] Such banditry merged easily with mass peasant attacks on the livestock of intruding landlords, as it did with the houghing movement that swept Connaught, Mayo, Roscommon and Sligo with 'the energy of a regular insurrection' between 1711 and 1713.[22]

In the pastoral division of labour, the Scottish Highlands supplied the meat-hungry metropolis, and the Irish pastures became a larder for armies, sailors, servants and slaves of the British Empire. This was paralleled by a geographical division of banditry and robbery, which connected the *blackmailer* of the clans, the 'fairies' of Connaught and the highwaymen about London. The connections transpired on the drove roads, the salt licks and the fattening leas. The roads removing wealth became the roads introducing soldiers, for as MacFarlane, the nineteenth-century observer of banditry, wrote, 'the great civilizers of countries are your road-makers'.[23]

III

In London the changes were no less fundamental. At the death of Elizabeth I there were four main London markets: the horse, sheep and live cattle market at Smithfield, pre-eminent in all the kingdom;

---

[21] J. Cosgrave, *A Genuine History of the Lives and Actions of the Most Notorious Irish Highwaymen, Tories and Rapparees* (Wilmington, Delaware, 1799), pp. 7–31.
[22] W. E. H. Lecky, *A History of Ireland in the Eighteenth Century* (New York, 1893), vol. i, pp. 354–94; J. E. Walsh, *Ireland Sixty Years Ago* (Dublin, 1851).
[23] A. R. B. Haldane, *The Drove Roads of Scotland* (Newton Abbot, 1973); K. J. Bonser, *The Drovers: Who They Were and How They Went: An Epic of the English Countryside* (1970); C. MacFarlane, *The Lives and Exploits of Banditti and Robbers in all Parts of the World* (1837), p. 25.

the Stocks market by the Mansion House; Newgate Market, halfway between the prison and St Paul's; and Leadenhall Market, between the Royal Exchange and East India House. At these places the ancient conflict between town and country was carefully organized by centuries of municipal regulation, Royal Charter and customary practices that were designed to reduce the hostilities between those who produced food and those who did not. If a single sentence may summarize the complexity of this organization, it is that the necessities of the consumer held primacy over the profits of market traders. Indeed, legislation was designed to reduce the number of those who merely traded in order that the market might provide as direct an encounter between the producer and the consumer as possible. This was the regulated 'market ouvert', or 'open market', and is to be distinguished from the 'free market'.[24]

During the seventeenth and early eighteenth centuries the growth of the London population strained the capacities of these markets to handle the increase of provisioning. Of thirty-two applications to the Crown and the City to license new markets, only seven were granted: Clare Market (1653), Stepney Market (1664), Honey Lane Market (1667), the Fleet Market (1700), Woods Close Market (1706), Hungerford Market (1749) and Southwark Market (1755). The graziers, drovers, jobbers, carcass butchers, kidders, hagglers, etc. continued to use scores of other unlicensed places of business.

Just as the City of London could not control the marketing practices of the suburbs that fell outside its jurisdiction, so the guilds, which had traditionally governed the meat trades, could no longer effectively exercise their traditional responsibilities. In the seventeenth century the City encouraged marketing by country butchers and others not belonging to the Worshipful Company of Butchers in order to increase supplies and to lower prices. Pestered and hindered by the free butchers, the importance of Leadenhall – the countryman's market *par excellence* – increased as the City extended its trading days and prolonged its market hours. The

---

[24] A. B. Robertson, 'The Open Market in the City of London in the 18th Century', *East London Papers,* vol. i, no. 2 (October 1958), pp. 15–22; Ray Westerfield, *Middlemen in English Business, Particularly between 1660–1760* (New York, 1915); R. R. Sharpe, 'London Markets' (1887), typescript in Lond. CLRO, misc. MSS 187.7; E. P. Thompson, 'The Moral Economy of the English Crowd in the Eighteenth Century', *Past and Present,* no. 50 (February 1971); Alan Everitt, 'The Marketing of Agricultural Produce', in Joan Thirsk (ed.), *The Agrarian History of England and Wales,* vol. vi, 1500–1640 (Cambridge, 1967).

free butchers retained the authority over the markets within their jurisdiction – confirmed in their charter of 1749 – to punish by fine or imprisonment those who sold diseased meat; hawked meat outside the markets; combined to raise prices; regrated cattle or sheep; sold, drove or slaughtered meat on the Sabbath; or sold pork in the summer.[25] By the 1720s the Company's informers and beadles were ineffectual in enforcing these regulations. The Company petitioned unsuccessfully the City's Common Council against non-freemen and country people who used the markets without obeying the Company's regulations, and against the increasing number of labourers who sold meat without having first served an apprenticeship. By the 1740s the Company of Butchers was in debt (its plate was pledged), unable to collect quarterage and ignored by apprentices, who preferred to work in the suburbs.

As a result of these changes London consumers found themselves prey to filth and corruption. At stalls and pitchings, in cart and wagon, Londoners were offered kidneys that had been inflated with air, lamb and veal pricked or padded to increase their weight, ewes and wethers dressed to appear as lamb, and meat puffed up with 'stinking breath or with wind injected by sundry devices'. Slaughtering and scalding operations took place in premises adjacent to market shops. In 1720 the inhabitants of Newgate petitioned against them. Tripe and bowels were sold in side streets, and entrails exposed with wholesome flesh upon the stalls. In 1760 the inhabitants of East Cheap complained of the offal and entrails tossed into the streets. Dung, intestines and innards were often just left in the streets.[26]

A similar process of ineffectuality and crisis affected the Worshipful Company of Poulters. The charters of 1665 and 1692 presented model means for controlling the supply, quality and sale of poultry. Their provisions sought to regulate both the farmers and the dealers. However, freemen of other guilds and country people doing business in the suburbs could not be brought under the Company's control. By the second decade of the eighteenth century guild control of poultry-dealing, even within the limits of the City,

---

[25] P. E. Jones, *The Butchers of London* (1976); Arthur Pearce, *The History of the Butchers' Company* (1929), pp. 110–14. In 1740 twenty-five butchers were indicted for selling meat on the Sabbath, MRO, *Sessions of the Peace Rolls*, MJ/SR 2729–36.

[26] CLRO, Remembrancers Papers, misc. MSS 172.9; George Dodd, *The Food of London* (1856), pp. 218–68.

Honour buys no meat: By the 1730s wholesalers and dealers controlled the trade, unrestrained by the moral economy.

had been further eroded by the illicit trade in lodging-houses, inns and cook-shops, by the uncontrollable expansion of street-vendors and by changes at the main markets. At the end of the seventeenth century the main poultry market opened at 6 a.m. on Monday, Wednesday, Friday and Saturday for trade between country folk and London citizens. Higglers and retailers were prohibited from entering the markets until after the 11 a.m. bell. By the beginning of the next century the country people were complaining that they could no longer find early-morning accommodation. The stalls were all occupied by regrators, engrossers and hucksters. The markets thus ceased to be the classic site where country people and householders met to satisfy mutual need. As the Company's control over the markets slipped away, so did its control of apprenticeship to the trade: fewer apprentices became freemen, and the numbers of men and women binding themselves to a seven-year apprenticeship declined at a steady rate. Despite a final effort at mid-century to prosecute non-freemen, the Company of Poulters became increasingly, like the Company of Butchers, an honorific society.[27]

[27] P. E. Jones, *The Worshipful Company of Poulters of the City of London* (1965).

By the 1730s wholesalers and dealers controlled the trade, unrestrained by the moral economy. Middlemen bought and sold the livestock at informal and unregulated markets around London (in Barnet, Knightsbridge, Romford, Islington, Mile End, Southall and Hayes). These people were jobbers, brokers, salesmen and carcass butchers; to their opponents they were forestallers, engrossers and regrators – or to use the colloquial talk of the 1720s, 'tranters' and 'crockers'. The forestaller *buys before* the market or he *forbears* from bringing his goods to the market. The engrosser *buys up* the market. The regrator *buys in order to sell* again. The odium attached to such profiteers went back to Tudor times and before.[28]

An Act of Charles II proscribed regrating cattle within eighty miles of London. An Act of Queen Anne noted 'a pernicious practice . . . for one butcher to buy a greater quantity of fat cattle or sheep than he can vend, unless by selling them again to other butchers', and it prohibited the practice within ten miles of London.[29] In 1716 an observer noted that at Smithfield and the other markets the jobbers and forestallers had such 'Power and Insolence' that they could thin or glut the market, raise or lower the prices 'just as they please'. They met at inns and yards 'at the town's end, or perhaps within a Stone's Cart of the Market', where their bargains were struck – sometimes with corrupted municipal authorities who pretended to license them. In the course of a week, by continuous dealing, the price of a bullock might rise from 20s. to 30s., or a sheep from 3s. to 4s. Wagoners and carriers became dealers too, accelerating the tendency to retail meats outside the markets.[30] In 1718 the 'inhabitants of London and Westminster' noted that such private selling encouraged the theft of livestock in nearby fields, the clandestine slaughter of ewes and the selling of carcasses unfit for consumption.[31] In 1754 'a Gentleman of the Temple' argued that

[28] Anon., *A New Canting Dictionary* (1725); CLRO, 'Suggestions for a Plan to Regulate the Usage of Smithfield Market, and to Prevent Forestalling the Same', MS 85.12; John Mathews, *Remarks on the Cause and Progress of the Scarcity and Dearness of Cattle, Swine, Cheese, &c.* (1797).

[29] 22 & 23 Charles II, c. 19, and 7 Anne, c. 6.

[30] Anon., *An Essay to Prove; That Regrators, Engrossers, Forestallers, Hawkers and Jobbers of Corn, Cattle and Other Marketable Goods . . . are Destructive of Trade, Oppressive to the Poor, and a Common Nuisance to the Kingdom in General* (1716).

[31] Anon., *The Case of the Inhabitants of the Cities of London and Westminster, and the Suburbs thereof, as also the Inhabitants of the Adjacent Counties, relating to the Oppression they lye under by means of the Forestallers, Engrossers, and Jobbers of Cattle and Flesh-Provisions brought to the several Markets* (1718).

there was a direct connection between the increase of butchers and poulterers' shops and metropolitan theft, which arose because the 'Farmers of the Markets abused their Powers by exacting too large Rates on the Market People'.[32]

Since the 1670s the City of London had leased the markets to agents who regulated them and collected tolls in return for a rent to the City. By 1739 the City received £1,733 from Leadenhall alone, and the farmers increased their revenues by encouraging permanent stalls. The agent at Leadenhall doubled the rents. Those who used the market only once or twice a week, or those whose volume was small – country people with a basket of eggs or a haunch of venison – could no longer afford a corner shambles or a market pitching, and were driven out. One Smith with 'standings by the hole in the wall' refused to pay the increased rent from 5d. to 2s. His rack, hock, block and knives were taken under distress of non-payment. Sarah Archer, a 76-year-old, was forced out in 1725. Meanwhile, big dealers won increasing control of the markets. In 1730 one of them, a certain White, controlled 20 per cent of the calf trade. Two jobbers controlled 80 per cent of the Newgate hog trade. In 1760 a Smithfield salesman knew a jobber who controlled two-thirds of Newgate Market and set prices accordingly.[33]

Around 1720 more than a hundred London and country butchers petitioned the City, protesting that they had become ruined by the jobbers, who contrived with shopkeepers and alehouse-keepers to avoid public sales, used the market every day of the week at all hours, and were responsible for the sale of unwholesome meat. The petitioners and their families had been ruined and the country people 'wholly discouraged and disabled' by the forestallers.[34] The centralization of market power was made possible by the City authorities, who were supine before the violations of the regulated market ouvert, and by the meat and poultry guilds, which were impotent in the face of the class differentiation that was taking place

[32] Anon., *Public Nuisance Considered* (1754), pp. 17, 20–28; CLRO, 'James Brown's Queries ab't the Markett at Bear Key', (1722), MS 85.17.

[33] CLRO, *Account Book of the Entry Fines and Weekly and Yearly Rents for Stalls and Shops payd by the Market People to the Farmers of the Markets*, misc. MS 30.5; Market Copy Accounts, 1738–39, misc. MS 161.22; *Papers Relating to Leadenhall Market, 1720–1741*, Rawstorne Papers, misc. MSS 172.15; Miscellaneous Papers, small MS box 30, no. 4; and misc. MSS 172.5; *JHC* 30:787 (May 1766).

[34] CLRO, 'Petition of Butchers against Sales on other than Market Days' (c. 1720), MSS 85.5.

in the trades they had formerly regulated. Thus expelled from the markets, the former cutting butchers, poulterers, small dealers, herb women, drovers, carters, small-time higglers and kidders were forced either to scramble for meagre places in adjacent alleys – which in any case could not accommodate them all – or to become highway robbers (to 'Raise Contributions upon the Publick') employing that topographical and commercial knowledge that was essential in their former trade. The prevalence of butchers among the highway robbers of London during the first half of the eighteenth century has to be understood in the context of the death of the policy and customs of the market ouvert.

IV

The forces that caused the expropriation of Highland and Irish cattle communities also led to the introduction of capitalist organization of London meat markets. From Rob Roy to Redmond O'Hanlon to Sarah Archer, the formation of the 'home market' produced its victims and its bandits. In the forests of southern England the woodland communities underwent rapid changes in meat provisioning – in particular, venison, whose poachers, the Waltham 'Blacks', had a direct relationship with the London highwaymen.[35]

In 1735 the Ordinary of Newgate wrote:

It has for some years past been a Practice amongst a parcel of idle dissolute Fellows in defiance of the Laws, to associate themselves together in Parties, in order to rob Gentlemen's *Parks, Chases* &c., of Deer.

He was referring to the poaching in Windsor and Waltham forests, to repress which the infamous Waltham Black Act had been passed twelve years earlier. That Act had two evil consequences according to the Ordinary. First, it caused poachers to organize themselves in larger, more disciplined groups that could work at night and travel some distance; and, second, by driving many poaching people out of their communities or by sending them to gaol, it caused their networks to expand. Many, perhaps two score, of the Blacks of Hampshire and Windsor evaded arrest during the government man-hunts of the 1720s. In turning to London these veteran Blacks relied on the social infrastructures of the London provisioning trades –

[35] E. P. Thompson, *Whigs and Hunters: The Origin of the Black Act* (1975).

that is, upon the men and women with grievances who shared with highwaymen the close and familiar knowledge of the city markets, of the roads, of the inns, bridle-paths, hedge, copse and close that provided the settings of the London poultry, game and meat trades.

Joseph Rose, a 38-year-old blacksmith with a wife and several children, fell 'into Conversation and Intimacy of these People call'd "*Waltham Blacks*"', and for several years took an active role among the southern deer-stealers. Having eluded the Whig net that was cast over the Blacks he went to London and took a job as a gardener and cow-keeper in Kensington, which supplemented his activities as a highway robber. John Field was one of his companions on the road. He was also a blacksmith. Formerly, 'being tall of Stature', he had joined the Horse Grenadiers, and it was while he was serving with them that he had been taken up for deer-stealing. He was acquitted of the offence and joined Joseph Rose and Humphrey Walker in London. We know less about Walker, though he too had a wife and children and was a former deer-poacher. These three one-time deer-stealers joined a group of London men – William Bush, a labourer and soldier from Hackney, Samuel Gregory and John Wheeler, who would save his neck in 1735 when he turned evidence against the others. They robbed in the Company of Dick Turpin,[36] who became a legend in his own times.

Certainly the Government treated him as such: they offered a large reward in 1737 for his capture, and, when he was caught, had his trial removed from York to the Old Bailey, where it might serve a larger exemplary purpose. Nor is it difficult to understand why. His years on the highway had brought together several previously disconnected disturbances and illegalities – such as smuggling, poaching and blacking, as well as those that resulted from the changes in London provisioning. These activities had made such a 'noise' in town that after his hanging his memory easily assumed many of the attributes of the 'social bandit'. The ballad, 'Turpin's Appeal to the Judge', remains a beautiful statement of the bandit's justice:[37]

> He said, The Scriptures I fulfill'd,
> Though I this Life did lead,

---

[36] The Ordinary's *Account*, 4 June 1735, 10 March 1735. The group's targets were magistrates, vicars and farmers. Their scene of action included Walthamstow, Epping Forest, Surrey, Kent and Barking.
[37] *Folksongs of the Upper Thames* (1950), pp. 253–4, 275–7.

For when the Naked I beheld,
   I clothed them with speed:
Sometimes in Cloth and Winter-frieze,
   Sometimes in Russet-gray;
The Poor I fed, the Rich likewise
   I empty sent away.

Turpin was the son of an Essex farmer. He attended a common school and completed an apprenticeship to a Whitechapel butcher. He married Hester Palmer, the daughter of a 'decent family' in East Ham. Having finished his apprenticeship, he began stealing cattle in the Plaistow marshes, selling the hides at Waltham Abbey and the flesh in the London markets. A warrant out for his arrest, he escaped and joined an Essex gang of smugglers, with whom he worked until they were dispersed by the Riding Officers. 'He then connected himself with a gang of deer-stealers, the principal part of whose depredations were committed on Epping Forest and the parks in its neighbourhood.' With Gregory, Wheeler, Field, Walker and Rose, his forest comrades, he robbed the graziers coming to town for market and the houses of London merchants. The next, and last, four years of his life provided the incidents from which subsequent legend was made: his encounter on a Cambridge heath with the highwayman, Tom King ('What, dog eat dog? Come, come brother Turpin; if you don't know me, I know you, and shall be glad of your company'); the hidden cave in Epping Forest; the generosity to higglers and poachers; the midnight ride to York and the death of his mare, Black Bess; the disguise as John Palmer, Gentleman; the wanton shooting of his landlord's prize rooster; the betrayal of his identity by his former schoolmaster, who intercepted a letter to his brother; his proud bearing at his hanging, where the only sign of fear was his trembling leg, that he could still only by repeatedly stamping it on the scaffold. The throngs that had come from miles around to witness the terrible scene surged towards the gallows to rescue his corpse from the hovering surgeons. No sooner had they saved it than the rumours began that he had been resuscitated and was yet alive.[38]

His memory persisted in many contexts – a cultural legacy of the

---

[38] The Ordinary's *Account*, 2 November 1736; Gordon Maxwell, *The Highwayman's Heath: The Story in Fact and Fiction of Hounslow Heath* (1935); W. R. Powell (ed.), *A History of Essex*, Victoria County History, vol. iv (1966); PRO, SP, Domestic Papers, 36:47, fols. 36, 41, 477.

eighteenth century to world civilization. Thus in 1841 it was said that his fame was not unknown to any member of the male population above the age of ten. He was a special favourite of English gypsies who frequently named their children after him. In Tasmania, Australia, the Alleghenies and the Ozarks, the English transported felons and indentured servants maintained his memory in new and oppressive circumstances as a man who would 'rob from the rich to give to the poor'.[39]

The development of the commodity-form in meat-marketing was partly an effect of the defences that arose against highway robbery. This we may illustrate by the trial of Edward Bonner, a London plebeian. He served his apprenticeship to a Clare Market butcher. There he learned those elements of the trade that butchers everywhere must know: how to take a whole carcass and break it down, how to quarter meat on the swing, how to hone his knives by listening to the blade's pitch sing on his steel. As an apprentice he was also initiated into the customs of the young men who at Clare Market were every bit as clannish as the glass-blowers of Whitefriars or the instrument-makers of Clerkenwell: the boys built their own bonfires for Guy Fawkes' Day, they paraded noisily through the streets beating marrowbones upon their cleavers, they collected money to maintain their cutter for the summer races upon the Thames. Having completed his apprenticeship, Edward Bonner set up in business for himself at Newgate Market. He married and raised three children. In 1727 his trade fell off. 'Being in Debt, his Creditors pressing him for their Money ... he came to the Resolution of going on the highway.' The Ordinary of Newgate wrote of him, 'he made it his business to introduce himself unto Persons' Company who kept Markets and Fairs under pretence of Dealing with them, and so got acquainted with their Times of Receiving large Sums of Money'.[40]

[39] In 1816 in Tasmania a farmer compared bandits to Dick Turpin, see PRO, Colonial Office Papers, CO 201/89F. Australian ballad references to Turpin are in J. Meredith and H. Anderson, *Folksongs of Australia* (Melbourne, 1967). See also, the Melbourne *Argus* (18 December 1878). See Jeremiah O'Donovan, *A Brief Account of the Author's Interview with His Countrymen* (Pittsburgh, 1864), p. 13, for Turpin in the Alleghenies. Charles Mackay, *The Extraordinary Popular Delusions and the Madness of Crowds* (1841), p. 634; *The Journal of the Gypsy Lore Society*, 3rd series, vi, no. 2 (1927); Harry McShane, *No Mean Fighter* (1978), p. 6; Raphael Samuel, *East End Underworld: Chapters in the Life of Arthur Harding* (1981), p. 132; Martin Flash, *The Sinks of London Laid Open* (1848), p. 97.

[40] The Ordinary's *Account*, 27 September 1736.

The roast beef of old England was bought and sold over pot and pipe in what was the largest concentration of taverns in London, along St John's Street and surrounding Smithfield. At the Rose and Crown, the White Hart, the Windmill, the Swan and Two Necks, the Golden Lyon, the Cross Keys, the Bear and Ragged Staff, the Bell, the Hart's Horn, the Dolphin, the West Swan, the George, the Greyhound, the Ram or the Rose the commerce of meat was conducted in circumstances that could be fleeting, convivial, unregulated and deceptive. '[I]t is no uncommon thing to hear many, who by their outward Appearance one would not take to be worth a Groat, talk and deal for Thousands of Pounds; but these are often the Prey of some Sharper, of which Sort this Place swarms.'[41] A man raised in the trade, possessing a grievance against his creditors, with both the weight of family responsibility and the advantages of matrimonial connections in the trade, had both the motive and the opportunity to become such a Smithfield sharper. Edward Bonner robbed the graziers and country jobbers in the Highgate woods or in Epping Forest as they returned from Smithfield and the other London meat markets, Once he robbed a grazier on the turnpike road between Hayes and Uxbridge. When the grazier raised a hue and cry, Bonner fled to the woods. 'With great difficulty,' the story continues, 'he got to a house in a Common near Harrow-on-the-Hill where seeing only a woman and a Boy, he went in, and asking for some small beer, and telling her he had been arrested by Bailiffs and made his Escape from them, she readily gave him some.' Even at the end of the century more than a tenth of the county's acreage consisted of common lands; the Harrow weald and Uxbridge common were among the largest.

At the time of Bonner's escape 156 miles of the London–Oxford–Worcester road were turnpiked by nine different Acts of Parliament. The Tyburn–Uxbridge section of the road was turnpiked in 1715. The tension between the commercial society represented by turnpikes and the subsistence economy associated with waste, weald and common was profound, and could upon occasion burst forth in mass direct action, as occurred in the Hereford Turnpike Riot of 1736.[42] To escape, as Bonner did, from the hostility of the turnpike

---

[41] Anon., *The Foreigner's Guide; Or, A Necessary and Instructive Companion Both for the Foreigner and Native in their Tour through the Cities of London and Westminster* (1729).
[42] Middleton, op. cit., pp. 99, 104, 114; William Albert, *The Turnpike Road System*

to the friendliness of the common was made possible by the short distance between them. In 1798 Middleton was still arguing that the turnpike verge should be cleared of trees and hedges precisely in order to make such escapes more difficult.

Bonner escaped, but because his companion in this attempted robbery did not, Bonner's friends in Newgate Market arranged for his flight to Rotterdam, where he would be safe should he be impeached by his companion turning King's evidence. In 1736, after five years of highway robbery, Bonner was finally brought to trial at the Old Bailey. We can hear the arch, mischievous voice of Abraham Wells as he testifies:

'I live at Endfield Wash; I am a Butcher, I come to Smithfield, – in June, – in July, aye in July it was; I am no Scholar an't please you, my Lord, – but I came to buy a Bullock: I bought it, and up comes Mr Bonner, how do you do says he? How d'ye do Mr Bonner says I. What have you bought a Bullock says he; will you go in and drink says I? Yes says he. I bought the bullock of a Customer I deal with; I paid him for it, and paid him £10 I ow'd him: Mr Bonner was with me and saw me pay the Money; It was in July and we were in Company together 5 or 6 hours.'
'What then?'
'He was in my Company and saw me pay the Money, that's all.'

Other witnesses corroborated Wells: he was said to have paid an Essex farmer, Foiler, at 11 p.m. and to have stayed drinking at the Greyhound until 4 or 5 a.m. Another said that Bonner kept a shop in Newgate Market and dealt in pork and veal with Wells. A fifth witness, John Lyon, was a clerk who pretended to have witnessed Foiler's receipt for the bullock. The court called the keeper of the Greyhound and its money-taker. They gave a description of the method of transacting business: 'The Way of paying Money in Smithfield is thus: the Money Taker receives the Debt: the Master does not give the Receipt but the Money Taker gives it; 'tis set down in his Book, and he gives the Receipt.' The Money Taker, John Broughton, was asked if he recorded the Wells–Foiler transaction:

No, but I can tell by my Books, whether such a one paid for a bullock, I take the Money and set it down in my Book, for the Graziers, they don't take the Money themselves.

in England, 1663–1840 (Cambridge, 1972), pp. 34, 35, 41 and Appendix C; the Ordinary's *Account*, 11 August 1736.

Turpin leaps Hornsey tollgate: The turnpikes represented the most advanced technological form of land transport then known

This testimony effectively broke Bonner's alibi. In constructing it his witnesses ignored the fact that in major transactions, such as the purchase of a bullock, money did not serve to purchase goods in advance, but was a means of payment following the sale.[43]

'Cocky' Wager was his companion in the robbery, and it was to his sister Bonner had fenced a stolen watch and by whom he was able to send a message to Wager 'to get him out of the Nation'. Wager, like his father before him, was a Newgate Market butcher. He was married with two children. Partly responsible for his success as a highwayman were the attentions he paid to innkeepers, oastlers, stable-boys, wagoners, higglers and the turnpike-keepers of Kentish Town, Hornsey Lane, Endfield and Waltham. The turnpike-keeper at Battle Bridge in Waltham took a cut in his takings. At a different trial in 1736 an Old Bailey judge accused a witness, 'You Turnpike

[43] *The Proceedings*, September and December 1736.

keepers often know that Men travel the roads for these wicked Purposes, and you conceal them.'[44]

The turnpikes represented the most advanced technological form of land transport then known. Dick Turpin's mare cleared a five-barred gate ('flying giggers' they were called) at one of the turnpikes. According to Middleton more broad-wheeled vehicles passed along the Uxbridge–Tyburn road than any other in the country. Between 500 and 800 wagons a month passed through the Marylebone turnpike, as its records disclose. The toll-keepers and gatekeepers occupied a profitable and dangerous position in this system of transportation. The Marylebone keeper sold gin and tobacco from the turnpike house. He kept poultry in the yard and exempted from the tolls particular cow-keepers. The toll-keeper near Farthing Pye House in the New Road between Paddington and Tottenham Court was attacked, wounded and robbed in the summer of 1759. The London end of the Chester, Portsmouth, Dover, Harwich, Coventry, Bristol, Birmingham, Hereford and Manchester roads were all turnpiked between 1717 and 1730.[45]

Turnpikemen and gatekeepers were caught between two social forces. That is why Cocky Wager, himself the victim of centralizing market forces, treated them with consideration. He likewise refrained from robbing country higglers whose friendship he needed for locating the wealthy graziers – exactly the relationship that John Middleton warned against. Middleton said that the millers, ostlers, chandlers and small country dealers in eggs, butter and poultry who frequented the roads and public houses around London were notorious receivers of stolen goods (corn, hay, poultry) and gave encouragement to pilferers, highwaymen and poachers.

When Bonner was captured, it took five or six men at the Black-Spread Eagle in Paternoster Row to subdue him. A gun battle was narrowly avoided and the constable in charge made sure to take him immediately to the alderman's for fear of a rescue by a dozen or so journeymen carpenters. Cocky Wager was apprehended outside London and the headborough described the ride back to the City:

'Twas as much as we could do to get Wager home, though I made a man ride behind him, for he was very unruly, pulling the horse about, making

---

[44] The Ordinary's *Account*, 3 March 1737.
[45] Albert, op. cit., Appendix C.

Motions with his Hands at every Body that came near him, as if he was firing a Pistol, crying Phoo!

Cocky was very uneasy and curs'd and swore bitterly on the Road, and when we got to Town, the Mob was so great that I could not carry him direct to the Justices for fear of a Rescue, so I got him with much Difficulty to New Prison.

One understands that he deserved his nickname. From the forty or fifty cockpits of London a vicious animal combat provided the London proletariat with its language of courage and cowardice. Opponents were 'pitted against' each other. Some died 'game'. Others died 'dunghill' – expressions that described analogous behaviour of the condemned at the gallows. To be 'well-heeled', to 'turn tail', to 'get one's spurs on', to be 'cock-eyed', 'cocksure' or 'cocky' – the crazed passions of the pit lent to the criminal justice system its bloody vernacular.[46]

V

Highway robbery, like other acts of appropriation, posed problems concerning knowledge of targets, techniques of appropriation, methods of flight and means of disposal. Butchers and market people gained the experience from their workaday lives to solve them. Through friendly innkeepers or market gossip they would know, for instance, when a drover or grazier returned from market with gold or silver on his person. From years of carting or driving animals to market, they were familiar with the terrain. Their dealings in market and at cook-shops, victualling houses and inns provided them with numerous possibilities of sale and disposal. The economic processes that had squeezed many of them out of customary patterns of work or trade multiplied the possibilities of disposal. In several senses they were expert at undertaking that fatal leap by which some useful thing – in this case, game, poultry, livestock – was transformed into its 'value form' – money. Yet the money-form might advance or change in ways unknown to a butcher or highwayman.

We saw this in the flaw of the elaborately constructed alibi for Edward Bonner in 1736: the ignorance of the method of remitting payment at Smithfield led to his hanging. At the beginning of the eighteenth century some advocated changing the money-form for

---

[46] George Ryley Scott, *The History of Cockfighting* (n. d.).

the purpose of eliminating highway robbery; and at the end of the century some thought that it was change in banking practices that had caused the demise of the highwayman. Henry Mayhew, for example, wrote: 'Our railways and telegraphs, postal communications and currency arrangements, have put an end to the mounted highwaymen, such as Dick Turpin or Tom King.'[47] Defoe, in *An Essay on Projects* (1697), written in a decade that was the creative springtime of English experimentation with the money-form, advocated a system of 'County Banks' or 'Inland Exchanges'.

By which such a Correspondence with all the Trading Towns in *England* might be maintained, as that the whole Kingdom shou'd Trade with the Bank. Under the Direction of this Office a Publick Cashier shou'd be appointed in every County, to reside in the Capital Town as to Trade, and in some Counties more, through whose Hands all the Cash of the Revenue of the Gentry, and of Trade, shou'd be return'd on the Bank in *London*, and from the Bank again on their Cashier in every respective County or Town, at the small Exchange of $\frac{1}{2}$ *per Cent.* by which means all loss of Money carri'd upon the Road, to the encouragement of Robbers, and Ruining of the Country, who are Su'd for those Robberies, wou'd be more effectually prevented, than by all the Statutes against Highway-Men that are or can be made.

Thus, was provincial banking advocated and anticipated as a form of police.

Defoe was greatly interested in the conveyance of money. In 1728 in the authorial guise of a street robber he advised money-owners: 'When any Person's Business calls him into the Country, let him take but just Money enough to bear his Expenses; or if he's oblig'd to send large Sums into the Country, the safest Way is to send it by the Carrier.' He advised the rich traveller to avoid becoming too readily acquainted with innkeepers and ostlers, to keep away from strangers, to ride slowly and to encourage the 'Hue & Crie'. In the same book he observes the transactions of a butcher receiving payment for purchases at a cook-shop, a gentleman doing business at a bookseller's, and a nobleman purchasing some Flanders mares at Smithfield (where 'there are Rogues generally in every Degree'), all to the purpose of understanding the moment of maximum vulnerability in the interval between purchase and payment.[48] He adopts the guise of the thief in order to advise the merchant. The

[47] Henry Mayhew, *London Life and the London Poor*, vol. iv (1861–2), pp. 329–30.
[48] Daniel Defoe, *Street-Robberies Consider'd* (1728).

endeavour to eliminate the misappropriations of the highway led to the refinement of the techniques of purchase and payment by the more secure separation of them in time and in space. This became the origin of provincial banking.

In Wales two banking organizations were established to look after the remittances of cattle-dealers who did business in London and to protect the drovers from the depredations of the 'Gentlemen Collectors' of the highway. These were the bank of the Black Ox at Llandovery and the bank of the Black Sheep with branches at Aberystwyth and Tregaron. Formerly, Welsh drovers returned from London with large sums of money that made them the desirable targets of armed bands. By the end of the century the sums realized by Smithfield sales were paid into London accounts against debts owed for the rent of estates. In Scotland, in the first half of the century drovers dealt at the Crieff and Falkirk cattle trysts largely in gold and silver. After mid-century tents and sheds were erected where tellers from Edinburgh banks provided notes of credit. By the end of the century such banks had corresponding banks in London, if not in Smithfield itself, so that drovers were no longer endangered by carrying large sums of rhino. Such financial safe-guards increased the volume of trade and the speed of realization.[49]

'Going upon the Accompt' in the 1730s had two meanings: it referred to new forms of credit money and to highway robbery.[50] On the one hand, social relations in the eighteenth century often manifested themselves in a shortage of gold and silver money. When payment was in arrears – in tokens or in limiting forms of credit – labouring poor people tried other ways of obtaining payment – ways that might have 'customary sanction' or might not. When they resorted to highway robbery, this was called 'the Account'. On the other hand, the increase of commerce in both geographical range and volume of trade caused problems in the turnover of advanced capital – or 'cash-flow' problems. These were partly solved by new forms of credit – monies of 'account'. We have seen one of the ways these two meanings were interrelated: the butcher who

[49] L. S. Pressnell, *Country Banking in the Industrial Revolution* (1956), pp. 48–9; *Select Committee on the State of Smithfield Market*, 2nd report, House of Commons (July 1828); *Select Committee on Promissory Notes Under £5*, 1st report, House of Commons (1826); Haldane, op. cit., and Bonser, op. cit.; Francis Green, 'Early Banks in West Wales', *Transactions of the History Society of West Wales*, vol. vi (1917); S. G. Checkland, *Scottish Banking: A History: 1695–1973* (1975).
[50] The Ordinary's *Account*, 5–8 October 1733.

could no longer find a livelihood in the customary market ouvert because of the centralization of capitalist marketing was well suited from experience for robbing on the highway, or 'going upon the Accompt'. This in turn led the graziers, the jobbers, the drovers and the regraters to settle their transactions over a period of time – not with ready cash, but by methods of the 'Account'. The ironic parallel between criminal thievery and mercantile deceiving was thus more than a device of the polemicist's imagination. An actual, dynamic relation existed between them, as Daniel Defoe and Henry Mayhew both noted.

This was a class struggle that took place behind the backs of the producers – that is, it was a dialectical movement, neither consciously understood nor actually intended by the class actors, yet real enough to cause fundamental changes in the development of the money-form, the home market and the reification of human relations. The highwaymen about London took to the road from necessity, under a sense of grievance and with the knowledge of years in the meat-provisioning trades. While some had been only labourers in these trades, many had been skilled or independent. They were fathers, husbands and middle-aged; they had access to kinship networks often denied to more youthful offenders. They aspired to regain a lost independence by taking to commercial activities – smuggling, duffing, dealing, receiving, as well as highway robbery – on the netherside of 'legitimate' commerce. From a class perspective this put them in an ambivalent position. In aspiring to that proud, if temporary, status of 'Gentlemen of the Road', they did not question the inegalitarian hierarchy of their society. Yet their boldness of act and deed, in putting them outside the law as rebellious fugitives, revivified the 'animal spirits' of capitalism and became an essential part of the oppositional culture of working-class London, a serious obstacle to the formation of a tractable, obedient labour force. Therefore, it was not enough to hang them – the values they espoused or represented had to be challenged.

VI

Edward Bonner was hanged in 1736, the year that John Wesley sailed with Oglethorpe for Georgia, and was comforted during the storms at sea by psalm-singing Moravians. Cocky Wager was hanged in 1737, the year that George Whitefield began his extraordinary evangelical preaching in Wapping, Ludgate and Newgate. In 1739 Abraham Wells was hanged in London, and Dick Turpin in York. That year was notable alike for the first mass open-air 'preaching of terror' in London by Whitefield and for Charles Wesley's gaol ministry in Marshalsea and Newgate.[51] Against the background of a terrible winter, a renewed imperialist war and a Europe-wide famine, the Methodist evangelicals made a bid for the soul of the London mob, whose strongholds in the prisons and at the gallows they directly assaulted. The first years of London Methodism took place in a gallows drama with highwaymen and the condemned. 'The civil war in the soul' was fought between two sets of cultural values – Methodist and antinomian. With John Wesley's first visit to Newgate we can see the outlines of the conflict in the clarity of the initial skirmish.[52]

In September 1738, he visited the condemned prisoners of Newgate 'and offered them free salvation'. In November, he rode in a coach to Tyburn; he joined three carts of condemned prisoners and another coach containing George Whalley, an old carpenter, who had murdered his second wife four years earlier. Wesley drank tea at Tyburn and at the stops along the way, which distinguished him from the condemned, who traditionally drank ale or gin. Tea, indeed, became the drink of the Methodists, while gin was by far the most preferred pain-killer of the proletariat.[53]

In 1721, 6,000 houses in London sold gin; in 1736, 7,000; and by 1749 the number had leaped to 17,000. The 'orgy of spirit drinking', as M. Dorothy George described it, affected urban mortality rates. It reduced resistance to disease, it increased infant mortality (the foetal alcohol syndrome) and for many it became a substitute for food. It was cheap and warming, and it offered forgetfulness. However, it also destroyed work discipline. 'Our common people,' Defoe wrote in 1728, 'get so drunk on a Sunday they cannot work of a Day or two following. Nay, since the use of Geneva has become so common many get so often drunk they cannot work at all, but

---

[51] Luke Tyerman, *The Life of the Rev. George Whitefield* (1876), vol. i, pp. 40–85; Charles Wesley, *The Journal* (1849), vol. i, pp. 96, 117, 120; *The Journal of Rev. John Wesley*, Everyman edn (1906), p. 34.

[52] Bernard Semmel, *The Methodist Revolution* (New York, 1973), p. 27.

[53] *The Ordinary's Account*, 8 November 1738; Nehemiah Curnock (ed.), *The Journal of the Rev. John Wesley, A.M.*, vol. iii (1938) pp. 70–71, 100–106. Professor John Rule informs me that Wesley was an occasional beer drinker, and that the Methodists distinguished beer from spirits.

run from one irregularity to another, till at last they become arrant rogues.'[54] Parliament sought to reduce its availability by licensing with the Gin Act of 1736, but because this 'let loose a crew of desperate and wicked people who turn'd informers merely for the bread' it led to murder and riot.[55] Tea, on the other hand, was sobering, its caffeine was conducive to work discipline, and it became the drink of the weekly meetings of the small Methodist bands. In taking tea at Tyburn, Wesley signified a cultural battle.

At Newgate in September 1738 Wesley preached, and according to his journal, 'all Newgate sang with the cries of those whom the word of God cut to the heart'. From then on the Methodists tried to convince the condemned to praise the Lord all the way to their hanging. The preachings and the hymns were full of the imagery of cutting and bleeding – imagery suitable to one who would advise obedience to the soldiers and sailors hacked up in the battles of Maestricht (1748), Dettingen (1743), Fontenoy (1745) and Cartagena (1741). Wesley preached submission. In July 1739 when a press-gang seized a member of his congregation, he did not utter a word or lift a finger to prevent it.

At the November 1738 hanging Wesley does not record *what* he said, though he attempted to bring the prisoners 'under conviction of sin' and we know that beginning in this year his favourite text became: 'The Kingdom of God is not meat and drink; but righteousness, and peace, and joy in the Holy Ghost.' In his journal he leaves the impression that the preaching met with success: 'tears ran down the cheeks' of one of the condemned, he wrote. Yet the impression is misleading: the hanging deeply disturbed Wesley – his handwriting became shaky, he could not write in his journal on the following day – and its editor surmises that this Tyburn visit caused one of his periodical attacks of illness.

Wesley does not tell us who hanged or why they hanged or indicate that he knew much about any of them. We know little about the carpenter and the sailor who murdered their wives, or about the Hampstead blacksmith and Holborn bricklayer hanged for burglaries. We know more about the Dublin Quaker who had organized an extensive guinea clipping organization in London (about forty porters 'dogged' for him, 'the Bank Master'), and we

---

[54] *Augusta Triumphans*, pp. 45, 50; M. D. George, *London Life in the Eighteenth Century* (1965), ch. 1.
[55] Anon., *The Life and Times of Thomas Deveil* (1748), p. 39.

know that of the six highwaymen who were hanged at least two, John Fosset and Henry Fluellin, had robbed with Cocky Wager.

Fosset had been a weaver and a sailor; he was married, and frequently 'in want of Bread'. He robbed a coach in Ratcliff Highway. He often robbed with Thomas Raby, whose father kept a public house. Raby hanged for robberies on the highway in Hendon, Finchley and Kensington. They communicated 'in their own Dialect', which Fluellin took time to translate for the Ordinary of Newgate. 'Chiving the Frow' (cutting women's pockets), 'clacking the carriers' (robbing parcels from inn wagons), 'tale' (sword), 'scout' (watch), 'calm and shade' (hat and wig), 'outside toge' (cloak), 'brace of wedges' (pistols), 'ridges' (guineas) and 'Dancy Cock' (a drunk) were the part of the lexicon the Ordinary recorded. These men regarded themselves as 'Kings of the Pad', the most prestigious rank in the criminal's hierarchy.

Strong waters belonged to the highwaymen just as tea did to the Methodists. In 1728 the most frequently sung ballad among highwaymen was a celebration of drink:

> Now we are arriv'd to the *Boozing-Ken*,
>   And our Pockets are full of Cole;
> We pass for the best of Gentlemen,
>   When over a flowing Bowl,
>   Our Hearts are at ease,
>   We kiss who we please:
> On Death its a Folly to think;
>   May he hang in a Noose,
>   That this Health will refuse,
> Which I am now going to drink.[56]

The eighteenth-century cant ballads celebrated the coronation of the King of the Gypsies, praised the loves of men and the loves of women, cursed the constable, mocked the thief-catcher, boasted of the deeds of highwaymen, extolled life unentangled by property, shared the joy of freed prisoners and encouraged the life of the road. Many were about highwaymen and the meat trades, like 'The Two Jolly Butchers' or 'The Yorkshire Bite'.[57] Such songs were sung in the streets, at Bartholomew's Fair and in the raucous settings of lodging-houses and gin-shops. Later the Society for the Suppression of Vice tore from the walls halfpenny ballads of these kinds. Francis

---

[56] Anon., *Villainy Exploded* (1728).
[57] *Folksongs of the Upper Thames* (1950), pp. 253–4, 275–6.

Place was thick with this life as a youth, and when he broke from it he made no allowances. His brother-in-law was a market butcher who was sentenced to transportation to Van Diemen's Land for robbing a farmer on the Watford Road. Place interceded at the Home Office to frustrate his sister's effort to gain her husband a pardon.[58] But in his old age Place sought to document the 'Grossness' of his youth by remembering the ballads, such as 'Jack Chance', about the boy whose mind ran on something great – 'to pad the hoof' and 'go on the scamp'. He knew isolated snatches by heart. 'My horse and I did lightning fly/When we heard the sound of coaches'; 'It's from the rich I rob, and it's to the poor I give'; or 'Winter is acoming, we must feed on Spirits.'

These songs belonged to an antinomian culture that during the English Revolution was aggressively religious and political.[59] But ninety years later, in the 1730s, much of this culture was coded 'in their Dialect', and very little of it appeared in print as theology (in the song, says Turpin, 'I the Scriptures have fulfilled'), except when it was being opposed, as in the oft-quoted exchange between John Wesley and Stephen Timmins, the plebeian preacher who said 'I am not under the law,' and 'All is mine, since Christ is mine.' Otherwise, Wesley records its talk and actions. When a recent convert at Fetter Lane argued that he was 'no more bound to obey than the subjects of the King of England are bound to obey the laws of the King of France', or when a child interrupted Wesley in full flow, saying 'You preach more the Law than the Gospel', Wesley records that 'torrent of Antinomianism' that many recruits expected and which he earnestly opposed.

The antinomianism appeared not as a political grouping or religious sect, but in attitudes, in lifestyle, in habits, in drink and in song. It was opposed by an emotional somatics that was capable of producing a rebirth to a new kind of body. The convulsions, writhings, shakings, groanings and teeth gnashings of conversion appeared dangerous to one like David Hume, who saw in the furious and violent fanaticism the not-forgotten dangers of the

---

[58] *The Autobiography of Francis Place* (1771–1854), ed. Mary Thale (Cambridge, 1972), pp. 121, 132–5; Brit. Lib., Add. MSS 27, 825, *Francis Place Paper*, 'Grossness'.

[59] A. L. Morton, *The World of the Ranters: Religious Radicalism in the English Revolution* (1970).

revolutionary levelling.[60] He was mistaken, because the mass outdoor gatherings led not to riot or organized challenges to established authority, but to a multiplicity of single-sex small groups, where confessional therapeutics sustained the repression of 'Satan'. The Methodist leaders were vigilant against the *signs* of backsliding. Sixty-three members were expelled in 1743 for lying, cussing, fighting, idleness and drink, but most were expelled for 'lightness and carelessness'.[61] In the early years Methodism did not appeal to the mind, but this was its advantage, for it sought enthusiastically to change attitudes by creating a 'new birth' in the rough, direct, physical London mob, to create a new discipline, a new body language, new habits for a disciplined and subservient proletariat.

In London, at best, it achieved only partial victories within 'Satan's strongholds'. At Wesley's first visit to Tyburn he was able to say that one of the condemned felt a peace 'which passeth all understanding'. Much else he did not record. And indeed this first skirmish in 'the civil war in the soul' seems to have been more of a victory for the side choosing the liberty of locomotion, the satisfactions of meat and drink, the lightness and carelessness, even the fire-in-the-belly over the dread terrors, solemnity of heart and pie-in-the-sky of the Holy Ghost. Two nights before the hanging two of the highwaymen escaped from their cells and attempted unsuccessfully to release all the other prisoners, and at the hanging itself two of the highwaymen 'had white Cockades in their hats in token of their Triumph over this World'.

---

[60] David Hume, 'Of Superstition and Enthusiasm', in R. H. Green and T. H. Grose (eds), *The Philosophical Works of David Hume* (1878), vol. iii, pp. 144–50.
[61] John Wesley, op. cit., pp. 212, 499, 548.

PART THREE

Industry and Idleness in the Period of Manufacture,
1750–1776

The period begins with the Seven Years War and concludes with the War of American Independence. The competition between England and France for the command of world labour needs to be understood in terms of the struggle of world labourers against their European masters. Anti-imperial violence was widespread: the Battle of Plassey (1757) and the defeat of Mir Kasim (1763) in India; Tacky's Rebellion in Jamaica (1760); the Whiteboy Movement in Ireland (1761); Pontiac's Rising in Michigan (1763–6), the land wars in the Hudson Valley (1765–6), the Regulators in North Carolina (1765–9); the silver miners' strikes in Mexico (1766); the Saramaka Maroon Wars in Surinam (1768–72). At stake were huge amounts of international plunder, which appeared as a sudden and steep ascent in English 'overseas trades statistics'.

In the British Isles during this period there were developments that led to the recomposition of the agrarian labour force: 1) a vast number of Parliamentary Enclosure Acts were passed that affected a quarter of the arable land; 2) sheep were introduced into the Highlands, and the crofting system elsewhere into arable farming; and 3) there was an aggressive transition to cattle-ranching in Ireland. In the face of such expropriations, the agrarian populations had either to accept a short life consumed in the new manufactories that were replacing the 'idle' conditions of the putting-out system of production, or to choose between migration across the ocean, soldiering, sailoring or prostitution in the city.

In London the social life of this growing 'mobbish' population was controlled by the Bugging Act (1749), the Licensing Act (1751) and the Marriage Act (1754), which marked changes in wages, drinking and reproduction respectively. The 1760s saw further changes in London policing: the Middlesex and Westminster magistracies were unified, as 'secret service' money from the Treasury was paid to the London 'court magistrate'; the Bow Street office was opened, where a clerk began to record crimes; rotation offices were established; and the Horse Patrol began to guard the roads around London.

These changes at a social level accompanied a profound change at the level of production. To say that the factory was introduced in this period would be misleading if by 'factory' is meant machine production, but if the term is understood to mean a hierarchical organization of production under the eye of a single authority, then it calls attention to a major and decisive development. Non-monetary appropriations continued in the putting-out system, where they appeared as trade 'usages' or 'customs'. Chapter 7 examines five trades – watchmaking, shoemaking, hatting, tailoring and service – in order to describe the customary appropriation, the changes in the technical mode of production, and the use of the criminal sanction to discipline a working class to new procedures and new modes. The working class 'sauntered', as Adam Smith complained: 'The habit of sauntering and of indolent careless application ... is naturally, or necessarily acquired by every country workman who is obliged to change his work and his tools every half-hour.' The new working class was to become stupid, as Adam Ferguson recognized: 'Many mechanic arts, indeed, require no capacity; they succeed best under a total suppression of sentiment and reason; and ignorance is the mother of industry as well as of superstition.'[1]

Chapter 8 examines the silk industry in order to explain in detail how one form of workers' power – over materials of production – could actually halt the coming of the factory. The struggle of the silk-workers in Spitalfields was decisive to the future of industrial developments not only in London, but elsewhere in Britain. The riots and demonstrations led by these workers, and the retributive terror and counter-terror of hanging and stoning, led to two major discussions within the ruling élite about the future: the first concerned the factory, and the second concerned the law. The culture of the Spitalfields weavers included a paradoxical mixture of cant (the language of thieves) and erudition in maths, music and botany. This part of London would be the focus of London radicalism for several generations.

Chapter 9 considers a vital part of the proletariat in London – namely, the Irish. Called a 'lawless' population by English sources,

[1] Adam Smith, *The Wealth of Nations* (1776), I, p. 2; Adam Ferguson, *An Essay on Civil Society* (1767), p. 182.

its experience in Ireland with the law was an experience with terror, and in London, said the proverb, 'the name of an Irishman was enough to hang him'. Mass cooperative labour in canal-making, soldiering, harvesting, building and coal-heaving was often Irish. In London the Irish coal proletarians formed the vanguard of the river general strike in 1768. The song and music of the eighteenth-century Irish suggest that they were no more cowed by threats of death than were the Iroquois who so astonished British militarists. The growth of such attitudes encouraged parliamentary 'humanitarians' opposing the death penalty.

CHAPTER SEVEN

THE CAT LIKES CREAM: THE WAGING HAND IN FIVE TRADES

'Was it fit
To make my cream a perquisite
And steal to mend your wages?'

Matthew Prior, *The Widow and her Cat* (1709)

'The Waging Hand gets a Penny.'

Daniel Defoe, *Street-Robberies Consider'd* (1728)

I

In the seventeenth century watches were toys, ornaments, insignia of power or stores of wealth. In the eighteenth century the watch assumed new functions; it became a measure of labour time or a means of quantifying 'idleness'. England led the world in the measurement of time. Her watches were widely imitated in Holland, Switzerland and France, countries that no longer were pre-eminent in production or design. The gangster, Jonathan Wild, hired Captain Johnson to sail a packet to convey stolen watches to Holland, and 'Sir John' Pagan, a successful Chick Lane pickpocket, maintained a 'warehouse' for stolen watches, which he too conveyed to Holland.[1]

The importance of an abstract measure of minutes and hours to the work ethic and to the habit of punctuality required by industrial discipline has long been accepted. It was probably Marx who first recognized that 'idleness', more than anything else, was the form of resistance most effective in 'the period of manufacture'.[2] The creation of the 'detail labourer' who performed 'fractional work' in the workshop meant that the value-producing class became collective, since no single worker produced a whole commodity. Furthermore, the organization of proportionality in the workshop (the ratios of

[1] Gerald Howson, *The Thief-Taker General: The Rise and Fall of Jonathan Wild* (1970), p. 142; and the Ordinary's *Account*, 17 June 1747.
[2] Karl Marx, *Capital*, vol. i, trans. Ben Fowkes (1976), ch. xiv, 'Division of Labour and Manufacture'.

different categories of detail labourers necessary to keep all fully occupied) was assisted by a mechanical measure of labour time.

The specialization of tasks in watchmaking provided William Petty and other political economists with their favourite example of the division of labour. By the end of the century it was estimated that there were 120 different branches to the trade. The enumeration of some of these (dial-makers, case-makers, wheel-polishers, escapement-makers, movement-makers, pinion-makers, chain-makers, jewellers, enamellers, gilders, brass-wheel-makers, screw-polishers, figure-painters, etc.) required the longest sentence in Marx's *Capital*, to illustrate the characteristic of heterogeneous manufacture whereby the product was the result of the assembly of many different components rather than the successive application of different qualities of labour to the same material (homogeneous manufacture).[3] In watchmaking therefore the division of labour did not have to take place in a single workshop, but among many dispersed and small locations. In the eighteenth century such places were concentrated in the northern suburbs – in Clerkenwell and St Luke's, the location too of allied trades such as optical work, mathematical-instrument-making and jewellery. The interlocking nature of these hundreds of rooms and garrets was at least as complex as the 'wheels within wheels' of the watches themselves.

Perhaps 8,000 men and many fewer women (mainly chain-makers in the country) were employed in the trade. Campbell wrote: 'All the Branches require a Mechanic head, a light and nice Hand, to touch those delicate Instruments with which they make Pivots almost imperceptible; and a Strong Sight, there being scarce any Trade which requires a quicker Eye or steadier Hand.' Blindness was the chief occupational hazard. Wages for the detail workers were not high and were usually paid by the piece; Campbell offered a range between 12s. a week and 30s. Wages to the female chain-makers were much lower. The fractionation of labour permitted some mechanization: 'Invention of Engines for cutting the Teeth in the several Parts of the Movement, which were formerly cut by Hand' occurred in the eighteenth century. 'This has reduced the Expence of Workmanship and Time to a Trifle,' wrote Campbell.[4]

Of the hanged watchmakers some appear to illustrate the impoverished conditions of the trade, like Henry Webb, who,

[3] ibid., pp. 461–2.
[4] R. Campbell, *The London Tradesman* (1747), pp. 250–52.

being ill-used by his master, stole a steel tobacco box; or Anthony Walraven, whose 'Trade', we read, 'being upon the Decay, insomuch that he could not make a moderate Provision for his Family, put him upon other Measures to do it'. William Udall was born in Clerkenwell in 1717 and lived there – bred to read, write and make watches – until his hanging in 1739.[5] He devoted his time to 'idle Company, drinking, lewd women, and other vices'. He escaped the Bridewell several times. He escaped the debtor's prison in the Marshalsea. He was quick with hand and eye. When finally he was incarcerated in Newgate, his friends conveyed to him a spring saw, a keyhole saw and gimblets with which he was almost able to mill away the locks on the prison chapel. As an apprentice he had learnt from a journeyman chaser in the same shop how to scrape the insides of gold watches that had been brought in for mending. Udall would tinker with the insides of the watches and refashion their faces so that they could not be identified and then use them as payment to those who held him in debt. Later he learned how to defraud the goldsmiths by sleight of hand. William Udall was hanged for stealing a silver watch worth 40s.

Christopher Rawlins, a silversmith, stole a watch, valued at £3 by the jury, and pawned it for two guineas. James Attaway, a watch-movement-maker, having no money, stole £100 in silver plate, and was hanged. Joseph Golding, a goldsmith, pawned his clothes for a brace of pistols and stole a silver watch worth 30s. When he failed to provide testimony against his cohorts because he did not have the guinea the clerk demanded for writing the 'Information', he was hanged. John Lowden, a watchmaker, lost his job in 1739; he stole a silver watch valued at 40s. by the jury and at 35s. by the pawnbroker, and was hanged in 1742.[6] There is a suggestive similarity between what these condemned men had stolen and what they were trained to work with and produce – namely, watches and precious metals. We shall observe similar correspondence in some other trades – clothes and tailors, fabric and weavers, etc. Watchmakers are familiar with watches and with gold and silver. They may know how they are made and who makes their parts. These *correspondences* arise from different material *circuits*. The pawnbroker – 'mine uncle' – connected the circuits.

There were 250 large pawnbrokers in London during the 1740s

---

[5] The Ordinary's *Account*, 8 August 1750, 28 August 1724, 14 March 1739.
[6] ibid., 20 May 1728, 4 June 1770, 26 May 1738 and 7 April 1742.

and a great many smaller ones. The Charitable Corporation, a municipally sponsored broker of pledges, was dissolved in 1731 on charges of accepting stolen goods. In the 1740s a serious debate developed over pawnbrokers. One writer defended them by saying that if employers would pay their workmen on the completion of work, there would be no problem of their acting as 'fences' or 'locks' for stolen goods; thus he acknowledged the relation between wage-payment and the pawnbroker. Campbell knew they were necessary 'to the poor labouring Tradesman' and he could not comprehend 'how they can live without the Pawnbroker'. Yet, pointedly, he did not deny that they were usurers and receivers. In 1745 a group of large brokers had a Bill introduced in Parliament to protect them from 'divers Persons of ill Fame and Repute, who live in Garrets, Cellars, and other obscure Places, taking upon themselves the Name of Pawnbrokers'.[7] In 1757 the Pawning Act was passed, requiring that brokers be licensed and record all pledges received; in this way the Act sought to regulate the relation between the universal circuit of money and the micro-circuits of materials. The mere possession of money was sufficient grounds of suspicion. 'Watchmakers especially were accused of pawning valuable components,' writes Professor Rule.[8] Many of the hanged watchmakers dealt with pawnbrokers, who – however usurious they may have been – were not as fatal in their evaluations as the jurors.

The real language of commodities was to be found in the preamble to the Watch Fraud Act of 1754 (27 George II, c. 7):

Whereas many persons employed in the making of clocks and watches have of late been guilty of divers frauds and abuses by purloining, imbezilling, secreting, selling, pawning or otherwise unlawfully disposing of the clocks and watches, or such parts thereof, or the materials for making the same, with which they have been entrusted . . .'

The Act punished offenders with two weeks' hard labour in the house of correction. There were other circuits of gold in which the

---

[7] Solomon Kuznets, 'Pawnbroking', *International Encyclopedia of the Social Sciences* (1935); Anon., *An Apology for the Business of Pawnbroking* (1744); Anon., *Villainy Unmask'd* (1752); Campbell, op. cit., pp. 296–7. The cashier of the Charitable Corporation, George Robinson, MP for Marlow, disappeared with tens of thousands of pounds.

[8] GLCRO, Henry Norris, *Minute Book, 1730–1741* (no. 2), Muniment Room, Ac. 61.21; John Rule, *The Experience of Labour in Eighteenth Century English Industry* (1981), p. 133.

yellow substance was not money, but an input of production – for watchmaker, decorator (gold leaf), jeweller and bookbinder (top-edge gilt) – and these circuits expressed other social and material relations. The trial of a wire-drawer suggests how such a circuit might connect with the law.

On 17 July 1723 an alderman took an information against John Price, a servant to a Grub Street wire-drawer; he had taken small quantities of gold plate wash and sold them to a Cow Lane snuff-box-maker.[9] Goldsmiths and silversmiths were designations covering many trades – jewellers, snuff-box-makers, tweezer-case-makers, silver-turners, burnishers, gilders, chasers, beaters, wire-drawers and lace people. Skilled workers might earn 2s. 6d. to 3s. 6d. at day rates. Masters employed 'besides those in his shop, many Hands without', combining shop and domestic production. In refining and alloying, the mercury of the amalgamation process subjected the workers to 'Paralytic Disorders' and affected their nerves so as to 'render their Lives a Burthen to them'. The wire-drawer produced gold thread called 'purl' for the lace man: 'The Business of a Wire-drawer is purely mechanical; a Hobby-Horse is capable to execute their Business, since the whole of their Work is performed by Engine, which they have nothing to do but turn around.' (John Price was such a 'Hobby Horse'.) The lace man might then sell or put out the purl to the silver-thread-spinner, who, by intertwining purl and silk, made an embroiderer's thread called 'sleysy'. The lace man's shop had equipment consisting of wheels and spindles much like those at a rope-walk. 'Women are employed in this as well as Men, and may earn Twelve or Fifteen Shillings a Week honestly; but they are much given to pilfering the Stuff, and have a Trick of moistening the silk to make up the Deficiency by Weight.' The goldfinders purchased 'the Sweepings of the Gold-smith's Shops and Refiner's Ashes, or the Rubbish wherein Plate is supposed to have been melted'.[10] The ashes and rubbish were washed in water, mixed with mercury which attracted the metals, distilled, separated out and then melted into a 'Lump' and sold to the refiner. In 1747 it was said that 'there are but few Masters in this Way: they take no Apprentices, and use only common Labourers to do their Work'.

This was homogeneous manufacture in which the same

[9] CLRO, Sessions Papers, 1723.
[10] Campbell, op. cit., pp. 141–9.

substance – gold – was changed from rubbish, to purl, to sleysy, to embroiderer's thread, to the glitter of eighteenth-century clothing through the labours respectively of the goldfinder, the wire-drawer, the silver-spinner and the lace people. In this circuit the value of the gold might appear as rubbish or thread, as input or finished product, as waste or money.

The printed account of John Price's trial charged him with stealing 'Gold Waste' while the original information taken against him referred to 'gold plate wash'. Perhaps it was a significant difference. The jury valued it at 10d., so he was transported instead of hanged. This was the same jury that, upon William Gwyn's production of witnesses to testify to his 'character' as a ticket porter, acquitted him of 'stealing' 500 cwt. of tobacco. The jury's knowledge of the class relations and tensions in the circuits of gold and tobacco was comparable to the pawnbroker's. While one dealt in law and the other in money, they both needed an all but universal knowledge of the many materials making up eighteenth-century London, since in day-to-day existence so often they, not law nor money, defined the struggle between the élite and the labouring poor. In 1751 Thomas Clements, a watch-spring-maker, who had worked eleven years at wages of 18d. a week, 'turned upon the Lay' and stole thirty-six pairs of shoes which he sold to a well-known receiver and pawnbroker, Cardosa, for £1 13s.[11]

II

Martha Purdue's father was a shoemaker and her husband was a watchmaker. She went into service. Her master ruined her and she turned to prostitution. One of her customers charged her with 'privily Stealing' 25 guineas. She was discovered in a 'poor Garret wherein were a few Flocks and Rags, but no Bed', and she was hanged in October 1720.[12] The women of the town often connected circuits – that is, they generally mediated the elementary exchanges of materials. Sometimes this mediation took place in the family, sometimes in the street, sometimes in the flesh. In economic terms they preserved the unities between production and reproduction. In Martha's case neither the 'gentle craft' of shoemaking nor the

[11] The Ordinary's *Account*, 11 February 1751.
[12] ibid., 26 October 1720.

watchmaker's 'wheels within wheels' could provide her with what she needed, and family connections could not sustain her. Many who might be called watchmakers could hardly live, and a serious crisis also permeated the shoemaking industry.

Shoemakers provided a useful service to all who walked and needed protection from the grit and muck in their way. Their labour received scarcely even subsistence wages, as can easily be confirmed by the stories of some of the shoemakers hanged at Tyburn – of whom there were fifty-one in the period studied. There was Benjamin Stevens, a literate fifty-year-old, who worked twenty years for one master shoemaker. His wife took to 'dram drinking', because her 'husband's profession and his mean income obliged them to live in but an indifferent neighbourhood'. In April 1745 she spent all their money and she returned home drunk. He murdered her. A bad situation found a 'bad remedy', as the Ordinary commented, 'for a man to ruin himself both body and soul, because he won't wait the appointed time which heaven intends for his relief'. There were two young men: John Jennings, a clog-maker who 'lay about Streets and upon Stalls, for the space of half a year and then went to live with a Woman who cried Fish'; and his friend, Christopher Jordan, who worked for his father, a shoemaker, and who 'on Account of his great Want' twice attempted suicide in Newgate, where he was incarcerated for stealing a hat and a wig after begging had failed to relieve his wants. Fortunately, Jordan's fellow prisoners prevented him from killing himself. Unfortunately, he was hanged in April 1742 on the evidence of the parish beadle and watch and against the testimony of his neighbours – a coachman, a publican's servant and an unemployed frame-maker.[13]

The shoemaking trade consisted of countless divisions. It was divided according to the type of shoe: there were men's and women's, as well as purpose-made shoes for workers such as chairmen, night-soil men and slaughterhouse men. It was divided according to the size of the market: at one end there was the bespoke market and at the other a large market for 'sale shoes' that supplied the plantations and the soldiers. It was divided according to operation: the clickers cut the leather, the closers sewed the uppers, the makers joined these to the heel and sole. And it was divided according to the site of production – between shop masters on the one hand, and cellar, garret and stall masters on the other. This division

[13]ibid., 9 July 1745, 22 November 1742 and 7 April 1742.

corresponded to a class division between 600 or 700 shoemasters in the Cordwainers Company who ran large operations (one such master employed 162 people), and perhaps 30,000 journeymen, country workers, apprentices and cheap garret masters.[14]

Wages were low – 9s. or 10s. a week. Women and children laboured in shoe-closing and shoe-binding, and their wages were even lower. Anne Baker bore five children to a sailor before she was nineteen. When he went to sea, she was confined to the workhouse, which put her out to labour for a Rosemary Lane closer. She could not live on such an income, and took to street-walking. In January 1764 she stole a guinea and was hanged two months later. Service in a wealthy household or the sea became alternatives that were frequently taken by poor practitioners of the 'gentle craft' of shoemaking. William Heath, for example, made shoes at a street stall. He could read and write and had sailed to the West Indies. He was hanged in January 1733 for stealing four shirts, part of somebody's washing that had been hung out to dry.[15] The labour of a wife or 'tack' – as an unmarried woman partner was known in shoemakers' language – might not be paid at all, yet it was essential to the out-working journeyman, stallman or garret master.

Survival as a shoemaker required access to leather, which required credit or capital. If they were wanting, the shoemaker might 'exchange soles and heels for inferior stuff of half its value', or he might gain material by reducing the thickness of the leather put out to him on credit.[16] No shoemaker ever hanged for such ploys, but, according to the Ordinary, they constituted for many the first step on the road to Tyburn. John Norman, who was hanged in December 1731, began his career as a pickpocket and burglar by pilfering from his master. He followed 'no Employment whatsoever but living upon the common Plunder'. William Williams, a clog-maker, was hanged in March 1735; he progressed from pilfering to breaking and entering. Richard Turner was suspected by his master, a shoemaker in Fleet Street, of many such 'dishonesties'. He stole £53

[14] Campbell, op. cit., pp. 216–21; Henry Mayhew, *The Morning Chronicle*, republished in E. P. Thompson and Eileen Yeo (eds), *The Unknown Mayhew* (1971), pp. 228–80.
[15] The Ordinary's *Account*, 28 March 1764, 29 January 1733.
[16] John Brown, *Sixty Years' Gleanings from Life's Harvest* (Cambridge, 1858), an autobiography brought to light by Nicholas Mansfield, who supplies an interesting commentary in *History Workshop: A Journal of Socialist and Feminist Historians*, vol. viii (autumn 1979), pp. 129–37; Charles Johnstone, *Chrysal* (1760), vol. i, ch. 11.

worth of plate and went to the triple tree. His 'Woman of the Town' had expensive tastes, he said, but he remained true to her to the end, asking her at the tree to accept his shirt-studs 'as the last token of my Love'.[17] Shoemakers' tradition made the meaning of 'pilfering' or 'dishonesty' problematic. The patron saints of shoemakers, Crispin and Crispinian, fled Rome to live in Paris, where they preached the Gospel by day and made shoes for the unshod poor by night. Some said that to do this they stole the leather, others that angels supplied them. In AD 287 they were martyred and their bones, it was said, washed ashore at Romney Marsh.[18] The 'Woman of the Town' was an angel to Richard Turner, who in stealing £53 of plate did the devil's work.

Neither angels nor devils made shoes. The 'pilfering' may be called 'clicking'.

The clicker's share of the work must be done with the greatest nicety, so as to adapt the proportions of the leather he cuts to the measurement of the foot, or else, as a workman expressed it to me, 'there can be no *success* in a boot'.

It also had a more doubtful meaning. ' To click' was defined in 1725 as 'to snatch', as in 'I have Clickt the Nap from the Cull' (I took the hat from the man), while the 'clicker' was defined as

the Shoemaker's Journey-man, or Servant that cuts out all the Work. Among the *Canters*, used for the Person whom they interest to divide their Spoils, and proportion to every one his Share.[19]

Between the 'Son of Crispin' and the 'canter' there was a mixed, and double moral world, with Parliament and the master cordwainers on the one side, and debt, destitution and despair on the other. Here 'clicking' and 'clickers' were central to the material and the moral relationship of an increasingly bitter struggle.

In the spring of 1723 the master cordwainers of London petitioned

[17] The Ordinary's *Account*, 20 December 1731, 31 December 1734 and 21 December 1739.
[18] H. Delehaye, *The Legends of the Saints: An Introduction to Hagiography* (1907), pp. 36–9. *The New Schaff-Herzog Encyclopedia of Religious Knowledge* (New York, 1909), vol. iii, p. 306, refers interested readers to Bolland's *Acta Sanctorum* (Antwerp, 1643), vol. xi, pp. 495–540. See also Herbert Thurston and Donald Attwater (eds), *Butler's Lives of the Saints* (1956), vol. iv, p. 197.
[19] Mayhew, op. cit., and Anon., *A New Canting Dictionary* (1725).

the House of Commons for legislation to protect their interests in the putting out of materials to the journeymen. They complained against journeymen having leather 'for making up of Boots, Shoes, Slippers, and other Wares; who [would] frequently pawn, sell, detain, and exchange, the same, being good, and vendible, for bad'. Abraham Hazard complained that fancy shoes put out for lace trimmings that he valued at £3 would be pawned for 5s. William Hall found that only rarely were the materials that he put out returned in the shoes that had been wrought up. Charles Reynolds too complained against this practice of journeymen pawning the good leather and making the shoes with inferior materials. In 1723 the master cordwainers obtained the Clicking Act (9 George I, c. 27), which authorized, upon the complaint of a 'credible person' to one magistrate, the searching of journeymen's domiciles, actions by distress to recover materials and orders of compensation for damaged or lost material. Journeymen were prohibited from 'selling Wares made of Leather in Chambers and other obscure Places'.[20] Clicking was criminalized.

The trade began to reorganize in the wake of three labour disputes and a wages strike in 1736. The master cordwainers sought to reduce unregulated competition from garret masters by prosecuting the curriers and tanners who supplied them with leather. They attempted to obtain legislation that would prohibit the curriers from selling less than the whole hide, which few, except large capitalists, could afford. While they did not succeed in this, a new 'trade' arose within the shoemaking division of labour and leather – the leather-cutter, who removed the cutting of hides from the knives of the poor. In 1747 Campbell described the origins of the leather-cutter – 'a Tradesman lately started up'. The increase of the poor reduced the capital and credit each had to purchase leather, so the leather-cutter 'cut out their Soals and Upper-Leathers . . . in Bits that answer these Uses, according to the several Sizes, and [sold] them to the necessitous Shoemaker'.[21] A basis of clicking within the division of labour thus was removed.

Henry Cook's father became a leather-cutter and profited enough in the new trade to set up his son, after he had completed his apprenticeship, in a shoemaker's shop in Stratford. Henry Cook married, had four children, but fell so deeply in debt that, with the

---

[20] *JHC*, vol. xx (March 1723), pp. 161–80.
[21] Campbell, op. cit.

beadles and bailiffs hounding him, he took to highway robbery in 'a Gold laced Hat'. He was hanged in September 1741 – a lesson to small master shoemakers as well as to leather-cutters. Matthew Lee completed his shoemaking apprenticeship in Lincolnshire and came to London. 'Soon after his Arrival in this City, he found himself in a very painful and disagreeable Situation; for he had no Friends capable of supporting or even assisting him.' He stole a silver watch and was hanged in 1752. Quite a number of shoemakers continued to die with their boots on at the gallows: George Anderson, a Wapping shoemaker, in 1742; Anthony Westley, a Rag Fair cobbler, in 1751; Joseph Joyce, who in returning from the wars in 1749 had to 'live by his wits'.[22]

These were men who could not live within the circuits of leather that had recently been tightened. Most of them belonged to a shoemaking proletariat that had contributed to the formation early in the century of 'shop committees', and many were known for that heterodoxy that characterized the nineteenth-century radicals in the trade. There was George Purchase, a journeyman in Salisbury Court, who was hanged in 1716 for shouting in a riot, 'No Hanoverian! No King George!' Or there was Samuel Badham, who turned to beggary and the memorizing of sermons after the crisis of his wife's death that led him to abandon his mending trade. In the prison yard he practised a harsh kind of didactics to fellow prisoners who mocked him with their teasing questions:

Pray, says I to him, who was the first Pawnbroker? He could not answer me, so I asked him what he thought of Joseph, who took the Lands of the Egyptians in Pledge for Corn in the Time of Famine; and so I silenc'd him.[23]

III

In considering hats we move from the sole of the eighteenth-century personage to the emblematic addition to the stature. Hats were made from the felters' 'bats', which consisted of the soft, spicated fur of the beaver. The circuit of fur extended from the rivers and lakes of the central and eastern woodlands of North America, where

---

[22] The Ordinary's *Account*, 16 September 1741, 11 October 1752, 23 November 1763, 11 February 1751 and 13 July 1752.
[23] ibid., 21 September 1716 and 6 August 1740.

the Blackfeet thought the beaver possessed magic because 'he makes for us kettles, axes, swords, knives, and gives us food and drink without the trouble of cultivating the ground'; to the sailors and dockers of the Hudson Bay Company, who in order to handle the beaver pelts were required to post bonds of honesty, swear affidavits and submit to searches of their persons; to the stooping servants of this mercantile giant who were required at the end of auctions to sift through the leavings on the floor for strands of the downy under-fur; to the hot and nauseous atmosphere of the hatter's garret, where felt was made with vinegar, glue, mercury nitrate and beer grounds; to the work of intemperate 'grave-diggers, curates, and bishops' (as the body-makers, finishers and shapers were called). And all this so that what once had provided warm cover for four-footed aquatic builders might now enlarge the stature of two-footed holders of office.[24]

War, virtually continuous, extended and interrupted this circuit, and a class struggle in London created ever finer variations to it. The War of Spanish Succession stopped the trade. The removal of beaver-trapping from the St Lawrence drainage basin to the Saskatchewan plains increased its costs of transportation. Competition with the French reduced the share in some markets, and the price of hats jumped from 2s. 6d. in 1700 to 3s. 2d. in 1730. Shortly after the Company of Feltmakers was chartered in 1667, a dispute between the journeymen and masters broke out over the employment of 'foreigners', the responsibility for 'spoilt work' and the price list. The arrival of French hatters after the Revocation of the Edict of Nantes (1685) and their employment in the Battersea and Wandsworth suburbs intensifed the conflicts between the incorporated trade and the skinners and merchants who 'weighed out stuff' for suburban home workers outside the feltmakers' corporate jurisdiction. In the face of these conflicts the journeymen responded by either forming clubs and combinations of their own or migrating

[24] Murray G. Lawson, 'The Beaver Hat and the North American Fur Trade', in Malvina Bolus (ed.), *Peoples and Pelts: Selected Papers of the Second North American Fur Trade Conference* (Winnipeg, 1972), p. 31; Harold A. Innis, *The Fur in Canada: An Introduction to Canadian Economic History*, revised edn (Toronto, 1970), pp. 126–7; Beckles Wilson, *The Great Company, being a History of the Honourable Company of Merchant-Adventurers Trading into Hudson's Bay* (Toronto, 1899), vol. ii, pp. 35–9; John C. Ewers, *The Blackfeet, Raiders on the Northwestern Plains* (Norman, Oklahoma, 1958); J. H. Hawkins, *History of the Worshipful Company of the Art and Mistery of the Feltmakers of London* (1917).

to the plantations or going upon the 'tramp'. The 1732 Hat Act, passed in spite of complaints that hatters 'can scarce get work in that Business' nor 'get Bread to maintain their Families', attempted to curtail American production and enforce apprenticeship regulations in London.[25]

During the depths of this depression, the three-legged mare at Tyburn sent a number of hatters kicking into eternity. William Booth of St Giles-in-the-Fields worked for several years as a hatter in Monmouth Street. At the end of 1732 he joined his brother who worked for butchers at Smithfield and went robbing on the highway. They stole 35s., for which William Booth was hanged. Another Monmouth Street hatter, Samuel Steele, got work in agriculture or labouring for the masons when the hatting trade was slack. With a coal-heaver he took to street-robbing and was hanged in 1734. Jack the Hatter learned the trade from his father. In October 1733 he joined a leather-breeches-maker and together they 'went out upon the Account'. He was hanged at the age of twenty-two for stealing a leg of pork in Stepney Fields. William Bourn, a Dublin hatter, came to London 'for insight in his Business' and took up lodgings with an Irish family in Bishopsgate. He robbed a goldsmith and was hanged in 1726.[26]

The 1730s were a period of protective retrenchment, of numerous 'Awful Examples' at Tyburn, and of an assault upon the journeymen hatters' custom of 'bugging'. In 1785 Francis Grose defined 'bugging' as

a cant word among journeymen hatters, signifying the exchange of the dearest materials of which a hat is made for others of less value ... Bugging is stealing the beaver and substituting in lieu thereof an equal weight of some cheaper ingredient.

Bugging depended largely on the domestic system of production. A case in 1723 illustrates this. William Hudson, a journeyman hatter, worked for Joseph Best, who bought coney wool and beaver stuff from a large hat factor, James Carwell, on the credit of future manufactured hats. Best sent Hudson to Carwell to fetch a packet of wool. Hudson on his return 'used as he went along to take some of the said Stuff or Wool out of the paper'. He took between 8 and

---

[25] George Unwin, 'A Seventeenth Century Trade Union', *The Economic Journal*, vol. x (September 1900), pp. 394–403); 5 George II, c. 22 (1732).
[26] The Ordinary's *Account*, 29 January 1733, 11 February 1734 and 27 June 1726.

10 oz. at a time, which he then sold to another hatter for 4s.[27]

Another form of bugging occurred not when the journeyman intervened between the master and the factor but when he appropriated material during manufacture. In 1733, a year after the Hat Act, the master hatters and feltmakers mounted an attack upon this type of bugging. In August of that year the Company of Feltmakers appointed a committee 'to consider and advise with Councill or otherwise what Method is proper to be taken to prevent Journeymen and others from makeing away with Stuff weighed out to them by their Masters'.[28] The committee's report has not come to light. Perhaps legal prosecution was one of its recommendations, for a year later we read a petition by James Short

that your Petitioner was this Day tryed and convicted of petty larceny in stealing a smale Quantity of Beaver and Coney wool; that your Petitioner hath a Wife & four smale Children & nothing to maintain them but his hand Labour & hath been these six weeks confined in Gaol whereby your Petitioners family is reduced to great hardships & almost starving.

Public punishment would be his 'utter undoing', and he petitioned that it be avoided. The justices accepted Short's request: he was privately whipped in the Clerkenwell House of Correction and released, despite a petition from his former employer that the punishment 'in Terror of others ... may be executed as near the Place of the petitioner's Abode which is near the Bell Dock in Wapping as your Worships shall think fit'.[29]

In February 1747 the master feltmakers appointed another committee 'to consult ways and means to apply to Parliament for suppressing and detecting the Journeymen in relation to their taking of Stuff', and in the year following yet another committee was appointed to draft legislation that would assure 'the preventing of the Journeymen Bugging of Stuff'. Legislation soon followed in an 'Act for the more effectual preventing of frauds and abuses committed by persons employed in the manufacture of hats' – the Bugging Act of 1749 (22 George II, c. 27). A punishment of hard

[27] Francis Grose, *A Classical Dictionary of the Vulgar Tongue* (1785); CLRO, Sessions Papers, box 1723–5, 'The Examination of William Hudson, 23 Feb. 1723, before John Fryer'.
[28] Guildhall, Feltmakers Company, *Court Book*, vol. iii (1726–49), MS 1570/3, pp. 221–2.
[29] MRO, Sessions Papers, 'The Humble Petition of James Short, August 1734' and 'The Petition of John Busby, Hatter, August 1734', MJ/SP/34.

labour and whipping was provided. There is no reason to suppose that Act was successful, since no cases appeared at the Old Bailey in the years that followed, and eight years later, in 1757, the court of the Company of Feltmakers again had to consider the problem. They heard a motion which proposed offering a reward of £5 'to the person or persons who shall discover any journeyman hatter or other person who shall purloin or embezzle the stuff they shall be entrusted with, upon condition that such journeyman hatter or other person shall be convicted of such offence'.[30]

The Bugging Act has figured prominently in recent English legal historiography because, unlike earlier statutes forbidding customary forms of appropriation (in 1662, 1668, 1697, 1703, 1722, 1726 and 1740), it punished convicted offenders with two months' hard labour in the house of correction instead of fining offenders. A customary form of income was thus criminalized. Some legal historians, however, argue that corporal and confining punishments had been used earlier against offences of 'embezzlement'. This was indeed the case, and it provides a legal corrective to those who work with other evidence. The Bugging Act, like the Clicking Act preceding it or the Watch Scraping Acts following it, was designed to put an end to the customarily acknowledged appropriations of workers who had not yet been fully alienated from the means and materials of production.

Embezzlement has recently been defined by a historian of eighteenth-century law as 'the unauthorized appropriation of an employer's goods by his employee'. This definition begs two important issues:[31] Who is the authority that authorizes? Why is it assumed that the 'goods' belong to the employer? Concerning the first question, we must remember that the Bugging Act was passed by a handful of Parliament men at the instigation of feltmongers in connivance with some master hatters: these may well have seen several working hatters hang in the previous few years; in anticipation of larger shiploads of pelts they eagerly followed the news of Sullivan's march against the Iroquois confederation, and wrote

---

[30] Guildhall, Feltmakers Company, *Court Book*, vol. iii (1726–59), MS 1570/3, pp. 561, 603.
[31] John Styles, 'Embezzlement, Industry and the Law in England, 1500–1800', in Maxine Berg, Pat Hudson and Michael Sonenscher (eds), *Manufacture in Town and Country before the Factory* (Cambridge, 1983), p. 188.

to magistrates suggesting how punishments should be conducted 'in Terror of others'. The authority of working hatters was not consulted.

The second question raises the issue of *to whom* did the wasted fur belong. We have recently been reminded that 'under common law, a person who had physical custody of an object by consent of its owner could not commit larceny . . . Physical custody even protected the possessor against forcible dispossession by the owner of the property.'[32] The ownership of the beaver fur during many stages in its metamorphosis was in *dispute*, and it was to resolve that dispute in favour of the feltmongers and master hatters that the Bugging Act was passed. To apply twentieth-century legal meanings of embezzlement to eighteenth-century practices of production and appropriation is to obscure the terms of both this dispute and analogous ones. 'A man who has made such use of material that a hat is the result has made a hat. That is all he has made. He has not made a "right to property" in the hat, either for himself or anybody else.'[33]

Sometimes it is necessary to recall that a statute is only a piece of paper. The failure to appreciate this is the source of Dobson's error when he writes that the Act 'ended' bugging. In fact the Bugging Act resulted in no noticeable changes in London indictments or convictions, though it may have led to more newspaper stories, as Professor Styles suggests. The *London Evening Post* and the *General Advertiser* printed stories about the prosecution of Ann Edwards for receiving 'stolen goods' from a journeyman hatter.[34] Hatters continued to be hanged – in the year after the Act, Peter Oldfield, a Southwark hatter, for stealing a gold watch; and George Taylor, a Clerkenwell hatter, for stealing some linen – and bugging continued to be a serious problem for 'Makers and Vendors of Hats'.[35] In 1764 they alleged in a memorial to the Privy Council that exports had decreased owing to 'the great increase in the price of labour' and 'from a deceit and unfairness in their Fabrick'. Meanwhile, the working hatters became more organized: they struck against the

[32] Craig Becker, 'Property in the Workplace: Labor, Capital, and Crime in the Eighteenth Century British Woolen and Worsted Industry', *Virginia Law Review*, vol. lxix (1982), p. 1492.
[33] L. S. Bevington, 'Why I am an Expropriationist', *Liberty* (May 1894), p. 37.
[34] C. R. Dobson, *Masters and Journeymen: A Prehistory of Industrial Relations, 1717–1800* (1980), p. 29.
[35] The Ordinary's *Account*, 26 March 1750 and 3 October 1750.

masters in 1768; they federated their clubs in 1771; and they formed a congress in 1772. The masters responded by again petitioning for new legislation: 'The Petitioners are great and daily Sufferers by Journeymen who embezzle their Materials, and by the Buyers and Receivers of the same.' The Bugging Act of 1777 (17 George III, c. 56) was the result.[36] It extended the punishment for bugging from two weeks to three months of hard labour at the house of correction.

IV

Bejewelled by the watchmaker, grounded by the shoemaker, elevated by the hatter, the eighteenth-century personage was 'made' by the tailor. In tradesman's lore, it was thought that Prometheus was a tailor, for he too 'by his Art metamorphosed Mankind so that they appeared a new species of Being'. The classical story is one of theft: Epimetheus in distributing the qualities among creation overlooked man. Prometheus thus found him naked and, to rectify Epimetheus' blunder, stole the Arts from Hephaestus and Athena, who prosecuted him for theft. During the period of study nine tailors hanged at Tyburn, all for thefts. Their stories continue a familiar theme of customary appropriation, but with this development: tailors were among the first of the trades to form unions, in two waves of militance in 1720–21 and 1744–5.

John Wilkins, a tailor, was hanged in January 1747 for stealing a gown and a pair of breeches. The Ordinary of Newgate commented that he died having no friends and no money. In this respect he was typical of the generality of tailors. In 1728 a country observer referred to 'those wretched emblems of death and hunger, the Journeymen Taylors'. The first student of industrial pathology, Ramazzini, noted that the characteristic tailor was 'a crooked, hump-backed, lame figure'. He might have added that many were virtually blind from years of close-stitching by candlelight, since during the winter, which was the only time he could be sure of employment, much of the working day – 6 a.m. to 9 p.m. – occurred in darkness. It is true that the statutory working day had

[36] Acts of the Privy Council, *Colonial Series*, 1745–1766, pp. 637–8; *The Annual Register* (1768); *The Gentleman's Magazine* (1768); *Berrow's Worcester Journal* (August 1768); Sidney and Beatrice Webb, *The History of Trade Unionism*, 2nd edn (1902), pp. 29–30; *JHC*, vol. xxxvi, pp. 118–19.

been reduced by an hour as a result of the 1721 Combination Act (7 George I, c. 13). However, when there was a 'hurry' in the work, such as during births, weddings or funerals of the royal family when the Quality of the town dressed up anew, then overtime was common. Otherwise, for fifteen or twenty-five weeks in the year, the tailor was unemployed. This was when the gentry left town and it was the tailor's 'cucumber time', for it began in early summer. The Covent Garden vendors called out, 'Cucumbers two a penny, tailors twice as many.'[37]

The Combination Act fixed the day rate of wages at 2s. between 25 March and 24 June, and 1s. 8d. otherwise. The City, Westminster and Middlesex Quarter Sessions were empowered to revise these, and to avoid trouble at times of scarcity or high prices, they revised them upwards. By 1745 2s. $7\frac{1}{2}$d. was the norm for half the year, a norm that was enforced by direct strike action in 1737 and 1744. Even such rates, it was complained, fell below the subsistence needs of a single tailor – much less a family man – owing to the duration of cucumber time and to the practice of masters hiring men for only a portion of the day. In 1745 *The Case of the Journeymen Taylors and Journeymen Staymakers* published a budget:

	£	s.	d.
For breakfast, more than the master's allowance	0	0	$\frac{1}{2}$
For meat, drink and bread for dinner	0	0	6
On the shopboard, in the afternoon, a pint of beer	0	0	$1\frac{1}{2}$
Bread, cheese and beer for supper	0	0	3
One day's expenses	*0*	*0*	*11*
Sunday's expense	0	1	0
The other five days' expense	0	4	7
Lodging for a week	0	1	0
Washing for a week	0	0	8
Shaving for a week	0	0	4
A week's expenses	*0*	*8*	*6*

[37] Bernardino Ramazzini, *De Morbis Artificium: Diseases of Tradesmen*, 2nd edn (1750); 'B.E.', *Dictionary of the Canting Crew* (1700); William Hone, *Every Day Book* (1826–7), vol. ii, p. 848.

It is an extraordinary budget when compared with the budget presented in the last chapter whose weekly expenses for a 'labouring Man and his Family' are more than twice what is presented here. This is a budget without fruit, vegetables or herbs; without coals or candles; without clothing or utensils; and without medicine, schooling or fees for lying-in. It is a budget, however, that can be balanced against a tailor's average weekly wage – 9s. The journeymen complained in 1745 that their families could not subsist.[38] This was not, even on paper, a 'family wage'. Yet home-working journeymen relied on the assistance of wife and children.

The Combination Act had further repressive provisions: it stipulated a penalty of two months' hard labour in a house of correction not only for any tailor combining to increase wages or to reduce hours, but also for any unemployed journeyman tailors refusing work from a master requesting it. In 1745 the home-working journeymen said that it was 'very hard' to 'be dragg'd from thence like a slave at the will of any master, and sent to the House of Correction, or press'd for a recruit'. George Thomas was hanged the year after the poor tailors presented their case. He was a Welshman, a sometime soldier, and was hanged for stealing a pair of shoes.[39] In the pedagogy of public hanging his death was an answer to those tailors who in the year preceding had appealed to the spirit of 'the free-born Briton' and to the 46th article of Magna Carta, which forbade imprisonment without a jury of peers.

Eight of the nine other tailors hanged at Tyburn between 1703 and 1772 were not born in London. John Gardiner, for instance, was a twenty-year-old tailor from Suffolk. 'Two or three months ago, thinking to make some Advantage by the Mourning of her late Majesty, he came to London with Mortished who knew the Town better.' Isaac Mortished was a married father, a 36-year-old Cheshire tailor. They broke into the Society of Pewterers and stole a £100 bond and a 40s. promissory note, and both were hanged in 1738.[40] The masters encouraged such migration as a means of undermining the organization of the 'flints', as those tailors were called who at a house of call inscribed their name with a flint upon a slate. Those

---

[38] F. W. Galton, *Select Documents Illustrating the History of Trade Unionism*, vol. i, *The Tailoring Trade* (1896).
[39] The Ordinary's *Account*, 1 August 1746 and 21 January 1747.
[40] ibid., 18 March 1738.

who did not were 'dungs', which included the thousands of stallmen, country workers and women home-workers. In a 1764 dispute the masters recruited 800 tailors from the country, and 230 from France, Germany and Holland. Migrants brought their experiences.

Patrick Knowland, a Dublin tailor, fled with his family to London to escape a debt. In London he cried out old clothes in Monmouth Street and dealt in the slop trade at Rag Fair. He had a house in Whitechapel whose rental value was £8 per annum. With his son he had stolen three bed-sheets and fifteen napkins, while his son-in-law, a house painter from Dublin, had stolen a coat, stays and breeches which he sold to fences in Monmouth Street and Rag Fair. All three were sentenced to hang, and Knowland's wife and daughter were imprisoned in Newgate. The Ordinary was impressed by the son's appearance, describing the 'silver mounting upon his cloaths'. He also said of him: 'He minded his employment very little but went out upon the purchase of what he could get.' Knowland, who was fifty-five, and the two younger men were hanged in December 1731, an important year that brought to an end a phase of struggle in Dublin.[41]

Dublin journeymen tailors were the first Irish trades people to combine to form durable organizations promoting their own interests as wage-earners. The late 1720s were also years of severe dearth caused by a succession of harvest failures between 1726 and 1728. The crisis of subsistence produced a crisis of reproduction. Babies were abandoned by their parents. Children were orphaned. In 1728 the Irish parliament responded with an Act to protect foundlings. The journeymen tailors organized themselves in houses of call, they referred to their organization as a 'union', they celebrated St James's Day in street processions and festivals and they complained of unemployment. In 1730 the Irish parliament passed the first Combination Act, which forced the tailors into secrecy and quiescence.[42] It was, then, from famine, unemployment and political repression that the Knowland family and William Philips had fled upon coming to London. The experience marked them.

Father, mother, daughter, son and son-in-law were neck-deep in London's shadow economy of clothing. We do not know what became of the mother and daughter. Yet theirs was a family enterprise in every sense. Two had served their time as apprentices in

[41] ibid., 20 December 1731.
[42] Galton, op. cit., pp. 27–9.

tailoring. They worked in Monmouth Street and Rag Fair. Their house in Whitechapel was reputed to be a receiver's ken. Beginning with the banking crisis of 1725 the Dublin tailors published annual commemorative poems:

> The louse bites us, 'tis not deny'd.
> We bite our masters, when we are employ'd.
> And they bite all the world beside.

Some master tailors were hanged for biting 'the world'. One was William Philips, a Dubliner – and a man of daring and enterprise, for he escaped Newgate in 1728. In Limehouse he employed seven or eight men. He was hanged for highway robbery in 1735. Another was Richard Hughes, a 45-year-old man from Staffordshire. 'Grasping after the things of this world was his principal concern,' said the Ordinary. 'To improve himself in his profession', he required credit. To get credit, he forged a letter falsely attesting to possessing some South Sea Company shares, and he was hanged for this in May 1757, a year after the 'advertising tailors' had split the trade and the journeymen's clubs. A third was Thomas Jones of Monmouthshire, who cheated the mercers and drapers by pretending to be a tailor's foreman. He defrauded the wholesalers by purchasing cloth with false tokens.

At the centre of production was the 'shop', where a well-appointed room was reserved for measuring customers, and other rooms were used for cutting cloth, sewing seams, making buttonholes, stitching lace, applying trim, pressing and performing the finishing work which the elaborate fashions of the time required. In such manufacturing establishments the haughty master, as Henry Fielding explained, only took measure, and otherwise was at the mercy of his scissors-wielding workers, led by the foreman who cut and finished the work. 'This is the best Workman in the shop, and his Place the most profitable; for besides his Cabbage, he has generally a Guinea a Week, and the Drink-Money given by the Gentlemen on whom he waits to fit on their Cloths.'[43]

What is cabbage? It is part of the 'mystery' of a craft whose decisive action was the cutting of cloth (the word 'tailor' derives from the French *tailler*, 'to cut'). Eye and hand combine in a mystery which

---

[43] Campbell, op. cit., pp. 190–94; Henry Fielding, *A Journey from this World to the Next* (1742).

proverbially makes the man. The eye imagines the pieces that will, when stitched, make a garment; the hand and shears must then rend the fabric into the requisite pieces. The mercer's bolts had to be cut with minimal waste: whether a sleeve, cuff *and* collar, or only sleeve and cuff, would be cut from a piece was the essence of the craft. Remnants were (and are) called 'cabbage', as the shreds were rolled up in a cabbage-like ball and put under the shop-board. A dictionary in 1725 explained,

The Cloth they steal and purloin is called *Cabbage*, which oftentimes affords them Breeches and Wastecoats for themselves, as well as whole Suits for very young and new-breech'd Boys; and, at the least, Cloth for Women's Shoes, and Silk (especially among Women's Taylors, and Manteau-makers) sufficient to supply half the Ladies in Town.[44]

We recall that Jack Sheppard assumed that a master tailor kept his store of wealth in the form of cabbage. A more exact valuation appears in the following: 'A tailor's carrot-pated daughter in Exeter Street, purloined so much cabbage from that old thief her father, as came to the sum of fifteen shillings, and ventured it last week in the lottery.' Cabbage had become a synonym for the craftsman's income:

> A Taylor, good Lord, in the time of Vacation,
> When Cabbage was scarce and when Pocket was low,
> For the sake of good Liquor pretended a Passion,
>   To one that sold Ale in Cuckoldy Row:
> Now a louse made him Itch,
>   Here a Scratch, there a Stitch,
>   And sing Cucumber, Cucumber ho.[45]

And as late as 1778 it could be used by a popular dramatist as a commonly understood expletive and cry:

> The shop-board moves! The needles dance cross-leg'd!
> The threads entangled! Oh, cabbage, cucumbers!
> Cab-cab-bage-bage-Oh!

Of the many words of customary appropriation within the work setting, cabbage is the only one that appears in Samuel Johnson's 'authoritative' dictionary (1755). Besides the specific meaning of the tailors' shreds and patches, he considered it a general term for

---

[44] 'B. E.', op. cit.; Anon., *A New Canting Dictionary* (1725).
[45] Thomas D'Urfey, *Songs Compleat*, vol. vi, p. 292.

stealing, and he thought that the origin of the word arose from the practice of small cottagers encroaching upon the common lands to dig themselves cabbage patches. Of the tailors hanged at Tyburn, only one was London born. He was thirty when he was hanged for a burglary in 1727. His name was also Samuel Johnson, but he was called Cabbage Johnson.

With the exception of a single sentence in the journeymen tailors' *Case* (1745), we do not find references to cabbage in the evidences surviving of the tailors' trade-union struggles in 1721 and 1745. Even the exception refers not to cabbage but to 'perquisite'. 'The poor laborious journeymen are confined to sit double on the board; from six in the morning until eight at night, without any other gain or perquisite whatsoever than their wages.' Part of the reason, most certainly, was the journeymen's desire to avoid any imputation of criminality. '[I]t cannot be alledged that any of them was ever yet charged with being concern'd in the street robberies, and other disorders so much complain'd of in and about this great city of late,' they wrote in 1745,[46] and it appears to be true that the tailors who were hanged, though poor, were either dungs or small masters. Another reason for the omission, at least in the trade-union pamphleteering and the printed parliamentary discussions, is that cabbage was part of the labour process itself – a matter between the shears and the cloth, as it were – while money wages were not inherent to the labour process and belonged to master, man and magistrate alike. Cabbage may also have been a means of distinguishing between flints and dungs.

Cabbage, once created, entered a waste economy. The papermaking industry depended on rags and remnants. Rag-pickers belonged to a large, if ill-reputed, occupation. The economy of cloth wastes was centred about Monmouth Street and Rag Fair. It provided women with an independent though meagre income by which a seamstress (like Kate Keys, Sheppard's friend) or a receiver, such as Mrs Knowland, could combine many small favours into a living. The flints, on the other hand, belonging to 'the most militant and effective trade union in eighteenth-century England', distinguished themselves from the women, country people and stallmen who worked at piece-rates for a ready-made market in 'Soldier's Cloathes'. Flints – as we learn from Samuel Foote's drama *The Tailors: A Tragedy for Warm Weather* – regarded Tyburn as a

[46] *The Case of the Journeymen Taylors* (1745), reprinted in Galton, op. cit., p. 33.

shameful death, and it is true that, in relation to other trades and as a proportion to their own numbers, few tailors swung from the triple tree.

We should not over-emphasize the divisions between flints and dungs.

> It is well known, before these fatal broils,
> The Flints and Dungs in friendly intercourse
> Together work'd, together friendly drank;
> Hence all are known, his name, his habitation,
> His house of haunt, and each particular.

Cabbage remained a customary appropriation and when a tailor in 1810 referred to 'all the shop-board rights and privileges of the craft' cabbage may have been included.

V

It was the task of the domestic servants to effect the luxury and refinement of the upper classes. They served the chocolate and cooked the roast beef. They powdered the wigs. They fuelled the fires, dug the gardens, pressed the silk garments, organized town and country jaunts. They swept the dirt out of sight. Service to the upper class was one of the largest occupations of the metropolis. It was an occupation that had similarities with both manufacture and the domestic system. Like the former, its division of labour was advanced: butlers, footmen, postilions, coach-drivers, maids, cooks, washerwomen, scullions, valets and waiters combined to produce the upper-class lifestyle. Their work was closely supervised by a hierarchical pecking order that meant that no servant was too distant from the eyes and ears of a superior. The family of the worker was not present at the work site; employers preferred unmarried people. Professor Malcolmson found that of sixty-one defendants tried for infanticide at the Old Bailey between 1730 and 1744, thirty-five were servant maids, a figure explained by the prohibition of pregnancy among servants.[47] On the other hand, service shared some attributes of the putting-out system. There was much coming and going – to markets, to the pump, to neighbours and to shopkeepers

---

[47] R. W. Malcolmson, 'Infanticide in the Eighteenth Century', in J. S. Cockburn (ed.), *Crime in England, 1550–1800* (Princeton, 1977), p. 202.

and tradesmen. Tyburnography suggests that the relationship between employers and servants required virtually annual 'examples'
to enforce discipline. Of the sixty-two servants who were hanged
between 1703 and 1772 we know that twenty-one received this
penalty for robbing their masters. The Earl of Harrington, the Revd
Mr Gibbons, Sir Simon Stuart, the Marquis of Linsey, Nicholas
Fenwick, Esq., Sir John Smith, the Earl of Leicester and the Earl
of Torrington all sent their servants to the hanging tree.[48] These
servants came from Lincolnshire, Gloucestershire, Cambridgeshire,
Yorkshire, Shropshire, Nigeria, Aberdeen, Derbyshire, Paris,
Dublin and Wiltshire. They stole handkerchiefs, horses, silver
spoons, belt-buckles, clothing, a chocolate pot, a shaving box,
watches and a glass window. We shall examine a single case.

The victim was the third Earl of Harrington, known as Peter
Shambles because of a peculiarity of gait incurred from a wound at
Fontenoy during the charge of the Irish 'wild geese'. His military
service was rewarded with the office of the Lord Lieutenancy of
Ireland (1747–51), which enabled him to exact his revenge: his
administration was characterized by neglect, jobbery and peculation.
He married Caroline, daughter of Charles Fitzroy, a court beauty
who amused herself by visiting Newgate, where she comforted
James Maclean, 'the Gentleman Highwayman', prior to his hanging
in 1750.

   John Weskett committed the robbery with two accomplices,
Bradley, a livery servant who had previously robbed the chambers of
Henry Montague, Esq., and one Cooper, a failed Ratcliff Highway
cheesemonger with a chandler's shop in New Turn Stile, Holborn.
Weskett learned of the valuables in His Lordship's drawer from the
steward, one Bevel. It was the day the tradesmen came to collect
'what these people have long exacted by the tyranny of custom,
under the name of *perquisite*, at their going away'.[49]

   Weskett, Bradley and Cooper took a 'Chance' and milked Lord
Harrington of several thousand pounds. John Fielding, the court

---

[48] The Ordinary's *Account*, 17 March 1710, 31 January 1713, 24 September 1722,
12 September 1726, 22 March 1727, 23 December 1730, 26 July 1731, 3 March
1737, 22 December 1738, 18 January 1739, 13 February 1740, 14 September 1741,
24 December 1744, 13 July 1752, 16 April 1753, 31 December 1734, 7 June 1745,
17 March 1755 and 16 May 1770.
[49] ibid., 9 January 1765; *The Gentleman's Magazine*, January 1765.

magistrate, and his nationwide network of myrmidons spent two years in catching this erstwhile servant. They succeeded by tracking down one of the banknotes (from his Lordship's London clerk, to a Liverpool merchant, to a northern Ireland linen factor who had received it at the Chester Fair), by penetrating the many disguises and aliases of the thieves ('He was dressed like a gentleman but appeared somewhat under that standard in conversation,' as the linen factor said of the thin-faced, pock-marked man from whom he received the banknote), and by the betrayal of a 'woman of the town', whom Weskett had seduced under pretence of marriage. Bradley, 'apprehended in a sailor's habit at Wapping', turned King's evidence, exposing Cooper, who was transported for fourteen years, and Weskett, who was hanged with 'a white Ribbon in his Hat'.[50]

Weskett was caught and hanged in January 1765 in the midst of a struggle against the perquisites and vails of servants. We need to clarify the meaning of these forms of income. At law 'perquisite' referred to property acquired by means other than inheritance. Evidently, it had many meanings even in law, and 'under the tyranny of custom' it had a great many more. Many of these meanings appear to have belonged to monetary income deriving from office. In Johnstone's *Chrysal* a countess is told about a municipal office: 'The salary! The salary signified nothing, it is the perquisites! The perquisites are the thing! Do you think any place is valued by the salary?' Administrators, such as Pepys or Walpole, amassed huge fortunes to themselves from the perquisites of office. The Customs, the Treasury, the Navy and the Army similarly provided administrators with huge chunks of surplus under the name of perquisite. Servants distinguished perquisites from other incomes. Thus Smollett writes in *Humphrey Clinker*:

John Thomas is in good health, but sulky. The squire gave away an ould coat to a poor man; and John says how tis robbing him of his parquisites. I told him, by his agreement he was to receive no vails; but he says how there's a difference betwixt vails and parquisites; and so there is for sartain.

---

[50] Peter Shambles continued to use the gallows to discipline his servants: John James, his lordship's coachman, upon being dismissed and reduced to subsisting on a weekly allowance of 8s. from his mother, turned burglar and was hanged on St Valentine's Day, 1770, five years after Weskett's hanging. The Ordinary's *Account*, 14 February 1770.

Vails were of two kinds, and both were specific to household servants. They could be money or goods. A Swiss visitor to England explained how 'if you take a meal with a person of rank, you must give every one of the five or six footmen a coin when leaving . . . and should you fail to do this, you will be treated insolently the next time.'[51] Such vails, depending on the grandeur of the household and the generosity of its guests, could be substantial. Piggot Horton, a gentleman's servant, bagnio manager and actor – who was hanged for stealing the watch of Lord Mordington's cook – said that in a place providing only £4 a year wages, he was able to collect in two years' vails more than £100.[52] Otherwise, vails referred to a source of income that was non-monetary and related to the particular tasks of the servant. Thus, the butler customarily received old bottles and candle-ends. The cook customarily kept pan-drippings, bones and fat that found no place on the master's plate. The scullion took firings and small coals. The coachman took broken or worn carriage parts. 'Do not covet to have the Kitchen Stuff for your Vales,' advised *The Complete Servant Maid* in 1677, 'but rather ask the more wages.' Vails became an expected right rather than an unexpected gift. Household management consisted in the successful negotiation of tasks and vails. Arbuthnot described what could happen in a disorderly household:

[Y]our Cook-Maid is in a Combination with your Butcher, Poulterer and Fishmonger; your Butler purloins your Liquor, and your Brewer sells your Hogwash; your Baker cheats both in Weight and in Tale; even your Milkwoman and your Nursery-Maid have a Fellow-feeling; your Taylor, instead of Shreds cabbages whole Yards of Cloath . . .[53]

In the middle decades of the eighteenth century the transition of such incomes from an 'ancient form of largesse', as Jean Hecht described vails, to a regular wage-form reached a crisis. In 1757 an agreement was entered into 'by the Gentlemen of Ireland' to prevent vails-giving. In the next few years several county associations were formed in England to combat the practice, as Jonas Hanway noted in his *On the Custom of Vails-Giving in England* (1760). 'Thomas Trueman, a Footman' set forth his advice and sentiments in a

[51] César de Saussure, *A Foreign View of England in the Reigns of George I and George II* (1725–1730), trans. van Muyden (1902), p. 194.
[52] *The Ordinary's Account*, 12 June 1741.
[53] César de Saussure, op. cit., p. 194.

similarly titled work. These texts argued that vails created insolence in office. 'The Foundation of it is laid in generosity, but the super-structure is rank corruption.' Hanway noted that the practice began in generosity as a form of gift-giving, but since it had become a universal custom it was taken as a right and regarded as a supplement to wages. In what amounted to a reduction of income, the servants struck back against the employers. In 1761 the footmen assaulted gentlemen who declared themselves against the practice; they broke windows, hurled brickbats and threatened Lord Cornwallis. In 1764 they threw aqua fortis upon the clothes of employers refusing to provide vails, and later in the same year brawls and riots broke out at Ranelagh Gardens over the same issue.[54]

Discipline was attempted by organizing the recruitment of servants, and this was also a *police* matter. In 1749 the Fielding brothers established the Universal Register Office as a labour exchange where employers might examine prospective servants and study their character references. *The Public Advertizer*, also a police venture under Henry and John Fielding, provided information on the servant labour market. The Office and the newspaper were part of a broader attempt not only to organize the London labour market (the Marine Society, the Female Orphan Asylum, the workhouses), but also to aid the detection of crime and the recovery of stolen goods. Both *The Public Advertizer* and the Universal Register Office systematically collected information about stolen property and descriptions of suspected wrongdoers.[55] Otherwise the labour market for servants was a matter of word-of-mouth in which employers had little control, at least in London. The networks of information about employment were located below stairs. In 1744 a long-nosed observer described the 'Intrigues of our Servant-maids', their 'cabal-ling together' to raise wages from 30s. to 'six, seven, and eight

[54] Anon., *The Life and Times of Sir Thomas Deveil* (1748), pp. 60–61; *The Annual Register*, part 1 (1761); J. Jean Hecht, *The Domestic Servant Class in Eighteenth Century England* (1956), pp. 157–67; E. S. Turner, *What the Butler Saw: Two Hundred and Fifty Years of the Servant Problem* (1962), pp. 47–55; *The London Magazine*, May 1764.

[55] John Fielding, *Some Proper Cautions to the Merchants, Tradesmen, and Shopkeepers of the Cities of London and Westminster* (1776); R. Leslie-Melville, *The Life and Work of Sir John Fielding* (1934); John Fielding, *Plan for Preventing Robberies within 20 Miles of London* (1755); John Fielding, *Extracts from Such of the Penal Laws as Particularly relate to the Peace and Good Order of this Metropolis* (1761); *The Public Advertizer* (1763).

Pounds *per An*', how country maids are advised by 'A Committee of Servant-Wenches', how 'the Herb-Woman, or Chandler Woman, or some other old Intelligencers ... sets Madam Cock-a-Hoop and she thinks of nothing now but Vails and high Wages'.[56] In such ways did female intelligence use the labour market.

Of the 65 servants who were hanged at Tyburn between 1703 and 1772 20 were women, a proportion distinguishing service from all other occupations represented at the gallows. Alice Gray of Hampshire worked as a nurse, a washerwoman and at 'making up Cloaths for Souldiers' until she was hanged. Janas Walton of Lancashire worked for fifteen years as a London servant until she was hanged for stealing 16 yds. of silk from a shop. Mary Taylor, a servant from Worcestershire, was hanged for a brawl in Whitefriars, where she robbed a man of 12 moidores and his teeth. Sarah Malcolm, a Durham-born London servant and laundress, made famous by Hogarth's portrait, was hanged for murder. Susannah Broom, a 67-year-old woman from Oxfordshire, married a Rag Fair clothes-dealer whose slack seasons she made up for by chairing the Quality around; she was hanged for murdering her husband. Eleanor Mumpman, a Yorkshire servant, fell into housebreaking after she lost her place. Elizabeth Fox, servant and sailor's wife, went robbing with an unemployed journeyman. She 'walk'd the Street, robbed, stole, and taking every Thing she could lay hold on, being one of the most scandalous Creatures and notorious Pickpockets in Town'. Ann Gwyn, orphan, washerwoman, prostitute and servant, 'lived upon the Spill and Plunder of Mankind'. Margaret Greenaway, a servant and member of Black Boy Alley society, was hanged for stealing a hat. Elizabeth Stevens, hanged for pilfering laundry, worked by going to 'Scouring and Washing'.[57]

In addition to perquisites and vails, the eighteenth-century London servant had a rarely contested right to clothing. This may have been part of the livery or it may have been 'castings'. The degree to which clothing was exchanged, both as payment for service and within the street markets, affected techniques of stitchery: 'As little stitching as possible was done so that the expensive material

---

[56] Anon., *A Trip from St James's to the Royal Exchange* (1744).
[57] The Ordinary's *Account*, 2 May 1707, 19 September 1712, 20 May 1728, 5 March 1733, 21 December 1739, 24 November 1740, 18 March 1740, 7 November 1744 and 10 March 1735.

could more easily be unpicked to make up again.'[58] Clothing represented a store of wealth for many people: the circuit of clothing might intersect with circuits of money. Adam Smith noted this in *The Wealth of Nations*: 'The old clothes which another bestows upon him, he exchanges for other old clothes which suit him better, or for lodging, or for food, or for money, with which he can buy either food, clothes, or lodging, as he has occasion.' Similar notions, less abstractly presented, were chalked onto the walls of the condemned cell in Newgate by John Tarlton. Besides being a poet, he was an unemployed bricklayer who once had work rebuilding the Sessions House at the Old Bailey.

> Poverty God D——m you, what makes you haunt me so,
> I han't one Grigg [$\frac{1}{4}$d.] to help myself you know:
> Neither Shirt, Shoe, nor Hose,
> For I have pawn'd my Cloaths:
> I han't a Coat upon my Back,
> No, nor by G——d but half a Hat,
> Both Day and Night, thus Maxims runs,
> Forc'd to Eat dry crusts, instead of butter'd Buns.[59]

Clothing, with its utilities, wealth and fashion, appears to have been a larger and more prevalent circuit than that of any other eighteenth-century material, including money, as flipping through a stack of indictment bills for any gaol delivery sessions would confirm. Thus, in the Middlesex Sessions of April 1740 the misappropriated goods included: a silk night-gown, 7 gallons of cherry beer, a coat, a waistcoat, a pair of leather breeches, a linen apron, 2 flaxen sheets, a pair of buttons, a silver spoon, a cloth coat, a linen sheet, a cambric mob, 10 lbs. of roast beef, $1\frac{1}{2}$ lbs. of mutton, a damask tablecloth, a ream of paper, 3 pts. of rum, a quilted petticoat, a pair of slippers, 3 linen cloaks, 5 holland caps, 6 pairs of worsted stockings, a copper saucepan, 6 brass rings, a silver watch – and this is but a fraction of it.[60] Those whose customary income was in clothing and fabric had to have knowledge of the social networks by which clothing could be converted into lodging, food or money. 'Where Ladies govern there are secrets, and where there are secrets there are vails. I lived with a lady once who used to give her cloaths away every month,' Henry Fielding wrote.

★

[58] Anne Buck, *Dress in Eighteenth Century England* (1979), p. 160.
[59] *The Wealth of Nations* (1776) I, ii; the Ordinary's *Account*, 24 May 1736.
[60] MRO, 'Gaol Delivery Roll, 16 April 1740', MJ/GSR 2735.

A song warns us against fastidious distinctions between custom and law; it is a song that has its origins in the older melodies of English communism. The songstress is a servant.

> I furnish'd all my rooms, every one, every one
> I furnish'd all my rooms, every one
> I furnish'd all my rooms with mops, brushes, and hair brooms
> Wash balls and sweet perfumes, them I stole, them I stole.

> I sail'd up Holborn Hill, in a cart, in a cart
> I sail'd up Holborn Hill, in a cart.
> I sail'd up Holborn Hill, at St Giles's drunk my fill
> And at Tyburn made my will, in a cart, in a cart.

Thus a halfpenny ballad explains the how and who of those immaculate interiors that Gainsborough or Reynolds rendered in their academic hues. Here there are no nicely discerned distinctions between vails and perquisites. Wash balls and sweet perfumes, the guardians against London stink, were simply stolen. Yet, we also note the answer, thrice repeated, to the question, whose rooms? Theft and private property become two sides of a coin. The ironic morality would have been clear to anyone hearing the song, as it was to Francis Place (who recorded it), and explains why the associations against republicans and Levellers of the 1790s so vigorously prosecuted those singing ballads 'in praise of thieving and getting drunk'. The answer in bitter irony had been supplied fifty years earlier:

> But Property must be, Save the Queen, Save the Queen
> Allow'd in each degree, Save the Queen.
> And some were there that saw,
> Who have sworn to mend this flaw
> By force of common law, Save the Queen, Save the Queen.

And behind these lines, going back still earlier, we can detect 'The Digger Song' of the English Revolution, with its eleven stanzas against the landlords, the lawyers, the priests and Cavaliers:

> You noble Diggers all, stand up now, stand up now,
> You noble Diggers all, stand up now,
> The wast land to maintain, seeing Cavaliers by name
> Your digging does disdaine, and persons all defame,
> Stand up now, stand up now.

CHAPTER EIGHT

Silk Makes the Difference

Their Laws and Cloaths were equally
Objects of Mutability;
For, what was well done for a Time,
In half a year became a Crime.

Bernard Mandeville, *The Fable of the Bees* (1714)

Whether the very shreds shorn from woollen cloth, which are thrown away in Ireland, do not make a beautiful tapestry in France?

George Berkeley, *The Querist* (1735)

I

If the seventeenth century were the 'Age of Wool' and the nineteenth century the 'Age of Cotton', then the eighteenth was the 'Age of Silk'. It was the fabric of power and class command. Gainsborough painted not people so much as displays of silken extravagance. The painter's point of view requires us to look up to these subjects whose hands grasp or fondle the fabric, and whose lips seem to say: 'I have, thou hast not.' A single dress might cost £50 in materials alone.

We may contrast the consumer and the producer. The consumers were the ladies strolling in St James's Park, adorned in cascades of silk contrived with cuffs, flounces and bows to capture the wandering eye. Or they were the gentlemen in their silk stockings and waistcoats, their brocaded jackets and silken knee-breeches, bowing and scraping into lordly favour, awaiting the moment to give a command of battle or to sign a death warrant. The producer is rarely seen, but must be imagined: tens of thousands of men, women and children massed on the other side of London, winding, throwing, dyeing, weaving, drawing, cutting, designing, stitching in hundreds of attics and garrets down the alleys of Spitalfields and Bethnal Green, whose magistrates kept a close watch upon their alehouses – the Crown and Shuttle, the Mulberry Tree, the Three Jolly Weavers, the Throwers Arms, the Dyers Arms, the eight taverns called the Weavers Arms, and the three called the Robin

Hood and Little John.[1] A proverb summarized the contrast: 'We are all Adam's children, but silk makes the difference.'

There were two opposing standards of consumption in the eighteenth century. The first was a subsistence that bordered upon starvation. The second consisted of the 'superfluities' that distinguished rank, which 'habit and education' made necessary. Each was necessary to the other: poverty, subordination and humility confronted riches, domination and pride. One was an 'animal oeconomy' and the other was 'political necessary', as the moralists expressed it.[2]

Sixty-four of the men and women hanged at Tyburn for whom we have biographical records were silk-workers – winders, throwsters, dyers, but mostly weavers. Of all apprenticed victims hanged at Tyburn, the weavers were the most numerous, comprising almost 10 per cent of the sub-sample. In relation to other trade-specific surveys of London workers, this was not unusual. The records of bonded migrants to the Atlantic colonies and the taxed indentures of apprentices also make it clear that the silk-worker had a prominent place among the hundreds of London crafts and trades. That most of the hanged apprenticed workers were weavers indicates nothing more than the numerical importance of weavers within the London working class as a whole. These statistics suggest that silk-weavers were neither more nor less likely to be hanged than workers in other trades. Silk-workers were neither a crimogenic population, nor one that was more law-abiding than others.

If we introduce other evidence, such as that of indictment levels, the conclusion needs modification. Comparing the ratio of indictments to population in 1740, we find that some of the silk parishes like Shoreditch (1:222) or St Luke's (1:295) had ratios greater than the average for London as a whole, while others like St George's-in-the-East (1:532) or Spitalfields (1:739) had ratios substantially less than the London average. If we compare the two kinds of criminal statistics (the hanged and the indicted), we can obtain for the different London parishes a kind of punishment indicator. The percentage of indictments in 1740 in Spitalfields (2 per cent) was far less than the percentage of those from this parish who were hanged (9 per cent). A similar discrepancy in percentage between indictments and

---

[1] MRO, 'A Register or Kalender of All the Innkeepers . . . of the Tower Division . . . Sept. 1770', MR/LV, 8/68 (a–c).

[2] Sir James Steuart, *An Inquiry into the Principles of Political Oeconomy*, ed. A. S. Skinner, vol. i (Edinburgh, 1966), p. 270.

hangings may also be found in Clerkenwell, Aldgate and White-chapel – other parochial suburbs with concentrations of silk manu-facturing. However, in St Giles-in-the-Fields, St Martin-in-the-Fields, and St James's, Westminster, the percentage of indictments was greater than the percentage of the hanged. This difference suggests that the authorities were more prone to use hangings to intimidate the textile suburbs than the parishes of central London. The silk-fabricating parishes needed more frequent and drastic teach-ing from the Tyburn podium.

Tyburnography reveals some other features. Sixty per cent of the silk-weavers hanged at Tyburn between 1703 and 1772 were born in London (38), and of these 75 per cent (28) were from the north-east silk districts. Of those born outside London, 14 (22 per cent) were from Ireland (Dublin mainly) and 10 (16 per cent) were from France or of French parents. The remainder were from the Midlands or East Anglia. Tyburnography thus shows an element of migration and the international organization of the silk labour market. Thir-teen (20 per cent) of the hanged weavers had been in the Army, Navy or merchant marine; thus a substantial proportion of the population was well-travelled. It was also a young population: 10 (16 per cent) of the hanged weavers were teenagers and 46 (two-thirds) were hanged before their thirtieth birthday. The crimes for which they were hanged were mainly crimes of the mis-appropriation of property: 1 for horse-stealing, 1 for counterfeiting, 2 for stealing from a dwelling-house, 2 for privily stealing, 11 for burglary and 30 for robbery. Otherwise, the hanged weavers included 2 convicted of rape, 8 of murder, 2 for infanticide and 4 for returning too early from transportation.

The poverty of the weavers is what we first notice from the evidence of the hanged. Thomas Beck, hanged in 1732, had worked as a weaver's drawboy, earning 3s. a week. John Lancaster, hanged in 1748, was a journeyman velvet-weaver. He asked the Ordinary of Newgate: 'What signified working all Day for a Trifle?' Richard Quail, hanged in 1741, leaving a widow and orphan, was 'brought into great straits by the hard weather last year'. A year later James Buquois was hanged. He explained that 'when the Weaving Business was slack ... he was out of Work'. Michael Grant, also hanged in 1742, worked for several masters, leaving each every four to six months. Before disaster struck him, he had only just left his last master in a wages dispute. John Ross, hanged in 1750, took to highway robbery, 'having no way to get Money' for his wife and three children. Even notorious rogues like Black Isaac (Isaac Ashley), a man whose skill in stealing handkerchiefs was legendary, 'must have something to subsist on', as the Ordinary observed. It perhaps may be allowed that poverty was the background to Joseph Philip's crime (murder): this melancholy man 'did it only to be hang'd, for he mightily long'd to die'.[3] Tom Paine's comment applies:

A world of little cases are continually arising, which busy or affluent life knows not of, to open the first door to distress. Hunger is not among the postponable of wants, and a day, even a few hours, in such a condition, is often the crisis of a life of ruin. These circumstances, which are the general cause of the little thefts and pilferings that lead to greater, may be prevented.[4]

Wages in the silk industry varied considerably. The boys who wound the silk for the weavers received very little indeed, a few shillings a week at most, and a significant amount of silk was wound for no remuneration at all in the London workhouses. The silk was spun or 'thrown' by women employed in mills by the master throwsters, who 'give but small wages'. Journeymen weavers might earn anywhere from 5s. or 8s. a week — as among the London ribbon-weavers — to 18s. or a guinea a week, as among the more skilled branches of the trade. These rates assumed constant employment, and do not include working expenses such as the hire of drawboys and quill-winders, candles or the loom. In velvet-weaving, rent for the loom was 1s. a week. Statistically accurate averages of wages are impossible to obtain because there was so much variation in the kind of work, and in the rates different masters paid. Nevertheless, it would be safe to agree with the author of *The Parent's Directory* (1761), who wrote: 'The wages of weavers in general are but poor.' Yet we cannot leave the matter there, without mentioning two further considerations of decisive importance to the cycles of struggles led by the weavers.[5]

First, the wage appeared to be a price paid by the master to the

---

[3]For these hanged malefactors see the Ordinary's *Account* for the following hangings: 22 May 1732, 28 October 1748, 18 March 1741, 13 January 1742, 12 July 1742, 31 December 1750, 20 May 1728 and 1 August 1712.
[4]Thomas Paine, *The Rights of Man* (1791), ed. Henry Collins (1976), p. 268.
[5]For sources providing evidence about wage rates see R. Campbell, *The London Tradesman* (1747), and N. K. A. Rothstein, 'The Silk Industry in London, 1702–1766', MA thesis, University of London, 1960.

putting-out merchant for the finished piece, so the definition of the 'piece' was a crucial question. It was both a qualitative and a quantitative problem. The three basic weaves (plain, twill, satin), when applied to the variety of silk threads and other fabrics sometimes mixed with the silk, produced an astonishing variety of fabrics – mantuas, serges, satins, velvets, damasks, brocades, etc. – each of which had a customary price (a price list composed by the journeymen in 1768 was twenty-seven pages long). Agreement about what measure constituted a piece was not simple either, since the standards of measure were sometimes in dispute. The half-ell, for instance, might vary between 19 and 21 ins. It was not until 1806, Samuel Sholl tells us, that the yard was paid for at 37 ins.[6] Disputes took two major forms – those about the price of the pieces and those about their size (which determined what was 'wasted').

The weaver's work (and hence his ability to complete it quickly) depended upon other workers. Some were under his nose, others across the sea. Drawboys helped adjust the shifting heddles for complex patterns and quill-winders kept the shuttles full. The indidivual weaver could control such cooperation, but the supply of weft thread or 'shute' he could not. A weaver might spend much time in setting up his loom and the organzine thread of his warp for the design supplied by the pattern-maker ('building the harnesses' as it was called), and yet after such unproductive labour, he might have to wait several days for the dyer or the throwster to supply the weft. The absence of a smooth proportionality (throwing to dyeing to weaving) in what was technically a homogeneous manufacture was the result of several factors, including (1) the mixture of modes of production (domestic for weaving, the mill for throwing); (2) changes of fashion and the increasing multitude of fabrics; and (3) the uncertainties attendant on the international supply of raw silk.

Many of the hanged weavers were either born in France or were children of French parents. French Peter was born in Poitou, a weaver and a soldier, who was hanged for stealing some India

---

[6] Daniel Defoe, *A Plan of English Commerce* (1722), p. 293 provides some information about customary lengths and widths of silk pieces. Samuel Sholl's is one of the few autobiographies of a Spitalfields weaver, *A Short Historical Account of the Silk Manufacture in England with a Sketch of the First 58 Years of His Life* (1811), p. 6.

curtains; Stephen Delaforce, a weaver and a weaver's son, was hanged for returning from transportation; Judith Defour, a Spital-fields winder and daughter of a French weaver, was hanged for infanticide; Peter Merchie, a journeyman weaver, son of French parents, for stealing a half-guinea. The Parliamentary Committee of 1765 investigating the silk industry was fully aware that London and France belonged, in respect of wages and recruitment, to the same labour market, and heard evidence provided by those who had worked on both sides of the Channel.[7]

An important portion of the hanged weavers were from areas either of declining textile production such as East Anglia, or from the Midlands where the mix of different kinds of textile-making was being reorganized. From the former area came William Bol-ingbroke, a Norwich man with three children, and whose wife dealt at Rag Fair. From the latter area came William Kite (a silk-dyer from Wolverton), Henry Chaplin (a ribbon-weaver from Warwickshire), John Cooper (a Worcester weaver), Ann Ellard (a Nottinghamshire stocking-weaver) and James Aldridge (a Manchester weaver). Daniel Defoe noted that the wage struggles of East Anglia resulted in the migration of many unemployed weavers to London.[8] Several of these hanged malefactors were familiar with textile practices around Coventry, a place that was connected to Spitalfields by both the technical division of labour and by a workers' exchange of materials.

Irish workers were the most numerous of the non-London-born Spitalfields weavers: James Falconer, a Dublin weaver who had lived in France; Philip Murray, a Dublin broadcloth-weaver; John Singleton, an Ulster weaver who worked with his father in London; Richard Quail from Cork; Andrew Macmanus, a silk-thread-maker and dyer; John Burnham, a Dublin silk-weaver caught up in a press-gang riot; James Mallone, a Dublin man sent to London by his master; Dennis Brennan, an Irish weaver hanged for stealing a hat; William Purcel, an Irish weaver who pawned his tools to buy gin; Patrick Roney, a Dublin silk-weaver hanged for stealing a

---

[7] For the hanged weavers of Huguenot extraction, see the Ordinary's *Account*, 25 October 1704, 26 October 1720, 8 March 1734 and 9 July 1734.

[8] ibid., 22 December 1738, 17 December 1707, 28 September 1727, 22 November 1742, 18 May 1743 and 7 February 1750. Daniel Defoe stressed this area of recruitment of the weavers in *Giving Alms No Charity* (1704) and in *The Review*, 20 March 1705.

portmanteau; Hannah Dagoe, who worked for her husband and was hanged for robbing a silk-broker.[9]

A portion of the hanged weavers were veterans of army and naval life. French Peter fought in the 2nd Regiment of Foot Guards in King William's wars. John Thompson had served before the mast in Queen Anne's navy. Nathaniel Jackson served four years on Irish garrison duty. Henry Chaplin fought in the Army during the Rebellion of 1715. John Fosset spent four years at sea. James Aldridge served in the 3rd Regiment of Guards. Such service exposed the weavers to the risks of world-wide imperialism. Thus, John Dixon was at the taking of Havana in 1762 when a third of the Spanish fleet was destroyed and the loot was allotted according to rank, an admiral receiving £122,000 and a common seaman £3. John Ward, a gauze-weaver, a married man, often in the workhouse, took part in the lucrative seizure of Senegal in 1758 when plunder valued at more than £250,000 was taken. He was hanged for stealing a watch. Ward had also served five years with the East India Company. James Naylor, a Spitalfields weaver, was hanged for a murder that resulted from a dispute about 'pilfering' in the house where he lived and worked his loom. He too had been a soldier for five years in the service of the Company.[10]

The heterogeneous and cosmopolitan experience of the London silk-workers was related to the demise of the London Company of Weavers, whose authority to determine craft and trade conditions was undermined by the growth of silk-weaving suburbs in the north-east of London outside its jurisdiction. The increasing complexity of the industry's structure gave illegal interlopers or capitalist entrepreneurs new opportunities of manœuvre. The putting-out system permitted the dispersal of production to obscure holes and corners of the suburbs, and also encouraged the practice of taking out-of-door apprentices, 'learners' and 'unlawful boys, girls, journeymen and the like', whose conditions of work and living were oppressive and who were used, according to M. Dorothy George, to reduce the wages and prolong the hours of indoor apprentices

[9] The Ordinary's *Account,* 3 March 1737, 26 May 1738, 7 May 1740, 18 March 1741, 4 May 1741, 12 July 1742, 11 November 1751, 7 February 1750, 26 March 1750, 4 May 1763.
[10] Ibid., 4 May 1722, 18 September 1727, 8 November 1738, 24 May 1736, 7 February 1750, 11 June 1764, 13 February 1765, 29 May 1753.

and lawful journeymen.[11] The youths and 'unlawful' workers were subject to direct coercions within the parish and within the work-houses, many of which produced thrown or wound silk by unpaid labour. Joshua Gee built his fortune from workhouses of this type. Edmund Gilbert, a Bethnal Green master weaver, took 'friendless charity children' as apprentices. He was hanged in 1745 for beating one of them to death.[12]

The weavers would not be controlled by 'market mechanisms' governed by wages. Mandeville wrote in 1723:[13]

Everybody knows that there is a vast number of Journeymen Weavers ... who, if by four Days Labour in a Week they can maintain themselves, will hardly be perswaded to work the fifth; When Men shew such an extraordinary proclivity to Idleness and Pleasure, what reason have we to think that they would ever work ...

Defoe wrote:

[Y]ou cannot with safety hire a Workman by the Day, to almost any kind of Business, unless your Eye be upon him, not only part, but even all the time of his work.

Theirs is a one-sided view: what was 'idleness' to them was civilization to others. Thelwall remembered the pidgeons and tulips, so carefully tended on Mondays, that became the basis of the Columbarian Society and the Floricultural Society. The study of nature's microcosms, so prevalent in Spitalfields, was the seed-bed whence sprang le goût anglais, under such designers as Dandridge, Vansommer, Anna Maria Garthwaite and Phoebe Wright. The idleness was the basis too of the weavers' contributions to mathematics (Middleton, Dolland, Simpson) as well as the creation of their intricate madrigals. Patience, intricacy, concentration were alike the qualities of their labour and their idleness.[14]

---

[11] M. Dorothy George, op. cit., pp. 192–5. See also Alfred Plummer, The London Weavers' Company 1600–1970 (1972).
[12] The Ordinary's Account, 7 June 1745.
[13] The Fable of the Bees, p. 208.
[14] The Tribune, vol. xxix, 23 September 1795, quoted in E. P. Thompson, The Making of the English Working Class (1963), p. 43; Handloom Weavers' Commission, vol. ii (1840), p. 216; Natalie Rothstein, Spitalfields Silks, Victoria and Albert Museum (1975).

II

'Put a miller, a weaver and a tailor in a bag, and shake them; the first that comes out will be a thief.' 'To be as thick as thieves' meant exactly the same as to be 'as thick as inkle-weavers', for the inkle (or ribbon-weaver) worked on a very narrow loom. It was Lord Kames, the Scottish jurist, who transformed such wisdom into an axiom in his anthropology – mankind's 'remarkable propensity for appropriation'.[15] To Mandeville no trade or calling was without its cheats or deceits 'legitimated by custom'.[16] 'There are some latitudes,' wrote Defoe, 'like poetical licences in other cases, which a Tradesman is and must be allow'd, and which by the custom and usage of trade he may give himself a liberty in,' and yet 'pass with me for a very honest man'. These customs, latitudes or cheats arose either between the merchant and the master to whom the silk was put out for work, or between the master and his workers. Allowance was made for waste, or negotiated in either case.

The techniques of production appeared to be highly wasteful. In the throwing of silk 'the Waste of every pound of Raw Silk of 24 ounces is 4 in Winding, 5 in boiling, & 2 in Manufacturing', eleven ounces in all. In thrown silk of 15 ounces to the pound it is 6, 'viz. 4 by boiling and 2 in Manufacturing'. The waste of boiling that separated the gum from the filature was also significant. Once thrown and wound there was further waste in warping. It was computed in 1765 that '16 Ounces do not produce above 10 Ounces for the Loom'.[17] The throwsters' wastes consisted of filaments that were too short or knotted or otherwise unfit for doubling. The throwster appropriating such wastes had to turn the bunched and twisted skeins into reels for ferrets, stockings, garters and fringes, and this became a labour-intensive sub-trade. These wastes or – to give them their technical names – the noils, pinions and flocks might not undergo further labour but be used or sold as locks and tufts for quilting, stuffing of cushions and mattresses, or for the sizing of paper. Various wastes arose from the labour of weaving: there would be fents (remnants), whose size would depend on how the weaving was cut from the loom; thrums were the unwoven threads that attached the warp to the beam and could be anywhere from 9

[15] *Sketches of the History of Man* (Edinburgh, 1788), vol i, p. 117.
[16] Mandeville, op. cit., p. 64.
[17] *JHC*, vol. xxx (March 1765), pp. 208–19.

to 30 ins. in length. These wastes, in fact, had a great many uses. Carpets, rugs, quilts, mops, handkerchiefs, scarves, muffs, dressings for wounds, children's clothing, puppets, dolls, sailors' caps and May bonnets were made from them. If the weaver and family could not find a use for the fents and thrums, they could be sold, entering into a thick circuit of silk materials.

Wastes were exchanged at one of the plebeian markets for used clothing, the chief market being Rag Fair. Ned Ward, the West End wag, left a description of his walk there from Well Close Square. 'A little draggle-tail flat-cap' informed him it opened daily at two, when all the rag-pickers of town come to rake the dunghills of 'old shreds and patches'. The 'ragged regiments' came 'to barter scraps for patches'. Two pence or threepence was counted 'as considerable takings'. Cryers of old satin, taffeta or velvet, those swapping earthenware for old clothing, purveyors of pancakes and dumplings gathered in the afternoons in huge throngs. 'It was very current to change food for raiment, that is, such needful repairs as a beggar's breeches may want between the legs, or his coat at armpits or elbows.' The better clothes were kept hidden away for customers with 'ready money'. It was a largely moneyless economy. A whalebone salesman at the market was murdered by his wife, Susannah Broom, when he refused to contribute to the weekly rent of sixpence. Moneyless exchanges were called 'blood for blood'. The cant talk of Rag Fair inverted the usual price form: 'rag' meant farthing, and 'thrums' meant threepence.[18] Here 'pilferers' fenced their goods, such as James Cropp, the silk-dyer, or Michael Bewley, the handkerchief-weaver, who were both hanged at Tyburn.[19] Several times, according to Ned Ward, the magistracy attempted to suppress the market, but without success.

If the circuit of rags found its headquarters in Rag Fair, it drew upon networks that were nationwide. 'Large-scale dealers during the mid 1770s developed a regular market in Spitalfields ... for work materials embezzled and otherwise stolen from Norwich,' Professor Styles informs us.[20] In the silk division of labour, Coventry

---

[18] The Ordinary's *Account*, 21 December 1739. 'Great Britain, apart from its own immense store of rags, is the emporium for the rag trade of the whole world': Karl Marx, *Capital*, trans. Ben Fawkes, vol. i (1976), pp. 467–8. Rag-pickers were the medium for the spread of smallpox and other infectious diseases, as the nineteenth-century investigations into public health discovered.

[19] The Ordinary's *Account*, 18 May 1743 and 13 April 1743.

[20] John Styles, 'Embezzlement, Industry and the Law in England, 1500–1800', in

occupied an important position that was connected to London by pedlars and 'macklers' on the one hand and by swift coaches called 'machines' on the other. John Hewitt, an alderman, magistrate and thief-taker of Coventry, recorded some of the examinations he took in the mid 1760s.[21] John Carmichael turned evidence against some Coventry ribbon-weavers. He travelled around the weaving villages selling scissors and knives for silk ribbons. A pair of scissors and a shilling would buy four yards of figured ribbons. Five pairs of scissors were exchanged for 'about nine yards of love ribbons'. A single pair of scissors equalled two yards of sarsnet shot. Carrying on transactions such as these, he was able to turn evidence against ten people.

They characterized the transactions in interesting ways. Robert Serjeant exchanged a parcel of ribbon that he had woven from silk received from Messrs Clay & Lowe, 'but being soiled, or otherwise damaged, he kept it for his own use'. Richard Hemersely exchanged four yards of ribbon woven from silk received from Messrs Sherwood & Reynolds, but it was silk that was made by a 'learner'. Crew and Wale said on oath that since they had paid full value for the silk put out to them, there could be no question of embezzlement. Wale's son, William, agreed that he had sold a couple of yards of tenpenny sarsnet, but he had woven them himself from the overlayings in the warp. William Dennis sold small amounts of ribbons made from the silk put out to him, but it was done only to make up for deficiencies in their weighing. William Canbrill said that Carmichael had come to his house, that he did exchange some ribbon for 'a couple of knives', and that 'the silk which the same was made of, he had from Messrs Wilsons and other quantities to manufacture and work up, which he considered no crime. Farther this examinant saith not.' Pry and badger as he would, Hewitt could not draw the weavers any further. They kept their silence and their notions of labour and property to themselves. The petty officers and constables took their side, and it was only with difficulty and increases in pay that they agreed to execute the sentence of whipping.[22] Thomas Bayliss, convicted of 'embezzlement', was given 'a stroke or two on his back with his clothes on'.

Maxine Berg, Pat Hudson and Michael Sonenscher (eds), *Manufacture in Town and Country before the Factory* (Cambridge, 1983), p. 179.
[21] *A Journal of the Proceedings of J. Hewitt,* 2nd edn (1790).
[22] J. Hewitt, *Proceedings on the Silk Act* (1791), pp. 355–9.

The dispersion of production, inherent to the putting-out system, whether in the suburbs of London or in the countryside, required transport to bring together the components of fabrication. The people who did this, with stout shoes and amiable manner, were macklers, walking morts, bawdy baskets, chapmen, swigmen, brush toyles, Manchestermen, end-gatherers and the flashman who spoke in 'a sort of slang or canting dialect'. This itinerant population straddled the money economy and the economy of 'blood for blood'. From 1698 Parliament attempted to license them at the Board of Trade (£4 for pedestrians, £8 for mounted dealers). The Board hired ten country riding surveyors and two town surveyors to monitor the itinerant population. They were instructed to keep a book and send weekly reports to London. In 1771 the Board of Trade licensed 371 mounted pedlars and 1,207 pedlars and chapmen who went on foot. By the mid-eighteenth century turnpikes began to replace the pedlars' byways, and London was connected to Coventry by an enclosed, rattling coach, driven by a team of fast horses that conquered the distance with astonishing speed – the Coventry Machine. In February 1765 its proprietor went to see Alderman Hewitt to show him a package that he had received from a journeyman silk-dyer's wife. Hewitt opened it and found thirty-three ounces of silk. Hewitt discovered that for several years the coach had been used to convey illicit silk in Coventry to dyers, dealers and weavers in Shoreditch and Spitalfields. In the trials that followed – a result of the cooperation between Hewitt in Coventry and John Fielding in London – the journeyman weaver in Coventry was burnt-in-the-hand, a master silk-dyer was acquitted, and another London dyer was transported. The effectiveness of police, the change in the mode of transportation and the mounting pressures upon the domestic journeyman signified a change in the class dynamics of silk production. Parallel to these developments were legislative changes.

III

Three Acts at the end of the seventeenth century proscribed misappropriations in the silk industry. The preamble to the Silk Throwsters Act of 1662 stated the problem:

Whereas there is a necessity lying upon the silkthrowers, to deliver to their winders or doublers considerable quantities of silk, which being of a good value, is by evil-disposed persons many times unjustly, deceitfully, and falsely purloined, imbezilled, pawn'd, sold and detained ...

'Said persons' were to be punished with having to make restitution of the goods 'damnified'; otherwise they were to be put in the stocks or whipped. The Winders and Doublers Act of 1668 punished such offenders with imprisonment. In 1697 a third Act extended the legislation to include the misappropriations of 'agents, journeymen, and warpers'.[23] In the eighteenth century such legislation was further enlarged to include other materials and other stages of the labour process. The Weft and Thrum Act of 1701 prescribed fourteen days of hard labour in the house of correction for false reeling or taking wefts, thrums or ends. It also prohibited truck payment to workers. An Act of 1726 suggested that legislators knew that technological factors made these offences possible, and tried to regulate them by setting limits on the length of the warping bar for the main types of cloth, and by defining the extent of the allowed over-measure: 'the thrums at the end of the warping bars shall not exceed eighteen inches.' In weighing out the wool, the Act stated that the pound should consist of sixteen ounces. Finally, the Act prohibited the weaver from using ends, wefts, flocks or pinions for any sort of goods whatsoever.[24] An Act of 1740 extended this legislation further to materials that had 'actually been wrought, made up, or manufactured'.

The Bugging Act of 1749 and the Worsted Act of 1771 attempted to determine the interval between putting out materials and their return – twenty-one days under the former, and eight under the latter. Powers of search were increased by both Acts. Ordinary tasks of the labour process such as sweeping out the room, snipping weft ends, tying up the warp to the beam, became potentially criminal offences. The Worsted Act extended the legal definition of 'receiver' to anyone buying thrums. This legislation, comprehensive as it appears, was largely ineffective.

Struggle over the appropriation of the materials of labour was endemic in the eighteenth-century clothing and weaving districts. Julia de Lacy Mann, the historian of the West Country weavers,

[23] 13 & 14 Charles II, c. 15 (1662), 20 Charles II, c. 6 (1668), 8 & 9 William III, c. 36 (1697).
[24] 13 George I, c. 23 (1726).

found that embezzlement was 'almost universally practised by weavers who worked in their own homes'. Josiah Tucker, the ecclesiastical spokesman of the West Country merchants, complained about it frequently, associating the practice with the loafing, skulking habits of the weavers and the 'underground' markets of embezzled yarn or 'slinge'. In East Anglia, following the Peace of Utrecht, disputes over waste, truck payment, false reeling and short-weighting resulted in a continuous series of disturbances. During the 1750s in Manchester and Stockport the people resisted attempts to punish those found guilty of 'embezzlement'. In 1758 check-weavers went on strike, demanding standardized lengths for their pieces in order to prevent the false measuring practised by the putting-out masters. An historian of the English silk industry shows that it was the difficulty of removing these 'illicit practices' from the industry in London that led those in the silk-stocking trade to remove their capital to the Midlands. The mere enactment of statutes does not establish the reality that the law intends, yet for a historian it is from judicial records that much of our evidence comes. A perusal of these led M. Dorothy George to the conclusion that in London 'the silk was constantly being "embezzled"'. Such cases are frequent and suggestive in their ambiguities.

At the Old Bailey in August 1723, John Simpson and William Strettam of St Bride's were indicted for 'feloniously stealing' 6 lbs. of thread valued at 30s. 'It appeared by the Evidence, that the Prisoners were Employ'd as Servants to beat the Thread, and took Opportunity to steal it.' In May 1715 Mary Rogers was indicted for stealing 6 skeins of linen yarn in St Leonard's, Shoreditch.

It appear'd by the Evidence, that several Goods having been lost before, and these hanging out to whiten, the Ground was narrowly watch'd, and the Prisoner (who was a Servant to Mr Smith) was seen to take the yarn off; and being taken, it was found ty'd round her Middle under her Petticoat. She said she had wrought several Years for Mr Smith, and never did him any harm; and that her Accusers are worse then she,

The jury found her guilty of petty larceny only, and she was whipped. In October 1721 Elizabeth Miller of St Peter's Cheap was indicted for 'feloniously stealing 1 Ell of Silk value 6s. and 5 Yards of Cambrick value £3 in the Dwelling-House of John Davenport'. Davenport's wife deposed 'that the Prisoner lodg'd in their House, and that she [the wife] brought Home the piece of Silk ... About a Fortnight after, she saw the Prisoner offer it to Mrs Shudal behind

St Clement's Church.' She offered it for sale as a remnant. The jury found her guilty only to the value of 4s. 10d., so she was branded, not transported.[25]

The other two centres of silk production, France and Italy, experienced similar problems. In Lyons, London's sister city in silk production, the merchants' attempts to wrest from the weavers and throwsters the right to discarded thread caused popular revolts in 1744 and 1751. When Vaucanson led a technological attempt to abolish it, he was assaulted and stoned by the Lyons workers. In revenge he swore to design a machine 'by means of which an ass [could weave] a piece of flowered silk'.[26] In the Po Valley Italian silks were produced by workers far removed from the silk factories. The struggle to replace piece-rates with time-wages began at the end of the seventeenth century. Mills were opened, and mechanization became more advanced. The workers' right to the discard consequently was more uncertain than in England. But the lesson common to all three centres of European silk production was that criminalization by itself was not enough to combat the customary rights of appropriation.[27] Mechanical, organizational and geographical strategies were necessary accompaniments to strictly legal prohibitions.

IV

The 'insurrections', 'mutinies' and 'tumults' of the 1760s caused the pattern of investments in textiles to change fundamentally, as technological and architectural solutions were sought to the problems of working-class 'idleness' and 'dishonesty'. These 'tumults' also placed the system of police spying and ministerial invigilation under severe pressure, raising serious issues concerning liberty and the constitution; a theatre of terror and counter-terror in the location and manner of capital punishment was grimly played out in the London streets. The disorder forced the ruling class to consider the rate of exploitation and the methods of increasing surplus value,

[25] *The Proceedings*, May 1715, October 1721 and August 1723.
[26] Shelby T. McCloy, *French Inventions of the 18th Century* (Lexington, Kentucky, 1952), p. 98.
[27] Carlo Poni, 'Misura contro Misura: Come il Filo di Seta divenne Sottile e Rotondo', *Quaderni Storici,* no. 47 (August 1981), pp. 385–422.

and to discuss the rule of law within the various modes of production that during the decade came under the command of English banks and flags

By August 1762 the Spitalfields weavers had composed their first 'Book' of prices. For the next ten years this would be the social contract, supplying a standard against which their petitions to Parliament, demonstrations, marches and organizations could be measured. It was to force compliance with it that community humiliations, such as charivaries and stonings, and direct industrial sabotage were practised. In 1763, 2,000 weavers, armed with cutlasses and in disguise, proceeded to those looms working at underrates and cut the work from them. Thousands of copies of the Book were distributed. Several times the military was called out and detachments of the Guards were sent into Spitalfields to suppress the weavers. In 1764 several thousand poor weavers marched from Spitalfields to St James's, Westminster to petition King and Parliament for higher wages and against foreign imports of finished silks. In 1765 the harvest was poor and food prices rose. The workhouses in Spitalfields and Bethnal Green were overcrowded. A committee of journeymen found that 1,382 looms had been idled, and four times that many weavers were without work or pay. In 1766 Parliament prohibited the import of foreign silks and made it a felony without benefit of clergy to cut work from a loom (6 Geo. III, c. 28). None the less, the cuttings continued against weavers 'Breaking the Book'. By 1768 the workforce in silk had been reduced to 40 or 50 per cent of what it had been six years earlier. Government informers were active in the silk districts. The journeymen clubs became more effective in enforcing compliance with the Book (now twenty-seven pages long). The cuttings and charivaries continued. In 1769 weavers were setting their own prices in the food markets. Hundreds of looms were destroyed. Striking workers in other trades now joined the weavers. Armed clashes and open gunfire burst out between detachments of the Guards and the journeymen clubs. Increasing numbers of families were without food, without raiment, and without fire.[28]

[28] This summary of the silk-weavers' struggles during the 1760s depends upon N. K. A. Rothstein, op. cit.; Henry C. Randall, 'Public Disorder in England and Wales, 1765–1775', Ph.D. Thesis, University of North Carolina (1963); the press, particularly *Berrow's Worcester Journal*, *The Middlesex Journal*, *The Annual Register*

These 'tumults' took place against a background of worldwide rebellion. To the London weavers events in Bengal were of immediate material interest. The Battle of Plassey (1757) was the turning-point in the transition from merchant trading to the direct command over Bengali labour. In 1761 Pondicherry surrendered. In 1763 Mir Kasim was defeated. In 1764 Hector Munro suppressed a strike among sepoys by setting four 6-pounders on them. Twenty-four were killed.[29] In 1765 the East India Company obtained the *diwan*, enabling it to gather directly the Bengal revenues, thus replacing the Mogul Empire as the supreme sovereignty. In the same year Robert Clive instituted 'cruelties that hitherto stand perhaps unparalleled in the records of nations'. The husbandmen in this 'paradise of India' paid half their crop in rents. The castes of weavers and winders of silk suffered a fall in wages and incarceration in the 'factories' of Dacca and Murshidabad, as well as imprisonment, flogging and bond slavery, against which sometimes the only form of resistance was self-mutilation of thumbs and fingers.[30] The Company's policies caused the first imperialist famine in 1769; a third of the population perished. In the same year the amounts of raw silk imported into England from Bengal reached about 700,000 lbs., almost double the average imports of any previous year.[31] Thus was a dream of Hanoverian policy fulfilled: while attempts to establish a sericulture in Georgia, the Carolinas, Virginia and even Nova Scotia had failed, English silk capital found in Bengal a source of raw silk directly under its control. After 1766 Bengal replaced Italy and Turkey as the main source of raw silk. 'The English are scatter'd over the face of the Nations: are these Jerusalem's children?' asked Blake.[32]

The upheavals of imperialist competition in the Seven Years War, the rebellion of the dispossessed against the European powers and the growing danger of the weavers' insurrections within the metrop-

---

and *The Public Advertizer;* George Rudé, *Wilkes and Liberty: A Social Study of 1763 to 1774* (1962), chapter 6.

[29] Philip Mason, *A Matter of Honour: An Account of the India Army, Its Officers and Men* (1976), pp. 107–9.

[30] William Bolts, *Considerations on India Affairs* (1772), and P.J. Marshall, *East India Fortunes: The British in Bengal in the 18th Century* (1974).

[31] E. B. Schumpeter, *English Overseas Trade Statistics, 1697–1808* (Oxford, 1960), pp. 51, 55.

[32] *Jerusalem* (1804).

olis of London caused the thinking of Britain's ruling élite to change significantly, and 'Jerusalem' was not an idea within that thinking. Scots were at the forefront of the intellectual conjunctures of British capitalism in the 1760s when the foundations of the disciplines of sociology, law, anthropology, economics and history were laid.[33] In 1759 Adam Smith published *The Theory of Moral Sentiments* and William Robertson his *The History of Scotland*. In 1765 William Blackstone, encouraged by a Scot, Lord Mansfield, Lord Chief Justice, began publishing his *Commentaries on the Laws of England*. In 1767 Adam Ferguson published his *Essay on the History of Civil Society*. In 1771 Andrew Millar published his *Origins of the Distinction of Ranks,* and shortly after Lord Kames published *Sketches of the History of Man*. They attacked previous traditions (mercantilism, common law) and adapted older concepts (labour theory of value, property, freedom) to new systematic theories that both aided understanding of the class wars of the 1760s and legitimated as 'progress', 'law' or 'necessity' the emerging recomposition of international class relations. Concepts such as 'the mode of subsistence', upon which cultural, legal and religious superstructures were built (Ferguson), or 'manufacture' as sub-division of labour and the reduction of craft to machine-like activity (Smith), arose from an effort to understand the materialism of historical dynamics and to guide it. The systematic elaboration of the history and law of property, contract, trust and rights against the 'Gothick ignorance' of common law established flexible rules of class exploitation that were deeply imbued in moral philosophy and appeared to countless planters, writers, advocates and merchants as an Olympian code reconciling massacre, slavery and exploitation with the progress of history. The class war, whether fought in Spitalfields or Murshidabad, at the Old Bailey or the cutchery courts of Calcutta, was defended and analysed by seminal minds who, sitting upon Chairs of Law or Moral Philosophy, instructed tobacco lairds, nawabs, West Indiamen, slavers and Whig statesmen in the intricacies of 'civil society' and the theatre of thanatocracy. '[T]hey accumulate a World in which Man is by his Nature the Enemy of Man,' wrote Blake.

To William Blake the contradictions of Albion, where 'all the Arts

---

[33] Anand C. Chitnis, *The Scottish Enlightenment: A Social History* (1976) is a useful introduction.

of Life' are changed into 'the Arts of Death', was often expressed in imagery derived from the weaver's tools (loom, treadles, shuttle, weights, heddles) and materials (thread, woof, fibres, warp). For him the details of that labour process were a means of revolutionary expression. And indeed the weavers' struggles of the 1760s require us to consider both the sociology of their organization and the techniques of the labour process. The former interested the higher authorities, as is shown by a remarkably clear memorandum addressed to Shelburne, the Secretary of State, in November 1768. The author begins by noting the removal of silk capital to Glasgow, where wage rates are far less than in Spitalfields. He notes that this mobility of investment is made possible by the reduction in skill required in the various stages of silk production. He then acknowledges the 'temporary Convulsions' that arise as the London weavers resist the flight of capital. He describes the level of community organization:

[T]he Workmen have united into Combinations of a very dangerous & alarming Nature, they have form'd a Plan of greater Extent and More Singularity than ever has been yet done in Cases of Combinations of this kind. They amount to several thousands and are reduc'd to the most exact Discipline under their Leaders, they plant Centinels in all ye Neighbourhoods of Spital Fields and are ready to collect themselves upon any Alarm. They disguise themselves with Crapes and are arm'd with Cutlasses and other Weapons. They write threatening Letters in the form of humble Petitions to the Master Manufacturers and they deter by Threats those labourers from working at an under Price who would be otherwise glad to be employ'd. They enter in the Night such Houses where they have Intelligence any Work is carried on at an under Price and cut and destroy the Looms to the Damage often of several hundred pounds. It is said they are learning the discipline of regular Troops ... The few Persons who have occasionally been taken up and confin'd for Disorders and Assaults in the Streets have been immediately rescued. They have their Watch Words and a cant Language understood only by themselves.[34]

The working people of London developed a common linguistic culture that may be called 'thieves' cant', as long as it is realized that this was not the property of a small sub-culture of 'criminals'. It lent the weavers protection against invigilation by outsiders and police informers. This language very often required translation at

[34] The Shelburne Papers, vol. cxxxiii, fol. 331, William L. Clements Library, University of Michigan.

the Old Bailey if the judges were to understand the proceedings. This was true of several hanged weavers – Tom Beck, Mike Bewley and Chris Freeman, for instance. 'I cannot conceive, my friend,' said Lord Mansfield to a witness at King's Bench, 'what you mean by this sort of language, I do not understand it.' 'Not understand it!' the witness rejoined in surprise, 'Lord, what a flat you must be.' Cant, or the 'flash' language, had origins in Dutch, Latin, Romany, trade jargons and even Hindi, as George Borrow learned when he spoke of thieves to an apple-barrow woman whose son had been transported. 'Nay, dear!' she gently reprimanded him, 'Don't make use of bad language; we never calls them thieves here, but prigs and fakers.'[35] A description of two trials, the first of which raises questions of language, will illustrate the weavers' struggles and introduce new thinking about both thanatocracy and the mode of production.

The first trial was William Horsford's. With others on 9 August 1769, he broke a reed (£1) and a harness (5s.) and cut 100 yds. of 'silk manufactory' (£100), all the property of Joseph Horton, a silk mercer who never appeared in court. The actual victims were two poor master weavers, Thomas Poor and his wife Mary.[36] They lived in a small three-storey building in Stockingframe alley, off Bishopsgate Street, in the very heart of the silk-weaving district. The ground floor was a warehouse. In the chambers of the top storey there lived and worked three or four combers. On the storey in between, the Poors had a bedroom whose furnishings consisted of a bed, a chest of drawers and a chair. Their son, William, and one of the journeymen also slept in this room. Across the landing, on which opened the room of a lodger, Able Dowas, who watched the events of the night through a keyhole, was the weaving shop. It was 36 ft. long, containing seven looms, one of which the Poors owned and the others they rented from Horton. A window reached the length of the shop, permitting sunlight to illuminate the fine

---

[35] George Borrow, *Lavengro* (1851), Everyman edn (1961), pp. 190 ff.
[36] *The Proceedings,* 18–21 and 23 October 1769, 7–9 and 11 December 1769 contain the direct quotations. My account supplements the evidence of *The Proceedings* with newspapers, *Middlesex Journal, Lloyd's Evening Post* and *Berrow's Worcester Journal,* with depositions and examinations found in CLRO, *Sessions Papers,* bundle 1769, and with papers retained in the PRO, particularly State Papers (SP 37/7), Entry Books (SP 44/142) and War Office Outletters (WO 4/77) and the Tower Letter Books (WO 94/13).

work, or moonlight to identify the cutters ('It was light enough to see a rat at the time, was it to run across the passage,' said Thomas Poor). In the shop the other journeymen, three or four in number, slept in a chimney nook. Thomas and Mary Poor paid a rent of £8 a year, generally in monthly or quarterly payments as they were able. When the rent collector came to make distress upon their goods (in December they were £2 13s. 4d. behind), he found that 3 guineas was the most he could get for their movables, 'looms and all'.

At 11 p.m. Bill Duff, Mickey More, John Doyle, Pat Pickle, John Valloine, Andrew Mahoney, Joe Coleman, alias Jolly Dog, and William Horsford arrived, thundering and rapping at the outward door. They ascended the stairs, allowed Mary Poor some moments to put on her petticoats, and then entered the workshop. These 'cutters' demanded that the bestirred journeymen identify the work on each loom. Of the four owners only 'Mr Horton did not give a fair price for his work', so it was only his work that was cut. Thomas Poor surveyed the damage – the cane and bombazine were cut – and he brought into court the wrecked harness and reeds. He patiently described to the ignorant court the uses of these parts of the loom and the *various* owners of the several components of manufacture.

It was not until the middle of the next month that the Poors decided to inform on the cutters, people whom they had known, eaten and worked with for four and a half years. A code of silence had been in existence, and offenders had been forced to submit to the humiliation of a 'skimmington': mounted on an ass backwards they were driven through the streets, hooted and hollered at in a nasty kind of rough music. Fearing this or similar reprisals, the weeks after the cutting were a time of choice for Thomas and Mary Poor. Mary spent some of the time in negotiation, buying drinks for the cutters, waiting for them to buy her silence. One of them offered her 30 guineas. Neighbourhood gossip frightened her, and she hid herself for seventeen nights in Limehouse. There she learned that Mr Chauvet, the biggest capitalist in the district, had offered a reward of £500, so she asked a woman to write him a letter over her mark. 'She was both hungry and dry.' Thomas Poor made his choice. Sir John Fielding brought him and Horsford together at Bow Street. Horsford asked him in Irish to have compassion. Poor answered in English, 'You had no compassion when you destroyed me, and when you was of the Defiance Sloop.' Horsford responded in Irish, saying that Poor was 'doing this for the sake of money'.

The journeymen weavers were organized in several clubs. They went by a variety of names including the Combinators, the Committee Men, the Subscription Society, the Dreadnought Sloop, the Defiance Sloop and the Liberty Men. It was said that they were able to collect thousands of pounds by letters such as this one from 'the Conquering of Bold Defiance':

Gentlemen, Send your donations this Night to the Dolphin in New Cock Lane by one Man with this Letter and keep up your Bodies, as at this time you must either conquer and flourish or starve and perish, for if sufficient means is not used at this time to crush your enemies you are and will be for ever Bond Slaves.

At the trial Horsford defended himself, saying he had spent the evening in question drinking with the headborough of Shoreditch, himself a weaver. Another companion of that evening, John Fitzharris, spoke of their conversations at the Well and Bucket: 'We talked about Wilkes and trade. There was a gentleman, on the right side of the fireplace, who talked about geograffee.'

The trial of John Carmichael introduces some other themes. He was indicted for breaking into the dwelling-house of Robert Cromwell and stealing 20 lbs. of raw silk ($£15$), 20 lbs. of dyed silk ($£15$), 200 yds. of silk trimmings ($£5$) and 200 yds. of gimp. Although Cromwell described himself as a 'master weaver', he did no weaving himself but through his foreman put out silk from his ground-floor warehouse in White Cross Alley, Moorfields, to journeymen scattered from Hoxton to the end of Bishopsgate Street. On the night of 25 September a group of cutters including many who worked for Cromwell — such as Cox, Haines and Carmichael — gathered in a public house, where they planned their attack. Armed with cutlasses and pistols, carrying axes and sledge-hammers, they broke into Cromwell's warehouse, destroyed dyed silk in a case and raw silk hanging from a peg, and then took away silk pieces which they concealed in Hoxton and later sold, dividing the proceeds into 3 crowns per man.[37] Carmichael was acquainted with Mary Whisson, one of Cromwell's lodgers, who decided to 'scragg' on Carmichael several weeks following the cutting and robbery. Carmichael fled to Coventry but, owing to the swift communication

[37] *The Proceedings,* 25 September 1769.

between John Fielding and the Coventry magistrate and thief-taker John Hewitt, he was apprehended climbing a stile into a commons near Rugeley, Staffordshire, on his way to Ireland. Weymouth, the Secretary of State, rewarded Hewitt with £111 14s.

During the previous summer of 1768 the Government intercepted a letter from Dublin addressed 'To the Committee of Silk Weavers in London' and signed by seventeen Irish weavers. It thanks the London committee for its diligence in sending wage-rates. It declaims against the 'ungenerous Tempers', the 'Hearts ... like Adamant', and the 'designing Schemes' of the 'Tyrants', the silk masters. They make

it their Business, at unseasonable Hours, to go armed with Blunderbusses, Pistols, Swords & Cutlasses, heading the Army & Watch, & lodging whom they think proper in Newgate. For Instance, they first lodged Will Dalton, whom they still detain thro' their Insinuations; Next the above Persons lodged Mr Clarke for 5 Days & Mr Ready & Wife for harbouring what they call Combinators; and lastly James Lundy for 4 days.

The letter is long and, evidently, it was part of a larger correspondence between Dublin and Irish weavers in London. It is full of pride, determination, mutualism and useful warnings. For example:

They have got one Dan Clark, in Garden Lane, who swears what the Master Weavers require. He being an ignorant Master, the other makes him their Cat's Paw, & he has been Villain enough to swear false.

Between the writing of this letter and 12 September, Daniel Clarke returned to London. There we find him in Artillery Lane, Spitalfields, described as a pattern-drawer; he employed his wife and several journeymen at looms and had work put out to him by bigger masters. That night he was visited by a deputation from one of the committees which broke into his shop and wrecked a reed, some cane, a quill-wheel and tackle he used in weaving floral figures. When the cutters learned that Mrs Clarke was working under rate, two of them, William Eastman and a Scot named Robert Campbell, cut her work. 'Blast the b——h, we'll learn her to make Leopard Satin.' This was the way they showed that 'the Lyon has been too much for the Leopard'. Clarke had been in trouble with the committees before; he had been examined and tried in one of their courts at the Red Lion, whose authority was temporarily vindicated over the 'leopard'. Later Clarke testified against Eastman. His expenses in the Old Bailey trial were paid by Lewis Chauvet, who persuaded him to turn cat's-paw again, and risk the vengeance of Spitalfields.[38]

Lewis Chauvet was one of the richest silk manufacturers. He had been a master since 1741. In 1750 he employed 450 people. In 1769 he refused to pay the 6d. per loom demanded by the weavers' subscription societies. He paid his workers' wages in money that he had marked so that he could maintain greater surveillance over their transactions. At the end of August in two nights of rioting seventy of his looms were destroyed and more than £10,000 damage was done to his silk wares. Doyle and Valloine participated in this riot. Doyle had worked for 15s. a week, but had been without work for four months. Chauvet took the lead in militarizing the district. He hired, trained and armed his own private guard ('to repel this daring Banditti', shouted one of the newspapers).[39] He encouraged the War Office and those East End magistrates in contact with the troops barracked in the Tower to billet troops in Spitalfields (where they stayed in public houses and churches); they maintained a visible presence in the streets, and did not restrain themselves from exercising their arms against the weavers, among whom there were several casualties in the street fighting in October and November 1769. Except for such skirmishes, the Government avoided direct military confrontation and the possibility of massacre. The two Sheriffs of London, Townsend and Strawbridge, were both supporters of Wilkes, and preferred to wrap themselves in the mantle of restrained, constitutional punishments. The ruling class could not afford to risk a massacre against its metropolitan working class, whom it had managed by the visible exercise of the public hanging – the staged massacre of a few.

[38] *The Proceedings*, 6–9 and 11 December 1769, 25 September 1769.
[39] C. Amelungen in *Werkschutz und Betriebskriminalität* (Hamburg, 1960), p. 11, notes that the Wach-und-Schliesgesellschaft, a private, external security force in Hamburg founded in 1901, was the first in continental Europe. Karl Heinz Roth, *Die andere Arbeiterbewegung* (Munich, 1974), notes the existence of a silk police in the textile mills of the 1880s.

V

Thanks to the many hundreds who died game, died drunk, died stoned, died bold or intrepid or with words of innocence on their breath, the public hanging had very largely lost its ability to awe or terrorize the London multitudes. Many of the best minds of the English élite meditated upon it. Mandeville studied Dutch methods and published them to English readers. Fielding advised close attention to Aristotle's *Poetics*, as a technical manual on how to produce terror without pity. He advised privacy. Adam Smith meditated upon the manner in which North American 'savages' faced capital punishment; he discovered that their self-command and magnanimity was the result of having studied from adolescence a personal 'song of death'. Adam Ferguson was also impressed by the fortitude of native Americans, who were able to defy their tormentors and bring honour to themselves by their bearing during the execution of capital punishment.[40]

But there was also available much experience, some of it published, of effective methods of capital punishment. In India, we have noted, Hector Munro blasted strikers with cannon. If the hangman and the condemned were the players of a drama representing sovereignty and its enemy, then the spectators were meant to assume the role of an audience that received the lessons of the gallows passively. The major lesson the gallows were supposed to teach was the absolute, apodictic authority of law; it was a code governing the relationship between state and civil society, and in this respect hanging was to be distinguished from murder or massacre. But 'society' in Spitalfields had long ceased to be 'civil'.

The 'principal Inhabitants of Spitalfields' wanted the hanging of Doyle and Valloine to take place not at Tyburn, but in the silk neighbourhoods of Bethnal Green in order 'to strike Terror into the Rioters'. A temporary stay of execution was obtained by Townsend and Strawbridge, but in the end Lord Mansfield adjudicated in favour of the Crown and the masters. So, the two cutters were led on a three-hour procession from Newgate, across the City into Whitechapel, and then north to Bethnal Green within hailing

---

[40] Bernard Mandeville, *An Enquiry into the Causes of the Frequent Executions at Tyburn* (1725); Henry Fielding, *An Enquiry into the Causes of the Late Increase of Robbers,* 2nd edn (1751); Adam Smith, *The Theory of Moral Sentiments* (1759), 9th edn (1801); Adam Ferguson, *An Essay on the History of Civil Society* (1767).

distance of the Dolphin, where the Conquering of Bold Defiance had met. Led by the weavers' wives, the crowds kept up the spirits of the condemned. Valloine called to the people to 'remember your Promise'. Many expected a rescue, for one had been planned. At a watchword the crowd began heaving stones at the authorities. But the cutters were quickly dispatched without the ministrations of the clergymen – an Anglican and a Methodist – who were present to say prayers. Before Doyle expired, he uttered his final words: 'Let my blood lay to that wretched man who has purchased it with gold and them notorious wretches who swore it falsely away'[41] – an utterance that would not go unheeded. The crowd then tore down the gallows and re-erected them at Chauvet's factory in Crispin Street. Between 4,000 and 5,000 people joined in the action of smashing his windows and removing his furniture to fuel bonfires in the streets. A spy was seized, his hair shorn off, and he would have lost his ears too, had not the Foot Guards arrived to save him and disperse the crowd. That was 6 December 1769.[42] Ten days later the wives of Carmichael, Horsford and Eastman circulated handbills pleading clemency for their condemned husbands. Although their petition and march to Westminster failed in this objective, the authorities hanged them at Tyburn, not daring to further risk the ire of Spitalfields crowds.

At noon upon a cold and snowy day, 16 April 1771, Daniel Clarke and Benjamin West, a Fleet Street weaver who had once employed Clarke to draw patterns for him, went walking in Spitalfields. It had been sixteen months since the hanging of the cutters whom Clarke had sworn against, and he must have thought the people cowed or forgetful. He was recognized. 'There goes Clarke, that blood-selling rascal,' was the shout, and instantly a small crowd gathered to badger and pester him. He took to his heels and found temporary refuge in the house of Mary Snee. The currents of popular memory run deep; now they flooded to the surface. A

---

[41] *The Middlesex Journal,* December 1769; *Lloyd's Evening Post,* December 1769.
[42] The constitutional issues raised by the change in venue of the hanging are set forth in a series of letters to Lord Weymouth by Townsend and Strawbridge that may be found in PRO, SP, 44/142, fols. 232–4. The *Gentleman's Magazine,* December 1769, contains some of the debate. Descriptions of the actions of the hanging and the mock hanging following it are found in *Baldwin's London Weekly Journal,* December 1769. James Harris (ed.), *A Series of Letters of the First Earl of Malmesbury,* vol. i (1870), p. 180, contains an account in which some of the questions about Royal Prerogative and the actions at the hanging are discussed.

hundred people beset the house hurling maledictions. 'They would hang him, or burn him, or stone him,' said Mary Snee. He was cornered, stripped and dragged by his feet into the street, where he was led by the neck on a parade of humiliation. The crowds grew. Widow Horsford was seen to 'jump out of the loom' at the news. Clarke was cursed and dragged to the brick-fields. Children pelted him with dirt. Bespattered with muck, he was thrown into a pond where he was ducked within a breath of drowning. He was removed to a sandheap, buried, dug up and returned to the freezing water. It was estimated that the crowd numbered 3,000. While he could speak, he taunted his tormentors, saying 'he would take twenty of them'. Widow Horsford said, 'Clarke, Clarke, I am left a widow, my children is fatherless on account of you.' Clarke answered, 'Chauvet is worse than me,' and then he expired. A grim ending that would be remembered for generations.

The stoning was a counter-terror, a defiant and brazen answer to the manufacturers and magistrates and ministers for the hangings of 1769.[43] In this sort of feud the authorities preferred to have the last word. Justice Wilmot, whose house had carefully been avoided on the parade to the brick-fields, coordinated the search for culprits who might serve as examples. Henry Stroud, the brother-in-law to Eastman, and Campbell, a Scottish weaver with four children, were indicted for Clarke's murder. Campbell was apprehended while boarding a ship for the Indies. Working with the Secretary of State, holding off the manufacturers who wanted *all* the cutters brought to justice, Wilmot found it difficult to find witnesses. Many fled to Ireland, others disappeared. Witnesses had to be bought: a fruiterer testified in court that he had been offered £80; a brickyard labourer was paid £100 for supplying evidence against Stroud. In the event Wilmot was able to make a case with witnesses who begged the court for protection, who trembled in fright, who were attacked as they came out of court. Wilmot himself escaped the crowd's anger only by the swiftness of his coach's horses. A Bishopsgate man was overheard to say 'that if the Man then in Newgate is not cleared we will Murder'. Stroud and Campbell were hanged in Hare Street on 8 July 1771 – 'in the very heart of the residence of the perpetrators' –

[43] Besides newspaper accounts and the accounts provided in *The Proceedings* of the trials of Stroud and Campbell, the fullest evidence of the stoning of Clarke arose out of the Coroner's inquest, the depositions of which may be found in PRO, Treasury Solicitor, Papers, TS, 11/169.

a short distance from Wilmot's residence. A colonel's guard protected it. Sir David Lindsay commanded a hundred soldiers with bayonets fixed, deploying them around the gibbet.[44]

Thus did the alternating pageants of ritual murder come to an end: a hundred bayonets from the War Office protecting the hangman and the magistrates. The scapegoating of the class antagonism concluded with this powerful, official display of power in the streets, where usually the trill of shuttles would fill the air. Even had Campbell boarded that ship to the Indies he would have found in Bengal circumstances like those of Spitalfields, but more so. The famine of 1769–71 killed millions of farmers and weavers. Wages fell, factories were built; and, as the East India Company began to regulate production, an endemic dispute over 'ferreted' piece-goods, analogous to the clandestine waste economy in Spitalfields, bound the Bengal weavers in a litigious destitution. Dacoity flourished and merged with the Sinyasin Revolt, a guerrilla war led by ascetic 'holy men' who were hard-core liberation-seekers; their goal was entasis or 'breaking through to their ground of being'. Warren Hastings, in consultation with Lord Mansfield in England, supervised the operations against the Sinyasin and 'persuaded his colleagues that every convicted dacoit should be hanged in his own village'.[45] In England, however, in Hare Street, the 'dialogue' of terror had come to an end. Other dialogues continued.

VI

One 'dialogue' produced informed, reflective inquiries into the 'idleness' of the English working class; it touched upon technological change, investment patterns and industrial organization. Malachy Postlethwayt favoured an intensive but short working week as best guaranteed to produce profits and social peace, while the anonymous

[44] *The Annual Register* (1771); PRO, SP, 37/8, 84/16 (a–n); and *The Proceedings*, 2–5 July, 8–11 July 1771, parts 3 and 4.
[45] Ramkrishna Mukherjee, *The Rise and Fall of the East India Company* (New York, 1974), ch. 5; N. K. Sinha, *The Economic History of Bengal* (Calcutta, 1970), 2 vols; H. P. Ghose, *The Famine of 1770* (Calcutta, 1944); Hameeda Hossain, *The Company of Weavers of Bengal: The East India Company and the Organization of Textile Production in Bengal, 1750–1813* (Bombay, 1988), pp. 19, 156–62, 171; and Penderel Moon, *Warren Hastings and British India* (1947), pp. 70–73.

author of *An Essay on Trade and Commerce* (1770) preferred an extensive and long working week.

'Anon.' opposed the 'riotous and disorderly manner' of the 'mis-guided populace'. They could have found work were they willing to comply with 'reasonable terms'. Because they had insisted upon 'extravagant wages', the silk manufactories removed to Glasgow where 'frugality' and 'industry' prevailed, 'where manufacturing people were glad to labour six days for the same money [that they,] in Spitalfields, had received for the labour of three days only'. 'Anon.' is an apologist for the silk capitalists (even the Parliamentary Committee of 1765 was sympathetic to the weavers' plight), and he clearly appreciates capital's freedom – its ability to remove accumulated labour from the sources of its creation to new areas where higher rates of exploitation can prevail. He considers several policies to discipline Spitalfields, including (1) the importation of foreigners; (2) the imposition of higher taxes on working-class 'superfluities'; and (3) the use of police, by which he meant an effective code of laws to abolish gaming, drinking, skittle-playing, beggary, bastardy and idleness, 'so that constant labour may grow into a habit'. A fourth strategy is particularly interesting in the light of both English experience and the experience of Bengal. 'Master manufacturers know that there are various ways of rising and making fall the price of labour, besides that of altering its nominal value.' High food prices might bring about the discipline that would get six days' work a week at four days' pay, without any direct attempts to reduce the nominal wage. For this strategy to work, 'the two distinct interests of the Kingdom' – land and trade – must walk 'hand in hand'.[46]

Liberty. 'This high-sounding word operates like magic on the unthinking multitude.'

The lower sort of people in England, from a romantic notion of liberty, generally reject and oppose every thing that is forced upon them; and though, from a fear of punishment, you may oblige them to labour certain hours for certain wages, you cannot oblige them to do their work properly.[47]

The political economist understands that even if the wage–price scissors were able to cut down necessary labour, this would still not

[46] *Essay on Trade and Commerce* (1770), pp. vii-viii, 19, 50, 30, 56 and 61.
[47] ibid., p. 92.

guarantee 'proper' work. The stuffs of Spitalfields were 'generally short of what they are called, both as to lengths and breadths'. This was the world of fents, noils, thrums, rags and ends where the hand-worker, far from the searching eye of the mercer, might augment the 'value of necessary labour' – that is, *live* by those customary usages that characterized material relations.

'Anon.' realizes that punishment alone is not enough. In his paean of praise to the 'House of Terror', his thinking anticipates in theory that which was not yet generally realized in practice, a place where the principles of production and punishment can be united – namely, a factory. In the year 1769, according to Andrew Ure, the phil-osopher of the factory, 'Arkwright created order', for it was then that he took out a patent for the spinning-machine.[48] Both the theorist of the 'House of Terror' and the man who mechanized spinning were responding to the same class forces which they sum-marized by the word 'idleness', and which were led by the Spi-talfields weavers

> ... when with weaving sons of silk,
> Oppress'd with debts and hunger, rose in arms,
> They had divisions then, as we have now:
> What did they do? When e'er they found a man
> Doubting or faltr'ing, him strait compelled:
> Hence, soon a formidable band arose,
> And all the sister trades were forc'd to join.
> Lo! their example points the way.

So Samuel Foote wrote of the tailors in 1778.[49]

As a result of the struggles among weavers in the 1760s, many were forced to migrate to escape the hardness of life: they went as indentured servants to America, they became sailors in the East India fleet, they returned to Ireland as tramps. And a certain number of them were hanged. Yet the struggle had not been a complete failure. Its greatest accomplishment was the pressure that induced Parliament in 1773 to pass the first Spitalfields Act (13 George III, c. 68). This introduced a system of binding collective bargaining between the workers and their employers. The magistrates for Middlesex, the City and Tower Hamlets were empowered to 'settle, regulate, and declare' the wages of the trade. In doing so, they

---

[48] Andrew Ure, *The Philosophy of Manufacture* (1835), p. 15.
[49] *The Tailors: A Tragedy for Warm Weather* (1778).

would consider the price of provisions and the balance of power between masters and workers.[50] In this respect, the long struggle beginning with the creation of the Book in 1762 ended with its vindication, since the Book became the social contract upon which the magistrates based their decisions. The threat of direct action persisted, despite the round of hangings and stonings of 1769–71. The workers' power was represented by the Spitalfields Act, and this is why William Pitt 'trembled at the very mention' of its repeal.

The years between 1763 and 1773 represented a transition period of class relations, during which older forms of conflict were replaced by new ones. The process of production shifted from a domestic or putting-out mode to manufacturing and the factory mode. The hand was replaced by the machine as the active principle in the ancient art of *lanificium*, overlooked by Minerva, Isis and Hindu deities. Before these years the divisions of labour had been re-connected by activities in the street into an open system of assembly. Afterwards assembly became increasingly closed behind factory walls.[51] Where once the little producer and the poor consumer met in Rag Fair in a thick economy of their own 'underworld', later they would find that the wastes that had sustained them were becoming distinct branches of a capitalist trade in by-products. Before this decade Spitalfields was a major centre of world production; afterwards the Midlands and the North replaced it. Where silk had before been the fabric clothing the class relation, afterwards it was replaced by cotton. This decade saw the transition from the 'vernacular' of silk to the 'language' of value. Before that date fents and thrums were an essential part of proletarian economies; after it money and the 'Book' dominated class relations. Purloining and customary usages became 'thievery' and 'embezzlement'.

After the 1770s the 'rights' and 'wrongs' of direct appropriations are more easily detected in the evidence than they had been before. In February 1782 Hannah Eaton, a thread-maker in a Whitechapel throwing mill, took a bobbin of Bengal silk and put it in her pocket. The man who turned the mill noticed this, and signalled to the

---

[50] Sir John Clapham, 'The Spitalfields Acts, 1773–1824', *The Economic Journal*, xxvi (1916), pp. 459–71.
[51] Stanley D. Chapman, 'The Textile Factory Before Arkwright: A Typology of Factory Development', *Business History*, vol. xlviii, no. 4 (winter 1974), and the same author's *The Early Factory Masters: The Transition to the Factory System in the Midlands Textile Industry* (1967) are good recent descriptions of the investments in the Midlands and the business problems with the first factories.

owner's wife. She called the constable, and the beadle had her seized and searched. Two other workers in the mill testified against Eaton before the magistrate.[52] Other evidence suggests that the 'rights' and 'wrongs' of appropriation had been internalized in the conscience of the young. The tender conscience of John Gray, a Spitalfields lad, was so upset by the knowledge that a fellow worker was stealing on the job that he was hospitalized in St Luke's, though the man who recounts this also thought it important to mention his long 'confinement to an uncongenial employment'.[53]

[52] GLCRO, OB/SP, 17 February 1782.
[53] Thomas Compton, Recollections of Spitalfields: An Honest Man and his Employers (1894), p. 46.

CHAPTER NINE

IF YOU PLEAD FOR YOUR LIFE, PLEAD IN IRISH

There's a big difference between a gallus story and a dirty deed.

J. M. Synge, *The Playboy of the Western World*

Frequently I test the roads on foot and I am used to being hard up without a penny in my purse for months.

O'Bruadair

I

The tension between the money-wage and the customary usages inherent in the trades of London at mid-century was beginning to find a resolution in the geographical mobility of capital, the reorganization of the mode of production and the mechanization of the labour. This was a slow process and cannot be fully understood without examining other forms of struggle by the London people, which this and the following chapter set out to do. In this chapter we consider the changes in Irish agrarian relations as a background to London migration; three characteristic types of Irish labour around London; the urban institutions of Irish mutualism; the vanguard of Irish workers during the insurrection of 1768; the relationship of the Whiteboy Movement in Ireland to the proletarian disturbances in London; and the cultural contribution of the London Irish to the subversion of thanatocratic power.

About 14 per cent (171) of the eighteenth-century people hanged at Tyburn were born in Ireland. Many were from Dublin. A third had begun an apprenticeship, of whom three-quarters completed this training. There were 109 Catholics, 7 Protestants; the religion of the remaining 53 Tyburn Irish is unknown. They were poor, and their poverty was determined by economic forces that often made no religious distinction. Their experience in Ireland and their collective achievement in London cannot be separated from a colonial experience of expropriation, even if this need not be interpreted in the strictly sectarian terms established by W. E. H. Lecky and J. A. Froude, the Victorian historians.[1] That there were some Catholic landowners or that the small farmers of Ulster and the Protestant artisans of Belfast and Dublin also suffered pauperization only complicates a process that modern scholarship still understands fundamentally as a huge expropriation. 'By 1700 14 per cent of all Irish land remained in Catholic hands, and by 1750 that proportion had fallen to 5 per cent.'[2] Yet Protestants represented only a fifth of the population. The cause of this expropriation was a combination of the infamous Penal Code, the famines (1726–7 and 1740–41) and the destruction of corporate land tenure and partible inheritance.

The hangman's noose and the woodsman's axe were the tools guaranteeing the Protestant Whig Ascendancy. It was their effects upon 'the residuary legatees' of a thousand-year-old culture that propelled multitudes of Irish souls across the water in a steady stream of migration. Sometimes, following a famine, this stream became a sudden torrent – many thousands, in 'long and miserable Passages', migrated to America after the famine of 1727. Despite incomplete and disputed records, it appears that in the eighteenth century between only a quarter and a fifth of the migrants were Catholic.[3] The 'Catholic Irish were a defeated, depressed, and leaderless people', Professor McCracken has written, and they may not have had the strength even to migrate.[4] From the evidence of those who did move and ended their days at Tyburn we can confirm neither the view that Professor Miller finds in the nineteenth century of self-pitying exile, resentful homelessness and romantic banishment, nor the opinion expressed by Thomas Carlyle and Frederick Engels of the Irish migrant as a mindless, if gregarious, brute.[5] Our evidence

---

[1] W. E. H. Lecky, *A History of Ireland in the Eighteenth Century*, 2nd edn (New York, 1893), and J. A. Froude, *The English in Ireland in the Eighteenth Century* (New York, 1874).

[2] Kerby A. Miller, *Emigrants and Exiles: Ireland and the Irish Exodus to North America* (New York, 1985), p. 21.

[3] ibid., p. 137.

[4] J. L. McCracken, 'The Social Structure and Social Life, 1714–60', in T. W. Moody and W. E. Vaughan (eds), *A New History of Ireland*, vol. iv, *Eighteenth-Century Ireland, 1691–1800* (1986), p. 53.

[5] Thomas Carlyle, *Chartism* (1839), pp. 28–31, and Frederick Engels, *The Conditions of the Working Class in England*, trans. W. O. Henderson and W. H. Chaloner (New York, 1958), pp. 105–6.

suggests that the Irish in London were less responsible for Irish nationalism or the stereotypes of alcoholism and recklessness than they were for a decisive contribution to the formation of an urban proletariat. Shy, sly and silent, by the eighteenth century secretiveness had become a weapon in the armoury of this subjugated people, whom we may approach first by language.

Having robbed the oppressed of land, the oppressor then banished their language, music and poetry. The result was a 'hidden Ireland' expressing itself in a foreign language, acting outside the law.[6] In 1688 the English attempted to silence the Irish national instrument – the harp. Irish songs, it was said in 1683, had become 'the doleful lamentations ... of a conquered people'.[7] Early in the eighteenth century the bardic contests and poetic meetings – the 'sessions' – were suppressed by the Penal Code. In consequence, the Irish language was 'banished from the castle of the chieftain to the cottage of the vassal', whence in hard times it migrated to England and thrived in the boozing kens of London. In the metropolis, it became a language of supplication. We remember that at the Old Bailey William Horsford, the journeyman weaver, reverted to Irish in pleading with Thomas Poor to have compassion upon his life. 'If you plead for your life, plead in Irish,' was the proverbial testament to this power.

The English language, as known at first in Ireland, had the opposite power. The seventeenth-century bard, Eamoun an Duna, records the first English words an Irish-speaking person would learn:

> Transport, transplant, *mo mheabhair ar Bhearla*
> Shoot him, kill him, strip him, tear him.
> A tory, hack him, hang him, rebel,
> A rogue, thief, a priest, a papist.

The language of violence was often the language of law. 'The only imposing institution with which the people came at all into contact was the law-court: with the law and its forms they then began to associate all ideas of ceremony, judgments and authority.'[8] Backed by violence and repeated by incantation, the ceremonious qualities

[6] Daniel Corkery, *The Hidden Ireland: A Study of Gaelic Munster in the 18th Century* (Dublin, 1925).
[7] Brian Boydell, 'Music before 1700', in Moody and Vaughan, op. cit., p. 565.
[8] Alan Bliss, 'The English Language in Early Modern Ireland', ibid., p. 555, and also R. A. Steward Macalister, *The Secret Languages of Ireland* (1937).

of legal vocabulary enlarged the language of lamentation, as 'whereas' so often did in law and in dirge.

Many were the bad men and women hanged at Tyburn who spoke better Irish than English: a Belfast man, formerly a captain of an Irish regiment in French service, who hanged in 1733; a Dublin weaver hanged the same year for raping his master's daughter; a veteran of the siege of Londonderry hanged in 1731 for killing the doorkeeper of a Haymarket gaming house; a Dublin footman hanged in 1744 for robbing Alderman Heathcote of his sword and belt; and Katherine Lineham, hanged in 1741. From the likes of her acquaintances, she knew nothing but Irish and bad. At seventeen she married an eighteen-year-old butcher's apprentice in Dublin. They came to London and 'associated themselves', the Ordinary wrote, 'with the Refuse of their own Nation about Rag Fair and the Hundreds of Drury'. A year later her husband was hanged because with Teddy Brian, Henry Smith and 'John of Gaunt' he attacked Squire Patten, the High Bailiff of Westminster, robbing him of his gold-headed cane of office. During the month between his trial and hanging Katherine waited every day at the Press Yard door to see her husband pass between his cell and the chapel of the condemned. As a 'hempen widow' she kept company at the Cart and Horse in Broad Street, St Giles, where 'they all spoke Irish'. She robbed with Ruggety Madge, Redman Keogh and Macdonnel. When the latter was taken, she visited him twice daily, taking him victuals and drink. To save his neck, he impeached the others. Katherine walked by the tumbril from Newgate to Tyburn to see and comfort her friend, Ruggety Madge. She saw George Stacey hang too, attending him at the tree. Finally, she herself 'danced in the Sheriff's picture frame' in January 1741.[9] This kind of evidence suggests the distinct presence in London of an Irish mutualism that was reinforced and protected by its language.

The language had a power to frighten English speakers. In 1725 the printer and shorthand writer of the Old Bailey *Proceedings* attempted a phonetic representation of Irish speech – 'O my Shoul I wash got pretty drunk, and wash going very shoberly along the Old-Bailey' – and for this they were summoned to appear before the Court of Common Council for 'the lewd and indecent manner

---

[9] The Ordinary's *Account*, 13 February 1727, 24 November 1731, 5 October 1744, 29 January 1733, 6 October 1733, 5 October 1744, 31 July 1741, 16 May 1750, 24 November 1740, 18 March 1741.

of printing the last Sessions papers'.[10] In the 1790s a serjeant's party entered an Irish ken in London to apprehend two deserters. Charging with fixed bayonets they succeeded.

But the worst was when we got out into the street; the whole district had become alarmed, and hundreds came pouring down upon us – men, women, and children. Women, did I say! – they looked fiends, half naked, with their hair hanging down over their bosoms; they tore up the very pavement to hurl at us, sticks rang about our ears, stones, and Irish – I liked the Irish worst of all, it sounded so horrid, especially as I did not understand it. It's a bad language.'[11]

II

The labour market of London, to which many Irish migrants 'piked', was exceptionally free. As Lot Cavenagh, the Dublin-born high-wayman, explained in the condemned cell before he was hanged, 'I proceeded on my Way to London, that great and famous City, which may truly be said, like the Sea and the Gallows, to refuse none.'[12] London was dominated by a mode of production called 'manufacture'. It required two types of workers. First there were those consigned to a specialized, partial task, using a single, refined tool, and contributing only partially to the completion of the finished product. Any of the trades examined in the last two chapters provide ready examples of such 'fractionated' workers. Secondly, there were the 'unskilled'. These were employed in gang forms of cooperation – building, dock work, road construction – or, lacking a background of apprenticeship, in the stepping and fetching within and without the manufactory. This labour grew in direct proportion to the division of craft labour. The first type of work was regular, uniform, continuous and sure; the second type was casual, undeveloped, incontinent, inebriated and promiscuous. The first worker was a 'hand worker'; and the second, a 'back worker' – with it or

---

[10] *The Proceedings*, 7–10 April 1725, and Michael Harris, 'Trials and Criminal Biographies: A Case Study in Distribution', in Robin Myers and Michael Harris (eds), *Sale and Distribution of Books from 1700* (Oxford, 1982), pp. 10 and 31.
[11] George Borrow, *Lavengro* (1851), Everyman edn (1961).
[12] The Ordinary's *Account*, 13 April 1743.

on it. Back worker and hand worker were necessary and complementary to the two-sided nature of work under manufacture.

The 'booleying' life of the wandering Irish worker was characterized by a picaresque refusal of regular work in London: the men became sailors, soldiers, harvest workers, canal-diggers, builders and coal-heavers; the women became prostitutes, laundresses, seamstresses, scullions and ballad-singers. These workers had few of the values of the Protestant work ethic. Urban workers observed St Monday. Arthur Young complained that Irish women refused to make hay. William Petty complained of the numbers of holidays: there were forty-nine more than English law allowed, including St

An Irish street-seller

Patrick's Day, 'his wife's and his wife's mother's'. Swift expressed the view in 1724 that half the souls in Ireland lived by begging or thieving. The desultory, sauntering habits of the Irish were an obstacle to the work discipline required for accumulation. Irish refusal to work was so widespread that what was elsewhere called 'the fruits of industry' in Ireland was called 'luck'.[13]

Proletarian labours in London were characterized by high turn-over, by the absence of guild fellowships, by ethnic heterogeneity, and by working conditions that were seasonal, dangerous and subject to harsh discipline. The productive power of such social labour arose from the assembly of many people in one place at one time. Individually weak and pitiful, as a collective mass this labour had power and posed danger. 'A body of men working in concert has hands and eyes both before and behind, and is, to a certain degree, omnipresent.'[14] Many of the Irish workers in London were employed as crafts persons, and they as often had emerged from craft experiences in Dublin or Cork. But it was the 'back workers' who had the more prominent presence – out-of-doors, gangs in fields, at building sites, and, most powerfully, upon the docks of the Thames, where in 1768 – that *annus mirabilis* – the social power of cooperative labour showed itself clearly as the collective power of an urban proletariat. To understand this we shall consider three determinate forms of the eighteenth-century Irish experience of mass, cooperative labour: agricultural work, soldiering and coal-heaving.

III

Many of those who lost their land went to England to work on the land owned by others. 'Spalpeen' is an Irish term for an itinerant

[13] This summary depends upon George O'Brien, *The Economic History of Ireland in the Eighteenth Century* (Dublin, 1918), ch. 3 especially, and upon more recent studies, namely L. M. Cullen, *An Economic History of Ireland since 1660* (1972), and the articles by Joel Mokyr, 'Uncertainty and Prefamine Irish Agriculture', and S. J. Connolly, 'Religion, Work-Discipline and Economic Attitudes: The Case of Ireland' found in T. M. Devine and David Dickson (eds), *Ireland and Scotland, 1600–1850: Parallels and Contrasts in Economic and Social Development* (Edinburgh, 1983); E. Estyn Evans, *The Personality of Ireland: Habitat, Heritage, and History* (1973), p. 79.
[14] Karl Marx, *Capital*, trans. Ben Fowkes, vol. i (1976), p. 317.

country labourer. Bands of spalpeens became a familiar sight in England at harvest-time. Of the Irish country workers hanged at Tyburn, most were hanged in the 1740s. Patrick Brown was dismissed from the July hay harvest in Hampstead. He retaliated against his employer by stealing his silver spurs. The gentleman had him hanged in September 1741, a timely example to the seasonal influx of spalpeens. Patrick Hayes from Kilkenny worked for weekly wages feeding cattle in St Pancras. He stole the keys and spectacles of the dairy farmer, and was hanged in August 1746. Bryan Cooley reaped hay in season. He stole a cane worth 5s. and was hanged in April 1743. His wife and four children came over from Ireland to comfort him before his hanging. William Bruce from Armagh 'came out of Ireland to look for work as far as Islington'. He stole a wig and a silk handkerchief; he was caught in a Barnet barn and hanged in August 1746. Patrick Kelly of Connaught was fifty years old with a wife and several children, many of whom were in London workhouses. He was a hay-maker and hanged for coinage. 'They file them down to the Letters, and file the Britannia quite off,' explained the Ordinary. Kelly said, 'I should not want an Estate if I had but a Quarter of what they have cheated poor People of.'[15]

These men and women had experienced the famine of 1740–41 – *bliadhain an áir* (the year of the slaughter), when mankind was 'the colour of the dock and nettles they feed on'. A country gentleman recorded what he had seen:

I have seen the labourer endeavoring to work at his spade, but fainting for want of food, and forced to quit it. I have seen the aged father eating grass like a beast, and in the anguish of his soul wishing for dissolution. I have seen the helpless orphan exposed on the dung-hill, and none to take him in for fear of infection; and I have seen the hungry infant sucking at the breast of the already expired parent.[16]

With such experience behind them the Irish itinerant population in London was used to being without money. Thomas Gent, who left Dublin for Chester in 1710 as a young apprentice, possessed a shilling. This made him a rich man in comparison to his companions, who on the trek to London were obliged to steal a goose for

[15] The Ordinary's *Account*, 13 April 1748, 16 September 1741, 3 July 1749, 13 April 1743, 1 August 1746 and *The Proceedings*, 14–19 January 1743.
[16] Anon., *Letter from a Country Gentleman in the Province of Munster to His Grace the Lord Primate* (Dublin, 1741); Michael Drake, 'Irish Demographic Crisis of 1740–41', *Historical Studies*, no. 6 (1968), p. 36.

supper.[17] Henry Fielding emptied two Shoreditch houses of more than seventy Irish people who among them did not have 'One Shilling'.[18] At mid-century an analyst of London crime listed as its third cause 'the mischief of Importing so many poor Irish every Year, under pretence of hay-making'. He recommended a system of import passes for the Irish coming to England as spalpeen harvesters.[19]

The recommendation was not heeded. And not only did English hay continue to be cut by Irish spalpeens, but also English wages. In London, to reduce the prevailing rate in building work, Irishmen were used. English builders, who preferred 'rather to be hang'd than starved', attacked Irish hod-carriers hired in 1736 to rebuild St Leonard's, Shoreditch.[20] A government spy left an account of how the 'common people' 'linked together in Clubbs for the Mutual Subsistance and Support of one another'. The undercutting of wages has not given the Irish labourer an enviable position in the historiography of the labour market in England.

Some of the Irish hanged at Tyburn knew Greek and Latin – such as Robert Haynes, a gallant of the Foot Guards, or Robert Irwin, a veteran of the siege of Londonderry, or Luke Ryley, the highwayman who robbed the Lord Mayor of London. Such classicists recall the tradition of Irish learning, and its devaluation by the eighteenth century. Learning, letters and music were not unknown to the spalpeen. Owen Roe O'Sullivan, the poet, was a landless Irish earth-delver. One of his longest and most well-known poems is about putting a new handle on his spade.[21]

> At the close of day, should my limbs be tired or sore,
> And the steward gibe that my spade-work is nothing worth,
> Gently I'll speak of Death's adventurous ways
> Or of Grecian battles in Troy, where princes fell!

[17] *The Life of Thomas Gent, Esq.* (1832), p. 5.
[18] Henry Fielding, *An Enquiry into the Causes of the Late Increase of Robbers*, 2nd edn (1751), pp. 141–3.
[19] 'A Citizen of London', *The Vices of London and Westminster* (1751), pp. 17–20.
[20] The account of these riots relied upon Anon., *Spitalfields and Shoreditch in an Uproar: Or, the Devil to Pay with the English and Irish* (1736), and a long report to the Prime Minister, Sir Robert Walpole, 'An Account of Some Particulars of the Late Riot in Shoreditch'. C(H)MSS, Cambridge University Library.
[21] Quoted in Daniel Corkery, *The Hidden Ireland: A Study of Gaelic Munster in the Eighteenth Century* (Dublin, 1925), pp. 9, 105.

The devaluation of learning was a consequence of the destruction of the Irish chiefs, whose poets, once aristocratic, were plunged into proletarian life. The poetry of 'hidden Ireland' therefore combined elevated diction with 'low' subject-matter, and provided a unique acknowledgement of the value of human labour. 'The Roving Worker' was a popular ballad in nineteenth-century Ireland.[22] The words date from the fall of Limerick (1694). To the familiar themes of Irish eighteenth-century balladry – departure from the homeland, separation from a loved one, and redemption through the Irish brigades – it adds familiarity with the tools and ways of the agricultural workers' lot:

> No more shall flail swing o'er my head,
> Nor my hand a spade-shaft cover,
> But the Banner of France will float instead,
> And the Pike stand by the Rover!

IV

Eight per cent of the Irish hanged at Tyburn had been soldiers. Many had served apprenticeships as tailors, weavers or shoemakers. Others were labouring country people. Such men comprised the 'wild geese' who left their homeland to form Irish regiments in European armies. It has been estimated that between 1691 and 1745, 450,000 Irishmen entered French military service – an exaggeration certainly, yet the number was significant. 'A good many became highwaymen and robbers.'[23] William Macklaughlane, a Belfast man, fought with the French regiments in the West Indies. James Carter, hanged in 1727 for stealing a silver tankard, had served in the French armies for five years. John Maloney, hanged for stealing a watch in 1722, had fought in Sicily and Messina for the Spanish. John Norton, hanged in 1705 for stealing a piece of damask, had fought all over Europe for twelve years. Recruitment of soldiers for Irish continental regiments took place in Ireland – where English ministerial policy actually found it useful since it rid a discontented population of the young, the rebellious and the energetic – and in London itself, where at the Rising Sun in Lincoln's Inn Fields, for

[22] Kathleen Hoagland (ed.), *1000 Years of Irish Poetry* (New York, 1953), pp. 184–5.
[23] Maurice Hennessy, *The Wild Geese: The Irish Soldier in Exile* (1973), p. 49.

instance, a gosling might join the wild geese at a promised rate of 7½d. a day – a wage competitive with that offered by English paymasters.[24]

Unlike the mercenary freebooters of the previous century, the soldier of the eighteenth century belonged to an army that was proletarian in two important respects. First, it was a waged army. Besides numerous customary allowances for food, drink and clothing, the soldier was supposed to receive a daily wage for his service. The payment of this was perhaps the most important step that a prudent general could take to ensure discipline. Second, the army's fighting power was cooperative in virtually every aspect: artillery entailed hierarchical cooperation among men of different skills; siegework required the simple cooperation among vast numbers that was comparable to canal-digging or road-making; marching and encamping were no less cooperative enterprises. Fighting power depended upon the success of rote-learning and repetitive drill of even the meanest individual soldier, who in the eighteenth century was armed with a weapon whose exercise, in the English army, required thirty-six different orders of command.[25] Maurice de Saxe, the French commander at Fontenoy, may introduce the most important aspect of eighteenth-century warfare. 'Military discipline,' he wrote in words quoted at the English Military Academy at Woolwich,[26]

is the soul of all armies; and unless it be established amongst them with great prudence, and supported with unshaken resolution, they are no better than so many contemptible heaps of rabble, which are more dangerous to the very state that maintains them, than even its declared enemies.

Observing that idleness, 'the instability of the human heart' and fatigue were the enemies of discipline and order, he wrote that 'it is absolutely necessary to make the soldier work'. He concentrated upon the comfort of the meanest unit of the army, the soldier, and

[24] John Cornelius O'Callaghan provides estimates of the numbers of 'wild geese' in his History of the Irish Brigades in the Service of France (Glasgow, 1870), p. 163. See also, John J. Silk, 'The Irish Abroad, 1534–1691', in T. W. Moody (ed.), A New History of Ireland, vol. iii, Early Modern Ireland, 1534–1659 (1976); the Ordinary's Account, 29 January 1733, 3 November 1725, 18 July 1722 and 7 February 1705; Lecky, op. cit., vol. i, p. 420.
[25] Major R. E. Scouller, The Armies of Queen Anne (Oxford, 1966), passim.
[26] George Smith, An Universal Military Dictionary (1779) and Maurice de Saxe, Reveries; Or, Memoirs upon the Art of War, trans. William Fawcett (1757), p. 79.

upon the soldier's lowest part, his feet. 'The principal part of all discipline depends upon the legs,' he wrote.

A great many of the wild geese moved earth as sappers and pioneers rather than shot each other as fusiliers or grenadiers; they were as familiar with the spade as the musket. Numberless men deserted. The Ordinary of Newgate wrote in 1735 that 'in the last short war [the War of Polish Succession] almost the one half of them went off and came over to England'. He was referring to those such as Peter Matthews, a Dublin shoemaker, who deserted at Phillipsburg, and Thomas Dwyer, a Tipperary country boy, who deserted at Fort Kiel. Before his hanging Dwyer was 'miserably poor and naked and complain'd for want of a Coat'. Then there was William Rine, a country worker from Munster, who deserted and was later hanged in London, and James Ryan, a poor farming man from the west of Ireland who was also at Phillipsburg, 'where finding there was little to be had but red hot Cannon Ball Bullets, he thought fit to desert'. Macmahon, a countryman from the north-west of Ireland, Gerald Farrell, a husbandman from Kildare, James Falconer, a Cork weaver, deserted too. Many of these men re-grouped in Flanders and made their way to London, where they became highwaymen and pickpockets. 'Among all these People that have sworn, there's not one but what are Irish,' said the judge at the Old Bailey. 'All Guilty. Death.'[27]

'Fontenoy ranks among the most murderous battles of the eight-eenth century,' its historian has written.[28] It was fought on 11 May 1745. The English were commanded by the Duke of Cumberland, who would become known as 'the Butcher' for his behaviour to the defeated Highlanders at the Battle of Culloden fought a year later. At Fontenoy, a General Hawley earned a popular sobriquet, 'the Hangman', after his notions of discipline. The French were commanded by de Saxe. His forces included six Irish regiments which were kept fresh until the end of the battle when, with slogans ('Remember Limerick!' 'Saxon Perfidy!') and tunes ('The White Cockade') prohibited in Ireland or England, they withstood Semple's Highlanders, defeated the Coldstream Guards and routed the

---

[27] The Ordinary's *Account*, 22 September 1735, 27 September 1736, 2 November 1736, 3 March 1737 and 3 March 1736.
[28] Francis Henry Skrine, *Fontenoy and Great Britain's Share in the War of the Austrian Succession, 1741–1748* (1906), p. 50.

exhausted Hanoverian troops.[29] While the victory loomed large in subsequent nationalist historiography, the ballad that came out of a battle has loomed larger.[30]

> You haven't an arm and you haven't a leg,
>   Hurroo! Hurroo!
> You haven't an arm and you haven't a leg,
>   Hurroo! Hurroo!
> You're an eyeless, noseless, chickenless egg;
>   You'll have to put with a bowl to beg:
>   Och, Johnny, I hardly knew ye!

Some Irish fought against the Hanoverians whenever possible. Such a one was Thomas Reynolds, hanged on 7 November 1750. He was in London on a 'furloe' to recruit men for the Irish brigade. He had served in Flanders. He had been at the siege of Fort William during the 1745 rebellion. He had seen his patron fall at Culloden (1746). Other Irish soldiers fought only to live, regardless of the colours on the standard. James Leonard, a Dublin shoemaker, for instance, was a drummer in George II's service at Gibraltar before he joined a Spanish regiment in Cadiz. Even when the experience of soldiering put men on opposite sides in war, life was such in London that their previous experience could make them effective allies. John Cassady was an Irish Catholic countryman; Robert Hunt was a Dublin Protestant. Cassady was a veteran of French Irish regiments; Hunt belonged to the British Grenadiers. In London they shared booty in stealing silver buckles and watches; they shared drink and dance at an Irish club ('a common Two Penny Hop'); they shared an enemy in Robert Rhodes, a notorious thief-taker; and they shared a veneration for St Patrick, whose day they sought to celebrate in 1740 by calling upon forty free Irish people to rescue them from the condemned wards of Newgate.

---

[29] This account of the battle draws upon Skrine, op. cit., O'Callaghan, op. cit., and John Mitchell, *The History of Ireland, Ancient and Modern, being a Continuation of the History of the Abbé MacGeoghegan* (New York, 1868); Hennessy, op. cit., p. 68. MacGeoghegan was the Chaplain to Dillon's Regiment of the Irish Brigades at Fontenoy. Adam Ferguson, the moral philosopher and historical materialist, provided spiritual encouragement to Cumberland's Highlanders, whom he addressed in Gaelic.

[30] Kathleen Hoagland (ed.), *1000 Years of Irish Poetry* (New York, 1953), pp. 271–3; J. G. Simms, 'The Irish on the Continent, 1691–1800', in Moody and Vaughan (eds), op. cit., p. 634.

V

Many Irishmen tried to escape from Newgate, like William Phillips, the Dublin tailor who escaped in 1728, or John Maxworth, alias Parliament Jack, who was nearly killed in an escape attempt in 1736, or James Hayes, who twice attempted to escape, once almost killing the turnkey, and once causing Newgate to be closed to all visitors. At his trial he had to be chained to prevent his assaulting the Lord Mayor, and he sailed up Holborn Hill double-ironed and handcuffed. Bryan Smith attempted to escape at Tyburn when, at the moment of his hanging, the crowd hindered the horses from pulling the cart from beneath his feet. George Ward was a Dublin house carpenter who belonged to 'a gang of young fellows' called the 'Cavanebale'. When the constables took up street-walkers, this gang set them at liberty, and locked up the officers of justice in their place. 'After the same manners they used to relieve Thieves, Robbers, or Highwaymen.'[31] A successful rescue of Irish prisoners in 1749 led to a large Government-sponsored manhunt that revealed the Dublin–London network of the Irish diaspora. Professor Clark has recently suggested that by mid-century the detailed course of events in the urban politics of Dublin and London were parallel and must be explained together. He suggested, furthermore, that the Irish example served frequently as an 'unacknowledged precedent' to the English. Although he wrote of parliamentary politics, the evidence is beginning to suggest that the same may be said of proletarian politics.[32]

The story begins with James Sinclair, a Scottish estate owner, a Member of Parliament, general and the Governor of Cork. He was commander of English forces in Flanders after Fontenoy, when the wild geese successfully plundered a clothing depot. He led an unsuccessful expedition in 1746 upon the French East India fleet off the coast of Brittany, and he was the employer of the philosopher David Hume. On 23 January, as Sinclair 'was going to pay his Compliments' to the Prince of Wales upon his birthday, he

---

[31] The Ordinary's *Account*, 30 April 1725, 24 May 1736, 22 November 1735, 11 August 1736, 3 July 1749.
[32] J. C. D. Clark, 'Whig Tactics and Parliamentary Precedent: The English Management of Irish Politics, 1754–1756', *Historical Journal*, vol. xxi (1978), p. 276; R. B. McDowell, *Ireland in the Age of Imperialism and Revolution, 1760–1801* (1979), p. 23.

discovered that his watch was missing. Two Irishmen, Thomas Topin and William Harper, were apprehended for stealing it and were locked up in the Westminster Gatehouse. The next evening twenty men armed with pistols and cutlasses attacked the prison, wounding three turnkeys and freeing Harper. Tobin was left chained to the floor since the imminent arrival of 'a party of the Guards' did not allow them sufficient time to file off his leg-irons. Nevertheless, 'they went off in Triumph and swore they would make a second Visit with Blunderbusses'. The Crown issued a proclamation against the rescuers and offered a reward of £100 for their capture.

John Bryan, a Covent Garden bricklayer, turned evidence against twelve of his former accomplices. Many were subsequently hanged.[33] There was James Field, who was a Dublin man and passed most of his life before the mast, upon privateers and merchantmen in the West Indies. In London he was a respected boxer. Although several warrants were out against him, 'the Officers were afraid of him, and if they met him in the Street, they pass'd him by without Notice'. He often acted as a bouncer at an Irish public house in Drury Lane called the Fox. Joseph Dowdell was born in Wicklow, where he served an apprenticeship to a leather-breeches-maker before moving to Dublin. He shipped aboard a Liverpool privateer. He resided at the Fox and lived by picking gentlemen's pockets in the Covent Garden piazza. Garret Lawler was born in Dublin. He was a butcher's apprentice. He broke his indentures, fled to Liverpool, piked to the start, and lived there by sharping and playing 'Old Nobb'. Thomas Masterton served an apprenticeship to a wig-maker in Dublin, and then took journeyman's work in Coventry. He moved to London and went upon the lay, picking pockets and breaking houses. Thomas Quinn, also a Dubliner, faithfully served an apprenticeship to a buckle-maker. He was a prominent figure in Dublin's 'Liberty & Ormond' riots. He went to sea in the West Indies trade. Unshipped in London, he joined the fraternity at the Fox and was caught for his participation in the rescue of Harper. The Fox was a place for refreshment and education. Dowdell trained Alexander Byrne, a Dublin gentleman's servant, in pocket-picking. Byrne was hanged in 1751. Daniel Thorowood, alias Dan the Baker, learned his trade in Dublin and his thieving in London. He was

[33] MRO, Sessions Papers, MJ/SP (September 1749), 'The Information of John Bryan'; *The Penny-London Post*, 20–23 January 1749; *The Worcester Journal*, 26 January 1749; *The London Gazette*, 31 January–4 February 1749; *DNB*.

hanged in 1751 with Richard Holland for stealing a gold watch. Holland was close to Field. Holland and Dan the Baker were caught at the Fox.[34]

W. E. H. Lecky noted the quasi-ritualized forms of violent disorder common to Dublin working people during the 1730s and 1740s, the feuds between students and tradesmen, butchers and weavers, Ormond Boys and Liberty Boys. Despite the paucity of research into Dublin plebeian culture, we know that it opposed much of officially constituted authority.[35] In July 1735 one journeyman's club captured a 'fellow that made it his Business to Swear against People for Committing Riots', Paul Farrel, known as Gallows Paul. By previous agreement he was turned over to another club, which cut out his tongue, castrated him and hanged him in Dublin's Weavers Square. A similar end befell Tim Kenney, a bailiff, and Mat Meakins, a constable.[36] The class war of the eighteenth century was bloody. The practice of justice by the Dublin proletariat favoured mutilation, scarring and ham-stringing, as did their 'betters'. The Irishmen hanged at Tyburn do not provide examples of disciplined behaviour. At his sentencing Patrick Demsey, the sailor and highwayman, 'was so wicked as to get himself drunk, and appear'd with all that Impudence and wicked Behaviour as astonish'd every Beholder; and as if in Defiance of all Law and Justice, wore his Hat in Court'. William Fleming, the Dublin highwayman, amused himself at his arrest by singing 'The Miller and the Highwayman'. When sentenced to hang he said, 'Damn my Eyes, if I do but live to see Bartholomew Fair and Southwark Fair over, I don't care if I am hanged.' Nor were the Irish women hanged at Tyburn models of feminine compliance. Ann Berry, the weaver, 'had resolution enough to put off all Female Softness and take to her the Roughness of the Robber'. Margaret Watson of Dublin was 'a wild, light-headed Girl, of disobedient Temper [who] regarded no Instructions'. Hannah Dagoe of Dublin, a milliner in London, was hanged for stealing a watch on St Patrick's Day. Being 'a lusty, strong, bold spirited woman' she was not easily hanged, knocking

---

[34] The Ordinary's *Account*, 31 December 1750, 13 April 1743, 19 December 1733, 2 October 1734, 17 June 1751.
[35] W. E. H. Lecky, *A History of Ireland in the Eighteenth Century*, 2nd edn (New York, 1893), vol. i, p. 322; J. A. Froude, *The English in Ireland in the Eighteenth Century* (New York, 1874), vol. i, p. 573.
[36] George Borrow, op. cit.

the hangman out of the cart before a company of Sheriff's officers subdued her so the hangman could do his work in earnest.[37]

Strong backbones, collective audacity, the inversion of class-based justice, the frequent practice of the art of escape, the bloody violence of soldiering, the rejection of feminine compliance, the clandestine social life of the public house and secret communication between London and Dublin thus seem to have been some of the characteristics of the London Irish at mid-century. To these we may add an undercurrent of Old Testament communism which was hinted at by the hanging of May 1750. Thirteen men and boys were carried to the gallows in four tumbrils. Of these three were Irish, four were sailors. Several tradesmen were represented – a postilion, a shoemaker, a butcher, a wig-maker, a coachman and an ivory-turner. A seventeen-year-old, said to be the son of William Harper, was hanged for stealing two gold rings. When he came to the tree, the Ordinary wrote, 'he talked to the Mob ... with as much Ease and Unconcern as a Man would do that was going to a Jubilee'.[38] In Jewish tradition the fiftieth year – or jubilee – was a time of emancipation and the restitution of land. In the evolution of the London proletariat the danger represented by the Irish did not go unnoticed. The principal London magistrate, Henry Fielding, regarded the presence of thousands of Irish in London as 'a Nuisance which will appear to be big with every moral and political Mischief'.[39] In the light of the strike of 1768 his remark appears prophetic. Fielding sought to reduce the danger by a policy of licensing such places as the Fox. Within a few years that policy and capacity for the moral and political mischief of the London Irish were to be tested by the coal-heavers.

VI

The importance of coal in eighteenth-century London can scarcely be over-emphasized. The ubiquitous dust infiltrated everything, from the throats of the men who shovelled it below the decks of the Newcastle colliers to the bronchial tubes of West End scullery

[37] The Ordinary's *Account*, 13 April 1743, 7 February 1750, 23 March 1752, 24 November 1740, 4 May 1763.
[38] ibid., 16 May 1750.
[39] Henry Fielding, *An Enquiry into the Causes of the Late Increase of Robbers*, 2nd edn (1751), p. 143; the Ordinary's *Account*, 11 November 1751, 29 July 1751.

maids. The small coalman with his sacks, or his cart and dray, was a common street figure.[40] One could not cross a London parish at the time the Rocque brothers made their map of London without passing two or three coal-yards. Among the bills of indictment attached to any Sessions of the gaol calendar, there is usually one or two for the theft of coal, just as there are two or three for the theft of food. The life and health of the people depended upon a regular supply of coal at low prices. Warmth, like nourishment, was a universal requirement. The boiling of soups, the baking of bread, the brewing of beer, the roasting of beef needed coal.[41]

The coal-heaver shovelled coal. He worked in gangs assembled by 'undertakers', contractors who 'undertook' to unload the collier ships. Between 400 and 900 men working in gangs of sixteen or

Coal-porters filling wagons at Coal Wharf

[40] John Ashton, *Social Life in the Reign of Queen Anne* (1883), pp. 54–5.
[41] Raymond Smith, *Sea-Coal for London: History of the Coal Factors in the London Market* (1961), pp. 70 ff.

eighteen, arranged in ascending platforms between the hold and the deck, removed the black cargoes to barges whose shallower draughts enabled them to dock alongside the coal wharfs. It was 'the greatest labour perhaps, performed by any man'.[42] Seven pints of liquid a day at least was required to replenish lost fluid. Work was uncertain. Wages varied between 14d. and 2s. a man per score (756 bushels) of coals unloaded. Deductions from wages by the undertakers (who assembled gangs at waterfront public houses) included 6d. to 9d. a day for drink, 1s. to 18d. for 'Commission money', 1d. for the undertakers' drawer, 1d. for his maid and ½d. rent on the shovel per chaldron unloaded. Two men monopolized the shovels. The same men controlled the supply of ash handles. A new coal shovel cost between 3s. 6d. and 5s. 6d.[43] The undertakers rented them at 300 per cent return. Slow-downs or strikes were swiftly punished by fines or worse: in 1751 when Harry Cummerfoot, 'a poor labouring Coalheaver', slowed down work to bargain for higher pay, he was committed to prison.[44] In the seventeenth century the heavers were protected by the Fellowship Porters and the Billingsgate Porters. These lost their efficacy by the 1690s, when sailors, soldiers and other non-freemen were permitted to compete for the work. The City of London was unsuccessful in organizing the heavers, and it opposed efforts at self-organization. The undertakers defeated some 'Articles of Agreement' drawn up by the heavers in 1739 to care for the sick, the lame, the widowed and the orphaned.[45] The high turnover is indicated by Tyburnography: Robert Elements was a carter, coal-heaver and highwayman. Edward Wentland was a jag-boot-maker, grenadier, East India sailor and coal-heaver. Tom Travis was a coal-heaver, sailor and Newcastle collier. Phil Wilson worked in the rope-walks, sailed to Norway, Virginia and the West Indies, and heaved coals. Lawrence Lee, an Irishman, heaved coals until he 'could bear it no longer'.[46] Injury, seasonal work and oppressive working conditions not only caused coal-heavers to take other kinds of work such as sailoring, harvesting, soldiering and

[42] Henry Mayhew, *London Labour and the London Poor* (1861), vol. iv, pp. 366 ff.
[43] T. S. Ashton and Joseph Sykes, *The Coal Industry of the Eighteenth Century*, 2nd edn (Manchester, 1964).
[44] 'An Impartial By-Stander', *The Case of Mr. R—ds* (1758), p. 9.
[45] Walter Stern, *The Porters of London* (1960), p. 108.
[46] The Ordinary's *Account*, 26 July 1732, 22 May 1732, 17 March 1755, 1 October 1753, 21 November 1743, 3 July 1749.

building, but also lent to the occupation its despicable reputation among settled artisans, like Francis Place, whose father-in-law, a Whitefriars coal-porter, died of drink.

The varieties of measuring coal encouraged pilfering, 'indirect Practises' and corrupt dealing. In theory, there were 3 bushels to 1 sack, 3 sacks to 1 vat, 4 vats to 1 chaldron and 21 chaldrons to 1 score. In practice, these units varied according to several factors: whether 'strike measure' or 'heap measure' was applied; whether Mr Savidge, the maker of vats, was uniform in his work; how the sacks were patched and mended; who measured the 'heap'; whether the twenty-first chaldron (called the 'Ingrain', and a perquisite of the London hangman) was included on shipboard or on the quayside; whether scorage (a shilling allowance) had been paid by the ship-master to the buyer; whether the merchants paid 'winking money' to the deputy meters of the City Coal Office; whether the coals were dry or wetted (when soaked they could swell like beans). Peculation and defalcation were rampant. A deputy meter was almost hounded out of office for refilling a vat the labourers had struck off. A labourer threatened to throw overboard a meter who complained of vats too greatly struck. 'There are particular gangs of Coal-Heavers,' we read, who have become 'so unruly that no Words of Threats will compel them to fill the Vatts'.[47] Spillages enabled children to collect coals from the river mud when the tide was out, the mudlarking that Mayhew describes. Some of the heavers hanged at Tyburn began life this way. Edward Joynes, who was hanged in December 1739, was a Shadwell glazier, sometimes a coal-heaver, and known for his 'indirect Practises' and pilfering. George Lloyd was a coal-heaver hanged on 3 October 1750 and called a 'Thames pilferer', as was Will Wright, hanged the same day. John Ryley, seventeen years old when he was hanged in 1747, was a carman who pilfered coals. A poor woman of St James's, named Rebecca Hart, stole coals. She provided the magistrate with her thoughts about it: 'It was no Sin in the Poor to rob the Rich,

---

[47] T. W. Willan, *The English Coasting Trade, 1600–1750* (Manchester, 1938) contains an appendix, 'Note on the Interpretation of Measurements of Coal', that is helpful. For Savidge's fraudulent vats, see the complaints reported in CLRO, *Repertories of the Court of Aldermen*, vol. cxl, fols. 405, 435, 460. Otherwise see, Henry Humpherus, *History of the Origin and Progress of the Company of Watermen and Lightermen*, vol. ii (1887), p. 200, and Anon., *Frauds and Abuses of the Coal Dealers Detected* (1747).

and that if is was, J— C— had died to procure the Pardon of all such Sinners.'[48]

VII

The evidence of the gallows suggests interesting 'knots' in the social relations to river life. Many of the hanged had worked 'the water lay'. Captain Keeble, who was hanged in 1743, robbed up and down the river: North Sea smacks, barges, West India sugarmen, lighters – any vessel moored in the dense river tiers were fish to his net. Cock-Eye Jemmy was his lieutenant. Their thefts were so frequent, their appropriations so efficient, that the shipmasters hired their own guards against them in the 1730s. John Fosset, living with his mother and sister in a Whitechapel garret and often 'in want of Bread', robbed with Captain Keeble. John Glew Gulliford hanged for his riverside depredations with Captain Keeble. He said, 'We all entered into an Agreement to go upon the River, and take anything we could get.' He got a firkin of butter and another sentence to Annapolis, where he had been transported twice before. This 'knot' helped sailors dispose of their 'little parcels', for these river boys knew the ladies of Rag Fair – Betty Barefoot, Jemmy Johnson, Moll James and Black Peg. Their 'Agreement' to 'take anything' followed the rejection two years earlier of an agreement for a coal-heavers' friendly society.

David Brown, a cabin-boy on a West Indiaman and sailor on a collier, from Newcastle (the 'Black Indies'), was hanged in 1751. The Ordinary mentioned his friends – gallows birds all – a list of whom suggests the breadth of such networks. James Newton, apprenticed to a holland trader and familiar with the Baltic, lodged in Cable Street and heaved coals. Michael Soss worked for rope-makers, hackling hemp and tarring junks; he had lived in Stepney and in New England. Applegarth was a Chatham sailor. William Tild, a Deptford lad, lost his father at sea, left his apprenticeship and fell into company that 'taught him how to provide for himself'. Anthony Byrne, a victualler, sawyer and sailor, was hanged with him. Richard Holland, waterman, sailor and coal-heaver, robbed the Billingsgate coal-factors. 'Sometimes he was dress'd as gay as

[48] The Ordinary's *Account*, 21 December 1739, 6 March 1732, 3 October 1750, 31 July 1747.

might be, and sometimes like the dirty Scoundrel he was.' Holland robbed with James Field, the Irishman who guarded the Fox. Holland knew Anthony Whittle, a New England sailor who had shipped with another Irishman, Bowen – also concerned in the Harper rescue. Holland also robbed with Benjamin Beckenfield, who was hanged on the last day of 1750 for stealing a hat.

In 1741 the Ordinary of Newgate explained how the Irish 'knots' of St Luke's and Shoreditch were dangerous associations. They would help each other in mutual defence. Charles Rogers, an unchurched, illiterate, tradeless coal-heaver, robbed a Customs officer, who later recognized him at a victualling house. Rather than lend him assistance, the 'ill Characters' of Whitechapel menaced the officer, and it took a substantial party of constables to make the arrest. Thieving provided its own kind of insurance. Thus when Russell Parnel, a rope-maker and coal-heaver, faced the gallows his reputation as a 'prime Hand' stood him well; his friends gave him subsistence in gaol, 'furnished him with a proper Dress to be hanged in' and provided his funeral.[49] When 'Agreements' existed and 'insurance' was provided, thieving offered to some an irresistible freedom. David Brown enlisted William Holmes with succinctly expressed speech:[50]

Go with me and do as I do and Money shall never be wanting. I live well upon the Lay and have everything at Command. We cannot be hanged more than once, and there's an End.

VIII

Starvation stalked the City in 1768. The price of bread had doubled. The price of meat had increased by a third. Crowds forced street-vendors to sell vegetables at reasonable prices. The Whitechapel butchers 'suffered prodigiously'. Elsewhere butchers 'were oblig'd to secrete their meat'. Corn-factors were attacked and their wagons stopped. The corn-dealers hid their plate, boarded up their coffee-houses and closed the Stock Exchange. On 11 May sailors assembled at the Stock Exchange 'and would not suffer any Person except their own Body to enter it'. Wage-workers withheld their labour. The

---

[49] ibid., 23 October 1751, 11 November 1751, 11 February 1751, 31 December 1750, 29 July 1751, 13 January 1752.
[50] ibid., 11 November 1751.

sailors and glass-grinders petitioned, shoemakers held mass meetings and the bargemen stopped work. The leaders of the tailors were imprisoned 'for irritating their Brethren to Insurrection, abusing their Masters, and refusing to work at the stated prices'.[51]

The mood was becoming desperate. Thomas Davis, for instance, said he 'did not care who they killed, rather than his family should starve'. When a 'Gentleman' asked a young man whether it was foolish for people to risk their lives, he was answered: 'Master, Provisions are high and Trade is dead, that we are half starving and it is as well to die at once, as die by Inches.'[52] It was feared that the 'Soldiery may become a Political Reverberatory Furnace' convincing the world 'that the Voice of the People is the Voice of God'. Soldiers were flogged and their discipline held. Two Piccadilly ballad-mongers who sang 'in praise of Liberty' were apprehended by the 'Peace Officers' and then rescued by a mob. In June, when the convicts sentenced to transportation were conveyed from Newgate to a 'close lighter' in Blackfriars, it was observed of the ninety-two that 'the major Part appeared very merry, and had Cockades with "Wilkes & Liberty" in their Hats'. Four months later another group of convicts were observed to be 'extremely merry' on a similar occasion: they 'huzza'd and declared they were going to a Place where they might soon regain their lost Liberty'.[53]

In many ways, the riots of the spring and early summer of 1768 appear to be classic instances of the eighteenth-century mob in action. There were the forms (petitioning, marching, illuminations, the smashing of windows) and the heterogeneity of the trades (tailors, shoemakers, carpenters, etc.). Another feature was the subordination of the mob's demands and actions to the middle-class reform movement led by John Wilkes,[54] although at several points

[51] CLRO, 'The Information of James Brown', Sessions Papers, bundle 1768.
[52] T. S. Ashton, *Economic Fluctuations in England, 1700–1800* (1959), p. 181; William Beveridge, et al., *Prices and Wages in England from the Twelfth to the Nineteenth Century*, vol. i, *Price Tables: Mercantile Era* (1939), p. 292; *Berrow's Worcester Journal*, 19 May 1768; *The Westminster Journal*, 14 May 1768; and the *Public Advertizer*, 14 May 1768.
[53] *Berrow's Worcester Journal*, 9 May 1768, 12 May 1768, 23 May 1768, 26 May 1768, 7 July 1768, 6 October 1768; *The Westminster Journal*, 7 May 1768, 14 May 1768; *The Public Advertizer*, 10 May 1768.
[54] George Rudé, *Wilkes and Liberty: A Social Study of 1763 to 1774* (1962), especially ch. 6; and Walter J. Shelton, *English Hunger and Industrial Disorders: A Study of Social Conflict during the First Decade of George III's Reign* (1973).

this movement seemed to be on the verge of losing control. 'The Extremities to which the Cry of Liberty is carried, seemed to threaten the Destruction of all Civil Society,' as one newspaper put it. Indeed, the extremities need to be seen as something new, unlicensed, insurrectionary, armed and proletarian. In 'striking' the sails the river workers prevented the ships from sailing. By hoisting the red flag of battle they signalled their intentions to their brothers. The artisans joined but did not lead these events; the river workers did, closing shipping and leading a ragged municipal strike, thus generalizing the term 'strike' and giving the red flag as a permanent bequest to the future proletarian movement. In July 'A Spectator' observed the pattern of the last few months: 'Thus Sailors, Taylors, Coopers, Lightermen, Watermen, &c. follow one another, the adventurous Coalheavers leading the Van.'[55]

The heavers suffered grievances particular to their work. In 1757 they petitioned Parliament against the undertakers who had 'artfully insinuated themselves into the Favour of the Masters of ships employed in the Colliery'. Undertakers often were 'considerable Owners in the coal ships'. As often they were 'established Ale-house keepers, and as such their Habitations are the sole Places of Rendezvous for those Labourers'. In 1758 the Coal Act (31 George II, c. 76) was passed despite the bribes of the undertakers to defeat it. The Act placed the heavers under the 'care and management' of the alderman of Billingsgate Ward. His clerk registered coal-heavers, allocated gangs to ship captains, received and distributed money for wages, and maintained a sickness and burial fund financed by a deduction from wages of 2s. in the pound.[56] The undertakers in response introduced the practice of 'whipping' coal. Whippers worked in reduced gangs of nine. Four 'firemen' in the hold loaded a basket. On deck four 'up-and-down-men' grasped a rope and with it climbed up a flight of steps called the 'way'; then, holding fast to the rope, they threw themselves from the top of the way to the deck. They thus 'whipped' the basket up from the hold. Whipping the coal, while requiring a greater outlay in baskets, tackle and cordage, in reducing gang size and the time necessary to 'unliver'

[55] Berrow's Worcester Journal, 12 May 1768 and The Public Advertizer, 21 July 1768.
[56] 'An Impartial By-Stander', op. cit., p. 4; JHC, vol. xxviii, p. 73 (9 February 1758). See JHC, vol. xxvii, p. 859 ff. (April and May 1757), and vol. xxviii, pp. 73 (9 February 1758), 202 (19 April 1758), 259 (30 May 1758) and 264 (2 June 1758).

(as it was called) a collier ship undermined the protections of the Coal Act.

In 1767, Ralph Hodgson, a Shadwell magistrate, organized another system of registration which succeeded in delivering the coal-heavers 'from those harpies who had hitherto kept them at such hard and scanty bread'. Hodgson represented a paternalist style of magistracy; he recognized that 'by a kind of prescription of custom' coal-heaving was 'deemed the property of the coalheavers'. This style was opposed by William Beckford, the alderman of Billingsgate Ward. His was the style of the slave master.[57] Indeed, he was the largest slave-holder in Jamaica, one of the richest men

A gang of coal-whippers at work

[57] M. D. George, *London Life in the Eighteenth Century*, p. 2, and Shelton, op. cit., p. 168. See also 'The Present State of the Coalheavers explained and considered', a report from one of the Government's spies, 30 June 1768, *Shelburne Papers*, vol. cxxx, William L. Clements Library, University of Michigan.

in the world, and a leader of the sugar interest. Beckford hired two 'clerks', Metcalf and Green, to counter-attack. The undertakers sought out Irish workers: 'One new Device they found out to reduce the Men's Wages for their own Emolument was to invite Numbers of men from Ireland, whom for some time they got to work at what rate they pleased.' The Irish immigrants formed clubs whose members 'were sworn to be always aiding & assisting to his Fellow Members'. One of these was called 'the Bucks', and another 'the Brothers'.

The murderous struggles that followed in 1768 between the coal-heavers and the new-style magistracy was organized around and through the riverside taverns. The tavern, even more than the parish, was the elemental unit of social life in London. The arduous nature of coal-heaving necessitated a close relationship with beer. The organization of the coal-heaving gangs, no less, required the public house. Since taverns were places of food and drink, control of them, especially during times of scarcity, was control of the river proletariat. That is why the magistrate's licensing power was so important, and why it was so precisely exercised during the months of riot in 1768. On the one hand, parasitic undertakers forced the coal-heavers to drink their wages away at their public house; on the other hand, the coal-heavers had taverns supporting them. It is tempting to compare this unit of urban social life with the 'knots' of river pirates (such as Captain Keeble's), or with the travelling harvest gangs of spalpeens, or with the camaraderie taught to the veterans of war. It is tempting also to see in such associations a parallel to the unit of traditional Irish kinship (*derbfine*), or traditional Irish agrarian settlement (*clachan*), or traditional Irish work reciprocity (*meitheall*), because they are also relatively small associations, based upon common purpose and mutualism – and were largely Irish in the sense that Gaelic could be freely spoken. While it is a temptation not all historians have resisted (Ellis sees a continuity between the 'knot' and the *sept*), on the basis of the evidence of the Tyburn gallows we resist it. While the same economic forces pulverized traditional Irish agrarian associations that recreated group associations in the infantry, the harvest gang and river tavern, these were not the same kind of organization, even though cooperative solidarity was common to them all.[58]

[58] P. Beresford Ellis, *A History of the Irish Working Class* (1972), p. 60; Maurice Craig, *Dublin, 1660–1860* (Dublin, 1969); the Ordinary's *Account*, 4 May 1741.

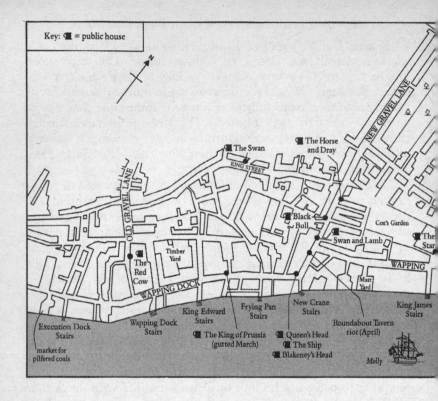

Metcalf was the keeper of the Salutation Inn; Green kept the Roundabout Tavern. The 'Bucks' met at the Horse and Dray; the 'Brothers' at the Star or the Pewter Dish. A dozen other taverns became involved directly in the struggle. At the end of February 1768 the Salutation Inn was mobbed and pulled down. In March, Ralph Hodgson, 'though not an Irishman', joined the St Patrick's Day parade with 'a green Herb in his Hat called a Shamrogge'. The undertakers allied with the constabulary, the headboroughs and the magistracy to get Hodgson dismissed. Green organized scab labour from the Roundabout Tavern. It was attacked in April with gunfire. A shoemaker bled to death on the pavement, a coal-heaver took a bullet in the head, 'dropped down backwards, and never stirred'. The taverns were besieged, their furnishings destroyed. Gunfire was frequent. Green was acquitted of murder. Those testifying for him were mobbed and one witness had her jaw broken. The coal-heavers were as violent in word as in deed. 'They would have Green's Heart

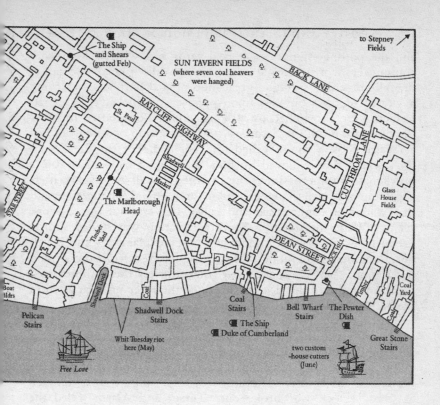

The Ship
and Shears
(gutted Feb)

SUN TAVERN FIELDS
(where seven coal heavers
were hanged)

to Stepney
Fields

BACK LANE

RATCLIFF HIGHWAY

St Paul

CUTTHROAT LANE

Shadwell
Market

The Marlborough
Head

Glass
House
Fields

Timber Yard

DEAN STREET

COCK HILL

Timber

Coal
Yard

Shadwell Dock

Coal

Coal
Stairs

Bell Wharf
Stairs

The Pewter
Dish

Boat
Bldrs

Pelican
Stairs

Shadwell Dock
Stairs

The Ship
Duke of Cumberland

Great Stone
Stairs

Whit Tuesday riot
here (May)

two custom
-house cutters
(June)

Free Love

and Liver and Do for him'; 'they would have him joint from joint';
'they would have his heart and liver, and cut him in pieces and hang
him on his sign'; 'they would hang him over his sign Post & cut
him into Beef Stakes'. From the perspective of the hungry, angry
people of the East End lodging-houses, the broad-backed, strong-
armed Irish coal-heaver, with sooty countenance, who could draw
on the collective power of the tavern with *its* society and *its* secrets,
would be an imposing figure. In 1768 he was awesome: by bringing
river traffic to a stand-still, he stopped the imperialist artery.[59]

In early May the coal-heavers extended their activities to include
the stopping of coal carts on land, the petitioning of wharfingers

[59] Benjamin Franklin, *The Gentleman's Magazine*, April 1768; Dermot Walsh,
'Alcoholism and the Irish', in MacMarshall (ed.), *Beliefs, Behaviors, and Alcoholic
Beverages: A Cross-Cultural Survey* (Ann Arbor, 1980); the Ordinary's *Account*, 21
December 1739, and *The Proceedings*, 5–10 December 1739.

and the posting of notices at coal-yards and wharfs. Men who continued to work at the old wage-rates were disciplined – Benjamin Franklin describes seeing a 'great mob of coal porters . . . carrying a wretch of their business upon poles to be ducked'. The coal-heavers were also joined by striking sailors. Between them, river shipping was dead. On Saturday, 7 May, a group of sailors entered a tavern, took a room, called for beer and sent for the keeper 'N.', whom they believed 'to be a Seaman's friend'. He wrote a proclamation for a mass meeting. It urged that all mates, carpenters and seamen, as well as owners and masters, attend the meeting; and that watermen, lightermen and ballast-heavers 'not go to work till our Wages be settled'. The proclamation was signed simply 'Seamen' – 'our own common title', they explained – and if it is not a democratic republic that is to be inferred from the closing declaration, 'No W—, No K—', nevertheless these abbreviated negations indicate the decisive break of the river proletariat from the 'Wilkes and Liberty' agitation.[60]

The Secretary of War readied the Guards. The Admiralty assigned armed cutters to the Pool. On Wednesday the merchants meeting at Cornhill acquiesced in some of the demands. The alliance between sailors and coal-heavers fell apart after the arrival on 20 May of the Newcastle collier fleet. The crews of these ships were employed as scabs.[61] Dock war broke out. 'Terror and Alarm' filled the neighbourhoods. Scores were killed. The coal-heavers sang:

> Five pounds for a sailor's head
> and twenty for a master's;
> We will cut the lightermen's throats
> and murder all the meters.

When sailors began to unliver coal at Shadwell dock on Whit Tuesday, the heavers attacked, and in the tumult that followed John Beattie, an apprentice sailor aboard the *Free Love* (James Cook's first ship), aged twenty-four, was wounded and died a fortnight later. With the river proletariat split over this shedding of blood the

---

[60] Franklin, op. cit.; *Berrow's Worcester Journal*, 5 May, 12 May, 19 May 1768; *The Public Advertizer*, 12 May, 13 May, 19 May 1768; 'Memorials of a Dialogue betwixt several Seamen, a certain Victualler and a S—l Master in the Late Riot', *Shelburne Papers*, vol. cxxx, William L. Clements Library, University of Michigan.
[61] *Calendar of Home Office Papers of the Reign of George III, 1766–1769*, pp. 336, 337, 341, 342, 395.

Government retaliated. Troops were posted in Shadwell. Cutters patrolled the Pool. Rewards were advertised. Country magistrates were notified to be on the look-out for fugitives returning to Ireland. Taverns suspected of containing arms were raided. Nine coalheavers were indicted for Beattie's murder. Four were apprehended in Staffordshire and escorted back to London by the 10th Regiment of Dragoons. They were James Murphy, James Duggan, Malachy Doyle and a certain Davis. Their trial opened on 6 July. The Government prepared its case carefully, drawing on the reports of its spies. The defendants were not without their supporters: two former employers of Davis spoke to his good character; a victualler and the keeper of the Swan spoke for Dogan; seven Shadwell witnesses spoke on behalf of Murphy; and Doyle was given good character by two former landlords and his current landlady. Nevertheless, James Murphy and James Duggan were found guilty and sentenced to be hanged.[62]

Hanged they were, on St Monday, 11 July, at Tyburn. Murphy's right hand, after he had swung, was stroked upon a child suffering from scrofula. Since their crime had been murder, they were sentenced also to be dissected at Surgeon's Hall. The Sheriff, fearing a rescue of their bodies, returned to the City via Fleet Street, thus avoiding St Giles-in-the-Fields, an Irish quarter, that lay across the more direct route. He did not want the Irish wake to be held in an anatomy theatre. The wake, in any case, was 'an unfortunate custom', according to M. Dorothy George, exercising a judgement shared by the Catholic Church in Ireland, which by mid-century began vigorously to oppose this and other 'heathenish' customs.[63] Nevertheless, on Monday night at Surgeon's Hall Irish keeners assembled 'with great Exclamations, with Bewailing'. We do not know what they said. The Irish language was especially suited to

---

[62] *Berrow's Worcester Journal*, 23 June 1768; *The Proceedings*, 6–13 July 1768; PRO, Treasury Solicitor, Papers, TS, 11/818/2696, and WO, 4, *Outletters*, 83/46, fol. 483; the Ordinary's *Account*, 17 March 1755; George, op. cit., p. 239; CLRO, 'The Information of James Becket', *Sessions Bundle*, June 1768; *A Journal of the Proceedings of J. Hewitt, Senior Alderman of the City of Coventry in his Duty as a Magistrate During a Period of Thirty Years and Upwards*, 2nd edn (1790), pp. 352–3.
[63] Sean O Suilleabhain, *Irish Wake Amusements* (Cork, 1967); J. L. McCracken, 'The Ecclesiastical Structure, 1714–60', p. 99 and Brian O Cuiv, 'Irish Language and Literature, 1691–1845', pp. 409–10, in Moody and Vaughan, op. cit.; and Thomas Crofton Crocker, *Researches in the South of Ireland*, ch. 9 (1824); Kerby Miller, op. cit., p. 80.

the extemporary lament. The violent deaths of Whiteboys in Ireland during the previous years were the subject of many elegies, laments and ballads. Thomas Crofton Croker wrote, 'keens are a medium through which the disaffected circulate their mischievous principles'. And not just keens. The games at wakes, such as Leaping the Besom, Hearing Confessions, Frumso Framso, Dividing the Meat, Hiding the Robber, the Spy, Listing for a Soldier, Coining the Money, the Mock Court – to name a few – circulated both 'mischievous principles' and the mischief itself, as not uncommonly a nocturnal wake might include attacking the property of an unpopular landlord. The wake of Murphy and Duggan, therefore, was watched by the authorities, and 'the Irish Howl lasted 'till near Two in the Morning'.[64]

Their hanging and the more spectacular hanging that was to follow in two weeks' time were for the instruction of Anglo-Irish workers within the metropolis and without. The Solicitor-General estimated that two-thirds of the coal-heavers were Irish. Certainly many of their names were: Kelly, Murphy, Kinshelo, Doyle, Magoury, Mahoney, McCone, MacDaniel. 'The name of an Irishman is enough to hang him,' was a proverbial summation of Old Bailey justice. It was widely thought that the leadership of the coal-heavers were 'of the Gang of White Boys in Ireland, driven out from thence for the most Enormous Crimes, as they have bragg'd and given it out themselves', to quote the Solicitor-General. In June it was reported that some coal-heavers 'called Whiteboys robbed and ill-treated divers persons in Stepney Fields'. At the end of the month, the newspapers reported: 'Near one hundred Irish Coal-heavers (called the Boys) have made their Escape.' In Samuel Foote's dramatic representation of the strikes of 1768–9 he assumed that the Irish were Whiteboys and trained to arms 'from earliest youth'.[65] That particular was an exaggeration, obviously, and yet so frequent is the mention of the Whiteboys in connection with the coal-heavers that the subject is worth consideration.

---

[64] *The Westminster Journal*, 16 July 1768; *Berrow's Worcester Journal*, 23 June 1768, 14 July 1768; PRO, Treasury Solicitor, Papers, TS, 11/818/2696; Sean J. Connolly, *Priests and People in Pre-Famine Ireland, 1780–1845* (Dublin, 1982); Brian O Cuiv, op. cit., pp. 409–10.
[65] Samuel Foote, *The Tailors; A Tragedy for Warm Weather* (1778), p. 31.

IX

The Whiteboy 'outrages', the name given to the largest and longest of agrarian rebellions in Ireland, lasted intermittently from 1761 to 1785. The actions of these Levellers, as the Whiteboys were sometimes called, took place in a period of increased expropriation and accumulation, intensified by the demands of two world wars. Following the Williamite confiscations of the 1690s the forests, and the human culture dependent upon them, were very largely destroyed. The agrarian policy introduced into Ireland promoted the use of land for cattle-raising rather than for growing food that could feed the population.[66] These long-term tendencies were exacerbated by the 'agricultural prosperity' that followed the bad harvests of 1757. The prices of pastoral commodities – beef, pork, butter – rose steeply to meet the provisioning needs of the British Army during the Seven Years War and to expand supplies to colonies in the Caribbean and North America. With the outbreak of cattle disease in continental Europe, and the passage in 1759 of the Cattle Exportation Act, the value of Irish land increased greatly. The tendency inherent in Irish agrarian policy that had already created two famines now received impetus that created, on the one hand, many small fortunes for sharp cattle-dealers, urban victuallers and rapacious landlords, and, on the other hand, a mass of dispossessed people who were no longer quite so willing to accept 'misfortune'. The poorest of the cottiers who had derived subsistence from a potato patch or cow kept on the common land suddenly found that even these were to be denied, as landlords evicted them in search of new grazing lands and erected walls, hedges and fences to keep their herds in and these former tenants out. Against this, the Irish cottier reacted with what Lecky called 'an insurrection of despair'.[67]

[66] The following summary of the Whiteboy Movement draws upon W. E. H. Lecky, *A History of Ireland in the Eighteenth Century*, new edn (New York, 1893), vol. ii, ch. 3; Angus Calder, *Revolutionary Europe: The Rise of the English-speaking Empires from the Fifteenth Century to the 1780s* (New York, 1981), pp. 672 ff.; Sam Clark and J. S. Donnelly, Jr (eds), *Irish Peasants: Violence and Political Unrest, 1780–1914* (Madison, Wisconsin, 1983); and James S. Donnelly, Jr, 'The Whiteboy Movement, 1761–5', *Irish Historical Studies*, vol. xxi, no. 81 (March 1978), pp. 20–54.
[67] Lecky, op. cit., vol. ii, p. 226; Richard Musgrave writes that the Whiteboy Movement began in 1759 – see *Memoirs of the Different Rebellions in Ireland*, 3rd edn (Dublin, 1802), vol. i, pp. 36–54. See also, M. R. Beames, 'Peasant Movements: Ireland, 1785–1795', *Journal of Peasant Studies*, vol. ii, no. 4 (July 1975), pp. 502–6.

In October 1761, bands of 200–400 people, dressed in white frocks and white cockades, threw down fences enclosing lands in Limerick. In the following years the Movement quickly spread to Cork, Tipperary and Waterford, and adopted actions designed to redress other grievances, such as the manifold tithes (of potatoes, of agistment, of turf, of furze) imposed by an alien religious establishment. The export of provisions was hindered, prisoners were rescued, gaols opened, garrisons attacked, apprentices released, cattle maimed, wasteland ploughed, and everywhere walls and fences torn down. The Movement was cloaked in anonymity and mystery. It was conducted 'under the sanction of being fairies'. It was led by mythological figures such as Captain Right, Slasher, Thumper, Cropper, Madcap Setfire and Queen Sive.[68] The frequent employment of secret oaths distinguished the Whiteboy Movement from previous episodes of mass unrest, and contributed to endowing 'hidden Ireland' with insurrectionary potential. One historian has argued that the Whiteboys and subsequent agrarian societies 'may have prevented the type of wholesale eviction which took place in Scotland in the last half of the eighteenth century'.[69]

While the Whiteboy Movement began in rural and agrarian settings, it ought not to be interpreted exclusively as 'agrarian unrest'. Certainly most members of the Movement were cottiers and agricultural labourers, but there were also craftsmen from the towns, who contributed to both the leadership and the rank-and-file. The modern historian of the movement stresses the influence of the weavers, who were notable for their strong journeyman combinations, the militance of their strikes in the 1760s and their familiarity with conacre rents, tithes and low agricultural wages.[70] Just as the creation of a landless proletariat is a corollary to the expropriation of land, so the experience of that struggle will move with the wandering proletariat thus created. A historian of the transported convicts to Australia wrote: 'The Whiteboy Associations were, in a sense, a vast trades union.' Whiteboy sabotage, according to Constantia Maxwell, contributed to the violence of Dublin jour-

---

[68] Called 'Rightboys' in Munster – see T. W. Moody (ed.), *A New History of Ireland*, vol. viii, *A Chronology of Irish History to 1976* (1982); J. A. Froude, *The English in Ireland in the 18th Century* (New York, 1874), vol. ii, p. 25.
[69] Maureen Wall, 'The Whiteboys', in T. D. Williams (ed.), *Secret Societies of Ireland* (Dublin, 1973), p. 24.
[70] Donnelly, op. cit., p. 39.

neymen. The friendly society of Philadelphia's ship carpenters, its historian avers, was associated with the Whiteboys. Therefore, when we consider the terms of exchange between England and Ireland in the late 1760s that included £1½ million in remittances to absentee landlords, £3 million of exports and thousands of hungry labouring people, we need to add to such material commerce a cultural exchange: broader than choleric playwrights or sad balladeers, it included the rebellious organizations of 'hidden Ireland' that surfaced in London in 1768 with such great effect. 'England has sown her laws like dragon's teeth,' said the Chief Baron of the Irish Exchequer, 'and they have sprung up, armed men.'[71]

X

The London Irish had by 1768 an unparalleled knowledge of arms and armed struggle. They contributed to an insurrectionary impulse within the London working class. At the same time, as a consequence, the Irish had close knowledge of violent death. The intimacy of that knowledge was expressed in vivid euphemisms designed to reduce the terror of hanging. Seven coal-heavers received the 'cramp jaw' at the Old Bailey only after a new interpretation was placed upon the Waltham Black Act. The seven danced 'a new jig without music' on 26 July 1768. This particular 'crack neck assembly' was located in Sun Tavern Fields, Shadwell, where the river people had held their mass meeting a few months before. The move from Tyburn was designed to terrify the poor and working people of the river parishes. The 'breath stopper' was witnessed by 50,000 spectators, perhaps the largest crowd at such a scene since the hanging of the Earl of Ferrers eight years earlier. The Government anticipated disorders, if not rescue attempts, when these seven were to dance 'tuxt de ert and de skies'. From 6 a.m. more than 600 soldiers patrolled the streets of Wapping and Shadwell. The Sheriff

<hr>

[71] Constantia Maxwell, *Dublin Under the Georges, 1714–1830* (1936), p. 270; A. G. L. Shaw, *Convicts and Colonies: A Study of Penal Transportation from Great Britain to Australia and Other Parts of the British Empire* (1966), p. 173; James H. Huston, 'An Investigation of the Inarticulate: Philadelphia's White Oaks', *The William and Mary Quarterly*, vol. xviii, no. 1 (January 1971); Thomas Prior, *A List of Absentees of Ireland*, 3rd edn (Dublin 1769), John Philip Reid, *In a Defiant Stance: The Conditions of Law in Massachusetts Bay, the Irish Comparison, and the Coming of the American Revolution* (Philadelphia, 1977), p. 142.

ordered all the constables of the Tower and Holborn divisions to assemble at the hanging site and to come armed with their staves. Thomas Turlis, the hangman, had stolen coal from a neighbour's cellar five years earlier. But, that his work might not be interrupted, the Sheriff quickly obtained a pardon for him. He did his duty upon the coal-heavers, sent 'a-spinning like a whirligig'. Once they had 'peaceably' exited the world, many of the spectators may have gone for a drink as was customary:[72]

> Wid a facer we coddled our blood
> For de wind id blows cold from de gibbett.

The hanging of these seven was the second of the last twelve months to be directly related to the emerging forms of labour relations. A year earlier, at Elizabeth Brownrigg's hanging at Tyburn in September 1767, the crowds had exalted. She was found guilty of murdering her apprentice. She had maintained a house to which parish orphans were sent for discipline, correction and work. Her hanging, thus, had helped to limit the exploitation of children by London employers. The hanging at Sun Tavern Fields, therefore, was a setback. It taught a hard lesson about collective bargaining: attempts to counteract the rise in the price of provisions by improving wage rates would not be allowed. The paternal policy towards labour relations represented by Hodgson had no place in river commerce.

With the hanging at Sun Tavern Fields the insurrectionary vanguard of the river proletariat was broken. The 'universal sullenness' that had worried Benjamin Franklin had passed. The midsummer hay harvest was good, the prospect of a bountiful grain harvest was bright, and corn imports were being unloaded. In August, when 102 ships arrived safely in the Thames, having weathered severe gales in the Yarmouth roads, disturbances did not interrupt their unloading. As for coal-heaving, some major changes were in order. The Government kept troops billeted in Wapping throughout September, although these troops hazarded their lives if they unlivered coal (two were murdered for doing this). The Admiralty kept its sloops and cutters in the river to protect outward-bound ships. The Secretary of State received a memorandum that included some radical proposals for the reorganization of coal-heaving: abolition

---

[72] *The Public Advertizer*, 25, 26, 27 July 1768; and Horace Bleackley, *The Hangmen of England* (1929), p. 90.

of middlemen; direct hiring by collier captains; payment of wages on board ship instead of in the tavern; penalties for docking wages or quitting work in the middle of a job. Nothing came of this. The coal wharfingers advertised for 300 men at a guinea a week, and Alderman Beckford agreed to advance wages after the Sun Tavern Fields hanging from 20d. per score to 2s. per score. The collier masters refused these rates, continuing to pay 18d. and hiring sailors.[73]

Ralph Hodgson lost his commission on the Middlesex Bench, retired to another part of town and wrote his memoirs. John Green had to give up the Roundabout Tavern. He moved to Lambeth and lived upon a pension from the Secret Service of £280 per annum. In 1779 he applied for preferment in the Middlesex Volunteers. Alderman Beckford became Lord Mayor of London, the Jamaican plantocrat now a master of wage-slaves as well as slave-slaves. Benjamin Franklin interrupted his studies of electricity in the late summer of 1768 to rewrite the Lord's Prayer. Instead of 'Thy will be done' he proposed 'May thy laws be obeyed'. Instead of 'Give us this day our daily bread' – a phrase he objected to because it 'seems to put a Claim of Right' – he substituted 'Provide for us this Day as thou hast hitherto daily done.' It is doubtful that these alterations would have caught on in the devotions of the river people, who, judging from the reception they offered John Wesley when he came to preach at an East End rope-walk a few years later, fiercely adhered to their own notions. They dumped him in a pond, swearing 'they would hear no such Doctrine as Damnation'.[74] Unfrightened by damnation, the London mob was even less intimidated by hanging.

To the consternation of ascendant legal authority in Ireland, the cottier was 'not terrified by the gallows'. This had recently been demonstrated. The hangings of twenty-six people in Cork, Waterford, Clonmel and Kilkenny for various Whiteboy offences during the 1760s failed to terrify the populace. The condemned proclaimed their innocence. The hanging of the Newmarket Whiteboys inspired poetry of vengeance. The wake of a Kilkenny Whiteboy was pub-

---

[73] Berrow's Worcester Journal, 26 May, 4 August, 1 September 1768; The Public Advertizer, 8 August 1768.
[74] Benjamin Franklin, Papers, ed. William B. Willcox, vol. xv, p. 301 (New Haven, 1982); John Norris, Shelburne and Reform (1963), pp. 191–3; Robert Wearmouth, Methodism and the Common People in the 18th Century (1943), p. 158.

licly funded. At Cork the Whiteboys mounted the gallows in their white frocks. Aggravation of the penalty by further degradation of the bodies – the head of a certain O'Sullivan was stuck on a pike, the breasts of the Kilkenny hanged were scored – only made matters worse. When Father Sheehy was hanged in 1766 the people treated the earth over his grave as holy ground; some years later his executioner was murdered by the populace.[75] Darby Browne swore at the gallows 'to be true to Sive and her children'. James Buxton mounted the gallows saying he had tried to put a 'stop to the oppressive and arbitrary valuation of tithe jobbers'.

Gallows terror being insufficient in Ireland to destroy the Whiteboy Movement, the Government responded by passing the first Coercion Act (1765). But this too made little impression and the first Whiteboy Movement was only defeated by an epidemic of smallpox, bad harvests and mass starvation.[76] It is not suggested that the Ascendancy in Ireland, or London, preferred the weapon of starvation to hanging, or that it 'conspired' to substitute the one for the other, but, as we saw in the previous chapter, the efficacy of high prices and dearth had been noted. In the far more turbulent 1790s the massacre of battle would replace the 'legal massacre' of hanging. Meanwhile, associations of armed, largely Protestant, middle-class men, called Volunteers, were formed in Ireland, whose duties were to suppress Whiteboys in the countryside and labour combinations in the town.[77]

By the end of the eighteenth century the Irish had established a new genre of song – the execution ballad. Such ballads were written in a slang or cant that was common to proletarians in port cities throughout the north Atlantic. They were coarse and lewd. The first English compilations of 'Irish Minstrelsy' refused to print them on the grounds of their deleterious influence on morals, and even J. E. Walsh reprinted selections from 'The Night Before Poor Larry was Stretched' only as an example of that song's 'utter laxity of all discipline and want of decency'. Yet, these ballads – particularly the six that make up the Larry Caffrey cycle – are of much interest. They tell of outwitting the thief-takers. They spell out curses against

[75] Lecky, op. cit., vol. ii, pp. 41–5.
[76] James S. Donnelly, Jr., 'The Whiteboy Movement, 1761–5', *Irish Historical Studies*, vol. xxi, no. 81 (March 1978), pp. 47–53.
[77] R. B. McDowell, 'Colonial Nationalism and the Winning of Parliamentary Independence', T. W. Moody, op. cit., p. 222.

the hangman and judges. They compare the law to the devil. They concoct intrigues of resurrection. They have philosophy:

> His brain-box hung all a-one side,
> And no distiller's pig could be blinder
> But dat is what we all cum to.

They have religion:

> Dough sure it's de best way to die
> De Devil a better a livin'!
> For sure, when de gallows is high,
> Your journey is shorter to heaven.

They have diagnostics:

His eyes were swell'd in his brain-box, like two scalded goose-berries in a mutton tart, and his grinders rattled in his jaw-wags, for all de world like a pair of white-headed fortune-tellers in an elbow shaker's bone box.

Solemnity, rectitude and 'delicacy' are noticeable only by their complete absence.[78] If death was an escape from oppression, the funeral was a celebration by the oppressed. The demographic explosion of mid-century has been studied by historians without much reference to women's attitudes to the labour of childbirth. Yet it was their experience that is summarized in the saying, 'Sing a song at a wake, and shed a tear when a child is born.' The corpse at the wake with pipe in his mouth and playing-cards in his hand was no longer beast, brute, drone or savage. The traditional anarchy of the 'pagan' wake had become an occasion to display a fearless defiance towards the repressive terror of official punishment. Such attitudes contributed to the subversion of thanatocratic power in London. Having danced the 'Kilmainham minuet', the corpse, no longer alive in the struggles of life and not yet consecrated by the

---

[78] James Hardiman, *Irish Minstrelsy; Or, Bardic Remains of Ireland with English Poetical Translations* (1831); J. E. Walsh, *Ireland Sixty Years Ago*, 3rd edn (Dublin, 1851), pp. 68–9; James N. Nealy, *The Mercier Book of Old Irish Street Ballads* (Cork, 1967); Donal O'Sullivan, 'Dublin Slang Songs, with Music', *Dublin Historical Record*, vol. i, no. 3 (September 1938), pp. 75–93; and Dr George Caffentzis, 'Cynical Content, Vision, and Momentum: George Berkeley's Philosophy of Money' (Calabar, Nigeria, 1985).

rites of Christian burial, was the cause for bringing forth drink and smoke, song and dance, kisses and love.

> When he came to de nubbing chit,
>   He was tuck'd up so nate and so pritty;
> The rumbler shov'd off from his feet,
>   And he died vid his face to de city.
> He kick'd too, but date was all pride,
>   For soon you may know 'twas all over;
> And when date de noose was untied,
>   At home why we wak'd him in clover,
>   And sent him to take a ground sweat.

PART FOUR

THE CRISIS OF
THANATOCRACY
IN THE ERA OF REVOLUTION,
1776–1800

Arnold Toynbee concluded the lecture that introduced the expression, 'industrial revolution', with the observation that its effects 'prove that free competition may produce wealth without producing well-being'.[1] Indeed, the wealth was *based* upon inequality and riches *meant* poverty. The problem, as Adam Ferguson stated in 1792, was to direct the poverty into the labour that would produce opulence. The 'competition' thus had to be organized. It was the wage system that became the fulcrum around which class relations revolved. The wage ceased to be invariable in the organization of social production and became both an indicator of class relations and a highly dynamic variable of exploitation. It operated to lengthen the working day, intensify labour by speed-up and invigilation, to produce competition within the labour markets, and finally to create a new moral and political stratification of the labouring poor.

Economic historians have been cognizant of the non-monetary relations between employers and employees in eighteenth-century Britain. Employers used truck payment as a means of avoiding guild or trade-union wage standards. Scottish salters and coal-miners 'arled' their children to a form of bondage that was not proscribed until 1799. Edwin Gay and E. Lipson have stressed how the removal of production to the master's premises (manufacture) ended the architectural and temporal circumstances that made misappropriation favourable to workers. Middlemen were eliminated, transaction time was reduced and close supervision was made constant. The intimate histories of the first English industrialists reveal the struggle at the most advanced sites of industrialization. Thus in 1772 as Wedgwood was expanding production at his Etruria works he found the 'Villainy' of his servants so widespread that he had to 'to sweep the House of every servant we have in it, Male and Female, some from the field Men, and others from the Works'.

[1] *Lectures on the Industrial Revolution* (Rivington, 1884), lecture viii, p. 93.

Matthew Boulton and John Watt unaccountably lost copper at their steam-engine factory; they dismissed several workmen for insubordination, who returned on Christmas Day of 1800 to rob the works. Non-monetary appropriation, or 'custom', has been closely studied in English agriculture, and it is there that the relationship between enclosure and custom finds its fullest expression. Mantoux wrote that the abolition of turbary, pannage, estovers and other common agrarian rights was the direct result of enclosure, which thus destroyed a class that had lived 'on the borders of [private] property rights'.[2]

A similar attack on customary rights occurred in London, with the difference that the metropolitan setting, despite the variety of trades and employments, enabled 'large bands of labourers', to quote John Millar, through 'constant intercourse' and 'with great rapidity' to communicate until the 'movements of the whole mass proceed with the uniformity of a machine'. To counter the tendency, the labour process itself had to be revolutionized, and this is precisely what Joseph Bramah, Samuel Bentham and William Vaughan set out to do with various mechanical innovations, as we shall see in the next three chapters. Toynbee, in considering the distinguishing characteristic of the period, placed an emphasis upon 'competition' rather than 'mechanization', and like him we shall focus on social rather than technical relations. For it was 'crime' that these tinkerers, entrepreneurs and inventors sought to abolish.

The Gordon Riots represented a watershed in London class relations. For the first time an international proletariat directly attacked the imperial ruling class at its major institutions, and so gave that class a serious fright. Thenceforth, the articulations of punishment and discipline underwent widespread changes, not the least of which was the abolition of the Tyburn hangings. This was the crisis of the thanatocracy – the form of state power that had

---

[2] George W. Hilton, *The Truck System including a History of the British Truck Acts, 1465–1960* (1960), p. 41; Jacob Viner, *Guide to John Rae's Life of Adam Smith* (New York, 1965), p. 110; Edwin Gay, 'The Putting-Out System', *International Encyclopedia of the Social Sciences*, vol. xiii (1935), pp. 6–11; E. Lipson, *The History of the Woollen and Worsted Industries* (1921), pp. 50–69; Ann Finer and George Savage (eds), *The Selected Letters of Josiah Wedgwood* (1965); Birmingham Central Reference Library, Boulton & Watt MSS, 'The Examination of William Fouldes, 10 April 1801'; Paul Mantoux, *The Industrial Revolution in the Eighteenth Century: An Outline of the Beginnings of the Modern Factory System in England* (1928), pp. 148–51.

for two centuries maintained discipline in the capital by periodic massacres at the gallows.[3] Thereafter, under the impetus of the changes in the labour process, the London proletariat was recomposed, whereby changes of disciplinary punishment and changes in the material relations of production were managed by a more closely studied allocation of wages. This is what gave the most brutish tyrants of the period their significance: Governor Wall had whipped a man to death for demanding 'short allowance' money; Captain Bligh fell victim to mutiny for repeated violation of material custom at sea.

[3] David D. Cooper, *The Lesson of the Scaffold: The Public Execution Controversy in Victorian England* (Athens, Ohio, 1974).

CHAPTER TEN

THE DELIVERY OF NEWGATE, 6 JUNE 1780

> Albion rose from where he laboured at the Mill with
> Slaves. Giving himself for the Nations he danc'd the
> dance of Eternal Death.
>
> William Blake

> From thence they proceeded to Newgate and gave
> them Five Minutes Law.
>
> *The Proceedings*, 28 June 1780

I

The Gordon Riots of 4–9 June 1780 were the most serious municipal insurrection of the eighteenth century. Parliament and the Bank of England were attacked; aristocrats found their houses demolished and their persons besieged. London parks became military encampments; strategic points were defended by artillery; the municipal bourgeoisie armed itself. Between 400 and 500 people were killed.[1]

The riots were named after Lord George Gordon, a Scottish peer who led the Protestant Association, a mass organization dedicated to the repeal of an Act passed two years earlier for the 'Relief of Roman Catholics'. Until the work of Dr George Rudé the riots were interpreted only as the misguided actions of an ignorant, drunken mob. Dr Rudé's study of the economic background both of the rioters and of their targets demonstrated that the rioters were not a criminal mob, but, on the whole, journeymen or wage-earners, and that their targets were chosen less because of their

---

[1] J. Paul de Castro, *The Gordon Riots* (1926), and Christopher Hibbert, *King Mob: The Story of Lord George Gordon and the Riots of 1780* (1958) are two good monographical introductions. They may be supplemented by the materials in John Stevenson, *Popular Disturbances in England, 1700–1870* (1979), and Tony Hayter, *The Army and the Crowd in Mid-Georgian London* (1978).

religious affiliation than because of their wealth.[2] His interpretation of the riots is the starting-point of our account, which, however, considers only two episodes – the successful attack on Newgate Prison and the attack on Lord Mansfield's house in Bloomsbury Square. Many other episodes of that week of apocalyptic actions are omitted – the freeing of prisoners in other gaols; attacks upon the properties of industrialists (Malo, the silk manufacturer; Desormeaux, the dyer; Mahood, the army clothier); the demolition of the houses of other judges; the indignities meted out to aristocrats; and the many incidents of looting. But the study of these two episodes, at either end, so to speak, of the 'criminal justice system', can illustrate some important themes about the riots, such as the disposition of force and terror among the classes of London, and the global dynamics of the London working class.

Chapter 1 introduced the theme of excarceration by telling of one man's daring escapes in 1722 from Newgate. The liberation of hundreds of prisoners on a single night in 1780 is an extension of that theme from an individual to a mass scale. Many of the historical themes introduced in that chapter appear again in this – slavery, wage-payment, criminalization. But the London working class of 1780 had experiences of war, slavery and revolution that substantially changed its nature. It was larger, more international. Moreover, the ruling class found that it could no longer rely upon the micro-dramas of the individual or small group hanging to terrorize the London population in general or to set examples to particular groups.

One witness to the attack on Newgate paid sixpence to watch it burn from the roof of a nearby house. 'Here I saw a new species of gaol delivery. The captives marched out with all the humours of war, accompanied by a musical band of rattling fetters.' This 'new species of gaol delivery' was more fully described by the Suffolk poet, George Crabbe, who saw the firing of Richard Akerman the Keeper's house, the destruction of the gates and roof, and the prisoners' escape from the 'volcanoe'. 'Not Orpheus himself had more courage or better luck.'[3] It was a glorious day for the London working class, who despised Newgate. Its inhabitants were said 'to

[2] George Rudé, 'The Gordon Riots: A Study of the Rioters and their Victims', reprinted in the same author's *Paris and London in the 18th Century: Studies in Popular Protest* (1970).
[3] Revd George Crabbe, *The Poetical Works*, vol. i (1884), p. 83.

The burning, plundering and destruction of Newgate

polish the King's iron with their eyebrows'. It was likened to a place of learning as 'the boarding school', 'City College', or, in reference to the childhood legend of the London merchant, 'Whittington's College', or simply the 'Whit'. It was likened to a drinking establishment as 'the Chequer Inn', 'the King's Head Tavern', 'the Sheriff's Hotel', 'the Stone Tavern' or 'the Stone Jug'. It was called the 'Quod', the 'Queer Ken', the 'Nark', or, in a less sarcastic register, the 'Trib' (short for tribulation), the 'Old Start', the 'Little Ease' or 'Limbo'.

Exact estimates of the number of prisoners freed on the night of 6–7 June 1780 must vary because of the confusion that took place and because, in addition to the main City and Middlesex prisons, many smaller places of confinement were forcibly opened – more than twenty crimping houses (where impressed sailors were confined prior to embarkation) and spunging houses (where debtors were held at the pleasure of their creditors). Newgate was the largest and most terrible dungeon. The excarceration of its inmates took place amid such fire and destruction that spectators were left with an idea 'as if not only the whole metropolis was burning, but all nations yielding to the final consummation of all things'. Within a few days there was printed a list of 117 prisoners 'delivered from the Gaol of Newgate', their offences, and the dates when they were tried at the Old Bailey. It has been possible to discover the trial records of 37 women and 43 men who were on this list. They represented several nationalities – English, Italian, German, Jewish, Irish and Afro-American. Legally, their crimes are easily summarized: 5 were charged with crimes against the person – a rapist, a bigamist, an anonymous-letter-writer and 2 murderers – and 2 were charged with perjury; otherwise the overwhelming majority were imprisoned for crimes against property – 2 arsonists, 5 counterfeiters, 6 burglars, 10 highway robbers, and 50 larcenists. As an economic class, they were the have-nots.

Among 50 larcenists who were delivered on 6 June 1780 there were 8 men and 2 women housebreakers. The art of robbing houses was called the 'rum lay'. It was further divided into the 'crack lay' (getting into a house by force) and the 'dub lay' (entering a house by means of keys). Those in Newgate were generally 'rum dubbers'. In the years preceding 1780 this art was much practised. A Parliamentary Committee collected evidence showing that the frequency of London burglaries had increased by a factor of eight between 1766 and 1770, and that the value of the goods stolen had increased by a factor of fourteen – a striking improvement in yield. As the material civilization of the urban bourgeoisie became more refined, its belongings – ever increasing in variety and number – became arranged with a view to display and security. The control of space is the essence of private property, and its architecture became more complex: yards, fences, railings and gates formed an outer perimeter; stair-wells, doors, rooms and closets an inner one; bureaux, chests, cabinets, cases, desks and drawers protected the articles of private property themselves. Each space was controlled by locks, and access to each required a key.

The Newgate rum dubbers had studied these social, architectural and technical problems. Sometimes, the solutions were astonishing. William Russell was sentenced to death because he broke and entered the dwelling-house of a man who left the key to his house with a woman across the street who made his bed. He returned to find that the back-door bolt had been wrenched off, but that the gate to his back garden was still securely padlocked. William Bagnall was a watch-spring-maker who had been in constant employment for six years. He was found guilty of many indictments that generally involved breaking and entering tailors' shops. The wife of Bagnall's prosecutor was astonished to find the door of their house locked and the key still on the inside *after* the lock had been picked and the shop robbed. James Steward, William Trubshaw and William Millions broke into the chambers of a Lincoln's Inn lawyer, picking the lock of the front door and each of the interior rooms. Millions was apprehended with fifty different keys in his possession; Trubshaw with thirty, as well as a dark lantern, a tinder-box and a screwdriver. The possession of many keys was itself a sign of guilt. Although James Cremer, a sailor, did not have a place to lay his head in London, none the less 'there was a great bunch of picklock keys' found in his pocket, as the Court was told. With them he broke into a Billingsgate beerhouse in the middle of the night and stole some beer-pots. For this he was sentenced to death.[4]

The picking instruments might be as simple as an iron screw, which Mary Hatfield, a waitress in a public house, and Mary Hicks had used to enter the room of a fruit-seller in their tenement. They stole her stuff petticoat and two cotton gowns. The clothes were pawned, and easily identified since they had been made from remnants. Said the fruit-seller: 'I cut it out foolishly; it is longer and wider on One Side than the other.' Experience in an old iron shop could provide the secret knowledge of locks and keys. James Penticross, a man who had lived seven years in America as a convict labourer, worked at such a shop in Peter Street. He took 36 yds. of silk ribbon and 48 yds. of silk gauze from a Smithfield coachman's warehouse. The owner had developed daily habits of inventory control. The warehouseman said, 'I do not book the goods over night'; instead in the mornings he used his keys. These did not work one morning; Penticross was apprehended with one that did.

Sarah Stilwell was a servant to a Charing Cross silk mercer. She took from him 10 yds. of bombazine, 11 yds. of silk, and a large remnant. They were recovered from a pawnbroker's. She was caught with many keys in her pockets – keys to the locks of boxes kept out of doors, and to those chests kept below stairs. She replaced the misappropriated fabrics with the pawnbrokers' duplicates, putting the latter in the locked chests that had contained the former,

[4] See *The Proceedings* for the following dates: 20 October 1779, 5 April 1780, 10 May 1780 and 19 May 1779.

suggesting a kind of loan. She was sentenced to die. The war between the haves and have-nots of London had changed since Jack Sheppard's time. It had become more secretive, nocturnal and dependent upon knowledge of locks and keys.[5]

The cases of the two escaped murderers whose trials we know about suggest two contrasting kinds of violence – violence within the working class and violence against its oppressor. Albert Love killed his wife during a quarrel in their Shadwell neighbourhood. 'Don't believe him, for he is a savage,' she had shouted to the neighbours. The second murder arose out of a quarrel between Mary Adey and a neighbour. The neighbour sent to Bow Street for a constable. When the constable arrived, he attempted to settle matters by taking Mary Adey's husband for impressment into the armed forces. Mary Adey killed the constable.[6]

Men and women reacted to their impoverished circumstances in different ways. Deprived of the social power of money, men might resort to their training in violence – as did the deserter from the Army, James Humphreys, who robbed the silver watch and chain from a keeper of a tripe and offal shop as he was going across St Pancras fields. Irishmen were experienced, often, with livestock and horse-dealing, and so we find Kennet M'Kensie and Pat Doyle in Newgate for the theft of a bay gelding. Or men might rely upon the respectability of tradesmen, who might in court testify to 'good character', as a painter, a butcher, a baker, a chandler, a grocer and some tailors did to the 'character' of James Lake, a Goodge Street tailor who took to the highway, well-mounted with pistol in hand, after his business had suffered.[7]

In general, women lacked such freedom of action and conse-quently resorted to different methods. The work that Mary Jones did in a St Giles' slum manufactory 'in making umbrellas' produced insufficient wages 'to make up her rent' in Beaufort Buildings. She robbed a fellow lodger of her linen gown and then sold it to an old clothes-dealer. Alice Bellamy had 'a great deal of distress to pay her rent', since she had been out of work from the house where she

[5]ibid., 10 May 1780, 5 April 1780, 20 October 1779.
[6]For the two murders, see ibid., 15 September 1779 and 10 May 1780. See also, Terence McClaughlin, *Dirt, A Social History as Seen Through the Uses and Abuses of Dirt* (New York, 1971).
[7] *The Proceedings,* 5 April 1780, 7 July 1779.

used to char. She took and pawned a pottage pot. While the outdoor robberies of men required alacrity, physical strength, boldness, bravura and speed, women tended to work indoors and relied upon quiet, intelligence, stealth and quickness. Mary Dyer found a door open one evening to a house in Charing Cross. She entered and found time to take some bedlinen and bread, before the mistress of the house found her hiding under the kitchen table with a loaf under each arm. She was taken to Justice Hyde's house where she was committed to Newgate. Not long after she was delivered on 6 June, Justice Hyde's house was burned.[8]

Many of the delivered prisoners had committed work-related crimes. Some were household servants, like Sarah Budge who stole property from her master and mistress, or David Davis who, following six years' service to a Ludgate linen-draper, took 26 yds. of printed linen. Others were out-of-place servants like Francis Thompson who robbed a man of a guinea near the Stratford waterworks. Some had committed crimes that arose from the inherent and material antagonisms of London work relations. Joseph Naylor, for instance, took 4 lbs. of sugar and 5 lbs. of currants from his employer, an India House grocer, after he had been dismissed in a wages dispute. Andrew Breeme paid rent to a German 'advertizing tailor' who supervised a tailor's lodging large enough for six workers. Breene burnt the house down. Ann Wood, a laundress, slept and worked in the same room as her employers, Patrick and Ann Bewley. She robbed them of a kettle, three flat irons and twenty linen caps. William Dawson was a skilled watch-case-maker. He was imprisoned for counterfeiting the stamp of the Goldsmith's Company. Mary Williams worked with her husband, a ragged labouring man, in a Long Acre back room. At night they laboured with aqua fortis, scouring sand and other ingredients to make the 'pickle' that permitted them to 'silver' base coins. When she ran away with another man, her husband swore an information against 'her crimes'.[9]

After Susannah Flood robbed the owner of a house on fire of 3 guineas, 3 half-crowns and 7s. under pretence of 'saving his Goods' from the flames, she sought to elude the chase that ensued from the cry of 'Stop Thief!' by seeking refuge in one of the numerous used

[8] ibid., 10 May 1780, 3 December 1777 and 12 January 1780.
[9] ibid., 15 September 1779, 5 April 1780, 10 May 1780, 3 June 1778 and 12 January 1780.

clothing shops of Monmouth Street. She chose a 'sank' or 'centipee', as they were called, a place where a tailor employed numerous people in the mass production of soldier's clothes. A salesman from Leadenhall Market testified against Sarah Lynch:

I went in after my hat; they shut the door, and pulled up their clothes, and wanted me to do with them, and the prisoner unbuttoned my breeches, and took the bag of money out of my pocket.

She had been languishing in Newgate since October 1778. Since prostitution was criminalized by legal practice, the buyers of sexual favours had, in effect, the power of imprisonment over the sellers. Esther Hale was charged with the theft of 10 guineas *after* she refused to accompany a recruiting sergeant to a bagnio. According to him, he was innocently gazing upon the waterworks from London Bridge when 'the Prisoner came and stood by me, and unbuttoned both the buttons of my breeches, and took my purse out', a purse containing his colonel's recruiting money. 'They were very roomy breeches,' he continued, 'made two years ago when they wore them very large, macaroni breeches I believe they call them.'[10] Abigail Perfect was put in Newgate by the Steward to a captain of a man-of-war. In April at midnight and 'not quite sober' he lodged with her at the suggestion of a watchman named Tankard. In the morning he found that his watch, knee-buckles and shoe-buckles were missing. He called the constable, who shook Abigail until a guinea dropped from her mouth. She then swore, said the steward, 'as much ever I heard a sailor in my life time'. The process of criminalization, or 'blaming the victim', is also illustrated by the trial of Mary Cunningham, 'a misfortunate girl of the town'. Her services were bought by a 'gentleman' who paid her in bad shillings; she was imprisoned for recirculating them. The physical strength of a man, 'a little the worse for liquor', was employed against 'an unfortunate, unhappy girl' named Mary Jones, who was knocked down – 'like a dog', she said – and then accused of stealing his silver watch after she had agreed 'to go with him [if] he would give me something'.[11]

On occasion a group of women might employ superior strength

[10] Ruth Paley, 'The Middlesex Justices Act of 1792: Its Origins and Effects', Ph.D. thesis, University of Reading, 1983, pp. 93 ff; *Proceedings*, 21 October 1778 and 23 February 1780.
[11] ibid., 10 May 1780 and 15 September 1779.

against a single and sober man, as the story of Lucy Johnson, alias Black Lucy, illustrates. She was one of the many Afro-American women 'of the Town'. James Boswell, a frequent purchaser of sexual services, tells of the Afro-American brothel frequented by the Earl of Pembroke. Lucy Johnson did not work there. Like all so-called 'luxury trades', there was a huge variety of working conditions, levels of pay and requirements of skill. In the 1770s at the best end of the trade someone like Black Herriot could be found working. She was a Jamaican slave and mother of a plantocrat's children. In London she became widowed and penniless. To support her children, she joined the 'company', or the 'sisters', and by her skills soon obtained seventy regular customers, of whom at least twenty were members of the House of Lords. Black Lucy belonged to the worst end of the 'company'. She offered to sell her dead husband's waistcoat to a Suffolk schoolmaster who in June 1779 was looking for a chestwarmer among the old clothes-vendors of Chick Lane. He agreed, for this purpose, to accompany her to a lodging-house kept by an Irish woman, Hannah Doyle. Once inside, Lucy Johnson threw him to the ground and, with the help of several other women, ripped open his breeches, and took from him a guinea and eight half-crowns. Later in prison she offered to 'make it up' with him. The schoolmaster refused, so she was tried, found guilty, sentenced to hang, and would have been had she not been delivered on 6 June.

To sum up: those who were delivered from Newgate were of the propertyless class. Most were in detention for acts against those with property. The prisoners were delivered at a time when across the ocean a war was being fought for independence and the pursuit of happiness. There were at least two white men in Newgate with American connections: John Hudson, a Pennsylvania apprentice and clerk who had come to London to escape 'the trouble in America', and James Major, whose position in the London office of the Customs placed him at one of the tenderest points of contact between the merchants on either side of the Atlantic. Hudson stole a banknote from a Fenchurch Street grocer. James Major had written an anonymous letter signed 'A True-Born Englishman'. In examining the events that took place on 6 June, we can see, I think, evidence that the revolutionary war had affected the actions of many that night, both inside and outside the prison walls. To the poet of the American Revolution, Philip Freneau, a decisive experience had been his own imprisonment in a British ship in May and June 1780.[12]

II

Hundreds of people took part in the delivery of Newgate. Who were they? What were their motives? How did they do it? To answer these questions we have three kinds of evidence: first, the reports of eyewitnesses (four poets – Johnson, Cowper, Crabbe, Blake); second, an engraving called 'An Exact Representation of the Burning, Plundering, and Destruction of Newgate', and, third, the court records of those who were brought to trial for the delivery.[13] The descriptions of the poets are affected by the shock of the spectacle – raging fire, billowing smoke – and by their fears as property-holders. The engraving depicts several interesting incidents in the behaviour of the mob: a blacksmith removing a thief's shackles; drinking from pots and bottles; the distribution of leaflets; the approach of the fire-engines; the insignia of cockade and flag; the victory trophies of chains and keys; the street fights against the constabulary where the arms are clubs, wheel-spokes, pikes, axes and cutlasses. It is a scene, neither orderly nor horrific, in which a hundred countenances are watching and gestures both brutal and tender are performed. The court records permit us to approach more closely a few individuals whose stories can help us understand the nature, as revealed in action, of this London working class. Of course, they were not 'typical' cases. They were singled out, but singled out as 'examples'.

Six men were indicted and tried for the prison riot. Two are characteristic of the London streets: a marketman and a sailor.[14] Richard Hyde was the sailor. One of the Newgate turnkeys signed an information against him. Hyde had insulted the turnkey, calling him 'one of Akerman's Thieves', and threatened him by saying he would 'cut his Throat and kill his Master'. Sailors broke Richard

[12] Philip Freneau, *Poems*, ed. Fred Lewis Pattee, vol. ii (New York, 1903), pp. 18–39.

[13] 'An Exact Representation . . .' was published in 1781, and has been republished as a 'Jackdaw' by Jonathan Cape (ed. Judith Kazantzis). Relevant judicial records may be found in CLRO, Sessions Files, SF, 1087, Indictment Bills, Gaol Calendars, Recognizances and Sessions Papers.

[14] *The Proceedings*, 28 June 1780.

Akerman's shutters. It took quite a time to force them open, and even then they opened only a crack. It was a sailor who forced himself, 'neck and heels', into the window, thus opening the way for many to follow into the prison-keeper's house, whence were obtained the keys for the gaol's main gate.

Quite a number of sailors must have taken part in the delivery of Newgate, for cutlasses and marlin spikes were frequently mentioned as being weapons in the armoury of the crowd. It had been a terrible year for sailors – the winter was cold and they had endured six years of war in which the press-gangs marauded the streets. So it was not surprising that this traditional element of the London mob was especially active on 6 June. Besides Richard Hyde, we can glimpse another mariner tried for his crimes during the riots. William Brown was tried for stealing a shilling from Carter Daking, a Bishopsgate cheesemonger.[15] Daking was in his compting-house, looking out of the window. Brown approached him with his hat in hand, and said:

Damn your eyes and limbs, put a shilling into my hat, or by God I have a party that can destroy your house presently.

Daking asked, 'What is the shilling for?' To which Brown replied that it was

for his men and his soldiers if he would keep the blood within his mouth, that if he did not give a shilling immediately, he would bring his men and take Mr Daking's house down.

To save his house and teeth Daking opened the window and paid the shilling. Brown was to be hanged for accepting it. At his trial he was defended by a victualler who said that Brown 'was so much in liquor that he did not know what he was about'. The victualler had known Brown 'ever since he went out in the *Serapis*'. Since that battle he had made his way back to London and lived with his brother having 'no visible way of getting his livelyhood'. The remainder of the trial record reads:

Prisoner. I was wounded in the engagement with Paul Jones, and I loose my senses when I have drank a little. I have done a great deal of good to the nation, my lord, and I hope you will save my life and let me serve his majesty again.

GUILTY. (*Death.*)

[15] ibid., and PRO, State Papers, SP, 37/21, no. 150, fol. 204, 'Petition of William Brown'.

Brown had fought in one of the most famous naval engagements of the American war, the battle between HMS *Serapis*, commanded by Captain Pearson, and the *Bonhomme Richard*, commanded by John Paul Jones. The latter's cruise around Ireland and Scotland with a polyglot crew had been the cause of much trepidation. John Paul Jones stimulated the Scottish bourgeoisie to form a 'citizen's' militia, made the coal-masters of Newcastle fear for the safety of their London ships, and provided excellent fare to the ballad-mongers who liked to compare him to Robin Hood and Dick Turpin. The battle off Flamborough Head, Yorkshire, lasted most of the day and night of 23 September 1779.[16] The *Bonhomme Richard* suffered 150 casualties, and HMS *Serapis* over 100. Pearson struck his Red Ensign in defeat, and Jones took 500 prisoners – including Brown – and sailed with them and his prizes to France. It was from there that Brown made his way back to London, a penniless veteran.

The marketman was George Sims, 'the Tripeman', a familiar person of the streets.[17] He lived in Westminster, where he lodged with Mr Smith, a tripe-dealer in St James's Market. Sims bought the inferior parts of the meat – the guts, innards and offal – from the cutting butchers. Indeed, he had a reputation for being forward in street quarrels, and we may imagine that a street-hawker of meat in such hungry times would often have had to know how to defend himself. He knew the markets, he knew the streets. He shared a room with his wife and a man whose working day ended at 8 p.m. His wife sometimes worked, but not always. Before Sims left for Newgate he had had 'words' about his wife being out of work. He led a 'vast concourse of people' to Newgate, shouting along the way, '*Newgate a-hoy!*', and gathering weapons, spokes, spikes and sledges. '*D—n his eyes, or d—n his blood he would have the gates down.*' Sims persisted and was seen with Akerman's bedding ('I saw the feathers fly') setting fire first to the Chapel of the Condemned and then to other wards of the prison. A prosecution witness said that he had heard him say that 'they were going to release the prisoners'. In his defence Sims claimed that with the exception of one turnkey he knew nobody in Newgate. Perhaps this was true, although of those released, two lived in, by and through the London meat trade. There was Eleanor Whiston, a 49-year-old live-in servant of a Fleet

---

[16] Samuel Eliot Morrison, *John Paul Jones: A Sailor's Biography* (Boston, 1959).
[17] *The Proceedings*, 28 June 1780.

Street butcher ('she is a w—e,' claimed his wife), whom she robbed of 40 guineas. She had two sisters living near by, and was known to many in the neighbourhood. Or Sims may have run across Joseph Briley, an Islington cattle-drover, two of whose children were in the workhouse, and who stole cows from his master of fifteen years, and was known for his 'rap' with the market people and the milkwomen.[18]

Richard Hyde, the sailor, and George Sims, the marketman, the first two Newgate deliverers we have considered, belonged to essential London industries – shipping and livestock. Although these occupations seem to be completely different in nature – the one rural, the other oceanic – they none the less shared in common the experiences of poverty, travel and mobility. Hyde was used to the obedience and discipline exacted by the Royal Navy, but neither he nor Sims had had any kind of interaction with the upper classes. In this, they may be distinguished from the next two deliverers of Newgate whom we shall consider. Francis Mockford and Thomas Haycock had both been waiters at a Westminster coffee-house, the St Alban's Tavern, where they attended a particular, and wealthy, clientele of West End gentlemen with whose manner and conversation they were as familiar as with the pots, pans and conversations of the kitchen.[19]

Mockford lodged with a wine-vault-keeper in Market Lane, behind the opera house. At the St Alban's Tavern he was well-valued by those he served; when the tavern was sold, several gentlemen offered Mockford £600 to take the business over. At Alderman Woodridge's request, Mockford cleared a way through the mob so that the fire-engines could approach Newgate. Witnesses testified that it was Mockford who brandished the gaol keys at the main gate of Newgate as if they were more symbols of power than instruments to be used. In fact, the *sight* of them caused the turnkey to open the gate. Mockford's action made a vivid impression upon eyewitnesses. The engraver of 'An Exact Representation' depicts a padlock and pair of 'great Keys' lodged upon the tine of a pitch-fork held aloft at Newgate.

Mockford did not stay at Newgate that evening to see all the

[18] ibid., 10 May 1780 and 12 January 1780.
[19] ibid., 28 June 1780.

prisoners released (not fully accomplished until near midnight), but returned in a hackney coach to his lodging-house, where he boldly announced to his fellow lodgers, 'I have got the keys of Newgate.' He put them on the table as he spoke and called for rum and water.[20] The presence of the keys was the cause of considerable fear. One judge at Mockford's trial suggested, 'You would not touch them for fear they would contaminate you?' and the landlord emphatically agreed: 'I would not come near them.' The magistrate who first examined Mockford said that Mockford had later disposed of the 'great Keys' of Newgate by walking out to the middle of Westminster Bridge and tossing them into the Thames. A key can tell a story. It is a clue. It has a power, and the nature of this power, as a guardian of space and of private property, was regarded by many as magical.

Thomas Haycock was with Mockford at Newgate, as he was at the St Alban's Tavern. He began the night of 6 June at the Houses of Parliament, then went to Justice Hyde's house at the end of Drury Lane, then helped organize the 'divisions' or 'bands', the arming of people and the approach to Newgate. To the tavern-keepers and householders of his neighbourhood he was known as 'Mad Tom'. After the prisoners had been let out, he returned alone to the West End, to the Bell in St James's Market where a tallow-chandler overheard him say that 'he was the first man to enter Newgate' and that he had 'let out all the prisoners'. Mad Tom would perhaps have had personal sympathy with the prisoners because he himself had several times suffered confinement at the hands of his neighbours. Indeed once they had restrained him in a strait-jacket, saying,

Tom, you have no property to lose, when you have lost that coat on your back you have lost all you are worth.

In this era of the American Revolution, it is noteworthy that it is a Lockean axiom that was chosen to be repeated at Mad Tom's trial for his life. That it had to be told was taken at the Old Bailey as evidence of his 'madness'.[21] Yet we need not take it in the same way. A 'Mad Tom' was a slang term in the eighteenth century designating one who only pretended to be mad, and perhaps Thomas Haycock found in madness a disguise enabling him to retain his own voice amid those that he so often heard. Whatever the case

[20] PRO, SP, 37/21, no. 179, fol. 245, 'The Information of Robert Gibson'.
[21] The Proceedings, 28 June 1780. His madness is stressed by those seeking his pardon, PRO, SP, 37/21, nos. 84, 170, 171.

may have been before the delivery of Newgate, after it, at his trial, Thomas Haycock uttered the most lucid interpretation of his actions and the events of the night of 6 June. On being asked why he participated in the delivery, he simply answered, 'The Cause', as if the 'cause' were obvious and need not be explained. Yet the judges were perplexed and asked him what was the cause. He replied: '*There should not be a prison standing on the morrow in London.*'

The relationship between the two answers raises some questions. The first assumes familiarity with a discussion about 'the cause', and the second answer is an elaboration of the first, and thus provides a hint about the discussion. Mad Tom does not answer the question with the libertarian rhetoric that had become common in the 1770s, nor does he answer it historically, by references, for instance, to the 'cause' of Wat Tyler or Jack Straw, leaders of the Peasants' Revolt of 1381, the last time that the prisoners of London had been liberated by the mass actions of the dispossessed, and the prisons ransacked and destroyed. Wat Tyler was on the minds of many. Indeed, Lord George Gordon in his conversations with other peers that week refrained from relinquishing his leadership on the grounds that 'there might spring up some Wat Tyler who would not have patience to commune with Government, and might very possibly chuse to embroil the nation in civil war'.[22] The Peasants' Revolt had figured in Cockney tradition from at least Elizabethan times. It was frequently depicted in the outdoors theatre of Bartholomew Fair, and accounts were also published in several editions of inexpensive chap-books (following 1750), when the ancient question was asked again:[23]

> When Adam delved and Eve span
> Who was then the gentleman?

Mad Tom went on to describe what happened after the crowd had armed themselves with crows, hammers and chisels in Long Acre: 'From thence they proceeded to Newgate, and gave them Five Minutes Law!' Did this mean liberation or retribution? Was he referring to the prisoners or their keepers? Is the remark one of

[22] De Castro, op. cit., pp. 19–20; Lloyd I. Rudolf, 'The Eighteenth Century Mob in America and Europe', *American Quarterly*, vol. xi, no. 9 (winter 1959).
[23] The narrations of the revolt are contained in *English Historical Documents, 1327–1485* (1969), pp. 127–37. That the revolt was alive in eighteenth-century memory is demonstrated by the many editions of Anon., *The History of Wat Tyler and Jacke Straw* (1750 and later).

ironic sarcasm? Was this a notion of law that he had derived from
the talk overheard in the kitchen or the dining-rooms of St Alban's
Tavern? Had he participated in the discussions of democracy that
took place at the Bell, the tavern of abolitionists and parliamentary
reformers of the London working class? The transcriber of the
remark found it potent and dangerous; he found it necessary to
disassociate himself from it by emphasizing in the printed *Proceedings*
of the trial that 'that was his expression', making sure that no reader
would mistake the author of this succinct interpretation of events.

Mockford and Haycock suggest broader themes by their actions
and words about the delivery of Newgate that in their ways express
some of the characteristics of the eighteenth-century mob. Mockford was a success among his patrons – a man who usually kept his
shoes clean and must have been well-spoken. But on 6 June it is
his actions rather than his words that command our attention.
Conversely, Haycock, a man of misplaced actions who would often
be forcibly restrained by the gentry of St James's Square, was to
utter at his trial words worth pondering: the awkward simpleton
found his voice.

The last two deliverers of Newgate we shall consider were John
Glover and Benjamin Bowsey. Their indictments described them
as 'not having the Fear of God before their Eyes but being moved
and seduced by the Instigation of the Devil'.[24] They were Afro-
Americans and former slaves. Their activities at Newgate were
decisive, and for that reason their importance to the history of
Atlantic working people can be likened to the more well-known
leaders of the Afro-London population, Ottobah Cugoano and
Olaudah Equiano, whose fame partly arises because they were
writers. Glover and Bowsey were activists.

John Glover lived in Westminster, where he was reputed to be a
'quiet, sober, honest' man. He worked as a servant to one Philips,
Esq., a lawyer who during the afternoon of 6 June sent Glover to
his chambers in Lincoln's Inn to fetch some papers. The streets were
full of people and news: the day before 'the Mobbing of the Lords'
had taken place, petitioners were returning from Parliament, ballad-
singers were exhausting their talents, and the clerks and lawyers of
the Inns of Court had begun to arm themselves to do duty against

---

[24] *The Proceedings*, 28 June 1780; CLRO, Sessions Files, Indictment bills, Gaol
Book, vol. xxviii, for June 1780.

the mob. Ignatius Sancho, a well-to-do African grocer, was in Westminster that evening. He describes in a letter how he saw 'at least a hundred thousand poor, miserable, ragged rabble ... besides half as many women and children, all parading the streets – the bridge – the Park – ready for any and every mischief'.[25] It was a day on which no one could avoid taking sides. Instead of fetching the papers, Glover joined one of the columns heading towards Newgate. Its approach filled him with determination – on Snow Hill he was seen striking the cobblestones with a gun barrel and shouting: *'Now Newgate!'* He was one of the first people to show his face at the 'chequers of the gate'. He addressed its keeper as follows: 'Damn you, Open the Gate or we will Burn you down and have Everybody out' – a threat he made good, for he was later observed 'to be the most active Person Particularly in piling up combustible matters against the Door and putting fire thereto'. At his trial there were questions concerning his identity. Witnesses agreed that he wore 'a rough, short jacket, and had a round hat with dirty silver lace upon it', but there was some confusion about the hue of his skin. One turnkey doubted he was black, another preferred to call him a 'Copper Coloured Person', and a third said he had seen 'Several Blacks and Tawnies', which solved whatever doubts may have existed in the minds of judges and jurors about the man setting fire to Newgate and the John Glover standing before them.

The London black community consisted of between 10,000 and 20,000 people – 6–7 per cent of the population.[26] This population was active during the week of 6 June. Later, Ottobah Cugoano would speak for this community when he said 'the voice of our complaint implies a vengeance'. But such voices were also the voices of 6 June. While Glover and others were busy at Newgate, Charlotte Gardiner, 'a negro', marched with a mob ('among whom were two men with bells, and another with frying pan and tongs') to the house of Mr Levarty, a publican, in St Katherine's Lane, near Tower Hill. Charlotte Gardiner was a leader of this march. She shouted

---

[25] Ignatius Sancho, *Letters* (1782), republished in Francis D. Adams and Barry Sanders (eds), *Three Black Writers in Eighteenth Century England* (Belmont, California, 1971).

[26] Discussions of the size of the London black population may be found in Fryer, op. cit.; James Walvin, *The Black Presence: A Documentary History of the Negro in England, 1555–1860* (New York, 1971); Folarin O. Shyllon, *Black People in Britain* (1977), and by the same author, *Black Slaves in Britain* (1974).

A crippled black sailor: The London black community numbered between 10,000 and 20,000, 6–7 per cent of the population

encouragement ('Huzza, well done, my boys – knock it down, down with it') and directions ('Bring more wood to the fire'), as well as taking two brass candlesticks from Levarty's dining-room. She did not even attempt to defend herself at the Old Bailey, and on 4 July she was found guilty and sentenced to death. One week later she was hanged. The night before her hanging, a badly mounted, solitary highwayman, described as a 'mulatto', robbed the passengers of the carriage plying Gunnersbury Lane of 'every portable article, watches, snuff boxes, etwee cases, rings, &c.'. Such appropriations, no less than the delivery of Newgate, were expressions of that avenging justice that Ottobah Cugoano found equally among his people of the Atlantic diaspora and the Jehovah whose words to Moses and the prophets he had often studied.[27]

John Glover was identified well enough at the Old Bailey for hanging purposes. For historical purposes, his identification, like that of the nameless millions of the African diaspora, is problematic. He, and they, lived with a double identity, represented by a free, African name and a slave English name. Cugoano was known to the English as 'John Steward'. Equiano was known as 'Gustavus Vasa'. The African name was associated with a location and with a community of kin. The English names were 'given' (Equiano had to have his beaten into him) and these were often Roman or pet names. As a result of the revolutionary struggle for freedom by slaves during the War of American Independence, such name changes frequently occurred. Professor Gary Nash has illustrated one such change. One of the crew of the *Bonhomme Richard* was a West Indies black man who had signed articles with John Paul Jones in Philadelphia. Neither his African nor his slave name is known; 'but this Afro-American mariner fought lustily in the epic battle against the *Serapis*, losing a leg during the sanguinary fray, and sometime thereafter renamed himself Paul Jones'.[28] Might John Glover have chosen his name for similar reasons?

The merchant and shipowner of Salem, Massachusetts and early

---

[27] Ottobah Cugoano, *Thoughts and Sentiments on the Evil and Wicked Traffic of the Slavery and Commerce of the Human Species* (1787), republished in Adams and Sanders (eds), op. cit., p. 106; and for a report of Gardiner's activities, *The London Chronicle*, 4–8 July 1780.

[28] Gary Nash, 'Forging Freedom: The Emancipation Experience in the Northern Seaport Cities, 1775–1820', in Ira Berlin and Ronald Hoffman (eds), *Slavery and Freedom in the Age of the American Revolution* (Virginia, 1983); Herbert Gutman, *The Black Family in Slavery and Freedom, 1750–1925* (New York, 1976).

member of the Marblehead Committee of Correspondence, General John Glover, raised a regiment in 1775 among the multi-ethnic mariners and fishermen of this important Atlantic port. The 21st Regiment (later, the 14th Continentals) provided transport for Washington's Delaware Crossing (1776) and performed amphibious duties for the Continental Army at Lake Champlain after the Battle of Saratoga (1777). It was known for its maritime experiences, its 'amusements and tricks', and for the presence of black soldiers, a fact that led to racial violence with soldiers from segregated units. Marblehead had long included an identifiable black population, which lived in 'Niger Marsh' and was buried in the 'Negro Burial Ground', except for veterans of the war, such as Black Joe, who were buried on a hill with other revolutionary casualties. Two black men appearing on General Glover's regimental rolls, 'Romeo' and 'Caesar Bartlett', were captured by the British and held prisoner aboard the brig *Fancy* in August 1777. In a list of *Massachusetts Soldiers and Sailors in the War of the Revolution* several 'John' or 'Jonathan' Glovers are listed as deserted or captured before 1780, and some are described as of dark complexion.[29] In the list of Negroes residing in Marblehead that was prepared in 1788 in compliance with an order from the Massachusetts legislature there are eighty names, one of which is written, 'glov-'. It is possible, therefore, that John Glover, the deliverer of Newgate, was one of the captured prisoners from General John Glover's regiment, and that he named himself after this man and retained kin in Marblehead, Massachusetts. Be that as it may, Glover was also a competent sailor (Captain Pultney of the man-of-war the *Sylph* said 'he should be glad to have him as one of his crew') and a literate legal researcher who in his own defence searched the Old Bailey *Proceedings* to discover that there existed criminal records of the two men who testified against him and that one of them, Lee, returned before his sentence of transportation was finished to become Akerman's servant.[30]

---

[29] *Massachusetts Soldiers and Sailors in the War of the Revolution* (Boston, 1899), vol. vi, pp. 508–9.

[30] N. P. Sanborn, *General John Glover and his Marblehead Regiment in the Revolutionary War* (1903); George Athan Billias, *General John Glover and his Marblehead Mariners* (Boston, 1958); *Dictionary of American Biography* (New York, 1931), vol. vii, pp. 331–2; Samuel Road, *History and Traditions of Marblehead* (1958); New England Historical and Genealogical Library, 'Massachusetts Tax Valuation List (1771)'. PRO, SP, 37/21, no. 248, fol. 334.

The problem of identification arises again when we consider a sixth deliverer of Newgate. Benjamin Bowsey was a man who came as close as any to being the leader of the 6 June delivery. He was the 'bell wether'. He was singular in appearance, dressed in 'a light brownish coat, a round hat, and a red waistcoat'. When he was hatless it was observed that 'the curles were out if he had any; and his hair smooth on his head'. What was most striking about Bowsey was neither his dress nor his colour, but his voice, which could excite both confidence and indignation. He was among the first to enter Akerman's house, where he was observed through an upstairs window searching a bureau drawer and putting things into a bundle. Bowsey then left the house and joined a party of thirty. They approached the prison, marching three abreast, armed with spokes, crows and paving mattocks. Bowsey was indicted on three counts: one for riot, one for pulling down Akerman's house, and one for breaking, entering and stealing. The third count records what he took from Akerman's house: nine pairs of silk stockings; a silk handkerchief; a cotton handkerchief; a muslin ruffle; a leather-bound book with a silver clasp, and a 'double Iron Key'. Some hours later Bowsey returned to his lodgings, where he displayed his new possessions to Ann Lesar, who shared his lodging. She was a needlewoman, and removed from the pairs of silk stockings the initials 'R. A.' that identified them as belonging to the Keeper of Newgate; on three of the pairs she stitched instead the initials 'B. B.' She knew or said nothing about the book which contained 'banker's cheques', and similarly 'never knew the meaning of the key'. It was 'a remarkable key', which particularly interested her interrogators, having a crown on the handle and Akerman's name 'at the length of it'. Bowsey did not rest the night at these lodgings. He returned to 'No. 3, in Berner's Street', where he had first worked upon coming to England. One of the servants was a black man named John Northington, who helped to welcome him 'in the servant's hall', where he passed the night.

Bowsey was an Afro-American. Robert Gates, a fellow servant, had known him 'from the second day after he came to England, which is six years ago' and Gates had known the person he worked for in America. On 6 June Bowsey was employed by a man whose name in the *Proceedings* was printed as 'Dr Sandiman', but in the newspapers as 'Dr Saunders'. If his employer was Richard Saunders (1720–85), the army surgeon, who had served his regiment in

Minorca, Cuba and America, it may be that Bowsey was West Indian.[31] On the other hand, it may be that he was a continental American, because variants of his name – 'Bowsa', 'Bowzer' – are frequently found in post-revolutionary times among the black maritime workers of Baltimore and Philadelphia.[32] 'Bowsey' or its main variants do not appear in lists of free, southern black names between 1619 and 1799, nor is it found in lists of free, northern 'patriot' blacks in the period 1700–1800. Many slaves deserted the plantations of their American masters during the Revolutionary War, especially after John Murray – Earl of Dunmore and the Royal Governor of Virginia – issued a proclamation in November 1775 promising freedom to all indented servants and slaves who joined His Majesty's troops. 'The number of Negroes who fled to the British,' according to Professor Benjamin Quarles, 'ran into the tens of thousands.' However, since it appears that Bowsey had come to England in 1774, he could not have done so in the mass exodus caused by Dunmore's proclamation. The only American record of the 1770s that bears the name is in a register of the 5th and 11th Virginia Regiments of the Continental Line, where a Giles Bowsey is listed as a soldier. Benjamin Bowsey may have been a Virginian. Having been sentenced to death, Bowsey submitted to the Sheriff's interrogation in his scramble to escape the noose. He identified six other rioters, which gained him some respite from hanging. He also seemed willing to cooperate with those, such as Alderman Woodridge, who were attempting to find the conspiratorial hand of 'some dark designing foes to this happy country' (one witness swore 'he saw a man on horseback'). Despite swearing that one Captain Lloyd, 'a Gent of America', had given him a guinea ('but for what purp[ose] or on what account the said Bowsey did not say'), he could not wheedle himself a pardon and was hanged.[33]

---

[31] DNB.

[32] James de T. Abajian, Blacks in Selected Newspapers, Censuses and Other Sources: An Index to Names and Subjects (Boston, 1977), vol. i, A–F, pp. 215–16.

[33] Newbell Niles Pucket and Murray Helles, Black Names in America: Origins and Usage (Boston, 1975), pp. 21–8; Mary Beth Norton, 'The Fate of Some Black Loyalists of the American Revolution', The Journal of Negro History, vol. lviii, no. 4 (1973); Benjamin Quarles, The Negro in the American Revolution (Chapel Hill, 1961); John Gwathmey, Historical Register of Virginians in the Revolution: Soldiers, Sailors, Marines, 1775–1783 (Dietz, Virginia, 1938), p. 83; Mullin, op. cit.; PRO, SP, 37/20, no. 228, fol. 218; no. 226, fols. 316–17; no. 229, fol. 320; no. 219, fol. 306; SP 37/21, no. 289.

Among Londoners by 1780 the American experience was as important a feature as the Irish experience or the traditions of particular trades, sects and neighbourhoods. In the dramaturgy of the delivery of Newgate we have recounted the actions of six men. Two – the sailor and the marketman – were familiar figures of the eighteenth-century mob. Two were servants to the West End gentry, familiar with the humours and manner of the Quality. Two were Afro-Americans who brought to London a living memory of the experience of slavery, and whose own community in London underwent changes in the decade preceding 1780.

Slaves, ex-slaves, Africans or Afro-Americans achieved out-standing prominence in London by 1780 – as drummers, horn-players, fiddlers, prostitutes, cooks, boxers and writers.[34] To the body of London they made significant contributions to the ear, the chin, the genitalia, pockets, tongue and mind. Because of their often intimate knowledge of so many ruling-class personages, they were familiar with their parts. From the tastier parts of the upper crust to the filthiest scum in the pot, the Afro-Americans came to know the London population. Moreover, they posed a significant political challenge to the ruling class, whose ideology consequently needed to be reformed.

The coherence (learned on plantation and shipboard) of the Afro-American population posed a police problem in London. It ex-pressed itself in clubs for dancing, music, eating and drinking, and in gatherings of American runaways and London servants. The chairman of the Westminster Quarter Session, John Fielding, was alarmed at the growing size of this population.[35] The plantocrats, he wrote,

bring them to England as cheap servants having no right to wages; they no sooner arrive here than they put themselves on a footing with other servants, become intoxicated with liberty, grow refractory, and either by persuasion of others or from their own inclinations, begin to expect wages according to their own opinion of their merits; and as there are already a great number of black men and women who made themselves trouble-some and dangerous to the families who have brought them over as to get themselves discharged, these enter into societies and make it their business to corrupt and dissatisfy the mind of every black servant that comes to England.

[34] Fryer, op. cit., ch. 4.
[35] John Fielding, *Extracts from the Penal Laws* (1768).

Fielding's account of Afro-American immigration is significant for its emphasis upon mobility and wages. Such Afro-Americans as Bill Richmond, the bare-knuckled champion brought over from New York by the sporting captain of a man-of-war, and Black Herriot, the acclaimed courtesan with a House of Lords clientele, indicate the genius of individual Afro-American talents in aristocratic settings. But the achievements of the black community as a whole depended upon what it could accomplish within the few parts of the labour market to which it had access. Most Afro-Americans were consigned to the kitchen or ship. They were too poor to be much influenced by the municipal ordinance forbidding them to take up apprenticeship indentures. Nor were they able to find a strategic material, such as the Irish for a time had found in coal, to use as a means of purchase and power. The English laws of servitude were unclear, so in addition to poverty and isolation, Afro-American servants in London suffered severer restrictions upon their mobility than any other category of worker, with the exception of parish children. In the 1750s they began to run away in significant numbers; and in the 1760s they began to demand wages. Hence the foundations were laid for the famed Somerset Case (1772) and the legislative movement to abolish slavery in England and elsewhere. What the Afro-American community was beginning to assert by the 1770s was the freedom of a proletarian – money and mobility.[36]

By the mid 1770s, as well as itself, this community had organized Granville Sharp and the English abolitionists. In March 1780 Tom Paine was writing the preamble to the Pennsylvania Slave Emancipation Act – 'at this particular time particularly', he wrote. The Afro-American population of London was tied to African people throughout the Atlantic by kinship, language and shared experience on plantation and shipboard. In this, it was a pan-African community.

Indeed the working-class population of London as a whole may be likened to a popular drink of the time, called 'All Nations': the dregs of all the different spirits sold in a dram shop were put together in a single vessel.[37]

---

[36] Douglas Lorimer, 'Black Slaves and English Liberty: A Re-examination of Racial Slavery in England', paper presented to the International Conference on the History of Blacks in Britain (September 1981), quoted in Fryer, op. cit., pp. 203 and 541.
[37] Francis Grose, A Classical Dictionary of the Vulgar Tongue (1785).

III

The delivery of Newgate and other lock-ups in London was not the only attack upon the law. Several magistrates' houses were demolished. Almost as well known as the delivery of Newgate was the attack upon the house and belongings of William Murray, Earl of Mansfield, Lord Chief Justice of the King's Bench, and the most powerful jurist in the world. He was a Scot, the possessor of a 'silver tongue' (he received elocution lessons from Alexander Pope), and when he smiled Junius felt 'an involuntary emotion to guard myself against mischief'.[38]

A few hours after the burning of Newgate, the railings surrounding Mansfield's house in Bloomsbury Square were torn down. Pictures were destroyed, windows were broken and furniture was thrown into the street. Two hundred of Mansfield's notebooks were consumed by fire.[39] He and his wife suffered the indignity of having to quit their house by the back door. The soldiery arrived some two hours after the assault had commenced and killed several people.

Mansfield has an important place in English legal history. He favoured the royal prerogative. He disencumbered the entailed estates of Scotland. He advised colonial governors when making legal decisions on no account to give reasons for their judgments. He invented legal fictions that enabled English courts to have jurisdiction in places where English law had not yet been introduced. He is remembered among legal historians for adapting English common law to 'the needs of a rapidly expanding commerce and manufacture'. He did this in two ways. First, he empanelled a special jury of merchants and businessmen who taught him the customs and usages of trade. With their advice he made laws, where none had existed, for the buying and selling of commodities, the affreightment of ships, marine insurance, bills of exchange and promissory notes. He benefited financially and it was said of him that he 'never knew the difference between total destitution and an income of £3,000 a year'. Second, he took the usages of commerce

---

[38] John Lord Campbell, *The Lives of the Chief Justices of England*, vol. ii (Philadelphia, 1851), pp. 253 ff.; *The Letters of Junius* (1786 edn), letters nos. 41 and 68.
[39] Professor James C. Oldman of the Georgetown University Law Center (Washington, DC) is writing a study of Mansfield, and has access to his papers. It is not at all clear which books and papers were destroyed. That some of them may have included documents whose production in court would be dangerous to some defendants cannot be excluded.

and, inspired by his study of Justinian's code of Roman law and continental codes, made them into law by judicial fiat. 'Lovers of liberty' criticized him for this on the grounds that it required an abandonment of common law which was the protector of liberty. For that reason Junius considered him 'the very worst and most dangerous man in the Kingdom'. Mansfield thus adapted a legal system that had arisen in feudalism to the requirements of a ruling class aspiring to world conquest and indebted to merchants and capitalists.[40]

The attack on his house was therefore an attack upon the leading exponent of British imperialism. Mansfield had shown by legal casuistry that the rule of private property and the accumulation of wealth were the zenith of civilization. That his 'proof' appeared to comply with natural reason as well as to the practices of the Roman Empire was all the better. The destruction of Mansfield's house inspired William Cowper, an advocate as well as a poet, to write some 'pretty verses' for the occasion, in which he compared 'the vandals of our isle' to the vandals who destroyed the Roman Empire. The fall of the Roman Empire was on the minds of many that week, and its historian, Edward Gibbon, altered the plan of his *Decline and Fall*. He changed his history to include a consideration of the Justinian code and he added some general observations comparing the Roman with European civilization. He thought that the European 'system of arts, and laws, and manners' – or machines, prisons and ideology – could preserve 'civilization' from the calamities and convulsions of savages abroad and at home.[41] Others compared the attack on Mansfield's house to the 'Republican phrenzy' and the 'levelling spirit' of the English Revolution which marks 'every property . . . a considerable booty'. Quite a number of people were tried on their lives for the attack. We can observe six of these 'vandals' filled with 'that levelling spirit' in the records of the Old Bailey.[42]

Sarah Collogan was sentenced to a year in prison because she

---

[40] Campbell, op. cit.; Allan Harding, *A Social History of English Law* (1966); Junius, op. cit.
[41] Edward Gibbon, *The Decline and Fall of the Roman Empire* (1776–88), ch. 38; and *Letters*, ed. J. E. Norton, vol. ii (1956), pp. 242–5; H. G. Wells, *The Outline of History* (1920), ch. 25, sect. 11.
[42] *The London Chronicle*, 6–8 June 1780; Campbell, op.cit., vol. iii (1851), p. 430.

was found wearing a printed cotton gown belonging to Elizabeth Murray, the judge's niece. An Irish woman, Elizabeth Trimmings, was tried for possessing five china dishes belonging to Mansfield's table service. Elizabeth Grant, the servant to a Flemish dealer at an old-iron shop, was tried for having in her possession a copper pot and a copper plate-warmer. John Gray, a man who walked with the aid of a crutch, was seen leaving Bloomsbury Square with a bottle of his Lordship's booze. He was a 32-year-old wool-comber from Taunton, Somerset, whose mind, according to some of the town's principal inhabitants, became disordered in 1777 or 1778: it was then that he had said 'he shou'd never be hungry any more', 'he shou'd subsist without food'; and he believed himself 'divinely commissioned to deliver to the world some important message', which he wrote down and travelled to London to publish. He was sentenced to death, leaving a widow and two young children in Taunton.[43] Laetitia Holland was sentenced to death for having in her possession two petticoats belonging to Lady Mansfield. Mary Gardiner actually boasted about the petticoats she acquired, and her loose tongue got her in trouble. According to the testimony of a publican who overheard her, when asked whether the clothing belonged to Lady Mansfield, she said: 'They *were* Lady Mansfield's and she thought she had a right to wear them as she had got them' (emphasis added). With the mention of the word 'right' the court's attention concentrated, and the judge interrogated the witness closely to ascertain that these in fact were the words she used. The publican repeated them. Nobody thought to ask Mary what she meant by this 'right'. Had she made or repaired these garments? Had she laundered them? Had they once been exchanged or come into her possession as a result of a domestic indiscretion?[44]

In the 1770s the language of liberty was often expressed in terms of 'rights'. In a public house it took courage to speak of some rights. In law, the language of rights implied a language of wrongs. The rights and wrongs of law were systematized by one of Mansfield's associates, William Blackstone. He died in January 1780 and thus could not have heard Mary Gardiner's particular assertion of right. His *Commentaries on the Laws of England* were published between

[43] PRO, SP, 37/21, no. 250.
[44] The accounts of most of those tried for criminal offences at Mansfield's house were published in *The Proceedings* of 28 June 1780 and 13 September 1780.

1767 and 1769. This work had originally stated that a slave coming to England became free upon arrival. Under Mansfield's direction this formulation was revised to say that the master 'probably' (3rd edition) or 'possibly' (4th edition) retained the right to the slave's unpaid service.[45]

Mansfield was both feared and hated in eighteenth-century London. His name passed quickly into parlance: spikes atop the wall of King's Bench Prison were known as 'Lord Mansfield's Teeth'.[46] Although some of his contributions to law (negotiable instruments, for example) would not have interested Mary Gardiner, his judgments at the Old Bailey would have been very widely known. Between 1757 and 1768 he attended that court at least once a year. Usually he would attend the April and October Sessions – the two months of the year when the indictment bills were piled highest and judgments were passed speedily. He presided at seventeen Sessions. His biographer carefully notes that 'he was somewhat severe in the punishments he inflicted'. We may be precise. At his Sessions 29 people were branded, 448 were transported and 102 were hanged. What became of the 448 people he transported to America, or what became of the friends and relations of the 102 people he caused to be hanged, is not easily known. Some may have been in Newgate Street or Bloomsbury Square on the night of 6–7 June.[47]

IV

'When H. G. Wells looked back to this period, with its enclosure of land, with its introduction of factories and prisons, he wrote of a 'new barbarism' threatening the English gentleman 'within an easy walk perhaps of his own door'.[48] Certainly, this was true, but, as Jeremy Bentham found, it was not necessary to venture outside to encounter such 'barbarism'. Jeremy Bentham, jurist, economist and

[45] Blackstone's equivocations in the various editions of his *Commentaries* are summarized in Fryer, op. cit., p. 121. See also Duncan Kennedy, 'The Structure of Blackstone's Commentaries', *Buffalo Law Review*, vol. xxviii, no. 3 (1979), pp. 205–379.

[46] Grose, op. cit.

[47] Campbell, op. cit. To arrive at this tabulation of Mansfield's sentencing I located among the ninety-six Proceedings published between 1757 and 1769 the nineteen times that Mansfield sat on the Bench.

[48] H. G. Wells, *The Outline of History* (1920), ch. 25, sect. 11.

political scientist, had an orderly mind that has been compared to a haunted house. Indeed, there was a skeleton in it. In the late 1770s this descendant of lawyers and pawnbrokers was busy at his desk writing legal codes, legislative principles and schemes for punishments.

In 1775 or 1777 Bentham completed a manuscript that would be called when it was published many years later *The Rationale of Punishment*. In it he argued against capital punishment, using a form of reasoning that already resembled the cost–benefit analysis for which he is famed. He studied the 'utility' of life and death, both in the abstract and as applied to affairs in his own household.[49] In 1774 Bentham engaged the services of a man named John Franks; he worked in the household as a footman and kitchen orderly. He was allowed 'board wages'. Franks confessed that owing to a household accident, he damaged two silver teaspoons. Mrs Bentham placed them in a drawer of the writing-table in the study. In May 1779 Franks was discharged from Bentham's service because, as Bentham explained, 'he got connected with an infamous woman'. Being old and blind, Franks was unable to sign articles aboard a privateer. On Boxing Day 1779 Bentham was away receiving his quarterly rents. On 28 December, the Feast of the Holy Innocents, he returned to find his shutters broken and his writing-table rifled. When Franks was apprehended with the two silver spoons, he said: 'This is all the money me got, me swear a robbery against you if you take my money away.'[50] Why did Franks say 'me'? Why did he say 'my money'? It had been Boxing Day, a traditional time of payment to servants as part of the holiday exchange.

Franks was tried at the Old Bailey for 'burglarously breaking and entering the dwelling house of Jeremiah Bentham, Esq.'. On 12 January 1780 Mr and Mrs Bentham went to the Old Bailey to testify against Franks, and as a result he was found guilty and sentenced to be hanged. In the two months between the sentence and his failure to obtain a pardon excarceratory actions of the London proletariat were many and fierce. In January 80 pressed men plotted an escape from a Wapping crimping house; in February 2 men (one had

---

[49] Hugo Adam Bedau, 'Bentham's Utilitarian Critique of the Death Penalty', *The Journal of Criminal Law and Criminology*, vol. lxxiv, no. 3 (fall 1983). See also, Michael Ignatieff, *A Just Measure of Pain: The Penitentiary in the Industrial Revolution, 1750–1850* (New York, 1978).

[50] *The Proceedings*, 12 January 1780.

served with General Howe in America) escaped from a river hulk, and 8 men escaped Clerkenwell Bridewell; in March 3 men, deserters from the 60th Regiment of Foot, were taken, swearing 'they would be the death of any man who should attempt to handcuff them'. In April the Recorder of London announced the fate of the capital convicts: some were permitted to enlist in the Jamaica Regiment, one was sent to hard labour, two Moorfields rioters 'were granted their enlargement', but Franks was to be hanged.[51]

Wednesday, 12 April 1780, was the day the new directors of the Bank of England were elected; it was the day the Easter Law Term began; and it was the day that the grey-haired Franks was hanged, reading 'his last repentant prayers with spectacles'. Thus, the end of a 'new Barbarian' – an ancient man, a lover and a servant to the famous penologist and utilitarian. Was Bentham's prosecution of Franks motivated by considerations of 'morals' and his disapproval of the woman with whom he became connected? Was his prosecution motivated by a strategy against customary forms of wages? Was it motivated by calculations of the utilities of life and death? Or were the spoons, like the petticoats of Lady Mansfield, so closely related to the 'personage' of this man, who dreamed of his own 'sanctity' and 'importance', that only hanging, as if by magic, could repair the damage? Bentham was much excited by the Gordon Riots; he joined the Lincoln's Inn militia and wrote of himself, 'I was a military hero for a night.'[52] The time was decisive to his theories of punishment.

The time was also decisive to the articulation of British coercion, military and civil. Regiments were raised with a view to divide and rule. County militias were raised to mobilize the property-holders. In Ireland the Volunteer Movement – an armed guard of property-holders – was used against the Whiteboys and, following the news of the Gordon Riots, deployed in Dublin's weaving districts to overawe its proletarian inhabitants. In the metropolis the London Military Foot Association was formed against the rioters and in subsequent years provided service against footpads, fugitives and

---

[51] *The London Chronicle,* 8–11 April 1780.
[52] Gertrude Himmelfarb, 'The Haunted House of Jeremiah Bentham', *Victorian Minds* (New York, 1968), emphasizes the ghostly aspect of Bentham; see also M. P. Mack, *Jeremy Bentham: An Odyssey of Ideas* (1963); his activities during this week are easily observed through his *Correspondence,* edited by Timothy L. S. Sprigge, vol. ii, *1777–1780* (1968).

prison rioters.[53] The civil system of class coercion also changed. On the one hand, the American War denied the option of transporting felons to American servitude, and, on the other, the transportation to Botany Bay had not yet started. Parliament considered transporting felons to west Africa, but rejected the idea for fear of an alliance between London malefactors and 'neighbouring Negroes'. The hulks in the Thames provided only a temporary (and precarious) substitute for transportation.

The last hanging at Tyburn was in 1783. Thenceforth, the exemplary and spectacular cross-city procession of the condemned was abolished, and hangings took place within the more easily controlled confines of Newgate. In September 1781 the City of London argued to the Secretary of State that the official and ancient terror of a Tyburn procession no longer deterred wrongdoers, but only hardened them in brutality. Edmund Burke in the summer of 1780 sought to avoid another massacre, this one at the gallows, for fear it would irritate rather than humble 'the lower and middling people'. Postponement, mercy and the dispersal of the locations of hangings, he argued, was necessary.[54] His efforts succeeded. When possible, the London Sheriffs avoided the mass gatherings of the Tyburn hanging (see Table 9). Free pardons were given to 'delivered' malefactors who voluntarily surrendered themselves, and the hangman, Edward Dennis, was pardoned for his role during the riots. Temporary gallows were erected in neighbouring streets, and traditional officers of the City, as well as the armed 'Gentlemen of the London Association', preserved order at these dispersed hangings.[55]

Knowledge of the hangings was restricted by such dispersal. The crowds were necessarily smaller. The days were not holidays. There was less scope for word of mouth. Knowledge was restricted in another way. The printed biographies of the condemned were not published at the hangings, so the condemned were denied this means of communicating with London. The Ordinary's *Account of the Behaviour, Confession, and Dying Words of the Malefactors who were*

[53]J. R. Western, *The English Militia in the 18th Century* (1956); Tony Hayter, *The Army and the Crowd in Mid-Georgian England* (1978); William Blizard, *Desultory Reflections on Police, with an Essay on the Means of Preventing Crimes and Amending Criminals* (1785). *The London Chronicle*, 4–6 April 1780, summarizes parliamentary debates on the organization of the military during this crisis.

[54]Edmund Burke, *Works*, 5th edn, vol. vi (Boston, 1877), pp. 241–53.

[55]Horace Bleackley, *The Hangmen of England* (1929); and for the tabulation of the 'thanatopography' see *The London Chronicle*.

TABLE 9:

Sites of hangings of those who took part in the riots of 6–7 June 1780

	Name of Rioter	Site of Hanging
Tuesday, 11 June 1780	William M'Donald	Tower Hill
	Mary Roberts	Tower Hill
	Charlotte Gardiner	Tower Hill
	William Brown	Bishopsgate
	William Pateman	Coleman Street
Wednesday, 12 June 1780	Thomas Taplin	Bow Street
	Richard Roberts	Bow Street
	James Henry	Holborn
Thursday, 20 June 1780	John Glover	Newgate
	James Jackson	Newgate
	Benjamin Bowsey	Newgate
	Samuel Solomons	Whitechapel
	John Gamble	Bethnal Green
Friday, 21 June 1780	Thomas Price	Old Street
	James Burns	Old Street
	Benjamin Waters	Old Street
	Jonathan Stacy	White's Alley, Moorfields
	George Staples	Coleman Street
Saturday, 22 June 1780	Charles Kent	Bloomsbury Square
	Laetitia Holland	Bloomsbury Square
	John Gray	Bloomsbury Square

Executed at Tyburn was replaced by a publication sold at a higher price and designed for a small and different audience; the proportion of the condemned's words to the tendentious, lurid and coloured words of interpretation supplied by the various editors was smaller. Moreover, this 'Newgate Calendar' or 'Malefactors Register' published fewer lives, failed to arrange them in chronological sequence, and hardly ever published the 'debates' and discussions that had taken place within Newgate prior to the hanging.[56]

In these two ways the publicity of a London hanging began to be restricted in the 1770s. During the same decade John Howard's investigations of English prisons began to obtain their first legislative results. Popham's two bills requiring periodical cleaning of prisons and abolishing garnish payments were passed in 1774. The year preceding the delivery of Newgate, William Blackstone and William Eden drafted the Penitentiary Act, which was comprehensive and systematic. Periodic inspection, abolition of fees, sanitation, segregation by age, segregation by gender, non-intercourse among prisoners and a continuous regimen of labour discipline were the new principles advocated by the 'reformers' and provided for in this Act.[57]

V

The Gordon Riots stimulated a new theory and practice of securing private possessions. The delivery of Newgate demonstrated some weaknesses in the practice of confinement. Many of those delivered had demonstrated weaknesses in the practice of locking things up. Joseph Bramah, pre-eminent among technicians of the household in the last quarter of the eighteenth century, not long after the riots published a book describing a revolutionary change in locksmithery, *A Dissertation on the Construction of Locks*. The theory of locks had remained fundamentally unchanged since Etruscan times – more than two millennia. Such changes as had occurred in European locksmithery concerned either the keyhole, which was often disguised by rich ornamentation of symbolic or magical figures, or the fixed wards within the lock, which became increasingly more complex. However, in the 1780s Joseph Bramah revolutionized the mechanics of the lock by introducing movable wards, which allowed for infinite variation. The secret of his lock could no more be ascertained 'than a seal be copied from its impression on a fluid, or the course of a ship be discovered by tracing it on the surface of the waves'.[58]

[56] Peter Linebaugh, 'The Ordinary of Newgate and his *Account*', in J. S. Cockburn (ed.), *Crime in England 1550–1800* (Princeton, 1977).

[57] Ignatieff, op. cit., pp. 93–6.

[58] Bramah's *Dissertation* is dated '1781'. Siegfried Giedion, *Mechanization Takes Command: A Contribution to Anonymous History* (New York, 1948), pp. 51–77.

Bramah placed his discovery in historical perspective. He concluded from a review of previous locks that the 'morals' of former times were less 'depraved'. He offered a methodology to the student of history, suggesting that 'the progress of a disposition to rob' may be better traced 'in the works of art for security and defence than on any other principle or ground of reasoning'. 'Modern depredation,' he believed, had become 'a system' employing 'art' and 'force' with such skill and power that resistance was defied. 'The idea of constructing a Lock, that might resist every application, and effort of art, was first suggested to me ... by the alarming increase of house robberies.' The enemies of the house might be 'foreign invaders' or 'domestic enemies', for servants had to have access to keys. Indeed, the hierarchy of servants within the household corresponded to their security responsibilities. Servants had the knowledge and the time to study the operation of locks. Specialists in the 'dub lay' needed this information. Often it was supplied by female servants, and perhaps it was in fond acknowledgement of that dependence that the 'rub dubbers' called their lock-picking tools by such names as Kate or Bess or Betty.[59]

Those in possession of keys possessed a power whose meaning is by no means restricted to the technology of opening and closing. It will be recalled that Ann Lesar, Benjamin Bowsey's fellow lodger, in reply to a close interrogation about the key he had brought back from Newgate, said: 'I never knew the *meaning* of the key' (emphasis added). Mockford had only to *show* the keys of Newgate to the turnkey to cause him with his keys, on the other side of the gate, to open it. The keys were the mob's trophy; brandished and held aloft, they were a rallying-point. Mockford's landlord refused to touch the keys for fear of contamination, and Mockford, we recall, later disposed of them by throwing them into the Thames. What were some of the 'meanings' of keys in the eighteenth century?

Keys were associated with magic and the devil. The art of lock-picking was known as the 'Black Art'. The most common lock-picking tool was called a 'charm'.[60] In the minds of many, secret, nocturnal household thefts were associated with witchcraft. The property-holder suffering from fear, ignorance and loss might turn on 'domestic enemies' as practitioners of magic. The grocer's servant who had robbed his master attempted to explain the theft to the

---

[59] Bramah, op. cit., and Grose, op. cit.
[60] ibid.

Old Bailey by saying 'The Devil was in him'. After Moses Foneskta and companions had robbed the Plaistow coach of six linen shirts, they were pursued to Petticoat Lane, where they disappeared 'as if *be witched*'. Bowsey and Glover were indicted for having been seduced by the Devil.

Book-and-key divination located lost property. The names of suspected people were written on separate pieces of paper. These were then inserted one at a time into the hollow stem of a key which itself rested upon a book (often the Bible). The book would become agitated when the guilty person's name was inserted in the key. Joanna Turner, a pious gentlewoman, recalled in her memoirs how she was detected by this method when she stole a shilling at her boarding school in the 1740s.[61]

In Portuguese West Africa, royalty was often represented by fetishes or prestige goods contained in a locked box. In Madagascar the key was thought to contain the essence of royal domination that could make fences, walls and doors secret and inaccessible. In religious tradition, keys mediated between a known physical realm and an unknown spiritual realm: Iphigenia was key-bearer to Artemis; Jesus gave Peter the 'power of the keys'. Keys thus were attributed with many of the magical powers that had formerly belonged to various totems. Sir George Frazer cited a vast number of instances, from the Pacific, India and Africa, to show how various totems (*pomali* in Malaya, *ooroo* in Celebes, *fady* in Madagascar, etc.) guarded wealth against transgressors. Thus, he demonstrated that 'superstition has strengthened the respect for private property'. Our evidence must modify this conclusion, for if the key had little-understood social meanings (as distinct from technical properties) in eighteenth-century London, these were none the less thought to be able to subvert respect for private property and, after 6 June 1780, the defences of private property.

The subversive possibilities of the key were represented in the Christian religion, not by Jesus' gift to Peter, but by the voice recorded in the Book of Revelations 20:1–3 that inspired the oppressed of the English Revolution and the slave revolts of the eighteenth century. It is a key that turns the world upside-down:

Then I saw an angel coming down from heaven with the key of the abyss

---

[61] Fryer, op. cit., p. 221; *The Proceedings*, 12 January, 5 April and 10 May 1780; Keith Thomas, *Religion and the Decline of Magic* (1977), p. 221.

and a great chain in his hands. He seized the dragon, that serpent of old, the Devil or Satan, and chained him up for a thousand years.

The 1780s were apocalyptic times, and were mirrored in as equally apocalyptic writing. 1780 was an important year for William Blake. He was twenty-three years old. He had become 'all my own' – he had achieved freedom from apprenticeship. His father, a hosier, was pro-American; his mother was Irish. His associate, Thomas Hollis, was a Miltonic republican. Blake read *Paradise Lost* at the age of ten. On 6 June 1780 Blake helped to deliver Newgate prison.[62] Blake expressed his vision of the experience of the Gordon Riots through a traditional English apocalyptic myth. Milton's last epic, *Samson Agonistes*, told of Samson's enslavement to the Phoenician imperialists. It was a story with parallels to the forms of defeat suffered by English revolutionaries at the end of Milton's life.[63] Samson moaned:

> ... O Glorious strength
> Put to the labour of a Beast, debas't
> Lower than bondslave! Promise was that I
> Should Israel from Philistian yoke deliver;
> Ask for this great Deliverer now, and find him
> Eyeless in Gazà at the Mill with slaves,
> Himself in bonds under Philistian yoke.
> (*Samson Agonistes*, 36–42)

When Blake engraved his image called 'Albion Rose' (as it was inscribed in its final version) he thought back to both Milton and the apocalyptic meanings of 1780.[64] The image of a naked man, limbs fully extended, hair formed in sun-like flames, was 'invented' in 1780. On this plate Blake engraved these lines that allude to Milton's:

> Albion rose from where he labour'd at the Mill
>   with Slaves
> Giving himself for the Nations he danc'd the dance
>   of Eternal Death.

Thus, we are invited to compare the delivery of Newgate with the central action of Samson, who in pulling down 'the whole roof'

---

[62] David Erdman, *Blake: Prophet Against Empire: A Poet's Interpretation of the History of his Own Times*, 3rd edn (Princeton, 1977), pp. 7–11.
[63] Christopher Hill, *Milton and the English Revolution* (1978).
[64] Robert N. Essick, *William Blake, Printmaker* (Princeton, 1980), pp. 70–78.

'Albion Rose from where he labour'd at the Mill with Slaves', by Blake

upon the heads of

> Lords, ladies, captains, counsellors, or priests,
> Their choice nobility and flower
> > (*Samson Agonistes*, 1653–4)

discriminated in his destruction because, as Milton carefully adds,

'The vulgar only 'scaped who stood without.' This image of liberation, one of the most powerful graphic renditions of human freedom, remains a document of 1780 and London. Its allusions to slavery, Africa, confinement, escape, death, destruction, revolution and freedom were at once documentary and prophetic.

CHAPTER ELEVEN

SHIPS AND CHIPS: TECHNOLOGICAL REPRESSION AND THE ORIGIN OF THE WAGE

> I will gather chips here
> to make a fire for you in fere
> And for to dight your dinner
> Against you come in.
>
> Japheth's Wife in *Noah's Flood*
> (The Chester Pageant, fourteenth century)

I

'Morals reformed – health preserved – industry invigorated – instruction diffused – public burthens lightened – economy seated, as it were, upon a rock – the Gordian knot of the Poor Laws not cut, but untied – all by the simple idea in Architecture!' These are the opening lines to Jeremy Bentham's *Panopticon; Or, the Inspection House*.[1] He thought he had found 'a new mode of obtaining power of mind over mind, in a quantity hither-to without example'. Whether the purpose be 'that of punishing the incorrigible, guarding the insane, reforming the vicious, confining the suspected, employing the idle, curing the sick [or] instructing the willing', he felt so certain that this 'simple idea in Architecture' could accomplish it that he spent most of his adult life trying to improve it.

The idea is perhaps now well known. Simply stated, the notion was that of a central inspection house from which radiated spokes (as it were) that contained the 'cells' in which any of a variety of activities might be carried out. The plan was meant to embody several different principles. First, is the centrality of control. Second, is the apparent omnipresence of the inspection. Third, is the invisibility of the inspector, situated in such a position that he can see all and none can see him. Finally, is the principle of isolation that makes it impossible for those confined to communicate with one another. Bentham's life-long obsession has been interpreted in psychological

---

[1] First drafted as a series of letters in 1787, it was published in 1791. See John Bowring (ed.), *The Works of Jeremy Bentham* (New York, 1962), vol. iv., pp. 39 ff.

terms (Gertrude Himmelfarb's 'haunted house') or as a social meta-
phor of total control (Foucault's 'carceral archipelago').[2] Neither
interpretation accounts for the origin of the idea.

The panopticon was not in fact Jeremy Bentham's idea, but that
of his brother, Samuel. He was born in 1757. In 1770, when Samuel
began his apprenticeship to a Woolwich shipwright, Woolwich
being one of the six Royal Navy dockyards (Sheerness, Chatham,
Deptford, Plymouth and Portsmouth were the others), Jeremy took
it upon himself to direct the education of his brother in the principles
of algebra and Euclid and to encourage in every way his talent for
mechanical improvement and invention.[3] Samuel spent less time
with axe or adze than with books. Unwilling to work 'alongside',
he was excluded from both craft solidarities and networks of preferment.[4] He thought the shipwrights were 'old-fashion'd'. Jeremy
consoled him. 'As to the old Shipwrights,' Jeremy stated, 'if the air
blowing upon them . . . would give them cold, he [may] make each
of them the present of an umbrella'.[5]

In 1779, unable to get an appointment in any of the royal dockyards, Samuel Bentham toured continental yards and arrived in
Russia at a time of imperialist ambition that enabled him to plan
and organize a shipyard in Krichev, on an estate recently sequestered
by Prince Potemkin.[6] He relied upon serf labour – which, although

---

[2] Bentham did not neglect the problems of fortification against external threats.
The lesson of the Gordon Riots was one that he also saw architecturally. The
panopticon was carefully designed to repel both hostile enterprises from within
and 'clandestine enteprises from without'. See ibid., vol. iv, pp. 105 ff. For the
many uses that the panopticon might have, at least in Bentham's imagination, his
manuscripts need to be consulted at University College, London: Bentham MSS,
vol. vii, fols. 53–106. Gertrude Himmelfarb, 'The Haunted House of Jeremy
Bentham', *Victorian Minds* (New York, 1968), and Michel Foucault, *Discipline
and Punish: The Birth of the Prison*, trans. Alan Sheridan (1977).

[3] Timothy L. S. Sprigge (ed.), *The Correspondence of Jeremy Bentham* (1968), vol.
i, p. 136.

[4] ibid., vol. ii, pp. 108 ff; M. S. Bentham, *The Life of Brigadier-General Sir Samuel
Bentham* (1862), p. 189; Sprigge, *Correspondence*, vol. i, p. 157; vol. ii, pp. 156, 176.

[5] ibid., vol. i, pp. 164–7.

[6] Matthew S. Anderson, 'Samuel Bentham in Russia, 1779–1791', *The American
Slavic and East European Review*, vol. xv (1956), pp. 157–72; Ian R. Christie,
'Samuel Bentham and the Western Colony at Krichev, 1784–1791', *The Slavonic
and East European Review*, vol. xlviii (April 1970), pp. 232–47. The most vivid
account of Samuel's Russian period is to be found in vol. iii of Jeremy's *Correspondence*.

numerous, was ill-disciplined – and about a score of workers from the armament factories of Carron. This combination of the recalcitrant serfs and the 'Newcastle mob – hirelings from that rabble town' did not work out: drunkenness, arson, theft, idleness, intrigue and sabotage prevailed. In 1786, when Jeremy visited, he found 'that the Russian Utopia was little better than a madhouse'. That summer the smith's shop was burnt to the ground, and one of the glass houses shared a similar fate.

The brothers concentrated. Jeremy wrote to William Pitt proposing that English convicts be sent to Russia. Samuel, meanwhile, had been tinkering. 'My brother,' Jeremy wrote,

has hit upon a very singular new and I think important (though simple) idea in Architecture ... The architectural idea [in the plan of what we] call an Inspection-house is that of a circular building so contrived that any number of persons may therein be kept in such a situation as either to be, or what comes nearly to the same thing, to seem to themselves to be, constantly under the eye of a person or persons occupying a station in the centre of what we call the Inspector's Lodge.[7]

They could not put this panopticon into practice: Potemkin sold his estates, war with Turkey broke out, and the Bentham brothers left Russia without knowing whether the singular architectural idea would transform a 'madhouse' into a 'utopia', but determined with their experience to put the idea into practice in England.

In London, in the outbuildings of his brother's house, Samuel occupied himself constructing models of the panopticon, while Jeremy in the main building drafted revisions of the plan and wrote letters advancing the idea to influential people. By the 1790s Samuel's considerable experience of mechanical design and shipbuilding, together with his equally important experience of the problems of controlling a large, insubordinate workforce, came to be recognized. In 1795 he was appointed Inspector-General of the Naval Works.

[7] *Correspondence*, vol. iii, p. 501. Even in the first drafts of the panopticon literature Jeremy was careful to specify that all parts of the building be fire-proofed.

II

Any study of working-class power must begin by considering the form and value of payment. For most workers in the eighteenth century the payments were not made in money, or, when they were, such payments were only one of several forms. This was true of Russian serf labour, American slave labour, Irish agricultural labour and the metropolitan labour in London trades. Other factors such as the length and intensity of the working day, the characteristic technologies of production, the methods of circulating the materials of labour in and out of production, the ways in which the final product was appropriated – these too were either determined by the methods of payment to the producers or related to them in a common structure of social and material relations. In eighteenth-century London, just as the necessary value of labour often appeared as 'crime', so the surplus value of the ruling class appeared as 'corruption', and nowhere perhaps was this more in evidence than in the dockyards.

The pay books of any of the six main naval dockyards are readily available and can provide what appear to be the day rates of all the categories of labour employed. These were numerous. A list of them will suggest the magnitude of the problems in the heterogeneous division of labour in what was, perhaps, the largest of eighteenth-century British enterprises. Deptford Yard employed shipwrights, quarterboys, caulkers, oakum boys, joiners, house-carpenters, wheelwrights, plumbers, pitch heaters, blockmakers, bricklayers' labourers, sailmakers, scavelmen, riggers, riggers' labourmen, armourers, smiths, compass-makers. The yard as a whole might employ 900 men and boys during peace and 1,100 to 1,200 during wartime.

Each trade could consist of several grades of worker with corresponding day rates, ranging from 3s. for a master boatbuilder to 1s. for a labourer.[8] In addition to day rates, there were certain forms of overtime pay. These were measured in 'tides' – periods of an hour and a half. The tide rate for shipwrights, joiners, carpenters, caulkers, bricklayers and wheelwrights was sixpence. For labourers and sawyers it amounted to threepence. Overtime was also measured according to 'nights' – that is, the full day rate was paid for five

<hr />

[8] B. M. Ranft, 'Labour Relations in the Royal Dockyards in 1739', *The Mariner's Mirror*, vol. xvii, no. 4 (November 1961), p. 290.

hours' work at the end of the normal working day.[9]

Let us look first at some *additions* to the base rate. The system of apprenticeship was controlled by the craftsmen, not the dockyard officers, and worked in such a way as to reduce the burden of work and increase the income of the 'skilled' worker to whom the apprentice's wages were paid. Apprentices were also expected to pay £2 2s. 'footing'; the penalty for non-payment was flogging with a hand-saw.[10] The officers of the Royal Naval dockyards often managed yards or supply houses of their own. At Deptford they were in a position to requisition the labour of the yard for their own purposes, so payment on these private accounts must be added to the workers' wage.[11] Against these additions several types of *deductions* from the nominal monetary wage have to be made. The salary of the surgeon resident at Deptford was paid from the men's wages. In some yards the salary of a resident clergyman was supplied by docking the workers' pay.[12] Pay clerks accepted a customary fee from workers before entering the amount of work time in the pay book. Finally, disciplinary deductions were common. Loitering, tippling, playing football or cricket, absence from the mid-morning or mid-afternoon calls, 'baseying' (bounding the walls during the working day) were all common offences punished by deductions from the monetary wage.[13]

The form and frequency of the payment of nominal wages encouraged a system of real payment whose effect was to reduce the money wages even further. In the seventeenth century, wage-payments at Deptford were often several years in arrears. While this appears to have improved *somewhat* in the eighteenth century, it was still an important enough matter to fight about, as the Deptford workers did in 1762, when wages were fifteen months behind.[14] Wages were paid only twice a year (*if* they were paid) and when the dockyard workers complained about this in the 1739 strike the

[9] R. D. Merriman (ed.), *Queen Anne's Navy: Documents Concerning the Administration of the Navy of Queen Anne, 1702–1714*, Navy Record Society (1961), p. 121.
[10] M. D. George, op. cit., p. 282; Daniel A. Baugh, *British Naval Administration in the Age of Walpole* (Princeton, 1965), p. 318.
[11] John Ehrman, *The Navy in the War of William III, 1689–1697* (Cambridge, 1953), p. 94.
[12] Merriman, op. cit., p. 109.
[13] M. Oppenheim, 'The Royal Dockyards', in William Page (ed.), *The Victorian History of the County of Kent*, vol. ii (1926), p. 376.
[14] Baugh, op. cit., pp. 316 ff.

Navy Board chastised them for their 'enormities'. If the officers at Deptford Yard wished to discharge a man they would regard an absence as grounds for marking him 'run' (deserted) and thus deny him his accumulated wages. Long arrears in payment, therefore, were a means of limiting turnover in the yard. Professional wage-buyers and creditors exerted considerable influence in Parliament, and so Deptford Yard rarely actually discharged a man without at least having his creditors repaid.[15] In cases where the wage was paid to the men – instead of being merely a wage of account settled between the Navy Office and the Deptford creditors – Navy tickets, not specie, passed hands. In theory these were redeemable at face value some several miles up the river at the Navy Office in London. In fact, during the first half of the eighteenth century they were redeemed at a usurious discount of between 24 and 50 per cent.[16] Before he entered the business of pirating Bibles, the noted phil-anthropist Thomas Guy made money by discounting Navy tickets at Deptford. While an initial inspection of pay books suggests the prevalence of money payment, a closer examination challenges such an assumption. The paymaster of the Navy treasury noted 'it has for time immemorial been customary' not to disburse copper money.

The inefficiencies of shipbuilding in both private and Royal Naval dockyards arose from the widespread corruption that flourished at all levels of dockyard organization, from the Commissioners of the Navy Board down to the bottom man in the sawyer's pit. It was observed of dockyard workers that their dwellings were constructed of materials formerly of His Majesty's Naval Stores, and after the naval defeats of the War of American Independence it was remarked that more ships were lost piecemeal in women's aprons than to enemy action at sea. The note of exaggeration in such remarks emphasizes the fact that dockyard inefficiency meant meat and drink for shipyard workers and their families.[17] The Mariner's Jewel (1724) advised the purser: 'All that you deliver by weight or measure, you must keep back the 8th part for waste.'

The nominal monetary wage was not at this time a matter of much contention. For the first half of the eighteenth century cer-tainly the wage-rates of the main categories of trades did not change

[15] Ehrman, op. cit., p. 92.
[16] Oppenheim, op. cit., p. 376. In 1762 the discount had dropped to 7.5 per cent.
[17] Robert G. Albion, Forests and Sea Power: The Timber Problems of the Royal Navy 1652–1862 (Cambridge, Mass., 1926), pp. 87–8.

at Deptford (or at any of the other Royal Naval dockyards).[18] But against this stability in wages must be set the vigour of protracted struggle that defended the men's control over the pace of work, the materials of labour and the structure of the labour force in the yards. In these fields of contention the men enjoyed a power — especially in wartime — that compensated for the low nominal monetary wage. Slow-downs, absenteeism, tippling and baseying were complained of constantly by Deptford Yard supervisors.[19]

At the beginning of the century the Navy Board sought to limit the winter working day to eight hours, not in order to reduce payment of tides or nights, but to eliminate 'the roguery and villainy they commit when it is beginning to grow dark'.[20] One twilight evening in 1694 the commissioner of the Chatham Yard observed 'the horrid consternation' of workers carrying out 'spikes, nails, bolts, lead, rope'.[21] Hemp and cordage were easy to take. Only the removal of large amounts would be discovered: in 1702, for example, a shipwright was stopped for 'accidentally' packing 36 lbs. of cordage in his tool-box. Copper and brass fittings were valuable items. Smuggled treenails provided the initial capital of more than one private shipbuilding enterprise. In 1729 sailmaking, which had been contracted out, took place within the Deptford Yard, and as a result canvas soon provided plentiful business for the small marine dealers outside the dockyard walls. Sailmakers would also cut out canvas and sew up breeches in the yard to sell to shipwrights and seamen for slops.[22]

Even those who were to gain a reputation for transforming the Navy into an efficient enterprise owed their wealth and power to the widespread corruption — this was as true of Phineas Pett and his sons as it was of Samuel Pepys, who made £14,000 at the Navy Board.[23] The chief remuneration of the yard workers was not their

[18] Baugh, op. cit., table 19, p. 309 for wage-rates in 1748, rates that were substantially the same in 1749; see PRO Adm., 42/540, Deptford Yard Pay Books.

[19] Ehrman, op. cit., pp. 90–92, and Baugh, op. cit., pp. 310 ff.

[20] Oppenheim, op. cit., p. 353.

[21] H. E. Richardson, 'Wages of Shipwrights in HM Dockyards, 1496–1788', *The Mariner's Mirror*, vol. xxxiii, no. 4 (October 1947), p. 270.

[22] Oppenheim, op. cit., pp. 363–4, 347.

[23] W. G. Perrin (ed.), *The Autobiography of Phineas Pett*, Royal Navy Record Society, vol. li (1918). Pett failed to reject bad timber; he repaired ships that ought to have been junked; he maintained his own personal storehouse with 'full scope withal to embezzle what he list'. James II 'protested very earnestly the cross

monetary wage, nor such dockyard materials as hemp or cordage. 'Noah's sons' worked in a circuit of wood. The perennial problem of the Admiralty and the basis of life for the men and women of the dockyards was 'chips'.

III

What were chips? What were they worth? Broadly speaking, they consisted of wood scraps and waste created during the work of hewing, chopping and sawing ship timbers. The term refers not to the wood itself but to the right of the worker to appropriate a certain amount of it – a prescriptive right since 1634. The amount of wood taken as chips depended upon the balance of forces between the dockyard workers and the Navy Board. Unlike wages, chips were negotiable and this itself was an ambiguity that benefited the men who under cover of chips might make away with all types of goods. 'There be nothing so frequent in our Minutes,' sighed an official of the Navy Board, 'as Orders respecting Chips.' When the 'chip-women' of Portsmouth were forbidden access to the yards, they rioted in protest.[24]

In 1662 it was ruled that chips could consist only in what could be carried out by one worker one day a week, a ruling that was a dead letter from the start. In 1702 the Deptford men maintained the right to take chips out of the yard three times a day and to enlist the assistance of their families in the appropriation. In 1730 the Admiralty defined chips as those 'lawfully made with Axes and Adzes, but not any sawn ends of Slabs of old Wood of any Kind'. In 1739 the Navy Board said that dockyard workers were entitled only to 'such Chips as shall be split out by their tools'. In 1752 a regulation attempted to limit the amount of chips to those that could be carried out of the yard untied under one arm. In 1764 we learn that at Deptford 'what is called the Poor, were allowed into the Yard twice a week to gather "Offal timber"'. In 1767 letters were published which explained the 'many Evils' arising from 'upwards of two thousand, mostly Women' who entered the dock-yards on Wednesdays and Saturdays 'to take from thence the small

---

grain was in the men and not in the timber'. Arthur Bryant, *Samuel Pepys*, 3 vols (Cambridge, 1933–39), vol. i, pp. 171–221.
[24] Oppenheim, op. cit., p. 347; *Lloyds Evening Post*, 3–6 September 1771.

Chips and Gleanings of the Yard'.[25] It was ordered that women be allowed to partake only of the small chips and sweepings, and these were twice weekly carted to the yard gates so that the women were prevented from entering the yard itself. The custom was used to shorten the working day. In 1783 the Navy Office reported: 'The Custom hitherto has been for the Men to leave off Work perhaps Half an Hour before Bell ringing, and even during Working Hours, to cut up clandestinely useful Timber to complete their Bundles, which are frequently sold as high as 1s. each.'[26]

In 1795 Samuel Bentham took lodgings by the Portsmouth Yard gatehouse in order to make precise calculations of the amount of chips (each piece less than three feet) that were taken from the yard. He learned that they provided not only one of the main sources of fuel for the poor, but also the characteristic architectural features of the neighbourhood: 'Stairs were just under three feet wide; doors, shutters, cupboards, and so forth were formed of wood in pieces just under three feet long.'[27] To those having a right to this prescriptive custom, chips were an essential part of their ecology – in housing, in energy, in cooking, in furnishings. The intensity of the practice varied with living conditions, prices and nominal wages. It represented both a substantial source of income to yard workers and a serious loss to the Navy. Deptford workers in the seventeenth century said they could not live without the practice. Later historians have agreed.[28] It was a perquisite providing between a third and a half of weekly earnings. Yeoman Lott, a Measurer of the Clerk of the Cheque at Deptford Yard (1752–63), who knew as much about this at Deptford as anyone in the 1740s and 1760s, thought that there was a direct relation between the amount of chips taken and real wages. The price of provisions was 10 per cent higher in Deptford, he said, than in other Royal Naval dockyards, and it was this that in his experience accounted for the more serious extent of Deptford depredations. The amount and value of chips are more easily documented as a loss to the Navy than as fuel, furnishings, etc. to the workers. The most expressive statement of loss – based on computations made once at the beginning of the century and again

[25] Oppenheim, op. cit., pp. 358, 370; Baugh, op. cit., p. 321. Yeoman Lott, *An Account of the Proposals made for the Benefit of His Majesty's Naval Service* (1777), p. 8.
[26] *JHC*, op. cit.
[27] M. S. Bentham, op. cit., p. 143.
[28] Baugh, op. cit., ch. 6; Albion, op. cit., pp. 80 ff; Ehrman, op. cit., p. 95.
[29] William Sutherland, *The Ship-Builder's Assistant* (1711), p. 7. His grandfather

twenty years later – was that only a sixth of the timber entering
Deptford Yard left it afloat.[29] There were many others. In the last
decade of the century the loss from all Royal Naval dockyards was
officially estimated at £500,000 a year. Unofficially the loss was
believed to be nearer four times that amount. Yeoman Lott conducted an experiment between 1768 and 1770 designed to determine
the monetary loss caused by the taking of chips. He found that in
the construction of a third-rate vessel (74 guns), the proportion of
lawful chips to the 'neat Content' of timber in the ship ought to be
4:11 and it was *this* proportion that he sought to re-establish. In
practice he learned that 60 per cent of all grades of timber ordered
for the construction of a third-rate found its way out of the dockyard
in the guise of chips.[30]

Time and again the Navy sought to replace the privilege with an
increase in the nominal wage. In 1663 the wage was increased by a
penny a day for this purpose; but the men took the penny and
kept the chips.[31] In 1783 it was proposed that fourpence a day to
shipwrights and twopence a day to carpenters 'be entered an extra
Sum on the Pay Books, as in lieu of Chips, that the Perquisite may
never on any Pretence come into future use'.[32] This too failed.
Indeed it is safe to say that any attempt to compound for the chips
that did not at the same time abolish the basis of the dockyard
workers' power in the job was doomed to fail. Yeoman Lott tried
this partial solution, indeed he devoted the best part of ten years at
Deptford in the attempt. In 1757 he presented the Admiralty with
his plan of allowing 'Artificers of His Majesty's Yards an Equivalent
in Lieu of their Perquisite Chips'. In 1767 he published a pamphlet
called *Important Hints towards an Amendment of the Royal Dock-
Yards*. In 1770 he investigated the dockyards of Amsterdam and
Rotterdam. Though proposing an across-the-board wage increase
of sixpence a day, his proposal at every step met with the concerted
opposition of the artificers. 'He has been,' as he stated in his petition
to the Admiralty in 1768, 'a great Sufferer, to the frequent Hazard

---

[29] William Sutherland, *The Ship-Builder's Assistant* (1711), p. 7. His grandfather
was foreman of shipwrights at Deptford for thirty years. He had himself worked
for fifteen years in the inspection of work at Portsmouth and Deptford. See also
William Sutherland, *Britain's Glory: Or, Shipbuilding Unveil'd*, 2nd edn (1726),
introduction.

[30] Lott, op. cit., pp. 33–6.

[31] Oppenheim, op. cit.

[32] *JHC*, op. cit.

of his Person and Employment, and the manifest Injury of his Property.' He was expelled from Deptford. No one would give him a job at Chatham or Woolwich – the two other Royal Naval dockyards on the Thames. When he found work as an agent for the Royal Hospital at Plymouth, his life there became one of continuous trouble. His garden plot was 'intirely destroyed and laid waste'.

The Navy's failures were the yard workers' victories – achieved by 'mutiny', 'commotion' and 'insurrection'. At the beginning of war in 1739 the Deptford workers, together with those of the other naval yards, went out on strike because the Navy had attempted to reduce night and tide work, as well as the number of chips the men could take by requiring them to unbundle their loads as they departed work in the evening. Another issue concerned whether chips were to be carried out under the arm or upon the shoulder. In June 1755 the shipwrights and carpenters of Chatham struck and boycotted the gates to prevent their perquisites from being 'injured'.[33] In October 1758 a similar issue caused the Deptford workers to strike again. In April 1768 shipwrights fought the marines over 'a Bundle of Chips', their 'Custom'.[34] The striking workers at Chatham stated: 'There is not a man amongst us who would not freely die for King and Country, but we will not tamely suffer ourselves to be made slaves to any particular man's whim, *for we are free-born subjects*.'[35] Although magistrates were summoned to read the Riot Act to the men refusing to enter the yards, the strike was finally settled by the Navy Board capitulating to the men's demands.

Thus, chips became associated with some deeply held working-class ideas of freedom and slavery. As a form of value, chips were not as desirable, useful or versatile as money, yet like money they fluctuated with prices, as the shipbuilding communities struggled to live. The Navy regarded chips as a problem of inventory control or of materials handling. In 1726 William Sutherland, author of a leading British work on shipbuilding, calculated that by abolishing the chips of the workers in order to build ships 'with another ship's chips' more than £93,000 might be saved a year, and this was an estimate based only on so-called 'rightful chips'. This was also the reason why virtually all eighteenth-century British treatises

---

[33] Oppenheim, op. cit., p. 373.
[34] *Berrow's Worcester Journal*, 5 May 1768.
[35] Ranft, op. cit., pp. 285 ff.

on shipbuilding began with the problem of timber supply and handling.[36]

IV

The eighteenth-century shipyard is an example of heterogeneous cooperation – that is, its internal division of labour was characterized by a series of discrete operations separated by time, place and the nature of the tools and materials. Each operation was physically independent of the others. Each required its own shops, its own tools and its own labour force. Daniel Defoe compared the shipyard to 'a well order'd city; and tho' you see the whole place . . . in the utmost hurry, yet you see no confusions, every man knows his business'.[37] In the production of the ship we can identify four main stages: the preparation of materials; the fabrication of materials into components; assembly; making watertight. We shall consider each of these stages.

The preparation of materials consisted of two activities that were organized in such a way as to maximize the opportunity of appropriating chips – namely, the *delivery* of timber and its subsequent *conversion* into various shapes and sizes. Virtually all who wrote on the subject wished that the timber might be roughly converted to size in the forests before it was brought to the yards. Snodgrass, a leading builder for the East India Company, considered 'that timber ought always to be cut to its proper shape as near as convenient to the place where it grows'. William Sutherland thought that such a practice would reduce carriage costs alone by five-sixths.[38] But such a plan required close communication between the yards and the areas of forest supply, and accurate specifications for the required timbers. Neither circumstance existed: communication was made difficult by scattered sources of supply that were as far apart as the Baltic and New Hampshire; and accurate specifications required a degree of standardization that did not yet exist. Any large warship would require about 2,000 oak trees in its construction. The *Royal*

---

[36] Sutherland, *Britain's Glory* (1726), for example, begins with a chapter entitled 'Observations for Regulating the Price of Timber'.
[37] T. S. Ashton, *An Economic History of England: Eighteenth Century* (1955), p. 113.
[38] Sutherland, op. cit., p. 7.

George, a ship of 100 guns launched in 1756, required 2,309 loads (a load = fifty cubic feet) of straight oak and 2,306 loads of compass (curved grain) oak. Before 1771, little attention was paid to the seasoning of timber – large stocks were laid up in the yard, the thick stuff and sawn planks were not properly stacked or separated by battens. Knees and other joining pieces were rarely stored in drying sheds. Some blamed the weakness of British ships upon the practice of using green timbers instead of well-seasoned wood in construction – a practice that was said to have resulted from the men taking the mature timber for chips and leaving the green stuff for production.

The conversion of logs into rough timber took place in the various saw-houses scattered about Deptford Yard. In terms of the volume of wasted timber it was perhaps in the process of rough conversion in the sawyer's pit that most of the largest chips were created. (Samuel Bentham was one of the first to consider the construction of steam-powered saw-mills in order to avoid such waste.) The whip saw used for rough or planking work possessed a broad blade of 7 or 8 ft. in length that was supported in a wooden frame. Two men operated it. The topman sharpened the teeth, marked the timber with a chalked line along its length, and held the tiller. The pitman held the box end of the saw and worked from the bottom of the sawyer's pit – a cavity dug in the ground about 12 ft. long, 6 ft. deep and 2 ft. wide. He also positioned the log on its rollers. The work was arduous. It was also impressive: 'It's really very admirable to see how Two Men should so nicely and exactly strike their Stroke, and at the same time not see one another.'[39] It was precisely the arduous and 'nice' nature of the work that made it vulnerable to increased exploitation. 'A sawyer's no robber – What he takes from one side he gives to the other,' as the saying went. As easily as he might be no robber, he might be one as well. As a result, sawyers were the first category of workers in the shipyards to be placed on piece-rates. Towards the end of the seventeenth century some sawyering knowledge was published. Sutherland devoted six pages to the problems of timber measurement and saw-tooth design. The sawyers determined the rate of work, because they and not the officers determined the dryness or greenness of the timber. Furthermore, 'Men's Notions differ mightily on this Particular of Converting Timber to the best Advantage',

[39] ibid., p. 60.

THE SAWYER

A sawyer

depending on the grain of the piece and the shape of the piece to be sawn, with the result that none but the sawyers were in a position to decide, and this became another source of their using piece-rates to good advantage as well as producing 'waste'. When in 1768 a steam-powered saw-mill was constructed only a few miles from Deptford, it was no sooner completed than it was destroyed. A generation would pass before another such attempt was made in the London area.

In the fabrication of components the shipwright exercised his art and craft as one of 'Noah's Sons'. His 'mystery' had been appreciated for centuries: it defied the law that heavy solids should sink and it delivered 'man' from the deluge (in some English traditions, Mrs Noah refused to enter the ark). Edmund Bushnell wrote in *The Compleat Ship-Wright* (1664): 'Yet their knowledge they desire to keep to themselves, or at least among so small a number as they can.' Knowledge of shipbuilding could not be obtained from books, and it is doubtful that books – except those containing mathematical tables – could have been of much assistance at all prior to the 1770s. From the shipwright's point of view the gap between imagination and reality was mediated not by print, but by pricking-out. The mould-loft was the *sanctum sanctorum* where the imagination found practical exercise. There on a vast floor the shipwright worked on his knees, laying out his patterns, tacking them on the floor, setting his fairing lines, and 'proving the frames', so that the proportions of the components – the transoms, keels, futtocks, knees, etc. – would remain true to the whole. From the shape and dimensions of a single piece an experienced shipwright could imagine the shape and dimensions of the finished ship.[40]

Once the shipwright had laid out his patterns, the next step was to fashion the roughly converted timber into components. This was also an art, since the components were not standardized. His tools were the adze and the axe. Adze work was close to the feet and toes. It was a 'universal paring instrument'.[41] As sharp as a razor and as heavy as shot, its use required delicacy and strength. A skilled shipwright, like Kline Falkenham, son and grandson of shipwrights, 'can take a chip off as thin as a piece of paper'. The futtocks provided the rib-like frame of the hull. For a large vessel a futtock might be 11 ins. thick and 18 ft long. Some would have double curves in their length. Each had to be hewn out of rough timbers by axe and adze. They were strongest, of course, when the natural grain of the wood ran with the curve of the final piece. Especially true in the construction of these timbers, but a rule that might apply to all of eighteenth-century shipbuilding, was the fact that the larger the individual component piece the more the skill required in its handling and fabrication – also the greater the loss caused by an error.

[40] As Kline Falkenham was able to show me at the Lunenberg shipyards (Nova Scotia) on 3 June 1981 in the mould-loft where he had laid out the HMS *Bounty* for the second MGM film.
[41] John Fincham, *A History of Naval Architecture* (1851), p. 81.

In 1726 it was estimated that in the construction of a futtock or ship's beam the proportion of wood in the piece to the rough timber from which it was fashioned was 7:25 – a proportion that gives us an idea of how chips were inherent in the work.[42] The ship's knees were pieces of timber that attached the cross-beams to the frame of the hull. To fashion the ship's knees was especially challenging because the shipwright had usually to cut across the grain. The first English shipbuilding manuals paid special attention to the methods of forming knees from blocks of wood so as to minimize the wasted pieces.[43]

In the assembly of components we shall look at only two methods of attachment that afforded scope for 'waste': scarphing and treenailing. The first method involved cutting the ends of the futtocks so that they would overlap one another by six or seven feet without increasing the thickness at the join. It can be easily imagined how an error or misjudgement with the adze might 'waste' one of these graceful parts.[44] The second method of attachment depended on the treenail. A treenail was a cylindrical piece of wood that was used to attach the outer and inner planking to the ship's frame or to attach various parts of the frame itself together. Many thousands of them were necessary to the construction of any ship. They were made from oak, generally from pieces towards the top of the tree where wood was most likely to be free of knots. The treenail had to be straight-grained so that it would not fracture upon being driven in. The oak was first sawn into appropriate lengths. Then it was split (finding the grain) into thinner pieces before being worked with the spike shave. Finally it was shaped with the router plane or moot. This was a tool that consisted of two adjustable halves (so that it could be used for different diameters) with a throat plated to resist wear. 'Great part of the Piece [was] wasted for the sake of the But' – that is, for the tapered conical head. Often the middle part of the treenail was thinned somewhat so that it did not have actually to cut the wood (often itself of oak) that it was driven into. During the first half of the century a man might get 6s. for making 1,000 treenails a foot long, and 30s. for 1,000 a yard long. The scope for

---

[42] Sutherland, op. cit., pp. 36–7.
[43] ibid., pp. 129–30.
[44] Scarphing methods are described in George Dodd, *Days at the Factories; Or, the Manufacturing Industry of Great Britain Described* (1843), p. 463.

waste was huge. William Sutherland found that about £5,000 was lost a year in treenail-making.[45]

The holes in the timbers designed to receive the treenail were bored with a long-pod auger whose bit might be one or two inches across, a 'shell' less likely to 'wander' or follow the grain. The auger's cross-handle was of considerable length so that greater torque could be applied. Extreme care was required in matching auger to treenail: if the match were too tight the planking or framing timbers might be split or weakened, if it was too loose the ship would soon leak. Besides skill in judgement, great strength was required: the wood was often hard, the depth that had to be bored sometimes exceeded four feet, and always the men were placed in awkward positions – now standing on the scaffolding, high above the ground, now horizontal, working close to the keel.[46] In driving treenails William Sutherland 'observed very great Controversies'.[47] The percussion of the hammers had to be exactly true, otherwise planks might split, frame timbers weaken and neighbouring treenails loosen.

The work of making watertight was performed by the caulker. His tools consisted of hammer and pitch-pot; his materials were oakum, leather, pitch and tar. With these he filled the seams between the planks. Seams might vary greatly in depth – from a few inches to many feet – and they were often located in awkward places. Beneath the hull, for instance, the caulker had to prise open seams resting on his back and hammering upwards. These workers resisted Sutherland's attempt to find objective criteria for measuring their work: 'The Caulkers will allow that there can be no Rules given: but Caulking must *of Necessity depend wholly upon the Judgement of the Workman, or true Breed Caulkers, as they term themselves.*' Sutherland, not himself a caulker, had his own opinions. 'I have really seen several experienc'd Caulkers at some times ease their stroke, and at other times force it, and yet in the very same Seam, and in a short Distance, which by any reasonable Man cannot be allowed for good

---

[45] ibid., p. 486; Sutherland, op. cit., pp. 51–2.
[46] R. A. Salaman, *Dictionary of Tools used in the Woodworking and Allied Trades, c. 1700–1970* (1975). A magnificent volume of social history! See also Nathaniel G. Clark, *A Scale of Prices for Job Work, On Old Ships ... for the Shipwrights of the River Thames* (1825).
[47] Sutherland, op. cit., p. 54.

Work.' He sighed the sigh of productivity specialists: 'You may constantly attend on the Working Man, and he may also seem very forward in his employment, and yet but to very little purpose.'[48] The caulker's hammer drove the pledgets of oakum between the seams of the ship's timbers. 'You got to be at it day and night' to learn to use one properly. The caulker judged how hard to hit by listening to the sound the hammer made on impact.

Like the shipwright, the eighteenth-century caulker shrouded his knowledge in sacred mystery, and this was the first thing that the caulkers made certain that William Sutherland understood. 'The caulkers in Sacred History are termed wise Men of Gebal.' The reference is to Ezekiel 27:9, in which the prophet in exile preaches against Tyre: 'The ancients of Gebal and the wise men thereof were in thee thy caulkers.' In this tradition the wise man and the craftsman were identical, sharing a Faustian combination of technical know-ledge and demiurgic power. Many must have been the instances in storms or high seas when mariners thought of these 'wise men'. Yet the age of the Enlightenment sought to distil the practical knowledge of the 'craftsman' from the mysterious airs of the 'wise man' where wisdom was a form of 'idleness', or in this case, resistance to the introduction of piece-rates.

Our examples of the preparation, fabrication, assembly and sealing of a ship suggest a few conclusions. First, the meanings of waste, raw material and finished product were unclear. Second, the mean-ings were often opposed. What were chips to one were ships to another, and vice versa. Third, such techniques and skills as we have indicated had determinable consequences upon the design, reliability and longevity of the ships, and hence upon the relative strength of the fleet of the Royal Navy against that of other maritime powers.

V

'The English navy was, in fact, in a very bad condition as regarded the building of ships,' wrote a nineteenth-century authority on the

[48] John Fincham, *A History of Naval Architecture* (1851), p. 81; William Sutherland, *Britain's Glory; Or Ship-Building Unveil'd being a General Directory for Building and Compleating the Said Machines* (1726).

history of naval architecture.[49] Another wrote of English ships: 'They were crank, in general heavy sailors, of ill stowage, confined, and inconvenient in the hour of battle.'[50] Ships did not last as long as those of other fleets. Such improvements in design that were made owed more to what was learned from captured enemy vessels than to the ingenuity or talent of English shipwrights.

In 1738 Sir John Norris attempted to have the shipwrights standardize ship design.

Every particular ship has been built, or re-built, according to different proposed dimensions. Those of the same class or denomination have been built of unequal size and proportions: so that the furniture and stores for one ship have not fitted another of the same rank; which has been the cause of infinite inconveniences to the service, as well as of a great increase in the expense of the navy.[51]

More was affected than furniture and stores. Two ships of the same rate could contain widely differing amounts of timber, even in their frames. The 74-gun *Thunderer* used nearly eighty loads more of timber in her construction than did the *Princess Amelia*, a ship that was actually in a class *above* the *Thunderer*. In 1685 it was stated at Chatham Yard: 'Were it not better done to have a certain size, figure, kind and value of ornament for every sort of boat of every rate, well digested and established as a standing rule not to be departed from?'[52] The relation between wasted timber and unstandardized design was well known. In 1726 Sutherland devoted his major text, *Britain's Glory*, to the thesis that by reducing the lost timber from five-sixths to a half he might at the same time build ships that lasted thirty years instead of twelve.

Little progress was made in the science of shipbuilding in eighteenth-century England. 'Success, in all probability, was more attributable to a coincidence of blunders innocently committed ... than to any regular and established system resulting from theoretical knowledge and studious application.' Such was the harsh judgement of John Charnock in 1800. Malachy Postlethwayt and Fincham made similar points contrasting science to experience.[53] At the

[49] Fincham, op. cit., p. 81.
[50] John Charnock, *History of Marine Architecture* (1800), vol. iii, p. 106.
[51] ibid., p. 123.
[52] Bryant, op. cit., vol. iii, p. 197.
[53] Charnock, op. cit., vol. iii, p. 52; Malachy Postlethwayt, *The Universal Dictionary of Trade and Commerce*, 3rd edn (1766), vol. ii, article called 'Shipping'; Fincham, op. cit., p. 177.

beginning of the century Sutherland wrote: 'But the Qualifications requisite to make any Man a Master are really so many, as well in the Theory as in the Practick Part, that it's almost impossible such Qualifications should be concentrat'd.' Earlier he had written: 'Out of the vast number of Shipwrights that are in England, there are scarce two of one Opinion; so that our occupation, altho' very useful, is no other than a Notion.' 'For was it demanded of our celebrated Shipwrights, what the Body of a Ship is, the Answer would be, An irregular confus'd Body.'[54]

If we can summarize these views of ship construction as either empirical ('coincidence of blunders', 'experience') or systematic ('theoretical knowledge,' 'science'), then it is important that we recognize that in the history of eighteenth-century English ship-building the former was associated with the working artificers and the latter with those like Sutherland, Snodgrass and Bentham, who, though intellectually systematic, were opponents to the practices of the yards, and the workers' circuit of wood. By the 1770s and the American war it had become clear that the seaworthiness and fighting qualities of the English ships depended upon the social and material nexus of chips. In the American war, the Royal Navy suffered a loss of 200 ships sunk or captured by the Continental Navy, and losses of an additional 600 vessels to privateers. Moreover, it was the sluggishness of the British fleet that prevented it from arriving before the French at Yorktown in order to cover Cornwallis's retreat.

VI

'The efficiency of a yard ... depended not only on its equipment but also on its organization, and particularly on the control which could be exercised over the workmen.' In this way the historian of the Navy of William III summed up the problem.[55] The naval authorities attempted seven solutions.

First, inventory identification. At the Restoration, when James, Duke of York, assumed the office of Lord High Admiral, his first

---

[54] Sutherland, op. cit., p. xxv; Sutherland, *The Ship-Builder's Assistant* (1711), p. 28.
[55] Ehrman, op. cit., p. 88.

action was to promulgate a rule designed to detect the theft of naval stores: timber and metal goods were to be stamped with a broad arrow; cordage and sailcloth belonging to the Navy were to be marked by a strand of characteristic thread.[56] But as all marine stores regardless of their owners came to be marked in this way the purpose of the regulation was defeated. 'An Act for the better preventing the imbezlement of his Majesty's Stores of War' (9 & 10 Wiliam III, c. 41) passed in 1698 made the practice of marking private stores with the King's sign (the broad arrow on timber, a blue streak in canvas, and a contrary thread in cordage) illegal and punishable by forfeiture of the goods and a £200 fine. In 1722 another Act made this one perpetual and allowed judges considerably more discretion in punishment: in addition to forfeiture and fine, they could now pass sentences of whipping, imprisonment or consignment to the workhouse.[57] By the 1760s the phrase 'red sail-yard docker' became a cant term referring to those who made a living by smuggling the King's naval stores.[58]

Second, fortification. Access to the yards was controlled by enclosing them. Unlike the fortifications surrounding Sheerness or Portsmouth with their bastioned tracing, counter-guards and mortared curtains, the lines formed by the Woolwich and Deptford brick walls were simplicity itself, interrupted only by a walled corridor at the main gate, an architecture designed to contain an enemy within not to repel one without. In 1670 the enclosure of work at Chatham behind brick walls was accomplished against the opposition of the shipwrights. Those at Deptford had been enclosed earlier though not with great effect.[59] At the accession of George I the private passages through the walls backing the houses of the yard officers were bricked up.

Third, security personnel. Access and egress were decisive. A gate is only as strong as its porter. The duties of the Master Porter at Deptford, besides attending the gate, included ringing the work bell at proper times, controlling the walls and private passages through them, preventing baseying, and – in the absence of the Master Shipwright or his assistants – searching 'all shipwrights and

[56] Oppenheim, op. cit., p. 351.
[57] 9 George I, c. 8.
[58] George Parker, *A View of Society*, vol. ii (1781), and Francis Grose, *A Classical Dictionary of the Vulgar Tongue* (1785).
[59] John Hollond, *Two Discourses of the Navy*, Navy Record Society 1896, pp. 97–8.

caulkers going out of the Yard and to take from them all timber, plank or which under the pretence of chips, he may find them carrying with them'.[60] He was assisted in this work by the form of the gate, a sluice, that forced the flow of departing men to trickle, so to speak, rather than flood out. Opposite the porter's office was another department responsible for general security – the Watch. There were 87 on the pay books in 1749 – the third most numerous (behind shipwrights and labourers) of 23 categories of labour employed at Deptford.[61] Rotated in day and night shifts, their job was to patrol the walls and to guard against night-time depredations. Paid but a shilling and a penny a day, they colluded with those they were supposed to watch. As a result the Navy Board in 1764 posted a permanent detachment of marines at Deptford to guard the yard.

Fourth, recruitment. Attempts to improve efficiency by controlling the recruitment to the yards also failed. Shipbuilders in the sixteenth and seventeenth centuries had often been impressed to work in the yards, though by the middle of the seventeenth century voluntary enlistment had become the rule. In the eighteenth century forced labour in the Thames yards appeared to have been important only during the Queen Anne wars.[62] In 1739 and 1755 the apprenticeship system was attacked but the strikes of those years defeated attempts at the 'dilution' of labour. 'Servants,' as Commodore Steward informed Lord Sandwich, provided 'a large supply of active good young workmen by which means you were enabled at all times when mutinous or disorderly behaviour took place to discharge those principally concerned, and in that way supported proper subordination'.[63]

Fifth, divestment. On 4 August 1783 the Navy Board issued the following order to the yards: 'You are not to suffer any person to pass out of the Dock gates with Great Coats, large Trousers, or any

---

[60] *Parliamentary Papers*, vol. vii (1806), Sixth Report, pp. 323–38. The investigation of the Deptford Yard was conducted in the summer of 1787.

[61] PRO Adm., 42/408 (Deptford Ordinary, 1748–9). Both Baugh, op. cit., and Ranft, op. cit., omit the watch from their summaries of the structure of the Deptford labour force.

[62] E. P. Jupp, *An Historical Account of the Worshipful Company of Carpenters of the City of London* (1848), pp. 183–7, and N. Macleod, 'The Shipwrights of the Royal Dockyards', *The Mariner's Mirror*, vol. xi (July 1925), pp. 282–3; *Journals of the House of Lords*, vol. xxvii, pp. 649 and 661 (February 1752).

[63] Oppenheim, op. cit., p. 379.

other Dress that can conceal stores of any kind ... No trousers are to be used by the labourers employed in the storehouses.' This remained in force throughout the Napoleonic Wars. The 'King's armour' was thus kept by 'unaccommodated man'.[64]

Sixth, criminalization. Over our trouserless, thrice-watched, walled and incarcerated shipbuilder was cast, as a last resort, the shadow of the gallows. An Act of 1589 was brought 'against the imbezelling of armour, habiliments of war and victuals'. An Act of 1670 (22 Charles II, c. 5), by removing benefit of clergy, imposed a mandatory punishment of death.[65] No one in London or Middlesex was hanged under these Acts during the first half of the eighteenth century; the Admiralty preferred to exercise less drastic violence. In the seventeenth century the construction of stocks and a whipping post inside the Chatham and Deptford yards was to no avail: they were no sooner built than torn to pieces. Statutes passed during the reigns of the first and second Georges enlisted the magistracy and the criminal sanction in the fight against 'filching' – 1 George I, c. 25 (1714) and 17 George II, c. 40 (1749).

When Lord Sandwich took his seat on the Admiralty Board in 1749, one of his first acts was to visit all the Royal Naval dockyards and rope-walks. With his brother Lords of the Admiralty he found in June that 'gross negligence, irregularities, waste, and embezzlement were so palpable, that their Lordships ordered an advertisement to be set up in various parts of all the yards, offering encouragement and protection to such as should discover any misdemeanours'.[66] Placards were stuck up. They had little effect. From the evidence of the Kent judicial records (the Deptford and Chatham yards were within the county of Kent), it appears that, if the Acts were used at all, they were not used against those appropriating timber products. During the 1720s there are no examinations, confessions or depositions in the records against the misappropriation of naval stores of any kind at the yards. In the mid and late 1730s the picture changes. In 1736 a master shipwright informs against a bricklayer for taking sheet lead. The next year a foreman turns in a shipwright taking an

---

[64] Richardson, op. cit., p. 379; Roger Morris, *The Royal Dockyards During the Revolutionary and Napoleonic Wars* (Leicester, 1983), p. 94.

[65] Blackstone, *Commentaries*, bk. 4, ch. 7, sect. 4, treats the felony as an instance of those 'Injurious to the King's Prerogative'.

[66] John Barrow, *The Life of George Lord Anson* (1839), pp. 214–16.

iron eye bolt.[67] These two cases are notable for not involving misappropriations of timber. Thus, despite the new Acts that were passed, it is clear that the men's power in the yard was great enough to enforce their definition of 'lawful Chips' despite the newly expanded criminal sanction.

We find no evidence in the judicial repositories for 1754–6 and 1767–8 that the criminal sanction was used against the yard workers' appropriations. But in the 1770s the situation changes somewhat. A Deptford caulker informs against a 'labourer being in want of Money' caught taking 'some Working Tools'. Many examinations and depositions survive for the 1770s against shipbuilding-related crimes that take place *outside* the yard or within the confines of *private* yards or on board ships moored in the river waiting to be hauled into dry dock for hogging, careening or other major repairs. In December 1774 at Deptford Yard we find the first instance of the use of the criminal sanction against those appropriating timbers, when a worker was caught cutting a hole in the oar-maker's store-house.[68] In 1775, when Lord Sandwich sought to introduce task work into the yards, the judicial records are full of accounts of the yard workers threatening and assaulting their officers, but there is nothing about any punishment for the appropriation of chips. Nevertheless, it appears that in the following years the criminal sanction was increasingly used; foremen, clerks, porters and surveyors were now inspecting even the 'bundles of chips' though not apprehending the men carrying them if they contained nothing but wooden chips.[69] By the 1790s the courts began to restrict those entitled to chips, and punishment became frequent. William Page was sentenced to six months in a house of correction for 'feloniously stealing'. 'I took him by the collar,' said the shipbuilder. 'Says I, what have you got under your arm. He said, chips. I told him, not being a ship-wright, he was not entitled to them.'[70]

Seventh, task work. The abolition of day rates of pay and the introduction of 'task work' amounted to the most systematic attempt to remove the right to chips. In 1752 the Admiralty rebuked

[67]KRO, Q/SB, Sessions Papers, 6 December 1737. Our sample for the 1720s included only the years 1721, 1722, 1723, 1728 and 1729. See also the depositions of 20 November 1738, 18 December 1739, 23 August 1739 and 16 August 1739.
[68]ibid., 5 December 1774, 14 December 1769, 3 January 1770, 18 June 1770, 10 August 1770, 9 August 1770.
[69]ibid., 20 July 1775 and 18 July 1775.
[70]Morris, op. cit., p. 94, and *The Proceedings*, 10 January 1798.

the Navy Board for failing to execute its positive injunction that task work be introduced throughout the yards. The scheme was a favourite with Lord Sandwich, who, faced with the parliamentary investigation into the conduct of the Navy during the American war, had cause to elaborate at length on the issue and account for its failure. He calculated that a shipwright working on time with double tides might make 4s. 2d. a day. With task work, the working week would be five hours shorter and wages 5s. 3d. a day.[71]

In August 1775 the Lords Commissioners of the Admiralty received a comprehensive 'Scheme of Task Work for Shipwrights', which provides us with some evidence about how the system was supposed to work. The document was based upon the limited experience of the previous year at Deptford Yard, where two frigates, *America* and *Culloden*, were built under conditions of task work. Under this pay scheme, the workers were to be reorganized. They were to work in gangs of twenty, supervised by a quarterman or fireman who would set the tasks, determine the time for completing the task, keep track of raw materials, and see that the work was performed 'in a substantial, workmanlike manner ... particularly for the well-driving of the Treenails ... and for the goodness of Materials'. People called 'Single stationed Men' were to keep track of the materials. Despite the view expressed in the 'Scheme' that its execution would benefit 'the Public and the Workman', the men at Deptford 'were not inclined to it'.[72]

In 1775 Sandwich reported that 'factions, enthusiasm, obstinacy, and ignorance ... kept the artificers in dire opposition to work in that mode'. An issue of power was at stake, as the *Annual Register* in its report of the coordinated strikes against task work recognized: the system would put it 'in the power of any petty officers to deprive them of the hard-earned reward of their labour'.[73] Lord Sandwich appreciated this fact too and wistfully remarked: 'In this country of liberty, the idea of forcing people to work in a manner they dislike would not be generally approved, and might occasion great uneasiness, possible general commotions.' The simplification of

---

[71] G. R. Barnes and J. H. Owen (eds), *The Private Papers of John, Earl of Sandwich, First Lord of the Admiralty, 1771–1782*, Navy Record Society, vol. iv (1938), pp. 363 ff.
[72] *Shelburne Papers*, vol. xliv, 'Dockyard Artificers and Stores', fol. 7 (22 August 1775), William L. Clements Library, University of Michigan.
[73] *Annual Register* (1775), pp. 168–9.

superintendence, the intensification of labour, the control over the materials of labour, and the reduction of income that would have followed in the wake of the operation of task work could not be attained without first being able to determine the meaning of the 'task' itself. The only way that that could be achieved was by revolutionizing the labour process – that is, by a fundamental change in the relations between men, instruments of production and the materials of production. We may now return to Samuel Bentham.

VII

We left Samuel Bentham in the outbuildings of his brother's Westminster property. There he tinkered with his wood-planing mill, the panopticon and other inventions. In 1794 Jeremy and Samuel Bentham testified before a House committee that was considering a 'Bill for preventing frauds and embezzlements in dockyards'. They were concerned to 'introduce Good Morals among the lower Orders of the People'. This could be established only by reducing their income, whose form, they said, produced bad morals. 'Few Servants after they live a Short Time in London and get a Taste for its amusements and Consequently a Desire to possess Money to gratify their new wants but are corrupted by the ready means they find of obtaining it at these Iron Shops.'[74] The number of such shops had increased twelvefold over the past twenty-five years. Regular manufactories were established for the removal of the coloured strand from the King's cordage, others for the purpose of knocking off the broad arrow from copper bolts, new spikes, nails, hoops and copper sheathing. All stores, shops, inns, taverns and lodging-houses were supposed to be inspected, licensed and monitored by a newly formed police. Yet the Benthams agreed that in the circumstances of 1794 'any attack at the present crisis on so large a Body of fraudulent People would be dangerous to the State', because 'they hold Political Opinions favourable to any Set of Men who are at present hostile to the Government'.[75]

Counter-revolutionary war was the 'present crisis', and it demanded ships. Samuel Bentham's attack could not appear political. Yet, while an attack through the labour process seemed indirect, it had

[74] University College, London, Bentham MSS, box 149, pp. 14, 18, 17.
[75] ibid., p. 1.

profound effects. Appointed Inspector-General of the Naval Works in 1795, his genius of mechanical command found realization; he became 'the great innovator ... of dockyard development'. In her memoir of his life, Samuel's widow introduces his first actions in the yards in a significant way: 'He therefore began by classing the several *operations* requisite in the shaping and working up of materials of whatever kind, wholly disregarding the customary artificial arrangement according to trades.' Once this had been done, he was able to contrive machines 'independently of the need for skill or manual dexterity in the workman'.[76] He was able to 'reform abuses' by revolutionizing every aspect of the management and work of the shipyard. He systematically classed operations according to 'the materials to be wrought' 'without regard to the popular divisions of trades' and for the purpose of introducing machines.[77]

His largest creation was the 'floating dam'. By making the dock capable of receiving a fully loaded ship, masts, rigging, fittings, armaments, furniture and stores no longer had to be removed from the ship in its transition from river to dry dock. It had taken five or six days for 700 men to strip a ship for dry dock, and then as much time again to fit her out when the repairs were completed. The floating dam, however, together with his improved method for mooring vessels alongside the quay, saved the time and expense of this exercise, and also removed one of the main occasions for embezzlement.[78]

He introduced a new method of joining wood, which he called, with delicate spelling, 'coqueing'. This produced a mortise-and-tenon join – a 'coque'. 'The most important advantage obtained by this invention is the very great additional strength given to the parts of ships so combined' – and other considerations were that such a method would save 25 per cent in wages, that it admitted the use of smaller timber, and that it removed the necessity of hewing out the scarphs. Furthermore, as the task itself was simplified, it became possible to design engines for making the coques and effective tools for sinking them.[79]

[76] M. S. Bentham, op. cit., p. 98; Morris, op. cit., pp. 46–54, summarizes his technological achievements.
[77] Samuel Bentham, *Services Rendered in the Civil Department of the Navy in Investigating and Bringing to Office Notice Abuses and Imperfections* (1813), p. 140.
[78] ibid., pp. 50 and 54; M. S. Bentham, op. cit., p. 148.
[79] Samuel Bentham, op. cit., pp. 86, 138–9.

He designed new treenails that were less likely to wound the wood, and more likely to resist moisture or decay. They could be made by machine and, owing to their greater joining effectiveness, fewer of them were needed for any ship. Therefore, fewer workers were needed, and those who remained could not find opportunity for making chips. He made better mooting machines and pointing tools. His invention of a separate punch for the hammering of treenails prevented them from splitting. He designed, made and introduced auger shanks possessing a universal joint, thus eliminating opportunities for chips that treenail-borers had theretofore enjoyed.[80]

In the reformation of abuses there really seemed to be no part of the ship's construction that Bentham did not touch upon. He said that he did 'away with the uses of Knees, and introduced in their stead for connecting the deck to the sides, a thick String-piece along the sides of the Vessels, under the beams'. (He was not the first to have 'done away with Knees'. Gabriel Snodgrass had caused a great change in them in the 1770s for the ships of the East India Company.[81]) Bentham made other 'improvements' that accorded with what he called the 'principle of inter-convertibility'; he attempted to apply this principle to every part of the ship in its construction, fitting and furnishing. A strict proportionality among the rates would not only have standardized ships of a particular class but would have made some parts of all rates interchangeable.[82]

Bentham realized that the biggest revolution in shipbuilding would come with the replacement of wood by metal. He was far too sensible to expect that this could be done at a stroke, so he contented himself with the provision of a millwright's shop at each yard and the mechanization of tools. He introduced several wood-working machines capable of planing, rebating, mortising and sawing in curved, winding and transverse directions. But of more importance than these were the carefully planned steps taken to introduce a steam-powered saw-mill for the conversion of rough timber – a process more responsible than any other for eliminating chips. He was well aware that such an innovation had its dangers, for it had been the 'machinations of sawyers' that had destroyed Dingley's steam-powered saw-mill in 1768. The first such engine was for the purpose of pumping up clear water for the men to

[80] ibid., pp. 86–7, 139–40.
[81] Westcott Abell, *The Shipwright's Tale* (1948), p. 95.
[82] Samuel Bentham, op. cit., pp. 111–13.

drink. When it was demonstrated – and for the novelty Lord Hugh Seymour came down from London – the machine's piston-rod broke. A copper nail had been placed in the cylinder.[83] Perhaps it was reasons such as this that led Sir Thomas Trowbridge to say, 'All the master shipwrights ought to be *hanged*, every one of them, without exception.'[84]

Such changes permitted Bentham to alter the job structure of the yards, and with it the wage structure. First, he attempted to reduce the denominations of artificers as much as possible. Second, within each denomination he established two or three classes according 'to their degrees of ability, diligence and good behaviour'. Thus social tractability was tied directly to the wage rate.[85] He established the principle of 'INCESSANT WORK', as he wrote it – namely twenty-four-hour shift work.[86] He devised and introduced as many closely covered docks as possible. These changes permitted the introduction of piece-work in 1801–3, which even though it was met by a great strike had nevertheless come to stay. Bentham alone was not responsible for the change, nor did it occur at a single stroke. Shipbuilders suffered an array of repression. A blacklist circulated from 1795; embezzlement was again criminalized in 1800; in addition to 1,100 made redundant by the peace with France, 450 shipwrights were discharged for disciplinary reasons in 1801; the artillery was deployed against rioting shipwrights the same year. So the technological repressions of Bentham were clearly assisted by other forms of repression, and when 'chip money' of 3d. a day for labourers and 6d. a day for shipwrights was introduced in July 1801 the ancient custom of chips had been decisively defeated.[87]

Bentham was deeply committed to crushing the power of ship-yard workers, not just in his day but for the future. Therefore he paid close attention to the abolition of the ship workers' apprenticeship system. He wished to establish 'Naval Seminaries' that would divide knowledge according to class: 'the common workman' and the 'superior officers' would attend different branches. Courses in mathematics, physics and other sciences necessary to the building and sailing of ships would become mandatory. When it was objected

[83] ibid., p. 144.
[84] ibid., p. 216.
[85] ibid., p. 192.
[86] ibid., pp. 15, 54–5.
[87] Morris, op. cit., pp. 121–3.

that an increase in the number of men competent to do shipbuilding work would mean more trouble, Bentham answered: 'It is well known that an increase of the number of workpeople in any business is the most effectual bar to combinations.' As all would have to study the shaping and designing and working of metal, the way to the full removal of wood was clear, and an era of metal ships made possible. John Fincham wrote: 'In addition to the ... intelligence necessary to official competency, their sentiments and associations ... would fit them to command with proper effect.'[88] In other words, class despotism in the yards would now be fully planned and grounded less on force than on 'rationality'. Science and command were now allied, and the productive power of the yard would thenceforth appear to be less the result of the cooperation of workers than a force of capital.

We propose to take all the important decisions and planning which vitally affect the output of the shop out of the hands of the workmen, and centralise them in a few men, each of whom is especially trained in the art of making those decisions and in seeing that they are carried out, each man having his own particular function in which he is supreme, and not interfering with the functions of other men.[89]

The words are not those of Samuel Bentham, but of Frederick Winslow Taylor writing a century later. The comparison with Taylor may have struck the reader before this point. Both Bentham and Taylor were early in life confronted with the forms of workers' power in a labour process characterized by the combination and cooperation of many detailed labourers and in which the technical organization of production was not separable from the forms of workers' self-organization. Both devoted much of their life to developing a system of management that would destroy that relation, and would instead complete the despotism of capital in the process of production. Both understood that essential to that task was the development of tools of adequate measurement, so that an objective standard of the amount of work completed, independent from the judgement of the worker, could be introduced – one of Bentham's earliest contributions was the 'curvature', a device for accurately measuring amounts of sawn curved timber. Both recognized that only when the 'task' itself had come under the control of

[88] Fincham, op. cit., pp. 174–7.
[89] F. W. Taylor, *The Art of Cutting Metals* (New York, 1906), sect. 124.

capitalist definitions could a system of piece-rates be established that would at once greatly increase profitability and raise wages. Both knew too that an increase of wages was fully consistent with an increase in the rate of exploitation. Finally, each was aware that before mechanization could be satisfactorily introduced a prior revolution in the labour process was required.

Between Sutherland's 'Notions' of 1724 and Bentham's 'system' eighty years later there were many developments. These were the result of a serious, protracted struggle, whose consequences in ship design, in nautical engineering, in mechanical operations, in productivity – perhaps even in the victories of the Navy during the Napoleonic Wars – are well known. Out of historical context they may appear to be improvements, but in context only the most interested or apologetic could view Bentham's mechanical reorganizations unequivocally as such. John Charnock published an encyclopaedic three-volume *History of Marine Architecture* in 1800. In it he described many of the 'discoveries' that had lately been introduced in ship-building. He reflected that 'avarice, luxury, and ambition' were the moral qualities that promoted the technical changes. The application of changes, he observed, had two important effects. First, they 'augmented the general inquietude of man'. Second, they promoted 'those horrid scenes of slaughter or desecration which, during so many ages, have disgraced the universe'.

While Charnock presented a historical context for understanding technological change in ship construction, the context he chose was one of moral philosophy. Such philosophic moralism has its own limitations. Its moral categories can be as general and distant as the categories of political economy; the language of 'depravity', 'luxury' or 'avarice' can be as alien to the antagonistic actualities of production as the language of 'improvement' and 'efficiency'. The 'language of chips' arose from within the struggle; its morality and its economies were far different from Bentham's or Charnock's. If they belonged to a 'republic of letters' the chip men and women belonged to a 'republic of wood'. Their profession was no less intelligible than philosophy or engineering – at least to those admitted to it. It had its ways of doing things – its arts and mysteries, its circuits of exchange and barter, its solutions to the ecological and energy crises of working people, its social structures between men and women, adults and children, the healthy and the infirm, and as we have seen, its characteristic ships.

CHAPTER TWELVE

———

SUGAR AND POLICE: THE LONDON WORKING CLASS IN THE 1790S

Every house a den, every man bound: the shadows are
    fill'd
With Spectres, and the windows wove over with
    curses of iron:
Over the doors, 'Thou shalt not,' & over the chimneys
    'Fear' is written:
With bands of iron round their necks fasten'd into
    the walls   ·
The citizens, in leaden gyves the inhabitants of suburbs
Walk heavy; soft and bent are the bones of villagers.

William Blake, 'Europe' (1794)

Is not this earth our common also, as well as it is the
common of brutes? May we not eat herbs, berries, or
nuts as well as other creatures? Have we not a right to
hunt and prowl for prey with she-wolves? And have
we not a right to fish with she-otters? Or may we not
dig coals or cut wood for fuel? Nay, does nature
provide a luxuriant and abundant feast for all her
numerous tribes of animals except us? As if sorrow
were our portion alone, and as if we and our helpless
babes came into this world only to weep over each
other?

Thomas Spence, The Rights of Infants (1797)

The modern history of Punch and Judy, the epitome of Cockney
entertainment, begins in 1790 when the Italian, Giovanni Piccinni,
a street puppeteer, arrived in London and set up shop in Drury Lane
with his Irish wife. He directed a portable street show that became,
as the modern historian of the show concludes, typical of 'the
new popular culture of the industrial revolution'. For us the show

summarizes in the motions of the plebeian puppeteer the emotions of a class riven with unresolvable contradiction.[1]

It was an oral performance full of the wit and wisdom of proletarian London. It depended on audience participation. It was performed frequently at Bartholomew Fair and other popular urban spaces. Despite the attack upon the Fair with its 'scenes of dissipation, riot, and confusion, which annually disgrace the metropolis of England', attempts to suppress the show never succeeded, partly because of the customary belief that the Punchman had the right to perform in any churchyard or in any side street for twenty minutes without interference.[2]

Punch at first seems to be the perfect archetype of the picaresque proletarian, full of appetite, life and laughter:

> Mr Punch is one jolly good fellow,
> His dress is all scarlet and yellow,
> And if now and then he gets mellow,
> It's only among good friends.
> His money most freely he spends;
> To laugh and grow fat he intends.

Yet the Punch and Judy show is violent: its exemplar of action is one of punching; the episodes consist of a succession of homicides. The show expressed class rage against family, police, courtiers, physicians and householders in a wilful display of murderous fantasy. Towards the end of the slaughter an officer with a warrant and a constable come to imprison Punch. He knocks them down, but, joined by Jack Ketch, the hangman, they overpower him. The gallows are erected. Punch pretends the gallows is an apple tree, the constable an apple-stealer, and the coffin an apple basket. So Ketch puts his own head in the noose to teach Punch how to do it, and Punch hangs the hangman.

> They're out! they're out! I've done the trick!
> Jack Ketch is dead – I'm free;
> I do not care, now, if Old Nick
> Himself should come for me.

---

[1] Robert Leach, *The Punch and Judy Show: History, Tradition and Meaning* (Athens, Georgia, 1985), p. 37. Quotations from Piccinni's show are from *The Tragical Comedy or Comical Tragedy of Punch and Judy* (Cambridge, 1926).

[2] *The Observer*, 10 September 1797.

Indeed, this was a historic victory for the London working class. The regime of hanging was coming to a close after the abolition of Tyburn and with the growth of alternatives such as imprisonment and transportation to Botany Bay.[3] To be sure, the hanging sentences continued to be tolled at the Old Bailey – 67 in 1790, 83 in 1791, 93 in 1792 – but many of these were commuted. Although rule by hanging persisted elsewhere, in London Punch might rejoice, for Jack Ketch, if not quite dead, was dying. Yet, this victory was purchased at a terrible price: Punch, in murdering friend and foe alike, suggests to us that the London working class was doing Jack Ketch's job for him. This chapter explores the association between the transformation of punishments and the imposition of the wage.

It is to Michel Foucault's credit that he understood that the legal and penal reforms at the end of the eighteenth century represented not a new sensibility but another policy towards the 'tolerated illegalities of the *Ancien Régime*'.[4] Yet his phrase 'tolerated illegalities' prejudges a relationship in which employers aggressively and systematically attacked, and in the end successfully expropriated, rights and usages that employees had customarily practised. While the term 'custom' presents its own problems, it does not presuppose the success of the expropriators and we therefore use it. An account of the judicial repression of custom is found in the Old Bailey *Proceedings*, which recapitulate the struggles recounted among different classes of London workers in the previous chapters. They are roughly indicated by Table 10.[5]

The data of the misappropriated things of the workplace strike us for the variety of materials: coal, beaver fur, timber, silk, sugar, pins and needles, pewter tedges, tobacco, calico, coffee, indigo, cochineal, lead type, beer, tea, planes and saws, silver and gold. The struggles over the material circuits of production of the previous decades became subject to a judicial onslaught in the 1790s.

The coal-heaver indicted for stealing from a barge said: 'I heaved out the coals ... and they gave me 1s. and the sweepings out.' The jeweller's servant who was transported for taking two ounces of

---

[3] Within a month of the landing of the first convicts (January 1788) five men were hanged. Frank Crowley (ed.), *A Documentary History of Australia*, vol. i, *Colonial Australia, 1788–1840* (Melbourne, 1980), p. 5.

[4] Michel Foucault, *Discipline and Punish: The Birth of the Prison*, trans. Alan Sheridan (1977), pp. 82–3.

[5] This data is gathered from the Old Bailey *Proceedings* from the first Sessions of 1790 to the last of 1799.

TABLE 10:

Old Bailey prosecutions against

misappropriations by employees during the

1790s

1790	16	1795	7
1791	10	1796	11
1792	14	1797	8
1793	23	1798	14
1794	10	1799	1

gold said: 'They are what I picked up sweeping the shop, the back storehouse, and places about at several times.' 'Sweeping' – the word is resplendent with the commonest, humblest labour: what every man, woman and child would know, for who had not swept a floor clean?[6]

The distinctions made in the defences could be subtle, as by the carman whose master was a soap-maker and whose wife was a laundress. 'My master used to make exceeding good weight; and when I have carried quantities of soap home, the over-weight I have brought home to my own house, but I never took a piece off my master's premises.' To the court much had to be explained. For instance: the rum had to sit for a week before it was drawn from the vats for the wholesale trade, so that it might be 'perfectly fine'. During this time, it was examined by the 'dip', when an allowance was made of 2 gallons. This was called the 'flow'. The warehouse labourers wore leather aprons; this was 'a common appendage to men in that line of business'. Bladders were another such appendage. The cooper and foreman had fallen sick; the warehouse labourers helped themselves on Saturday night to 16 gallons' flow. Chatfield & Chatfield, the owners, had much trouble getting witnesses: they got a boy, Richard Bunce, who was much frightened and began to cry, 'because I am brought here to condemn these men'.[7]

The trials spanned the range of professions, from the oldest to the

[6] ibid., 15 December 1792 and 9 January 1793.
[7] ibid., 14 September 1796 and 2 December 1795.

most advanced, from prostitution to the famous needle-making extolled in Adam Smith's fable of capitalist productivity. Mary Cheeseman was the servant to a Rosemary Lane shoemaker who swore a theft against her after she refused to submit to his advances. The red morocco children's shoes were gifts, she said, which she pawned in Cable Street. She was transported for seven years. James Tingay was a labourer who did the 'finishing' at a needle-producing shop. He took 3,000 needles.[8]

By the 1790s such informal customs (sweepings, overweight, gifts, the flow) had become a known and accepted part of the class relationship, recognized and negotiated by propertied people such as might be found on jury panels, who were not, therefore, deaf to pleas based upon them. Robert Dixon, a journeyman printer indicted for stealing a book from a Strand bookseller, was acquitted by a jury that understood that 'a practice ... prevails among compositors and pressmen of retaining a copy of every book they work upon'. Two plumbers indicted by the churchwardens of St Sepulchre's for stealing lead from the roof they were hired to repair were acquitted on the grounds of 'it being customary in the trade for them to take such lead at a reduced price'.[9]

In workshops across London, as the *Proceedings* makes clear, there was a kind of 'collective bargaining' over the materials of production. The prosecutor of a cooper was asked: 'Perhaps you have never heard of such a thing as perquisites of the little tare that might drop from the casks?' He answered, 'There were no perquisites of coffee; they have beer.' Ann Priestly worked in the cellar as a tobacco-stripper. She had five children, and a litigious, zealous master. She was indicted for stealing 6 lbs. of tobacco. The master said, 'We are in the constant habit of allowing them every Saturday night a quantity of tobacco or snuff, which ever they like, in order to keep them from pilfering.' The jurors understood, and sentenced her to three months in the house of correction. Nathaniel Harris was a porter in a calico warehouse. He considered the wrappers and packing cases as perquisites ('We cut them up for firewood, some of them, not all'), but his employer did not ('You are a damned rascal, you ought to be hanged'), and despite five witnesses testifying in favour of his character, he was found guilty and transported for seven years. Thomas Hayes, four years a calico-glazer, who cut the

[8] ibid., 17 September 1794 and 31 October 1792.
[9] *The Observer*, 25 September 1796 and 15 January 1797.

fag-ends from the pieces, said it was common in the haste of business to make mistakes: 'I accidentally cut off two folds instead of one.' His master was asked: 'Do you allow your men any perquisites?' 'None,' he answered, and so he too was transported for seven years.

Frequently, defendants refrained from defences of custom, and spoke of family care instead. Philip Bramley, a cooper, 'found this coffee scattered upon the floor, and I thought, as I had a large family, and I did not know that it belonged to any body, I might as well have some'. Another cooper explained that in work they could not help but spill some 'raw dirty coffee', which he thought to take and to clean since he had 'a very large family, four children'. 'I have a wife and two children and work very hard for my bread besides stealing tobacco,' said John Kirby, who worked at a Tower Hill warehouse. Joseph Lockley, a journeyman hatter, had a wife and three children. 'My Lord, I had three rabbit-skins at home, which I intended to convert into a hat for one of my children.' 'My Lord, I have a very large family, and have had the palsy several times,' pleaded the printer's labourer who took three pieces of type.

In other cases we note an entrepreneurial or retaliatory edge. Sam Young, a youthful carpenter, stole a plane and cabinet-saw at a job site in order to stock himself for the West Indies. Martha Howell took two calico towels after she was dismissed from service without wages. A black woman, Susannah, took calico from her mistress, Lady Polly, whom she had served for nine years without wages, and was transported for seven years. A fifty-year-old brewer's labourer, indicted for taking a pint of twopenny ale, said: 'Well then, hang me for a little small beer.' He was punished by six months in the house of correction. George Cowland's defence in taking a cheese from the Custom House Key was that the constable there had 'transported above forty people in the last two years'.[10]

While the prosecution of such customs included the breadth of London trades, two commodities particularly were subject to vigorous, innovative repression – namely, silk and sugar. The criminalization of customary takings by silk-workers during the 1790s became more extensive in the tribunals of summary justice and more severe as measured by the numbers remanded for trial at the Old Bailey. Of the 17 cases of silk theft at the court, 13 appeared

---

[10] *The Proceedings*, 15 February 1792, 14 September 1796, 15 February 1792, 15 February 1797, 28 October 1795, 16 September 1795, 14 February 1798 and 7 December 1791.

between 1790 and 1793. In 1790 a man was tried for concealing 6 oz. of silk in his 'petticoat trousers' while unloading a Bengal merchantman. Another was tried for concealing 6 oz. of raw silk taken while working in a dyer's skeining room. William Young, 'the streetsman' for a master dyer, in employment for twenty-six years, was accused of short-weighting the skeins he worked up at home, a charge he did not deny but blamed his wife. Women windsters were often accused. Bez Ozeland, a weekly servant, took some black warp silk on her birthday. She slept and worked in a single room. She was forty-two years old. Her husband was at sea. She was found guilty and sentenced to death. Sarah Slade stole 6 oz. of wound silk from a windster. 'I have got three small children ... I went up this court to make water, and there lay this silk scattered about.' In 1797 one of the 'police officers' of the East India Company warehouse apprehended a weaver, William Athill, with 13 lbs. of raw silk. 'I unpinned the lugs of the bale, and brought it away in my hat and breeches,' as he had done for thirteen years.[11]

By the 1790s Spitalfields had become a byword for poverty. The workhouses of Spitalfields and Bethnal Green were overflowing with desperation. The private charities to relieve the weavers were inadequate, though 'almost every church and chapel in the metropolis ... made a collection'. The master weavers were attacked in print for gaining 'large fortunes by the labour of these men'. The silk-workers posed dangers to the authorities by their trade committees, by their democratic assemblies and by their traditions of militant heterodoxy. Three well-known radicals of the decade had close associations with Spitalfields or the silk trade. Mary Wollstonecraft was born there; her grandfather was a handkerchief-weaver, and her father a capitalist weaver, landlord, parish officer and captain in the militia. John Thelwall, the radical elocutionist who refused to doff his hat to the Prime Minister, was the son of a silk mercer. William Blake lived next door to an asylum for female orphans, where he heard their sorrows in the whirling wheels of silk-throwing.[12]

---

[11] ibid., 16 April 1790, 8 July 1790, 15 September 1790, 8 December 1790, 12 January 1791, 14 September 1791, 15 February 1792, 31 October 1792, 20 February 1793, 30 October 1793, 30 April 1794, 13 January 1796, 22 June 1796 and 12 July 1797.

[12] William Hale, *An Appeal to the Public in Defence of the Spitalfields Acts* (1822),

The economics of the silk industry and the political organizations of the workers presented themselves as a police problem. The man who developed the theory and practice of policing the industry was the Scottish textile factor, Patrick Colquhoun. His early experience was essential to his London success, for in the developing lowlands of Scotland he was experienced in both the transatlantic commerce of the cotton trade (he had lived in Virginia) and the details of the disciplining of the spinners and weavers of Paisley. Thus, he knew the meaning of the 'division of labour' in both senses – namely, as commerce (the social division of labour) and as fractionization (the specialization of tasks). In 1789 he moved to London, where his countryman, Henry Dundas, the Home Secretary (1791–4), was his patron.

Colquhoun cut his teeth in Spitalfields. By November 1792 he had organized spies to infiltrate the 'mischievous Confederacies' of the silk districts. As a sitting magistrate he dealt swiftly with instances of silk takings. The master manufacturers of Spitalfields had formed a committee for preventing and punishing 'Embezzlement and other Offences in the Silk Manufactory'. In October 1793 the committee thanked the Home Office for its 'Police System', for establishing a 'judicial Tribunal' for the prosecution of offending workers, and for checking the 'System of depredations which heretofore occasioned a loss of many thousands per annum to the silk Manufacturers'. Colquhoun was particularly thanked by Desormeaux, a large silk-dyer, and an active force on the committee. The 'embezzlement' of small amounts of silk gave way, under this combination of invigilation and prosecution, to daring, daylight robberies. In the winter of 1795 Desormeaux was robbed of 651 lbs. of thrown silk which was being carted to his warehouse.[13]

But silk was the product of a depressed industry, catering largely for a domestic market. Of more importance to the police of the metropolis were coffee, tea and sugar. These were the products of empire, they were the basis of the industrialization of England, and their transportation depended on the strategic shipping industry.

The Thames was the jugular vein of the British Empire. London,

---

p. 21; the *DNB*; Claire Tomalin, *The Life and Death of Mary Wollstonecraft* (1974), pp. 2–4.
[13] Radzinowicz, op. cit., vol. iii (1956), pp. 214–27; Patrick Colquhoun, *A Treatise on the Commerce and Police of the River Thames* (1800), pp. 519–20; *The Proceedings*, 2 December 1795.

the largest city in the western hemisphere, containing by 1800 nearly a million souls, was both the capital of England and the centre of an empire that embraced the workshops of Bengal, the plantations of the Caribbean, the 'factories' of West Africa and the forests of North America. The Thames was tidal for ninety miles from its mouth in the North Sea to the quays and wharfs of the Pool. Through these waters passed the wealth of the Empire. A Scottish plantation master of St Nevis wrote of the Thames,[14]

> Thou art king of streams;
> Delighted Commerce broods upon thy wave;
> And every quarter of this sea-girt globe
> To thee due tribute pays.

The commerce 'brooded', as indeed it might, for it was an exchange of violence for narcotics: upriver came either unnourishing hunger suppressants such as tobacco and sugar, or deceiving stimulants such as coffee and tea, while downriver sailed vessels carrying soldiers, marines, convicts, sailors, migrants, gunpowder, cannon, Bibles and sharp-edged tools.

Sugar was transformed during the second part of the eighteenth century from an upper-class luxury to a working-class necessity. British per capita sugar consumption rose from 4 lbs. a year in 1700 to 18 lbs. a year in 1800. Imports ascended gradually during the first half of the century, and then at mid-century they began to climb steeply from about 1 million cwt. to 2 million cwt. at the opening of the War of American Independence. After a precipitous decline during that war, imports recovered and rose rapidly during the next two decades, reaching more than 3.7 million cwt. in 1799.[15]

Sugar is an exciting, cheap calorie, lending to the body sudden sources of energy that are as productive as they are unstable. It is a sweetener to the bitter substances of industrial diet – tea, coffee and chocolate. It saves time and fuel in food preparation. It deadens pangs of hunger. Yet it also drains the body of precious vitamins and minerals, causing 'fatigue, nervousness, depression, [and] apprehension'. Jeremy Bentham, following a famine year in 1796, wrote a little piece of home economics called *Errors of the Present Practice of Cooking*. English cookery had too much labour and too

---

[14] James Grainger, *The Sugar-Cane: A Poem* (1764), p. 160.
[15] Noel Deerr, *The History of Sugar*, vol. ii (1949), pp. 530–32; Elizabeth B. Schumpeter, *English Overseas Trade Statistics, 1697–1808* (Oxford, 1960), pp. 61–2.

much flour. He advised making up bread with treacle in order to save on butter and to disguise the taste and colour of adulterated flour. By such advice, sucrose, 'the favoured child of capitalism', became a staple ingredient in the factory and the workhouse.[16]

The commerce of the Thames 'brooded' too in memory of the conditions of production, as the plantation master of St Nevis must have known. The day began with 'the cracking of whips, the smothered cries, and the indistinct groans of the Negroes, who never see the day break but to curse it'. The most lucrative colony in the world and the keystone of colonial slavery in the Caribbean was St Domingo. Human labour was concentrated there as it had never before been. In the 1760s 10,000 West African slaves were imported each year; in the 1770s the number rose to 27,000; by the end of the 1780s, 40,000 slaves were imported annually and production in the island since 1780 had nearly doubled. Thus, by 1791 half a million slaves were employed in these 'factories of the field'. 'The course of sugar history', to quote Noel Deerr, was altered on the night of 14 August 1791, when a female priestess trembled and shook, setting in motion a revolution against slavery, European rule and the plantation. The slaves demanded a system of *trois jours* (three days for the master and three days for themselves). In thirteen years they would have become victorious, free, independent and possessors of their own lands, defeating three imperial armies.[17]

The struggle against the Haitian revolution had profound commercial, demographic and social consequences in all of Europe and perhaps none more prominently than on the civilization on the banks of the Thames.[18] In September 1793 the British Army invaded. The campaigns of the next five years cost Britain £10 million and 100,000 casualties. The largest expeditionary force ever to sail from Britain departed in 1796 for the West Indies, where a maroon war had broken out in Jamaica and six other islands were in revolt. Sugar production fell to 20 per cent of pre-war levels. St Domingo was

[16] Sidney W. Mintz, *Sweetness and Power: The Place of Sugar in Modern History* (New York, 1985), p. 214; William Duffy, *Sugar Blues* (New York, 1975), pp. 46, 70, 137.

[17] Bryan Edwards, *An Historical Survey of the Island of Saint Domingo* (1796), p. 164; Deerr, op. cit., p. 317; Alfred Métraux, *Voodoo in Haiti*, trans. Hugo Charteris (New York, 1959), p. 32; and Thomas D. Ott, *The Haitian Revolution, 1789–1804* (Tennessee, 1973), p. 15.

[18] C. L. R. James, *The Black Jacobins: Toussaint L'Ouverture and the San Domingo Revolution*, 2nd edn (New York, 1963).

'the burial ground of Great Britain'. 'The amount of blood and treasure drained from England by that miserable island of St Domingo will never, I think, be truly known,' wrote Fortesque, the historian of the British Army. 'After long and careful thought and study I have come to the conclusion that the West India campaigns, both to windward and leeward, which were the essence of Pitt's military policy, cost England in Army and Navy little fewer than one hundred thousand men, about one-half of them dead, the remainder permanently unfitted for service.' In December 1796 the 32nd Regiment sailed with 650 men for St Domingo and by February only 80 were fit for service. A Scottish surgeon at Port au Prince wrote of the patients' 'low, muttering, grim, melancholy which is lost in meditating wrath, without an attempt to move'. 'The eye has an expression,' he continued, 'of anguish unspeakable, and a languor in its movement, an inclination to shut out all objects.' In London a correspondent to the *Observer* wrote: 'There is scarcely a family in the Country that has not to deplore the loss of some devoted relative.'[19] The anger, grief, powerlessness and 'meditating wrath' found representation in the Punch and Judy show as homicidal contradiction. Punch calls for a doctor, whom he battles with his stick ('physic'), and tosses away dead. A black servant complains of the noise, and is rewarded by a drumming with bell, organ, fiddle and trumpet.[20]

The international circuit of sugar brought the violence of its social relations back to London, where indeed it had begun. In the fate of the West India regiments the violence of the criminal sanction had come full circle. After 1778 English magistrates were given discretion to punish offenders by assigning them to the colours, 'being Loose, Idle, Disorderly, and fit to serve the King'. Many London convicts and 'idle disorderly persons' were consigned to river tenders for service in the West Indies, and a number survived,

[19] *The Observer*, 2 October 1796; John Fortesque, *A History of the British Army*, vol. iv, part 1, *1789–1801* (1915); *Journal of Lieutenant Howard*, February 1796–February 1798, Boston Public Library, MS, fAm.6; David Patrick Geggus, *Slavery, War, and Revolution: The British Occupation of Saint Domingue, 1793–1798* (Oxford, 1982), *passim*.
[20] Hector McLean, *An Inquiry into the Nature and Causes of the Great Mortality Among the Troops at St Domingo* (1797), pp. 12, 29; Colin Chisholm, *An Essay on the Malignant Pestilential Fever* (Philadelphia, 1799), p. 205; Peter Fryer, *Staying Power: The History of Black People in Britain* (1984), pp. 79–89.

hints of their experiences being given at the Old Bailey.[21] Matthias Knuckley sailed as a felon with forty-three others to Martinique and then to Haiti in the notorious 60th Regiment. He was marooned. He returned to St Giles-in-the-Fields, was caught, sentenced to hang and pardoned on condition of rejoining the 60th. William Bateman was transported in 1787 for stealing a wooden boat. He was confined for seven months in Newgate, then three years in the Woolwich hulks. 'I thought it very hard to be a slave in my own country, working morning, noon, and night.' He escaped to sea, lived in revolutionary France and returned to London.[22] Sarah Pearson was transported for stealing some rings. She and her shipmates mutinied because the captain intended to convey them to Honduras. Henry Boxer, who was sentenced to death for robbing a Danish sailor, was offered a pardon if he would join a man-of-war. He sailed in Lord Howe's fleet, got sick at Torbay, was captured in St Domingo, escaped a French prison, made his way to Jamaica, fell sick, sailed to Liverpool aboard the *Lottery Guineaman*, and made his way to London, where he worked as a press-gang bully.

Young men did not enlist willingly. Cheats and terror were employed to get them in, and once in servitude they were isolated, enclosed, transported and subjected to the rapacity of cruel officers. Considerable propaganda and successful agitation in London against these abuses culminated in the Crimp House Riots of August 1794, when several thousand people assembled to liberate 'recruits' from crimping houses in Charing Cross, Holborn and Cripplegate. The authorities feared that the disorders would put an end to the recruiting service. The Lord Mayor, having 'a just Abhorrence of the present Attempts to renew the Riots of 1780', cooperated with the constabulary, the militia and the War Office in a coordinated military response. The riots were preceded by the distribution of handbills — 'Soldiers! now is the time to acquire glory! protect crimping! murder those of your fellow creatures that dare resist it! fire on the friends of freedom! destroy liberty! and prepare chains for yourselves and children!' — and by William Cobbett's brilliant twopenny pamphlet, *The Soldier's Friend*, whose starting-point was the soldier's

[21] Roger Norman Buckley, *Slaves in Red Coats: The British West India Regiments, 1795–1815* (New Haven, 1979), p. 3.
[22] *The Proceedings*, 15 December 1792, 14 September 1796, 25 October 1797 and several cases of hangings for those returning from a sentence of transportation to the regiments of the West Indies — for instance, see *The Proceedings*, 4 July 1798.

pay (3s. a week but more than a shilling in arrears).[23]

As thousands of people left London to suppress slave rebellion in the West Indies, so hundreds of Afro-Americans came to London: these were the two sides of the human migrations attendant upon the sugar circuit.[24] Individuals, like Benjamin Bowsey, brought an audacious and insurrectionary element to the roughly understood feint and probe of London rioting. During 1792, when meat prices were extravagantly high, when there was 'murmuring among the people' and a riot in Fleet Market, the authorities were particularly watchful of the black population. It was Richard Blakeman, a 27-year-old black man, who was whipped and imprisoned for taking 13 lbs. of beef from a Fleet Market butcher's stall. In the 1780s four Afro-American Londoners were among the first convicts transported to Botany Bay. The infamous mutiny on the *Hermione* (August 1797) was caused, amid shadowy talk by United Irishmen and revolutionary Jacobins, by the death of one black man (falling from the foretop), and the assassination of its captain by another black man.[25] Authorities took precautions during the 1790s: 'We have directed all the Blacks and People of Colour in health at Portsmouth to be removed into the Captivity and Vigilant Prison Ships' (December 1796).[26]

Boxing was the one career really open to talents; it was the one stage where the last might be first. The 'sweet science' was dominated by those who in the hierarchy of labour were the lowest. There were the Jews (Daniel Mendoza), the Irish (Simon Byrne), the dockers (James Burke) and especially the former Afro-American slaves: Joe Leashley the first recorded black champion (1791); Bill Richmond of New York, who taught royalty as well as Hazlitt 'the art of self-defence'; Tom Molineaux of Virginia, who learned to fight on the docks and square-riggers; Sam Robinson, another black New York docker; and Harry Sutton, a Baltimore and Deptford docker. In 1792, a black man, Mungo, broke the jaw of a Newington

---

[23] PRO, HO, 42/33, 21 August 1794; *The Proceedings*, 17 September 1794, 16 September 1795 and 4 December 1793; Olivia Smith, *The Politics of Language, 1791–1819* (Oxford, 1984), pp. 77–9.

[24] Fryer, op. cit.; Folarin O. Shyllon, *Black People in Britain, 1555–1833* (1977).

[25] *The Observer*, 6 May 1792; *The Proceedings*, 5 December 1792; John Cobley, *The Crimes of the First Fleet Convicts* (Sydney, 1970), pp. 46, 56, 192, 203; Dudley Pope, *The Black Ship* (New York, 1964), p. 142.

[26] John Fielding, *Extracts from the Penal Laws* (1768); W. Branch Johnson, *The English Prison Hulks* (1957), pp. 52–67.

carpenter during a Kennington Common battle. The superintendent of the prison hulks kept Little White, a black man, to box prisoners to death.[27]

The Afro-American community in London produced two leaders who were remarkable for their persistence in legal struggles, for the eloquence of their writings and for their pan-African appeal. They also gave much help to the other London ethnic populations in their struggle. Ottobah Cugoano, from Ghana, a slave in Grenada, was one of its leaders. The literature of Afro-American freedom knows few passages excelling his in the stern denunciation of oppression, in the prophetic certitude of liberation, or in grace and magnanimity of expression. He mastered the political economy of money and understood its tricks, including the irrationality of the wage-form, and therefore urged that the price of provisions be regulated so that the poor could live 'without being oppressed and screwed down to work for nothing'. In Cugoano an endangered agrarian custom becomes a symbol in his lamentation for his homeland: 'Woe is me! alas Africa! for I am as the last gleanings of the summer fruit, as the grape gleanings of the vintage, where no cluster is to eat.'[28]

Olaudah Equiano was born in Nigeria. He was a slave on a sugar plantation in Barbados, and on a tobacco plantation in Virginia. His years at sea provided him with a refined knowledge of the material customs of the sailor's 'privileges'. He was a leading London activist, prodding Granville Sharpe and assisting the Sierra Leone expedition. The mass experience of which Equiano was a personification placed the Afro-American at the tip of the arrow of time. In early 1792 he helped Thomas Hardy link up with the Sheffield abolitionists and the Corresponding Society, thus extending the constitutional discussion of reform from plebeian to proletarian contexts nationwide. Edward Thompson has considered this the starting-point in 'the making of the English working class', though he omits mention of Equiano.[29] Bearing in mind Equiano's decisive role in the effort, it

[27] Fryer, op. cit., appendix 1, 'Prize Fighters, 1791–1902'; W. Branch Johnson, op. cit., pp. 66–7; *The Observer*, 12 February 1792.
[28] *Thoughts and Sentiments on the Evil and Wicked Traffic of the Slavery and Commerce of the Human Species* (1787), reprinted in Francis D. Adams and Barry Sanders (eds), *Three Black Writers in Eighteenth Century England* (Belmont, California, 1971), p. 80.
[29] *The Interesting Narrative of the Life of Olaudah Equiano, or Gustavus Vasa, the African* (1789), and Brit. Lib., Add. MS, 27811, London Corresponding Society, vol. i, letter of 18 April 1792. Thompson's oversight is a result of relying on

would be more accurate to say 'the working class in England'.

In 1794, 3,663 deep-water ships arrived in the Port of London. While this was three times as many as the port served in 1702, the facilities of the port had not changed. The sugar fleet arrived in the five months between May and October, sailing again in the autumn. In 1756, 203 West Indiamen arrived, each carrying on average 295 hogsheads; in 1794, there were 433 West Indiamen, carrying on average 282 hogsheads. The traffic was accompanied by an exciting market, prices varying in the 1790s between 27s. and 87s. a hundredweight. The war raised insurance costs. Higher duties were imposed. Speed in unloading was of the essence. Petty charges, warehouse rent and loss of weight reduced the price per hundredweight by a shilling a month. Hogsheads on deck sold for several shillings more than those in the hold. Fortunes were made.[30] The international drug and slave cartel, or 'West India interest', became a dominant partner in the Bank of England and a powerful influence in Parliament. The imperial traffic was bedevilled by its river workers. The 74 prosecutions brought against them provide a guide to global wealth: 26 involved the theft of sugar; 15 tea; 9 coffee; 7 tobacco; 7 coal; 3 indigo; 2 rum; and 1 each of chintz, logwood, cochineal, copper and anchors.

A laden, homeward-bound West Indiaman drew about 17 ft. The difference between high and low tide varied between 13 and 18 ft. The ships therefore could not moor alongside the quays, and instead moored mid-river in tiers of seven or eight ships. Cargoes were unloaded into lighters, whose shallow draught permitted them to approach the Legal Quays at low tide. The Legal Quays were only 1,419 ft. in length. Warehouse and apron space was also limited, so sugar hogsheads were stacked seven or eight high on the open wharf. These conditions resulted in delays.[31] In 1794, when the Jamaica fleet arrived, it was delayed at Deptford for six days 'on Account of the crouded State of the Pool'. Eight to ten days were necessary to unload a ship even when lighters were available. Ships forced to unload downriver might have to wait four to six weeks to have their cargoes reach the quays. On the quays the sugar hogsheads

---

Hardy's printed *Memoir* (1832), which, unlike his contemporary writings, omits mention of his former room-mate and friend.

[30] *Second Report from the Select Committee Upon the Improvement of the Port of London* (1799), *Parliamentary Papers*, vol. xxiii, no. 154, pp. 42, 55, 59, 69, 99.

[31] Joseph G. Broodbank, *History of the Port of London*, vol. i (1921), *passim*.

rested two to four weeks before warehousing. The Committee of the West India Merchants made such delays the principal complaint in their memorials. The delays were the primary cause of the 'plunderage' of their cargoes. This was the third way that the commerce of the Thames 'brooded'.

'A Hogshead is not deemed plundered till it has lost a certain Weight, which I think is about Two Cwt. of the Plantation Weight,' said John Inglis, a merchant with thirty years' experience. There was an allowance of 12 lbs. sampling. Samples were taken two or three times. A weight of 10–14 lbs. was allowed for 'drainage', and 1 cwt. for tare. These were allowed or unavoidable losses, and did not constitute 'plunder'. The Customs Commissioners said the port was 'subject to great Losses' from 'clandestine Proceedings'. A landing surveyor said that plunderage from the West India ships was at a 'magnitude as to call loudly for redress'. A West India merchant with nineteen years in the trade estimated that the merchants lost between £200,000 and £300,000 a year.[32]

In reaction to the plunderage from the moored ships, a combination of merchants, engineers and magistrates produced a two-pronged counter-attack:[33] a river police was created and the enclosure movement was extended in the creation of the London wet docks. The former appears to be direct, subjective repression; the latter to be indirect, objective repression. Michel Foucault accepts the apparent separation between increased wealth attendant upon greater capital investment and the armed attack upon the illegalities of the lower strata of society. In London, however, as we now shall show, they were logically and historically related, accumulation of particular wealth and criminalization of particular workers being two sides of the same coin.[34] To understand this, we need to examine the labour of the river and the docks.

River work employed more people than any other London industry. Colquhoun estimated that 120,000 people were directly

[32] C. Northcote Parkinson, *The Trade Winds: A Study of British Overseas Trade During the French Wars, 1793–1815* (1948), p. 168; Lillian M. Penson, *The Colonial Agents of the British West Indies: A Study in Colonial Administration Mainly in the Eighteenth Century* (1924), pp. 196–207; Colquhoun, op. cit., appendix 3.

[33] William Vaughan, *On Wet Docks, Quays, and Warehouses for the Port of London* (1793), and *A Letter to a Friend on Commerce and Free Ports and London Docks* (1796); William Tatham, *The Political Economy of Inland Navigation* (1799); and Samuel Smiles, *Lives of the Engineers*, vol. ii (1862), p. 196.

[34] Foucault, op. cit., p. 85.

employed, and 500,000 indirectly. Thus, overall, perhaps a third of
the adult labour force of London was employed in river work. It
was a young proletariat in that it grew rapidly and directly with
the expansion of commerce. Turnover was high, as we see in the
judicial records, which note many instances of weavers who turned
to river work in hard times. It was both cooperative labour and
heterogeneous labour in that many different skills were required to
work together to bring in and unload the ships.

There were lumpers. 'To lump' meant two things: to contract to
unload ships, or to pilfer around the docks. The double meaning
expressed the two sides of the exploitation. On the one hand, the
lumpers' labour of trucking on the quay, slinging by fall, hauling
by skid, signalling, manipulating winches and cranes, setting up
derricks and unstowing the cargo was dangerous, unsteady work:
slipping on wet surfaces, getting entangled in cordage or swinging
heavy loads resulted in fractures, hernias, rope burns and lacerations.
Since the master lumpers (often publicans) pocketed the chief part
of the lumping dues, the working lumper had little choice but to
connive in the breaking of the cargo to line his own pocket. The
master lumpers competed for 'game' ships. Ships' mates turned a
blind eye, if not a helping hand. The parsimony of the shipowners
in not feeding the lumpers required them to go ashore two or three
times a day for their drink and food. This was a secondary cause of
the pilferage. Another cause was a changed job definition that
required the lumpers to 'strike Yards and Top-Masts, get up the
Derrick' and prepare the ship's decks for unloading.

Ralph Walker, a veteran ship's captain in the Jamaica trade,
explained:

The Foreman of the Lumpers came into the Hold, and told me that I did
not know my own Interest in sending the Casks up in good Order, for
there would be nothing left for the Sweepings of the Hold ... and that I
was doing them an Injustice, as they had nothing for washing down the
Decks, coiling down the Cables, &c., except the Sweepings of the Hold.

Mr Ogle, the wharfinger and broker who owned a fifth of the
Legal Quays, testified to Parliament that he himself paid 'a Lumper
for discharging a Ship's Cargo, a Sum which I knew would not
more than pay One Third of the Wages of the Men'. While Colquhoun stressed those cases where a lumper remunerated himself
especially handsomely – he said 3 or 4 guineas might be earned a
night, he recalled the lumper who kept both a mistress and a riding

horse 'out of the profits of his delinquency' – less interested sources agreed that 'they could not subsist without (what they are pleased to Term) Perquisites'. John Drinkald, a shipowner, explained to parliamentary investigators:[35]

'Lumpers, they were paid by the ship owner, at as low a price as they could get, some of the men and master lumpers used to think they had a right to take sugar.'
    'They all helped themselves to make up for short wages?'
    'Yes'.
    'Therefore, this, which used to be called plunderage, was at least in a considerable degree, a mode of paying wages?'
    'It certainly was an understood thing.'

There were lightermen. The lightermen worked the flat-bottomed river craft that conveyed the sugar hogsheads to the quays. It took a minimum of four hours to load a lighter and two and a half hours to discharge it. Six hundred lighters were licensed for the unloading of foreign merchandise. The lightermen observed frequent holidays and were infamous for their lack of punctuality. What they took they called 'wastage' or 'leakage'. They were paid by the West India merchants, but owing to the crowded state of both the river and the quays they often had to wait in the river, and thus their single most serious grievance was demurrage. In 1792 they doubled their fees from 6d. to 12d. a hogshead, yet even this did not remove the main cause of plunderage from lighters – the lack of payment. They were known as a conniving, cantankerous group, the cause of many delays and missed markets for the ever-hungry brokers. In 1791, for instance, 1,500 sugar hogsheads blockaded the Legal Quays for six weeks. 'It was clear that mere police regulations would be unequal to meet the difficulty.' In 1812 some lightermen were tried at the Old Bailey for stealing tea. 'The tea that was found on me I bought of a seaman. It was his private stock,' said one. Proud, independent, their craft often idle, the lightermen were mobile merchants on their own account, hustling and dealing among the other river workers.[36]

[35] Charles B. Barnes, *The Longshoremen* (New York, 1915); Tatham, op. cit., p. 233; Walter M. Stern, *The Porters of London* (1960), p. 64; Colquhoun, op. cit., p. 210; *Report from the Committee Appointed to Enquire into the Best Mode of Providing Sufficient Accommodation for the Increased Trade and Shipping of the Port of London, Parliamentary Papers*, vol. xxvii (1795–6), p. 100.
[36] Colquhoun, op. cit., p. 20; Vaughan, op. cit., pp. 9–10; *The Proceedings*, 2 December 1812.

There were gangsmen. At the quay, wharf and warehouse gangsmen handled and shifted the heavy burdens. A contemporary authority on hydraulic engineering said: 'With respect to the Gangsmen taking the Sweepings, it has been a Perquisite usually allowed them, insomuch as to be considered Part Payment from the Merchants for their Labour.' Mr Ogle explained to Parliament how their sweepings might arise:

Instead of the drawing Holes (which are in general large enough to admit a Man's Hand) being immediately stopped, not One in Ten is so done; consequently they are open to petty theft in the Warehouses by the numerous Labourers necessarily employed therein by the Wharfingers; which would be prevented if the Coopers observed the Resolutions and stopped the Holes.[37]

There were coopers. They were the most craft-conscious workers of the river, whose hand skills gave them an authority among the river trades lasting into the twentieth century. Their skills impressed Virginia Woolf: 'The light stroke on either side of the barrel which makes the bung start has been arrived at by years of trial and experiment. It is the quickest, the most effective of actions. Dexterity can go no further.' They provided drink to other workers ('Can I have a drink, Mr Cooper?'); they lorded about with their 'scribing irons' (openers!). At the base of this power were ancient customs – 'sucking the monkey' and 'tapping the Admiral' – mentioned in Chaucer and Xenophon. The coopers united the two stages of offloading – on the river and on the quay – and their position was thus vital for the provision of sweepings to the lumpers and gangsmen. Within the division of labour, theirs was strategic to the livelihood of all. The chairman of the Wharfingers believed them to have been the major cause of *all* river plunderage.[38]

In the sale of a hogshead, two samples of 7 lbs. each (one for the buyer, one for the seller) were permitted. The sweeper brushed off the top of the hogshead after the cooper had opened the cask for sampling. These sweepings were collected in a receiving hogshead called 'the Devil'. Every cooper had his 'accommodation' tub. By 1796 the coopers' sampling allowance had grown to 26 lbs. per hogshead 'with the Consent and Privity of the Merchant; and is considered by him as Part Payment for his Services; and without it,

[37] *Parliamentary Papers*, op. cit., p. 100.
[38] Virginia Woolf, 'The Docks of London', *The London Scene* (New York, 1975), p. 14; *Parliamentary Papers*, op. cit., p. 19.

A cooper

or some equivalent, he would not perform the Labour he now does'. Cooperage rates varied between 6d. and 1s. 6d. per hogshead, yet such rates 'will not pay for the Labour of the Coopers employed', let alone for the hoops and nails. When offered a pay rise, the coopers refused for fear that the 'samplings' would be removed.[39]

Colquhoun placed an entirely different cast upon the custom. 'Since the chief object,' he wrote, 'of this class being plunder alone, they created work for themselves, for the purpose not only of affording abundant resources for Pillage, by the spillings of the casks, but also to keep as many of them as possible on board.' Despite the

[39] Bob Gilding, *The Journeymen Coopers of East London*, History Workshop Pamphlet, no. 4 (1971), *passim*.

construction of the wet docks, the coopers' work was not significantly changed, and hence their powerful position in the division of labour was not so easily removed. In the 1790s they formed the 'Hand in Hand', a trade union. They conducted a successful strike in 1811. Their waxers and samplings were preserved. They continued to 'tap the Admiral' or 'suck the monkey'. It was only in the strike of 1821, when a system of seniority and licensed identification was instituted in the West India Docks, that the sugar coopers lost many of their 'privileges'.[40]

While at least 18 men were tried at the Old Bailey during the 1790s for feloniously taking sugar from the river quays or moored ships, prosecutions at the Old Bailey were insufficient to repress the plunderage. Generally, small amounts were taken – 6 lbs. in a handkerchief, 8 lbs. in the breeches, 7 lbs. in a hat, 8 lbs. in a smock frock – but there were larger takings as well: 50 lbs. in bags athwart the stern, 75 lbs. in bags over the bow. The men were identified by occupation. There was 1 publican, 2 watermen, 1 warehouse porter, 1 ship's mate, 5 soldiers and 8 lumpers. Of these only 3 were acquitted; 2 were whipped, 6 were imprisoned in Newgate or the house of correction, and 3 were transported to Botany Bay. The men were in their thirties or older.

The circumstances of their apprehension throw light on methods of working, the organization of labour and a security system that depended upon watchmen, 'elders' and informers. Lumpers were searched or 'rubbed down'. Anderson's employer noticed him coming out of the cellar: 'His hands appeared sugary.' Rogers was stopped at Chester Quay warehouse: 'I said, soldier, where have you been at work? He said the capstan. I saw his hands all over sugar.' An informer weighing sugar at Galley Quay caught Richard Bromfield lying between two broken sugar hogsheads 'with a hat full of sugar under his arm'. James Gillett took sugar out of bag no. 848 and concealed it in his handkerchief. He defended himself at his trial by saying 'he had got the gripes, and that he took it to sweeten a little beer with'. He denied taking it from the bag, saying 'the sugar laid all abroad'. The informer who collared him had fingered five others. It was widely believed that he was paid a guinea for every one he accused. Another informer, William Lambert, 'laid on a shelf in the lump room' to watch the warehouse labourers, two

[40] Colquhoun, op. cit., p. 79, and George Pattison, 'The Coopers' Strike at the West India Dock, 1821', *Mariner's Mirror*, vol. lv (1969), pp. 171–2.

of whom he brought to trial for taking 'bastard sugar' from a cask and hiding it in their waistcoats and frocks.[41]

Judicial records tend to individualize struggles that are otherwise collective in nature, though there are some exceptions. The prosecution of a wherryman, Joseph Jesson, and a porter, Benjamin Payne, shows how the criminal appropriation of sugar exactly parallels the riverside division of labour. One afternoon a hogshead of sugar was hauled from the hold to the deck of a West Indiaman, the *Rose*. Its staves fell out, and then the sugar. The cooper repaired the hogshead and put 40 lbs. of the spilled sugar into a box. A wherry under the oars of Jesson came up to the lighter that was receiving the sugar, took the box, and made for shore, where Payne waited 'with his knot'. He and two lumpers lifted the box out of the wherry and conveyed it to a public house, the Queen Catherine. 'It is not customary for lumpers to pay any thing till they have disposed of their goods,' Elijah Melkin, a witness, explained. Melkin then sent for a constable and had Jesson and Payne arrested. From cooper to wherryman to porter to lumper – so far the exact course of the legitimate cooperation of tasks. Then the course diverged – to publican to constable to the Old Bailey and to Botany Bay.[42]

Bird was a lumper, Chambers a waterman, and Annis was keeper of the Black Boy in Wapping. Bird handed three bags of sugar over the bow to Chambers, who conveyed them to Annis tending a lighter. This was the action described by John Branham, a 'stag' or professional informer for Patrick Colquhoun. His testimony convicted all three. He also informed against James Flowers and John Coulhurst, who took sugar from the *Bushy Park*. Branham deserted one of His Majesty's ships in 1780, and was punished by confinement in a tender. In 1790 he went to work for the Customs, but lost this employment for bad language and taking sugar. By 1797 Branham appears as a waterman in the pay of Colquhoun and the West India merchants. He also belonged to a Wapping 'boat society' which organized insurance and repairs for its members, who paid 2d. a week. The club refused to pay damage to Branham when his boat was stove in 'upon the grounds that it was wilfully done'. Flowers was steward of the club, which had its 'articles' and received

---

[41] *The Proceedings*, 15 September 1790, 24 February 1790, 7 December 1791, 4 December 1793, 2 December 1795, 30 November 1796, 20 September 1797 and 18 April 1798.
[42] ibid., 28 October 1795.

its 'affidavits'. When Branham informed against Flowers there was much pushing and shoving, 'this, that, and the other, and waterman's language'. Branham again applied to the club for money, on St Stephen's Day, 1797, and when it was denied, he seized the boat belonging to the son of the club's housekeeper. At the next meeting of the club Branham was removed by 'the voice of all the whole people'. Yet, he continued to 'stag'. The jury did not credit his testimony and Flowers and Coulhurst were acquitted.[43]

The construction of the West India Docks on what had formerly been habitable land was the hydraulic answer to the customary plunder of the river working class. George Hibbert, the Chairman of the West India merchants, recollected the conversations that led to the mammoth, masonry enclosures:

The plunderage which took place before the goods were brought to the King's Beam, was very extensive; it was carried on by combination, and with very great art, and it was at the same time ... very difficult of detection; it was easy to commit it, and very difficult to detect it: then our consideration was this, let us bring the ship as quickly as possible from sea to the wharf, where she shall deliver her goods, and let her discharge with the least interruption possible; let us devise also a way of delivering the cargo which shall not be liable to what we suffer now, either in the occasional delivery of ships by their crews (which was a rare thing) or by lumpers. This was the conversation which led, afterwards, to the construction of the West India Docks.[44]

Like the hydraulic works of ancient river civilization, the new docks and canals of London required vision of terrific scope and power over huge amounts of labour. 'It was chiefly due to the energy and persistence of one man, Mr William Vaughan', that the docks were constructed, writes the authority on the Port of London. Vaughan worked with the most ambitious industrialists of the day – William Jessop designed the lifting cranes and John Rennie designed the double iron doors, the spacious vaults and the railway and wagon system. Vaughan was descended from a line of London and Boston merchants and Jamaican planters. He was a pupil of Dr Priestley, he was acquainted with Benjamin Franklin and was a friend of Matthew Boulton. His colleague, William Tatham, no less experienced in conditions of American commerce and

---

[43] ibid., 18 April 1798.
[44] Report from the Select Committee ... on Foreign Trade. West India Docks (1823), Parliamentary Papers, vol. iv, p. 143.

production, was amazed by the 'unbounded wealth' of the British Empire, but shocked that so little attention was paid to the '*centripetal* facilities of the amazing transfer of wealth'.[45]

In March 1794 the West India merchants met for the first time to discuss the building of wet docks. In the summer of 1797, £500,000 was raised; another £500,000 was raised in the following year, and in 1799 a further £750,000. The West India Dock Company was formed in 1799. It excavated 295 acres in the Isle of Dogs. The dock was opened in 1802 with accommodation for 600 vessels. Its perimeter was guarded by a gap of 100 ft. between it and the nearest building; a moat 6 ft. deep and 12 ft. wide; and a wall 30 ft. high.

The wet docks removed dependence on the tides. Turnaround time was reduced. Warehouse and apron space increased. The docks were insulated by high walls that 'would give convenience and security to property . . . they would at once strike at the root of all those illicit practices which plunder the proprietor . . . and also check those receiving houses and cellars up and down the river, which form so great a part of our river plunderage'. Stations of 'business, inspection, and control' were established. Commercially the docks were a success. Unloading time was reduced from twenty-five days to fifteen days. Shipping costs were reduced by 40 per cent. Lighterage was abolished. Night work was made possible. The concourse of uncontrolled traffic and people was eliminated. Workers could easily be rubbed down. Control over samplings, tare, drainage, sweepings and scrapings was established. These advantages were reflected in the weight of the hogshead: the difference between its ship and landing weight fell from 27 lbs. in 1797 to 8 lbs. in 1822. The savings were not the result of the docks only.

'*Walls, locks, bars* are of little avail against evil propensities of the mind,' wrote Colquhoun, which is affected only by 'the strong and overawing hand of power'.[46] Until the establishment of the Marine Police Office in 1798 there had been no paid, centrally directed and armed police force in London. The Rotation Offices and Horse Patrol of 1763 protected the Quality at their gaming-houses and tea-rooms. The Bow Street Foot Patrol of 1782 had a limited range both geographically and jurisdictionally. The Honourable Artillery Company was used in extraordinary instances, such as the Gordon

---

[45] Broodbank, op. cit., vol. i, pp. 78–89; Tatham, op. cit., p. 146.
[46] Colquhoun, op. cit., p. 266.

Riots. The Middlesex Stipendiary Magistrates Act of 1792 helped to centralize intelligence gathering and to remove some of the corruption of the Bench. Otherwise, law enforcement in London was divided between the parochial watch and constabulary on the one hand, and the Army on the other hand. The Marine Police Office was a milestone in metropolitan policing and in the history of the wage-form.[47]

The West India Merchants' Committee had long employed informal security guards on the quays, a practice that grew out of its reward system of 1765 and 1767. Its resolutions of 1789 remained a starting-point as well as a standard. These prohibited 'all perquisites arising from Sweepings of Sugar'. They prohibited ship workers from going on shore during the day and they required that lumpers 'be victualled on board, and searched when they go on shore at night'. Captains were to board ships in the evening, crews were to be 'kept under Eye and Command'. The only open hatch was to be the working hatch. No boat was to be fastened to the ship. No damaged casks were to be loaded into a lighter. Watchmen were to be armed. Sweepings were not permitted to the gangsmen. Only one sample was allowed and once taken the hogshead was to be sealed immediately. Although these resolutions were several times published, amended and revised, they remained a dead letter.[48]

John Harriott blew the breath of life into them in the summer of 1797 when this magistrate, a farmer and underwriter at Lloyds, submitted a plan for the establishment of a Thames police office to the Home Secretary. Alone he did not succeed, but when he began working with Patrick Colquhoun, they were able within a year to open the office. 'We seized the bull by the horns, and never quitted our hold for upwards of two years. It was a labour not unworthy of Heracles, and we succeeded by our joint efforts, in bringing into reasonable order some thousands of men, who had long considered plunder as a privilege.'[49]

Colquhoun was the London agent for the planters of St Vincent, Nevis, Dominica and the Virgin Islands. He worked tirelessly for the West India Merchants' Committee in London. He worked

---

[47] Ruth Paley, 'The Middlesex Justices Act of 1792: Its Origins and Effects', Ph.D. thesis, University of Reading, 1983.

[48] These are reprinted in Colquhoun, op. cit., appendix 5.

[49] John Harriott, *Struggles Through Life: Exemplified in the Various Travels and Adventures in Europe, Asia, Africa, and America* (1809), vol. ii, pp. 259–60.

closely with the Home Secretary and the House of Commons, testifying frequently to the Finance Committee on the subject of police and drafting its legislation on that subject. Edmund Burke, Edward Gibbon and Adam Smith were visitors to his home. He collaborated closely with Jeremy Bentham on police schemes and reformation of the dockyards. If a single individual could be said to have been the planner and theorist of class struggle in the metropolis it would be he. Melville Lee called him the 'architect' of the police. The Webbs called him its 'inventor'. His influence goes far beyond the establishment of the Marine Police Office, because his books, although written for the practical purpose of establishing a police force, contain that combination of law, economics, flattery and class hatred that together have exercised a powerful influence upon subsequent conceptions of law and order.[50]

His conception of class relations was at once cosmic and dialectical. London was the greatest manufacturing and commercial city in 'the known world'. Its riches were greater than anything 'in the Universe'. Yet, he stated axiomatically, where riches flow there is an accession of crime. The 'progressive increase of Crimes' is 'the constant and never-failing attendant on the accumulation of Wealth'. '*Commercial Riches* and *Criminal Offences* have grown together.' Property and acts of pillage are logically and necessarily connected. He speaks, not for the West India merchants and planters, but for the 'community', the 'nation', 'humanity', the 'civilized world', 'society', the 'law'. His attitude was Newtonian in its obsession with enumerating the 'flux' of wealth and crime. He measures exports, imports, river traffic, ocean traffic, profits and losses. He seeks to do the same with the working class, whose lodging-houses, street-sellers, horse-dealers, pawnbrokers, stable-keepers, second-hand sellers, hawkers, pedlars, public houses, old-iron shops he wished to count, register and license.

'Police in this Country,' he writes, 'may be considered as a *new Science*; in the PREVENTION and DETECTION OF CRIMES, and in those other Functions which relate to INTERNAL REGULATIONS for the well ordering and comfort of Civil Society.' This was the classic conception of 'police' because it combined law

---

[50] Patrick Colquhoun, *Treatise on the Police of the Metropolis* (1795), *The State of Indigence* (1799) and *A Treatise on the Commerce and Police of the River Thames* (1800); W. L. Melville Lee, *A History of Police in England* (1901), p. 219; Sidney and Beatrice Webb, *The Poor Law*, p. 403.

and economics, the protection of property and the protection of production. It is the conception that Colquhoun learned from the Scottish élite such as Adam Smith, whose *Wealth of Nations* first appeared as 'Lectures on Police', or William Robertson, who distinguished feudal from commercial societies by the presence of 'police'. Smith's pupil, Adam Ferguson, had argued in 1792 that 'national felicity' depended on 'labour rightly directed'. That 'Wealth comes from inequality' was the first principle of his 'Moral and Political Science'.[51]

Colquhoun sees the working class as an epidemic: the mass of labourers are 'contaminated', one group of workers 'infect' another. Hence he proposes a police to sanitize class relations. He sees the working class as a military enemy whose 'various detachments and subdivisions ... [form] the general army of Delinquents'. 'Opportunities are watched and intelligence procured with a degree of vigilance similar to that which marks the conduct of a skilful General.' The London working class has spun a 'system', a 'monstrous System of Depredation', a 'General System of Pillage'. It is 'disciplined in acts of Criminal Warfare'. It forms 'conspiracies'; it comprises a 'phalanx'. The working class is also uncivilized, possessing 'unruly passions', 'rapacious desires', 'evil propensities', 'noxious qualities', 'vicious and bad habits', and its moral turpitude needs the 'humane improvement' by police.

'Poverty' was necessary to wealth ('It is the lot of man – it is the source of *Wealth*'). 'Indigence' on the other hand is 'the evil'. It is the condition of 'idleness', the root of all problems, producing 'a disposition to moral and criminal offences'. 'Idleness' is both a moral category and an economic one: it is the refusal to accept exploitation. This refusal is measured by the 'losses' of the West India merchants (during a decade of unprecedented profit and trade). The conflation of morality and economics is found also in Colquhoun's taxonomy of depredation, which, in fact, apart from diction, is identical to the riverside division of labour, so watermen became 'night plunderers', coopers became 'light horsemen', lumpers become 'heavy horsemen', porters and gangsmen become 'scuffle hunters', etc. Colquhoun employs a rhetorical strategy that criminalizes the river proletariat. The semantic trick enables his readers both to extol the division of labour and to despise the divided labourers. The rhe-

[51] William Robertson, *The History of Scotland* (Philadelphia, 1811), vol. i, p. 161; and Adam Ferguson, *Principles of Moral and Political Science* (1792).

torical freedom permitting this sleight of hand is necessary to the double vision of the bourgeoisie, which fears and dreads the working class while simultaneously understanding that labour is 'the foundation of all value'.[52] Dr Johnson noted that the diction of the labouring class was casual and mutable, and he called it 'fugitive cant', thus performing a semantic criminalization. He therefore excluded the diction of labour from his dictionary as 'unworthy of preservation'. Such ignorance was a luxury that could not be afforded by those who needed to understand the proletarians, such as police, army captains and engineers. Captain Grose's *Dictionary of the Vulgar Tongue*, whose third edition was published in 1796, does not mention the terms of Colquhoun's opprobrium. He was unfamiliar with river work. Colquhoun's semantic strategy was an old one, originating in the first cant dictionaries of the sixteenth century. They divide the working class into a dangerous, incomprehensible, secret underworld, and an honest, plain-spoken, orderly world of labouring dependents. By the 1790s the association between civilization and correct English implied that speakers of vulgar English were 'savage' – the term Harriott used to describe river workers. Colquhoun added particularity to this generalization.

Colquhoun was not given to making distinctions between 'custom' and 'crime', and where he was forced to acknowledge them his goal was only to abolish the difference.

What was at first considered as the wages of turpitude, at length assumes the form, and is viewed in the light of a fair perquisite of office. In this manner abuses multiply, and the ingenuity of man is ever fertile in finding some palliative. Custom and example sanction the greatest enormities: which at length become fortified by immemorial and progressive usage: it is no wonder, therefore, that the superior Officers find it an Herculean labour to cleanse the Augean stable.[53]

The relations of appropriation give to labour a unity that is apprehended according to various capitalist interests. We can distinguish three. First, are the technologists, like Samuel Bentham or William Vaughan, who see the working class as the producers of things, because they wish to increase productivity by revolutionizing the tools of labour. Second, are the economists, like Adam Smith or David Ricardo, to whom the working class is a quantitative

[52] David Ricardo, *Principles of Political Economy and Taxation*, ed. R. M. Hartwell (1971), p. 63.
[53] Colquhoun, *Treatise on the Police of the Metropolis* (1795), p. 252.

aspect of capital, the producers of a value according to the duration of their labour. Third, are the police, like Colquhoun and Harriott, who see the working class as the producers of idleness, drunkenness and disorder. Customary appropriations appear as inefficiency or waste to the technologist, as an inventory loss or transaction cost to the economists, and a depredation or crime to the police. They therefore wage war against the working class.

The Marine Police Office at no. 259 Wapping New Stairs was divided between a police department and a department for lumpers. The latter paid wages, the former prevented plunder. It had a two-fold object: 'To procure a speedy and regular discharge of West India ships by registered and approved Lumpers, under the control of the Office; and to protect the Property in every stage of the Discharge, from the moment the Ship arrives at her Moorings to the final delivery of the Goods at the King's Beam.' The office maintained a register of lumpers, and provided an assembly point for lumping gangs. Fifty constables were hired, armed and serving in rotation, whose principal duty was to search the lumpers every evening when they came ashore. The policemen were paid 5s. a day – a large sum when it is considered that soldiers were paid at best 3s. a week and that weekly 'necessaries' in 1795 for a family of four cost 19s. The police officers were armed with cutlasses as well as staffs of office. They enforced a working day of an additional hour. No lumper was permitted to go on shore during the working day. Their meals were to be taken on board, half an hour for breakfast, and an hour for dinner. The Police Office organized payment of wages. Previously the master lumper was the only person paid, and he allowed the 'men to remunerate themselves by Plunder'. Upon depositing a fee of 2s. a ton, the owners were 'relieved of the trouble of paying the Lumpers weekly'. The police enforced piece-rates at 11d. per hogshead of sugar, 7d. for a tierce, 2d. for a bag, etc. 'The Lumping Rates have been ultimately settled on the lowest Terms, for which honest labour can be procured for daily wages.'

They also enforced a dress code, for working-class 'equipage' was designed for customary takings. A sorter at the East India Company warehouse took china in the skirts of his coat. A tea-chest-nailer had 'a large piece of leather sewed to the waistband of his breeches'. A coffee-cooper carried samples in his knee-breeches and his hat. Others secreted their plunder in hidden pockets, bladders and bags. The instructions to the police officers commanded that when the Lumpers come on board to begin to discharge, your attention must be particularly directed to their dress, to see that they have no frocks, nor wide trowsers, jemmies, or under-waistcoats with pouches; and that no bags or empty stockings are brought on board either by Lumpers, Coopers, or any other Persons, not forgetting to examine the Crowns of their Hats.[54]

Years later Herman Melville suffered the indignity of a dockyard search. Joe Bloomberg remembered his first day at the London docks: 'At the end of the day I was going home with a friend ... when the Dock Police stopped us and asked had we anything on us we shouldn't have. I replied "Yes". I showed him my hands that were a mass of blisters. "I never came in with these but I'm going home with them." '[55]

The probity of the police was maintained by inspection, rotation and much oath-taking – an oath of office, an oath of vigilance, an oath of fidelity and an oath of allegiance. Their essence and purpose, however, was to remove customary taking.

As soon as you enter the Ship which is assigned to you, it must be your first duty to see that the printed paper now delivered, entitled A CAUTION, be nailed, pasted, or fastened to the Main-Mast; and that you suffer no person to remove or take it down, until the Ship is completely unladed; and that you, or your colleague, read it aloud every morning, while the lumpers are at breakfast, or when they come first on board, that those who cannot read it themselves may not pretend ignorance; and that you also paste up, and read in the same manner the caution against *Sweepings* and *Scrapings*, that no person may be allowed to appropriate, to their own use, any article whatsoever, whether sugar, coffee, or anything else, which may drop into the hold from the casks and packages.[56]

In the evening of 16 October 1798 a large mob attacked the Marine Police Office in Wapping High Street. A police officer had taken Charles Eyres and another coal-heaver 'in custody for having coal in their possession'. John Harriott and Patrick Colquhoun summarily found them guilty and fined them 40s., not a sum easily to hand for a river worker. The magistrates knew what was at stake. Harriott himself wrote that they regarded the coal as a perquisite, 'a custom of their predecessors', that they had 'fair title to such

[54] *The Proceedings*, 24 February 1790 and 8 June 1791.
[55] Joe Bloomberg, *Looking Back – A Docker's Life* (1979), p. 17.
[56] Reprinted in Colquhoun, *A Treatise on the Commerce and Police of the River Thames*, p. 649.

coals'. They 'had long been in the constant practice of each man taking his sack, containing two or three bushels of coals, whenever he went on shore from the ship he was unloading'. *'Custom* was their invariable plea,' he wrote. To Harriott the 1,400 Irish coal-heavers were 'an unruly set of beings' and 'half savage'. The two magistrates understood that the custom was river-wide and product-wide; if they broke it at one point, it would be easier to remove it all over. For their part, the coal-heavers also understood that this was a moment of truth for river workers generally.[57]

Feeling ran high on the river. The context was one of defeat. The memory of the Great Mutiny of the year before still lived, for it had been caused by many of the same issues: wages to the sailors were two or three years in arrears, and what the sailors ate and drank was served at bad measure of 13 oz. to the pound. Although good measure prevailed after the mutiny, in the summer of 1797 at least thirty-six sailors were hanged from the yard-arms of the Fleet. In the spring of 1798 the Irish Rebellion began – 'the Rising of the Moon' – whose point was supplied by the Protestant urban demo-crats and whose heft was supplied by the rural Catholic cottier, who, R. A. Salaman reminds us, 'was not a serf – he was much nearer akin to a slave'. The rising was to fail despite its desperation and 'the Gaelic sea network' that united Irish people below decks. In the spring the London radicals were imprisoned, the treason trials of the United Irishmen began, and the hope of a coordinated republican rising in the three kingdoms was dashed when Napoleon decided to invade Egypt not Ireland. By late summer 1798 the repressions began in earnest: 30,000 peasants were slaughtered by staged hangings, unstaged massacres and 'hunting the croppies'. And the migrations began to Prussia, to Glasgow, to the Caribbean and to the Thames, carrying with them their news, songs and struggles.[58]

On 25 August an Irish river worker, Joseph Leahey, was murdered by a press-gang. He lodged in Spruce's Island, an Irish part of Wapping. All through the summer 'there have been quarrels between coal-heavers and press-gangs'. Indeed, the struggle in London was wider: eleven of the mutineers, including the 'rebel

[57] Harriott, op. cit., p. 261.
[58] James Dugan, *The Great Mutiny* (1965); R. A. Salaman, *The History and Social Influence of the Potato*, revised edn (1985), p. 266; Thomas Pakenham, *The Year of Liberty: The Great Irish Rebellion of 1798* (1972); and Albert Goodwin, *The Friends of Liberty: The English Democratic Movement in the Age of the French Revolution* (Cambridge, Mass., 1979), pp. 436–49.

captain' of the 'Sandwich', escaped from Cold Bath Fields. The military prisoners in the Savoy rioted for several days. The day of Leahey's death, 25 August, was a Saturday and pay-day for the coal-heavers. Three or four press-gangs prowled in Wapping. The press-gang claimed in court to have been stoned, 'bobbed' and frightened by Irish imprecations. Stones and brickbats flew about in a 'perfect riot'. The press-gang retaliated by 'doing one of them' – that is, by stabbing Leahey in the kidneys. He expired. His assailants were found guilty of manslaughter at the Old Bailey in the middle of September. They were discharged and fined 1s. each.[59]

This was not a sum to inspire faith in justice, particularly when contrasted with the 40s. fine against Charles Eyres. Therefore, when the Police Office was attacked, the slogans were: 'Here goes for the forty' (tossing a paving-stone), and 'We will have the money back, or else we will have the house down.' The besieged magistrates roused themselves to action. Harriott (feeling 'young again') ordered out the pistols. Colquhoun read the Riot Act. An officer, along with a lumper's foreman, named Gabriel Franks, gave chase to the mob down to a cooperage at Dung Wharf. In the dark, a man was shot dead. The body was taken to Execution Dock, where the dockers thought it was Branham, the river 'stag' ('d—n his eyes, we have got him dead at last'). But it was Gabriel Franks. James Eyres, the brother of Charles, was taken up, tried for murder, found guilty and hanged.[60] Thus, in the first battle for the establishment of a police force, Jack Ketch remained a necessary last resort.

We must emphasize the historic importance of the River Thames Police. It was the first police force in London's history that was under the command of a centralized state authority. In this it was distinct from the parochial Watch and Constabulary. Police historians are thus correct in seeing it as the forerunner of the 1829 Metropolitan Police Act (establishing the 'Bobbies' or 'Peelers') and the County Constabulary Act of 1836, both of which were decisive in the formation of a centralized monopoly of internal violence. The River Thames Police is also historically significant because it accepted direct responsibility for the payment of wages to the lumping gangs of the West India Fleet. They set piece-rates, they managed accounting and they disbursed monies. They were

[59] *The Proceedings*, 12 September 1798; *The Observer*, 8 April, 20 May 1798.
[60] ibid., 9 January 1799.

therefore directly responsible for the quantitative exploitation of the river working class.

In determining who would receive wages, the River Police also determined wagelessness. Customary remuneration required a community-wide network of marine-store-dealers, grocers, inn- and alehouse-keepers, landlords and brothel-owners with whom the river workers might barter or exchange their takings. Such men and women, in providing food, drink, love and lodging, were an essential part of the urban economy of the poor. Old rag and iron shops, orange boys, petty retailers, barrow-women, street-dealers, copemen and receivers were unlicensed. Prostitutes thrived upon those who took their income from the maritime employments. Chatting about common friends in Liverpool and taking off the pants of a seafaring man she had picked up, Catherine Davies, who also did his washing, swallowed six of the sailor's guineas.[61]

The underground or non-monetary community was physically destroyed to make way for the docks. To paraphrase Sir Thomas More's famous dictum about sheep and enclosure, where once East End people had lived by the water, after the construction of the docks the water lived upon them. Of more significance than the submergence of the riverside neighbourhoods, which, however gigantic as labour, remained geographically limited, was the criminalization of the dockers' customary takings. This introduced a moralizing discourse on honesty and wickedness – that came to characterize police, legislative and economic policies – to ever-widening segments of working-class London until by 1867 James Greenwood considered it one of the seven curses of London: 'Many men adopt a sort of hobbling compromise, walking as it were with one foot on the path of rectitude, and the other in the miry way of petty theft.'[62]

Thus, the historic function of the River Thames Police was less the apprehension of criminals or the detection of crime – and this was well understood by Colquhoun, whose emphasis was always on the *prevention* of crimes and the *renovation* of morals – than it was, paradoxical as it may appear, the creation of crime or the practical redefining of its meaning. The eighteenth-century view regarded the police function as not so much to defend private

---

[61] *The Proceedings*, 2 December 1795.
[62] James Greenwood, *The Seven Curses of London* (1867, Garland reprint 1984), p. 169.

property (though this of course was included) as to create and then to sustain the class relations in the production of private property. This is a point that is omitted in the otherwise useful account by Professor David Philips: 'the urban shopkeeper wanted something which would efficiently protect his commercial property' is his explanation of the origin of this police. The formulation is too broad in that it might equally apply to the shopkeepers of the 1690s, and it is too narrow because the policy and the practice of police at the end of the 1790s was to protect the production of property in addition to its commerce, hence employers of all kinds, as well as shopkeepers, welcomed the police.[63]

When Professor Philips writes, 'There was hostility to the idea of a professional police from the newly-emerging organized working class, for whom such a force was seen as a new agency of political repression,' we must carefully define what is meant by 'the newly-emerging organized working class'. If in the early phase it refers to the London Corresponding Society and its plebeian allies, then that hostility in the 1790s was directed against the spying, double-dealing and political terror of police such as Colquhoun organized in Spitalfields in 1792. Otherwise, rarely do the radical 'Jacks' of the 1790s mention proletarian customary usages, and the exceptions are exotic or agrarian. In passing, Wollstonecraft observes the necessity of perquisites in a letter from Scandinavia.[64] Thomas Spence recounted at his trial for sedition in 1801 an earlier episode when a forester apprehended him gathering nuts in woods belonging to the Duke of Portland. Nowhere has evidence come to light of actual defence of the customs.

The subject was complex: in point of law it was confused ('multiple differences in minute particulars', according to a Scottish jurist; 'the accumulated legacy of a multiplicity of local legislative initiatives', according to Professor Styles), and in point of fact direct appropriations ranged along a continuum from judicially recognized 'incorporeal hereditaments', to 'usages of the trade', to 'allowances of the master', to informally accepted entitlements, to payment for

[63] David Philips, '"A New Engine of Power and Authority": The Institutionalization of Law-Enforcement in England, 1780–1830', in V. A. C. Gatrell, Bruce Lenman and Geoffrey Parker (eds), *Crime and the Law: The Social History of Crime in Western Europe since 1500* (1980), p. 178.
[64] *Letters Written ... in Sweden, Norway, and Denmark* (1796), quoted in Janet M. Todd (ed.), *A Wollstonecraft Anthology* (1977), p. 163.

particular work, to a 'gift', to substitution for wages in truck, to compensation against distress, to 'an understood thing'.[65] Even where we might most expect a vigorous defence and counter-attack from those who opposed private property in land or capital, like Thomas Spence, 'the unfee'd advocate of the disinherited seed of Adam', we are struck by the contrast between the abstract, intellectualized argument for the national 'common', and the massive, desperate experience of those taking direct action in appropriating to themselves part of the product of their labour. What accounts for this distance between idea and activity, between principle and practice? Repression (fear, militarization and self-censorship) is part of the answer. In September 1800, when food riots broke out in north, south, west and east London, the militia, the army, the volunteer corps and the associations were mobilized to repress them.[66] Spence wrote at the same time:

The other Day one of the Labourers belonging to the East India Warehouses, being in my company, and, knowing he could confide in me, opened his Mind pretty freely concerning the present riots, and told me that several of their people had been discharged for saying they would bite of the Bullets from their Cartridges, if they were ordered to fire at the Mob.[67]

Spence's reaction is either ironic ('Must not one's privileges be very great in a Country where we dare not pluck a Hazel Nut?'), or it retreats to a vivid but allegorical communism, as in his meditation following his conversation with the warehouse worker:

A Worm pays no Rent: the Earth while he lives is his Portion, and he riots in untaxed Luxuries. And if perchance a Crow or other Creature, should pick him up, why this is only Death, which must come in some shape or other to us all as well as he. But in this respect he had the Advantage of us that while he lived he paid no Rent!

To repression we must add money as a cause of the disconnections of the counter-revolution of the late 1790s. To succeed the police required the active cooperation of a sector of the working class.

[65] John Styles, 'Embezzlement, Industry and the Law in England, 1500–1800', in Maxine Berg, Pat Hudson and Michael Sonenscher (eds), *Manufacture in Town and Country before the Factory* (Cambridge, 1983), pp. 192–3.
[66] *The Observer*, 21 September 1800 and *The Times*, 16–20, 22, 23 September 1800.
[67] Thomas Spence, *The Restorer of Society to its Natural State* (1801), pp. 33–4.

Those with access to money wages became active disciplinarians of the wageless, a bitter result of the counter-revolution of the 1790s. The reduction of real income by direct physical attack upon the dockers' income, and the separation of the struggle in the labour process from that outside of it, produced the preconditions of the monetary wage upon which the hierarchies of power within the working class rested. The contradiction helps to explain that 'jolly good fellow', the homicidal Mr Punch. Punch summons Judy, who brings their baby. When it makes a mess, he beats it and throws it away, dancing all the while. Judy attempts to defend the child, so Punch belabours her until she's quite dead. He sings.

Excepting children, women were the weakest part of the London working class, and their voices are faint indeed. Professor Joan Scott listens attentively for evidence of 'artisan women', and in finding none suggests that the category, 'working class', is a gendered (male) category.[68] This is to throw out the baby with the bath water. Mary Wollstonecraft was also an attentive listener – listening indeed was her excellence as an artisan. At the very end of her life, when 'the world appeared a vast prison', she wrote Jemima's story, which was published posthumously. It is a proletarian story. Jemima 'had been hunted from hole to hole as if she had been a beast of prey or infected with a moral plague'. Her infancy was passed in a cellar. She existed but to curse. She was apprenticed to a Methodist Wapping slop-seller who beat her, fed her on table refuse and raped her. 'I stole now, from absolute necessity, bread.' She accepted the beastly views of those hating her class as true of herself: 'I was the filching cat, the ravenous dog, the dumb brute, who must bear all.' She took to whoring ('Detesting my nightly occupation, though valuing ... my independence'), and then became a washerwoman, working from one in the morning till eight at night, 'condemned to labour, like a machine'. She injured herself at the tub, and 'began to consider the rich and poor as natural enemies, and became a thief from principle'.[69] This is the language of the class struggle at its least mediated. Jemima had once been servant to a Hampstead intellectual who read aloud to her the 'radical' tracts of the period, and it was perhaps that experience that led her to talk of 'principle'. Otherwise her experience, like that of the majority of men and women of the

---

[68] Joan Wallach Scott, *Gender and the Politics of History* (New York, 1988), pp. 72–6.
[69] *The Wrongs of Woman: Or, Maria: a Fragment* (1798).

London working class described in these pages, was expressed in action.

For the radical craftsmen whose traditions included both dissent and at least dialogue with the tribunes of the 'Age of Reason', it was a competitive decade in which the skills and independence of many were degraded to sweated conditions, and others became active in self-help organizations, trade unions, radical democratic associations. The skilled London artisan faced one political defeat after another with legislation proscribing public assemblies, seditious publications and trade-union combinations in the anti-Jacobin hysteria of the decade. Yet as the new century began parts of this proletariat had access to a wage.

In its political action, and sometimes in its written expressions, this sector of the working class had little choice but to accept the revolution in class relations. It acquiesced in the technological recompositions of the labour process in exchange for a system of wage-payment. This is seen most clearly in the history of the shipwrights and their trade combination, the St Helena's Society. The strike of May 1800, led by John Gast, accepted on the one hand the collective bargaining of time and money. A handbill was posted on the dock wall of Chatham Yard contrasting the prices of 'the Necessaries of Life' in 1775, 1795 and 1801 – in twenty-five years they had tripled. On the other hand, Gast accepted the policing duties of the waged workers against those who continued to subsist in the economy of chips.[70] But we see it elsewhere in other variations. The capitalists in the hatter's trade found technological repression less successful in getting rid of bugging than the geographical relocation of investments to Cheshire and Lancashire, the substitution of new materials of production (silk for beaver stuff) and the incarceration of fabrication behind factory walls.[71] The shoemakers resented competition from veterans and ex-servants who 'scabbed', and so they began in the 1790s to police themselves by their Society rules, which punished 'sotting and swearing', the observation of St Monday, and (in Rule XXI) the purloining of the 'master's stuff'.[72]

[70] Peter Linebaugh, 'Labour History without the Labour Process: A Note on John Gast and His Times', *Social History*, vol. vii, no. 3 (October 1982); PRO, HO, 28/27, In-Letters from Admiralty.
[71] P. M. Giles, 'The Felt-hatting Industry, c. 1500–1850, with special reference to Lancashire and Cheshire', *Transactions of the Lancashire and Cheshire Antiquarian Society*, vol. lxix (1959).
[72] *Rules of the Society of Journeymen Boot and Shoe Makers*, quoted in A. Aspinall

Tailoring too was transformed, and the material conditions of production that had formerly permitted the tailor his 'cabbage' were removed. By the 1790s cutting by pattern had ceased to be the exclusive practice of secretive masters, and had become widespread with the publication of printed patterns that provided exact directions as to how to cut each piece, and illustrations showing the most economical way to lay out the patterns of the cloth. When the journeymen masons went on strike for a wage increase in May 1796, they argued that 'their trade is exempt from any of those perquisites which enrich the other artisans, and that their wages are not adequate to their labour and the dearness of provisions'.[73]

This transformation of the material and social relations of production was reflected in the radical ideology of this sector of the working class. 'Wages' and 'rights of man' became ineluctably associated among the English Jacobins. At the formation of the London Corresponding Society in 1792 a relationship between rights, wages and property was expressed axiomatically: 'The Wages of every Man are his right.'[74] Yet, in a historically significant ambiguity, this 'democratic' organization boasting of its 'Members unlimited' in fact excluded those not 'in possession of his reason [or] incapacitated by crimes'. John Gast argued that 'the produce of his labour, to the mechanic, is surely as much an estate or inheritance to him as the right of ownership over a large tract of land, is to its lordly proprietor'. This was an argument adduced against the wage cut of 1800 when the shipwrights went on strike 'to enable us to provide for ourselves and families, in that manner, which every man has a right to expect from the produce of his labour'.[75] The same thought concludes Cobbett's powerful pamphlet, *The Soldier's Friend* (1791): 'I would have you look upon nothing that you receive as a *Favour* or a *Bounty* from Kings, Queens, or Princes; you receive the wages of your servitude; it is your property, confirmed to you by Acts of the Legislature of your Country.' The London artisan, his back against the wall, cried out that his 'skill' or his 'labour' was his property, thus asserting his independence against paternalism

---

(ed.), *The Early English Trade Unions; Documents from the Home Office Papers* (1949), pp. 81–7.
[73] Norah Waugh, *The Cut of Men's Clothes 1600–1900* (New York, 1964), pp. 91 ff.; *The Observer*, 8 May 1796.
[74] Brit. Lib., Add. MSS, 27812, London Corresponding Society, Minute Book, p. 25 (October 1792).
[75] John Gast, *Calumny Defeated* (1802).

while turning his back against those other sectors of the class without that 'tract of land'.

Just as 'the rights of man' presupposed doctrines of legal 'wrongs', so the monetary abstracting of human labour as wages presupposed criminalizing customary appropriation. In the first paragraph of *Common Sense* Tom Paine wrote: 'A long habit of not thinking a thing *wrong* gives it a superficial appearance of being *right* and raises at first a formidable outcry in defence of custom.' The London tradesmen associated the discourse of 'custom' with the 'gothick' or feudal constitution which had degenerated into the 'old Corruption' of George III. To them 'revolutionary democracy' meant the acceptance of class relations based upon reason and wages. What this meant in terms of actual class practices is revealed by Francis Place's reading of William Godwin's *Enquiry Concerning Political Justice*. It strengthened his determination to become independent of journeyman work, to become his own boss, and to boss others.

From Godwin he learned that the essence of the wage system is accountability. This meant that the worker was predictable; it meant that the worker's value was capable of quantitative measurement; it meant that the worker was responsible for losses of materials during production; it meant that money rationalized class society. None of this was possible under the *ancien régime*. The immunities and prerogatives to which the utilitarian objected were the material basis of a class relation where custom, licence, usage, perquisite, 'pillage and plunder' prevailed. These Godwin compared to the 'little peculium' of the slave, ancient and modern, which should be sacrificed to the public interest. At the time Place read Godwin, he worked under an Irish foreman whom Place disliked because, first, he was an 'ingrate', and second, he was less knowledgeable than Place, a tailor, in 'cutting out and making the most of materials'. The absence of strict reciprocity in exchange (ingratitude) and the inefficient techniques of materials handling were the essence of the 'irregular' life and the cabbage exchange of the eighteenth century. As a master tailor and boss of thirty-two workers Place became a firm opponent of piece-work done by journeymen in their own rooms, where they were less likely to be accountable than working under their master's nose.[76]

---

[76] Francis Place, *Autobiography*, ed. Mary Thale (Cambridge, 1971), p. 136. See also Place's evidence to the Select Committee on Tailors (1811), republished in F. W. Galton, *Select Documents Illustrating the History of Trade Unionism*, vol. i,

The lifestyles promoted by such radical London artisans fore-shadowed the discipline of the industrial worker: punctuality and obedience to the factory clock; acceptance of a new diet of sugar and potatoes, and new drinks in tea and coffee; a continuous working day, where dinner was moved from the afternoon to the evening or night-time; it meant a new language in refraining from profanity; it meant cleanliness and sanitation; and it meant the punctilious recognition of *meum et tuum* even when property was socialized in production. These were the marks of 'respectability'.[77] At their base, I am suggesting, was the power of the wage, which concealed the division between unpaid and paid labour, between men and women, adults and children, slaves and free, a division which as a result became deeper and more violent.

As Punch puts an end to wife and child, black servant and blind beggar, doctor and courtier, constable and hangman, he puts an end to the society that gave rise to the repressions of gender, race, class and law. This, so to speak, is the revolutionary side to Punch. In exercising his murderous rage against women, children, beggars and black people, Punch recapitulates, in the little motions of the puppeteer, larger, actual divisions within the London working class as a whole, in which rape, infanticide and the suppression of slave rebellion were mass experiences, recognizable and undeniable.[78] The media of action in Punch and Judy are the stick and wit. Each could become anything Punch wanted, affirming, as it were, that both the tools and the words of the 1790s were human creations. Action contradicted words – the gallows became an orchard, the fiddle a mortal weapon, the stick became 'physic'. Words mean what those with power say they mean. The stick is Punch's dictionary. Old Nick does appear ('I know you have a great deal of business when you come to London'), a combat ensues, as terrific as Christian's struggle against Apollyon, and Punch is triumphant. 'Huzza! Huzza! the Devil's dead!' and the show is over.

The Tailoring Trade (1896), p. 127; William Godwin, *Enquiry Concerning Political Justice* (1798), Isaac Kramnick (ed.), 1976, p. 466.

[77] Gunther Lottes, *Aufklarung und plebejisches Publikim zur Theorie und Praxis des englischen Radikalismus im spaten 18. Jahrhundert* (Oldenbourg: München, 1979), pp. 207–19.

[78] Anna Clark, *Women's Silence. Men's Violence: Sexual Assault in England, 1770–1845* (1987).

BIBLIOGRAPHY

JUDICIAL REPOSITORIES

CORPORATION OF LONDON RECORD OFFICE

Account Book of the Entry Fines and Weekly and Yearly Rents for Stalls and Shops payed by the Market People to the Farmers of the Markets, misc. MS 30.5

'The Case of the Tacklehouse Porters of the Twelve Primary Companies' (1707), box 1, shelf 149

'The Case of the Ticket Porters against the Tacklehouse Porters Presented to the Court of Aldermen' (1707), box 5, shelf 149

Index to London Indictments, 1714–1755

'James Brown's Queries ab't. the Markett at Bear Key' (1722), MS 85.17

Market Copy Accounts, 1738–9, misc. MS 161.22

Miscellaneous Papers, small MS box 30, no. 4 and misc. MSS 172.5

Papers Relating to Leadenhall Market, 1720–1741

'Petition of Butchers against Sales on other than Market Days' (c. 1720), MSS 85.5

'The Porters Case Book, 1716–1724'

Rawstorne Papers, misc. MSS 172.15

Remembrancers Papers, misc. MSS 172.9

Repertories of the Court of Aldermen

Sessions Files

Sessions Papers

Sharpe, R. R., 'London Markets' (1887), misc. MSS 187.7

GREATER LONDON COUNCIL RECORD OFFICE

A Register or Kalendar of all the Innkeepers of the Tower Division, MR/LV, 8/68 (a–c)

Norris, Henry, *Minute Book, 1730–1741* (no. 2), Ac. 61.21

St Pancras, *Register of Burials, 1689–1729*, P90/PAN/1/3

KENT RECORD OFFICE

Sessions Papers, Q/SB

MIDDLESEX RECORD OFFICE

Calendar of Indictments, MJ/CJ
Hardy, W.J. (ed.), *A Calendar of the Middlesex Sessions Books and
    Orders of Court, 1639–1751*
  Middlesex Gaol Delivery Registers
Justice's Qualification Oaths, MJP/Q
Middlesex Commissions of the Peace, MJP/CP
Middlesex Gaol Delivery Books, MJ/GDB
Middlesex Orders of Court Books, MJ/OC
Middlesex Process Registers of Indictments, MJ/SBP
Middlesex Sessions of Gaol Delivery Rolls, MJ/GDR
Middlesex Sessions Papers, MJ/SP
Middlesex Sessions of the Peace Rolls, MJ/SR
The Minute Book of Brentford Petty Sessions
Westminster Instruction Books for Indictments, WJ/SBJ
Westminster Sessions Papers, WJ/SP
Westminster Sessions of the Peace Rolls, WJ/SR

PUBLIC RECORD OFFICE

Admiralty Oyer and Terminer Records, HCA 1/57
Admiralty Papers, Adm. 1/4129
Chatham Papers, 30/81
Colonial Office Papers, CO 201/89F
Courts Martial Proceedings, WO 71/20
Deptford Ordinary, Adm. 42/408
Deptford Yard Pay Books, Adm. 42/540
Navy Board Records, Adm. 106/2181
Secretary of War, Outletters, WO 4
Ship's Pay Books, Adm. 33/350–83
State Papers Domestic, George I, SP 35
State Papers Domestic, George II, SP 36
State Papers, Entry Books, SP 44/81
Tower of London, Garrison Papers, WO 94
Treasury Solicitor, Papers, TS 11

MANUSCRIPT COLLECTIONS

BOSTON PUBLIC LIBRARY

Journal of Lieutenant Howard, MS fAm.6

BRITISH LIBRARY

Add. MSS. 27,825, Francis Place Papers, 'Grossness'
Add. MSS. 27,826, Francis Place Papers
Add. MSS. 35,142, Francis Place, *Autobiography*
Add. MSS. 27,811, London Corresponding Society

BIRMINGHAM CENTRAL REFERENCE LIBRARY

Boulton & Watt MSS

CAMBRIDGE UNIVERSITY LIBRARY

Cholmondeley Houghton Papers
'An Account of Some Particulars of the late Riot in Shoreditch'

WILLIAM L. CLEMENTS LIBRARY, UNIVERSITY OF MICHIGAN

Concerning the High Price of Provisions
Dockyard Artificer and Stores, vol. xliv
'Memorials of a Dialogue betwixt several Seamen and a certain
　　Victualler & S—l Master in the late Riot'
Shelburne Papers

GUILDHALL

Feltmakers Company, Court Book, 1726–9, vol. iii, MS 1570/3
Stephen Monteage, *The Diary*, MSS 205
St Andrew's, Holborn, *Register of Burials*
Society of Genealogists, *The Apprentices of Great Britain, 1710–1762,
　　extracted from the Inland Revenue Books at the Public Record Office*,
　　33 vols. (1921–8)

UNIVERSITY COLLEGE LIBRARY, LONDON

Bentham MSS

NEWSPAPERS

The Annual Register
Applebee's Original Weekly
    Journal
The Argus (Melbourne)
Baldwin's London Weekly Journal
Berrow's Worcester Journal
The British Journal
The Colony (Norfolk,
    Massachusetts)
The Craftsman
The Daily Post
The Gentleman's Magazine

Lloyd's Evening Post
The London Chronicle
The London Gazette
The London Magazine
The Middlesex Journal
The Observer
The Penny–London Post
The Public Advertiser
Reade's Weekly Journal
The Weekly Journal or Saturday
    Post

PERIODICAL PUBLICATIONS OF CRIMINAL ADMINISTRATION

The Ordinary of Newgate, His Account of the Behaviour, Confession, and Dying Words of the Malefactors Who were Executed at Tyburn, 1703–72

The Whole Proceedings upon the King's Commission of Oyer and Terminer and Gaol Delivery for the City of London and also the Gaol Delivery for the County of Middlesex, 1714–1800

PARLIAMENTARY PAPERS

Report from the Committee Appointed to Enquire into the Best Mode of Providing Sufficient Accommodation for the Increased Trade and Shipping of the Port of London (1795–6)

Second Report from the Select Committee Upon the Improvement of the Port of London (1799)

Report from the Select Committee ... on Foreign Trade. West India Docks (1823)

The Journals of the House of Commons

The Journals of the House of Lords

Calendar of State Papers, Colonial Series, America and the West Indies, vols. xxxiii–xxxv (1722–7), xxxvii (1730), xxxix (1732)

A Handlist of Proclamations Issued by Royal and other Constitutional

Authorities, 1714–1910, Bibliotheca Lindesiana, vol. viii (Wigan, 1913)

Acts of the Privy Council, Colonial Series 1745–1766

Handloom Weavers' Commission, vol. ii (1840)

House of Commons, Select Committee on Promissory Notes Under £5, 1st report (1826)

House of Commons, Select Committee on the State of Smithfield Market, 2nd report (July, 1828)

BOOKS PUBLISHED BEFORE 1810

'A Citizen of London', The Vices of London and Westminster (1751)

'An Impartial By-Stander', The Case of Mr R—ds (1758)

Anon., A Genuine Narrative of all the Street Robberies Committed since October last by James Dalton (1728)

Anon., A Letter from a Member of Parliament for a Borough in the West ... Concerning the Excise Bill (1733)

Anon., A Narrative of All the Robberies, Escapes, &c. of John Sheppard (1724)

Anon., A New Canting Dictionary (1725)

Anon., A Trip from St James's to the Royal Exchange (1744)

Anon., A True Narrative of All the Proceedings Against the Weavers (1675)

Anon., An Apology for the Business of Pawnbroking (1744)

Anon., An Essay on Bulk Tobacco (1692)

Anon., An Essay to Prove: That Regrators, Engrossers, Forestallers, Hawkers and Jobbers of Corn, Cattle and other Marketable Goods ... are Destructive of Trade, Oppressive to the Poor, and a Common Nuisance to the Kingdom in General (1716)

Anon., An Oration on the Oppression of Jailors which was Spoken in the Fleet Prison on the 20th February 1731 (1731)

Anon., The Beggar's Wedding; Or, Rackall the Gaol Keeper Outwitted (1729)

Anon., Black Tom (1686), reprinted in Roger Thompson (ed.), Samuel Pepys' Penny Merriments (New York, 1977)

Anon., The Case of the Inhabitants of the Cities of London and Westminster, and the Suburbs thereof, as also the Inhabitants of the Adjacent Counties, Relating to the Oppression They Lye under by Means of *the Forestallers, Engrossers, and Jobbers of Cattle and Flesh-Provisions brought to the several Markets* (1718)

Anon., *The Case of the Journeyman Taylors* (1745)

Anon., *The Declaration of John Matthews Deliver'd to a Friend Two Days before his Death* (1719)

Anon., *Essay on Trade and Commerce* (1770)

Anon., *The Foreigner's Guide: Or, A Necessary and Instructive Companion Both for the Foreigner and Native in their Tour through the Cities of London and Westminster* (1729)

Anon., *Frauds and Abuses of the Coal Dealers Detected* (1747)

Anon., *The Genuine and Authentick Account of the Life and Transactions of William Parsons, Esq.* (1751)

Anon., *The History of Wat Tyler and Jacke Straw, Chap-Book* (1750)

Anon., *Letter from a Country Gentleman in the Province of Munster to His Grace the Lord Primate* (Dublin, 1741)

Anon., *The Life and Times of Sir Thomas Deveil* (1748)

Anon., *Public Nuisance Considered* (1754)

Anon., *Robin Hood and Little John* (1730)

Anon., *Select Trials at the Sessions-House in the Old Bailey*, 4 vols. (1742)

Anon., *Spitalfields and Shoreditch in an Uproar; Or, the Devil to Pay with the English and Irish* (1736)

Anon., *Tricks of the Town Laid Open; Or, a Companion for Country Gentlemen* (1747)

Anon., *Villainy Exploded* (1728)

Anon., *Wat Tyler and Jack Straw: Or, the Mob Reformers, Or, the Comical Humours of Justice Wantbrains* (1730)

Anon., *The Whole Life and Conversation, Birth, Parentage, and Education of John Sutton* (1711)

Antoril, Andre João, *Cultura e opulencia do Brasil* (Lisbon, 1711)

Barrington, Daines, *Observations on the More Antient Statutes* (1766)

'B.E.', *Dictionary of the Canting Crew* (1700)

Behn, Aphra, *Oroonoko* (1688)

Bellers, John, *Essays About the Poor, Manufactures, Trade, Plantations and Immorality* (1698)

Bentham, Jeremy, *Panopticon; Or, the Inspection House* (1787)
    Errors of the Present Practice of Cooking (1796)

Bentham, M. S., *The Life of Brigadier-General Sir Samuel Bentham* (1862)

Bentham, Samuel, *Services Rendered in the Civil Department of the*

Navy in Investigating and Bringing to Official Notice Abuses and Imperfections (1813)

Berkeley, George, *The Querist* (1735)

Bird, T., *Lieutenant Bird's Letter from the Shades to Thomas Bambridge in Newgate* (1729)

Blackstone, William, *Commentaries on the Laws of England* (1765–9)

Blizard, William, *Desultory Reflections on Police, with an Essay on the Means of Preventing Crimes and Amending Criminals* (1785)

Bluett, Thomas, *Some Memoirs of the Life of Job, the Son of Solomon* (1734)

Bohum, W., *Privilegia Londini*, 3rd edn (1723)

Bolts, William, *Considerations on India Affairs* (1772)

Bowring, John (ed.), *The Works of Jeremy Bentham* (New York, 1962)

Bramah, Joseph, *A Dissertation on the Construction of Locks* (1781)

Bunyan, John, *The Pilgrim's Progress* (1684)

Burke, Edmund, *Works*, 5th edn (Boston, 1877)

Burrington, George, *An Answer to Dr William Brakenridge's Letter* (1757)

Burt, Captain Edmund, *The Compleat Ship-Wright* (1664)

Burt, Edward, *Letters from a Gentleman in the North of Scotland* (1754)

Butler, Herbert Thurston and Donald Attwater (eds), *Butler's Lives of the Saints* (1956)

Cadogan, William, *Essay on the Nursing and Management of Children* (1750)

Campbell, R., *The London Tradesman* (1747)

Carew, Bampfylde-Moore, *The Life and Adventures of Bampfylde-Moore Carew noted Devonshire stroller and Dog-stealer during his passage to the plantations in America* (1749)

Chambers, E., *Encyclopædia; Or, An Universal Dictionary of the Arts and Sciences* (1728)

Charnock, John, *History of Marine Architecture*, 3 vols. (1800)

Chisholm, Colin, *An Essay on the Malignant Pestilential Fever* (Philadelphia, 1799)

Colquhoun, Patrick, *The State of Indigence* (1799)
  A Treatise on the Commerce and Police of the River Thames (1800)
  Treatise on the Police of the Metropolis (1795)

Coppe, Abiezer, *A Fiery Flying Roll: A Word from the Lord to all the Great Ones of the Earth* (1649)

Cosgrave, J., *A Genuine History of the Lives and Actions of the Most*

Notorious Irish Highwaymen, Tories and Rapparees (Wilmington, Delaware, 1799)

Crabbe, George, *The Poetical Works* (1884)

Crowley, Frank (ed.), *A Documentary History of Australia*, vol. i, *Colonial Australia, 1788–1840* (Melbourne, 1980)

Cugoano, Ottobah, *Thoughts and Sentiments on the Evil and Wicked Traffic of the Slavery and Commerce of the Human Species* (1787)

Defoe, Daniel, *Augusta Triumphans* (1728)

　A Brief History of the Poor Palatine Refugees (1709)

　The Complete English Tradesman (1726)

　Giving Alms No Charity (1704)

　The Great Law of Subordination Consider'd (1724)

　The History of the Remarkable Life of John Sheppard (1724)

　A Plan of English Commerce (1722)

　The Review (1705)

　Street-Robberies Consider'd (1728)

　A Tour through the Whole Island of Great Britain, 2 vols. (1724–7)

D'Urfey, Thomas, *Collin's Walk Through London and Westminster* (1690)

Edolis, William, *Letters from America, Historical and Descriptive* (1792)

Edwards, Bryan, *An Historical Survey of the Island of Saint Domingo* (1796)

Entick, John, *A New and Accurate History and Survey of London, Westminster, Southwark and Places Adjacent* (1766)

Equiano, Olaudah, *The Interesting Narrative of the Life of Olaudah Equiano or Gustavus Vasa, the African, Written by Himself* (1789)

Exquemelin, A. O., *The Buccaneers of America*, trans. Alexis Brown (1969)

Falconer, William, *An Universal Dictionary of the Marine* (1769)

Ferguson, Adam, *An Essay on the History of Civil Society* (1767)

　Principles of Moral and Political Science (1792)

Fielding, Henry, *An Enquiry into the Causes of the Late Increase of Robbers*, 2nd edn (1751)

　A Journal of a Voyage to Lisbon (1754)

　A Journey from this World to the Next (1742)

Fielding, John, *A Brief Description of the Cities of London and Westminster* (1776)

　Extracts from Such of the Penal Laws as Particularly relate to the Peace and Good Order of this Metropolis (1761)

　Extracts from the Penal Laws (1768)

　Plan for Preventing Robberies within 20 Miles of London (1755)

Some Proper Cautions to the Merchants, Tradesmen, and Shopkeepers of the Cities of London and Westminster (1776)

Fletcher, Andrew, *An Account of a Conversation Concerning a Right Regulation of Governments for the Common Good of Mankind* (1703)

Two Discourses Concerning the Affairs of Scotland (1698)

Foote, Samuel, *The Tailors; A Tragedy for Warm Weather* (1778)

Franklin, Benjamin, *Papers*, ed. William B. Willcox (New Haven, 1982)

Freneau, Philip, *Poems*, ed. Fred Lewis Pattee (New York, 1903)

Gast, John, *Calumny Defeated* (1802)

Gay, John, *The Poetical Works of John Gay*, ed. G. C. Faber (1969)

'G. E.', *Authentick Memoirs of the Life and Surprising Adventures of John Sheppard by Way of Familiar Letters from a Gentleman in Town*, 2nd edn (1724)

Gent, Thomas, *The Life of Thomas Gent, Esq.* (1832)

Gibbon, Edward, *The Decline and Fall of the Roman Empire* (1776–88)

Letters, ed. J. E. Norton (1956)

Godwin, William, *Enquiry Concerning Political Justice* (1798), ed. Isaac Kramnick (1976)

Grainger, James, *The Sugar-Cane: A Poem* (1764)

Hale, Matthew, *A Discourse Touching Provision for the Poor* (1683)

Pleas of the Crown (1682)

Hanway, Jonas, *On the Custom of Vails-Giving in England* (1760)

Harriott, John, *Struggles Through Life: Exemplified in the Various Travels and Adventures in Europe, Asia, Africa, and America*, 2 vols. (1809)

Hawles, John, *The Englishman's Right: A Dialogue Between a Barrister-at-Law and a Juryman*, 8th edn (1771)

Hewitt, J., *A Journal of the Proceedings of J. Hewitt*, 2nd edn (1790)

Proceedings on the Silk Act (1791)

Hodgson, Ralph, *The Conduct of Ralph Hodgson, Esq.; One of His Majesty's Justices of the Peace for the County of Middlesex in the Affair of the Coal-Heavers* (1768)

Holcroft, Thomas, *Life*, ed. Elbridge Colby (1925)

Hone, William, *Every Day Book*, 2 vols. (1826–7)

Horsmanden, Daniel, *The New York Conspiracy. Or a History of the Negro Plot* (1810)

Houghton, John, *Husbandry and Trade Improv'd*, 4 vols., 2nd edn (1728)

Howard, John, *The State of the Prisons in England and Wales*, 2nd edn (1780)

Hume, David, *Philosophical Works*, eds T. H. Green and T. H.Grose, 4 vols. (1878)

Hutton, W., *The History of Derby* (1791)

Janssen, Stephen Theodore, *Tables of Death Sentences* (1772)

Johnson, Captain Charles, *A General History of the Pyrates* (1724)

Johnstone, Charles, *Chrysal* (1760)

Junius, *Letters* (1786)

Kames, Lord, *Sketches of the History of Man* (Edinburgh, 1788)

King, Charles, *The British Merchant or Commerce Preserv'd* (1721)

King, Gregory, *Natural and Political Observations and Conclusions upon the State and Condition of England* (1696)

Lind, Dr, James, *Essay on Diseases Incidental to Europeans in Hot Climates* (1768)
  Treatise of the Scurvy (1753)

Locke, John, *Second Treatise of Civil Government* (1690)

Lott, Yeoman, *An Account of the Proposals Made for the Benefit of His Majesty's Naval Service* (1777)
  Important Hints Towards an Amendment of the Royal Dockyards (1767)

Lucas, Theophilus, *Authentick Memoirs Relating to the Lives ... of the Gamesters and Sharpers*, 2nd edn (1744)

McArthur, John, *Principles and Practices of Naval and Military Courts Martial* (1792)

McLean, Hector, *An Inquiry into the Nature and Causes of the Great Mortality Among the Troops at St Domingo* (1797)

Mandeville, Bernard, *An Enquiry into the Causes of the Frequent Executions at Tyburn* (1725)
  The Fable of the Bees: Or, Private Vices, Publick Benefits (1714), ed. Philip Harth (1970)

Marryott, Matthew, *An Account of Workhouses* (1730)

Mathews, John, *Remarks on the Cause and Progress of the Scarcity and Dearness of Cattle, Swine, Cheese, &c.* (1797)

Middleton, John, *A View of the Agriculture in Middlesex* (1798)

Misson, H., *Memoirs and Observations in his Travels Over England* (1719)

Muralt, Béat Louis de, *Letters Describing the Character and Customs of the English and French Nations* (1726)

Newton, Isaac, *Correspondence*, ed. J. F. Scott (Cambridge, 1967)

Oglethorpe, James Edward, *The Sailors' Advocate* (1728)

O'Rahilly, Egan, *Poems*, eds P. Dineen and T. O'Donoghue (1911)

Paine, Thomas, *The Rights of Man* (1791), ed. Henry Collins (1976)

Parker, George, *A View of Society*, 2 vols. (1781)

Pearce, William, *General View of the Agriculture in Berkshire* (1794)

Pett, Phineas, *Autobiography*, ed. W. G. Perrin, Navy Records Society, vol. li (1918)
  Economic Writings, ed. C. H. Hull, 2 vols (1899)

Petty, William, *Political Arithmetick* (1690)

Place, Francis, *Autobiography*, ed. Mary Thale (Cambridge, 1971)

Postlethwayt, Malachy, *The Universal Dictionary of Trade and Commerce*, 3rd edn (1766)

Prior, Matthew, *The Widow and her Cat* (1709)

Prior, Thomas, *A List of Absentees of Ireland*, 3rd edn (Dublin, 1769)

Pugh, Matthew, *The Humble Petition of Matthew Pugh, Late Steward to the Poor Prisoners in the King's Bench* (1732?)

Ramazzini, Bernardino, *De Morbis Artificium: Diseases of Tradesmen*, 2nd edn (1750)

Ramsay, John, *Account of the Life, Adventures, and Transactions of Robert Ramsay, alias Sir Robert Gray* (1742)

Robertson, William, *The History of Scotland* (Philadelphia, 1759)

Sancho, Ignatius, *Letters* (1782)

Sandwich, Earl of, *Private Papers*, eds G. R. Barnes and J. H. Owen, Navy Record Society, vol. iv (1938)

Saussure, César de, *A Foreign View of England in the Reigns of George I and George II* (1725–30), trans. van Muyden (1902)

Saxe, Maurice de, *Reveries; Or, Memoirs upon the Art of War*, trans. William Fawcett (1757)

Shaw, William, *Select Tracts and Documents Illustrative of English Monetary History, 1626–1730* (1896)

Shepeard, James, *Some Reasons Why It Should Not Be Expected the Government Would Permit the Speech or Paper of James Shepeard which He Delivered at the Place of Execution to be Printed* (1718)

Smith, Adam, *The Theory of Moral Sentiments* (1759), 9th edn (1801)
  The Wealth of Nations (1776)

Smith, Alexander, *A Complete History of the Lives and Robberies of the Most Notorious Highwaymen* (1719)

Smith, George, *An Universal Military Dictionary* (1779)

Smollett, Tobias, *A Complete History of England*, 3rd edn (1760)
  Roderick Random (1748), ed. Paul-Gabriel Bouće (1979)

Snelgrave, William, *A New Account of Some Parts of Guinea and the Slave Trade* (1734)

Spence, Thomas, *The Restorer of Society to its Natural State* (1801)

Sprigge, Timothy L. S. (ed.), *Correspondence of Jeremy Bentham*, vol. ii, *1777–1780* (1968)

Steuart, Sir James, *An Inquiry into the Principles of Political Oeconomy*, ed. A. S. Skinner, 2 vols (Edinburgh, 1966)

Sutherland, William, *Britain's Glory: Or, Shipbuilding Unveil'd*, 2nd edn (1726)

    The Ship-Builder's Assistant (1711)

Swift, Jonathan, *Directions to Servants* (1745)

    A Discourse Concerning the Mechanical Operation of the Spirit (1704)

    A Short View of the State of Ireland (1727–8)

Tatham, William, *An Historical and Practical Essay on the Culture and Commerce of Tobacco* (1800)

    The Political Economy of Inland Navigation (1799)

Told, Silas, *Life*, 3rd edn (1796)

Tower, Joseph, *Observations on the Rights and Duty of Juries in Trials for Libels* (1784)

Trueman, Thomas, *The Custom of Vails Giving* (176?)

Tucker, Josiah, *The Elements of Commerce and Theory of Taxes* (1755)

Vanderlint, Jacob, *Money Answers All Things* (1734)

Vaughan, William, *A Letter to a Friend on Commerce and Free Ports and London Docks* (1796)

    On Wet Docks, Quays, and Warehouses for the Port of London (1793)

Walker, Thomas, *The Quaker's Opera; Or, the Escapes of Jack Sheppard* (1728)

Walwyn, William, *The English Soldier's Standard* (1649)

Ward, Ned, *The Wooden World Dissected* (1707)

Webster, William, *Arithmetick in Epitome* (1715)

Wedgwood, Josiah, *Selected Letters*, eds Ann Finer and George Savage (1965)

Wells, Edmund, *The Young Gentleman's Course in Mathematics* (1714)

Wesley, Charles, *The Journal* (1849)

Wesley, John, *The Journal*, ed. Nehemiah Curnock, 3 vols (1938)

Winstanley, Gerrard, *The Law of Freedom in a Platform or True Magistracy Restored* (1652), reprinted in George Sabine (ed.), *The Works of Gerrard Winstanley* (Ithaca, New York, 1941)

Wollstonecraft, Mary, *The Wrongs of Woman; Or, Maria: A Fragment* (1798)

PUBLISHED COLLECTIONS OF DOCUMENTS

Aspinall, A. (ed.), *The Early English Trade Unions: Documents from the Home Office Papers* (1949)

Bromley, J. S. (ed.), *The Manning of the Royal Navy: Selected Public Pamphlets, 1693–1873*, Navy Record Society (1968)

Browne, William H. (ed.), *Archives of Maryland: Proceedings and Acts* (Baltimore, 1894)

Calendar of Home Office Papers of the Reign of George III, 1766–1769

Galton, F. W., *Select Documents Illustrating the History of Trade Unionism*, vol. i, *The Tailoring Trade* (1896)

Hening, William W., *The Statutes at Large Being a Collection of All the Laws of Virginia* (1823)

Lloyd, Christopher (ed.), *The Health of Seamen: Selections from the Works of Dr James Lind, Sir Gilbert Blane, and Dr Thomas Trotter*, Navy Record Society, vol. cvii (1965)

Merriman, R. D. (ed.), *Queen Anne's Navy: Documents Concerning the Administration of the Navy of Queen Anne, 1702–1714*, Navy Record Society (1961)

Walvin, James, *The Black Presence: A Documentary History of the Negro in England, 1555–1860* (New York, 1971)

Williams, Eric (ed.), *Documents of West Indian History*, vol. i, *1492–1655* (Port of Spain, 1963)

BOOKS PUBLISHED AFTER 1810

Abajian, James de T., *Blacks in Selected Newspapers, Censuses and Other Sources: An Index to Names and Subjects* (Boston, 1977)

Abell, Westcott, *The Shipwright's Trade* (1948)

Adams, Francis D. and Sanders, Barry (eds), *Three Black Writers in Eighteenth Century England* (Belmont, California, 1971)

Albert, William, *The Turnpike Road System in England, 1663–1840* (Cambridge, 1972)

Albion, Robert G., *Forests and Sea Power: The Timber Problems of the Royal Navy, 1652–1862* (Cambridge, Mass., 1926)

Altick, Richard, *The Shows of London* (Cambridge, Mass., 1978)

Amelungen, C., *Werkschutz und Betriebskriminalität* (Hamburg, 1960)

Amnesty International, *When the State Kills ... The Death Penalty: A Human Rights Issue* (1989)

Appleby, Joyce Oldham, *Economic Thought and Ideology in Seventeenth Century England* (Princeton, 1978)

Ashton, John, *The Fleet: Its River, Prison and Marriages* (1887)
Social Life in the Reign of Queen Anne (1883)

Ashton, T. S., *Economic Fluctuations in England, 1700–1800* (1959)

Ashton, T. S. and Joseph Sykes, *The Coal Industry of the Eighteenth Century*, 2nd edn (Manchester, 1964)

Barnes, Charles B., *The Longshoremen* (New York, 1915)

Barrow, John, *The Life of George Lord Anson* (1839)

Baugh, Daniel A., *British Naval Administration in the Age of Walpole* (Princeton, 1965)

Beattie, J. M., *Crime and the Courts in England, 1660–1800* (Princeton, 1986)

Beck, William T. and Ball, T. Frederick, *The London Friends' Meetings: Showing the Rise of the Society of Friends in London* (1869)

Beier, A. L., Cannadine, David and Rosenheim, James M. (eds), *The First Modern Society: Essays in English History in Honour of Lawrence Stone* (1989)

Beier, A. L. and Finlay, Roger, *London, 1500–1700: The Making of the Metropolis* (1986)

Beloff, Max, *Public Order and Popular Disturbances, 1660–1714* (1938)

Berg, Maxine, Hudson, Pat and Sonenscher, Michael (eds), *Manufacture in Town and Country before the Factory* (Cambridge, 1983)

Berlin, Ira and Hoffman, Ronald (eds), *Slavery and Freedom in the Age of the American Revolution* (Virginia, 1983)

Beveridge, William, et al., *Prices and Wages in England from the Twelfth to the Nineteenth Century*, vol. i, *Price Tables: Mercantile Era* (1939)

Billias, George Athan, *General John Glover and his Marblehead Mariners* (Boston, 1958)

Bleackley, Horace, *The Hangmen of England* (1929)
Jack Sheppard (Edinburgh, 1933)

Bloch, Ivan, *Sexual Life in England*, trans. William H. Forster (1958)

Bloomberg, Joe, *Looking Back: A Docker's Life* (1979)

Bolam, David, *Unbroken Community* (Saffron Walden, 1952)

Bonora, Beth and Elissa Krauss, *Jurywork: Systematic Techniques* (New York, 1979)

Bonser, K. J., *The Drovers: Who They Were and How They Went: An Epic of the English Countryside* (1970)

Borrow, George, *Lavengro* (1851), Everyman edn (1961)

Bowen, Frank C., *Sea Slang: A Dictionary of Old-Timers' Expressions and Epithets* (n.d.)

Brailsford, H. N., *The Levellers and the English Revolution* (Stanford, California, 1961)

Brewer, John and John Styles (eds), *An Ungovernable People: The English and Their Law in the Seventeenth and Eighteenth Centuries* (1980)

Bridenbaugh, Carl and Roberta, *No Peace Beyond the Line: The English in the Caribbean, 1624–1690* (New York, 1972)

Broodbank, Joseph G., *History of the Port of London*, 2 vols (1921)

Brown, John, *A Memoir of Robert Blincoe, an Orphan Boy: Sent from the Workhouse of St Pancras, London, at Seven Years of Age, to Endure the Horrors of a Cotton-Mill* (Manchester, 1832), republished by Caliban Books (1977)

Brown, John, *Sixty Years' Gleanings from Life's Harvest* (Cambridge, 1858)

Bruce, Philip, *Economic History of Virginia in the Seventeenth Century* (New York, 1896)

Bryant, Arthur, *Samuel Pepys*, 3 vols. (Cambridge, 1933–9)

Buck, Anne, *Dress in Eighteenth Century England* (1979)

Buckley, Roger Norman, *Slaves in Red Coats: The British West India Regiments, 1795–1815* (New Haven, 1979)

Burke, Peter, *Popular Culture in Early Modern Europe* (New York, 1978)

Burn, John, *The Fleet Register, Comprising the History of Fleet Marriages* (1833)

Caffentzis, C. G., *Clipped Coins, Abused Words and Civil Government: John Locke's Philosophy of Money* (New York, 1989)

Calder, Angus, *Revolutionary Empire: The Rise of the English-speaking Empires from the Fifteenth Century to the 1780s* (New York, 1981)

Calvet, Louis-Jean, *Les Langues Véhiculaires* (Paris, 1981)

Campbell, John Lord, *The Lives of the Chief Justices of England* (Philadelphia, 1851)

Capp, B. S., *The Fifth Monarchy Men: A Study in Seventeenth Century English Millenarianism* (1972)

Carlyle, Thomas, *Chartism* (1839)

Castro, J. Paul de, *The Gordon Riots* (1926)

Chandler, F. W., *The Literature of Roguery*, 2 vols (New York, 1907)

Chapman, Stanley D., *The Early Factory Masters: The Transition to the Factory System in the Midlands Textile Industry* (1967)

Checkland, S. G., *Scottish Banking: A History: 1695–1973* (1975)

Chitnis, Anand C., *The Scottish Enlightenment: A Social History* (1976)

Clark, Anna, *Women's Silence. Men's Violence: Sexual Assault in England, 1770–1845* (1987)

Clark, G. N., *The Later Stuarts, 1660–1714* (1944)

Clark, Nathaniel G., *A Scale of Prices for Job Work, on Old Ships ... for the Shipwrights of the River Thames* (1825)

Clark, Sam and Donnelly, James S., Jr. (eds), *Irish Peasants: Violence and Political Unrest, 1780–1914* (Madison, Wisconsin, 1983)

Cobley, John, *The Crimes of the First Fleet Convicts* (Sydney, 1970)

Cockburn, J. S. (ed.), *Crime in England, 1550–1800* (Princeton, 1977)

Colletti, Lucio, *From Rousseau to Lenin* (New York, 1972)

Compton, Thomas, *Recollections of Spitalfields: An Honest Man and his Employers* (1894)

Connolly, James, *Labour in Irish History* (Dublin, 1910)

Connolly, Sean J., *Priests and People in Pre-Famine Ireland, 1780–1845* (Dublin, 1982)

Cooper, David D., *The Lesson of the Scaffold: The Public Execution Controversy in Victorian England* (Athens, Ohio, 1974)

Corkery, Daniel, *The Hidden Ireland: A Study of Gaelic Munster in the 18th Century* (Dublin, 1925)

Coyne, Franklin, *The Development of the Cooperage Industry in the United States, 1620–1940* (Chicago, 1940)

Craig, Maurice, *Dublin 1660–1860* (Dublin, 1969)

Crocker, Thomas Crofton, *Researches in the South of Ireland* (1824)

Cullen, L. M., *An Economic History of Ireland since 1660* (1972)

Davis, K. G., *The Royal African Company* (1957)

Davis, Ralph, *The Rise of the English Shipping Industry in the 17th and 18th Centuries* (1962)

Deerr, Noel, *The History of Sugar*, 2 vols (1949)

Delehaye, H., *The Legends of the Saints: An Introduction to Hagiography* (1907)

Devine, T. M. and Dickson, David (eds), *Ireland and Scotland, 1600–1850: Parallels and Contrasts in Economic and Social Development* (Edinburgh, 1983)

Dillard, J. H., *All-American English* (1975)

Dobson, Austin, *Eighteenth Century Vignettes* (Oxford, 1923)

Dobson, C. R., *Masters and Journeymen: A Prehistory of Industrial Relations, 1717–1800* (1980)

Dodd, George, *Days at the Factories; Or, the Manufacturing Industry of Great Britain Described* (1843)

The Food of London (1856)

DuBois, W. E. B., *The Suppression of the African Slave Trade* (New York, 1896)

Duffy, William, *Sugar Blues* (New York, 1975)

Dugan, James, *The Great Mutiny* (1965)

Dunlop, O. Jocelyn, *English Apprenticeship and Child Labour: A History* (New York, 1912)

Dunn, Richard S., *Sugar and Slaves: The Rise of the Planter Class in the English West Indies, 1624–1730* (Chapel Hill, 1972)

Ehrman, John, *The Navy in the War of William III, 1689–1697* (Cambridge, 1953)

Ellis, P. Beresford, *A History of the Irish Working Class* (1972)

Engels, Frederick, *The Condition of the Working Class in England*, trans. W. O. Henderson and W. H. Chaloner (New York, 1958)

Erdman, David, *Blake: Prophet Against Empire: A Poet's Interpretation of the History of His Own Times*, 3rd edn (Princeton, 1977)

Essick, Robert N., *William Blake, Printmaker* (Princeton, 1980)

Evans, E. Estyn, *The Personality of Ireland: Habitat, Heritage, and History* (1973)

Evans, Robin, *The Fabrication of Virtue: English Prison Architecture, 1750–1840* (Cambridge, 1982)

Ewers, John C., *The Blackfeet, Raiders on the Northwestern Plains* (Norman, Oklahoma, 1958)

Faller, Lincoln B., *Turned to Account: The Forms and Functions of Criminal Biography in Late Seventeenth and Early Eighteenth century England* (Cambridge, 1987)

Feaveryear, Albert, *The Pound Sterling: A History of English Money* (1963)

Fincham, John, *A History of Naval Architecture* (1851)

Fisher, Chris, *Custom, Work and Market Capitalism: The Forest of Dean Colliers, 1788–1888* (1981)

Fisher, William, *The Forest of Essex: Its History, Laws, Administration and Ancient Customs* (1887)

Flash, Martin, *The Sinks of London Laid Open* (1848)

Fortesque, John, *A History of the British Army*, vol. iv, part 1, *1789–1801* (1915)

Foss, Edward, *The Judges of England*, 7 vols (1864)

Foucault, Michel, *Discipline and Punish: The Birth of the Prison*, trans. Alan Sheridan (1977)

Fox Bourne, H. R., *John Locke: A Biography*, 2 vols (1876)

Froude, J. A., *The English in Ireland in the Eighteenth Century* (New York, 1874)

Fryer, Peter, *Staying Power: The History of Black People in Britain* (1984)

Furniss, Edgar, *The Position of the Laborer in a System of Nationalism: A Study in the Labor Theories of the Later English Mercantilists* (New York, 1920)

Gardiner, S. R., *History of the Commonwealth and Protectorate, 1649– 1656*, vol. i (1903)

Gatrell, V. A. C., Lenman, Bruce and Parker, Geoffrey (eds), *Crime and the Law: The Social History of Crime in Western Europe since 1500* (1980)

Geggus, David Patrick, *Slavery, War, and Revolution: The British Occupation of Saint Domingue, 1793–1798* (Oxford, 1982)

George, M. Dorothy, *London Life in the Eighteenth Century* (1965)

Giedion, Siegfried, *Mechanization Takes Command: A Contribution to Anonymous History* (New York, 1948)

Gilding, Bob, *The Journeyman Coopers of East London*, History Workshop Pamphlet, no. 4 (1971)

Gillis, John, *For Better, For Worse: British Marriages, 1600 to the Present* (New York, 1985)

Goodwin, Albert, *The Friends of Liberty: The English Democratic Movement in the Age of the French Revolution* (Cambridge, Mass., 1979)

Goreau, Angeline, *Reconstructing Aphra: A Social Biography of Aphra Behn* (New York, 1980)

Gray, Lewis C., *History of Agriculture in the Southern United States to 1860* (Washington DC, 1933)

Green, Thomas A., *Verdict According to Conscience: Perspectives on the English Criminal Trial Jury, 1200–1800* (Chicago, 1985)

Greenwood, James, *The Seven Curses of London* (1867)

Gutman, Herbert, *The Black Family in Slavery and Freedom, 1750– 1925* (New York, 1976)

Gwathmey, John, *Historical Register of Virginians in the Revolution: Soldiers, Sailors, Marines, 1775–1783* (Dietz, Virginia, 1938)

Haldane, A. R. B., *The Drove Roads of Scotland* (Newton Abbot, 1973)

Hale, William, *An Appeal to the Public in Defence of the Spitalfields Acts* (1822)

Hardiman, James, *Irish Minstrelsy: Or, Bardic Remains of Ireland with English Poetical Translations* (1831)

Harding, Allan, *A Social History of English Law* (1966)

Hawkins, J. H., *History of the Worshipful Company of the Art and Mistery of the Feltmakers of London* (1917)

Hay, Douglas, et al., *Albion's Fatal Tree: Crime and Society in Eighteenth Century England* (1975)

Hayter, Tony, *The Army and the Crowd in Mid-Georgian London* (1978)

Hecht, J. Jean, *The Domestic Servant Class in Eighteenth Century England* (1956)

Heckscher, Eli F., *Mercantilism*, 2 vols (1935)

Herndon, G. Melvin, *William Tatham and the Culture of Tobacco* (Florida, 1969)

Hibbert, Christopher, *King Mob: The Story of Lord George Gordon and the Riots of 1780* (1958)

Hill, Christopher, *The Experience of Defeat: Milton and Some Contemporaries* (1984)

   Milton and the English Revolution (1978)

   Puritanism and Revolution (1958)

Hilton, George W., *The Truck System including a History of the British Truck Acts, 1465–1960* (1960)

Himmelfarb, Gertrude, *Victorian Minds* (New York, 1968)

Hoagland, Kathleen (ed.), *1000 Years of Irish Poetry* (New York, 1953)

Hohman, Elmo Paul, *Seamen Ashore* (New Haven, 1952)

Hollond, John, *Two Discourses of the Navy*, Navy Record Society (1896)

Hoon, Elizabeth, *The Organization of the English Customs System, 1697–1786* (New York, 1938)

Hossain, Hameeda, *The Company of Weavers of Bengal: The East India Company and the Organization of Textile Production in Bengal, 1750–1813* (Bombay, 1988)

Howe, Ellie, *The London Compositor 1785–1900* (1947)

Howson, Gerald, *The Thief-Taker General: The Rise and Fall of Jonathan Wild* (1970)

Humpherus, Henry, *History of the Origin and Progress of the Company of Watermen and Lightermen*, 2 vols (1887)

Ignatieff, Michael, *A Just Measure of Pain: The Penitentiary in the Industrial Revolution, 1750–1850* (New York, 1978)

Inglis, Brian, *Poverty and the Industrial Revolution* (1971)

Innis, Harold A., *The Fur in Canada: An Introduction to Canadian Economic History*, revised edn (Toronto, 1970)

Insurance Company of North America, *Ports of the World: A Guide to Cargo Loss Control*, 10th edn (Philadelphia, 1976)

International Labour Conference, *Maximum Permissible Weight to be Carried by One Worker*, Report VI, 1 & 2 (Geneva, 1966)

Jackson, K. H. (ed.), *A Celtic Miscellany: Translations from the Celtic Literatures* (1971)

James, C. L. R., *The Black Jacobins: Toussaint l'Ouverture and the San Domingo Revolution*, 2nd edn (New York, 1963)

Jarvis, Robert C., *Customs Letter-Books of the Port of Liverpool, 1711– 1813*, Chatham Society, 3rd series, vol. xi (Manchester, 1954)

Johnson, W. Branch, *The English Prison Hulks* (1957)

Jones, P. E., *The Butchers of London* (1976)
The Worshipful Company of Poulters of the City of London (1965)

Jupp, E. P., *An Historical Account of the Worshipful Company of Carpenters of the City of London* (1848)

Kaminkow, Jack and Marion, *A List of Emigrants from England to America, 1718–1759* (Baltimore, 1964)
Original Lists of Emigrants in Bondage from London to the American Colonies, 1719–1744 (Baltimore, 1967)

Kaviraj, Narahari, *A Peasant Uprising in Bengal, 1783: The First Formidable Peasant Uprising against the Rule of the East India Company* (New Delhi, 1972)

Kerridge, Eric, *The Agricultural Revolution* (1967)

King, Peter, *The Development of the English Economy to 1750* (1971)

Kisch, Bruno, *Scales and Weights: An Historical Outline* (1965)

Knoop, Douglas and Jones, G. P., *The London Mason in the Seventeenth Century* (Manchester, 1935)

Kramer, Stella, *The English Craft Gilds: Studies in their Progress and Decline* (New York, 1927)

Kramnick, Isaac, *Bolingbroke and His Circle: The Politics of Nostalgia in the Age of Walpole* (Cambridge, Mass., 1968)

Langford, Paul, *The Excise Crisis: Society and Politics in the Age of Walpole* (1975)

Lascelles, E. C. P. and Bullock, S. S., *Dock Labour and Decasualisation* (1924)

Leach, Robert, *The Punch and Judy Show: History, Tradition and Meaning* (Athens, Georgia, 1985)

Lecky, W. E. H., *A History of Ireland in the Eighteenth Century*, 5 vols (New York, 1893)

Lehmann, Joseph, *The Model Major-General: A Biography of Field Marshal Lord Wolseley* (Boston, 1964)

Leslie-Melville, R., *The Life and Work of Sir John Fielding* (1934)

Li, Ming-Hsun, *The Great Recoinage of 1696 to 1699* (1963)

Lipson, E., *The History of the Woollen and Worsted Industries* (1921)

Longmate, Norman, *The Workhouse* (1974)

Lottes, Gunther, *Aufklarung und plebejisches Publikim zur Theorie und Praxis des englischen Radikalismus im spaten 18. Jahrhundert* (Oldenbourg: München, 1979)

Lyons, Frederick J., *Jonathan Wild: Prince of Robbers* (New York, 1936)

Macalister, R. A. Steward, *The Secret Languages of Ireland* (1937)

McClaughlin, Terence, *Dirt: A Social History as Seen Through the Uses and Abuses of Dirt* (New York, 1971)

McCloy, Shelby T., *French Inventions of the 18th Century* (Lexington, Kentucky, 1952)

McDowell, R. B., *Ireland in the Age of Imperialism and Revolution, 1760–1801* (1979)

MacFarlane, C., *The Lives and Exploits of Banditti and Robbers in all Parts of the World* (1837)

MacGoeghegan, James and Mitchell, John, *The History of Ireland, Ancient and Modern* (New York, 1868)

Mack, M. P., *Jeremy Bentham: An Odyssey of Ideas* (1963)

Mackay, Charles, *The Extraordinary Popular Delusions and the Madness of Crowds* (1841)

McMullan, John L., *The Canting Crew: London's Criminal Underworld, 1550–1700* (New Brunswick, 1984)

McShane, Harry, *No Mean Fighter* (1978)

Maitland, F. W. and Montague, F. C., *A Sketch of English Legal History* (1915)

Mantoux, Paul, *The Industrial Revolution in the Eighteenth Century: An Outline of the Beginnings of the Modern Factory System in England* (1928)

Manuel, Frank E., *A Portrait of Isaac Newton* (Cambridge, 1968)

Marshall, Mac (ed.), *Beliefs, Behaviors, and Alcoholic Beverages: A Cross-Cultural Survey* (Ann Arbor, 1980)

Marshall, P. J., *East India Fortunes: The British in Bengal in the 18th Century* (1974)

Marx, Karl, *Capital*, trans. Ben Fowkes, vol. i (1976)

Marx, Karl and Frederick Engels, *The Communist Manifesto* (1848)

Mason, Philip, *A Matter of Honour: An Account of the India Army, Its Officers and Men* (1976)

Massachusetts Soldiers and Sailors in the War of the Revolution (Boston, 1899)

Masur, Louis P., *Rites of Execution: Capital Punishment and the Transformation of American Culture, 1776–1865* (1989)

Maxwell, Constantia, *Dublin Under the Georges, 1714–1830* (1936)

Maxwell, Gordon, *The Highwayman's Heath: The Story in Fact and Fiction of Hounslow Heath* (1935)

Mayhew, Henry, *London Labour and the London Poor*, 4 vols (1861)

Meredith, J. and Anderson, H., *Folksongs of Australia* (Melbourne, 1967)

Métraux, Alfred, *Voodoo in Haiti*, trans. Hugo Charteris (New York, 1959)

Michinton, W. E. (ed.), *The Growth of English Overseas Trade in the Seventeenth and Eighteenth Centuries* (1969)

Middleton, Arthur Pierce, *Tobacco Coast: A Maritime History of the Chesapeake Bay in the Colonial Era* (Virginia, 1953)

Miller, Kerby A., *Emigrants and Exiles: Ireland and the Irish Exodus to North America* (New York, 1985)

Mintz, Sidney W., *Sweetness and Power: The Place of Sugar in Modern History* (New York, 1985)

Moody, T.W. (ed.), *A New History of Ireland*, vol. iii, *Early Modern Ireland 1534–1659* (1976), and vol. viii, *A Chronology of Irish History to 1976* (1982)

Moon, Penderel, *Warren Hastings and British India* (1947)

Morris, Roger, *The Royal Docklands During the Revolutionary and Napoleonic Wars* (Leicester, 1983)

Morris, William, *Signs of Change* (1888)

Morrison, Samuel Eliot, *John Paul Jones: A Sailor's Biography* (Boston, 1959)

Morton, A. L., *The World of the Ranters: Religious Radicalism in the English Revolution* (1970)

Mukherjee, Ramkrishna, *The Rise and Fall of the East India Company* (New York, 1974)

Myers, Robin and Michael Harris (eds), *Sale and Distribution of Books from 1700* (Oxford, 1982)

Nealy, James N., *The Mercier Book of Old Irish Street Ballads* (Cork, 1967)

Norris, John, *Shelburne and Reform* (1963)

O'Brien, George, *The Economic History of Ireland in the Eighteenth Century* (Dublin, 1918)

O'Callaghan, John Cornelius, *History of the Irish Brigades in the Service of France* (Glasgow, 1870)

O'Donovan, Jeremiah, *A Brief Account of the Author's Interview with His Countrymen* (Pittsburgh, 1864)

Ogg, David, *England in the Reigns of James II and William III* (1955)

Ott, Thomas D., *The Haitian Revolution, 1789–1804* (Tennessee, 1973)

Pakenham, Thomas, *The Year of Liberty: The Great Irish Rebellion of 1798* (1972)

Parkinson, C. Northcote, *The Trade Winds: A Study of British Overseas Trade During the French Wars, 1793–1815* (1948)

Pearce, Arthur, *The History of the Butchers' Company* (1929)

Penson, Lillian M., *The Colonial Agents of the British West Indies: A Study in Colonial Administration Mainly in the Eighteenth Century* (1924)

Piccinni, Giovanni, *The Tragical Comedy or Comical Tragedy of Punch and Judy* (Cambridge, 1926)

Pinchbeck, Ivy, *Women Workers and the Industrial Revolution, 1750–1850*, 3rd edn (1981)

Plumb, J. H., *Sir Robert Walpole*, 2 vols (1960)

Plummer, Alfred, *The London Weavers' Company, 1600–1970* (1972)

Pope, Dudley, *The Black Ship* (New York, 1964)

Powell, W. R. (ed.), *A History of Essex*, Victorian County History, vol. iv (1966)

Pressnell, L. S., *Country Banking in the Industrial Revolution* (1956)

Price, Jacob M., *France and the Chesapeake* (Ann Arbor, 1973)

Pucket, Newbell Niles and Helles, Murray, *Black Names in America: Origins and Usage* (Boston, 1975)

Quarles, Benjamin, *The Negro in the American Revolution* (Chapel Hill, 1961)

Radzinowicz, Leon, *A History of Criminal Law and Its Administration*, 4 vols (1948–68)

Rediker, Marcus, *Between the Devil and the Deep Blue Sea: Merchant Seamen, Pirates, and the Anglo-American Maritime World, 1700–1750* (Cambridge, 1987)

Reid, John Philip, *In a Defiant Stance: The Conditions of Law in Massachusetts Bay, the Irish Comparison, and the Coming of the American Revolution* (Philadelphia, 1977)

Ribton-Turner, C. J., *A History of Vagrants and Vagrancy and Beggars and Begging* (1887)

Ricardo, David, *Principles of Political Economy and Taxation*, ed. R. M. Hartwell (1971)

Robert, Joseph C., *The Story of Tobacco in America* (New York, 1952)

Robinson, William, *The History and Antiquities of the Parish of Hackney*, 2 vols (1842)

Rock, Paul and McIntosh, Mary (eds), *Deviance and Social Control* (1974)

Rosenfeld, Sybil, *The Theatre of the London Fairs in the 18th Century* (Cambridge, 1960)

Roth, Karl Heinz, *Die 'andere Arbeiterbewegung* (Munich, 1974)

Rothstein, Natalie, *Spitalfields Silks* (Victoria and Albert Museum, 1975)

Rudé, George, *Criminal and Victim: Crime and Society in Early Nineteenth-Century England* (1985)

Paris and London in the 18th Century: Studies in Popular Protest (1970)

Wilkes and Liberty: A Social Study of 1763 to 1774 (1962)

Rule, John, *The Experience of Labour in Eighteenth Century English Industry* (1981)

Rüsche, Georg and Kirchheimer, Otto, *Punishment and the Social Structure* (New York, 1939)

Saadawi, Nawal el, *Woman at Point Zero*, trans. Dr Sherif Hetata (1983)

Sainte Croix, G. E. M. de, *The Class Struggle in the Ancient Greek World from the Archaic Age to the Arab Conquests* (Ithaca, New York, 1981)

Salaman, R. A., *Dictionary of Tools Used in the Woodworking and Allied Trades, c. 1700–1970* (1975)

Salaman, Redcliffe N., *The History and Social Influence of the Potato*, revised edn (1985)

Salgado, Gamini, *The Elizabethan Underworld* (1977)

Samuel, Raphael, *East End Underworld: Chapters in the Life of Arthur Harding* (1981)

Sanborn, N. P., *General John Glover and his Marblehead Regiment in the Revolutionary War* (1903)

Schumpeter, Elizabeth Boody, *English Overseas Trade Statistics, 1697–1808* (Oxford, 1960)

Schwartz, Hillel, *The French Prophets: The History of a Millenarian Group in Eighteenth Century London* (Berkeley, 1980)

Scott, Arthur P., *Criminal Law in Colonial Virginia* (Chicago, 1930)

Scott, George Ryley, *The History of Cockfighting* (n.d.)

Scouller, Major R. E., *The Armies of Queen Anne* (Oxford, 1966)

Semmel, Bernard, *The Methodist Revolution* (New York, 1973)

Shaw, A. G. L., *Convicts and Colonies: A Study of Penal Transportation from Great Britain to Australia and Other Parts of the British Empire* (1966)

Shearman, Montague, *Athletics and Football* (1887)

Shelton, Walter J., *English Hunger and Industrial Disorders: A Study of Social Conflict during the First Decade of George III's Reign* (1973)

Sheppard, F. H. W. (ed.), *Spitalfields and Mile End New Town* (1957), vol. xvii, *Survey of London*

Sholl, Samuel, *A Short Historical Account of the Silk Manufacture in England with a Sketch of the First 58 Years of His Life* (1811)

Shyllon, Folarin O., *Black People in Britain, 1555–1833* (1977)
Black Slaves in Britain (1974)

Skrine, Francis Henry, *Fontenoy and Great Britain's Share in the War of the Austrian Succession, 1741–1748* (1906)

Smiles, Samuel, *Lives of the Engineers* 3 vols (1862)

Smith, Abbot Emerson, *Colonists in Bondage: White Servitude and Convict Labor in America, 1607–1776* (New York, 1971)

Smith, Olivia, *The Politics of Language, 1791–1819* (Oxford, 1984)

Smith, Raymond, *Sea-Coal for London: History of the Coal Factors in the London Market* (1961)

Smout, T. C., *A History of the Scottish People, 1560–1830* (1969)

Snyder, Francis and Douglas Hay (eds), *Labour, Law, and Crime: An Historical Perspective* (1987)

Sombart, Werner, *Luxury and Capitalism* (Ann Arbor, 1967)
The Quintessence of Capitalism: A Study of the History and Psychology of the Modern Business Man, trans. M. Epstein (New York, 1967)

Stephens, James Fitzjames, *A History of the Criminal Law in England*, 3 vols (1883)

Stern, Walter M., *The Porters of London* (1960)

Stevenson, John, *Popular Disturbances in England, 1700–1870* (1979)

Suilleabhain, Sean O., *Irish Wake Amusements* (Cork, 1967)

Surrey Record Society, *Surrey Apprentices from the Registers in the Public Record Office, 1711–1731* (1928)

Sydney, William Connor, *England and the English in the Eighteenth Century: Chapters in the Social History of the Times*, 2 vols (1891)

Taylor, F. W., *The Art of Cutting Metals* (New York, 1906)

Teignmouth, Lord and Harper, Charles G., *The Smugglers* (1923)

Thomas, Keith, *Religion and the Decline of Magic* (1977)

Thompson, E. P., *The Making of the English Working Class* (1963)
Whigs and Hunters: The Origin of the Black Act (1975)

Thompson, E. P. and Yeo, Eileen (eds), *The Unknown Mayhew* (1971)

Thornton, Peter, *Baroque and Rococo Silks* (1965)

Thring, Theodore, *Thring's Criminal Law of the Navy*, 2nd edn (1877)

Tomalin, Claire, *The Life and Death of Mary Wollstonecraft* (1974)

Toynbee, Arnold, *Lectures on the Industrial Revolution* (Rivington, 1884)

Turner, E. S., *What the Butler Saw: Two Hundred and Fifty Years of the Servant Problem* (1962)

Tyerman, Luke, *The Life of the Rev. George Whitefield*, 2 vols (1876)

Ure, Andrew, *The Philosophy of Manufacture* (1835)

Vilar, Pierre, *A History of Gold and Money, 1450–1920* (1976)

Viner, Jacob, *Guide to John Rae's Life of Adam Smith* (New York, 1965)

Walsh, J. E., *Ireland Sixty Years Ago*, 3rd edn (Dublin, 1851)

Warner, Frank, *The Silk Industry of the United Kingdom: Its Origins and Development* (1921)

Watts, Michael R., *The Dissenters: From the Reformation to the French Revolution* (Oxford, 1978)

Waugh, Norah, *The Cut of Men's Clothes, 1600–1900* (New York, 1964)

Wearmouth, Robert, *Methodism and the Common People in the 18th Century* (1943)

Webb, Igor, *From Custom to Capital: The English Novel and the Industrial Revolution* (1981)

Webb, Sidney and Beatrice, *English Local Government from the Revolution to the Municipal Corporations Act* (1906–1929)

Wells, H. G., *The Outline of History, Being a Plain History of the Life of Mankind* (1920)

Westerfield, Ray, *Middlemen in English Business, Particularly between 1660–1760* (New York, 1915)

Western, J. R, *The English Militia in the 18th Century* (1956)

Westfall, Richard S., *Never at Rest: A Biography of Isaac Newton* (Cambridge, 1986)

Willan, T. W., *The English Coasting Trade, 1600–1750* (Manchester, 1938)

Williams, T. D. (ed.), *Secret Societies of Ireland* (Dublin, 1973)

Wilson, Beckles, *The Great Company being a History of the Honourable Company of Merchant-Adventurers Trading into Hudson's Bay* (Toronto, 1899)

Wood, Peter H., *Black Majority: Negroes in Colonial South Carolina from 1670 through the Stono Rebellion* (New York, 1974)

Woodruff, Philip, *The Founders of Modern India* (New York, 1954)

Woolf, Virginia, *The London Scene* (New York, 1975)

Wright, Louis B. (ed.), *Letters of Robert Carter, 1720–1727: The Commercial Interests of a Virginia Gentleman* (San Marino, California, 1940)

Wroth, Warwick, *The London Pleasure Gardens* (1896)

Wyckoff, Vertrees J., *Tobacco Regulation in Colonial Maryland* (Baltimore, 1936)

ARTICLES

Anderson, Matthew S., 'Samuel Bentham in Russia, 1779–1791', *The American Slavic and East European Review*, vol. xv (1956)

Basset, John Spencer, 'The Relation between the Virginia Planter and the London Merchant', *Report of the American Historical Association* (1901)

Becker, Craig, 'Property in the Workplace: Labor, Capital, and Crime in the Eighteenth Century British Woolen and Worsted Industry', *Virginia Law Review*, vol. lxix (1982)

Bedau, Hugo Adam, 'Bentham's Utilitarian Critique of the Death Penalty', *The Journal of Criminal Law and Criminology*, vol. lxxiv, no. 3 (fall 1983)

Beloff, Max, 'A London Apprentice's Notebook, 1703–1705', *History*, new series, vol. xxvii (June–September 1942)

Bevington, L. S., 'Why I am an Expropriationist', *Liberty* (May 1894)

Chapman, Stanley D., 'The Textile Factory Before Arkwright: A Typology of Factory Development', *Business History*, vol. xlviii, no. 4 (winter 1974)

Christie, Ian R., 'Samuel Bentham and the Western Colony at Krichev, 1784–1791', *The Slavonic and East European Review*, vol. xlviii (April 1970)

Clapham, Sir John, 'The Spitalfields Acts, 1773–1824', *The Economic Journal*, vol. xxvi (1916)

Clark, J. C. D., 'Whig Tactics and Parliamentary Precedent: The

English Management of Irish Politics, 1754–1756', *Historical Journal*, vol. xxi (1978)

Curtis, T. C. and Speck, W. A., 'The Societies for the Reformation of Manners: A Case Study in the Theory and Practice of Moral Reform', *Literature and History*, vol. iii (1976)

Davis, Ralph, 'Seaman's Sixpences: An Index of Commercial Activity, 1697–1828', *Economica*, new series, vol. xiii, no. 92 (November 1956)

Donnan, Elizabeth, 'Eighteenth Century English Merchants: Micajah Perry', *Journal of Economic and Business History*, vol. iv (1931–2)

Donnelly, James S., Jr., 'The Whiteboy Movement, 1761–5', *Irish Historical Studies*, vol. xxi, no. 81 (March 1978)

Dunn, Richard M., 'The London Weavers' Riot of 1675', *Guildhall Studies in London History*, vol. i (October 1973–April 1975)

Ekrich, A. Roger, 'Bound for America: A Profile of British Convicts Transported to the Colonies, 1718–1775', *The William and Mary Quarterly* 3rd series, no. 42 (1985)

Everitt, Alan, 'The Marketing of Agricultural Produce', in Joan Thirsk (ed.), *The Agrarian History of England and Wales*, vol. vi, *1500–1640* (Cambridge, 1967)

Fisher, F. J., 'The Development of the London Food Market, 1540–1640', *Economic History Review*, vol. v, no. 2 (April 1935)

Giles, P. M., 'The Felt-Hatting Industry, c. 1500–1850, with special reference to Lancashire and Cheshire', *Transactions of the Lancashire and Cheshire Antiquarian Society*, vol. lxix (1959)

Glass, D. V., 'Socio-economic Status and Occupations in the City of London at the end of the Seventeenth Century', in A. E. J. Hollaender and William Kellaway (eds), *Studies in London History* (1969)

Gray, Stanley and V. J. Wyckoff, 'The International Tobacco Trade in the Seventeenth Century', *The Southern Economic Journal*, vol. vii, no. 1 (July 1940)

Green, Francis, 'Early Banks in West Wales', *Transactions of the History Society of West Wales*, vol. vi (1917)

Hausman, William J. and Neufeld, John L., 'Excise Anatomized: The Political Economy of Walpole's 1733 Tax Scheme', *The Journal of European Economic History*, vol. x, no. 1 (spring 1981)

Hay, Douglas, 'War, Dearth and Theft in the Eighteenth Century: The Record of the English Courts', *Past and Present*, no. 95 (May 1982)

Herz, Gerald B., 'The English Silk Industry in the Eighteenth Century', *The English Historical Review*, vol. xxiv (October 1909)

Huston, James H., 'An Investigation of the Inarticulate: Philadelphia's White Oaks', *The William and Mary Quarterly*, vol. xviii, no. 1 (January 1971)

Innes, Joanna and Styles, John, "The Crime Wave", Recent Writings on Crime and Criminal Justice in Eighteenth-Century England', *Journal of British Studies*, no. 25 (October 1986)

Jernegan, Marcus W., 'Slavery and the Beginnings of Industrialism in the American Colonies', *American Historical Reviw*, vol. xxv, no. 1 (October 1919)

Kalman, H. D., 'Rebuilding Newgate Prison', *Architectural History*, vol. xii (1969)

Kellett, J. R., 'The Breakdown of Guild and Corporate Control over the Handicrafts and Retail Trade in London', *Economic History Review*, 2nd series, vol. x, no. 3 (1958)

Kennedy, Duncan, 'The Role of Law in Economic Thought: Essays on the Fetishism of Commodities', *The American University Law Review*, vol. xxxiv, no. 4 (summer 1985)

'The Structure of Blackstone's *Commentaries*', *Buffalo Law Review*, vol. xxviii, no. 3 (1979)

Kuznets, Solomon, 'Pawnbroking', in *International Encyclopedia of the Social Sciences* (1936)

Ladd, Doris M., 'Finding their Own Voices: Mexican Miners and Strikers, 1766', History Department, University of Hawaii (n.d.)

Langbein, John, 'Albion's Fatal Flaws', *Past and Present*, no. 98 (February 1983)

'The Criminal Trial before the Lawyers', *The University of Chicago Law Review*, vol. xlv (winter 1978)

Lawson, Murray G., 'The Beaver Hat and the North American Fur Trade', in Malvina Bolus (ed.), *People and Pelts: Selected Papers of the Second North American Fur Trade Conference* (Winnipeg, 1972)

Linebaugh, Peter, 'All the Atlantic Mountains Shook', *Labour/Le Travail* (winter 1982)

'Labour History without the Labour Process: A Note on John Gast and His Times', *Social History*, vol. vii, no. 3 (October 1982)

'(Marxist) Social History and (Conservative) Legal History', *New York University Law Review*, vol. lx, no. 2 (May 1985)

Macleod, N., 'The Shipwrights of the Royal Dockyards', *The Mariner's Mirror*, vol. xi (July 1925)

Mansfield, Nicholas, *History Workshop: A Journal of Socialist and Feminist Historians*, vol. viii (autumn 1979)

Mars, Gerald, 'Dock Pilferage: A Case Study in Occupational Theft', in Paul Rock and Mary McIntosh (eds), *Deviance and Social Control* (1974)

Medick, Hans, 'The Proto-industrial Family Economy: The Structural Function of Household and Family during the Transition from Peasant Society to Industrial Capitalism', *Social History*, vol. iii (October 1976)

Meusel, Alfred, 'Proletariat', in *International Encyclopedia of the Social Sciences*, 1st edn (New York, 1936)

Millward, R., 'The Emergence of Wage Labour in Early Modern England', *Explorations in Economic History*, no. 18 (1981)

Nash, Gary, 'Forging Freedom: The Emancipation Experience in the Northern Seaport Cities, 1775–1820', in Ira Berlin and Ronald Hoffman (eds), *Slavery and Freedom in the Age of the American Revolution* (Virginia, 1983)

Norton, Mary Beth, 'The Fate of Some Black Loyalists of the American Revolution', *The Journal of Negro History*, vol. lviii, no. 4 (1973)

Oppenheim, M., 'The Royal Dockyards', in William Page (ed.), *The Victorian History of the County of Kent*, vol. ii (1926)

O'Sullivan, Donal, 'Dublin Slang Songs with Music', *Dublin Historical Record*, vol. i, no. 3 (September 1938)

Pattison, George, 'The Coopers' Strike at the West India Dock, 1821', *The Mariner's Mirror*, vol. lv (1969)

Pearl, Valerie, 'Puritans and Poor Relief: The London Workhouse, 1649–1660', in Donald Pennington and Keith Thomas (eds), *Puritans and Revolutionaries: Essays in 17th Century History* (1978)

Petrovitch, Porphyre, 'Recherches sur la criminalité à Paris dans la seconde moitié du xviiie siècle', in *Crimes et criminalité en France, 17ᵉ–18ᵉ siècles*, eds A. Abbiateci et al., *Cahiers des Annales*, vol. xxxiii (Paris, 1971)

Philips, George L., 'Two Seventeenth Century Flue-Fakers, Toolers, and Rampsmen', *Folklore: Transactions of the Folk-Lore Society*, vol. lxii, no. 2 (June 1951)

Poni, Carlo, 'Misura contro Misura: Come il Filo di Seta divenne Sottile e Rotondo', *Quaderni Storici*, no. 47 (August 1981)

Pound, J. F., 'The Social Structure and Trade Structure of Norwich, 1525–1575', *Past and Present*, no. 34 (July 1966)

Price, Jacob M., 'The Rise of Glasgow in the Chesapeake Tobacco Trade, 1707–1775', in Peter L. Payner (ed.), *Studies in Scottish Business History* (1967)

Ranft, B. M. 'Labour Relations in the Royal Dockyards in 1739', *The Mariner's Mirror*, vol. xlvii, no. 4 (November 1961)

Richardson, H. E., 'Wages of Shipwrights in HM Dockyards, 1496–1788', *The Mariner's Mirror*, vol. xxxiii, no. 4 (October 1947)

Rive, Alfred, 'The Consumption of Tobacco since 1600', *The Economic Journal*, Economic History Series, vol. i (January 1926)

Robertson, A. B., 'The Open Market in the City of London in the 18th Century', *East London Papers*, vol. i, no. 2 (October 1958)

Rogers, Nicholas, 'Popular Protest in Early Hanoverian London', *Past and Present*, no. 79 (May 1987)

Rudolf, Lloyd I., 'The Eighteenth Century Mob in America and Europe', *American Quarterly*, vol. xi, no. 4 (winter 1959)

Schwarz, L. D., 'Social Class and Social Geography: The Middle Classes in London at the End of the Eighteenth Century', *Social History*, vol. vii, no. 2 (May 1982)

Sharpe, J. A., '"Last Dying Speeches": Religion, Ideology, and Public Executions in Seventeenth Century England', *Past and Present*, no. 107 (1985)

Sioussat, George L., 'Virginia and the English Commercial System, 1730–1733', *Report of the American Historical Association* (1905)

Spate, O. H. K., 'The Growth of London', in H. C. Darby (ed.), *Historical Geography of England Before 1800* (Cambridge, 1936)

Stavisky, Leonard P., 'Negro Craftsmanship in Early America', *American Historical Review*, vol. liv, no. 2 (January 1949)

'The Origins of Negro Craftsmanship in Colonial America', *Journal of Negro History*, vol. xxxii, no. 4 (October 1947)

Thompson, E. P., 'The Moral Economy of the English Crowd in the Eighteenth Century', *Past and Present*, no. 50 (February 1971)

Turner, E. R., 'The Excise Scheme of 1733', *The English Historical Review*, vol. xlii (January 1927)

Unwin, George, 'A Seventeenth Century Trade Union', *The Economic Journal*, vol. x (September 1900)

Van Klaveren, Jacob, 'Fiscalism, Mercantilism, and Corruption', in D. C. Coleman (ed.), *Revisions in Mercantilism* (1969)

Walsh, Dermot, 'Alcoholism and the Irish', in Mac Marshall (ed.),

Beliefs, Behaviors, and Alcoholic Beverages: A Cross-Cultural Survey (Ann Arbor, 1980)

Wrigley, E. A., 'A Simple Model of London's Importance in Changing English Society and Economy, 1650–1750', *Past and Present*, no. 37 (1967)

UNIVERSITY THESES

Hemphill, John, 'Virginia and the English Commercial System, 1681–1733', unpublished Ph.D. thesis, Princeton University, 1964

Kulikoff, Allan, 'Tobacco and Slaves: Population, Economy and Society in Eighteenth Century Prince George's County, Maryland', unpublished Ph.D. thesis, Brandeis University, 1975

Linebaugh, Peter, 'Tyburn: A Study of Crime and the Labouring Poor in London During the First Half of the Eighteenth Century', Ph.D. thesis, Centre for the Study of Social History, University of Warwick, 1975

Neeson, Jeanette, 'Common Right and Enclosure in 18th Century Northamptonshire', Ph.D. thesis, University of Warwick, 1977

Paley, Ruth, 'The Middlesex Justices Act of 1792: Its Origins and Effects', Ph.D. thesis, University of Reading, 1983

Randall, Henry C., 'Public Disorder in England and Wales, 1765–1775', unpublished Ph.D. thesis, University of North Carolina, 1963

Rothstein, N. K. A., 'The Silk Industry in London, 1702–1766', MA thesis, University of London, 1960

INDEX

Account, see Ordinary of Newgate

Actes and Monuments of These Latter and Perilous Dayes (Foxe), 74

Afro-Americans: Anglicized names, 341; culture, 134–7, 169; deserting slaves, 354–5; leaders, 415; Newgate delivery, in, 341–2, 348–55; prostitutes, 341; servants, 356; sugar trade, from, 414. *See also* slavery

agriculture: cattle economy, 194–5; Enclosure Acts, 221; improvement, 187–8; London's relation to, 99–100

Albion's Fatal Tree, (Hay, Linebaugh, Thompson, (eds.)), xvii–xviii, xix, xxii, xxiii

America: bonded emigrants, 102; transportation, 123. *See also* Afro-Americans

Angier, Humphry, 94–5

antinomianism, 217

apprentices: butchers, 199, 205; condemned, 98, 101–2, 105; Irish, 238; meaning, 62; Negroes, 137

arithmetic: 174–5; political, 48. *See also* metrology

army: condemned soldiers, 96–7; criminality, 44; crimping, 413; discipline, 298–9; 310; Gordon Riots, in, 333, 357, 425–6; hangings, at, 321; incompetence, 47; Irish soldiers, 297–300; punishment, as, 411–13;

Spitalfields riots, 279, 283; strikes of, 316, 322; wages, 297–8; West Indies (1793), 411–12

Articles of War, 53

bailiffs, 56–7

ballads, 216–17, 324–6

Bambridge, Thomas, 180

Bank of England, 47, 51, 54, 162, 333; West India interest, 416

banking system, 210–13

Barrow, Robert, 136–7

Bartholomew Fair, 18–19, 30, 40, 216, 347, 403

Beattie, Prof. J. M., 52

Beckford, Alderman William, 312–13, 323

Beggar's Opera (Gay), 40, 143

Behn, Aphra, 66

Bellers, John, 13, 68, 69

benefit of clergy, 53, 54, 65, 66

Bentham, Jeremy: cooking, on, 410–11; Gordon Riots, on, 372n; penal reform, on, 360–61; police schemes, 427; prison reform, 371–3

Bentham, Samuel: dockyard reforms, 383, 390, 396–401, 429; prison reform, 372–3

Black Act, *see* Waltham Black Act

Black Boy Alley gang, 149–50

Black Rolls, 58

Blackstone, William, 273, 359–60, 365

Blake, William, 4, 122, 273–4, 342, 368–70, 402, 408

Blincoe, Robert, 12

Bliss, Thomas, 180

Blood Money: 52, 54; Act (1692), 59

Bonner, Edward, 205–8, 210, 213

'Blueskin', 27, 34–5, 40

book and key divination, 367

Botany Bay, 414

Boulton, Matthew, 330

Bowsey, Benjamin, 353–4, 414

boxing, 414

Bramah, Joseph, 330, 365–6

Britain's Glory (Sutherland), 389

British Empire, 47, 409–10

British nation, 116–17

Brownrigg, Elizabeth, 322

bugging, 237–41, 268. *See also* custom

Bunyan, John, 71–2. *See also* *Pilgrim's Progress*

Burke, Edmund 363, 427

Burt, Captain Edward, 195

butchers: apprentices, 199, 205; Company, 197–9; free, 198; highwaymen, as, 184–92, 202, 205; middlemen, 200–202; numbers of, 201; poulters, 198–9; status of, 184–5

Byrd, William, 155

cabbage (tailor's remnants), 24–8, 251. *See also* custom

capital punishment: Articles of War, 53; awesomeness, loss of, 280; class attitudes to, 54; extent of, 50; methods of, 280; modern

capital punishment – *contd.*
day, xv–xvi; money, relation to, 54; new offences, 52, 53–4, 74; pardoning power, 52; sovereignty, as element of, 50–51; tariff of punishment, in, 17–18, 73. *See also* benefit of clergy; hangings; Ireland; Waltham Black Act

capitalism: accumulation, 10, 34, 46–7; credit monies, 51–2; criminality, and, xxi; development of, xxv–xxvi; needs of, xxiv. *See also* economics.

Capp, Prof. B. S., 11

Carlyle, Thomas, 289

Carmichael, John, 277–9, 281

Carter, Robert, 155, 156

Cary, John, 68

cattle, *see* agriculture; butchers; Ireland and Irish

Chandler, F. W., 119

Charitable Corporation, 228

Charles II, 44, 45, 56, 77, 120

Charnock, John, 389, 401

Chauvet, Lewis, 279, 281, 282

Child, Josiah, 4

childbirth, 147–9, 248

Childs, Joshua, 68

Civic Government, Two Treatises of (Locke), 42, 48

Clark, Sir George, 44

Clark, Prof. J. C. D., 301

Clarke, Daniel, 278, 281–2

class distinction: xxiii–xxv, 14; Colquhoun on, 427; exploitation by law, 273; hanging, and, 54; highwaymen as epitome of struggle, 213; income divisions, 78; judicial process, in, 74; law as mask for, xxii–xxiii; measurement of, 49; middle, 78–9; police's role, 434–5; Spitalfield riots, in, 270–83. *See also* criminal class; proletariat; ruling class; working class

Clerkenwell, 25–7, 35, 69, 226

Clive, Robert (of India), 272

clothing: dockers', 430–31; sale and exchange, 253–4; theft of, 359

coal trade: Coal Act (1758), 311; heavers, 306–7, 311–18, 322–3, 432–3; importance of, 304–6; measuring, 307; pilfering, 307–8; wages, 306

Cobbett, William, 413–14, 439

cock-fighting, 210

coinage offences: clipping, 51, 54, 55; Coinage Act (1696), 51; counterfeiting, 55, 96; money police, 56; unsound coinage, 67; Wapping Mint, 57

collective bargaining, 285–6

Colquhoun, Patrick: 421, 423, 425; police, and, 426–8, 434; working class, on, 428–30

combinations (trade unions), 17, 18, 242, 274, 438

commodity: money, 51; producing society, 82

common lands, 206–7

Compleat Ship-Wright, The (Bushnell), 385

confessions, *see* Ordinary of Newgate . . .

Cook, Henry, 185–6, 234–5

coopers, 163–7

Coram, Thomas, 148

Cordwainers Company, 232

Cottington, John, 120

counterfeiting, *see* coinage offences

Coventry, 261, 266, 267

Cowper, William, Earl, 78

Cowper, William (poet), 342

Crabbe, George, 334, 342

Craftsman, The (periodical), 115, 179

crime, *see* criminalization; punishment; robbery

criminal class: birthplaces, 92–4, 107–10; occupations, 103–10; poor as, xxi, 71–2

criminalization: custom, of,

429, 434; dockers' chips, 393–4; poor, of, 71–2

Crimp House Riots (1794), 413

Cromwell, Oliver, 42, 44, 120

Cugoano, Ottobah, 348, 349–50, 415

Cumberland, William Augustus, Duke of, 299

custom (perquisites): attacks on, 329–31; attitude, change of, 286–7; Bugging Act (1749), 238–9; criminalization, 404–7, 429, 434; dockyards, from, 376–8, 393–4, 399; factories, from, 329–30; informers, 172; justification for, 435–6; maintenance of, 182; Port of London, 418–24, 430–32; quasi-legality, 172–3; servants' vails, 250–55; sugar, 173; tailors' cabbage, 245–8; tobacco, 159–60, 170–73; tradesmen, 249; wages, relation to, 418–24, 431–2, 435–6; weavers', 264–70

Customs, Board of: Act of Frauds (1662), 259, 273; allowances, 175; attacks against, 173, 176; bonded warehouses, 178; Commissioners, 417; officers, 173–4; paper work, 174; Riding Officers, 159

Dawkins, William, 155, 156

Defence of Public Stews (Mandeville), 146

Defoe, Daniel: 37, 85; drink, on, 214–15; idleness, on, 54, 263; money-form, on, 211–12; poor, on, 4, 58; trade, on, 10; workhouses, on, 13

Dekker, Thomas, 71

Diver, Kenny (Mary Young), 143, 151

Dobson, C. R., 240

dockers, see river workers
dockyards: Bentham's reforms, 396–401; Chatham, 391, 393; chips, 378–82, 393–5 (criminalization), 393–4; Deptford, 374–82, 391–2, 395; security, 391–2; task work, 394–5; theft from, 391; trousers banned, 392–3; waste, 393, 399
Dodd, Judge Samuel, 77
domestic service: birthplaces, 249; clothing, 253–4; division of labour, 248; hanged servants, 98, 253; hierarchy, 248; infanticide, 248; labour market, 252; perquisites (vails), 250–5; robbery of employers, 249
Doyle, John, 276, 279–81
drinking: gin, 214–15; highwaymen and, 216; Licensing Act (1751), 221; Newgate, in, 29
Dutch Wars, 44–5
dying words, see Ordinary of Newgate . . .

East India Company, 19–20, 46, 68, 272, 283, 382, 398
Eastman, William, 278, 282
economics: coinage, 51; competition, 329, 330; demand, 193; flight of capital, 274; food prices, 309; foreign trade, 445–6; freedom of proletariat, 122; labour as source of value, 48–9; moneyless, 265; science, as, 49; truck payments, 329; wealth (consumption, and), 97–8; (inequality, and), 329, 428; working class, 429–30. See also capitalism; labour; money; wages
Eden, William, 365
Edgworth Bess (Elizabeth Lyon), 15, 16, 21–2, 25, 28, 30
Ellis, P. Beresford, 313

embezzlement, 239. See also custom; robbery
Enclosure Acts, 221
Encyclopédie (Diderot), 64
Engels, Frederick, 7, 289
English Revolution, 4, 39, 42, 52, 73
Equiano, Olaudah, 136, 169–70, 348, 351, 415
escape, see excarceration
Essay Concerning Human Understanding, An (Locke), 48, 60
Essay on the Nursing and Management of Children (Cadogan), 147
Essay on Trade and Commerce (anon.), 284
excarceration: Gordon Riots, after, 361–2; meaning, xxvi, 3; theme of, 23, 30. See also freedom; Newgate delivery; Sheppard, Jack
Excise, 178–82. See also Customs, Board of

Fable of the Bees (Mandeville (q.v.)), 33–4, 54–5, 115–16
factories, see manufacture
families: budgets, 55, 190–91, 243; care of, as defence, 407; domestic servants, 248; orphanages, 149; proletarian, 146. See also marriage
Ferguson, Adam, 222, 273, 280, 329, 428
Field, John, 203, 204
Fielding, Henry, 135, 245, 252, 254, 280, 296, 304
Fielding, John, 135, 249–50, 252, 355
Fiery Flying Roll, A . . . (Cope), 184
Fifth Monarchy Men, 11, 58
Figgs, John, 33
Fineham, John, 389
Firmin, Thomas, 68
Fleet marriages, 141–2, 149
Fleet prison, 180
Fletcher, Andrew, 47
Fluellin, Henry, 216

Fontenoy, battle of (1745), 229–30
foreign trade, see London; trade
Forward, Jonathan, 154, 181, 182
Fosset, John, 216
Foucault, Michel, xxvi, 3, 404, 417
foundlings, 148–9, 244. See also workhouses
Fox, Elizabeth, 140
Franklin, Benjamin, 323, 424
Franks, John, 361
Freame, John, 13
freedom: concept of, xxvi, 72–3; custom and, 381; ex-slaves, 360; popular support for, 40–41; press-gangs, 67–8; proletariat, of, 122. See also excarceration
Friendly Societies, 65
Froude, J. A., 289

Gardiner, Mary, 359
Gast, John, 438
Gay, Edwin, 329
Gay, John, 40, 57, 184
George, Isaac, 135–6
George, M. Dorothy, xix, 192, 262, 269, 317
Georgia (USA), 180
Gibbon, Edward, 358, 427
Gilbert, Edmund, 263
Glasgow, 155–6
Glover, John, 348–51
Godwin, William, 440
'Going upon the Accompt', meaning, 212
gold speculation, 45
goldsmiths, 228–9
Gordon, Lord George, 333, 347
Gordon Riots (1780): Blake on, 368–70; events of, 333–56, 357–8; hangings after, 363. See also Newgate delivery
Gregory, Samuel, 203, 204

habeas corpus, 72

Haiti, 411
Hale, Sir Matthew, 53, 4, 55, 68
hanging: days, 91; language of condemned, 216–17; post-Gordon Riots, 363–4; publicity restricted, 363–4; regime ends, 403–4. See also capital punishment; Ireland and the Irish; Tyburn
Hanoverian oligarchy, 77
Hanway, Joseph, 251
Harmon, Thomas, 71
Harrington, William Stanhope, Earl of (Peter Shambles), 249–50
Harriott, John, 426, 431
Hastings, Warren, 283
hatmaking, 235–41; bugging, 237–41; French competition, 236; hanged hatmakers, 237; Hat Act (1732), 237
Hawles, Sir John, 84, 85
Haycock, Thomas (Mad Tom), 346–8
Hazard, Paul, 49
Hecht, Jean, 251
Herriot, 'Black', 34, 356
Hewitt, John, 266, 267, 278
highwaymen, 184–218: aspirations of, 189, 213; butchers and, 184–213; classic defence, 187, 203–5, 217; Dick Turpin, 203–5; money-form, as cause of, 210–12; setting for, 187–9
Hill, Christopher, 14, 42, 49
Hodgson, Ralph, 312, 323
Hogarth, William, 180
Horsford, William, 275–7, 281–2, 290
Howard, John, 365
Hume, David, 217–18
Humphreys, Sir William, 77
Humphry Clinker (Smollett), 98, 250. See also Smollett, Tobias
Hutton, William, 23–4
Hyde, John, 181

idleness: concept of, 14, 263, 270; working class, 222
imprisonment: allowances for prisoners, 151; post-Gordon Riots, 365. See also Newgate; prisons
Indian silk trade, 271–2, 280, 283
industrial revolution, 329–30. See also manufacture
industry, idleness, and, 221–3
infant mortality, 149
infanticide, 148–9, 248
Ireland and the Irish: agrarian policy, 288–9, 318–19; apprentices, 288; cattle trade, 195, 196, 318–19; clubs, 313–14; Dublin/London similarities, 312–13; famines, 295, 319; hanged Irish, 288, 297, 302–3, 318 (birthplace of condemned), 92 (defiance to execution), 323–5 (euphemisms for hanging), 321 (execution ballads), 324–6 (occupations of condemned), 95–6; Irish penal code, 53; Irish Rebellion (1798), 432; labourers, 223, 292–7; land-holding, 289; language, 290–92, 317; lawlessness, 195–6, 222–3, 290; migration, 48, 432 (America), 289–90 (London), 288; Newgate escapes, in, 301; penal restrictions on, 94; poverty, 295, 319, 432; silk-weavers, 10–11, 261, 278; soldiers, 297–300; strike of, 17, 68, 313–17; subjugation of, 47, 289, 323; tailors, 244; undercutting wages, 295–6, 313; vails (customary perquisites), 251; wakes, 317–18; Whiteboys, 318–21; work ethic, lack of, 48
Italian silk production, 270

James, C. L. R., 65
Jefferies, Richard, Judge, 77, 85
Jenkins, Stephen, 189–90
Johnson, Dr Samuel, 74, 122, 130, 246–7, 342, 429
Jones, John Paul, 343–4
judges: juries, influence over, 83–4; Old Bailey, 77–8; public interest in, 90
juries: composition of, 84–5; corrupt, 85; function of, 83, 85–6; independence, lack of, 83–4; 'pious perjury', 83, 85; public interest in, 90; qualifications, 78; special, 357; valuers, as, 79, 230

Kames, Henry Home, Lord, 264, 273
Keys, Kate, 22
keys, significance of, 366–8
King, Charles, 10
King, Gregory, 88–9
King (of Ockham), Peter, Baron, 77
King, Tom, 204, 211
Kneebone (wollen draper), 9, 13, 27
Knowland, Patrick, 244

labour: 'abstract', 69; Bentham's reforms, 396–401; child, 69, 229; collective, 65; division of, 15–16, 64, 66, 226, 248, 286 (dockyards), 374–5, 382 (London's role), 94 (silk trade), 265–6 (social/specialization distinction), 409 (town and country), 99–101; dock, 417–22; employment-related crimes, 339–40; industrial revolution, in, 330; international, 116; management, 400; market, 252, 292; mobility of, 284; recruitment, 64; relations, emergence of, 322; source

labour – contd.
of value, as, 48–9; surplus,
73; task-work, 394–6; time
measurement, 225–6;
unskilled, 292; value
theory, 121, 139. See also
manufacture; wages;
working class

Lacqueur, Prof. Thomas,
xvii–xviii

Lade, John, 19–20

larceny: meaning, 54;
petty/grand distinction,
82, 154

last words, see Ordinary of
Newgate . . .

law: contempt of proletariat
for, 150; criminal
adminstration, 52, 74;
enforcement, 426;
judge/jury as makers of, 82;
jurists, 273; money
offences, 56–7; procedure,
79; rewards system, 52. See
also Old Bailey; police

Lecky, W. E. H., 47, 289

Levellers, 11, 12, 39, 43, 58,
255, 318

liberty: Blackstone on, 122;
common law and, 358. See
also freedom; Wilks, John

Lilburne, John, 11, 82

Lipson, E., 329

Locke, John, 42, 48; money,
on, 51, 60; poverty, on, 51;
property, on, 49, 53, 54;
sovereignty, on, 50;
workhouses, on, 69

locks, significance of, 336–8,
365–6

Lockyer, Robert, 39

London: cosmopolis, as, 96,
133, 137, 170, 356;
Empire's hub, 409–10;
fashionable, 97; Fire of,
133; guilds, 197; health,
142; highways, 194;
judicial process in, 74–88;
markets, 187, 193;
migratory movement, 92–
6, 142, 244–5, 258, 261;
port, 125–6, 416–22 (West
India Dock), 424–5; social

topography, 100, 110, 149–
50; surroundings, 99;
tavern, 206; trades, 69–71,
133

London Corresponding
Society, 439

London Tradesman, The
(Campbell), 226

Lott, Yeoman, 380–81

Lovell, Salathiel, 77

Lyon, Elizabeth, 22

Macclesfield, Thomas Parker,
Earl of, 40

MacFarlane, C., 196

Macgregor, Rob Roy, 195,
202

Maclean, James, 249

MacPherson, John, 196

McCracken, Prof. J. L., 289

Maitland, F. W., 52

Making of the English Working
Class (Thompson), xvii

Malcolmson, Prof. R. W.,
248

Malefactors Register, 364

Mandeville, Bernard de, 33–
4, 54–5, 115–16, 131, 146,
263, 280

Mansfield, William Murray,
Earl of, 273, 275, 280, 283,
284; jurist, as, 357–60

manufacture: detail labourers,
225–6; factory system, 222,
286 (pilfering, effect on),
329, 438; French
competition, 221;
heterogeneous/
homogeneous distinction,
226, 229–30; London, 98–9;
organization, 64–5; Smith
on, 273; unskilled, 292

markets: capitalism in, 202;
middlemen, 200;
organization, 196–7;
ouvert, 197, 202, 213;
poachers' haven, 203;
powerful traders, 201;
prices, 200; regrating cattle,
200; regulation, 197–8,
200–201; Smithfield, 196–
7, 200; taverns, trading in,
206–8; venison, 202–3

marriage: Fleet, 141–2, 149;
'leaping the sword', 141;
Marriage Act (1753), 149,
221; sailors, and, 139–42;
working-class, 140–41

maroon villages, 189

Marryott, Matthew, 13

Mason, John, 12

Marx, Karl, xvii–xviii, 225,
226

Maxwell, Constantia, 320–21

Mayhew, Henry, 8, 25

meat: cattle thefts, 200;
eating, 192–3; market
system, 187, 193–4, 197–8;
poultry, 198–9; prices, 200;
unwholesomeness, 198,
200. See also butchers;
markets

Meffs, John, 123, 151

Melville, Herman, 431

Methodism, 71: aims of, 218;
drink, and, 214–15;
Georgia, 180; hanging,
attitude to, 215; London,
137–8. See also religion

metrology: coal, 307;
hogsheads, 163–6; tobacco,
162–3

Middleton, John, 99, 188, 209

Millar, Andrew, 273

Milton, John, allegories on
freedom, 4, 42, 43–4

minters, 57–8, 68. See also
coinage offences

mobs: Excise Bill, 179–81;
riots of 1768, 310–11; social
class, as, 38; statutory
control, 221. See also
Gordon Riots

Mockford, Francis, 345–6,
348, 366

Moll Flanders (Defoe), 120

money: artisans' income,
191–2; cash transactions,
210–13; commodity, 51;
corruption by, 115–17;
forms of, 56; inducement
to work, as, 54–5; law
enforcement, 56–7;
moneyless economy, 265–
6; sailors and, 131–2; theft
of, and punishment, 80–82;

money – *contd.*
  violence from lack of, 338;
  Walpole, under, 115–17.
  See also coinage offences;
  wages
Money Answers All Things
  (Vanderbilt), 190
Montague, Charles (Earl of
  Halifax), 51
Morris, William, 64, 65
Munro, Hector, 272, 280
Mutiny Act (1689), 44

'nailing people', 20–21
Napoleon I, 432
Nash, Prof. Gary, 351
Navy: Board, 374–82;
  discipline, 53. *See also*
  dockyards; sailors;
  shipbuilding
New Law of Righteousness, The
  (Winstanley) 42
New York, 136
Newgate: 'Calendar', 364;
  delivery, 333–56 (Blake
  on), 368–70 (prisoners
  delivered), 334–42 (trials
  following), 342–54; design,
  29; drink in, 29; 'Garland',
  39–40; hangings in, 363;
  overcrowding, 59; regime,
  28–30; Sheppard in, 28–30,
  31, 33
Newton, Sir Isaac, 49, 52, 55,
  60
North, Roger, 4

Ogg, David, 44, 55
Olgethorpe, James, 67, 180,
  213
O'Hanlon, Redmond, 196,
  202
Old Bailey: buildings, 77–8;
  jurors, 78–86; Session
  House, 76–7; spectators,
  86–8
*Ordinary of Newgate, The, His
  Account of the Behaviour,
  Confession, and Dying
  Words of the Malefactors . . .:*
  censorship, 91; Gordon

Riots, after, 363–4;
  prostitutes, and, 145; sale
  of, 143; source, as, xix–xx,
  xxi, 88–9, 120
orphanages, 149
O'Sullivan, Owen Roe, 296

Pagan, 'Sir John', 225
Page, William, 30–31
Paine, Tom, 259, 356, 440
Paradise Lost (Milton), 43–4,
  48, 60
Patterson, William, 47
pawnbrokers, 220, 227–8, 235
Pearce, Thomas, 176
Peasants' Revolt (1381), 347
penal reform, *see* punishment
Pepys, Samuel, 250, 377
perquisites, *see* custom
Perry, Micajah, 155–7, 162,
  169, 181, 182
Pett, Phineas, 377 and n.
Petty, William, 4, 47, 48–9,
  55, 88, 126, 226
Philips, Prof. David, 435
Philips, William, 244–5
picaros, 119–22: butchers as,
  186–7; proletarians
  compared, 151–2
Pilgrim's Progress (Bunyan
  (q.v.)), 52, 58, 59–60, 85,
  150
Pinks, Thomas, 190
Pitt, William, 286, 373
Place, Francis, 20, 143, 216–
  17, 255, 440
plantations: Customs Board
  in, 159; insurrection in,
  177–8; methods employed,
  65–6; tobacco workers,
  169, 177
poaching, 202
police: Afro-Americans, and,
  355; Bow Street Foot
  Patrol, 221, 425; class
  relations, maintenance of,
  434–5; Colquhoun and,
  426–8; dock, 430–31;
  effectiveness, 267;
  Fielding's role, 252;
  money, 57–8, 211; moral,
  58; property, protection of,

434–5; Riding Officers,
  159, 162; river, 417, 425,
  433–4; 'secret service'
  money, 221; self-policing
  by traders, 438; silk trade,
  in, 409; spying, 270; strikes
  of 1768, in, 314; thief, 58;
  Walpole, under, 116
Political Arthimetic (Petty), 48
Pollexfen, Sir Henry, 4
Postlethwayt, Malachy, 159,
  283, 389
Pound, Prof. E., 103
Pratt, John, Judge, 77
press-gangs, 67–8, 129
Price, John, 229–30
prisons: Bentham's reforms,
  371–3; conditions in, 179;
  Fleet, 180; Penitentiary
  Act, 365; reform, 180, 371–
  3; ships, 414, 415. *See also*
  Newgate
proletariat: 'deep sea', 123–42;
  family relationships, 146;
  law, attitude to, 150;
  meaning, 121–2; property,
  and, 121–2; reproduction,
  139–40; self-organization,
  151; Walpole, under, 119–
  52. *See also* picaros
property: bailment, 63;
  crimes against, 341;
  growth of, xxi; law
  development on, 273;
  offences, 56–8; police role,
  434–5; proletariat and,
  121–2; protection by locks,
  365–8, 372n; punishment,
  relation to, 79–82; respect
  for, xx; slaves as, 52–3;
  social meaning, 79; theft
  and, 255; values in larceny
  cases, 79–82; wage
  relationship, 439
prostitution: material
  exchange, 230; persecution
  of, 58–9, 340–41;
  prevalence of, 145–7;
  sailors and, 434
Protectorate, 42–3
Public Advertiser, The, 252
Punch and Judy, 402–4
punishment: army service as,

punishment – *contd.*
411–13; jury's role, 85–6;
methods available, 16–17;
money, relationship with,
80–82; Old Bailey, 74–7;
prison ships, 414, 415;
property, relationship
with, 79–80; reform, 404;
vagrants, 47. *See also* capital
punishment; prisons;
transportation

Puritanism, 58. *See also*
religion

putting out, 62–4

Quaker's Opera, The
(Walker), 7, 29–30, 40

Raby, Thomas, 216
Rag Fair, 126, 247, 253, 263,
291
Rainborough, Thomas, 121
Randolph family, 155
Randolph, Sir John, 177, 182
Rationale of Punishment, The
(Bentham), 361
reason: dawn of Age of, 48;
thieves beyond, 54
red flag, 311
Rediker, Prof. Marcus, 129
religion: antinomianism,
217–18; foreign influences,
70–71; Gordon Riots, 333;
non-conformism, 71;
sectaries, 9, 10–11, 85. *See
also* Methodism
reproduction, proletarian,
139–40
Restoration, 43, 53
Reynolds, Charles, 234
Ricardo, David, 429
Riding Officers, 58, 159, 204
Rights of Infants, The
(Spence), 402
Riot Act (1715), 16–17, 18
river workers: customary
practices, 170–76; docks
supplant homes, 434; dress
code, 430–31; exploitation,
169, 172; hanged workers,
308–9; language, 429;
policing, 430–34; riots of

1768, 432–3, 436; strike of,
17, 68, 311; thieving, 308–
9; Walpole's attacks on,
178–80
robbery: entrepreneurial
spirit of, 3–4; house
burglary, 336; keys,
significance of, 366–7; laws
against, 54, 65; lock
improvements, 365–6;
Locke on, 49; popular view
of, 40; prevalence of, 50;
punishment for (money),
80–82 (property) 79–80;
ruling class view of, 49–50;
women as receivers, 145.
See also crime; custom;
larceny
Robertson, William, 273, 428
Roderick Random (Smollett),
119, 130, 134–5, 141, 193
Rogers, Prof. Nicholas, 78
Rose, Joseph, 203, 204
Royal Navy, *see* Navy
Rudé, Dr George, 108, 333
Ruggety Madge, 140
ruling class: aims of, 70;
idleness, attitude to, 14;
legal authority, as, xxiii;
plundering by, 8, 28;
proletariat, attitude to, 122;
robbery, view of, 49–50;
Spitalfields riots, 279
Ryan, James, 126, 150

sailors: 'deep sea proletariat',
123–42; discipline, 130–31;
diseases, 130; hanged, 96–7;
language, 134–5, 151; life at
sea, 66, 130; manning of
ships, 66; money,
signficance of, 131, 137;
nationalities, 133–6;
Newgate delivery, in, 343;
numbers, 125; press-gangs,
67, 129; rebelliousness,
136–7; recruitment, 67,
128; skills of, 130; strike of
1768, 311, 314, 316; trade,
role in, 126–7; wages, 127–
8, 432 (additional earnings),
128; 'widow's men', 142;

women and, 139–42. *See
also* dockyards;
shipbuilding
Samson Agonistes (Milton), 42,
368
Sandwich, John Montagu,
4th Earl of, 392, 393, 395
Saxe, Marshal Maurice de,
298, 299
Scotland: agriculture, 195;
banditry, 195; banking
system, 212; cattle exports,
195, 196; Clearances, 221;
economists, 273; Rob
Roy, 195; sheep farming,
221; silk manufacture, 284;
tobacco imports, 156;
vagrancy, 47
sectarians, 10–11
servants, *see* domestic servants
Shaddon, William, 154
Shadwell, 317
Shadwell, Thomas, 57
Sharp, Granville, 356
Shelburne, William, Earl of,
274
Shepeard, James, 90
Sheppard, Jack:
apprenticeship, 14; criminal
life, 14–16, 21–2, 24–5, 27,
246; escapes, xxvi, 3, 21, 23,
25, 27, 30–31, 33–7;
execution, 38–9; notoriety,
7–9, 14, 31–3, 38, 40–41;
philosophy of, 33–4;
printed works on, 39–41;
women, 21–2, 145
Sheppard, Tom, 22, 34–5
shipbuilding: caulkers, 387–8;
chips (custom), 378–82,
393–4 (decline of), 438
(money in lieu), 399;
design, 389; machines
introduced, 398–9; St
Helena's Society, 438;
sawyers, 383–4;
shipwrights, 384–6; strike
of 1800, 438; timber
requirements, 382–4;
treenailing, 386; waste,
378–82, 386–7, 389
shoemaking, 231–5:
journeymen, 234; leather-

shoemaking – *contd.*
cutters, 234; radicalism in, 235; self-policing, 438; strike of, 17, 36, 234; women in, 232

silk trade: 'Book' of prices, 271; combinations, 274; customs (perquisites), 264–70 (decline of), 438 (judicial repression), 407 (policing), 409; division of labour, 265–6; encouragement of, 20; exchange system, 265–6; foreign imports, 271–2; growth of, 10–12; hanged workers, 257–62; imports, 19–20, 68; itinerant dealers, 267; London parishes, 257; poverty in, 258–9; Spitalfields weavers, 10–11, 19–20, 68 (riots), 270–83; statutory control, 267–8; structure, 262–3, 267; techniques, 264–5; wages, 259–60; waste, 264–5; working conditions, 24

silversmiths, 228–9

Sinclair, James, 301

Skinner, John, 172, 181

slavery: abolition movement, 356, 415; code, 52–3; deserting slaves, 354–5; establishment of, 45–6; freedom in England, 360; rebellions against, 136–8, 411–14; sailors' attitude to, 136; plantations, 65–6; tobacco trade, in, 156

Smee, Mary, 281–2

Smith, Adam: 97, 178–9, 193, 222, 254, 273, 427, 428, 429; capital punishment, on, 280

Smollett, Tobias, 98, 115, 119, 120, 130, 134–5, 141, 193, 250

smuggling, 156, 159, 161

Snodgrass, Gabriel, 398

social contract, hanging as renewal of, xx

Society for the Propagation of Christian Knowledge, 58

sociology of condemned: age, 101; birthplaces, 92–4, 108–11; employment, 94–101 (apprentices), 101–2 (sailors), 123–42 (trades), 103–9; methodology, 88–91; mutual support, 149–50; non-Londoners, 95–7; procreation, 139–45; seasonal spread of indictments, 131–3; sources, 91

South Sea Bubble, 47, 54, 158

sovereignty, Locke on, 50–51

Spate, O. H. K., 110

Spence, Thomas, 436

Spitalfields, 10–11, 19, 68; poverty, 408; riots, 270–83 (effect of), 284–7

starvation, 309, 324

Stephens, James Fitzjames, 53

street culture, 89–90

street-sellers, 144–5, 199

strikes, 234, 309, 438. *See also* trade unions

Stroud, Henry, 282

Styles, Prof. John, xxiv, 240, 265

sugar: consumption, 410; market, 416; pilfering, 417, 420–24; port facilities, 416–17; West Indies war (1793), 411–12

Sun Tavern Fields, 321–3

Sutherland, William, 380n, 387–8, 389–90, 401

Swift, Jonathan, 94, 148

Sykes, James, 22–3

tailoring: cabbage (perquisites), 245–8, 439; hanged tailors, 243–4; Irish tailors, 244–5; liveries, 253–4; working hours, 241–2. *See also* textile industry

Tailors, The: A Tragedy for Warm Weather (Foote), 247–8

Tatham, William, 153, 168, 424

taverns: meat sales in, 206; riverside, 313–14; silk trade, and, 256–7

Taylor, Frederick Winslow, 400

tea, 121, 215

textile industry: apprentices, 106; depression in, 55; regional specialization, 99; working conditions, 23–4. *See also* silk trade

thanatocracy, 50, 53–4

theatre, 18–19, 40

theft, *see* custom; larceny; robbery

Thelwall, John, 408

thief-takers, 27–8, 33, 59, 150. *See also* Blood Money; Wild, Jonathan

thieves' cant, 72, 274–5

Thompson, Edward, xvii, 415

Thornhill, James, 237

Timmins, Stephen, 217

tinkers, 71

tobacco trade: abuses in, 155, 158, 164; Bulk Tobacco Act (1699), 161; customs and excise, 159–60, 161–2, 178–82; depression in, 157–8; freight costs, 156, 157; French monopoly, 178; hogsheads, 163–7; imports, 156–7, 159 (Scottish), 156; packing techniques, 160–61, 166–8; plantations, 177–8; porters, 167; smuggling, 156, 159, 161; statutory control, 177–80; theft, 153–4, 160, 164, 166, 168 (custom, as), 170–79

Told, Silas, 137–8

Towers, Charles, 91

Toynbee, Arnold, 329, 330

Tracy, Robert, Judge, 77

trade: cash problems, 212–13; classification, 103–10; foreign markets, 44–6, 115, 126–7, 221; French competition, 236; growth under Walpole, 116–17; overseas, 221. *See also* specific trades

trade unions: collective bargaining, 285–6; combinations, 17, 18, 242, 274, 438; money-wages, 438; self-organisation, 64–

trade unions – *contd.*
5; tailoring, 241, 244, 247.
See also strikes
transport, *see* London
highways; turnpikes
transportation: Botany Bay,
414; business
arrangements, 154; end of,
363; Georgia, 180; illegal
return from, 154;
Mansfield, under, 360;
Transportation Act (1719),
17, 18; women, 59, 142
Trowbridge, Sir Thomas, 399
Tucker, Josiah, 188
Turlis, Thomas, 321
turnpikes: Hereford riots
(1736), 206; keepers abet
highwaymen, 208–9; trade,
role in, 267
Turpin, Dick, 203–5, 208,
209, 214, 217
Tyburn: class struggle,
symbol of, xvii, xix;
crowd, xvii–xviii; hangings
abolished, xxv, 363;
procession to, xxv, 330;
Tyburnography, 89
Tyler, Wat, 347

Udall, William, 227
Universal Register Office,
252
urbanization, 70
Ure, Andrew, 285

vagabonds, 71–2
vails (servants' perquisites),
250–55
Valloine, John, 276, 279, 280–
81
Vanderlint, Jacob, 190–93
Vaucanson, Jacques de, 270
Vaughan, William, 330, 424,
429

Wager, 'Cocky', 208, 209–10,
213
wages: army, 297–8; Bugging
Act (1749), 221; coal trade,
306; collective bargaining,
285–6; custom (perquisites)

and, 288, 378–82, 418–24,
431–2, 435–6; dock
workers, 430, 431–4;
domestic servants, 252–3;
imposition of, 404; Irish,
295–6, 313; lowness of, 4,
8; manufacturers', 64;
mechanization, effect of,
400–401; money, 60, 436–
8; need, balance with, 54–
5; non-monetary, 251;
origin of, 371–401;
pawnbrokers and, 228;
piece-, 63, 226, 259–60,
263, 383, 440; right to, 439;
sailors, 127–8; strike of
1768, after, 322; tailoring,
242–3; task work, 394–6;
truck payments, 329;
watch industry, 226;
weavers', 20, 259–60, 263;
working conditions,
relation to, 367–9. *See also*
families; budgets
Walker, Humphrey, 203, 204
Walker, Ralph, 418
Walpole, Horace, 182, 250
Walpole, Robert, xxiii, 40,
115, 178–82
Waltham Black Act (1723),
18, 52, 120, 202, 321
Waltham Forest Blacks, 202–
3
Walwyn, William, 11, 28
Wapping Mint, 57–8
watchmaking, 225–31;
hanged watchmakers, 226–
7; Watch Fraud Act (1754),
228
Watt, John, 330
Wealth of Nations (Smith),
254, 428
weaving, *see* silk trade
Wedgwood, Josiah, 329
weights and measures, *see*
arithmetic; metrology
Wells, Abraham, 207, 214
Weskett, John, 249–50
Wesley, Charles, 214
Wesley, John, 213–15, 218,
323
West, Benjamin, 281
West Indies: constitution, 52–

3; Merchants' Committee,
416, 424, 426; wealth,
source of, 45; West India
Dock, 424–5. *See also*
plantations
Wheeler, John, 203
Whigs, property, views on,
49–50
White, James, 153–4, 156,
160, 169, 170, 182
White, Mary (Cut-and-
Come-Again), 145, 150
Whiteboys, 318–21, 323–4
Whitefield, George, 213–14
Wild, Jonathan, 27–8, 35, 59,
120, 123, 225
Wilkes, John, 279, 310, 316
William III, 47, 52, 53–4, 65
Wilmot, Justice, 282–3
Windsor forest, 202
Winstanley, Gerrard, 28, 30,
58, 73
wire-drawers, 229
Wollstonecroft (Godwin),
Mary, 408, 435, 437
women: acquittal of, 85;
birthplaces of condemned,
143; 'breeders' on
plantations, 66; childbirth,
147–9; condition of, 143–4;
dockyard chips, 378–9;
Irish, hanged, 303–4;
migration, 142–3; poverty
and theft, 338–41;
punishment of, 59;
receivers, as, 145; sailors,
and, 139–42; shoemaking,
in, 232; street-sellers, as,
144–5; working class, 437.
See also marriage;
prostitution
work: ethic, 61; forms of, 61–
7; working week, 283–4.
See also labour; wages;
workhouses
workhouses: Bishopsgate,
11–12; foundation of, 68;
infants in, 149; life in, 12–
13, 408; social control,
means of, 9, 13; system of
work, 69; weaving, 263;
Workhouse Act (1723),
17–18

working-class: Colquhoun
  on, 429; crime and, xxii, 8;
  language of, 429–30; law,
  attitude to, xxiii; money
  wages, 436–8; origins, 415,
440–41; police role, 434–5;
power of, 374; 1790s, in,
402–41; Thompson on,
xvii, 415; women, 437. *See
also* class distinction

Young, Mary (Jenny Diver),
  143, 151